Decolonizing African Studies

Rochester Studies in African History and the Diaspora

Toyin Falola, Series Editor
The Jacob and Frances Sanger Mossiker Chair in the Humanities
and University Distinguished Teaching Professor
University of Texas at Austin

Recent Titles

Youth and Popular Culture in Africa: Media, Music, and Politics
Edited by Paul Ugor

African Migration Narratives: Politics, Race, and Space
Edited by Cajetan Iheka and Jack Taylor

Ethics and Society in Nigeria: Identity, History, Political Theory
Nimi Wariboko

African Islands: Leading Edges of Empire and Globalization
Edited by Toyin Falola, R. Joseph Parrott, and Danielle Porter-Sanchez

Catholicism and the Making of Politics in Central Mozambique, 1940–1986
Eric Morier-Genoud

Liberated Africans and the Abolition of the Slave Trade, 1807–1896
Edited by Richard Anderson and Henry B. Lovejoy

The Other Abyssinians:
The Northern Oromo and the Creation of Modern Ethiopia, 1855–1913
Brian J. Yates

Nigeria's Digital Diaspora: Citizen Media, Democracy, and Participation
Farooq A. Kperogi

West African Masking Traditions: History, Memory, and Transnationalism
Raphael Chijioke Njoku

Cultivating Their Own: Agriculture in Western Kenya during the "Development" Era
Muey C. Saeteurn

A complete list of titles in the Rochester Studies in African History and the Diaspora series may be found on our website, www.urpress.com

Decolonizing African Studies

Knowledge Production, Agency, and Voice

Toyin Falola

UNIVERSITY OF ROCHESTER PRESS

Copyright © 2022 by the Author

All rights reserved. Except as permitted under current legislation, no part of this work may be photocopied, stored in a retrieval system, published, performed in public, adapted, broadcast, transmitted, recorded, or reproduced in any form or by any means, without the prior permission of the copyright owner.

First published 2022

University of Rochester Press
668 Mt. Hope Avenue, Rochester, NY 14620, USA
www.urpress.com
and Boydell & Brewer Limited
PO Box 9, Woodbridge, Suffolk IP12 3DF, UK
www.boydellandbrewer.com

ISBN-13: 978-1-64825-027-9
ISSN: 1092-5228

Library of Congress Cataloging-in-Publication Data

Names: Falola, Toyin, author.
Title: Decolonizing African studies : epistemologies, ontologies, and agencies / by Toyin Falola.
Other titles: Rochester studies in African history and the diaspora ; 93. 1092-5228
Description: Rochester, NY : University of Rochester Press, 2021. | Series: Rochester studies in African history and the diaspora, 1092-5228 ; 93 | Includes bibliographical references and index. | Contents: Introduction: The Decolonial Moments — Epistemologies and Methodologies — Decoloniality and Decolonizing Knowledge — Eurocentrism and Intellectual Imperialism — Epistemologies of Intellectual Liberation — Decolonizing Knowledge in Africa — Decolonizing Research Methodology — Oral Tradition: Cultural Analysis and Epistemic Value — Agencies and Voices — Voices of Decolonization — Voices of Decoloniality — Decoloniality: A Critique — Women's Voices on Decolonization — Empowering Marginal Voices: LGBTQ and African Studies — Intellectual Spaces — Decolonizing the African Academy — Decolonizing Knowledge Through Language — Decolonizing of African Literature — Identity and the African Feminist Writers — Decolonizing African Aesthetics — Decolonizing African History — Decolonizing Africa Religion — Decolonizing African Philosophy — African Futurism.
Identifiers: LCCN 2021028316 (print) | LCCN 2021028317 (ebook) | ISBN 9781648250279 (hardback) | ISBN 9781800103900 (ebook other) | ISBN 9781800103917 (epub)
Subjects: LCSH: Decolonization—Africa. | Postcolonialism—Africa. | Africa—History—Study and teaching.
Classification: LCC DT31 .F28 2021 (print) | LCC DT31 (ebook) | DDC 960—dc23
LC record available at https://lccn.loc.gov/2021028316
LC ebook record available at https://lccn.loc.gov/2021028317

This publication is printed on acid-free paper.
Printed in the United States of America.

To Samuel Oloruntoba, a passionate Pan-Africanist

Contents

Acknowledgments ix

Introduction: The Decolonial Moments 1

Part One: Knowledge Production

1. Decoloniality and Decolonizing Knowledge 27
2. Eurocentrism and Intellectual Imperialism 45
3. Epistemologies of Intellectual Liberation 75
4. Decolonizing Knowledge in Africa 101
5. Decolonizing Research Methodologies 126
6. Oral Tradition: Cultural Analysis and Epistemic Value 150

Part Two: Agencies and Voices

7. Voices of Decolonization 197
8. Voices of Decoloniality 243
9. Decoloniality: A Critique 276
10. Women's Voices on Decolonization 294
11. Empowering Marginal Voices: LGBTQ and African Studies 326

Part Three: The Disciplines

12. Decolonizing the African Academy 349
13. Decolonizing Knowledge through Language 380
14. Decolonizing of African Literature 411
15. Identity and the African Feminist Writer 438
16. Decolonizing African Aesthetics 480
17. Decolonizing African History 511

18. Decolonizing African Religion   538
19. Decolonizing African Philosophy   566
20. African Futurism   595

   Bibliography   623

   Index   667

Acknowledgments

The idea of writing this long book owes to many institutions, colleagues, and scholars. It was a product of invitations to give public lectures and run workshops on frontiers of history, African affairs, and African studies. The significant elements that informed this book are the dominance of the Western-universal knowledge system, which must be challenged, the methods to challenge it, the specific areas to be challenged, and the critical voices that have offered alternatives. The book is particularly informed by the recognition that there will never be one approach to decolonizing knowledge. The book presents decolonization in many ways over various disciplines. There will be the usual contestations, as this book will form the basis of multiple debates, including critical objections to some of my statements. Thought patterns and knowledge systems are, by nature, multiplex and multiplural. For example, a decolonial critique does not necessarily satisfy feminist views, and feminist discourse is not necessarily in agreement with nationalist critique.

I decided to write this book in Amsterdam after a productive meeting on October 11, 2018, with the graduate students and professors at the Huizinga Research Institute and Graduate School of Cultural History and the Netherlands Institute of Cultural Analysis (NICA). I have to thank, once again, the organizers of that vibrant workshop, the Masterclass and Public Lecture on the "Academy and the Idea of Decolonization," notably Larissa Schulte Nordholt of Leiden University and Marleen Reichgelt of Radboud University. Both were ably supported by Murat Aydemir of NICA and Paul Koopman of Huizinga. I enjoyed vibrant panel discussions with Professor Dr. Marieke Bloembergen of the Royal Institute of Southeast Asian and Caribbean Studies, Dr. Karwan Fatha-Black of Leiden University, and Mitchell Esajas of the Black Archives and the New Urban Collective. Carlos Flores Terán of the University of Groningen offered enthusiastic responses.

I gave lectures on different parts of this book in over a dozen countries. The agenda was to potentially recast discussions within African studies, as many continue to grapple with the idea of decolonizing various fields and disciplines. I cannot remember all the names, but I appreciate the support and assistance of many people who facilitated the trips, ran various errands, and managed hundreds of email communications. The various campuses offered space to discuss different chapters in this book. Seeing the growing demand and request for lectures, discourses, and debates on decoloniality/decolonization made it apparent that there is an urgent need to address this in a scholarly body of work. Not only will it be a "manual" for researchers and academics, but it will also be a legacy and a trigger for sustained discussions on the theme, helping to acculturate the practice of epistemic decoloniality gradually.

It was indeed a challenging book to write. Among the scholars and teachers who read different chapters or/and proposals were: Kayode Olagunju, Njomo Bankonba, Sifiso Majuba, Kwame Tanko, Moses Ochonu, Abikal Borah, Samuel Ojo Oloruntoba, Bola Dauda, Adeshina Afolayan, Adanna Ogbona, Michael Afolayan, Damilare Osunlakin, Biko Agozino, Bashir Salau, Serges Kamga, Martins Olusanya, Tyler Fleming, Damilare Bello, Tolulope Oke, Wale Luqman, Temitope Olabisi, Olajumoke Yacob-Haliso, Devon Hiaso, Sabelo Ndlovu-Getshani, and Anna Lee Carothers.

What can I say other than express profound gratitude? I recognize all the scholars listed above for their critical comments and scholarly objections where necessary but also their strong endorsements of the project. Many communications occurred in the middle of the night when honest people were supposed to be fast asleep. I was always awake, seven days a week, eighteen hours a day, consumed by the passion for engaging in debates, and responding to critical reviews and making amendments. As I was vigorously challenged politically by the Left and Right and by students and professors, the project became more complicated. A student in Kenya asked me: "What is wrong with universalism?" Another one followed up with: "Why do you use Western scholarship to criticize Western ideas?" Of course, you will see many references in this book generated by Western scholars. Ideas are not necessarily binary. The discussion moved to how hegemonic ideas can be modified and applied and sometimes hard to dismantle. I was never short of words, but I was rarely able to satisfy everyone.

Many times, when ideas and differing or unpopular approaches popped up, I consulted with the scholars mentioned above—many of them solidified several of the caveats I made in my decolonization proposals. As seen in the book, some include the belief that Afrocentricity does not necessarily preach the abandonment of all aspects of Western knowledge and epistemology. Afrocentrism's struggle seeks the acknowledgment and incorporation of the uniqueness of African scholarship in global epistemology through pluriversality. When good heads meet, ideas are generated. The idea to critique decoloniality itself within the context of material constraints on African institutions in the current debased global capitalist framework, and how these realities complicate any decolonial agenda, both in the educational and broader cultural arenas, was trialed with a couple of these noble minds, seeing its originality in the discourse of decoloniality. They quite agreed that this was circumspect though noteworthy and should be given more attention. However, my critique of decoloniality does not erode the necessity to correct Africa's problems of underdevelopment and break away from existing, failing structures in order to embrace an alternative path.

The publishers contracted brilliant evaluators whose stellar peer reviews made this a better book. Many of these evaluations exude pure brilliance and fair assessment; while many were accepted, a few could only be adjusted or were not amenable to change. Cutting the length of the book, for instance, was one suggestion that could not just be implemented as proffered if the book was to maintain its sanctity, inclusivity, and integrity as well as the "independence" of the chapters.

This acknowledgment would not be complete without due salutation to scholars who have made specific efforts toward addressing some aspects of decolonization/decoloniality, generating the process of undoing the ills of colonialism and coloniality, and creating the theoretical framework that contains the body of knowledge under which epistemic disobedience and justice is anchored. I devoted four chapters in total to give an overview of some of their excellent contributions. Their contributions and inclusion here affirm that some criticisms you will read in this book about Western hegemony and the monopoly of knowledge production are major concerns that have long been central to the African methodologies of scholars from differing disciplinary backgrounds within African studies.

Lastly, I acknowledge the desire and thirst for both knowledge and a path to decolonizing African studies among my esteemed readers. The book would not have been conceived if there were no intended users, especially African academics living and working on the continent, but not exclusively so. Governments, agencies, and civil organizations' efforts to eliminate the vestiges of colonization in several sectors on the continent need to be fully supported and encouraged by books of this nature. Many sections of the book also make meaningful suggestions on executing decolonial policies to resolve the struggles at hand. African governments and organizations can only implement these credible suggestions, and agency in the struggles—although academic—can only be won through all parties' collaborative efforts.

It will be "mission accomplished" if this book provokes debates on mental decolonization, shifting paradigms on decoloniality, conversations on gender and knowledge production, the increasing role of the LGBTQ communities in African studies, and more.

Austin, Texas
December 2020

Introduction

The Decolonial Moments

The conceptualization and study of the past have followed a pattern of classifying events into groups with common threads: sources, periods, themes, and geographical locations. This pattern of classification is informed by the need to obtain chronologically delivered accounts that facilitate analytical approaches but also aid the ease of access and comprehension. As a methodology in historical study, this classification serves as a handy guide in navigating through the vast area of knowledge that is historical evolution.

African studies has had several such defining periods in the course of its evolution. These are represented by the various titles each epoch bears; thus, the broad divisions into ancient and modern periods.[1] To the ancient times belonged the civilizations of Egypt, Kush, Ethiopia, and the Sudanic empires that existed both in the BCE period and later. This was followed by an era of external invasions, conquest, and conversions coming from the Middle East and Europe, which also marked the start of Christian and then Muslim influence on the continent. These held sway up until the arrival of European ships, this time on the southern shores of Africa, to herald the beginning of what historians now call the "early modern." The modern periods (from the 1500s) of African history belong to the expansion of capitalism and Western modernity, which included the transatlantic slave trade, mercantilism, imperialism, colonialism, apartheid, neocolonialism, and globalization.

---

1 These periods in African studies are further divided into antiquity (the period before written records), early (written) history, colonial history, postcolonial history, and contemporary history. It should be remarked that some of these are European temporal frames imagined as universal and imposed on African history.

African studies has been taught in many different forms by a multitude of different scholars with different worldviews and agendas.[2] This has resulted in the availability of other representations of African cultures and the past. Although the discipline of African studies was not recognized as an academic field in Western universities, African American "organic" intellectuals have presented the history of Africa in ways that contributed to the elevation of Black pride.[3] In the periods 1500 to 1950, imperial historiography stood as African historiography until decolonization activities brought about a new African historiography.

The labels "decolonizing" and "de-colonial moments" encapsulate defining moments within the period after the Second World War, from the start of political decolonization (the 1950s) to the present time. The era concerns the identification of watershed moments in the course of the advancement of decolonization. Simply put, it is the presentation of a decolonization timeline with highlighted moments of bulk academic and political movements such as:

- the emergence of a new African historiography/perspective, the modernization theory, Pan-Africanist, and national liberation movements of the 1950s and 1960s;

- the birth of the underdevelopment and dependency theory and the rise of Marxism as a political ideology and intellectual epistemology in the 1970s and 1980s;

- the postapartheid Africa and the rise of an African renaissance and emphasis on African political thought in the 1990s; and

- the "Rhodes Must Fall" ("fallism") movement in South Africa and the Black Lives Matter protests in the twenty-first century, 2015 and 2020 respectively, continuing the unfinished business of epistemological and racial decolonization.

This book adheres to a chronological sequence of mass decolonization events that have marked the progress of liberation movements since its

---

2   This paragraph and the one that follows were adopted as the central feature of a Seminar, University of Cape Town, South Africa. "Toyin Falola: The Decolonial Moments," http://www.huma.uct.ac.za/event/toyin-falola-decolonial-moments.

3   Du Bois, *Africa, Its Geography*; Du Bois, *Africa: Its Place*.

inception. The movements fed the rise of the African academy and the decolonizing agenda of an emergent academic elite. The period would cover academic political decolonization moments like the nationalist liberation movements of the 1950s to the 1970s; the ideological and theoretical contests between the 1970s and 1980s; the postapartheid African renaissance of the 1990s, and the popular movements (Rhodes Must Fall and Black Lives Matter) of the twenty-first century.

The Nationalist Liberation Movements and "Decolonizing" the Academy: 1950s–1970s

The nature and focus of African studies took a different turn most noticeably in the 1950s after the Second World War.[4] This new African historiography, as it has come to be known, rose in protest of the existing colonial historiography, which cast Africa as ahistorical, incapable of development, and on the margins of world history. The challenge of the imperial historiographical hegemony by this crop of African and Africanist historians is "in a sense development of, and a significant factor in, the intensification of national liberation movements."[5] In other words, it was a part of the process of decolonization.[6]

The decolonization of African history involved questioning the processes, constructing the theoretical and conceptual base, and setting the methodology through which the fallacious conclusions that characterized colonial historiography were derived. The approach to dispelling these false notions by investigating beyond the limitations of the previous scholarship and proving the existence of a historical African past necessitated a successful demonstration. In Africa, this involved developing

---

4 Davidson, *Africa Awakening;* and Dike, *Trade and Politics*, are two such revolutionary publications that exemplified the change in the narrative of African historiography and the nature of African studies.
5 Ogot, *General History of Africa*, 71.
6 It must be noted, as a criticism of nationalist historiography by such scholars as K. O. Dike and J. F. Ade-Ajayi or comparative continental history by Basil Davidson, that although their works are "decolonizing," they replicated the form of universal histories. They certainly inserted African voices but were unable to write histories that generated uniquely African ideas of history.

new and multidisciplinary methods and adopting hitherto relevant but disregarded (oral) sources for the reconstruction of African history—demonstrating a more complete and objective account of Africa's past. In Europe and North America, this resulted in the reevaluation of the place of African history and its study[7] as a relevant academic field.

Political independence created a supportive environment for the new African historiography to flourish. Newly independent governments funded the establishment of African universities, departments of history, research institutes, national archives, and museums of antiquity. The activity generated in Africa in this period led to the emergence of its dominant schools of thought, like (prominently) the Ibadan School of History, which decried the limitations of missionaries and colonial governments. Others were Makerere University in Uganda, the University of Ghana, and later in 1961, the Dar es Salaam School, which popularized the dependency approaches in Africa. African studies, since its reconstitution into the new African historiography, has acted as the vehicle for African decolonization, redefining the topics of relevance and even localizing Western epistemic frames. It has, through its achievements, changed the way the African past is conceived and studied.

The Ideological and Theoretical Contests of the 1970s to 1980s

The close connection between theory and practice in historiography, as well as between historical works with changing political and socioeconomic contours,[8] ensured that by the 1970s, popular nationalist movements had begun to decline with the euphoria of independence and its historiography. However, the still-existing imperial epistemological

---

7   It has been suggested (by the Hayter Report of 1961) that the recognition that African studies received in British institutions of learning was due to "political changes." In American institutions of learning in the 1960s and 1970s, the introduction of African studies is alleged to be a by-product of the recognition of the importance of area study programs in the Cold War. However, what remains undisputed is the contribution of Professor K. O. Dike's idea of a "multi-disciplinary approach" to African studies in its "legitimization" in academic circles.

8   Ogot, *General History of Africa*.

hegemony still influenced the nature of African studies as well as what came out as knowledge that was applied to the socio-economic realities of the period.

The independence/African nationalist historiography was faulted for its "elitist" focus and the "falsification of the past" and for presenting an oversimplified picture of an essentially equal and socially compact "traditional" society. The nationalist narratives of this historiography were said to have obscured the extent of its effectiveness in pursuance of independence in addressing Africa's sociocultural and economic complexities beyond political independence. The critics also alleged the nationalist historiography of adopting European analogical and teleological methods in the study of Africa's past in its "over-determining" attempt to counter European narratives, therefore, failing to probe further into precolonial historical realities of African material and social life. Thus, this historiography was problematic and increasingly became irrelevant, creating the need for new paradigms.[9]

The dependency theory was developed mainly as an alternative approach to tackling the new challenges. This theory, epitomized by Walter Rodney's influential *How Europe Underdeveloped Africa*, was also criticized for the unsuitability of its concepts in analyzing African history before the emergence of the capitalist world-system, the attention given to external structural factors as against internal ones, in the explanation of Africa's underdevelopment. This unsuitability of the dependency theory in addressing the vacuum left by the failure of the development decade and its modernization theory led to the rise of radical perspectives. These radical tendencies came variously in the form of Trump, dependency, feminist, and ecological and postcolonial traditions. Prominent among these in this period was the Marxist theory adopted by "radical" intellectuals to proffer alternative routes to Africa's socioeconomic liberation.

Popular from at least the mid-1970s to the late 1980s, Marxism as an ideology was identified not only as a theory but a morally superior social representation that offered a more efficient economic system, absent of the taints of economic exploitation and racialism associated with Western capitalist societies.[10] It was attractive to young intellectuals "dissatisfied with bourgeois and capitalist theories, processes, and practices of

---

9   Ogot, *General History of Africa*.
10 Hughes, "Appeal."

development in Africa and around the world, and who wanted to articulate an alternative version and paradigm of development."[11] At Ahmadu Bello University, in Zaria, Nigeria, a respected Marxist school emerged, using Marxism as a scientific method to study Africa, creating a cluster around an African perspective regarded as anticapitalist.[12]

During this period, there were intense arguments about the adoption of precapitalist modes of production. These modes were developed by French Marxist anthropologists and economists and embraced by several historians, contributing to a methodological and historical analysis. It primarily provided an alternative to European-derived laws of development and their ethnocentric analytical basis that were arbitrarily imposed on phenomena and had to be understood in their specific contexts. Although the Marxist and dependency theorists shared affinities in their emphasis on exploitative economic structures, they disagreed on the dynamics responsible for Africa's contemporary underdevelopment. By contrast, the latter identified the internal dynamics of African societies; the former pointed to the influence of external ones. The Marxists' contestations have been credited for enriching the theme of the "liberation struggle" by informing a critical reevaluation of themes covered in the periods of the nationalist historiography, which in turn led to the discussion of a "second liberation."

The Postapartheid African Renaissance of the 1990s

The fall of the apartheid regime in South Africa marked both the end of the struggle for political independence in Africa and another significant step toward recognition of the humanity and rights of all Black people in Africa and worldwide. This led to the reawakening of the idea of a "renascent Africa" originally proposed by Nnamdi Azikiwe and Cheikh Anta Diop. This time it was led by Thabo Mbeki, former president of

---

11 Ogot, *General History of Africa*.
12 The cast is minimal but highly influential. See, among others, works by Cabral, Samir Amin, Slovo, Ruth First, Stuart Hall, Eskor Toyo, Edwin Madunagu, Bala Usman, Bade Onimode, Ola Oni, Ngufi, Nzimiro, and Agozino.

South Africa. South Africa was host to an international conference on the African Renaissance in 1998.

This idea of an Africa rediscovered has been described as "a remembering" of a continent and a people who have suffered from "dismembering" effects of colonialism and "coloniality."[13] The idea covered a wide range of African liberation initiatives, from political decolonization to the Fallism liberation discourse. It also concerns revisiting the discourse on the various ways Africa can achieve socioeconomic liberation and development. African renaissance emphasized an Africanized system of knowledge production that can attend to the demands of African reality: that is, the decolonization of African studies through its educational institutions.

The Popular Rhodes Must Fall and Black Lives Matter Movements

The popular Rhodes Must Fall (RMF) protest movement in South Africa in 2015 and the Black Lives Matter (BLM) protests reoccurring in 2020 are symbolic of the long-time protest against Euro-American socioeconomic and racist systems that have taken on various titles (colonialism, neocolonialism, globalization, and postglobalization) over the years.

The RMF movement, which was initially directed at the statue of Cecil Rhodes, a physical representation of extant colonialist sentiments, soon led to a broader movement to decolonize African education. This was also echoed in the BLM movement, where both the physical and psychological representations of subjugation and inferiority of "Black" people were challenged in widespread protests in 2020. The politics of both the RMF and BLM have promoted the ideas of decoloniality, further opening the space for the insertion of the "epistemology of the South" in various academies. Although "decoloniality" has gained currency in recent years, the distinction between it and "decolonization" can be blurred.

---

13 Ndlovu-Gatsheni, "Revisiting."

Figure I.1. #RMF Statue Removal 05. Photograph by Desmond R. Bowles. Used with permission.

Figure I.2. Justice for Jamar protest march, Minneapolis, Minnesota, November 15, 2015. Photograph by Fibonnaci Blue. Creative Commons License CC BY SA 2.0.

Decoloniality and Epistemologies of the South

Decolonizing the epistemology of the Global South (of which Africa is a major component), which concerns the removal of the provisions of coloniality (the continuation of colonial-like relations after the dismantlement of direct colonialism[14]) in the knowledge production processes of Africa, has been a preoccupation of Africanist intellectuals in the twentieth and twenty-first centuries. The successive periods of anticolonial struggles have led to the point where attention has been on cognitive freedoms from Western-dictated patterns and directions. This is mostly in response to the realization of the continuous impingement of neocolonial structures and modes of power on African identity formations, nation-building projects, and knowledge production.[15]

African academics and Africanists such as Ngugi wa Thiong'o, Basil Davidson, Claude Ake, Chinweizu, Mueni wa Muiu, and Guy Martin have criticized the continuous use of foreign Euro-American ideas and institutions in Africa. For their part, Latin American scholars such as Arturo Escobar, Anibal Quijano, and Walter Mignolo have also strongly pushed their drive for "alternative knowledge as part of their revolt against the oppressive character of the racially-organized, hegemonic, patriarchal and capitalist world order alongside Euro-American epistemological fundamentalism that denies the existence of knowledge from the non-Western parts of the world."[16] These calls from intellectuals from the Global South for the decolonization of epistemologies has, in Africa, taken the expression of a need for the Africanization of its educational institutions beyond their personnel.

The movement for the decolonization of African epistemologies involves devising a system of knowledge production where thought processes are informed by the observable social and ecological interaction that is reality—the thinker's reality (in this case, an African). Therefore, knowledge produced is sensitive to the complexities and nuances of the African continent, against Western hegemonic thought traditions that reduce African academics and universities to a mere conduit for inculcating Western knowledge, values, and worldviews. Take, for example, the

---

14 Ndlovu-Gatsheni, "Revisiting," 2.
15 Ndlovu-Gatsheni, *Coloniality*.
16 Ndlovu-Gatsheni, *Coloniality*, viii.

modernization theory, which interpreted the processes of social and economic development in a "natural" manner that placed Western nations at the apex of economic growth and Africa at the lowest level in a linear sacrosanct trajectory. These and other such Western-celebrated theories, when imported and adopted, impede African developmental attempts, akin to fitting "round pegs in square holes."

We currently live in a slightly different era in African liberation struggles. The struggle has moved almost entirely to academic fields—with an emphasis on the ever-growing importance of research in developing ways to break free of the African socioeconomic squeeze fostered by capitalist structures. In this activity, Africanist intellectuals at the front can rarely afford to engage in knowledge production for the mere intellectual enjoyment of it; they have written extensively on decolonizing the epistemology of the Global South. At once theorists, ideologists, empiricists, and activists, these intellectuals have continued to rally for the reconstitution of African studies in a manner that reflects its realities through continued emphasis on the epistemological decolonization of the Global South.

Chapter Outline

This book encompasses both the decolonizing and decolonial epistemologies and privileges the African voices that have produced the best ideas on these various issues. The role of African studies (the perception and representation of the African past) has been central to different periods of liberation struggles. Having formed the basis for the justification of centuries of Euro-American socioeconomic onslaughts, African studies is the appropriate tool for reversing the economic damage sustained by Africa during these periods. The structure of Western hegemony throughout Africa was designed to dominate African knowledge production systems and its application to African realities in a bid to keep the continent perpetually reliant on the Global North. African studies' origins, however, means that the nature of African studies as a field remains problematic. African perspectives continue to be marginalized or excluded in research, and thus, African studies mostly continues to offer misrepresentations or misunderstandings of the continent. This book responds to the urgent need to eliminate the vestiges of colonialism within the academy and research methodologies and provides a balanced overview of what a feasible decoloniality should look like. In essence, the book endeavors to provide a blueprint for African studies to reconfigure itself for the twenty-first century. The text deploys a holistic approach by identifying and critiquing the limitations to decoloniality, examining the impediments that culminated in the failure of the late twentieth-century struggle for decoloniality, and the problems associated with current African trends that militate against adequate academic decoloniality.

The book is divided into twenty chapters that analyze the central problem—Eurocentric monopoly of knowledge and the exclusion or marginalization of African epistemology or perspectives in research methodologies—while also examining different scholarly voices of decolonization and decoloniality. Also looked at is the contribution and role of women in decoloniality, while following up with the decoloniality of different facets of African studies such as literature, language, the African academy, philosophy, aesthetics, history, and religion. The book culminates in declaring the way forward for decoloniality: African Futurism.

Chapter 1 addresses colonization, seen not only as a historical phenomenon but also as an ethnocentric one that has continued to dominate all aspects of contemporary life, especially monopolization of human epistemology. However, attempts to reverse decolonization and its implications in everyday life have been taking place in Africa since the mid-twentieth century. Such attempts have always encountered difficulties and hesitancy notwithstanding the questions of the best methodology to execute decolonization in the academy—or that of the paradoxical process of liberation within a mind that in itself has been colonized—all of which this chapter seeks to address. Some of the answers to these questions lie in the power of language, especially the role of the English and French languages in establishing and sustaining colonization. This issue raises the problem of how to liberate language as a tool of construction to be used by Africans themselves for self-expression. The decolonization of knowledge is not confined to an academic struggle in methodology but with an intense focus on the thinking process of gender segregation, "raciality," and promotion of inequality engendered by Western-introduced heteropatriarchy, white superiority, and rigidity of societal sexual roles. The chapter introduces the reader to the book's key concept of seeking to end exclusion of the subaltern from global academia with the acceptance and inclusion of global perspectives while also eliminating hierarchies in epistemology to create a balance and decolonize the collective African mind's framework. The chapter concludes with a proposed solution: a collaboration between the academy, the government, and the people as a whole.

Chapter 2 addresses Eurocentrism and its impact on African studies. The chapter generally explains how cultural or racial superiority of the West over non-Westerners as well as understanding them from a Western perspective, which is seen as standard—the justification for colonizing the backward and barbaric non-Westerners. The chapter also shows how Eurocentrism equates modernization with the Western way of life, color, style of governance, language, economy, fashion sense or culture, and infrastructural development. The belief that non-Westerners have no history until their encounter with colonialism still taints the field, thereby violating these peoples' origin, history, and humanity as well as offering a biased retelling of their past. The subject of Eurocentrism and its consequent phenomena of imperialism is further seen in the misinformed belief that climatological factors also contribute to the perceived inferiority of nonwhites in science, thinking, and beauty. Added to the above is the racial thinking that Africans are physically and biologically inferior to their Western counterparts. The current dilemma, however, is that all the above and more have morphed in modernity to be reflected in education and imperialist history. The chapter asserts that the solution lies in decolonization and decoloniality, that is, Africanizing Africa and the Western acceptance of "other" perspectives while experiencing Africa and engaging in the logical analysis of Africans. Decolonization faces not only the obstacle of resistance from the colonizers but also that of the colonized, who perhaps have accepted the normalcy of coloniality.

Chapter 3 critically examines the silence or exclusion of subalterns in Africa, Southeast Asia, South America, and women in academic publications, as well as its far-reaching implications in international relations, pedagogy, and policy. The silence about the inferiority of the subaltern in terms of global power and not population (in which the subaltern collectively is in the majority) is to justify the idea of Eurocentrism and validate the belief in the monopoly of knowledge and its centrality and universality. Consequently, these beliefs tainted aspects of African studies throughout the latter twentieth century, as the field was dominated by scholars from or based in the United States and Europe. Contrary to Eurocentric belief, the concept of decolonization is not limited to the liberation of the national sovereignty of colonial nations but is also about economic, political, and cultural issues. Indeed, coloniality is the barrier to the expression of subaltern epistemology: hence, the purpose of this chapter is to resolve these problematic issues, beginning first with looking at the difference between coloniality and colonization to advance the need for a decolonial approach to liberating knowledge. Then we can rationalize how epistemic violence requires decoloniality and how it could be prevented using a decolonial methodology before proceeding to identify the barriers to incorporating subaltern epistemologies in the academy and proffering appropriate solutions. Finally, the chapter advocates the empowerment of subaltern epistemologies by redefining knowledge. The chapter also explores questions pertinent to this process, such as whether or not subalterns can express themselves and overcome the many barriers in world systems. Examples of how Afrocentric methodology—African epistemologies or perspectives—could be applied include the social sciences (in the academia), in art as well as politics.

Chapter 4 attacks Eurocentric perspectives of knowledge that see everyday practices of non-Westerners as brutal, demonic, and backward while ignoring the value of their diverse characteristics. The chapter argues that these biases and misconceptions validate the imposition of their perceived superior knowledge system and methods to replace indigenous ones. However, as the chapter argues, the failings of this practice are that Western epistemology has not been able to cater for (all) the needs and nuances of the African continent—hence the call for Africanizing knowledge systems, language, and epistemology as the crucial step to reconstructing the history of the continent going forward. The core of this chapter is the adoption of the three-pronged fork of language, art, and creativity as the tools essential to the decolonization of knowledge and the collaborative adoption of African indigenous languages in learning and teaching is posited as the solution to the coloniality of knowledge.

To many scholars, the term "research" in the African context has been to ultimately allude to the era of colonialism and imperialism in Africa. This stance has contributed to the growing calls for (as well as institutional reluctance toward the use of) the indigenous methodology in research on Africa. As we learn in chapter 5, this is mainly in response to the Eurocentric approach of research on Africa, which has chiefly been the extraction of data and information from the continent and subjecting them to Western interpretation without sufficient interaction with the people being researched, thereby resulting in erroneous interpretation of facts owing to a lack of understanding of the peculiarities of the Other's cultural ethos. The African "Other" is silenced to emphasize the assumed superiority of the West and also to archive and alter its form. It is this act of collecting data and colonizing African research that has prompted the need for research to be redeemed, albeit with a rehabilitated purpose. Therefore, decolonizing research starts with tracing the Eurocentric methodologies of researching the subaltern cultural ethos, the explorative mechanism, and its consequent action of appropriation to impose colonial practice, a means to an end—subverting or breaking down this Eurocentric methodology imposition on the research of the Other. This chapter's goal—decolonizing research—includes challenging the Western monopoly of epistemological perspectives in research and resituating indigenous methodology at the center. The chapter also aims to establish a world of unbiased research of the Other, while also counterbalancing it with the traditional and modern way of knowing. This requires emphasizing the role of indigenous languages and cultures in research. Consequently, it also involves African studies scholars from outside the continent (i.e., North America, Europe) asking broader questions about their own biases.

Chapter 6 examines the importance of oral tradition in communicating knowledge. This tradition should not be underestimated, especially when it is the preferred mode of communication. While the Western methodology of research favors oral tradition in Western Classics, such as the *Iliad, Odyssey, Beowulf,* as well as the Qur'an and the Bible, the neglect of the same in African societies, which inarguably outnumber their Western counterparts, has called for its examination. This chapter provides a case study on how oral tradition goes beyond the intrinsic value of preserving culture to being crucial for decolonial research. The analysis of oral tradition includes its pattern in Africa vis-à-vis its general nature and social context as well as its recording and representation in the context of global neocolonialism. This demonstrates the immense importance of oral traditions in African cultures as a tool of epistemic liberation. As the chapter will show, oral traditions in African research methodology have suffered neglect for many of the same reasons African crafts have been rejected by the Western world—which sees art as something to be viewed for aesthetic values, studied, and preserved for display only. Language in Africa is diverse, and translation to English drains this language of cultural meaning and aesthetic value. The genres of oral tradition include epic, proverbs, poetry, folktales, myths, historical narratives, religious performances, such as the Egungun (masquerades) festival, and finally, jokes or riddles. The accuracy of oral tradition was also examined and likewise its relationship with colonialism. Oral tradition serves as a tool of epistemic liberation by being adopted in pedagogy from preschool to university; their importance transcends the humanities, as they can also be made to preserve indigenous solutions to health care, natural sciences, and so on.

Chapters 7 and 8 examine the significant advocates of decolonization and decoloniality and their diverse contributions. With the hegemony of the Global North hampering the progress of the Global South, the quest to decolonize is gradually becoming a cultural transgression in the Global South, hence the increase in scholarship bordering on decoloniality. These scholars include Walter Rodney, Achille Mbembe, V. Y. Mudimbe, Molefi Asante, Mahmood Mamdani, Archie Mafeje, Samir Amin, Claude Ake, Ali Mazrui, Ndlovu-Gatsheni, Walter Mignolo, Enrique Dussel, and Boaventura de Sousa Santos. The ideas of decolonization and decoloniality, like other intellectual ideas, have been birthed and furthered by people championing the cause. Chapter 7 subsequently explores the work of major scholars that have helped chart a path for African studies to advance. Walter Rodney's decolonization efforts focus on African socio-economy as he rejects the Eurocentric belief that Africans are incapable of managing their own natural and human resources, with a counter-analytical evaluation of how European activities of colonialism and imperialism are responsible for African underdevelopment. Similarly, Achille Mbembe questions the Eurocentric hegemonic monopoly of knowledge, which to him is not a sign of intellectualism and argues for pluriversalism—the global recognition of all other disregarded epistemology as valid—while calling for a radical African approach to resistance, dumping Western culture, and achieving epistemic decoloniality. Mbembe's significant contribution is on the question of the dual identity of Africans: one imposed on them by European imperialists and their original one as Africans. His solution to this, as found in his book, is the reinvention of

Africa; for him, this project of rebirth depends on Africans themselves. Molefi Asante's decolonial contributions are more prominent in his quest to revolutionize the academic landscape—Africanizing academic curricula—furthered by establishing a PhD program that later became known as Africology. Other scholars examined include Mahmood Mamdani, Archie Mafeje, Samir Amin, Claude Ake, and Ali Mazrui.

Chapter 8 discusses the voices of decoloniality. With the hegemony of the Global North predominantly hampering the progress of the Global South, the quest to decolonize is gradually becoming a cultural transgression in the Global South, hence the increase in scholarship oriented toward decoloniality. Sabelo Ndlovu-Gatsheni argues that Eurocentric ideals' insistence on rationality as the benchmark of humanity and civilization serves to alienate the Global South and dehumanize non-Europeans—creating a global hierarchy with Africa at the bottom of the ladder. This global coloniality is preserved through the colonial matrix of power, being, knowledge, and nature. Mignolo's contribution mainly addresses the composition of coloniality in present times while reflecting on the historical moments that created and preserved it. He identifies decoloniality—through his works—as a political project; his scholarship touches on how decoloniality can expose the logic of coloniality, the rhetoric of modernity, and the colonial epistemic difference he believes is responsible for Western dominance of knowledge and culture. Dussel contributes to the decolonial struggle through his works on the philosophy of liberation and transmodernity. In his view decoloniality can be achieved by the movement of the subalterns by reaching inward to affirm legacies rejected by Euro-modernity. Santos contributes to decoloniality with insight from the perspective of sociology and law while also establishing his premise in the crises of modernity and proposing a solution: the need for Global South critical thinkers to reflect inward and seek answers to the current concerns outside Euro-American modern centers and scientism.

Chapter 9 unconventionally attempts a critique of the idea of decolonizing knowledge (in isolation, as has been the focus of most epistemic decolonial scholars) by focusing on the problems attached to such an opinion. The chapter examines the danger of repeated failures by looking at the reality of the current economic and political situations as well as learning lessons from more conscious attempts at decolonialization, which started in the 1960s and ended in failure in the 1980s. This is prompted by the informed understanding that coloniality—engendered by postcolonialism is not only sustained in epistemology but as well in culture, economics, and politics. This chapter proposes an all-encompassing and holistic decoloniality—a joint venture by the academy, government, policymakers, and the people—having learned from the failures of the 1980s.

Studies in decolonization, like almost every other area of life, have marginalized women with men taking the lead role—creating the impression that women have contributed nothing to decolonization discourse. This is a great disservice to the efforts of female scholars from the Global South, such as Chandra Talpade Mohanty, Bolanle Awe, Simi Afonja, Nina Mba, Fatou Sow, Oyeronke Oyewumi, Filomina Steady, Amina Mama, Ayesha Imam, and others. Chapter 10, therefore, is committed to giving voice and recognition to the efforts of these women as well as examining their contributions to decoloniality. For example, Mohanty contributes to the social dichotomy created by the West in which Western women are seen as liberated, sophisticated, and in control of their lives. By contrast, women in the Third World are seen as oppressed without taking into consideration the uniqueness of the Other nor the resistance of women to patriarchy. Studied in this chapter is Oyewunmi, another scholar whose contribution specializes in the Eurocentric misconstrued generalization of women of the Oyo Yoruba (as a case study). In her argument, condemning Eurocentric "invention" of women, social hierarchy is not determined by gender but rather by social identity and position. This chapter study also examines the contradiction in Afrocentric scholarship: the marginalization of women. This is reflected in the work of Ayesha while counterbalancing it with Hunt's assertion that African historiography is not silent when it comes to women. This chapter concludes with an examination of organizations established for the promotion of women's interests: AAWORD, WORDOC, and DAWN.

Chapter 11 outlines the varied scholarly engagements surrounding the experiences of lesbian, gay, bisexual, transgender, and queer/questioning (LGBTQ) people in the world, particularly in Africa. The reality that sexual identity is a fluid and individual construction is still relatively alien to African academic culture and has created numerous pressing issues for nonheterosexual individuals. While male- and female-centric (feminists inclusive) ideas and arguments are considered, the exclusion of another category of humans not defined by gender (the LGBTQ community) becomes apparent. They are not only excluded from African society at large, but have been marginalized in African academia as well, with there being a paucity of materials in decolonial discourse on LGBTQ inclusivity.

Relying on the information presented by activist scholars, chapter 11 explores the human rights abuse issues that have remained the signature of homophobic laws, especially in Third World countries. An in-depth case is made for the theoretical fusion of the feminist and queer theories as an opportunity to examine the subject of sexual minorities, which sets the stage for a further exposition on sexual colonialism and the decolonization of sexual identities. However, the chapter chronicles other salient problems surrounding the subject. These include suicidality among young members of the LGBTQ community, issues concerning their sexual health, and the media's role in the positive representation of the queer community. Lastly, the chapter discusses concepts of political and religious homophobia as drivers of the African homophobic policy, while noting the positive benefits of religious acceptance of queer people, and the experiences of heterosexual parents with nonheterosexual children.

In chapter 12, the decoloniality of the African academy is discussed in depth. Education is seen as the knowledge hub of society—driving scientific and technological advancement. At the same time, research plays a fundamental role in producing new knowledge for universities as well as for sociocultural and economic development. However, as discussed in this chapter, the story in Africa is not just about poor infrastructural development: inadequate funding, lack of research interest and inadequate education policies, lack of independence and adequate support from the government, and outdated colonial curricula are all identified as factors responsible for the problems of Africa and the African university. These problems have resulted in calls for reform from African scholars as well as the need to decolonize the curriculum, given colonialism is responsible for the destruction of the local capacity to promote the knowledge system by replacing it with colonial education. This chapter seeks to resolve the issue of decolonizing the African academy by examining the history of universities in Africa and their impact on African studies, the knowledge being produced by these universities and their limitations in addressing African problems, and efforts and initiatives of postcolonial African scholars to achieve decolonization and transform African universities to respond to African needs. The chapter concludes with the recommendation of inclusion of African indigenous knowledge systems and language in the curricula, learning materials, and medicine.

Systematically following the previous essay, chapter 13 attempts a decoloniality of language. Frantz Fanon believes that Africans are subjected to Western culture through the imposition of Western languages—stripping Africans of their true identity and heritage. This has urged African scholars to seek decolonization of the African language, with the government adopting the usage of indigenous language for business. The 1962 conference at Makerere University in Kampala, Uganda, is credited with having triggered a formal discourse on the language question in Africa. The conference title alone, "A Conference of African Writers of English Expression," meant that African writers in indigenous languages were marginalized. This made Wali and Ngugi wa Thiong'o question the rationale behind using a foreign language to express African experience with a relativist viewpoint that views continued nonindigenous language usage as glorification of colonialism and portrays African language as inferior.

As the chapter will show, experimental research has proven that students taught in indigenous languages performed better in some cases owing to ease of comprehension. At the same time, use of a foreign language as the lingua franca tends to alienate the vast majority of the African population from contributing to national development. The interaction of foreign and indigenous languages notably has created middle-ground languages, such as Pidgin and Krio, in defiant response to domination by foreign languages. The onus is on the policymakers to decolonize language: with the common example of North Africa providing evidence of how indigenous language can be used effectively without losing the benefits that foreign languages can bring.

Chapter 14 complements the preceding one, critically examining the decolonization project in African literature and languages. Contributions to the decolonization project in Africa, since the end of colonialism, have been excellent on the whole. It is, therefore, necessary to state that scholarly work in postcolonial Africa has faced some scrutiny where intellectuals have examined how colonialism has had an ineradicable effect on Africans and how this can be remedied. The results are not just physical; they are also systemic and mental. Similarly, this chapter is dedicated to examining the ongoing decolonial project. In other words, the decolonizing project is not just a project to scrutinize the effects of colonialism on our political structures but also a way to help Africans rediscover their true identities. One of the main tasks of decolonization is not to compulsorily return Africans to precolonial lifestyles and beliefs; however, it is an attempt to help us all understand what it is like to be African. This chapter examines the efforts of the decolonization of African literature and languages, and it will also examine both literature and language. The chapter also explores the growing call for a rejection of Westernization and in its place, the adoption of traditional African literature and indigenous languages to help dismantle the vestiges of colonialism in Africa—especially as it pertains to African minds—before concluding by asking a critical question: is true decolonization of African literature and languages possible?

Chapter 15 serves to examine the uniqueness and relevance in the identity of African feminist writers especially given their focus on vibrant, heterogeneous, and dynamic local contexts—foregrounding the shifting and variant conceptions of feminist ideologies in Africa—thereby contributing to the decolonizing of knowledge about African women, gender, society, and nations. The chapter also explores the growth and development of feminism in Africa, as well as the different conceptualizations of feminism by African scholars and critics. This will provide insight into the new dialogue within feminist and gender studies in Africa and examine the ideology of selected works and authors with regard to feminism. It will also further explore the relevance of African feminist writers concerning the African woman and culture while examining the writer's responsibilities in ideological reformation and illumination of women's struggles. The chapter argues that the African feminist writer is a product of traditional and modern influences on gender issues and therefore quite relevant to present societies. It also argues that the classification of the feminist writer and her works reveal a nonhomogeneity in the various conceptions of feminism(s). The chapter points to the ambiguity surrounding the concept of feminism in Africa. It goes further to discuss the African feminist writer as a bridge between the modern and traditional practices that give women agency.

Chapter 16 is an in-depth examination of the various mediums promoting African culture and creative expressions within the African space. African creativity is not shaped by the influence of colonization,

Westernization, or globalization; it was an inherent characteristic that was found in the cultural heritage and precolonial creative expression. Thus, it is the creativity that is foregrounded here rather than the reaction to outside influences. Various themes such as African languages, African fashion, and African films are explored to show how they help to not only promote but also to sustain African culture, heritage, and creative expression. The importance of language in the promotion and reclaiming of African identity and culture is also touched upon here. The use of the African language started with oral literature in music and poems, yet, as this chapter shows, in the post-independence era, many African musicians such as Makeba, Chiwoniso, Malian Baliake Sissoko, Yvonne Chaka Chaka, and Asa use their music (and certain indigenous African musical instruments) to help promote its use. Fashion is at the heart of African creative expression, which has successfully evolved over the decades and centuries. Despite the presence of Western fashion, Africans have been able to explore the fashion world by using it to counter political domination and has, thus, become a unifying factor for homogenous and erogenous culture. The cultural and technological exploitation of Africa is further depicted in the chapter with the example of how films were used to convince Africans to fight in the Second World War. Actors like Tunde Kelani explore and promote the Yoruba culture while also making complementary use of the white man's technology—a typical example of how African artists have successfully helped to break the hold of colonization while comfortably combining their own indigenous styles with the fashionable trends of the West.

Chapter 17 aims to define the essence of the decolonization of African history: its origins, justification, processes, objectives, and anticipated outcomes. It starts by retracing the history of colonialism in Africa beginning with the transatlantic slave trade and the eventual partition of the 1880s, further examining the efforts of scholars in the late nineteenth century to decolonize African history. This is seen as the foundation upon which decolonization in every other sense gains a foothold—through supplying historical consciousness and knowledge of self-worth required to assert one's own indigenous culture. The chapter critiques the economic and political implications of capitalism, which has created economic inequality in Africa. Besides the economic problems created by underfunding, other issues identified include lack of political support, insufficient will, a lack of commitment by African scholars, and dwindling awareness of the general populace. Three phases of decolonization of African history are identified: the first was resistance to the imposition of colonialism (1880 to 1914) in the form of armed resistance; the second, starting in the 1950s, combined intellectual and armed struggle; while the final phase began in the postcolonial struggle of the 1970s. Prominent among scholars who set out to correct misconceptions about Africa is K. O. Dike, who restored a strong narrative to African history. The chapter delves into how oral tradition was promoted as a viable historical source but also how the interdisciplinary approach was embraced as methodology. Also examined are the institutions through which African history is being decolonized and the objective that the decolonizing of African history serves, while concluding with the impacts of the struggle, especially in African universities.

The focus of chapter 18 is on how African traditional religion (ATR) has suffered from the impact of colonialism into the twenty-first century. The coming of European culture and Christian religion impeded the growth of ATR. The chapter shows the desecration of ATR practices as a potent tool to un-Africanize Africans, while Europeans were oblivious of the positive contributions of ATR to African society in maintaining peace, encouraging political order, stabilizing the economy, and initiating moral values. Hence, the mission of this essay is to remove the misconceptions first by introducing the need to understand the African language as a means to understand the people and their practices. Also, the concept of God is examined from differing perspectives to explain the significance of ATR. The link between ATR and African medicine was also seen as false and was demonized. Then it was replaced with Western hospitals for healing. Decolonizing ATR in this context would mean showing how it is used not only for healing but also how it was the equal of Western science. However, the task of decolonizing religion, like other forms of decoloniality, is a governmental project—the recognition of ATR as a state religion. The study concludes with certain positive ATR practices and an explanation of their belief system.

Chapter 19 focuses on different schools of thought on African philosophy. The first, ethno-philosophers, believe that African philosophy is evident in people's religious beliefs, myths, proverbs, and in folkloric forms uncontaminated by Western ideas. The second believes it is the analysis of and the reflection on African social realities and conceptual systems as well as new resources of knowledge by contemporary philosophers. Others—Universalist philosophers—believe in the universality of philosophy, negating ethno-philosophy, which they see as debased. This chapter attempts a decoloniality of these philosophical approaches and notions to generate working philosophies and philosophical traditions for the current African reality. The language of learning and teaching is also examined followed by the need to accommodate courses that expose students to the diversity of African "truths" and realities.

Chapter 20 examines the concept of African Futurism. Some Afrocentric scholars believe neocolonial discourse is the right approach to achieve inclusive African emancipation centered on African identity, to provide cohesion and African episteme, and to proffer Afrocentric solutions to African socioeconomic problems. This allows for reinvention of the African identity and redirection of African developmental trajectory away from subjective tendencies. Seen as the advanced stage of decoloniality, African Futurism involves the application of "traditional" (indigenous) instruments of articulation and cohesion, such as Afro-spirituality, myths, folklores, and indigenous techno-scientific innovations deployed in their capacity to actualize future possibilities and sever ties with the Global North—its ontology and logocentrism. The main distinguishing factor between African Futurism and Afrofuturism is that while the former relates to the ideals and reality of Africans in the continent, the latter centers on the Western experience of diasporic Africans. This study examines the diverging African futurists' projection: whether the best solution for Africa is to adopt Western approaches owing to the advancements that Europe and North America have made or reject them entirely. The question of the African identity is also raised vis-à-vis how the African peoples can be unified in this common goal by awareness of the diversity of their race, language, beliefs, and historical experience. This unity becomes vital in light of the need for Africa to, for example, partake in the coming fourth industrial revolution. As hitherto pointed out, although the chapters are independent in their extensive discourse and analysis of their subject matter, they also inextricably complement one another. Hence, have an excellent explorative read.

Part One

Knowledge Production

Chapter One

Decoloniality and Decolonizing Knowledge

Colonization, as a historical-cum-ethnocentric phenomenon, does not merely exist in the past; instead, it is a living historical event that takes shape in institutions and, more importantly, also in ideologies and human knowledge. For hundreds of years colonization has been defined in terms that have gained global acceptance, including the contexts of established hierarchies of gender, race, and class; standards of success; and understandings in academia.

Since the mid-twentieth century, there have been numerous attempts (some of them a lot more earnest than others) at decolonization in our school systems, our everyday lives, and in universities. However, there have been predictable barriers and many unanswered questions. For instance, how may one best achieve decolonization? Furthermore, what does it even mean to decolonize? Should one approach decolonization through the use of language, curriculum adjustment, or complete system restructuring? But how can one participate in acts of decolonization when one's mind has been influenced by colonized ideals? Put another way, how can one consciously think in a decolonized fashion when all thought processes have been intrinsically colonized? This essay seeks to challenge mainstream perspectives on the philosophical requirements of decolonization.

Even if we do not wish to admit it, colonization has shaped even the very best of our institutions of learning and understandings of knowledge. Lewis R. Gordon, an American philosopher, posed an interesting question in 2014 related to this matter: if knowledge is colonized, was it ever free in the first place? Indeed, the general notion of "knowledge" is that it is only available in the context of modern Europe. Anything related to history, science, or discovery prior to encounters with modern Europe—or anything outside of Europe—has up until recently not been considered knowledge at all.[1] This notion is so ingrained in broader society and even in some academic fields that it cannot be described as anything other than evidence of a collectively colonized mind. This state of a European-based or Eurocentric mind is so central and powerful that it even affects how one perceives and uses language. As Gordon further noted, when one assesses language, the tendency is to consider roots and sources from European or Mediterranean areas (and only rarely Western Asia areas). However, in reality, the roots and sources that one traditionally considers to be either Latin or Greek can often have more ancient links to Egyptian or Km.tian (or other non-European or nonwhite) words. For example, the Egyptian word *Crethi* and the Km.tian word *kotket* can be discovered by way of the Hebrew word *Crethi*, which means "to cut."[2]

Through academic language as well, colonization has influenced all thought processes and methodologies that have consistently undercut nonwhite, nonmale groups. For example, aboriginal professors Bonita Lawrence and Enakshi Dua have even criticized antiracism scholarship for not being either inclusive or sensitive enough, particularly when it excludes aboriginal peoples' perspectives and culture.[3] The obvious answer to this crisis of exclusion would be to include more aboriginal voices like Lawrence's and Dua's so there is wider representation.

However, wider inclusion of aboriginal voices is not without its problems. Lawrence, even when conveying her own experience of racism, knows that she might not be able to speak for an entire indigenous population. Firstly, as an academic, she is already in a place of privilege that few experience in her community. As a result, her voice can never actually "speak for" her entire community. Secondly, not being a traditional elder, she does not represent the body of knowledge considered to be most significant for the aboriginal peoples. Thirdly, her language must be academic in nature in order to receive any credence. But this academic style is far removed from the nature of common aboriginal language—thus making matters of relevance and relatability all the more complicated.[4]

---

1 Gordon, "Disciplinary Decadence," 81.
2 Gordon, "Disciplinary Decadence," 84.
3 Lawrence and Dua, "Decolonizing Antiracism." 122.
4 Lawrence and Dua, "Decolonizing Antiracism," 122.

Lawrence has admitted that she often finds herself asking to whom she is even speaking as an academic.[5]

The issue of language is perhaps most critical when examining the process of decolonizing knowledge. Therefore, even with all of its merits or demerits, language cannot express every phenomenon because it has its own limitations. In the case of the English language in particular, ripe with colonized history and the mark of white men, the limitations are almost endless. Indeed, because white English-speaking males were the first to become academics, they could use the language to their advantage because the language was, in essence, designed chiefly for them. In such a way, with their privilege, they could continue to control and dictate just how language was to be understood and propagated beyond the walls of the university. They could also shape the histories of nonwhite, nonmale populations of various kinds and establish hierarchies of race, class, and gender—with white, heterosexual men of course being at the top of the hierarchy. All of this came from the simple yet resounding power of words. Language has a way of shaping not only histories but also the minds of those who read such histories.

Undoubtedly, words are powerful tools. But what happens when these tools can only be wielded by a select few, who in turn have the capability to write the stories about those without access to such tools? The aboriginal people, for example, are now presented with a dilemma. With this inherently colonized language construct, they can articulate to some extent the anguish they feel about not using tools designed for them. They can even try to reconstruct their histories. However, can they ever really completely attain their decolonization with a language never intended for their use? How can they feel comfortable in an atmosphere that was originally the invention of white heterosexual men? Arguably then, language must be reclaimed by nonwhite, nonmale populations. But this takes time, and the methods to completely reconstruct language are hardly intuitive.

Claudio Moreira and Marcelo Diversi are two academics from Brazil who have combated issues of colonized knowledge through communication and collaborative literature that transcend class structures. They have collaborated on several articles and a book. Each time they collaborate, they must decide whose name will be presented first in the final

---

5   Lawrence and Dua, "Decolonizing Antiracism," 122.

product. However, they make their decision in an unconventional way: according to fate. In the author's note in their first book, they wrote: "We write together, and we refuse to be forced into the positive reductionism that creates an illusion of order and rank in a collaboration marked by love, respect, and admiration for one another. So, we tossed a coin into the air."[6] Yes, a coin toss is all Moreira and Diversi (or Diversi and Moreira) use to decide order—with no semblance of the arbitrary hierarchy that has been grounded into academia. Moreira and Diversi are both Brazilians, but they are fully aware of being brought up on opposite sides of the class spectrum—something that makes their collaborative relationship all the more unusual. When they met in their teenage years, Moreira had graduated high school and started working in order to support his family and himself. Meanwhile, Diversi was attending university without any need for a job to help support his loved ones or himself. However, in spite of their differences, they both shared a passion for reshaping a system that favored riches and privilege. Consequently, in the evenings as young men, they would meet together to read poetry and revel in the idea of a public revolution.[7]

Soon, Diversi and Moriera decided to become writing partners and produce a revolution of their own. They knew they had much to learn from each other's experiences, and in their collaboration they sensed a microcosm of an ideal social utopia under the "vision of unconditional inclusiveness."[8] With their differences in upbringing yet similar passions, these writers feel they can participate in decolonization through their work because they intentionally discuss issues concerning Western ideologies.[9] They were initially discouraged from writing a book together because "junior scholars should write their own books, period."[10] But Moreira and Diversi knew that in their refusal to adhere to scholarly norms, they were decolonizing what was considered to be the standard.[11] They knew that in their collaboration, they could attest to "cooperative and collectivist

---

6 Moreira and Diversi, "Betweeners Speak Up," 399.
7 Moreira and Diversi, "Betweeners Speak Up," 400.
8 Moreira and Diversi, "Betweeners Speak Up," 401.
9 Moreira and Diversi, "Betweeners Speak Up."
10 Moreira and Diversi, "Betweeners Speak Up," 404.
11 Moreira and Diversi, "Betweeners Speak," 405.

principles"[12] and social democracy.[13] Moreira and Diversi believe that flipping a coin and "writing together is an act of resistance against the academic ranking system and the idea that better work comes from isolated individuals."[14] I argue that we can take Diversi and Moreira as an inspiration for what to pursue in the future. We should reach out to others and accept as many different points of view as possible. Furthermore, we should not insist upon useless hierarchies that reinforce the belief that only some are deserving of knowledge. Only when we include others can we bring some balance to knowledge and decolonize our collective mind's framework.

With some academic and everyday language considerations in mind, we should also turn to other academic methods of decolonization. Dr. Shose Kessi, a professor from the University of Cape Town, has studied decolonization, especially with regard to preventing sexual violence promoted by colonialist ideals. On July 25, 2017, she presented at a colloquium called "Decolonization, Pluriversality, and African-Situatedness in Sexuality and Sexuality-Related Violence Research and Advocacy" and explained that scholars must ask themselves three questions:

1. How has the history of colonization shaped society? (In Kessi's work, she asks herself how the history of colonization has shaped a society of sexual violence).
2. How do we as researchers and even everyday individuals reproduce this colonized history in our values and beliefs?
3. How do we resist and utilize alternatives to the colonized framework?[15]

According to Kessi, there are three organizing principles that allow this colonized history to be manifested in our present: capitalism, racism, and hetero-patriarchy.[16] These organizing principles work in all aspects of our lives—even in ways which go unnoticed because we have been programmed to find such principles as normal. In fact, our schemas have

---

12   Moreira and Diversi, "Missing Bodies."
13   Diversi and Moreira, *Betweener Talk*.
14   Diversi and Moreira, "Betweeners Speak," 405.
15   African Psychologies, "Decolonising Knowledge."
16   African Psychologies, "Decolonising Knowledge."

been developed by these organizing principles of colonialism since our infancy, and for this reason it takes extra effort to denounce them.

These organizing principles are validated by powerful institutions and entities like science and, most of all, the nation-state. Science, for example, allows for a pyramidal structure of class, race, and gender to emerge when it shows "evidence" of Africans having the lowest IQs, or of women and men as being fundamentally different physiologically and psychologically. However, from a decolonized point of view, this "evidence" is based only on presupposed prejudices and assumptions.[17] Strictly speaking, scientists may have accurately predicted certain patterns based on gender and race, which may have, in turn, caused these scientists to misinterpret the data that they saw or even to subconsciously rearrange the data to fit their own perspective. To be sure, even though we typically imagine "science" as an unfailing, unbiased discipline, this is not always the case. There can be faulty science. Unfortunately, this faulty science can also reproduce itself and lead to more faulty science, thereby confusing what is actually factual. Ultimately, this faulty science can become ingrained in the fabric of knowledge.

The nation-state is notorious about perpetuating racial, class, and gender hierarchies. After all, the nation-state in all its forms, founded on the binary of "we" and "them," has always found ways of defining what it means to be a "true" citizen and how to punish those who do not conform to this definition. It is no accident that men traditionally have more public access and women are confined to private access. The heterosexual family unit is universally considered to symbolize the balance of the nation-state. The woman has a fundamental role to play in this unit in the private sector, as in bringing up her children. In doing so, she is a key instiller of the nation-state's values and culture. Consequently, if a woman deviates from her role—let's say by not raising children or by identifying as lesbian—she is considered a threat to the nation-state. Indeed, "sexual appropriateness is always tied to ideas of reproduction."[18] This means that sexual choice is dictated by colonialism. If men or women go against their assigned heterosexual roles, they are considered to be unnatural citizens. The nation-state makes this clear through law and implicit culture,

---

17 African Psychologies, "Decolonising Knowledge."
18 African Psychologies, "Decolonising Knowledge."

which means that it condones sexual violence against such "unnatural citizens."[19]

Dr. Kessi maintained that there is no one perfect way to resist this colonized sexual violence or colonized culture because any answer comes with a great deal of self-reflection. However, there are some things to consider when conducting research from a decolonized perspective, which include the following contentions:

1. We must make sure that our research is outwardly focused and not internally focused. In other words, we must understand our place as researchers.
2. We must ask ourselves how our work counteracts colonialism by confirming that our research does not reproduce the same historical conventions that have been propagated, in some cases, for hundreds of years.
3. We must collect narratives from the people we are studying because ultimately the people are the true experts on their own lives. For this reason, having the right questions to ask our participants is essential. Without the right questions, the best narratives cannot shine through.
4. Research and activism are two inseparable, joint facets in decolonializing frameworks of knowledge.[20]

From Kessi, there are three vital notes that should be added below:

1. We cannot insert our own perspectives and experiences into others' perspectives and experiences—except if the perspectives and experiences coalesce at some critical nodal points.
2. In our research, by ensuring that our work does not simply repeat received biases, we are giving the marginalized a voice. By ensuring that we are activists, we are giving others the chance to be their own best advocate.
3. Because the inherently political nature of colonization is impossible to ignore, it is useful to consider the act of decolonizing as the act of creating "self-governing nation-states"[21]—in other words, states that are not bound by any tyrannical system that dictates all laws, customs, and interactions.

---

19 African Psychologies, "Decolonising Knowledge."
20 African Psychologies, "Decolonising Knowledge."
21 Hargreaves, *Decolonization*.

Joseph Achille Mbembe has some useful insight into how universities across all disciplines can decolonize knowledge. In 2017, at the Duke Franklin Humanities Institute, Mbembe presented his views on how universities must adapt to new knowledge in order to survive. According to Mbembe the university should be considered a "truly common and public good" and a "microcosm of a society in which each voice counts." He feels that "co-belonging makes sense." However, he also warned that universities are currently facing a lot of challenges, particularly generational ones. With today's youth, technology has become inculcated in their minds, creating an entirely "different self" that universities must acknowledge. Furthermore, knowledge today is unbounded and not nearly as rigid and limited to specific fields as it had been in previous generations. Knowledge now requires skill in many forms: reading, writing, interpreting images, and public speaking, for example. Necessarily, traditional teaching methods must be reimagined.[22]

Yet even with all of these challenges, Mbembe added that universities have reached a point of "heightened curiosity and experimentation" because Africans are finding increasingly that their experience of the world is not represented by current knowledge and must instead be examined through "new bodies of thought." Happily, at this time, knowledge itself is being questioned not just in Africa but also around the world, particularly with regard to matter, time, politics, and culture. Currently, the gap between the sciences and the humanities is closing, and there are more subfields within disciplines. The humanities used to teach that human beings are separate from the natural world because they are unique. However, as science and the studies of posthumanism and ethnography show, there is no great separation between objects and subjects. Even cognition, which was considered to be the most unique facet of human beings, can be replicated to some extent in machines that, like human beings, can make decisions.[23]

This expansion has brought about a vast number of academic journals, which indicates just how interrelated various disciplines in the humanities and sciences—of both the social and natural kind—have become. However, with this expansion comes complications. Now more than ever, with evidence that human beings are not particularly unique, academics

---

[22] Duke Franklin Humanities Institute, "Achille Mbembe."
[23] Duke Franklin Humanities Institute, "Achille Mbembe."

are faced once again with an ancient question: who or what exactly is the human being, particularly the human being who is not Western?[24]

Mbembe emphasized that, at this juncture in history, universities and academics must use three methods by which the "knowledge landscapes" as we know them can be altered. One, there must be a continuous critique of the assumptions found in Western thought. For example, as science has shown, nature is actually not fixed and is not necessarily measurable. Now that this critique has been presented and verified time and time again, there are steps that must be taken in order to establish more accurate truths. Two, there must be a "recategorization of the human" altogether—in a way that does not configure with standard thoughts. Three, the normalization of human sciences must occur.[25]

To these three points, Mbembe added two more considerations. According to Mbembe, activism is what allows all fields to relate to a common goal of decolonization. Furthermore, multivocality is the main goal of decolonization, for it allows us to care about people in a more "planetary" sense—in the context of people's individual natural environments.[26]

It is important to remember that a major tenet of decolonization must involve the inclusion of all kinds of stories—especially from those who have been historically marginalized. From such stories, history can in a sense be reclaimed, and notions of knowledge can be reconceptualized. Most notably, through stories from the marginalized, the most personal methods on the continuance of decolonization can be discovered.

Dr. Olivia U. Rutazibwa of Ghent University, who specializes on European Union (EU) human rights issues, has formed her own theory of decolonization after coming to terms with the realities of racism and her own racial identity during her student years. In 2011 at TEDx Flanders, Rutazibwa revealed her story and how it elucidated a theory of decolonization. As Rutazibwa explained to her audience, she grew up thinking that there was no such thing as racism, despite the fact that she was Rwandan and adopted by white Flemish parents. Her parents presented her—unconsciously—with two basic colonized notions: that anything is possible through hard work and that there is no such thing as unequal opportunity. Rutazibwa existed in this blissful ignorance until the spring

---

24 Duke Franklin Humanities Institute, "Achille Mbembe."
25 Duke Franklin Humanities Institute, "Achille Mbembe."
26 Duke Franklin Humanities Institute, "Achille Mbembe."

of 2006, when Hans Van Themsche infamously shot three individuals in Antwerp, Belgium, killing two of them. After this heinous deed, the people of Antwerp joined together in a march to protest this senseless violence. Rutazibwa further observed this march downtown alongside a white Belgian man. Under normal circumstances, Rutazibwa might have ignored this man, but it was the conversation between them that made him impossible to forget. The man first asked Rutazibwa where she was from. This was no surprise to Rutazibwa; for, even in her admitted ignorance, she knew that seeing a Black woman in Belgium was not a common occurrence. When she replied that she was from Belgium, the man asked, "But where are you really from?" Once again, Rutazibwa was not surprised. She told him that she was adopted in Rwanda by Flemish parents.[27]

At this point, Rutazibwa said, it became readily apparent to her that this conversation was entirely one-sided, for this man—as well-intentioned as he probably was—continued to ask questions and be unmoved by the responses. Rutazibwa knew the man saw her as a stereotype that fit within his own personal beliefs. When telling this story, Rutazibwa clarified for her audience in the following words:

> I am not telling you this story to make fun of this guy. . . . The reason I am telling this story is that it taught me a lot about the colonized mind. What struck me in this conversation with this guy is that he was seeing me because he came up to me and wanted to talk to me, but at the same time because of all the knowledge he had had during his life about people of color, he was incapable of hearing me or seeing me. So somehow, I was silenced.[28]

Shortly after this conversation, Rutazibwa moved to Italy to study racial issues in her PhD work. While completing her doctoral program, she made many friends of color. And she could not help but notice that even though these students were arguably upstanding citizens not just for being doctorate students but also because they were multilingual, they were continuously silenced by Italian society. They were essentially "treated like illiterates" and even pursued by the police. It is here where Rutazibwa experienced pure racism, which went beyond mere stereotyping. She also realized, most strikingly, that the "mindset" of society allowed blatant

---

27   TEDx Talks, "Decolonizer."
28   TEDx Talks, "Decolonizer."

racism not only to exist but also to be accepted. This mindset, she now understood, was a result of colonization, which, by her definition, is the silencing of others. This means that the process of decolonization must require an act of "desilencing" and "going after stories" that others have silenced for generations.[29]

In June of 2011, Rutazibwa and other European academics organized a conference in Frankfurt with the thematic title of "The Decolonization of the Social Sciences." It was in the hopes of unearthing stories that had been silenced and overshadowed by colonization for many years. These stories could not have been unearthed from library books that had already been influenced by the colonized mind or a conventionalized schema of the world. At this conference, Rutazibwa learned about theories on the stabilization of Africa from lesser-known African academics she had never heard of. Here, she realized, was a representation of the truest and purest form of decolonization, all made possible by the most fundamental agreement: the democratization of ideas. In relation to Africa and African scholarship, this means that even though convention has stated that the European Union should generate ways to "save" Africa, there are also ways for the African people to generate their own solutions. They simply need the voice and power to do so.[30]

Rutazibwa encourages the media to "dig deeper" for stories that are not as conventionalized, "mainstream," "sensationalized," or, indeed, colonized, by seeking out those in the general public and informing them of current pressing issues. In summary, Rutzibwa said decolonization is about the kind of information that is accessible to all—not a select few—in society. It is "not about political correctness or silencing yourself . . . it is actually the opposite. It is a call to dig deeper" and to really listen to others.[31]

Overall, academics have managed to create inventive ideas to define decolonization, separated as much as possible (within reason in the English language) from a colonized mindset. Simply put, the ideas do not stem from tired colonized ideologies. They are based on the perspectives of people who are on the "outside looking in," and they are conscious of multiculturalism. To continue this progress, more blending of the non-academic and academic spheres is needed. After all, it is not just academics

---

29   TEDx Talks, "Decoloniser."
30   TEDx Talks, "Decoloniser."
31   TEDx Talks, "Decoloniser."

who have been impacted by colonization. If academics prize decolonization and inclusion, they must extend their knowledge to the communities at large. This can be achieved through easier access to journals. These journals must also contain less academic jargon that is inherently colonized because, as this essay has established, language has power. If the language of knowledge is presented as academic jargon, power is only offered to a select, privileged few. If, on the other hand, knowledge is presented in lay terms, power can be distributed evenly throughout society.

With these steps, the colonized notion of privilege will further dissolve, and academics from nonwhite, nonheterosexual backgrounds will no longer feel the burden of speaking for all within their demographic. Furthermore, the average citizen will not feel so hesitant to participate in academic research because they will see academics as, in a sense, their own neighbors or allies—rather than lofty, intimidating elites. When this occurs, more accurate research on underprivileged communities can occur, and more stories of humanity in all its forms can be unearthed. Ultimately, it is through collaboration and compassion—not division and self-centeredness—that decolonization can become a reality.

Decoloniality in the Context of Colonization and Coloniality

Decoloniality, as a residual of colonized societies and interpersonal race framework,[32] stems from the historical imposition of both colonization and coloniality upon peoples of the world. Most pointedly, it deals with colonization as pursued by individuals and powers of European origin. European colonization extends its reach to varying portions of the globe, from the Americas to Asia, Australia, and most profoundly the African continent. Due to the European ability to cross hemispheres and spread their influence around the world, the European colonization conquest began around the fifteenth century.

Western-centered institutions, ideologies, and customs have been maintained with varying degrees of success across the borders of now-independent nations. The European powers were able to maintain their foundations in many countries that used this colonial structure to begin their re-ascendance to attempted self-sustainability. Through historical as well as geographic events, thought to be important milestones in

---

32 Bhambra, "Postcolonial."

the history of civilizations, the gain and loss of power in these regions impacted not only European interests but also the regions formerly under their control. Nevertheless, the continued pursuance of the subjugation of people, resources, and land continues well into the twenty-first century.

Colonization—defined as direct or sometimes indirect control of a nation's economic, political, and social infrastructure by an external power[33]—has long generated discussions regarding the current treatment, perception, development, and progress of increasingly diverse populations of individuals. These conversations often extend to champions of pluralism in the West through convergence, with both indigenous individuals and those of the diaspora. However, in engaging with the ideas surrounding colonialism, one must understand the behaviors as well as impacts resulting from the interaction of the powers.

Colonialism's effects are clearly outlined in the late Kenyan Professor Ali Mazrui's proposed six long-term consequences of colonialism.[34] Mazrui detailed the imposition of capitalism[35] upon the African nations, particularly through the African slave trade,[36] which led to negative perceptions regarding the African work ethic and African slaves and their descendants in other regions of the globe. Africa's entrance onto the world stage occurred in a Western context, with the continued division of its nations according to the stipulations of the Berlin Conference,[37] while being introduced to international law through the presence of European powers within the country. Mazrui's remaining points indicate the extent to which the perception of Africa and Africans as well as the experiences of the African people are European influenced, mainly through cultural elements such as language[38] and religion[39] and its philosophies.

The foregoing impacts, though characterized as a direct influence on the resources and political structures of the African nations during the age of colonialism, should not be misconstrued as a brief aberration in the history of the African continent. It is these interactions with colonial powers over several centuries that created the foundations for current African nations

---

33 Bhambra, "Postcolonial."
34 Ndlovu-Gatsheni, "Decoloniality."
35 Ndlovu-Gatsheni, "Decoloniality."
36 Ndlovu-Gatsheni, "Decoloniality."
37 Ndlovu-Gatsheni, "Decoloniality."
38 Ndlovu-Gatsheni, "Decoloniality."
39 Ndlovu-Gatsheni, "Decoloniality."

as well as the knowledge systems and beliefs of its people. Colonialism's advent of modernity as a justification for Europeans to subjugate African people examines not only the perception of the people and structures of the African continent but also the construction of modernity as a concept. Under the guise of modernity and civility, the colonizing nations were able to perpetrate the destruction of identities, languages, as well as customs and ideologies stemming from these facets of African culture.

Through the colonial perception of Africans as existing within ethnic- and kinship-based systems, as well as being underdeveloped and ill-convened, the colonial powers were able to facilitate the physical division of land and people as a means of accessing resources and establishing power institutions over subjugated groups of individuals. Colonialist actions prioritized a European agenda over African people's needs. The perpetuation of European languages as superior also supports this agenda, as not only were indigenous languages often disregarded, but formal relations between African and European individuals were marked by the advent of European languages in Africa over indigenous traditions. The introduction of Christianity to the various African nations introduced European thought and belief systems through the development of religious education and secular education characterized by religious ideologies.

Many of these adverse colonial effects were challenged in the rise of decolonization movements across the continent. Indigenous Africans assessed the strength of their own nations, asserted a right to their land and resources, and reasserted—and in some cases rediscovered—their own culture. However, many of the abovementioned effects were deeply rooted in not only just infrastructures but also in the minds of the individuals who remained in the matrix of postcolonial Africa. While the direct dominance of European powers had been challenged, removed, or overthrown in many nations, the government structure that replaced these European powers rekindled some of the same ideas and practices put in place by colonial systems. Issues such as religious tolerance, government accountability, racial classification (including apartheid), socioeconomic classifications, and equal access to resources for everyone remained tasks that many nations were unable to carry out without referencing Western policies that had been in place for so long.[40]

---

40 Bhambra, "Postcolonial."

These residual structures comprise what Ramon Grosfoguel has called the "mythology of decolonization."[41] This refers to the Euro/Euro-American perception of the complete eradication of the colonial regime and its influence from the modern state. Grosfoguel further examines the subscription to this myth as a concession to the current state of "coloniality"[42] within the dominated region. The prioritization and globalized adherence to the Eurocentric capitalist system that reveres profit making[43] divides the economic system into labor and capital.[44] Eurocentric capitalist systems also keep race relations between that of Europeans and non-Europeans unequal through means of slow or no economic mobility, one example of the sort of "coloniality" emphasized by Grosfoguel. Grosfoguel continues to examine the "capitalist/military/Christian/patriarchal/white/heterosexual/male"[45] perspective introduced to the colonized regions such as Africa that have persisted for centuries. Grosfoguel's concept of "hetararchies"[46] demonstrates the overall visual structures continued under coloniality. However, the internal judgments and perceptions of the world made by the African people and African nations have created a culture that is often in the image of European modernity.

In understanding these aspects of the current state of the African nation, one whose progress and development is viewed through the lens of Western ideology, it is then essential to determine how to deconstruct the "coloniality" often written off as the decolonized state. The decommissioning of the state of knowledge and perception of the minds of individuals with a history of colonialism such as that in Africa, faces the enormous challenge of not only reexamining the physical infrastructure of the state but also of the combination of perspectives of the overall systems of governance, society, and economy. While multiple calls have been made and attended to regarding the need for traditional African ideologies, such as those of kinship ties and a communal focus over individuality, with regard to systems of governance and economic policy, future

---

41 Ndlovu-Gatsheni, "Decoloniality," 485–96.
42 Grosfoguel, "Epistemic."
43 Grosfoguel, "Epistemic."
44 Grosfoguel, "Epistemic."
45 Grosfoguel, "Epistemic."
46 Ndlovu-Gatsheni, "Decoloniality."

leaders must first view the proliferation of knowledge as a stepping-stone to the development of such agencies. For example, the development of the tertiary education system within many countries of Africa mimics that of the European/Euro-American institutions with teachings of disequilibrium in global topics and Eurocentric research methodologies.[47] These research methodologies and technologies[48] that the African individual is exposed to are tied to the world order perpetuated by coloniality and must be challenged with perceptions originating from alternate regional customs, practices, and understandings. The spread of knowledge within education systems as well as interactions between individuals, groups, etc., facilitates examining the epistemological insights[49] with regard to topics of national structures, as well as social topics such as race, gender, and sexuality.

Many scholars and writers have examined the relationship between colonialism and imperialism in an effort to establish the knowledge of the coloniality that exists within the current state, as well as practicalize approaches to challenging these influences within the modern era. Samir Amin, in his interview with Amandy Aly Dieng,[50] expressed his support for the Dependency school and Latin America[51] as well as Immanuel Wallerstein's World Economy Concept.[52] These two ideologies expand on Amin's establishment of the relationship between imperialism and capitalism, in which Amin asserts the inherently imperialistic nature of capitalism.[53] To Amin, capitalism has progressed in a forward-cyclical nature. Amin further expands his views to say that it is this capitalist system that has prevented developing nations from becoming developed—and not even permitted to "catch up."[54]

Amin's regard for economics does not go without mention of key political changes and institutions necessary for the development of an

---

47 Ndlovu-Gatsheni, "Decoloniality."
48 Ndlovu-Gatsheni, "Decoloniality."
49 Grosfoguel, "Epistemic."
50 Dieng, "Samir Amin,"
51 Dieng, "Samir Amin."
52 Dieng, "Samir Amin."
53 Dieng, "Samir Amin."
54 Dieng, "Samir Amin."

alternate system, "twenty-first century socialism."[55] Through previous and current structures of democracy as well as a shift to an improved form of democracy, a forward advancement to the ideologies and structures of a more socialist system is possible as a substitute for the capitalist state.[56] The notions put forward by Amin not only demonstrate the value of intellectuals as a point along the revolutionary path to change but also the position of intellectuals as critics.[57]

Frantz Fanon, another well-known critic of the colonial system as well as of the role of capitalism and its effects on the African population, demonstrates the vitality of capitalism within the Western context and its alteration of the systems of the colonial and postcolonial state. Fanon's book *The Wretched of the Earth* depicts capitalism as the root of the troubles faced by previously colonized countries, while also extending its impact on politics and economy into the postcolonial state of African nations. Fanon indicates the similarities in the emergence of the state bourgeoisie[58] to that of the Western bourgeoisie or middle class, the division of labor, and the expansion of capital. The state bourgeoisie[59] in this way assisted in the perpetuation of numerous European social structures and capitalist conventions, the particular division of labor between subsets of the population, as well as a generally perceived racist attitude toward the community. Fanon asserts that the state mistreats and misguides the people for its own benefit in relation to the existence and influence of the state bourgeoisie.[60] It is with regard to this issue that Fanon puts a great responsibility upon the lower classes to stand and develop an alternate system in which they are not perceived as objects of capitalist manipulation. Fanon's argument places a burden on leadership and governance in managing the postcolonial state; the state must act as the source of inclusion and equal distribution of resources and kindle much-needed African Unity.

In many cases, the future with respect to the status of coloniality appears to be a joint venture between intellectuals, the government, and

---

55 Dieng, "Samir Amin."
56 Dieng, "Samir Amin."
57 Dieng, "Samir Amin."
58 Fanon, *Wretched*.
59 Fanon, *Wretched*.
60 Fanon, *Wretched*.

the people of the nation. Both Amin and Fanon recognize the complexity faced in the task of decoloniality just as another critic, Archie Mafeje from South Africa, acknowledges the value of the social sciences; but his focus is also concerned with the maintenance of state infrastructure.[61] Mafeje places emphasis on the variety and role of intellectuals in a society: his taxonomy includes the intellectual[62] who is able to rebel against the status quo; the Shanghaied organic intellectual,[63] who values monetary success rather than independent thought; and the transcendent intellectual,[64] who is opposed to the current state. Mafeje's perspective on this intellectual freedom sets him apart from many other academics, researchers, and theorists; his arguments place a heavy emphasis on the necessity of political action, which is long overdue for a revolution if future generations are to prosper.

---

61   Nyoka, "Archie Mafeje."
62   Nyoka, "Archie Mafeje."
63   Nyoka, "Archie Mafeje."
64   Nyoka, "Archie Mafeje."

Chapter Two

Eurocentrism and Intellectual Imperialism

Eurocentrism is a general phenomenon of interpreting the culture and backgrounds of non-European communities from a Western perspective. This may include consideration of non-European societies as inferior to their Western counterparts, viewing non-European histories through the lens of colonization and expansion of Western thought, and undervaluation of non-European ways of life. Eurocentrism, while having taken many forms throughout history, has been present since at least the fifth century BCE, when it was first documented in Greek historian Herodotus's writings when he refers to "barbaric Asian hordes . . . lacking European individuality" despite constructing beautiful architecture.[1] Scholars have also found that since the time of Herodotus, human beings have had a tendency to rank one another, and human beings from the Western world have implicitly or explicitly favored Western values and culture. Socrates, for example, said:

> Citizens, we shall say to them in our tale, you are brothers, yet God has framed you differently. Some of you have the power of command, and in the composition of these he has mingled gold, wherefore also they have the greatest honor; others he has made of silver, to be auxiliaries; others again who are to be husbandmen and craftsmen he has composed of brass and iron; and the species will generally be preserved in the children. . . . An oracle says that when a man of brass or iron guards the State, it will be destroyed.[2]

---

1 Bowersock and Bernal, "Black Athena."
2 Gould, *Mismeasure*.

With a Eurocentric lens, the ideals of successful humanity exist on a spectrum. At one end of the spectrum—associated with the highest human achievement—is the Western world that is considered to be the liberal, modern, civilized, and white society. At the other end of the spectrum—associated with lack of achievement—is the non-Western world that is considered to be the traditional, backward, barbarian, and Black/indigenous.[3] For anyone who possesses a Eurocentric worldview, words such as "modern," "civilized," "traditional," "backward," and "barbarian" are not all weighted; rather, these words constitute people and places that can be easily identified by any "reasonable" person. For instance, it is considered obvious to the Eurocentric person that a "modern" and "civilized" society necessarily has a strong economy; European-style forms of government, fashion, architecture, and etiquette; the most advanced technology; and a white population. Conversely, it is considered obvious to the Eurocentric person that a "traditional," "backward," and "barbarian" society necessarily has a weak economy; Eastern and Global Southern forms of government, fashion, architecture, and etiquette; less advanced technology; and a darker-skinned population. It might never occur to the Eurocentric person that different cultural norms exist and that certain Western standards may not be applicable in the non-Western world. Simply put, the Eurocentric person favors a world according to their own view, which includes a sort of psychological colonialism.

In fact, today a new sort of Eurocentric colonialism is alive not only psychologically but also literally, for it is not uncommon for the so-called modern and civilized Western and Anglo-American nations to try to "help" other nations achieve the Eurocentric standard of development. However, in doing so, these Western and Anglo-American nations are behaving in an exploitative manner and not taking into account the experiences and worldviews of the nations they are trying to fundamentally change.[4] For example, those who possess a Eurocentric mindset often deny the subjectivity of the words "progress," "advancement," or "development." For a Eurocentric person (colonizer), these words all represent one reality and one form of achievement; but to a colonized individual, these words can represent an entirely different reality.

---

3   Franzki, "Eurocentrism."
4   Franzki, "Eurocentrism."

Furthermore, Western and Anglo-American nations have violated the autonomy, views, and rights of colonized people by writing or shaping their history for them. The problem with this kind of historical subjectivity is that the colonized people are told they have no precolonial history. For example, as the historian and professor Hugh Trevor-Roper infamously said in the 1960s, "Perhaps, in the future, there will be some African history . . . but at present there is none: there is only the history of Europeans in Africa. The rest is darkness . . . and darkness is no subject of history."[5] Instantly, because of a few ignorant words from a Eurocentric mind, the entire story of Africa was erased. Even worse, Trevor-Roper painted an ugly picture in which only European history was considered important. In his eyes, Europeans saved the world from barbarity; European influence and ingenuity have "shaken the non-European world out of the past—out of barbarism in Africa. . . . The history of the world, for the last five centuries, in so far as it has significance, has been European history."[6]

Unfortunately, Trevor-Roper's blinkered historical views gained wide acceptance. African history, up until recently, was not considered to be a legitimate or extensive field of study in academia. Undoubtedly, much of the reason for this is because there was not much incentive, even from those who wrote African history textbooks, to advocate for an African history curriculum at universities. According to T. R. Batten, African history remained mostly static and uneventful prior to European invasion: "Throughout the long ages before Africa was controlled by European powers in the nineteenth century, there were few changes in African ways of living."[7] Even British colonial officials in Africa in the 1930s did not deem it necessary for African natives to learn about their own history. The colonial officials thought that "true" history—European history— should be taught to the natives instead. One colonial official said: "We must tell [the natives] the story of how the white man has come in his great ships to show the new ways of mining and planting, bringing also factories and cinemas, railways and motorlorries, which break up the old life."[8] Strangely, this was an interesting reversal of prior British colonial

---

5 Trevor-Roper, *Rise.*
6 Trevor-Roper, *Rise.*
7 Batten, *Past and Present.*
8 Matthews, *Black Treasure,* 273.

education policy before the 1930s, where it was considered important for African natives to know their own native history.[9]

It seems that any support for a truer account of African history being taught in any official educational setting was a short-lived spark of progressivism. Eurocentric attitudes that pushed aside African history mostly prevailed throughout much of the twentieth century. In fact, American universities have only offered "Black studies" courses for the past fifty years.[10] British universities have a similar story. According to the Historical Association, in 1968, only nineteen out of forty recorded British universities taught African history courses. These statistics remained the same in 1990—over twenty years later.[11] But Eurocentric attitudes have led to more than just exclusion of African studies. Asian, Latino, and Native American studies courses have also been offered in American universities only in the last half century.[12]

Just like with many stories of change, the origins of collegiate programs that dared to cover the stories and histories of people of color came from protest. In other words, the fight against Eurocentrism has never been readily accepted. In the United States, after the Higher Education Act of 1965 was passed and more students of color matriculated into largely white universities, students of color demanded more rights. The first-ever Black Student Union at San Francisco State College (now San Francisco State University) was especially forthcoming in its demands for change—particularly with its demands for the creation of a Black studies department. This Black Student Union's demonstrations lasted five months. The union even convinced not only Black students but also other students of color to walk out of academic areas and classes.[13] The protesting voices had such an impact on San Francisco State that finally, in 1968, Nathan Hare, a progressive professor who sided with the student protestors, created the nation's first Black studies program.[14] Along with the Black studies program came the College of Ethnic Studies at San Francisco State, which between 1968 and 1969, added programs and classes about not

---

9   Omolewa, "Educating" 267–87.
10 Beeson, "US Celebrates."
11 Bourne, "History," 240.
12 *Advancing Justice*; Escobar, "How 50 Years;" Lee, "Fifty Years."
13 Rogers, "Celebrating."
14 Beeson, "40th Anniversary."

just African Americans but also Asian Americans, Latino/a Americans, and Native Americans.[15]

Sure enough, students at other universities were just as restless for change. In 1968, Chicano students from California State University at Los Angeles joined the pivotal Chicano Movement in the 1960s that demanded more civil rights for Chicano people. These Chicano students instigated a formal walkout of their own, carrying signs that read "WE DEMAND SCHOOLS THAT TEACH" (specifically, schools that teach Chicano students about their heritage and that show Chicano students respect) and "WE ARE NOT DIRTY MEXICANS." Consequently, Cal State LA created the first Mexican American studies program[16] (preceding even San Francisco State's La Raza program in the College of Ethnic Studies by just a few months).[17] Thus began the rapid growth of ethnic studies programs across the United States.

Needless to say, there are still roadblocks. In 2010, Arizona lawmakers banned ethnic studies programs in their state.[18] Even though this ban was overturned in 2017,[19] criticisms of ethnic studies continue to echo, and ethnic studies programs still struggle just as the rest of the liberal arts do.[20] Victor Davis Hanson, a historian at the Hoover Institution, said that "universities have too often graduated zealous advocates [in ethnic studies programs] who [lack] the broad education necessary to achieve their predetermined politicized ends."[21] Journalist Gustavo Arellano once admitted that he used to think Chicano studies served to "[achieve] little more than inspiring third-generation Mexican Americans from Whittier to change their names to Xipe or Xochitl from Bryan or Yennifer."[22] Perhaps these sorts of attitudes explain why not all universities have ethnic studies programs. For instance, as of 2015, only thirty colleges and universities in the United States had an Asian American studies program, and only seventy colleges and universities in the United States offered

---

15   College of Ethnic Studies.
16   Escobar, "How 50 Years."
17   Latina/Latino Studies page at: http://latino.sfsu.edu/.
18   Escobar, "How 50 Years."
19   Escobar, "How 50 Years."
20   Dutt-Ballerstadt, "Academic."
21   Hansen, "In Defense."
22   Escobar, "How 50 Years."

Asian American studies classes.[23] Furthermore, most students who take ethnic studies classes are people of color,[24] thus suggesting that students from European or Anglo-American backgrounds find it unnecessary to take classes that do not constitute "the most important" part of history or society (or the parts that relate to them). Ultimately, Eurocentric attitudes remain the focus, and a Eurocentric narrative of history is far from being completely eradicated in the academic world.

Perhaps the worst consequence of the erasure and marginalizing of non-European history is that this revisionism has been presented as the absolute truth. The Westerners and Anglo-Americans who have done the erasing and minimizing have not taken into account how biased their representation of another people's history is.[25] This "truth" is indeed pernicious, for even universities and schools outside of North America and Europe have assumed subconsciously that North America and Europe are at "the center of history" and that North American and European stories need to be the focus of educational curricula.[26] Ultimately, Eurocentrism suppresses the voices of others, and it clings to global power by condemning and oppressing nations that do not comply with Eurocentric values and standards.[27]

Even though the word "Eurocentrism" may on the surface appear to be synonymous with racism, there are some important distinctions to consider—even though "Eurocentrism" and "racism" certainly can be related. While Eurocentrism promotes the European (or Western and Anglo-American) worldview, racism is a broader worldview that involves three things: the "belief in race as a biological concept," "the belief in the superiority of one's own race," and the rationalization of "institutional and cultural practices that formalize domination of one racial group over another."[28] This means that anyone, not just a white person, can be racist toward others—at least at the interpersonal level. For at the institutional level, people of color are not in positions of power to be racially discriminatory toward white people. However, if someone holds Eurocentric

---

23 *Advancing Justice.*
24 Escobar, "How 50 Years."
25 Franzki, "Eurocentrism"; and John Muthyala, "Reworlding America."
26 Franzki, "Eurocentrism."
27 Franzki, "Eurocentrism."
28 Awad, "Psych of Racism."

views, one necessarily thinks that European (or Western and Anglo-American) culture is superior. In summary, a person can have Eurocentric views and racist views, but the racist views for the Eurocentric person must be directed toward those who do not fit the Eurocentric mold. In many cases, this might also mean that the Eurocentric person favors whiteness over Blackness or brownness.

It should be mentioned also that one does not have to be from a stereotypically Eurocentric nation or be stereotypically white in appearance to have subconscious Eurocentric views. Indeed, a colonized individual may have lived under the regime of the colonizer for so long that they begin to fundamentally believe that the colonizer's culture is the superior culture. Consequently, the colonized individual may become deeply despondent or may be imbued with a sense of helplessness. This can be seen in beauty standards, for example. A recent meta-analysis study by Susan L. Bryant at Columbia University showed that American Black women are especially susceptible to feelings of low self-esteem when exposed to European, Anglo-American, and white beauty standards.[29] She found that families of color idealized lighter skin (without their full knowledge), and lighter skin was associated with more racial pride.[30] She also found that Black adolescent girls with the darkest skin and with hair the least like their Anglo-American female counterparts were most likely to be socially isolated and, as a result, have poorer academic achievement.[31] Even later in life, Black women who did not possess traditional European characteristics were less likely to be hired in the workplace.[32] All of these experiences explain why Black women in the United States are more likely to develop eating disorders, a negative body image, self-hatred, and depression.[33]

This is not to say that people of color are not conscious of the burden of Eurocentric values; they most certainly are. Studies have shown that people of color who are more aware of racial discrimination (either from personal experience or indirect experience) are more likely to have

---

29 Bryant, "Beauty Ideal," 80–91.
30 Raskin, Coard, and Breland, "Perceptions," 82.
31 Holcomb-McCoy and Moore-Thomas, "Empowering;" Robinson-Moore, "Beauty Standards," 82–83.
32 Robinson-Moore, "Beauty Standards."
33 Christine C. Iijima Hall, "Beauty."

mental health problems.[34] Notably, studies have also shown that racial pride and a strong sense of racial identity are helpful buffers against racial discrimination.[35] But of course, this means that a person of color must overcome the initial shock and pain of not feeling welcome in a society that does not favor them. This can be poignantly demonstrated in Austin Channing Brown's critically acclaimed book, *I'm Still Here: Black Dignity in a World Made for Whiteness*. Brown says: "I had to learn what it really means to love Blackness."[36] And of course she had to learn, for she grew up in a family that was acutely aware of racial prejudice and passed on this awareness to her. Brown's parents even gave her a traditionally white man's name so that employers could look at her résumé and not instantly toss it in the garbage.[37] Certainly, as she grew up, Brown experienced the pain of racial discrimination all on her own. Even though she attended the same church for years, regular attendees (most of whom were white) almost every Sunday asked her if she was new or, more offensively, if she was looking for the food pantry—all because she was Black.[38] All of these experiences and more contributed to Brown's sense of alienation from a world not designed for her. But through the exploration of her culture and her eventual willingness to ignore others' expectations, she found racial pride and, consequently, stability.[39]

Eurocentric beliefs and racism are alive and well in today's politics and leadership. One may look, for example, at former US President Donald Trump's infamous series of tweets on July 14, 2019, that were formally condemned by the House of Representatives[40] as being racist. Referring to four progressive, Democratic women of color in the US Congress—Rashida Tlaib, Alexandria Ocasio-Cortez, Ilhan Omar, and Ayanna Pressley—Trump tweeted:

---

34 Wallace, Nazroo, and Bécares, "Cumulative," 1294–1300.
35 Caldwell et al., "Racial Identity," 1322–36; Rowley et al., "Relationship," 713–24; Sellers et al., "Racial Identity Matters," 187–216.
36 Brown, *I'm Still Here*, 24.
37 Brown, *I'm Still Here*, 15.
38 Brown, *I'm Still Here*, 20.
39 Brown, *I'm Still Here*, 24–39.
40 The draft of the resolution may be accessed here: https://rules.house.gov/sites/democrats.rules.house.gov/files/BILLS-116hres489ih.pdf.

So interesting to see 'Progressive' Democrat Congresswomen, who originally came from countries whose governments are a complete and total catastrophe, the worst, most corrupt and inept anywhere in the world (if they even have a functioning government at all), now loudly and viciously telling the people of the United States, the greatest and most powerful Nation on earth, how our government is to be run. Why don't they go back and help fix the totally broken and crime infested places from which they came.[41]

This tweet is undoubtedly problematic and offensive in its Eurocentrism for several reasons. First, Omar is the only congresswoman of the four attacked who was actually born outside of the United States. She was born in Somalia and immigrated to the United States in 1997,[42] while Ocasio-Cortez is a "third-generation Bronxite" (in the state of New York),[43] Pressley is from the state of Ohio,[44] and Tlaib is from the state of Michigan.[45] This means that Trump instinctively associated these women with countries outside the United States, thereby showing how "true American-ness" is not embodied by these women. Trump simply suggested that these women were not "truly American" because they are women of color.

Second, Trump described these women's alleged countries of origin as "totally broken and crime infested," with "governments [that] are a total and complete catastrophe, the worst, most corrupt and inept anywhere in the world." Yet, as previously mentioned, only one woman of the four (Omar) was born outside the United States. Even so, Trump's intentions were clear: he used vitriolic language to deride these women of color's ethnic backgrounds and ancestral birthplaces that he considers to be inferior to his birthplace, the United States. On a further ironic note,

---

41 On January 8, 2021, Twitter permanently banned Trump from Twitter and his tweets may no longer be found there. They can be found in the Trump Archive, a publicly available and searchable database found here: thetrumparchive.com.
42 See Omar's campaign website: https://www.ilhanomar.com/about.
43 See Ocasio-Cortez's campaign website: https://ocasio-cortez.house.gov/about/biography.
44 See Pressley's campaign website: https://pressley.house.gov/about.
45 See Tlaib's campaign website: https://tlaib.house.gov/about.

Ocasio-Cortez's ancestors came from Puerto Rico,[46] a US territory. Once again, in Trump's mind, it appears that "United States" and "American" are very specific descriptions that do not involve Ocasio-Cortez, her ancestors, or Puerto Ricans in general.

Third, Trump described the US government as "the greatest and most powerful." Here, we see a striking example of a man describing the Eurocentric spectrum. For Trump, at one end of the spectrum is the United States, the epitome of "Anglo-American-ness" and success. At the other end are the unnamed, unspecified countries (that do not deserve clarification because, for Trump, "they are all the same") that are "un-American" and are associated with failure. Not only are Trump's remarks racist and xenophobic, but to assume that the United States is the greatest country in the world despite its own failings is an attitude rooted in the worst kind of Eurocentrism.[47] When reading Trump's above tweets, one cannot help but hear an unjustified superiority in his voice.

Let us now return to concepts of Eurocentrism more historically and generally. As mentioned above, Eurocentrism has not always taken the form of straightforward degradation or devaluing of nonwhite-majority countries but has also come in the form of stereotyping, romanticization, sexualization, or infantilization of individuals due to their non-European background or even of entire societies. While periods of European conquest or economic prosperity have typically correlated with more outspoken expression of Eurocentric beliefs, some basic beliefs have consistently informed these opinions.[48]

These beliefs include the idea that non-European societies are influenced by their climate, making them scientifically inferior. Georges-Louis Leclerc, Comte de Buffon, who was considered to be "the father of all thought in natural history in the second half of the 18th century,"[49] wrote that climate was the reason non-Europeans were considered less attractive than Europeans: "The most temperate climate lies between the 40th and 50th degree of latitude, and it produces the most handsome and beautiful men. It is from this climate that the ideas of the genuine color

---

46   Smith, "Ocasio-Cortez."
47   Bendix, "The US;" Desilver, "US Students."
48   Hugill and Blaut, "The Colonizers."
49   Mayr, *Growth*, 330.

of mankind, and the various degrees of beauty ought to be derived."[50] Other beliefs that contributed to Eurocentric attitudes include the idea that non-European religions, including Islam, are strange, and that those practicing these religions need to be "saved" by the truth of Christianity; that non-European societies are anti-individualistic and despotic, as well as cruel (often cited with examples including the archaic practice of sati in India and foot binding in China);[51] and the idea that non-Europeans are biologically inferior to Europeans.

Indeed, as early as the eighteenth century, researchers tried to provide "scientific" explanations for how those of African descent were physically and biologically inferior to those of European descent. Carl Linnaeus, from his observations of human beings (biased though they were), created his own human taxonomy that categorized humans based on their supposedly natural, innate tendencies. *Homo sapiens afer* (an African, Black human being) was "ruled by caprice," whereas the *Homo sapiens europaeus* (a European, white human being) was "ruled by customs"—the latter often being thought more praiseworthy than the former.[52] By the nineteenth century, polygenism emerged: a belief system that posits that Africans were descended from another race entirely.[53] David Hume, who followed this belief system, said that polygenism explained African people's lack of admirable qualities. In his estimation, "There never was a civilized nation of any other complexion than white. . . . No indigenous manufacturers amongst [non-whites], no arts, no sciences. . . . Not to mention our [European] colonies, there are negroe [*sic*] slaves dispersed . . . of which none ever discovered any symptoms of ingenuity."[54]

Furthermore, Samuel George Morton, a prominent American scientist who subscribed to polygenism, collected data to indicate that African skulls were smaller than European skulls, thus "proving" that Africans were of lesser intelligence. However, as Stephen Jay Gould found, Morton's data were actually "fudged" so as to accommodate his belief that Africans were less intelligent than Europeans.[55] It is also worth noting that smaller brain

---

50 Gould, *Mismeasure*, 71.
51 Wallerstein, "Eurocentrism," 94.
52 Linnaeus, *Systema Naturae*, 66.
53 Gould, *Mismeasure*, 71.
54 Popkin, "Philosophical," 71.
55 Gould, *Mismeasure*, 82–87.

size does not dictate intelligence or lack thereof across species.[56] Albert Einstein's brain, for example, was smaller than the average brain.[57]

Nevertheless, the most prominent instances of Eurocentrism in modern society are found in two forms: education and imperialist history. Eurocentrism in education has been manifested in various forms, as shown above—whether it is contempt for indigenous knowledge and knowledge systems or through disregard of inventions and discoveries from non-European societies (or even the misattributing of non-European inventions to European men). For example, nineteenth-century French zoologist Baron George Cuvier said that ancient Egyptians must have been white, for he could not imagine that such a respectable civilization could have been constructed by "the Negro."[58] Morton also believed in this position for a time, and later only slightly altered his view: that Egyptians who invented their civilization were neither Black nor white but rather some other race of their own. However, he maintained that the Egyptian slaves most certainly were Black because of their slave status.[59]

Furthermore, as recently as 2016, US Republican politician Steve King said in response to white people at a Republican convention being criticized for their rowdy behavior: "I'd ask you [MSNBC anchor Chris Hayes] to go back through history and figure out where are these contributions that have been made by . . . [nonwhite people]. Where did any other sub-group of people contribute more to civilization?"[60] King's comment is certainly reflective of his Eurocentric attitudes and his ignorance. But perhaps his education was Eurocentric, and he never learned that the Chinese invented paper[61] and gunpowder,[62] or that the Egyptians invented the first number system.[63]

The most institutional examples of Eurocentrism in academia can be found in the social sciences, especially in historiography and philosophy. Eurocentrism is, to some extent, intrinsic to contemporary education

---

56 Koch, "Does Brain."
57 Costadi, "Snapshots Explore."
58 Stocking, *Race, Culture, and Evolution*, 232.
59 Smedley and Smedley, *Race in North America*, 232.
60 Horwitz, "Dear Steve."
61 Aiken and Lu, "Historical Instances," 173.
62 Whipps, "How Gunpowder."
63 Chrisomalis, "Egyptian," 485–96.

systems since contemporary education systems are largely Western, and social science, in "accepted" academia, is largely a product of this Western, intrinsically Eurocentric system. In fact, according to Professor Immanuel Wallerstein, a prominent American sociologist, research in the social sciences was overwhelmingly located in only five countries until 1945: the United States, France, Britain, Germany, and Italy.[64] Furthermore, social sciences as a field was formally introduced in order to address European problems and histories at a point when European colonial conquest had essentially influenced broad global politics. It is unavoidable that the field is significantly focused on and influenced by Western thought and theory. Even following 1945, when the Cold War period brought more attention to decolonization and postcolonial movements, the small sample sizes of case studies conducted do not contain sufficient diversity to make the sweeping generalizations by the field valid. In fact, in a field such as the social sciences, to make such sweeping generalizations based on small, nondiverse sample studies is parochial, Wallerstein claims, because people's very natures are highly contingent upon the conditions and interactions they inhabit and are raised in.[65]

World historical studies also see a discrepancy in the amount of detail and information present from the sixteenth through the nineteenth centuries, again specifically in Europe, compared to the emphasis placed on this same period globally. The reverence with which this period is treated, especially in the context of colonialism and inventions of the period, is perhaps the prime example of modern historiography exhibiting Eurocentrism.

For example, the College Board—a US organization that administers Advanced Placement (AP) exams and curricula, as well as the SAT (formerly, Scholastic Aptitude Test)—in May 2018 released its plan for the new AP World History exam: to the dismay of many, the test and corresponding curriculum only covered history from the period 1450 AD onward. This new exam ignored essential historical events prior to 1450, such as the rise and expansion of West African kingdoms and the philosophy of Confucianism. In response to complaints about this new change,

---

64 Wallerstein, "Eurocentrism and Its Avatars," 95.
65 Wallerstein, "Eurocentrism," 97.

the College Board vowed to design the test and curriculum so that it covered more material prior to 1450 AD.[66]

Indeed, the new and improved test and curriculum for the new course called "AP World History: Modern," effective in the fall of 2019, covers 1200 AD to the present, rather than 1450 AD to the present. But while the material for the period 1200 to 1450 AD allows for a more respectable focus on communications and trade between global regions, developments in East Asia, Islam, state building in the Americas, and state building in Africa, problems still remain. First, thousands of years of history prior to 1200 AD are still omitted. Second, the College Board recommends that instructors break up the 1200 to 1450 AD period into two units, "The Global Tapestry" and "Networks of Exchange," and both of these units each will comprise 8 to 10 percent of questions on the AP exam. By comparison, the single unit of "Revolutions" from 1750 to 1900 that covers the Enlightenment, nationalism, and the industrial revolution constitutes 12 to 15 percent of questions on the students' exam. Moreover, after the "Revolutions" unit, the remaining units are heavily focused on Western nations' contributions and interactions with non-Western nations.[67] In the College Board's defense, however, it recently extended an offer to create an exam and curriculum for a course called AP World History: Ancient, depending on the amount of student and school interest.[68] Perhaps this is why the AP World History: Modern exam arguably retains a Eurocentric bent. But, even with the impending AP World History: Ancient exam, it is a shame to give students the impression that modern history for the most part belongs to the West.

Besides the AP World History Exam—now the AP World History Exam: Modern—the College Board offers courses on AP European History and AP United States History. However, it does not offer an exam or curriculum for any sort of history that concentrates on specific regions other than Europe and the United States.[69] Perhaps this is unsurprising, considering how most US states have low standards when it comes to history in school curricula. In most states, history is incorporated into the

---

66   Washington, "Diversity."
67   College Board, *AP World History.*
68   See https://apcentral.collegeboard.org/courses/ap-world-history/course/confirming-interest-in-ap-ancient.
69   Washington, "Diversity."

ELA (English Language Arts) curriculum,[70] and even if history is taught, "the field remains driven covertly by Western priorities . . . returning us often by non-Western routes to the idols of the old "Rise of the West" historiography."[71]

But of course, a Eurocentric bias in education—and the pushback against it—does not just occur in the United States. Savo Heleta recently wrote an article summarizing the effects of British influence on South African higher education curriculum. Not surprisingly, he found that in the South African university system, Eurocentrism has dominated and "required a whole way of thinking, a discourse in which everything that is advanced, good and civilised is defined and measured in European terms."[72] During the apartheid era, this bias toward Eurocentrism manifested in South African universities' administrations blatantly favoring white students over Black students[73] in order to encourage white supremacy and to bring up future white leaders to continue the mission of the colonialist society.[74] However, even after the apartheid era, Eurocentrism reigned in South Africa's higher education system in other insidious ways. According to Suren Pillay, the South African curriculum centers on "[the] idea of Europe, as a metaphor, and turns all [non-Europeans] into bit players or loiterers without intent on the stage of world history, either too lazy to do anything [themselves] or always late, and running behind to catch up with Western modernity."[75] Such a focus has remained since 1994, even after universities claimed they would redirect their mission toward something far less Eurocentric in nature.[76] Ultimately, this lack of action is a signal to students that their university "seeks to universalize the West and provincialize the rest."[77] As a result, decolonization activists have renewed pressure on South African universities to completely redesign their

---

70 Washington, "Diversity."
71 Drayton and Motadel, "Discussion," 8.
72 Kelley, "A Poetics," 27.
73 Bunting, "Higher Education."
74 Ramoupi, *African-Centered*, 5; and Pietsch, "Empire," 2.
75 Pillay, "Decolonizing," 3.
76 Pretoria Department of Education, *Report*.
77 Zeleza, "African Studies."

curriculum[78] and to specifically connect how discrimination and colonization of the past also affects South Africans in the present.[79]

Worldwide, there have been several efforts to correct this Eurocentric bias in education and historical coverage: redetermining the accuracy of this presentation of historical events; placing this timeframe in a wider context by extending the chronology and geographic range to put European achievements in "perspective" with other important global events and focusing on the negative, or at least "less than positive" impacts of European actions in this period.

Universalism, or the idea that certain truths are universally valid, has been the leading philosophy of modern science and thought.[80] While scientific and mathematical evidence have demonstrated that this is true in some fields, the infiltration of universalist thought into values and theology, for example, has proven problematic. Especially with regard to the spread of Christianity, with forced or coercive conversions being the colonial norm, no a priori evidence for the validity of Christian beliefs has been produced, making the religion no more or less valid than any other faith-based system. Universalist ideology applied in the case of such cultural knowledge has not only committed the Eurocentric transgression of assuming a universal Christian truth but also forcing Western cultural "truth" onto societies that had already adapted their systems of knowledge to fit their specific needs.[81] For example, the early Christian missionaries in the Niger Delta region and in modern-day Zimbabwe destroyed African religious shrines.[82]

While aspects of civilization and imperialist-based Eurocentrism have been previously explored through the lens of academia, the notion of being "civilized" itself has strongly Eurocentric implications. To expand on this subject, it is worth noting that the notion of being civilized is typically associated with modernity, democracy, capitalism, and the lifestyles of those inhabiting the Western Hemisphere. With modernity especially, we also see it associated with the advent, availability, and access

---

78 Heleta, "Decolonization," 5.
79 Garuba, "What Is an African Curriculum?" and Pillay, "Decolonizing," 5.
80 Ingram, "Universalism."
81 Ingram, "Universalism."
82 Chitakure, *African Traditional*, 77; and Nwabueze, *Visions & Revisions*, 176.

to technology, with capitalism and democracy, individualism, and certain social mannerisms. While these concepts in and of themselves are not wholly problematic, the fact that policies implemented based on these Eurocentric ideas are still in place *is* problematic. For example, the Monroe Doctrine, established by the United States in 1823, restricts European "rights to interfere" in Latin and South America, effectively claiming the Americas as part of the US "sphere of influence."[83] This almost parental approach to foreign relations with other sovereign countries and the wholesale carving up of global geographies into "spheres of influence" continues today. The manifestation of the concept of civilization against nations or cultures that Western powers deem "uncivilized" or different may have drifted away from imperialism but continues to assert itself.[84]

This modern-day twist on the traditional imperialistic form of Eurocentrism and concepts of civilization have not been without debate. During the Cold War, nonaligned nations consisted largely of newly decolonized nations that refused to take a side with the superpowers staking out "spheres of influence." Further, global leaders of postcolonial nations have repeatedly spoken of the necessity to "modernize" without giving up certain indigenous values and lifestyles. Specifically, as mentioned in "Eurocentrism and its Avatars" by Professor Wallerstein, the current prime minister of Malaysia has been vocal about ensuring that Malaysia's workforce is able to cope with advances in technology without absorbing all of the ideas and values that Western societies may hold regarding civilization.[85] The introduction of societies picking and choosing what values and attributes they wish to incorporate from the previous monolith of "civilization" is certainly a step forward in terms of combating Eurocentric perspectives and encouraging multiculturalism.

Orientalism occupies a cross-section of the previously discussed academic and implemented aspects of Eurocentrism. As an attitude and method of interpreting and distributing knowledge of non-European cultures, orientalism can be understood as a kind of counterpart to imperialist ideas on civilization. The discussion and awareness of orientalism gathered steam after Edward Said's publication in 1978 on the topic,

---

83   Arias, "Violence." 47–64.
84   Arias, "Violence."
85   Wallerstein, "Eurocentrism," 99.

where he broadly defines orientalism as a patronizing attitude toward non-Western societies.[86] More specifically, orientalists take it upon themselves to "learn" about non-Christian religions and non-Western societies but from the perspective that only Christianity and Western knowledge are valid. They approach non-Western societies with the preconception that non-Western knowledge is twisted, unnatural, and static. Non-Western societies, or "the Orient," were archaic and barbaric, whereas Western societies were modern and civilized. There are many problems with the orientalist approach: orientalism does not reflect reality and is highly prejudiced, among other flaws.[87] Orientalism is not just problematic within academia; the spread of orientalist attitudes beyond the confines of religion acted as a kind of propaganda that solidified and justified Eurocentrism and general imperialistic actions. For this reason, erasing and addressing orientalist attitudes, research, and justifications has been key in postcolonial research and movements.

Eurocentrism has taken many shapes and forms over the years: it has been the basis of colonialism and orientalism, but its influence has extended to historiography and philosophy. Orientalism has long been used to justify and consolidate European power and expansion, impacting the operation of global politics to date with Western hegemony. Identification and reification of Eurocentric attitudes and history are crucial to building an equitable, peaceful world, especially as we become more interconnected in the wake of globalization.

Ending Eurocentrism

The task of ending Eurocentrism appears to be an uphill battle when one considers the deep-seated assumptions already indelibly etched in the psychology of the average European and Anglo-American. Many Westerners believe in their inherent superiority over people of color because they were raised with that notion and grew up in a society marked by institutionalized racism. Consequently, they are beneficiaries of these lopsided conditions where they experience the nonwhite community being subjected to subhuman treatment and in most cases do not perceive any injustices.

---

86 Leong, *Orientalism*.
87 Leong, *Orientalism*.

The situation becomes more difficult when Westerners understand the maltreatment faced by this nonwhite demographic in schools, places of work (including seeing the high percentage of nonwhites in menial jobs), and even in the political system but nevertheless instinctively accept an unequal binary system of white and nonwhite. However, the problem does not lie only with the white community that already assumes white superiority in global society: this assumption has been unconsciously accepted by nonwhites as well. As a result, Eurocentrism and its destructive escapades is considered a normal part of a thriving society where the master-subordinate relationship is comfortably maintained.

In February 2020, Ahmaud Arbery, an African American, was shot dead by unmasked white Americans for violating no known law. From a surface analysis of this incident, one would probably find it unjustifiable. When considered carefully, one would understand that there is no reason for committing such a crime against another individual simply because the victim has a different skin color. A few months after the outrage and condemnation on social media of the act, another African American became a victim of police brutality. George Floyd, a loving father of three, was brutally murdered by police officers. One of these officers knelt on Floyd's neck for approximately eight minutes, which eventually caused Floyd to asphyxiate. Floyd's death caused much grief within the Black community and again sparked outrage around the world over unjustified killings of Black people.

The connection between the death of these two African Americans within the span of four months and the institutionalization of Eurocentrism may not be easily discernible. When one understands that many white Americans believe that the maltreatment of the nonwhite community reinforces the master-subordinate structure of Anglo-American society where nonwhites always occupy the inferior position, one connects the dots of the arrogance behind these condemnable acts. It should be reiterated that the killing of nonwhites in American society, as in the two cited cases, may be seen as extreme measures taken against the marginalized nonwhite community members to perpetuate Eurocentrism. There are limitless instances of unreported maltreatment that these communities are still subjected to. If there had not been a history of similar "successful" offensive actions against nonwhites, it would be difficult to indulge in such blatant insensitivity to human life and their well-being.

The society that sees nothing condemnable in these kinds of injustices cannot be trusted with solutions to the root problem: Eurocentrism.

The daily experiences faced by the nonwhite community in Anglo-American environments cannot compare to what non-European countries are subjected to by the European and Anglo-American countries who already consider themselves as standard-bearers and thus enforcers of modernity. For example, in 2019, Abu Bakr al-Baghdadi, the head of the Islamic State, was killed in an American operation in Syria. Of course, terrorism is a morally reprehensible political act that deserves collective and global condemnation. However, how a terrorist should be brought to justice should be a joint decision between the countries that feel victimized by the terrorist organizations and powerful countries who have the wherewithal to thwart the activities of these offensive groups. Anything short of this amounts to a hegemonic imposition.

We can therefore compliment France's position regarding Francophone African countries on the European hegemonic crusade. Within the context of a master-subordinate relationship, France subjected its ex-colonies to extreme financial subjugation that impeded their progress as nations. One can understand why Francophone countries deliberately accept unfavorable terms with France—for fear of devastating economic reprisals. In fact, the French discontent with resistance from their former colonies has been expressed through the alleged assassinations of Francophone African leaders like Larbi Ben M'Hidi and Larbi Tbessi of Algeria, who want to diminish France's influence in their country. They were met with brick walls of denial because Eurocentrism, to the colonialists, must be preserved at all costs. These countries were coerced to sign agreements that would always be to France's advantage, thereby making them modern colonies of the West. And the loud silence of the whole world is a silence of consent.

Even those Western citizens who perhaps condemn Eurocentrism and its destructive influences are directly or indirectly benefiting from the philosophy and its institutionalized system. As such, the pursuance of genuine retracement of the Eurocentric practices would be difficult for those who are the primary beneficiaries of the system. Eurocentrism began concurrently with the activity of enslavement and colonialism and then evolved to globalization and modernity, all of which are ways of continuing the hegemonic agenda. It is not ahistorical to assert that the Anglo-American and European ascension to economic development has the efforts of Africans to thank for this. Therefore, putting an end to Eurocentric philosophy does not mean that institutions and benefits attached to it would automatically be abolished. There are various factors that make ending Eurocentrism, especially from the perspective of Westerners, difficult but not insurmountable. Many African countries are rendered financially incapable of managing their affairs, as can be seen in the recent increase in the number of Africans seeking refuge or asylum in Anglo-American and European countries, which can be interpreted as a spill-over effect of long-standing colonialism. Another factor is that a number of Africans have internalized the accepted superiority of the West and are ashamed of their own culture and skin color. As Ronald Hall, a professor of social work at Michigan State University, observes:

> So even though dark skin is a feature of African-Americans, light skin continues to be the ideal because it's the one preferred by the dominant group: whites. The bleaching syndrome has three components. The first is psychological: This involves self-rejection of dark skin and other native characteristics. Second, it's sociological, in that it influences group behavior (hence the phenomenon of black celebrities bleaching their skin). The final aspect is physiological. The physiological is not limited to just bleaching the skin. It can also mean altering hair texture and eye color to mimic the dominant group.[88]

For Eurocentrism to experience a decline in global practice, the work starts by accepting that the arrangement enthroned by a Eurocentric philosophy is unhealthy for the progress of everyone, not just the African people. There is no amount of persuasion that would influence the beneficiaries of Eurocentrism to consider taking alternative routes to living when they have not accepted that their ways have inhibited the growth of other people. The underlying efforts of these beneficiaries of Eurocentrism can range from making deliberate sacrifices in denouncing Eurocentric ideas and values. Although this revolutionary action can be sparked by different factors, some of which are the occurrences of injustice that catch the interest of the masses and provoke them into different actions. For example, the killing of George Floyd recently in America led

---

88 Hall, "Black America's Bleaching Syndrome."

Figure 2.1. Black Lives Matter protesters kneel and raise their hands in London's Oxford Street, July 8, 2016. Photograph by Alisdare Hickson. Used with permission.

to Black Lives Matter protests being publicized on a global level, and it forced many countries to reconsider their adoration and celebration of past heroes who were on record as having participated in the slave trade. Following this development, a number of Anglo-American institutions have registered their apologies to victims of slavery.

The above suggestion pertains to the beneficiaries of Eurocentrism and its institutions. However, there are a number of things to be done to end Eurocentrism. First among them is the introduction of Afrocentrism to counter misconceptions of Anglo-American and European countries toward Africa. Even though the system has been criticized by European apologists and the targets themselves, Afrocentrism has been able to defend African identity from the Westernizing doctrines of hegemonic countries. Therefore, this work suggests applying a modest form of Afrocentric ideology, which affirms the existence of Europe and its greatness in the process of human collective development but offers viable alternatives that validate African contributions to global culture and its development. Europeans are quite aware that Africa is the "cradle of civilization," and this is why they reject the connection between contemporary Africans and the ancient Egyptians, even in the face of scientific evidence.

Contrary to the claims of scholars like Mary Lefkowitz, Clarence Walker, and Kwame Anthony Appiah that Afrocentrism is nothing more than the product of excessive fantasizing about African history, Afrocentrism has proven that it can accommodate alternative narratives about any group or race of people, as long as their Afrocentric histories are not marginalized in favor of other histories. By championing modest Afrocentric ideas, the long-time victims of Eurocentric narratives could seek an intellectual revolution that would educate them on their history and inspire the valuation of their Afrocentric identity. Unlike apologists for Eurocentrism and their orientalist rhetoric, in Afrocentrism non-Black communities are not derided for their skin color, and neither are they taunted for having no solid historical antecedents. Basically, Afrocentrism has merely acknowledged the relationship between the history of civilization and the involvement of the African race to reclaim their lost identity.

While not meant to tear down the integrity of Eurocentric philosophies, especially ones pertaining to their contributions to technology, modernity, and civilization, Afrocentric philosophies only promote African contributions to, and interpretations of, progress, modernity, and civilization. African scholars deserve to till the soil for the cultivation of ideas that would emancipate their people from the shackles of inferiority and marginalization they continue to be bound by since the start of colonialism and slavery. The refutation of second-class status imposed by Eurocentrism is necessary because it would invalidate the erroneous mindset of the West against Africans and reveal the true nefarious intentions behind such deliberate revisionist history. Many Africans demonstrate their acceptance of inferior status in the extreme ways they celebrate ideas derived from European and Anglo-American culture, and usually employ notions of Western progress as models for African affairs. Without knowing it, these groups of people have accepted their marginal status. Many such individuals have not even traveled to European countries, and yet they idealize European culture while ignorant of its historical and contemporary failings.

Afrocentrism therefore must reflect African politics in terms of the content of the philosophies needed to run African affairs. This must be built on an understanding that different people have unique social and political trajectories, which invariably demand approaches that are not universal but contextually based. This would lead to the decolonization of politics in the long term, providing African solutions to specific African dilemmas. For example, many African countries were left as pseudo-democracies when the European imperialists were forced to abandon their colonial projects. In the attempt of some of these ex-colonies to perhaps impress their ex-colonizers with their penchant for self-determination, many of them began the nation-building process without taking stock of the inherited identity and legacy left by the colonialists. This led to the confirmation of the European bias, as a number of African countries descended into violent conflicts immediately after independence and into their postcolonial eras.

From one disaster to another, these countries began to drag themselves in the murky water of internal strife, struggle, and conflict that continued to affect their ability to think deeply and devise the proper political philosophies with which to run their political affairs. Therefore, it is incumbent on African leaders to begin the process of ending Eurocentrism by being active and conscious about using Afrocentric approaches to their various challenges. One way to understand how Eurocentrism still has a stranglehold on African countries is by considering the approaches that many Africans employed to containing or stemming the spread of COVID-19. Social distancing, lockdown, and the wearing of face masks, although common practice in many parts of the world, are all methods devised by countries beyond the African continent. The truth is that European and Anglo-American countries have the financial capacity to operate effective approaches to fighting COVID, while a large number of African countries do not.

Without taking their own environmental issues into consideration before adopting these Western strategies, Africans suffered two serious consequences related to their Westernized COVID response. One, they did not bother testing the functionality of these methods on their countries' populations. This led to distrust from the masses, who were expected to strictly adhere to the COVID restrictions. Sure enough, within a short period, Africa's appropriation of the Eurocentric approach led to the spread of the virus in many African countries. The fact is, that many Africans cannot even survive two weeks in a lockdown situation. This is corroborated by the insufficient economic conditions of many of the countries to look after the population of more than a billion people during this emergency. In whatever angle from which the incidents were viewed, Eurocentric approaches to African challenges are ill-advised at best and impotent at worst.

Ending Eurocentrism seems difficult because of the various benefits that certain people, especially African political and religious leaders, gain from it. No doubt many organizations and interests benefit from peddling Eurocentrism. Suffice it to say therefore that Eurocentrism is a multibillion-dollar affair from which various bodies draw their economic power. This is because Western audiences usually anticipate bad news about nonwhite communities, which validates their superiority and affirms their imagined power.

Between the sixteenth and early twentieth centuries, the production of knowledge reinforced Eurocentric ideologies in every sphere. In the field of history, Eurocentric historians denied the existence of African history and declared that the African past was basically marred by barbarism, primitivity, and inconsequential conditions. Africans were thought to have no literary history worth studying or learning.

This attitude would also spread to science. There were data that "proved" that Africans were biologically designed to occupy inferior positions to their Western counterparts, as indicated elsewhere in this section. All these became the foundation upon which the Western audience developed their bias against Africans. Their psychology was formed by internalizing the distorted messages made available by Eurocentric historians and philosophers. Since this kind of thinking was profitable for the Western publishing industry and media outlets, the demand for distorted information increased. The relationship of the Western audience and their intellectual community was predominantly a business one and therefore determined what form of knowledge was produced.

Since most Europeans and Anglo-Americans will never visit Africa, it is important to provide the true image of Africans and Africa to these European audiences. Africa and her people are like every other ethnic group in the world, with considerable challenges and a gradual development process. Therefore, the circulation of negative news about the

African people seeks only to serve a provincial purpose where Africans would be portrayed negatively and depicted as a people in urgent need of European and Anglo-American intervention. Usually, this is untrue. The proliferation of this malicious content about Africans in the media and other outlets is why many in the West do not, in general, think highly of the African people.

When one considers the fact that a large number of Anglo-American and European citizens still believe that Africa is just one country rather than a whole continent, and in retrospect, that Africans are all primitive people, one would understand the reengineering projects that the West sought to achieve with Eurocentrism. These biased attitudes would therefore be reflected even in the comments of lettered people like the aforementioned Trevor-Roper and would surface in the racist opinions of former US President Donald Trump (as indicated elsewhere in this book), as well as feature in the master-subordinate relationship kept by the custodians of the Christian faith against the practitioners of African religion. Since the majority of these Western audiences basically remain in their geographical settings, whatever information they get about Africans is through secondary sources, which are mostly unreliable in many cases. Those in the Eurocentric bloc therefore cash in on this opportunity to project images that denigrate Africans for consumption by a European audience. The power to stop the circulation of such unfounded narratives about Africans does not lie with Africans themselves: this power must come from European and Anglo-American sources.

In essence, Eurocentrism will be less pervasive when the peddlers of the philosophy allow for true representation of events. It will end when Europeans and Anglo-Americans journey to Africa to have firsthand experiences. Eurocentrism would come to a halt when Western audiences engage in logical analysis of Africans, who are doing fine in their respective environments even in the Western world. The fact that many Africans are in important positions using their intellect to improve the conditions of places where they live dispels the assumption that they are inferior, a notion peddled by the Eurocentric historians. By rushing to showcase the bad deeds of Africans in diasporas and showing suspicious reluctance in informing the world about the commendable efforts of Africans who are leaders in various fields, Western media have therefore demonstrated their unapologetically Eurocentric bias. The perpetuation of these attitudes would make the hegemonic agenda of the West a little stronger.

The outright rejection of these Eurocentrist attitudes would provide the means for the African people to grow appropriately.

Eurocentrism will end when Western society understands the primacy of African decisions on African affairs. Africans do not need Eurocentric decisions to move their societies forward. There must be a change of mentality about the ways the Western world perceives the African people. The erroneous assumption that Africans are a people incapable of independent thinking is the main reason why the West continuously intervenes in African affairs, thereby imposing their ideologies in a way that inhibits the agency of the African people. Advancement in technology does not automatically qualify any group of people to become the global standard for moral, political, and social ethics. In fact, while technology remains crucial to steering the globe to another milestone of collective development, a moral society is indispensable to sustainable progress.

How do we therefore identify a good society? This is the question one should ask. A good society is one that identifies goals and devises ways in which such goals could be achieved without pressure. One of the reasons for the problems Africans face is that they instantaneously fell for the European model of progress and decided to model their development on that of the Anglo-American and European world. Africans abandoned their project of developing good social conduct to meet a world that is interconnected because of the advent of technology. As such, the Africans' problem started from their mindset toward development. From their leadership down to the average citizen, whatever does not bear the mark of Western notions of development is not respected. This is primarily the result of having the seed of Eurocentrism planted and germinated in their minds for a protracted period.

When the former US president Donald Trump made insulting comments about Africans, he alluded to the lagging development of their countries, taunting them because of their dissimilar perceptions of modernity and civilization. Apart from the fact that having such an orientation reinforces racism and promotes Eurocentrism, there is the possibility of these comments affecting how African Americans perceive themselves. Therefore, the politics of stereotyping the nonwhite community has been the main reason for the divisive culture that Eurocentrism actively validates. Apart from the distortion in the circulated narratives that Africans are a people stuck in a perpetual state of primitivism, the character assassination in peddling such Eurocentric bias and making important decisions that affect the race using unfounded arguments make it continuously difficult for Africans to maximize their potential. It should be reiterated that the political problems culminating in wars and internal conflicts that characterized African countries are residual events from the colonial world. Therefore, deriding Africans for not transforming their environment while still dealing with the legacy of wars is wholly unfair.

The identification of internal challenges and the provision of workable solutions should be the exclusive preserve of Africans themselves. Doing this would assist them in arranging their priorities accordingly, as issues that need moral solutions would not be met with scientific ones. Development is a long process with a logical progression of ideas, projects, and engagements. It is inconsequential to evade some steps in the quest for social development; otherwise, the result would not be worthwhile or sustainable. For example, many African countries had a history of social progression prior to the invasion of their continent by the combined forces of the Europeans and Arabs; they were forced to abandon these available structures and systems to concentrate on the Western style of growth. From education and medicine to philosophy and moral standards, all of these were subsumed under Eurocentric systems that in the long run did not bring the anticipated development. A number of African countries inherited from the colonialists a system of education that did not support the expression of human creativity, unlike their African systems where every member of the society actively participated in building its infrastructures. Such a system recorded the great contributions that Africa is said to make to scholarship generally.

There was division of social activities where people would apply different skills in building their society. There were architects who were responsible for developing the infrastructure, and they were evolving to meet the level of development and civilization envisioned by their environment. There were experts in metallurgy, who made materials needed for common purposes. This is in addition to those specifically concerned with the development of philosophy to be used by all the members of society for social advancement. Every major development of the African world is dedicated to different experts, who, like their counterparts in other places of the world, were evolving and improving on their knowledge with time. However, the West assumed that these people could not handle the responsibility of developing the African infrastructure. Going back to the precolonial way of doing things could not be guaranteed even if the project of decolonization became successful. The fact, however, remains that the people would begin to conceptualize development and contextualize it in ways that would impact their lives accordingly.

By and large, the eradication of Eurocentrism could happen earlier than imagined. There are no two sides that can give identical interpretations of an event even when they are in close proximity to the object. Apart from the human limitations of physical space, there are various biological characteristics that dictate what we see and how we see them. When we come to a global understanding of this simple truth, perhaps it would influence the way we see others who are geographically or culturally different from us.

To strengthen this argument, the imposition of a single perspective encourages the disparaging of the Other by subduing their interpretations through intellectual blackmail. Universalizing ideas, implicit in the habit of the West in their projection of wrong identity through harsh narratives on the nonwhite community, promote the supremacist ideology of the West at the expense of others, thereby foregrounding their hegemonic agenda in critical discourse. The globalist Europeans and their Anglo-American ideologues repudiate the idea that Africans are independently capable of instigating intellectual engagements that can produce worthwhile contributions to knowledge systems globally. Convinced of this baseless sentiment, the hegemonic West concludes bitterly that the African race collectively is engrossed in some form of inertia that robs them of intellectual viability and therefore disqualifies them of their right to take action concerning even their very own existence. Such supremacist ideology reverberates in racial comments reflected in such expressions as, "Africans are a people without writing," and "Africans are people without history," as projected even by learned Europeans like Trevor-Roper in the twentieth century. Obviously, it would be difficult for the people who actively rejected the ontological independence of Africa to therefore give any regard to their intellectual expressions.

Rather than suppress their voices and perspectives by making deprecatory and condemnatory comments, as found in the comments of lettered Europeans, the global intellectual society must deploy diplomacy and courtesy in their reactions to alternative perspectives. Peddling a singular Eurocentric perspective alienates others whose realities are constructed by these imposed Western ideas. The problem therefore is that the perspective of the West is effective only in answering European and Anglo-American questions. Its validity becomes questionable when dealing with African realities. Therefore, forcing the latter to express themselves with the imposed system would limit their expressiveness and influence their exponential growth generally. In other words, multiple perspectives are encouraged for the supremacy agenda of the West to be stopped. Africans must avoid being victims in this sort of global system, as they would continuously be exposed to constant harassment and denigration in the event that they do not offer credible alternatives to universalism.

Chapter Three

Epistemologies of Intellectual Liberation

> Wisdom is like a baobab tree,
> a single person's hand cannot embrace it
> —Akan Proverb

Introduction

Fifteen years ago, African scholars produced less than 0.5 percent of all academic publications globally.[1] This percentage is taken from select universities in Nigeria, South Africa, and Egypt. The pattern has remained stagnant since the 1980s, despite increased attention toward the African university.[2] Academic publications about Africa are numerous, but only a small percentage are by African scholars.[3] African studies is not the only area lacking in African voices; the pattern persists through all academic disciplines, from the humanities and politics to social sciences and hard science. The silence of the African voice has practical implications for fields such as international relations, pedagogy, and policy.[4] This academic gap is not the problem of Africa alone; there is a gap in the number of academic publications produced by subaltern academics

---

1 Zeleza, "Intellectual."
2 Mama, "Is It Ethical," 1–26.
3 Today, the internet is creating greater access, making academic work from Africa more visible to those who have the patience to seek it.
4 Ndlovu-Gatsheni, "Genealogies," 13–40.

internationally. I utilize the term "subaltern academics" to include those postcolonial nations of Southeast Asia, South America, and Africa as well as women.

Despite its frequent use in literature, there is an unspoken contradiction in the term "subaltern." The subaltern exists only in juxtaposition to a mainstream perspective. In the modern world order, the mainstream perspective is Eurocentrism. Europe's position as the mainstream perspective has roots in power, not majority opinion. Consider the size of the regions defined as "subaltern" such as Southeast Asia, Africa, Latin America, and Central America. These heavily populated areas make up a large percentage of the world's population.[5] The subaltern perspective is only subaltern in respect to global power and not by population. By population, the subaltern perspective is better defined as the "majority of the world" perspective.[6] These epistemic perspectives are so diverse they can only be put into one group in contrast with another group. The use of the term "subaltern" is inevitably tied to the global power structure. The creation of the term "subaltern epistemologies" is evidence of Eurocentric global power over academia.

The perspective that subaltern academics bring to the academic community are subaltern epistemologies. Epistemology is a field of philosophy that defines the nature of knowledge. Subaltern epistemologies have different philosophies on what can be known and the methodological approaches to validate knowledge. Traditional epistemology champions reason as the sole way to achieve knowledge. It reinforces the scientific method as the pathway to this validation of knowledge.[7] When subaltern epistemologies are silenced, we are given the illusion that there is only one way to knowing, one epistemology. This is an illusion, tied to the history of global powers and their agenda for knowledge production.[8] Traditional epistemology only validates one perspective: that of a singular epistemology. The silencing of subaltern epistemologies results in a singular Eurocentric story about knowledge production.

Chimamanda Adichie, an eloquent speaker, defined the effects of the global rejection of subaltern epistemologies in her TED talk, "The

---

5 *World Population Review*, "Continent."
6 Silver, "If You Shouldn't."
7 Arowosegbe, "African Studies, 308–21.
8 Ndlovu-Gatsheni, "Why Decoloniality, 10–15.

Danger of a Single Story." Adichie uses her experience being stereotyped as a Nigerian woman to explain the danger of stereotyping. She generalizes her experiences to explain how Western stories about other nations reduce those nations to only stories of poverty or victimization. She describes telling someone's story for them as the ultimate power of oppression.[9] The lack of subaltern academics published globally reflects Western dominance in academia.[10] The subalterns have their stories told for them, a modern manifestation of the oppression of the "majority world."

In the Western story, decolonization is equivalent to the liberation of colonial nations. Yet, many scholars question decolonization as indicative of liberation. Liberation is much more than just recognition of national sovereignty. Postcolonial nations are economically, politically, and culturally dependent on Western nations. This means that the academics of postcolonial nations fall in the jurisdiction of Western nations. At the time of "liberation" for postcolonial nations, the global academic systems were already set in a Eurocentric hierarchy. Postcolonial nations have political recognition, but now they need intellectual liberation.[11]

Coloniality is the barrier to the expression of subaltern epistemologies. The continued effects of colonialism have created a global academic system that devalues subaltern epistemologies and privileges the colonial agenda. Understanding the plight of subaltern epistemologies and finding solutions requires an understanding of coloniality.

In this chapter, I differentiate coloniality from colonization to advocate for a decolonial approach to knowledge. I explain the epistemic violence that requires decoloniality. Then, I describe Afrocentricity as an approach to decoloniality to prevent epistemic violence. I further this example by applying African epistemologies to various disciplines. I explain the barriers toward subaltern epistemologies in academics and propose how to overcome them. Finally, I advocate for a redefinition of knowledge to empower subaltern epistemologies.

---

9   TED, "The Danger of a Single Story."
10 Masaka, "Prospects," 284–301.
11 Arowosegbe, "Bias of Eurocentricism."

Epistemologies of the Global South

The traditional concept of epistemology developed from discussions between Aristotle and Plato about the nature of knowledge. Aristotle argued for a rationalist approach to knowledge, using reason to surpass the limits of the senses.[12] Plato argued for an empiricist perspective, using the senses to ground the creative limits of reason in reality.[13] Greek philosophy was the foundation for the rationalists' Enlightenment. Descartes built on empiricism by adding skepticism, the active questioning of knowledge.[14] Other enlightenment philosophers built upon the idea of truth as something that can be known through proper observation and reason, along with proper skepticism. Gettier formalized the philosophical definition of knowledge by defining it as a "justified true belief"[15]; Began and Bacon created the foundations to the scientific method;[16] and Karl Popper formalized definitions to science by debunking what he called "pseudoscience."[17] The result of the work of these and many other famous European epistemologists defines the global academic system.[18] This system depends on the use of the scientific method and university validation for knowledge to be validated.

The assumptions of European epistemology are that knowledge exists, the universe is predictable, and we can learn about the universe through study and skepticism. Epistemology exists in the framework of the Enlightenment, in that it is separate from religious or mystical ideas deemed unscientific.[19] Knowledge through European epistemology does not have to have a goal but contributes to knowledge of the universe. In many parts of the world, the concept of separating religion and science does not exist. Through its history, values, and goals, epistemology is regarded as distinctly European.

---

12 Aristotle, *Posterior Analytics*.
13 Plato, *Republic*.
14 Descartes and Lafleur, *Meditations*.
15 Gettier, "Is Justified," 121–23.
16 Bacon, *Novum Organum*.
17 Popper, *Conjectures*.
18 Schlesinger, *Disuniting*.
19 Arowosegbe, "Bias of Eurocentricism."

There are several patterns in subaltern epistemologies, generalizations to differentiate them from Western epistemology. An example is spirituality. Many peoples believe that the world we are living in is inseparable from the spiritual world. Thus, all phenomena are related to those of the spiritual world. The value of collectivism makes some peoples require a meaning to knowledge that helps the community, instead of knowing for the sake of knowing. Many cultures value experience of an individual above empirical evidence. Another epistemic pattern is ritual; through ritual—interrelated to spirituality and collectivism—people can know more about the spiritual and physical world.[20]

Generalizations are extremely limited because subaltern epistemologies are diverse. An example of a subaltern epistemic perspective is that of Ubuntu. Ubuntu is the African philosophy that focuses on the role of the individual within the whole. It is often compared to the phrase "I think, therefore I am," which defines humanity as those who can think. Ubuntu counters "I am because we are," meaning that humanity is defined as finding a role in society. Through this view, knowledge is known through the community and that which is useful for the community.[21] A very different epistemic perspective is *buen vivir*, the philosophy of the good life in South America. *Buen vivir* focuses on balance and interconnection between community, culture, and the environment. From this perspective, knowledge can come from any of those places and must be useful for them.[22] Another example is the Chinese and South Asian philosophy of Taoism, which focuses on unending change in life in which living things live in harmony with the earth.[23] The thing these philosophies have in common is that they all are seen as inherently subordinate in the Eurocentric epistemology.

Subaltern epistemologies also include the feminist perspective.[24] In 2018 only 30 percent of academic publications were by women.[25] Subaltern epistemologies speak for those who are systematically disenfranchised, whose voices are silenced. Internationally, this includes the voices

---

20   McDougal, "Africana Studies," 236–50.
21   Wu et al., "Perturbing," 504–19.
22   Hidalgo-Capitán and Cubillo-Guevara, "Deconstruction," 23–50.
23   Wu et al., "Perturbing."
24   McFadden, "African Feminist," 36–42.
25   *UNESCO*, "Just 30%."

of women. Women are discriminated against with respect to their economic, political, and cultural rights. This includes a lack of opportunity to pursue academic work. Especially vulnerable to epistemic rejection are women who come from non-Western cultures. These women experience intersectionality in aspects of their oppression. This means that their race and gender magnify the effects of oppression so that they are the most negatively affected.[26]

The rich amount of knowledge that the subaltern has to offer academia versus the low production and high barriers to subaltern academia leads to the question, "Can the subaltern speak?"[27] It is a question of whether the subaltern can overcome the system that works to silence their voices. In the next section of this chapter, I will describe the way in which European epistemologies came into their privileged positions in the academic hierarchy, the effects of this, and ways to work against the dominance of Eurocentrism.

Decolonization

Colonialism was the oppressive systematic migration of Europeans into other territories. These territories were officially "unclaimed" or "undiscovered," from the European perspective, and so Europeans made these territories their own. Decolonization was a political process in which Western nations granted many non-Western nations independence and integration into the modern political regime. It came out of the nationalist movements of many countries in the 1960s. This independence did not end the colonial matrix of power that had developed in the last few centuries. The colonial system of power has its origins in 1492 when Columbus started claiming the Americas for Spain. It continued through the Westphalian Peace Treaty when the modern nation-state system was created, defining areas of being and nonbeing that were open to conquest. It then escalated through formal colonization in the Berlin Conference. Colonial powers were solidified even after independence by the creation of the United Nations world political system, which underprivileges the role

---

26 Madhok, "Coloniality," 56–71.
27 Spivak and Morris, *Can the Subaltern*.

of postcolonial nations. Thus, these hundreds of years of global hierarchical processes were not destroyed by the formal independence of nations.[28]

The colonial matrix of power describes the long-lasting effects that were created during colonialism that supported its practice.[29] This includes Eurocentric ideas about economics, authority, gender, sexuality, and knowledge that have influenced practices and perceptions throughout the rest of the world.[30] Colonizing European nations did so under a "civilizing mission." This appealed to both religious and secular parties. To religious people, it meant spreading Christianity, and to others it meant curing those nations of their "backwardness."[31] From the perspective of a "civilizing mission," European epistemology is so-called correct knowledge that Europe alone was able to discover through the process of the Enlightenment. The Eurocentric nature of epistemology reinforces European political motivations of colonization.

Decolonization was able to officially give autonomy to the citizens of these decolonized countries. Yet, the colonial matrix of power, the ideology of colonialism, and their institutions remained. This includes a political hierarchy that privileges Europe and economic policies that perpetuate dependence on Europe by exporting raw materials. It also includes the social and cultural privilege of European institutions—including those of academia. Decolonization leads to liberation on paper, but the colonial matrix of power meant that national autonomy, including that of intellectual liberation, was far from achieved.

Decoloniality: The Context of Modernity and Neocolonialism

Decoloniality is the modern response to the colonial matrix of power. It was defined by Latin American scholars expressing their frustrations with the concept of postcolonialism. It advocates intellectual liberation, an ongoing process in which subaltern agents actively fight against contemporary colonial matrixes of power to retain their autonomy. Examples of coloniality after colonialism include the structural adjustment programs

---

28 Ndlovu-Gatsheni, "Why Decoloniality."
29 Mignolo, *The Darker Side*.
30 Ndlovu-Gatsheni, "Decolonising, 46–51.
31 Flikschuh, "Idea," 1–26.

(SAPs), the Washington Consensus, and apartheid. Coloniality encompasses all of the cultural, economic, and political control that Western nations continue to hold over postcolonial nations.[32] Key to this process is rejection of a hierarchy that privileges Eurocentric epistemologies. This civilizing mission marked the "invention of Africa." Africa was invented in the eyes of Europeans as a backward place that needed foreign intervention to thrive. It was characterized as a homogenous place despite the wide diversity of the continent.[33] Decoloniality moves toward the reinvention of Africa through her own perspective. This is not a story of failure but one that celebrates success and looks to the future.

The global hierarchy that privileges Western epistemology is an example of an ideology. In the view of Marxism, ideology is the work of the elite class that dominates the proletariat. The elite class spreads the ideology so that the working class will accept their inferior position in society instead of pushing against it. From this perspective, in the global hierarchy of knowledge, Western "knowledge" is the ideology used to control the proletariat. The UN system and Western ideas of neoliberalism are meant to be applied worldwide. Marxism is useful for understanding the relationship between oppression and ideology.[34] Still, Marxist ideas were applied to the subaltern by European philosopher Gramsci. The application of Marxism to postcolonial nations is a European framework for non-European problems.[35] Furthermore, the analysis of class alone simplifies coloniality and decontextualizes it.[36]

Another explanation for the global hierarchy of knowledge that privileges the Western epistemology is Legitimation Code Theory (LCT). LCT acknowledges the social and epistemic context in which knowledge develops. It is up to the person receiving the "knowledge" to determine whether it is legitimate or not. The legitimation of knowledge also takes place in social and epistemic contexts. People decide whether knowledge is legitimate or not by who it is coming from and how it came to be known.[37] LCT applied to the global knowledge hierarchy suggests

---

32   Ndlovu-Gatsheni, "Decoloniality," 485–96.
33   Mudimbe, *Invention*.
34   Nuruddin, "Africana Studies," 93–125.
35   Brennan, "Antonio Gramsci," 143–87.
36   Ndlovu-Gatsheni, "Why Are South African," 52–61.
37   Maton, "Progress," 157–78.

that Western knowledge is legitimized because it comes from the West and its scientific methods. It also suggests that global academia does not legitimize non-Western epistemologies because their methodology and academics are not seen as valuable. LCT and Marxism are both perspectives that can reinforce the idea of decoloniality but still focus on specifics instead of addressing the whole issue. They talk about coloniality in terms that are too general instead of describing how these individual peoples have been systematically oppressed throughout history.[38]

Colonialism created the colonial matrix of power, which consisted of institutions and ideology to support colonial rule. Decolonization was able to grant the independence of these nations and the removal of many Westerners. The colonial matrix of power that allowed the Western oppression of postcolonial nations continues through economic, political, and cultural means. If coloniality is able to define humanity through Western definitions of what it means to be human, then decoloniality must counter by redefining the nature of humanity through subaltern epistemologies.[39]

A key manifestation of this is Immanuel Kant's definition of man as capable of reason. By this logic, those who cannot reason are lesser men. Subaltern epistemologies do not always champion reason the same way European epistemology does. Other epistemologies may champion spirituality, collectivism, experience, or even ritual above reason. Through the perspective of Western epistemology, holding religion above reason justifies Western global domination by dehumanizing the subaltern.[40]

Decoloniality is related but separate from postmodernism. Postmodernism is a theory that does not see modernity as progress. It questions the concept that current ideas, creations, and systems are superior to those of the past. It seeks to redefine modernity, not as something progressive but as a snapshot of our current time.[41] Modernity through a postmodern perspective is dual in nature. It has a positive side involving consumerism and progress, while it has also seen the rise of global hierarchies.[42] One way that postmodernism is similar to decoloniality is that it redefines modernity. Coloniality defines modernity as that which is

---

38 Ndlovu-Gatsheni, "Decoloniality."
39 Desai and Sanya, "Towards Decolonial," 710–24.
40 Stikkers, "An Outline," 40–49.
41 Ndlovu-Gatsheni, "Why Decoloniality."
42 Ndlovu-Gatsheni, *Empire*.

Western—that which is advanced.[43] Postmodernism is a European questioning of whether "modernity" is true to its name; decoloniality invites non-European perspectives to actively work against the European foisting of oppressive modernity onto other nations.[44]

Decoloniality is also not cosmopolitanism. The vision of cosmopolitanism is the equitable blending of global cultures. It was a justification ideology made for the policy of globalization, in which markets were deregulated and profit became the sole indicator of national growth. This resulted in an economic system in which postcolonial nations relied on Western economics, culture, and politics. In other words, cosmopolitanism is a Western justification for the colonial matrix of power. Cosmopolitanism at its surface is diversity. In practice it is unidirectional, with Western domination across the world.[45] For example, Western culture permeates throughout all of Africa, yet how much of African culture is visible in America? This is an example of cosmopolitanism's unilateral nature. Diversity has to be true to its name and not an acceptance of the global hierarchy.

A similar pattern follows with diversity in research and academia. Research in academia cannot claim to be diverse without addressing the underlying issue of coloniality. This means that a field cannot simply acknowledge subaltern epistemologies, although it is a first step. Western academics must include the active input of researchers of subaltern epistemologies. At the same time, they must seek to point out manifestations of coloniality in their own epistemology and academia.[46] Subaltern epistemologies must not only be about the subaltern but include the subaltern experience of coloniality. This is how decoloniality can advocate for subaltern epistemologies.[47] This is not a singular process in which the story of the struggle between decoloniality and the colonial matrix of power is told. It is a story consisting of many stories from many culturally diverse perspectives. There is not a single answer to fight the problem of Western

---

43 Alcoff, "Mignolo's Epistemology," 79.
44 Grosfoguel, "Epistemic," 211–23.
45 Mignolo, "Cosmopolitanism," 111–27.
46 Alcoff, "Mignolo's Epistemology."
47 Grosfoguel, "Epistemic Decolonial."

epistemological dominance but rather a continuous process of legitimating subaltern epistemologies.[48]

I have described the way in which the modern global epistemic hierarchy was founded through ideological justification of colonialism: coloniality. Thus, the current system of knowledge that is globally accepted is not accepted for its merit but because of its relations to power. In this view, subaltern epistemologies—which make up much of the world—are neglected. The result is epistemic violence, epistemic limitations, and systematic humiliation of entire cultures. I will present two current models that can be utilized to bridge the gap between traditional and subaltern epistemologies: border thinking and constellation of knowledge.

Constellation of knowledge is an epistemic theory in which no one set of knowledge is legitimized above the rest. Instead of following a singular epistemology, diverse methodological and epistemic foundations can be legitimized. They coexist despite any paradoxes or dualities between them, all part of the larger picture of human knowledge.[49] This idea works toward legitimization of subaltern epistemologies. Yet, it does not actively account for the devaluation of knowledge created through the colonial matrix of power. Thus, much like the idea of cosmopolitanism, it fails to break down the system of hierarchy that controls modern academia.

Border thinking is an epistemic perspective that was first developed by Latin American feminist decolonial epistemologist Gloria Anzaldúa.[50] It was further integrated into the literature on decoloniality by Mignolo.[51] Border thinking uses geographical borders in both physical and symbolic ways. It works on the assumption that Western epistemologies are not able to cover all forms of knowledge. Some of these unknowns are explained through other subaltern epistemologies, which are covered up by the colonial matrix of power. The borders represent the paradoxes and dualities between these two forms of knowledge, which are necessary to both acknowledge and discuss. Border thinking dissipates the idea of a hierarchy of knowledge in which one culture is superior than another. Rather, it actively considers the cracks in the system of global knowledge

---

48 García, "Decoloniality."
49 De Sousa, "General Introduction," xvii–xxxiii.
50 Anzaldúa, *Borderlands*.
51 Mignolo, *Local Histories/Global*.

created because of coloniality and works to resolve them through legitimization of subaltern epistemologies.[52]

Epistemic Violence

To pursue a path of decoloniality, we must understand the consequences of the current hierarchy of knowledge that privileges European epistemologies. Epistemic violence is a consequence of coloniality in which local cultures are rejected in favor of Western epistemology. The result is disruption of local culture and creation of community trauma.[53] As mentioned previously, telling someone's story for them is the greatest form of control. An example is a nonprofit coming into a community and telling them that their systems of health care are inferior and that Western medicine is the only option. The message that the West sends such a culture is that they are unable to produce the right kind of knowledge. The result in the non-Western country is typically either total rejection of Westernization or rejection of one's own culture, both with uniquely negative consequences. Called "epistemicide," this undervaluing of a group's cultural knowledge causes individual and collective trauma.[54]

Western epistemology inherently contains the message that only a singular truth exists: that of Western science. The result is that when Western pedagogy is spread to nonwhite majority areas, the educational sector in these non-Western places takes an epistemic hit. In the Western paradigm, there is no room for additional cultural knowledge of subjects. The Eurocentric model of the university denies students the ability to contribute the unique knowledge they bring from their ethnic backgrounds.[55] To deny a group the ability to produce knowledge is to deny them the ability to be truly human and thus leads to epistemicide.[56]

One tangible example of epistemic violence would be mental health interventions in Sri Lanka. Interventions done with trauma victims in Sri Lanka worked to improve mental health using the medical model

---

52　Alcoff, "Mignolo's Epistemology."
53　Vazquez, "Translation," 27–44.
54　Masaka, "Prospects."
55　Morreira, "Steps towards Decolonial," 287–301.
56　Masaka, "Prospects."

of depression. For people in Sri Lanka who followed a Buddhist way of life, depression was unfamiliar to them as a concept. To the Buddhist, the Western terminology that is used to describe depression could also describe just an everyday devout Buddhist. Thus, trying to educate victims through a Western epistemology causes epistemic violence by devaluing their culture; this, on top of previous psychological damage, can cause extreme harm. Mental health interventions in Sri Lanka could instead focus on the culturally appropriate cures to depression that already exist, such as the Buddhist practice of meditation.[57]

Another example is Chicana women in Mexico. These women were part of a culture that was undervalued, their voices largely legitimized by Western epistemology. Femicide, the killing of women, is common in Mexico especially among Chicana women. These women are poor and are often blamed for their own deaths for engaging in risky behavior. The lack of action regarding their deaths is a symptom of a culture of epistemic violence involving Chicana women. Activists in the Chicana feminists' community work toward remembering the femicides and making the lost voices of those women heard.[58]

One tool of epistemic violence that is often overlooked is translation. Translation is not a simple exchange of words in a one-to-one ratio. It requires cultural knowledge to be able to understand the true meaning of words. Through translating works into English, Western epistemology is able to alter the voices of the subaltern. Instead of using translation as a tool of erasure, translation should be used in a more broadening way that expresses the opinions of the subaltern. In this way, translation can be used as a tool of border thinking, promoting the understanding of breaks in subaltern epistemologies because of coloniality and comparing subaltern and traditional epistemologies.[59] One practical way that this can be done is by including a summary of research in the native language of the peoples it is relevant to. This way, the translation is less vulnerable to interpretation and information can be more freely accessed across cultures.[60]

One tool of epistemic violence is language of instruction. On one hand, teaching children only through English devalues their own cultural

---

57 Watters, "Three Challenges," 237–56.
58 Galván, "Collective Memory," 343–57.
59 Vazquez, "Translation."
60 Lincoln and González, "Search," 784–805.

knowledge. It sends the innate message that knowledge can only be learned through the West. It also makes that information harder for children to understand, giving them an inferior understanding of knowledge as opposed to if they were able to use their own language.[61] On the other hand, English can provide valuable tools for young academics. It can give them access to the global economy; it also allows them to access more materials than would be available in their mother tongue alone, since more academic work and literature is available in English. The danger of a nonnative speaker teaching in English is alienation from one's culture. The danger of not teaching in English is continued disconnection from the global economy and lack of non-English pedagogical materials.

Teaching English is only one example of a Eurocentric pedagogy, one of the primary causes of epistemic violence around the world. Eurocentric pedagogy devalues subaltern perspectives on a variety of issues. The most well-known example is that of history. The phrase "history is told by the winners" is absolutely true, as powerful nations are able to spread their ideology and push their political agenda. An example is the history of African Americans in the United States. Few American public school history courses cover the horrors of slavery or the journey of African Americans to gain their freedom in America. It also hardly mentions their cultural background or Pan-Africanism. Additionally, US high school history courses rarely touch on the stories of African Americans; when they do, Black people are painted largely as victims of the Western slave trade, leaving out much of the story. Scholars have emphasized the importance of altering these curricula or providing supplementary curricula to African American students that work against Eurocentric education.[62]

Epistemic violence takes many forms. It occurs in schools, media, and nonprofit interventions. Epistemic violence causes community and individual trauma by devaluing the human capacity of a group to produce valid information. The result of epistemic violence to the subaltern is intergenerational physical, political, academic, and psychological oppression.

---

61 Morreira, "Steps towards Decolonial."
62 Carroll and Jamison, "African-Centered Psychology," 52–72.

Afrocentricity

This chapter has examined subaltern epistemologies in the context of postcolonial nations as well as feminism. The cure to the epistemic violence caused by oppression of the subaltern epistemologies is decoloniality, and decoloniality is achieved by first calling out the symptoms of Eurocentrism and continued coloniality. Then, epistemology must shift its focus to subaltern perspectives. A wonderful example of a framework to give voice to subaltern epistemologies is Afrocentricity. Afrocentricity requires the African diaspora to actively contextualize epistemology based on their own cultural values and ideologies.[63]

Afrocentrism works to acknowledge Africa's unique cultures. One definition of Afrocentrism defines three tenets of Afrocentrism: (1) cultural centeredness on African nations, (2) paradigmatic pluralism, allowing for the presence of multiple worldviews to exist, and (3) cultural liberation and agency—or respecting African culture and actively working to preserve it across nations.[64]

This study has described how decoloniality can be explained through Marxism. It also mentions that this perspective can also be Eurocentric. Yet, it is a useful model for explaining the relationship between global Western power and the dominance of Western epistemology. Some scholars say that this theory is worth utilizing in decoloniality discourse if viewed through Afrocentrism. Afrocentrism can adjust for the perspectives of the subaltern, but it does not mean that Western theories should be outright rejected. Rather, they can be grounded in Afrocentrism and blended into mainstream academia.[65]

A meta-analysis done in 2014 of different theories in Africana studies sought to identify patterns in their Afrocentric perspective. The research sought to extract these patterns for the purpose of identifying them with Afrocentric approaches. Researchers found nine important patterns that defined the Afrocentric perspective. These included "Recognition of the Necessity of Cultural Specificity, Prioritization of Africana Needs and Interests, Heterogeneous Collectivism, Collective Emancipation and Empowerment, Agency and Self Consciousness, Historical Location,

---

63 Mazama, "Afrocentric Paradigm," 387–405.
64 Schreiber, "Overcoming," 651–71.
65 Nuruddin, "Africana Studies."

Cultural Situating, Recognizing the Shaping Effects of Oppression and Liberation, and Intersectionality."[66] All these categories are focused on understanding the global Africana experience and can be used as tools to contextualize research and knowledge on African perspectives. The key is that Afrocentrism changes the foundations of research to include African values, working against the colonial matrix of power.

A Note on Postracialism

Postracialism is a concept utilized by the Western world and international politics that seeks to erase color from the general discourse. Postracialism uses peace rhetoric that argues against "tribalism" and seeks solidarity among all races. It is often equated with being "color-blind." One recent politician who took a postracial perspective was Barack Obama. Obama was the first Black president of the United States; he was the son of a Kenyan. An Afrocentric perspective would mean that Obama would have to accept that African American cultures are more closely tied to African than American cultures. However, Obama could not embrace his African heritage while appealing to the voters of white America. He argued that such statements are characteristic of tribalism and promote further divisions rather than peace. He had to embrace a policy of multiculturalism to gain the power to promote change.[67]

The problem with a postracial perspective is that it fails to correct for coloniality. Similar to the idea of cosmopolitanism, postracialism is an impossible narrative. The hierarchy of knowledge created by coloniality requires active dismantling. Not talking about race encourages silence. Pan-Africanism emphasizes race so that groups suffering from oppression can work together to find solutions. Afrocentricity is the tool of this global collaboration. The peace rhetoric and dream of postracialism is tempting, yet it is doomed to fail because it involves ignoring coloniality.

Key to Afrocentricity is how words are translated. When Western epistemology tries to analyze African ideas, it makes the key mistake of not using a "thick" translation. A thick translation takes into account the contextual information usually left out of the translation process. This

---

66 McDougal, "Africana Studies."
67 Austin, "Barack Obama," 113–28.

includes historical context, cultural connotations, social norms, religion, and geographical location. When Western epistemologies try to understand African concepts without an African epistemology, they make the mistake of thinking Africans use terminology in the same sense that they do.[68]

Afrocentric research has requirements, including the rejection of objectivity, rejection of distance between the researcher, and participant and holistic thinking. These tenets are key problems in Western research on Africa. Objectivity involves the inherent separation of religion and science that exists in Western epistemology. Researchers trying to survey participants objectively without any personal relation to them come off as rude. This will not prompt proper responses from African respondents. Finally, holistic thinking is necessary because African participants do not separate culture from other analytical categories unlike Western epistemology.[69] This means that research should reflect African perspectives about the interdependent nature of the universe. In many African ontologies, the world is seen as spiritual by nature, with physical manifestations that require it to be interpreted as such.[70]

Another key characteristic of research on African peoples is purposeful empiricism. African epistemologies value things for their role within society and how useful they are in solving problems for people. To conduct appropriate research in these areas, the people's needs must be considered as well as those of the researcher.[71]

Afrocentricity is able to legitimize African epistemologies and give them a voice. Through this, the global hierarchy of knowledge can accommodate African epistemologies. Afrocentricity and African epistemologies should always be used by those of African descent, whatever their area of research. Westerners studying African areas or peoples must always include African epistemic perspectives.[72]

---

68 Stikkers, "An Outline."
69 Schreiber, "Overcoming."
70 Carroll, "An Introduction," 257–70.
71 Carroll, "An Introduction."
72 Wiredu, "Toward Decolonizing," 17–46.

Applied African Epistemologies

Afrocentricity can be used to construct an African epistemic approach in any field. This section will outline some examples of how this is done to highlight the consistent ways that subaltern epistemologies are ignored across academia because of coloniality and ways to incorporate Afrocentricity to appropriate the research.

I have already described African epistemologies briefly by summarizing the way in which Western epistemologies can be contextualized through Afrocentricity. Some of the key pieces discussed were rejection of objectivity, purposeful research, and holistic thinking. The implication for these tenets of African validation of knowledge is that knowledge is validated through social and spiritual means, not through formal academic processes alone. The social means in which knowledge is validated is through experience delivered through intergenerational processes. Spiritual information is sometimes also related through these social processes and validated through interpretation of natural phenomena as well as paranormal ways such as visions. While African epistemologies are incredibly diverse throughout the continent, these patterns can be abstracted to better understand what direction African epistemologies take. In general, in African epistemologies wisdom is not divorced from knowledge.

Subaltern and Social Sciences

The social sciences comprise a field that requires African epistemologies. The social sciences in general have been cited by many scholars as using outdated frameworks.[73] These frameworks have low flexibility for shifts in social values over time, making them inapplicable to both changing times in Western nations and completely inapplicable to other cultures. The structure of the social sciences often builds on previous frameworks. Sociology and psychology, for example, use scientific methods to interpret patterns in social lives. Yet research methodology and theory for the social sciences developed in Western contexts. This is problematic when theories of the social sciences are applied to other cultures. Social reality

---

73   Chabal, *End of Conceit*.

is experienced and interpreted differently in different cultures.[74] As an example of the way in which African epistemologies are vital to understanding social phenomena in Africa, I will relate African epistemologies to female genital cutting (FGC).

The controversial nature of FGC, stemming from diverse cultural interpretations of the practice, are apparent in its name. Advocates for the abolition of the practice have long called it "female genital mutilation" (FGM). In this chapter, I use FGC as a more neutral terminology. These Western advocates often speak of the lifelong pain associated with the practice, health risks caused both during the surgery and afterward, and the psychological damage inflicted by this trauma. Western advocates use rhetoric that demonizes the women who perform the surgery, criticizing the tenets of a culture. The result is often the wholesale rejection of Western interventions.

An African epistemic perspective would notice several pieces missing from the Western narrative on FGC. First of all, FGC is an incredibly diverse practice administered in over twenty-eight African countries, each country performing the surgery in different ways, some safer than others. Next, demonizing the women who perform the surgery (or other women) is a symptom indicating that one misses the intersectionality of the practice, too. African women are subaltern in the sense of both their nationality and gender, leaving them vulnerable to such misunderstandings. Furthermore, FGC did not develop ex nihilo but rather from a series of complex historical and economic contexts. To call a quick end to the practice, demonizing the women who perform it, is to altogether ignore the perspective of the cultures that practice FGC.[75]

FGC undoubtedly has negative health consequences, as acknowledged by the World Health Organization, and is illegal in most countries in which it is practiced. Still, the way to work toward better female health practices is not by further alienating them through ignorance of their perspective and culture. Successful interventions to eliminate the practice have included education about the practice that allows the community to decide how to restructure itself so that these dangerous surgeries do not have to be carried out anymore. Thus, change must come from the African epistemic perspective with the agency of the people involved.

---

74 Carroll, "An Introduction."
75 Werunga et al., 150–64.

Art and Subaltern Epistemologies

Another field in the humanities that especially requires the insight of African epistemologies is art. The modern idea of what art was developed in Europe during the Renaissance. This defined art as something created for the purpose of aesthetics and displayed for the viewer to look upon and interpret. The art is commodified with a value and prestige placed upon it based on "expert" opinion. The global Eurocentric definition of art fails to validate the creative work of the subaltern.[76] In the context of Africa, especially key to this exclusion, is that of crafts. African peoples have historically made extremely decorative objects that are used in community, practice, or ritual. For example, a mask decorated to look like an ancestor has extreme ritual value as a manifestation of that ancestor. Another example is crafts such as basket weaving. These can take elaborate forms that are the expression of different cultural groups. Western definitions of art exclude these crafts from definitions of what constitutes art. Western art is consistent with capitalist views, while subaltern art does not always fit into this model.[77]

Besides definitions of what art is, there is also a Eurocentric point of view in art interpretation. Art interpretation in the West separates what is on the inside and outside of the mind. Art is expected to not only be something made only for viewing, but it must have a surface level and abstract meaning. Subaltern art does not need to have this meaning. Subaltern ideas about what art is do not focus on the duality of meaning in art but instead on the aesthetic value of it.[78]

Politics and Subaltern Epistemologies

African epistemologies can also be applied through politics. Political negotiations between Western and African nations take place under different epistemic values. Understanding the perspectives that each side is taking is helpful for successful negotiation. One aspect of African political discussions that differs from Western discussions is the prominence of

---

[76] Glăveanu and Sierra, "Creativity," 340–58.
[77] Shiner, *Invention*.
[78] Glăveanu and Sierra, "Creativity."

religion in politics. In Western nations, religion is seen as separate from politics except in special circumstances. There may be patterns in which religious groups support political parties, but the government doesn't work toward a religious goal. In many African nations this is not the case.

The government will use religious rhetoric and discuss their relations with other nations in relationship to their deity.[79] This might include the perspective of an epistemology based on the Bible or the Qur'an, or otherwise rhetoric of local religious values. African epistemologies also include the idea of cultural kingdoms. These kingdoms, defined by culture, legacy, and tradition, play a central role in national politics. Therefore, political discussions with many African nations require knowledge about the traditions and structures of these kingdoms.[80]

Decoloniality in International Relations

In addition to not taking the time to understand the rhetoric behind African political negotiations, international relations take place within the framework of coloniality. This is also how the theories within international relations developed: within the power relations of a system of colonialism. To move past the global political powers of coloniality, subaltern epistemic perspectives are integral to imagining new political orders.[81] International relations beyond the West are necessary to understand how to collaborate better politically.[82] One way to do this is to encourage the creation of regional international relations schools that focus on contextualizing international relations (IR) theories on their local cultures. The problematic implications of this model are that each school would be biased by nationalism instead of encouraged to pursue genuine international relations. The key is to not throw out preexisting international relations theories but instead offer different theories with new perspectives on the same issues.[83]

---

79 Ellis and Haar, "Religion," 385–401.
80 Skalník, "Chiefdoms."
81 Naylor et al., 199–209.
82 Acharya, "Dialogue and Discovery," 619–37.
83 Acharya, "Dialogue and Discovery."

A good example of decoloniality in politics is the rhetoric of Nelson Mandela. Mandela used his religious and cultural values to challenge the racist binary created by coloniality, apartheid being one of the most obvious examples. Through apartheid, even though the system of colonization was officially over, its legacy was apparent. The Western framework for this issue was one of binaries, a power struggle between Black and white. Nelson Mandela refused this framework and countered it with his own message of peace and racial harmony. He worked toward peaceful protests and imagined a world in which nations would work together to embrace the tenets of decoloniality.[84]

Every field of study has the opportunity to embrace African epistemic perspectives. They should always do so when studying Africa and are of African descent. It is key in a field of study when trying to incorporate other perspectives to take into account one's own cultural biases and create a more mindful approach.[85] Here I have described perspectives in African epistemologies and how they can be incorporated into various fields. Any subaltern epistemologies can follow the same route. A field cannot claim universality without taking into account subaltern epistemic perspectives. These can be incorporated through focusing on local cultures.

Biases in Subaltern Literature: Barriers to Subaltern Epistemologies

One of the main questions that decoloniality asks is this: how are we to create new solutions to world problems under the same framework that created them? This question reflects on the current global power structure and its production of knowledge that create the same effect. The solution, as outlined in this chapter, is that of a new epistemic framework. Yet again, the question is: how are we to create a new epistemic framework under the current institutional practices of academic and epistemic frameworks created by these institutions?

Subalterns are continually silenced by the systematic nature of coloniality. Even when academia has decided to work toward decoloniality and against the colonial matrix of power, this silencing still persists. The

---

84 Ndlovu-Gatsheni, *Decolonial*.
85 Haas, "Race, Rhetoric, and Technology," 277–310.

foundations of institutions such as the university and the global culture of academia retain the patterns of colonialism without the active help of members in that system. It takes much effort for academics to work against this system. Much of the literature on decoloniality is still written by Europeans, while subaltern perspectives are ignored. Subalterns are still being written about from the Eurocentric perspective rather than being heard themselves; in other words, their story is still being told for them.[86]

The challenge moving forward with subaltern epistemologies is that all work is done through our identities.[87] We cannot simply include the perspective of others but must deconstruct the Western identity to understand how and why it differs from the subaltern. The result will be a genuine attempt at listening to and relating to the subaltern.[88] Even in a radical field that seeks the opinion of the subaltern, such as in African studies, Eurocentrism is apparent. The academic system in which the field of African studies exists is a product of the academic system that came out of the Enlightenment. The power behind the construction of this field is Western, and the attention to African epistemologies is an afterthought. The assumptions behind studies of the subaltern must always be critically evaluated. The focus must be on full inclusion of the subaltern's voice instead of outsiders writing about them, as has been the case with many area studies programs in the past.[89]

Part of this challenge is the form in which the subaltern speaks. In many places, knowledge is written outside of formal academic journals. Oralities can often be more venerated than written information. This is especially true in Africa because cultures tend to embrace a community path toward learning. Another challenge for the subaltern is validation of their mediums of information. This is inevitably tied into subaltern epistemologies. Scholars in their respective fields must take into account all types of subaltern literature, including forms like oralities.[90]

A way to facilitate the expression of more subaltern epistemologies is the creation of more universities in non-Western areas. There was a huge wave of university creation during decolonization, yet many of these

---

86   Morris, *Can the Subaltern Speak?*
87   Appiah, *Ethics.*
88   Alcoff, "Mignolo's Epistemology."
89   Arowosegbe, "Bias of Eurocentrism."
90   Jegede, "Women, 253–66.

universities were created as partnerships with European universities. This is an example of the universities being simple transplants of the European idea of universities, instead of being an African invention. These colonial routes of universities along with modern corporate influences give them neoliberal and neocolonial biases.[91]

The African university often uses Western resources that are inappropriate for African epistemologies. They also use the Western system of dividing the disciplines that do not exist individually through all epistemologies, which makes the solving of practical problems difficult. Professors recruited by these universities must have a strong alliance with decoloniality in order to actively do reform work in their institutions.[92] This is not a new perspective on the African university; when African universities were first being established, scholars such as J. E. Casely Hayford and Edward Wilmot Blyden spoke for the creation of an African university from the perspective of Africanity in the 1870s. Such protests often have led only to the production of counterfacts to racism within the same epistemic framework in which they were made, instead of epistemic rebellion.[93]

For areas with a paucity of universities, as is the case with many African countries, the problem of funding remains an issue. Policymakers in those countries should be encouraged to invest in academia to promote development appropriate for each nation. In the meantime, nonacademic resources that attest to the epistemic foundations of those areas should be validated and incorporated into the literature. This can be done by framing investment in universities not through the detached, prestige motivated vision of the West, but by rhetoric of social responsibility.[94]

The Elusive Nature of Epistemology

The field of subaltern epistemologies challenges epistemology in the sense that (1) traditional epistemology is not the only way of knowing and (2) the underlying assumption of epistemology—that there is a single truth—is false. Epistemology is supposed to give an unbiased definition

---

91 Ndlovu-Gatsheni, "Decolonising."
92 Ndlovu-Gatsheni, "Decolonising."
93 Ndlovu-Gatsheni, "Decolonising."
94 Mama, "Is It Ethical to Study Africa?"

of the way in which we should know things and how knowledge is validated. It defines how we learn about the world through practical observations and reason, making emotional and religious observations secondary. Yet, the existence of alternative epistemologies shows that epistemology is not so simple. There is epistemic diversity, different definitions of what qualifies as knowledge shaped by cultural values. The myth of a singular epistemology only exists because colonial power relations used this ideology as justification for colonization. Decoloniality works to move past the idea of a singular epistemology, leaving room for a new, pluralist definition of epistemology.[95]

The trap of binaries is easy to fall into. In this chapter, I have often referred to binaries as Western or non-Western: the subaltern and the traditional. The field of epistemology developed through the philosophical conversation in ancient Greece. Yet these conversations did not take place separate from international philosophy; they were influenced by African, Asian, and other philosophies. Although the idea of epistemology arising from Western thought is tempting, it isn't entirely true.[96] Western epistemology is not entirely Western. Similarly, the accepted epistemology of various subaltern groups is not necessarily totally their own but rather what they have accepted. The collaborative nature of epistemologies is why none should be outright rejected. Instead, border-thinking must be used to see the limitations in all epistemologies: how they interact and how they can come together to help us better understand our world through new perspectives.[97]

The ideal way forward for academia is to move toward a model of various truths in which no one truth is accepted but various forms of knowledge—even contradictory ones—can coexist. The idea that African universities need to avoid mimicry and find new paths to development is not new.[98] The way to do this moving forward is through new conceptions about the nature of epistemology. This is a global cultural academic shift that requires the invitation and attention to subaltern perspectives done in a novel way. There are many challenges associated with this ideal. First, academics internationally are often held up to Eurocentric academic

---

95   de Sousa, "General Introduction."
96   Hutchings, "Dialogue," 639–47.
97   Alcoff, "Mignolo's Epistemology."
98   Fanon et al., *Wretched*.

standards in their field. Often, students must be conversant with Western academic ideas to advance their career far enough to produce knowledge. Instead of working toward accepting only students who meet Western standards, universities and journals must appreciate diverse qualifications for academics wishing to contribute to their field. Universities must reward professors and professionals who go against the grain and express subaltern epistemologies. Above all, universities must seek out areas where the subaltern is not heard and encourage the dissemination of their ideas. The colonial matrix of power works within the institutions of academia and requires active participation of all to be more inclusive of subaltern epistemologies.

Conclusion

Subaltern epistemologies have insufficient presence in modern academia. The colonial matrix of power has systematically disadvantaged subaltern scholars in the global academic system. Institutions of academia, the university, must actively promote the publication of subaltern epistemic work in order to counter this global system of oppression. The Akan proverb "wisdom is like a baobab tree, a single person's hand cannot embrace it," expresses the problematic nature of traditional epistemology. Every knowledge system is incomplete. Academia must be able to change the assumption behind epistemology, that there is a singular truth, in order to accept the idea of a constellation of knowledges.

Rather than destroying current Eurocentric academic work, border-thinking requires academics to acknowledge Western academia as incomplete. This encourages them to seek complementary perspectives to broaden their knowledge from diverse perspectives. The blending of knowledges from global perspectives will promote a more complete collection of knowledge by modern academia. Intellectual decolonization, if promoted by subaltern academics and supported by Western academics, is the path to true liberation of "postcolonial" nations.

Chapter Four

Decolonizing Knowledge in Africa

Introduction

Colonial rule in Africa has far-reaching implications for several areas of African society and knowledge systems. The process of colonialism in Africa exerted dominance on the continent's education system, and consequently, the African mind. Traditional medical practices, music, religion, leadership, judicial processes, resource management, and the overall economy were equally affected.[1] Formal education sectors discouraged indigenous knowledge systems in favor of hegemonic Western ones. Zegeye and Zamba explicitly state that "the category of 'knowledge' as a constructed and constituted discipline at European Universities recorded Europe's memories as the 'archaeology of knowledge.'"[2]

This "knowledge" through colonialism has been introduced and sustained in Africa, which was not a mere act of sharing one's understanding but rather a supercilious imposition of "superior" knowledge on a people whose culture was considered inferior. Most African systems were seen as driven by superstition rather than reason. No doubt this consideration of Africa lacks depth, given that precolonial African society possessed diverse cultural histories and educational structures.

Traditional medical practices and indigenous religious activities were demonized and replaced with "modern" Western medicine and religions. Western languages currently occupy prominent positions in sociocultural

---

1   Kaya et al., "African Indigenous," 30–44.
2   Zegeye and Vambe, "African Indigenous," 329–58.

and academic activities while a proficiency in indigenous languages is deemed an indicator of illiteracy. Western governance has been instituted at the expense of native governing systems; indigenous musical practices were relegated in favor of Western forms; traditional methods of conflict resolutions have equally been relegated to centralize Western judicial processes while the continent's economy and psycho-social outlook of the people is constantly being influenced by Western philosophy. In other words, although the colonizers no longer have governance over the continent, the legacy of colonialism continues to operate extensively within Africa.

For the past two decades, as noted by Horschemke, emphasis has been placed on the need to decolonize or rather challenge the hegemony of Western systems and philosophies.[3] This is primarily because these philosophies, practices, and knowledge systems were unable to cater to the diverse and multicultural needs of the continent. There is, therefore, a pressing need to adopt African knowledge systems, languages, and epistemologies to reinvent, self-regulate, and decolonize knowledge. Language is considered the organizing principle of knowledge systems and, therefore, possesses the capacity to condition the perception of knowledge in society: hence the necessity to explore the use of language in the mission of decolonizing African knowledge. Also crucial to this mission of decolonization is to focus on art and creativity, which tends to have a subliminal effect on the human psyche. As such, this study intends to explore the decolonization of knowledge in Africa using language and creativity.

Language and African Education

Education, or the imparting of knowledge, is a purely universal concept; however, formal or Western education in Africa is an example of direct consequences of colonialism. Considering the universality of the concept, the distinction of Western education lies in the method of dispensation. Precolonial African education was generally conducted informally, which in this context makes reference to the oral-based education system practiced at the time with language as the key agent of impartation.[4] This oral-based education implies that much of the people's history, traditions,

---

3   Horsthemke, "Indigenous Knowledge," 1–15.
4   Finnegan, *Oral Literature*.

and other knowledge systems were passed orally from generation to generation. A huge part of the educational materials and philosophies of the African people is laden in the people's oral traditions and customs.

African epistemologies and skills, some of which include traditional scientific medicine and technology, were also transmitted orally. These educational materials embedded in oral traditions were transmitted using the people's languages, which aside from imparting knowledge, helped learners acquire language skills that promote its use effectively and creatively.[5] However, the supposed absence of predominant writing culture for the purpose of documentation made provisions for the claims of African cultural, scientific, and epistemological deficiency, hence the quest to "civilize" and "educate" Africa.[6] Therefore, without indigenous African knowledge, the Europeans set out on their mission to "de-Africanize Africans in their ontological-epistemological, psycho-cultural, socio-linguistic and therefore, developmental categories," language being its most effective tool.[7]

The adoption of the colonizer's language for formal use in the continent, the installation of these languages in educational curricula, and as the language of instruction in schools around the continent all qualify as evidence of colonialism.[8] Language as noted by Ngugi "is the most important vehicle through which . . . power fascinated and held the soul prisoner. The bullet was the means of physical subjugation. Language was the means of spiritual subjugation."[9] Therefore, by bequeathing such authority to the colonizer's language, its culture automatically takes a hegemonic stance against that of the indigenous. This lends credence to the earlier claim that language is an effective vehicle for the transmission of culture.

In the field of education, language plays a primary role in the process of imparting knowledge given that a greater portion of the process involves intricate linguistic interactions between students and teachers. Aside from the possibility of simpler methods of assimilation and understanding in the case of indigenous language use, having a privileged status and use

---

5   Okeke, "Traditional Education," 15–26.
6   Akporobaro, *Introduction*.
7   Trudell and Schroeder, "Reading Methodologies," 165–80.
8   Bunyi, "Language," 133–54.
9   Ngugi, *Decolonizing*.

of the colonizer's language in the education process created a language hierarchy in the minds of students: hence, their assumption that foreign languages and invariably foreign cultures are superior to their own. Ngugi further expatiates this opinion by stating that "language possesses a dual character, it is both a means of communication and a carrier of culture."[10] Also, according to Trudell and Schroeder, "Learning to read and write is a psycholinguistic and social process."[11] In other words, the learner would most likely develop an affinity for the linguistic environment from which the knowledge they are ingesting emanates. Alexander, in his "English Unassailable but Unattainable: The Dilemma of Language Policy in South African Education," explores the social reluctance to overthrow dominant European languages and ideals, a situation that has been sustained by classist hierarchies, perceived economic advantages, and language policies that favor European languages within the continent. As chronicled by Alexander:

> It is an indisputable fact that in the post-colonial situation, the linguistic hierarchy built into the colonial system led to knowledge of the conquerors' language becoming a vital component of the 'cultural capital' of the neo-colonial elite. It was and remains their knowledge of English and/or French [for example] that sets them apart from the vast majority of their African compatriots and which keeps them and their offspring in the privileged middle and upper classes.[12]

This will, therefore, provide justification for the African scramble for European affectations and explain the presupposition that European capitalism, elitist mannerisms, and fluency in foreign languages like English is the symbol of literacy, success, and progress. In communities like Tharaka in central Kenya, English language is seen as the language of literacy and opportunity, hence the emphasis on English language in various schools in different communities.[13] Also, there seems to be an inextricable link between the colonizer's language and education in contemporary Africa. Mazuri substantiates this notion by opining that in the case of the English

---

10 Ngugi, *Decolonizing*, 87.
11 Trudell and Schroeder, "Reading Methodologies," 165–80.
12 Alexander, "English," 11.
13 Schroeder, "Mother Tongue," 379–89.

language in Kenya, "The command of the English language was often used as a criterion of one's level of education."[14]

Furthermore, it is pertinent to note that education throughout the African continent as we know it is unbearably Eurocentric. Higgs notes that much of what is regarded to be education within the continent is a reflection of European theories and methodologies: this is understandable, given the dominant use of European languages in education and communication across Africa.[15] Scholars like Ademowo categorize the majority of African languages as threatened with extinction, which implies that with the imminent death of these languages, if no protective measures are implemented, the cultures dependent on these languages for transmission are equally threatened.[16] Therefore, by relegating African languages to the background, European cultures, epistemologies, and educational paradigms are given hegemonic power at the expense of African cultures and indigenous knowledge systems. Understanding this implication brings to the forefront the need to decolonize education in Africa by addressing the dominant use of foreign languages at the expense of local languages in the education process.

Having established the far-reaching effects of language in conditioning the mind and transmitting culture and knowledge to a vast population, it is unsurprising that in the quest to decolonize African education, several scholars are calling for the centralization of African languages in education and institutions across the continent. For Mbembe, the teaching of African languages and their employment in instruction is crucial to the decolonization process.[17] In other words, in reclaiming Africa, there is need to centralize the use of African languages in learning and teaching. According to the 1953 and 2004 UNESCO publications of language and education, it is important to educate children in their local or familiar languages; they also underscore the primary role of language in teaching and learning.[18] For other scholars like Ademowo, indigenous languages should be employed alongside formal languages like English to facilitate

---

14 Mazrui, *Political Sociology*.
15 Higgs, "Towards an Indigenous," 445–58.
16 Ademowo, "Teaching Science," 50–63.
17 Mbembe, "Decolonizing."
18 UNESCO, *Use of Vernacular*.

cognition and assimilation among students.[19] In his opinion, multilingualism should not be viewed as an obstacle but could rather be harnessed for the processes of development. The centralization of indigenous languages could also encourage knowledge production, as language is clearly a vehicle for indigenous knowledge, conceptualization, and production.

With that being said, it is essential to note that Africa continues to lag behind in knowledge production particularly in areas like technoscientific development and even in social sciences across the globe.[20] This is unfortunate given that nowadays advancement in science and technology are determinants of infrastructural and sociocultural dominance. With these advancements and productivity comes a knowledge economy that is controlled by the producers of these marketable advancements. However, science and technology are not the only areas ailing from the dearth of knowledge production. Social sciences, as noted by Ademowo, are equally affected. With that established, Africa continues to be losing out in our rapidly evolving and technologizing societies worldwide. In an advocacy brief spearheaded by UNESCO in 2010, the abysmal output of Africa in terms of knowledge production is stated as follows:

> Africa has the smallest share in scholarly publishing, which is mirrored by the international Social Science Citation Index which, despite its cultural bias, covers the world's leading scholarly science and technical journals in more than 100 academic disciplines. Only one per cent of the citations in the Index are from Africa. The publicly accessible knowledge production of African scholars takes place outside Africa. The UNESCO Science Report of 2005 indicated that Africa is contributing only to 0.4 per cent of the international gross expenditure on research and development, and of this, South Africa covers 90 per cent.[21]

The above excerpt consolidates the claim of Africa's backwardness and marginalization from the rest of the world in the areas of knowledge production; Ademowo also notes her exemption from world governance and

---

19   Ademowo, "Teaching Science."
20   Ademowo, "Teaching Science."
21   UNESCO, *Why and How Africa.*

social dominance given her prolonged inability to measure up with the techno-scientific productivity of the West.[22]

Also, education is undoubtedly the foundation for a thriving knowledge economy. There is, however, a link between the continued sacralization of colonial languages in African education and polity and the seeming inability of Africa to break free from the shackles of their colonial past into a space of indigenous ingenuity and domestic knowledge production. This is true given that the promotion of colonial languages also promotes their epistemologies and educational paradigms, some of which do not mirror the realities of Africa. In justification of this notion, Abdi opines that colonial education's primary objective was to strip Africa of its essence and identity while promoting Eurocentric constructions of Africa and privileging European identity.[23] These constructions aimed at disparaging African epistemological and linguistic essence, as noted by Emeagwali and Dei, should clearly be separated from the African descriptions of indigenousness.[24] Therefore, it is not far-fetched to state that the continued sacralization of colonial languages, and inadvertently their cultural dispositions, places Africa at risk of perpetual underdevelopment.

Ngugi wa Thiong'o views decolonization as a process of inward searching where the consequent perspective is placed in relationship with a larger universal context. In his exact words, "to decolonize" in general means to engage in a continuous process where Africans "see themselves clearly in relationship to themselves and to other selves in the universe."[25] In essence, to truly embark on the decolonization of African education systems is to look inward and identify the far-reaching though subtle effects of the dominant use of the colonizer's language in the continent's education system. To address the issue is to thoroughly examine Africa's multilingualism while also interrogating educational policies and paradigms that favor this dominance.

Oftentimes, Africa's multilingualism shoulders the blame for the vast acceptance of colonial languages in African education. Because these languages are often viewed as the common ground for learners from diverse linguistic backgrounds (with rapid globalization as one of its

---

22 Ademowo, "Teaching Science."
23 Abdi, "Decolonizing," 64–82.
24 Emeagwali and Sefa Dei, *Introduction*.
25 Mbembe, "Decolonizing."

many justifications), dominant Western languages are assumed to guarantee successful global communication and upward economic mobility. Although, these arguments might hold some merit, Africa's multilingualism and cultural diversity should not be seen as divisive or isolating.

Rather, this diversity should be viewed as an asset toward positive indigenous education and knowledge production.[26] This notion complements the UNESCO 2010 opinion that the multiplicity of language and culture is often perceived to be a source of "communication barrier and viewed as synonymous with conflicts and tension. It is assumed that managing so many speech communities is problematic and costly."[27] Acknowledging and assuaging these fears is Kioko et al., who notes from a sociopolitical perspective that the issues of unity in society are often independent of language. Language simply serves as the tool through which existing division and conflict is communicated.[28]

The multilingual nature of the African space defines the African essence. Wolf examines multilingualism and multiculturalism as integral aspects of African society, embracing an introspective understanding of self.[29] The first step toward solving a problem is first identifying the problem and then the nonproblem. In other words, identifying that multilingualism is a nonproblem is recognizing that the problem lies in the inadvertent elimination of the African essence from education through the promotion of European ideals and its Eurocentric language policies. Therefore, one would see that the solution lies in creating a transformative education system that takes into consideration the needs of the people, which stems from their sociocultural and linguistic diversity. Also, multilingual strategies should be put in place to select suitable indigenous instructional media in schools while also identifying effective teaching techniques and a culturally essential curriculum.

This study, in line with the UNESCO 2010 report, recommends a dominant, relevant local language approach to teaching and learning while also providing space for international languages, which are equally relevant in the global scheme of things.[30] This juncture demands

---

26   UNESCO, *Why and How Africa*.
27   UNESCO, *Why and How Africa*.
28   Kioko et al., *Language*.
29   Wolff, *Pre-School*, 4.
30   UNESCO, *Why and How Africa*.

an assessment of the language debate between Ngugi wa Thiong'o and Chinua Achebe. Both renowned in the field of literature, they have differing views with regard to the linguistic aspect of decolonization. While the former clamors for an absolute adoption of indigenous languages in the creation of African literature, Achebe advocates for the personalization or domestication of the language to carry the weight of Africa's experiences, realities, and nuances.[31] Achebe's views tend to echo the current realities of postcolonial Africa. The idea of completely extricating the continent from Western languages and knowledge systems is almost impractical as societies are clearly interlaced; therefore, the problem does not lie within the incorporation of both languages in African education but rather with the extent of this incorporation in reference to indigenous African languages.

However, the emphasis remains on indigenous knowledge production, promotion of indigenous languages, and harnessing of existing multilingualism. Charity, they say, begins at home; the necessary complementarity between local and foreign languages can be achieved with a proportionate investment in local and international languages. In other words, this study does not outrightly condemn or discourage the teaching and learning of international/foreign languages but rather emphasizes an investment in Africa's local languages and the complementary use of both languages in education. To clarify the endorsement of this view is to examine research projects that reveal the resulting cognitive development of students and the expansion of African consciousness as well as improved knowledge production among teachers and learners. The subsequent research data that supports this endorsement serves as the foundation to request a change of language policy in education in contemporary Africa. After all, Fardon and Furniss are of the opinion that language policies and planning in Africa should draw insight from research that explores a relationship between language, education, state, and development.[32]

Research reports analyzed and presented by Kioko et al. in their article "Language and Education in Africa: Answering the Questions" reveals that emphasis on the use of local or familiar language in children's education in Africa shows a significant improvement in a child's success in formal education. Also, adopting a multilingual education policy in teaching

---

31   Ngugi, *Decolonising*.
32   Fardon and Furniss, *African Languages*.

and learning affords learners the opportunity of commencing learning in their most familiar language. Children can easily link their experiences and learning at home with the teachings in school; with that, the education system has factored in the students' realities and experiences in the process of learning.[33] With the ease and familiarity afforded by use of African languages on the continent, teachers have recorded improvement in students' writing, reading, and listening skills. It is also less cumbersome to acquire similar skills in other languages. The students' cognitive and retentive skills are also improved through this practice. That being said, it is imperative to stress that African languages also serve as veritable tools for the transmission of culture, therefore, thriving African students equals a culturally conscious productivity among those with solid cultural backgrounds.

From a sociopolitical standpoint, they note that although the promotion of Western languages comes from a fear of marginalization, language plays little to no role in marginalizing economies and countries. Kioko et al. assert that "languages are not what will hold Africa back from participation in the globalised world; rather self demeaning attitudes are by far the greater danger to development and entry into the world of the 21st century . . . It has been said that on no other continent in the world has the entire continent has the entire population had to attempt to make technological or informational progress through the medium of someone else's language."[34]

Furthermore, they note that the use of African languages in schools not only improves cognitive and academic performance but also creates positive sociocultural outcomes in various multicultural and multilinguistic communities. Okech lends credence to this notion by opining that multilingual education could provide resources for building knowledge economies by creating information demand in various languages.[35] It could also stimulate indigenous productivity and innovation that could attract global demand, thereby creating wealth and development for the painfully underdeveloped African continent.

Foreseeing an opposition to the endorsement of African languages as instructional languages in African schools—owing to a presupposition

---

33 Kioko et al., *Language*.
34 Kioko et al., *Language*.
35 Okech, "Multilingual," 117–25.

that African languages are hardly equipped for the technicalities of formal education—this study debunks notions of this deficiency. These anxieties and preconceptions, according to Kioko et al., are unfounded. African languages are equipped to transmit African epistemologies and philosophies and to also possess sophisticated linguistic patterns, systems, and vocabulary that convey contextual meaning.[36] African languages also possesses adaptive features that make it possible to adapt to inevitable changes in a progressive society. In order to do so, African languages, just like other human languages of the world, would likely borrow and domesticate its lexicons and idiomatic expressions from other languages across the globe. Such is the case of the English language, which is estimated to have borrowed from over eighty-four languages across continents including Africa.[37] To demonstrate this famed capacity of African languages, Kioko et al. submits that the Kiswahili language of Tanzania has been adopted for the teaching of all subjects in the curriculum of primary schools in the country, while many African languages are often used exclusively and effectively for broadcasts in various media platforms.[38]

However, if these demonstrations are deemed inadequate, the best way to improve the capacity of any language is to make it the language of instruction in education. That way, its users will have no choice but to expand such communication to fit into their various teaching and learning demands. As long as some, even policymakers, continue to show skepticism toward African languages' use in pedagogy: including in various subjects including science, mathematics, and technology, Africa stands the risk of never unlocking the wealth of knowledge and development that has shaped her languages.

Decolonizing Research and Scholarship in Africa

The first thought that comes to mind at the mention of research is that it is a systematic process of searching for knowledge. In the African or indigenous context as observed by Smith, it is rather associated with painful reminders of ugly histories and experience in the hands of colonizers.

---

36 Kioko et al., *Language*.
37 Jackson and Ze Amvela, *Words, Meaning and Vocabulary*.
38 Kioko et al., *Language*.

For her, there is a direct connection between the word "research" and European colonialism and imperialism. In her words, "'Research' is probably one of the dirtiest words in the indigenous world's vocabulary. When mentioned in many indigenous contexts, it stirs up silence, it conjures up bad memories; it raises a smile that is knowing and distrustful."[39] She examines the process of "research" as one that legitimated the colonizer, or "researcher," to draw unfounded conclusions about the indigenous person, which in the context of this work is the African.

In recent times, there have been counter-discourses from people from marginalized areas such as Africa; these responses involve a retelling of the African story by rewriting the continent's history, correcting faulty notions of gender and other misinterpreted areas; in other words, reframing the image of Africa and reclaiming her history and epistemologies. This exercise presents itself as a form of response that accounts for the bourgeoning chronicles of "The Empire Writing Back" in postcolonial Africa and beyond. As a blanket phrase for almost all counter-responses to colonial writings and assumptions of its former colonies, Achebe's "The Image of Africa" qualifies as one. Here, the writer explores the blatantly wrongheaded conclusions made about Africa even in contemporary times born out of sheer ignorance and notions of superiority on the part of most Westerners.[40] Smith addresses this ignorance by exploring the tendency of Western researchers to assume that they are sufficiently knowledgeable about Africa with only cursory second-hand experience of the continent.[41] Africa, Achebe describes, is to the West an image of direct juxtaposition to Europe, something that was accentuated in Conrad's novel, *The Heart of Darkness*. He sums up the work in the following words: "'Heart of Darkness' projects the image of Africa as 'the other world,' the antithesis of Europe and therefore of civilization, a place where man's vaunted intelligence and refinement are finally mocked by triumphant bestiality."[42]

Achebe's essay goes on to ponder and deconstruct Conrad's literature to point out unfounded claims about the African people, the denigration of Africa's language, and the blatant projections of Africa as a land of

---

39 Smith, *Decolonizing*, 1.
40 Achebe, "An Image."
41 Smith, *Decolonizing*, 1.
42 Achebe, "An Image."

barbarism. Achebe takes Conrad's work apart chapter by chapter to draw attention to the inherent disregard for Africa's history and culture. Just like Achebe, several other scholars and writers have invested in rewriting and correcting these shallow notions of the African people. This process is also a form of decolonization. However, this particular aspect focuses on deconstructing Western narratives and assumptions about Africa. Smith posits that "taking apart the story, revealing underlying texts, and giving voice to things that are often known intuitively does not help people to improve their current conditions. It provides words, perhaps, an insight that explains certain experiences—but it does not prevent someone from dying."[43]

If the above process is a form of decolonization, what then is decolonization and how can it be defined in encompassing terms. The following definition by Chilisa comes to mind:

> Decolonization is thus a process of conducting research in such a way that the worldviews of those who have suffered a long history of oppression and marginalization are given space to communicate from their frames of reference. It is a process that involves "researching back" to question how the disciplines-psychology, education, history, anthropology, sociology, or science-through an ideology of Othering have described and theorized about the colonized Other, and refused to let the colonized Other name and know from their frame of reference.[44]

This above definition provides a premise for subsequent suggestions in this section. Alongside the deconstruction of European narratives and scholarship on Africa, African scholars and researchers should devise culturally appropriate strategies and methodologies that are founded on indigenous values, worldviews, and language in order to challenge Eurocentric methodologies that denigrate indigenous experiences and knowledge systems.[45] In various areas of learning, efforts should be made to identify suitable decolonizing methodologies or effective principles and strategies for every research exercise, and researchers should also truly understand their function and role in researching indigenous societies. The preceding

---

43   Smith, *Decolonizing Methodologies*.
44   Chilisa, *Indigenous*, 14.
45   Keikelame and Swartz, "Decolonising," 1–7.

factors are geared toward aiding and informing the establishment of research paradigms and methodologies for both indigenous and nonindigenous researchers. However, in order to frame these paradigms adequately, the following questions by Edward Said should be brought to the fore: "Who writes? For whom is the writing being done? In what circumstances? These, it seems to me, are the questions whose answers provide us with ingredients making for a politics of interpretation."[46]

Also, cultural familiarity is crucial for exhaustive and efficient ethnographic or scientific research, which means relatability with the host community. In other words, researchers in question are expected to possess in-depth knowledge of the people's culture, values, and language. However, the possession of this quality does not guarantee a smooth investigative process. As observed by Smith, irrespective of the indigenous identity of some of the researchers, they still struggle with an insider-outsider status in several host communities, owing to unfavorable research experiences in some of these communities. Insider-outsider status refers to the conflicting position of the researcher in the host community. This is the case of researchers supposedly from similar linguistic and cultural backgrounds of the indigenous community being studied. Their affiliation with Western education and training inadvertently presents them as representatives of the rival group (Western/Eurocentric researchers).[47] The other type of researcher is one who shares no cultural or linguistic background; however, the insider-outsider status is still applicable because his or her self-categorization as indigenous or foreign is inconsequential and can only be determined by how much he or she is attuned to the indigenous space.

Factors like the aforementioned familiarity with culture, language, and values are necessary to create a platform for researchers to have access to relevant information and other necessary resources available within the host community. An understanding of the culture and values will provide the researcher with basic insight into the lives of the people; it will eliminate the possibility of any desecration that could anger the community. Also, the researcher will likely not look and act too much like an outsider. An understanding of the people's language will aid in communicating with members of the community while providing access to core research

---

46 Said, *Orientalism*.
47 Smith, *Decolonizing*, 1.

subjects and even establishing a rapport that could elicit trust, which is "a crucial indicator for sound relationships in a research process."[48]

Having a history of colonialism, slavery, and even apartheid in Africa has engendered a form of distrust toward explorers and ethnographic researchers. As noted by Keikaleme and Swartz, most respondents and local inhabitants expressed angry sentiments against researchers. Apparently, they have had a series of experiences with researchers who tend to extract knowledge without giving credit to their sources. To them, research is rooted in the colonial philosophy of taking as knowledge in itself, becoming a commodity of colonial enterprise. Alongside this knowledge were their resources, which were exploited and appropriated while people were demonized and shunned. This justifies the reservation of some indigenous persons encountered by Keikaleme and Swartz in the course of their research. In their exploration of epilepsy and examination of a possible collaboration between biomedical researchers and indigenous healers, they encountered the following as an example of one local response:

> This leader openly raised concerns about exploitation of their indigenous knowledge in research: Our concerns with research is that, we [traditional healers/leaders] willingly share our knowledge about the indigenous plants that we use to treat illnesses, but after the information has been given to researchers, we do not hear about the results and how plants have been processed into medicines; we do not see our names on the labels of the medicine bottles of the plants we have provided . . . (Traditional leader)[49]

This skepticism toward researchers will undoubtedly be impediment to a smooth interaction between researchers and the researched. Some of these participants also claim that most researchers have little or no regard for their everyday way of life as they tend to flaunt their "superior" knowledge. Therefore, to create indigenous paradigms for research, the idea of engendering trust between the researched community and the researcher is key.

Also important to the researcher is maintaining the interest, respect, and trust of the indigenous people. The researcher is already operating

---

48   Smith, *Decolonizing Methodologies*.
49   Keikelame and Swartz, "Decolonizing."

from an outsider-insider space and therefore needs to enforce a proportionate flow of power. There should be a "power with" and not a "power over" approach since both parties should make notable contributions to the research.[50] To achieve this, formal agreements should be drawn out by the research organization to protect the rights, dignity, and knowledge of participants and the studied communities.[51] It brings to mind the need for the proposition and development of appropriate codes of conduct and ethics that draw insight from Africa's own realities and experiences. Factors like power could be evaluated to provide suitable approaches to research in vulnerable and marginalized communities in Africa. It will explore the much-needed counterhegemonic and anticolonial position of research in African communities.

These examined concepts as factors will assist the creation of systematic approaches or paradigms that resonate and centralize the subaltern thought, philosophies, epistemologies, and society while also framing questions and issues that decentralize favored Western methodologies of research. Along with creating a process divorced from Eurocentric bias in order to approach indigenous knowledge or to create methodologies that are drawn from indigenous worldviews and knowledge systems, decolonization equally implies developing systems of knowledge derived from exploration of ancient indigenous knowledge and modern ways of knowing.

Haoua also warns that the decolonization process is not one for unfounded nationalist declarations, as it seems that most decolonization literatures appear to be attacks on Western paradigms and epistemologies.[52] Although decolonization is aimed at decentering Western paradigms, it is not a blind espousal of nationalist affiliations but rather a more inward examination of research to identify subtle oppressive currents and marginalizing ideologies in the adopted Western paradigms.

---

50 Keikelame and Swartz, "Decolonizing."
51 Keikelame and Swartz, "Decolonizing."
52 Hamza, "Decolonizing," 123–34.

Music and Decolonization Studies

The process of decolonization in Africa, which has been described as the centralization of indigenous knowledge and cultural heritage of the African people, cannot be exhaustively explored without examining the place of music and musicians in the process. Music is popularly described as food for the soul; it is a nonrepresentational and abstract art form that tends to have a powerful effect on the thoughts and feelings of people.[53] Its effects are, at best, subliminal. It is indeed a powerful, soothing, yet intense force that can be adopted for other purposes besides entertainment. It can be wielded to mobilize musicians to utilize their craft as weapons for political advocacy and cultural promotion. Contemporary musicians with African roots are well aware of the potency of music and have successfully promoted their cultural values and their political agendas aided by the boom in the music industry since the mid-twentieth century.[54] Promoting and maintaining traditional musical practices have been described by Ngugi as a form of resistance to mental colonialism.[55] This, therefore, qualifies music as an effective tool for decolonization in the African continent.

Given the hegemony of Western languages, philosophies, and other cultural forms in most postcolonial African societies, it is unsurprising that there is a proliferation of music recorded in colonial languages. Nevertheless, singing or listening to music in their native language allows for Africans to reclaim a sense of identity and culture in a postcolonial era.[56] Agawu further explores the primacy of language in scholarly discourses and the performance of music: "Without language, there would be no song; without song, African music would not exist. Language and music are thus tied as if by an umbilical cord. No one who ignores its linguistic aspects can hope to reach a profound understanding of African music."[57]

Having established that language possesses a dual character, which is to communicate and transmit culture, it is necessary to examine the use

---

53 Thaut, *Rhythm*.
54 Thaut, *Rhythm*, 58–59.
55 Ngugi, *Decolonising*.
56 Carter-Ényì and Carter-Ényì, "Decolonizing, 58–65.
57 Agawu, *African*, 113.

of indigenous African languages in music. The use of native African languages in songs by Africans in the continent and diaspora has led not just to the promotion of the people's cultural heritage; it has also catalyzed the preservation and revitalization of more than a thousand African languages.[58] Also, contemporary musicians as observed Ngugi tend to reinvent indigenous musical practices and songs by incorporating current realities and experiences of urban Africa; they also engender new African language expressions and words that effectively capture the experiences of modern African life.[59]

The resulting effect of this strategy is the revitalization of an African consciousness. Put succinctly, the reinvention and decolonization process engendered by contemporary musicians presents itself in the following expression: "The same song or composition may be presented in many different ways: in the vernacular or translation; in a different key; with new instruments; with a different beat; played fast or slow; a short or a long version; and so forth."[60] Exploring the life of Miriam Makeba of South Africa (Mama Africa), Quintina Carter-Enyi and Aaron Carter-Enyi examine the expression of decolonization using indigenous languages. Makeba is noted to have recorded most of her songs in various languages such as Xhosa, Zulu, Swahili, and other Niger-Congo languages. Once, her solo recording "Lakutshona Ilanga" (in Xhosa), having gained popularity in the United States, was given an English version—"You Tell Such Lovely Lies"—and she was asked to perform it. It was clearly not a translation, and the artist is noted to have been skeptical of the new version. She considered the song's lyrical composition to be incompatible with the somber mood of the Xhosa original.[61] Carter-Enyi and Carter-Enyi opine that the song clearly did not sit well with Makeba, as she did not sing any more songs in colonial languages irrespective of the growing demand for songs in English and the negative reaction from record companies and tour managers as a result of her decision.[62] Her unwavering stance even in the face of opposition communicated her regard for

---

58 Agawu, *African*.
59 Ngugi, *Decolonising*.
60 Carter-Ényì and Carter-Ényì, "Decolonizing."
61 Carter-Ényì and Carter-Ényì, "Decolonizing."
62 Carter-Ényì and Carter-Ényì, "Decolonizing."

African culture; it also expresses her conscious efforts to fight the colonial ambition to enslave the mind of the African using language.

Also, Makeba's agenda was not solely expressed using indigenous languages and sounds; she also employed the use of visual props, some of which include her clothing and appearance. [63] She often appeared on stage in African fabric and fashion while her hairstyle—"a close cut natural hair later known as the 'Afro' hairstyle"—is said to have drawn European attention. This provides credence to the notion that fashion and style offer ethnic representation and identity, which can go a long way in rewriting a people's narrative and providing insight into a people's culture and heritage.[64] Using her music, Makeba showcased her culture's oral tradition and instilled in the listener the desire to know more about her people. She also drew attention to some of the disapproving reactions of the West to unfamiliar indigenous linguistic expressions. She familiarized her audience with distinct African rhythms and sounds and does this with conviction. By reclaiming African music and language, Makeba effectively spread awareness about apartheid, race relations, and identity. In the following excerpt she examines the distinct sound in the Xhosa language that is often thought to be unintelligible and often attributed to primitivism:

> This next song . . . it's a Xhosa wedding song. Everywhere we go people often ask me 'how do you make that noise?' It used to offend me because it isn't a noise, it's my language. But I came to understand that they didn't understand that Xhosa is my language, and it's a written language. . . . Now, I'm sure everyone here knows that we in South Africa are still colonized. The colonizers of my country call this song 'a click song' simply because they find it rather difficult saying 'Qongqothwane.[65]

Makeba is, however, not the only African singer that has employed the use of indigenous languages in their music. Some others who did the same include Angélique Kidjo, Yvonne Chaka Chaka, and Asá.[66]

---

63 Carter-Ényì and Carter-Ényì, "Decolonizing."
64 Power, Tyler, and Disele, "Conserving,"
65 Dutch TV Studios, "Decolonizing."
66 Carter-Ényì and Carter-Ényì, "Decolonizing," 64.

Aside from the use of indigenous languages in music, Africans have also devised other decolonization strategies, such as the continued decline in the exclusive use of colonial languages in musical renditions. The use of these languages, such as English, in various formal institutions including the mass media has created a system of high and low culture; colonial language is associated with high culture, and the indigenous represents the low. With the multiplicity of ethnic groups and languages within Africa, it is nearly impossible to eliminate the use of these languages. Therefore, to appeal to a vast majority of Africans and non-Africans alike without advancing the colonial agenda, some musicians have opted for the use of domesticated variants of these colonial languages alongside indigenous expressions, techniques, and musical nuances in the production of contemporary music. With this, African music is reinvented and revitalized while consciousness and nationhood are nurtured through the inclusion of indigenous languages and dialects in contemporary African popular music.

Notably, musicians like Fela Anikulapo Kuti of Nigeria come to mind. Fela's music is politically conscious; it was more about the reconstitution of a national identity by holding leaders accountable. His musical expression can easily be categorized as one of sociopolitical activism. However, unlike Makeba, Fela employed the use of the domesticated variants of colonial English and Pidgin English as his language of expression. This can be viewed as a counterhegemonic approach, one that inadvertently engineered a middle ground for the high and low culture of English and indigenous languages, respectively. His music reflected the era of political consciousness and Pan-Africanism. The singer is noted by Carter-Enyi and Carter-Enyi to have attributed his use of Pidgin English instead of his native Yoruba to the spirit of eliminating the exclusivity of music.[67] The genre he helped pioneer is referred to as Afrobeat, while his promotion of Pidgin English and the infusion of indigenous style and language have earned him the position of a precursor and a huge influence on contemporary Nigerian hip-hop.[68] Although Fela was not the first person to engage with the indigenization of European English in Nigeria, other singers like Mojola Agbebi, Fela Sowande, and Akin Euba are noted to have preceded him in that direction. However, his music and its popularity added to the popularity and acceptance of Pidgin English in the country.

---

67   Carter-Ényì and Carter-Ényì, "Decolonizing," 64.
68   Olorunyomi, *Afrobeat!*

In the postcolonial Nigerian music scene, the use of Pidgin English gained popularity across diverse ethnic and linguistic groups and became the language of pop music in present Nigeria. Pidgin English is a domesticated version of the English language; it accommodates the various linguistic nuances of the Nigerian people and provides a middle ground between high and low culture. It serves as a language of decolonization given its capacity to express distinct cultural and contemporary realities of the African people as well. It echoes Ngugi's notion of innovation, of pushing new limits in music using language and incorporating new experiences, urban struggles, and the history of the people.[69] He further describes contemporary African music as true to its roots and heritage but also accommodating the realities of the present. In other words, although Pidgin English represents the vestiges of colonial incursion, it currently provides a counterhegemonic alternative not very different from the intentions of indigenous languages. Therefore, the use of Pidgin English, much like indigenous languages, elicits a sense of identity and nationhood to the Nigerian singer and listener. As a language of popular culture, Fela and a long list of contemporary Nigerian hip-hop artists have employed its use.

Having examined the decolonization practice in music practice, it is pertinent to examine African music scholarship to identify decolonization activities that have been in place in the study of music in Africa. Language forms a principal portion of every decolonization study, so naturally, Mapaya notes that studies of African music has always been conducted using the colonizer's language, and not surprisingly, many significant aspects of African music have remained inaccessible.[70] Songs naturally driven by language are incubators of culture. The message and composition of African music continue to be created in the same languages from one generation to another, preserving its cultural composition as well as the language of the music. With that said, it is imperative to emphasize the composition and study of African music in African languages to be able to provide access to the nonmaterial essence of African music, which continues to be out of reach.

Contemporary scholarship in Africa as previously established seems to be experiencing a revolution: many music scholars, such as Agawu,

---

69 Ngugi, *Decolonising*.
70 Mapaya, "Indigenous Language," 29–34.

Ekwueme, Euba, Nzewi, Akpabot, and many others have indexed the shift from Western-centered to a more Afrocentric scholarship in the field of music, eliminating erroneous notions of African music's incapacity to develop into a viable field of scholarship. With this, there is a centralization of African musical philosophies, devices, and theorizations inspired by African musical epistemologies and knowledge systems, while the essential functionality of African music is extensively harnessed.

Decolonizing of African Literature

The question of African literature calls to mind a series of debates as to what qualifies as African literature. Is it literature produced in Africa and about Africa? Or does the subject or theme have to be on Africa? Does it include literature by Blacks who are not from the continent? Must the language be an indigenous African language? Or can it include colonial languages like English, French, Portuguese, or Arabic? Aside from other questions raised, the subject of language continues to persist in decolonization studies. Like other areas of knowledge production, language is integral to determining the identity and ownership of literature. Some scholars like Obi Wali and Ngugi wa Thiong'o are of the opinion that literature written in colonial languages does not qualify as African literature. The use of colonial languages is associated with the propagation of cultural servitude as intended by colonialism.[71] However, this view does not ally with Achebe's conception of African literature; to him language use is hardly a parameter for defining African literature. He further states that although the process of colonialism came with dubious ambitions and racial prejudice, the English language is rather a useful inheritance that can be mastered and harnessed effectively to further the African cause. Indeed, according to Achebe, "We may go on resenting it because it came as part of a package deal which included many other items of doubtful value and the positive atrocity of racial arrogance and prejudice, which may yet set the world on fire. But let us not in rejecting the evil throw out the good with it."[72] Ngugi wa Thiong'o and Achebe's famed disagreement and debate on this subject matter have framed an approach for the discourse of identity and decolonization in African literature.

---

71 Onwuchekwa and Madubuike, "Towards the Decolonization," 29–57.
72 Achebe, "African."

Far from the debate between the two intellectuals, writers like Gordimer emphasize African consciousness in the discourse of African literature. For Gordimer, literature can be written in any language to qualify as African literature, but it has to reflect the writer's African consciousness and African experience.[73] Ngugi and Obi's school of thought therefore disqualifies works of reputable African literary artists and intellectuals like Chinua Achebe, Gabriel Okara, Christopher Okigbo, Wole Soyinka, Ben Okri, Chimamanda Adichie, Nadine Gordimer, Seffi Attah, and the list goes on. These writers have successfully conveyed the African experience using the colonizer's languages. Although there are other grounded sentiments against their literature that equally sets the stage for the discourse of decolonization in African literature.

With an extensive look at Nigerian poetry, Chinweizu et al. explore the problem of language and meaning in African poetry. They opine that Nigerian poetry, especially those associated with the University of Ibadan and the University of Nsukka in the early postindependence era, are guilty of using complex languages that are modeled after nineteenth- and sixteenth-century British writers. Their poetry is accused of being rife with "Latinisms and Shakespeareanisms" with structure and form that reflect the affectations of the colonizers.[74] To them, these British nuances leave no room for African originality since even imagery and forms are imported from the colonizer's culture while there is a desire to create literature similar to that of British novelists and poets. In a passionate analysis on poems written by J. P. Clark, Christopher Okigbo, and Michael Echeruo, Chinwezu et al. convey the following opinion:

> J. P. Clark's "Ivbie" is replete with such cliches and Shakespeareanisms as "thereby hangs a tale," "bade us hold our tongue/Bade us note," "sleep no more." In "Heavensgate" Christopher Okigbo writes: "Singeth jadum the minstrel.... Singeth jadum from Rockland." The poem is dotted with latinisms: Lustra; La- crimae Christi; Lumen mundi. Michael Echeruo's Mortality bristles with Corpus Christi formulas: iie nos inducas; ure igne; nobis quoque peccatoribus; qui tollis peccata nmundi; miserere; non sum dignus—"according to the order of Melchisedech."[75]

---

73 Gill, *Modern African*.
74 Onwuchekwa and Madubuike, "Towards the Decolonization," 29–57.
75 Onwuchekwa and Madubuike, "Towards the Decolonization," 29–57.

The above excerpt reveals the extent of a supposed Eurocentrism in the selected African literary works; it reflects the hegemony of European literary standards and the unconscious and unquestioned adoption of these standards and paradigms by African intellectuals. Besides, part of the appeal of European standards and values is that they are "one-size-fits-all," no? The sarcasm of the preceding sentence is clearly not lost on Chinweizu et al. since they carefully note that African literature derives from the oral traditions and cultural reservoirs of the African people and are not compatible with European cultural standards and values.[76] Achebe's *Things Fall Apart* best represents the type of literature that critics praise. The text embodies a precolonial African reality given the writer's ability to adapt the English language to the local Igbo context and his success in creating realistic characters and generous representations of the Igbo cultural values, proverbs, and idioms.

While interrogating the obscurantism of African literature, Chinweizu implies that it is imperative to note that the dictum of art for art's sake does not and should not apply to African literature. It emanates from the ashes of colonialism and should, therefore, present a functionality that aims to emphasize the African identity through an originality that is true to African culture and tradition. In the use of imageries, Clark, Okigbo, Echeruo, Okot, and Soyinka are accused of importing Greek mythological characters, alien religious symbols, and imageries that leave the reader wondering if there are no African equivalents. Some scholars will counter Chinweizu, et. al.'s opinions by first identifying that these writers were beneficiaries of European education and so naturally there will be some European influences. In other words, African literature is not homogenous. Diversity tends to define the African reality, and it is undoubtedly reflected in the varying approaches to literature produced in the continent.

Conclusion

The study of decolonization reveals the existence of an implicit Eurocentrism in Africa that can be traced to colonial activities in various spheres of African society. It is, however, essential to identify these

---

76   Onwuchekwa and Madubuike, "Towards the Decolonization," 29–57.

expressions of colonialism, especially given the dire need to decolonize knowledge—philosophies, language, epistemologies, and concepts—as it will inform and influence original methodologies and approaches to research and education. However, given how Western ideologies and methodologies are strongly woven into the global space, it is almost impossible to provide a solely African system and approach to knowledge production and research because the template used will likely be derived from the West given the continent's overdependence on Western thinkers for strategies and direction. Therefore, an attempt to decolonize without engaging in an inward and outward campaign for the centralization of African thought might just lead to a failed Western facsimile. In other words, the conceptualizations of Western scholars and thinkers will not proffer the necessary insight to create indigenous ideologies and methodologies to displace Western hegemony.

However, this is hardly an attempt to discourage African scholars in the decolonization process; it is rather to warn them of the implications of the expansive hegemony of Western ideologies and approaches and to encourage efforts toward a centralization of African thought. The complementarity of both Afrocentrism and Western approaches should be accepted, but the hegemony of concepts from Western scholars and other knowledge producers should be aggressively discouraged.

Chapter Five

Decolonizing Research Methodologies

If the notion that "research" has become a dirty word in the indigenous context[1] has found credence within the African or indigenous[2] knowledge universe, it is because the word itself is suspect, having been bound up with the history of colonialism and European imperialism in Third World countries, Africa included. The activity of research itself has been argued to be a prelude to loss, theft, cultural dominance, and an instrument of political control.[3] Hence, it references colonialism and imperialism for the reason that in the indigenous context, where it achieves functional relevance, it conjures a history of incursive violence, hegemonic force, cultural displacement, and historical reconstruction while also serving as a grim reminder of the colonial times as they are manifested in various aspects of indigenous reality.

To reinforce what Tihuwai Smith, Deloria, Pualani-Louis, Bekisizwe Ndimande, and other advocates of indigenous methodology in research continue to champion over time, research, especially scientific research—that branch of knowledge presumably founded, as conventional history tells us, on a Western philosophical knowledge foundation and believed to be instrumental in opening doors to other disciplines—is bounded in the extremes of colonialism. It often involves outsiders willing to "collect" without sufficient dialogue or empathy and establish generalizations that misinterpret data and objectify or alienate its producers from exercising

---

1 Smith, *Decolonizing*.
2 The term "indigenous" here refers to previously colonized people, especially of the Third World.
3 Overton, "Decolonizing," 598–99.

any control over the final products of research, all of which leads to cases of insensitivity. This thoughtlessness emerges from an insufficient knowledge of whatever indigenous phenomenon is being studied and the local contexts and processes that sustain it. It is for these reasons that research is often remembered vis-à-vis imperialism when the word comes up in the indigenous context.

I have used the word "presumably" previously as a placeholder and signifier because it works within the colonial agenda to blur the contributions of the Other, those existing on the margins of global knowledge as it exists today. This erasure is done is such systematic ways that global or universal knowledge is indeed at its core construed as Western, implying Europe and North America as being the sole knowledge powerhouses. The best way to make clear this appropriation is to explain the procedures through which the West was able to co-opt so much of the world's knowledge and culture as its own. Extraction of already existing knowledge from their indigenous sources to be rebranded as Western phenomena is only symptomatic of a systematic procedure of "taking" and "re-introducing" that characterized the imperialist enterprise.

Just as Smith argues, new knowledge sourced from outsider cultures transformed old ideas into new considerations of an increasingly expanding world; the validity of such specific knowledge forms in the face of exponential discoveries of indigenous epistemologies turned knowledge itself into a commodity for the colonial enterprise.[4] John Overton claims that research is not just an intellectual endeavor but one driven by commerce, through which careers and tenures have been secured through the misrepresentation of the Other.[5] Consequently, the merging of the intellectual and the commercial in the imperialist enterprise turned knowledge into a commodity.

No wonder, then, that notional conceptions about the indigenous Other, in the bid to expand the frontiers of knowledge as made necessary by the increasing cultural and socioeconomic explosion of the late seventeenth and eighteenth centuries, were reframed to fit the Enlightenment philosophies that would eventually usher in modernity. Industrial and scientific revolution, liberalism, and reliance on logic and personal conviction and search for logically derived knowledge recharged the

---

4 Smith, *Decolonizing*.
5 Smith, *Decolonizing*.

colonialist impulse to accommodate knowledge extraction as part of its imperialist strategy.

Consequently, forms of knowledge alien to the West, from Asia to Africa (but discovered through imperialist incursions into non-Western traditions) were eventually appropriated by the West. These indigenous contributions, of course, have been silenced throughout history for two chief reasons. Firstly, the West wanted to shore up their positional superiority,[6] which is always diametrically opposed to any substantial ascendancy of non-Western traditions. As put succinctly by Smith, indigenous objects of Western explorations, research, or scientific discoveries are considered to neither possess their own voice nor contribute to world culture in any significant measure except through a Western interpretation. This was the dominant ideology at the time, and such ideologies have permeated modern thought. The second reason is tied to an aside made earlier: to the West, objects possess neither a "life force, humanity, spirit of [their] own,"[7] and as such could not be conceived of as anything substantial. So, the philosophies, technologies, knowledge forms, and systems of thought "uncovered" by the West in these regions were archived as Western properties to be later reintroduced into the regions in altered forms.

Another angle from which the argument can be rendered is to see "coloniality" and modernity as inextricably linked, owing to the coterminous relationship between advancement in science and technology ushered by Enlightenment and the discovery of the New World. This led to expeditions, expansion, charting of slave routes to advance the slave trade in Africa, and extraction of cultural resources and knowledge—acts that eventually cleared the path connecting imperialism to colonialism. Coloniality, through research, notions and systems of civilization, worldviews, and exercise of knowledge continues to maintain power structures unfavorable to indigenous peoples.[8] These mechanisms are said to pre-

---

6   Said, *Orientalism*.
7   Smith, *Decolonizing*, 64.
8   The term "Indigenous people" or peoples, as each instance of use would determine, is both used in adjectival and (proper) nominal senses: the term refers to people embroiled in the struggle against colonialism in all its forms, from the indigenous people of North America, Australia, Africa, and elsewhere.

serve positions of dominance and subservience.[9] Indeed, when laid bare, one sees patterns of dominance in evidence from the colonial era.

Conditions like these have served as provocative influences for indigenous scholars who have decried the colonizing impact of research by referencing or referring to its history of "taking."[10] Perhaps, nowhere is this history of "taking" more apparent than in ethnography. This is because appropriate ethnographic research is ineffective without an object of study.[11] This object can range from social structure to human beings.[12] Ethnography is itself implicated by its methodologies: requiring theoretical formulations founded on Western epistemic categories, theoretical inferences informed by the same generalizations as a result of the insider-outsider dialectic and the absence of due reflexivity, and evaluation by a critical scholarly community that often exists outside the borders of the object of study—all of which privileges and superimposes the West as the bastion of knowledge over the producers of data. For scholars like Denzin and Lincoln, research is not only an act of imperialism but also accommodates practices with impositional undertones; it allows for appropriation and epistemological hegemony, an example of which is ethnographic research.[13]

For this reason and many more, ethnography has often been touted to be the poster child of neocolonialism or, more appropriately, a glamorization of cultural "collecting." It should also be considered that the mythology of Western dominance and superiority, entrenched in philosophical formulations—such as the "burden of the West," used in justifying colonialism—has not only been extended into present times but also entrenched into structures of knowing and identity, which covertly or overtly require indigenes to find space within it if they are to lay claims to being civilized. Essentially, the dichotomy between colonizer and colonized, with its attendant philosophies and implications, are still being replicated and maintained, even if in mediated forms, in the postcolony; this type of maintenance culture culminates in the perpetuation of the categories of dominance and subservience, especially, for instance, through research that aims to collect by positioning the researcher as the

---

9   Donahue and Kaylan, "Introduction," 124–37.
10 Whetung and Wakefield, "Colonial Conventions, 146–58.
11 Michrina, "Reflexive Ethnography," 212–14.
12 Michrina, "Reflexive Ethnography."
13 Ndimande, "Decolonizing," 215–26.

one in possession of critical tools of retrieval and preservation and the researched as the object in need of rescuing. Thus, one gets the reproduction of colonial relationships.

Stealing, collecting, and taking are appropriate terms for the exploitation that manifested in the eighteenth and nineteenth centuries under the guise of research, where cultural items, territories, resources, and environmental features were extracted from their spaces and timelines without appropriate permissions. That such thefts are labeled discoveries and are considered to have been rescued from indigenous peoples (and thus from cultural decay) by being given enduring value in a new form (as averred by a Western apologist, James Clifford),[14] not only betrays the regnant mindset at the time but also comments on to what extent research can be seen as an incursive and usurping tool by the victims of these blatant "takings." Smith pegs the rules of engagement structuring those activities responsible for barring indigenous peoples from being actively present in the debate that categorized them as objects.

Globalization, as it is today, is an advanced and retooled accumulation of these sorts of collectivist enterprises and imperialist impulses. Hence, what many postcolonial theorists and writers like Gayatri Spivak, the Bolekaja Critics, Frantz Fanon, Homi Bhabha, and Chakrabarty Dipesh, among many more, have ushered to the fore of postcolonial or decolonial discourse becomes legitimate and worthy of further championing. An example of this is Edward Said's take on Western discourse. To him, discourse generally seems to be supported by Western institutions, which inform the character of scholarly theorizations, cultural (modern/popular/postmodern) principles and vocabulary, and the colonial procedures of administration that have formed the covert and sometimes overt foundations of knowledge and sociopolitical institutions in former colonies and Third World regions.

To Said, these processes are all the more effective as a result of the symbiotic relationship and constant exchange between the scholarly process of "knowing" informing much of twenty-first-century knowledge, and the sort of imagining of the "Other" that popularly characterizes interracial posturing, discourse, and relationships. In the words of Said, what obtains in scholarly investigation pertaining to acquisition, dispensing, and rebranding of knowledge will expand with the support of corporate

---

14 Clifford, *Predicament*.

institutions who make "statements about it [the Other], authoriz[e] views of it, describe[e] it ... teach about it, settl[e] it, rul[e] over it." By so doing, the West retains its centripetal power of pulling all data toward it as the hub of world knowledge.

To see the matter for what it is requires us to see the situation as Smith does: "Within the enclaves of these acts the formal scholarly pursuits of knowledge and the informal, imaginative, anecdotal constructions of the Other are intertwined with each other and with the activity of research."[15] Research is for this reason a site of contestation, where knowledge merchants seek to redeem research of the "Other" from the policing gaze of the West by giving impetus to the subaltern, a position of marginality. This way, research is being redeemed by and through itself. Yet there is an irony to this, and the irony is manifested in the Western apparatus used in effecting this power shift.

The pedagogic tools and rules of research themselves are bound up in either first-order or second-order Eurocentrism. The logic unfolds this way: contexts, discourse, and strategies of colonialism survive in the condition of coloniality, which has found its way down to the public and private domains of the postcolony.[16] They constitute what Donahue et al. refer to as the "epistemic landscape of Western culture, politics, and philosophy."[17] This landscape is global and as such entrenched in the philosophy and manifestation of globalism and global thought/knowledge that holds modern society together.

The problem with research, especially the indigenous mold, as a tool of refracting the domineering energy of the West undisturbed within its methodologies, is the refusal—whether by deliberate posturing or uninformed oversight—by its practitioners to decenter the West as a cardinal point of reference for epistemological formulations and theorizing in the disciplines. This means that even postcolonial- and decolonial-oriented research, critiques, and posturing are themselves implicated in the conditions of coloniality by the Eurocentric methodologies or conceptual frameworks upon which they are organized. This second-order Eurocentrism is not limited to methodological frameworks or theorizing but also includes comparative philosophies that require discerning

---

15   Smith, *Decolonizing*, 3.
16   Donahue and Kaylan, "Introduction."
17   Smith, *Decolonizing*, 128.

the conceptual frameworks and operative terminologies conceived by Western scholars. Through such comparative juxtapositions, indigenous cultures from which research draws data and conclusions are objectified as sites of extraction and relegated to the margins of knowledge. To shed light on this condition, it is essential to quote Garfield at length:

> Given a powerful scholarly tradition practiced by the members of a politically and economically powerful group, it is indeed possible to come to know another culture by bringing it as an object under the lens of one's own intellectual microscope. In doing so, however, one transforms that body of knowledge in fundamental ways. Indeed, the transformation is so complete that if it is successful, the alien culture becomes relegated to a merely historical phenomenon. The authority as readers and interpreters of texts is shifted from those within the tradition to the alien experts. Alien commentaries gain ascendancy over traditional commentaries. The hermeneutic method of the conqueror becomes the standard means of reading the vanquished, and the vanquished tradition becomes, as the Ven. Geshe Ngawang Samten put it in conversation, "the domain of curators."[18]

Perhaps the situation is worse than it presents itself; the reason being that if Eurocentrism, expanded to mean both Europe and North America, was indeed as prevalent as it is in methodologies, philosophies, and approaches to cultural studies (especially, as discussed above, in ethnography) it would only make more sense that this condition of coloniality is entrenched in basic theoretical and knowledge categories in the disciplines. These include (but are not limited to) theoretical notions of cultural diversity and difference, which serve as ideological launch pads for many interdisciplinary and scholarly investigations along cultural lines. Were this to be the case, dislodging objectifying and limiting tendencies in research appropriating Eurocentric methodologies may be an arduous task. This is because: 1.There is a respectable truth in the assertion "that all cultural difference is colonial difference,"[19] if we were to approach that statement from the Othering tendencies of European exploitation of indigenous terrain[20]; 2.If the notion of culture, as it were, were suf-

---

18 Jay, *Empty Words,* 244.
19 Donahue and Kaylan, "Introduction," 131.
20 The mere situating of "the body" as the dominant category of understanding the human condition in scholarly theorizing and cultural studies of

fused with coloniality, as made apparent by the discourse of subalternity, marginality, and colonial othering, how then does research circumvent the privileging of Europe as a cardinal point of reference without canceling itself? More so, how are primary categories of analysis like epistemology and ethics extricated from the center, to be precise, divested of any forms of principal references to principles of Western philosophical discourse? These questions are sacrosanct to any discourse on decolonizing research methodologies.

Although merely scratching the surface, the foregoing testifies to the complex and intrinsic relationship research has with imperialism and colonialism. To make attempts at some kind of broad-spectrum sanitization is to begin with a decolonization strategy. Thus, it is impossible to attempt decolonizing without investigating, exploring, identifying, and exposing the colonialist and imperialist impulse regnant in scholarship and research as disciplines, bodies of knowledge, and tools of preservation. Just as Donahue et al. posit, "To reflect on coloniality is not to study the history of colonialism from the safety of a 'postcolonial' present. Rather, it requires one to interrogate ongoing legacies of colonialism [because] Postcolonial and decolonial studies... aim to make this contemporary condition of coloniality theoretically and empirically visible."[21]

To attempt to decolonize, as a result, is to engage in exposing, subverting, and picking apart the legacies of colonialism in modern times. To decolonize means different things to different scholars who have engaged the topic at several levels, like Fanon, Nigugi, Achebe, Smith, among a host of others. Regardless of the angle at which they have each approached the subject, one converging premise is that decolonization is a process that engages imperialism and colonialism in its subtle and overt manifestations. To paraphrase Smith, who has forcefully engaged this question in her seminal book on indigenous methodology, to decolonize is to engage both imperialism and colonialism at multiple levels and, especially for researchers, have a critical and nuanced understanding of

---

race or gender issues privileges a Western pedagogy that rests on visuality as a dominant mode of perception rather than orality, which is unique to many indigenous concepts.

21 Donahue and Kaylan, "Introduction," 124.

their undertones as they exist in the assumptions, motivations, and values sustaining research practices.[22]

To research is to refocus attention to a thing in the larger context of scholarship. In an indigenous context, to research would be to emphasize the presence or nature or an aspect of it using set principles and methods. Decolonizing research, therefore, would be to identify subversive approaches to researching aspects of native cultures: that is, research that promotes the continued dominance, exploitative mechanisms, and the appropriating designs that promote imperialist and colonial practices, knowledge, and methods over others. The manner in which this is done speaks to the purpose and process of decolonizing. As opined by Ndimande, the premises of decolonizing research are made apparent in terms of the goal they intend to achieve.[23]

The necessary question that must arise at this point to set in motion the requisite remedies is about the forms of present-day European colonialism and imperialism: In what ways have they been maintained in indigenous knowledge matrices that adversely affect indigenous methodologies of research and that require substantive and efficacious counterhegemonic or decolonizing strategies? Put differently, to what areas must attention be turned to mount successful campaigns that would return displaced indigenous epistemologies to the center of the discourse?

Decolonizing Research Methodology: Why?

It is not enough to agitate against the obvious or clandestine forms of oppression in a modern postcolonial framework. Activating the apparatus that seeks to decenter the West and situate the subaltern requires identifying, dismantling, and reorganizing the status quo. This reorganization comes in different patterns: shedding colonial skins and advancing native culture in all its productions. Decolonizing research is all the more important because it thrives in the philosophy of counterhegemonic posturing where scholars and academics invested in the anticolonial and anti-imperialist enterprise remodel research designs in a way

---

22 Smith, *Decolonizing*, 20.
23 Ndimande, "Decolonizing," 215–26.

that showcases a dialectical struggle with long-standing and colonizing practices in research into the indigenous sociocultural sphere.

Mounting a decolonizing campaign in research is essential for the benefit of challenging the Western gaze in research on indigenous peoples. It affords indigenous scholars a redemptive avenue within Western epistemology where they have internalized Western methodologies, deploying them in ways that do not essentially frame questions and issues in terms that resonate with indigenous worldviews. Like Hamza contends, the word itself accounts for a reality where indigenous peoples receive primary focus and where legacies of the indigenous are moved to the center of discourse.[24]

The goal is to not only establish a process where nonindigenous and indigenous researchers approach native cultures without biased Eurocentric views but to also generate indigenous models of knowledge production or research fueled in proportionate levels by both indigenous and modern ways of knowing. This is to eliminate any form of insularity in research, which itself is a colonizing apparatus, while also being conscious of the pitfall of merely replacing one set of provincial principles with another,[25] as a decolonized research design requires. By utilizing the colonizer's language as a tool of awareness in connecting with current trends of knowledge, the researcher would have achieved three things: overturn colonial heritage via a counterrevolutionary form by using the language of the colonizer against the colonizer (colonial gaze) in a way that fulfills the decolonizing imperative; connect through cross-cultural interactions; use the tools of colonization to continually situate, in the capacity of a primary agent, indigenous modes of knowledge beyond the provincial considering no culture is unchanging, particularly in a global context. This would not be at odds with Achebe's use of the English language, moving the marginalized from the sidelines to the center.

To reiterate the concerns of Hamza, decolonizing research methodologies requires for practicality the lessons of decolonization to avoid unchecked nationalism that does nothing to raise sociocultural consciousness in a sustained manner beyond simply being a reactionary stance. It means the researcher must turn inward at several points before, during, and after the research activity; this may mean exhuming and reframing

---

24 Hamza, "Decolonizing."
25 Fanon calls this the "logic of displacement."

native epistemologies for use, code-switching during interviews (especially for the native researcher), and taking into consideration the indigenous worldview in shaping specific and context-based research projects and questions.

Linguistic Turn: Decolonizing the Language of Research

Because it organizes reality in a deterministic way, language is often the first consideration in the decolonizing campaign. This is reflected in language being a form of logos or, as structuralists like Roland Barthes affirm, a transcendental signifier, from which meaning is sourced. At the forefront of knowledge production issues in Africa is the debate on the means of preserving and codifying the knowledge and cultural heritage of Africa, especially in ways that can debunk the European myths that have relegated it to the margins of civilization. One such hotspot of debate is in the area of language and literature. Yet, one thing is essential enough to be decipherable from the many arguments over the years: language in an indigenous context is more than a linguistic phenomenon or a communicative system; it is an identity and a source of heritage.

Where Fanon, referred to as the father of the "Indigenist Essentialist school,"[26] argues that speaking a colonizer's language means existing for the colonizer, considering the use of a language's syntax and morphology translates into imbibing to an extent the dynamics of its culture, supporting its civilization, and perpetuating the orchestrated death of indigenous culture.[27] Isaiah Ilo calls it the worst kind of assault on a people's consciousness,[28] that is, linguistic colonization. By adopting the language of the colonizer, the colonized can elevate themselves beyond their native culture, which is now demonized as uncivilized in relation to the extent of his/her adoption of the colonizer's culture. Obi Wali echoes Fanon's argument, although in a more extreme light, when he equates adoption of such foreign language and by extension its culture to the death of African imagination and culture.[29] To him, the media of

---

26 Ilo, "Language," 1–9.
27 Fanon, *Black Skin*.
28 Ilo, "Language," 2.
29 Wali, "Dead End," 13–16.

knowledge preservation, creation, and propagation should be unapologetically African. Any contravention is not a creative reinvention but the abortion of any foreseeable revolution in the future against neocolonialism, considering indigenous languages are the languages of the peasantry and the working class, who in history are more often than not the instigators of revolutions.[30]

Ngugi wa Thiong'o echoes the same thought when he framed language as the most significant apparatus with which colonizers captured the indigenous soul.[31] To divorce Africa from colonial moorings is to encourage cultural autonomy, and this can only be effective when cultural identity can be extricated from colonial and neoimperialist mechanisms of exploitation. Ngugi did not only advocate for the use of indigenous languages in documenting and construing African reality through literature and the disciplines but also the situating of messages of revolutionary unity and hope through content and strategy.[32] One such strategy is employing indigenous languages in research and research interviews. In fact, if Achebe and Ngugi, who occupy different positions on the language debate spectrum, have a common thread it would be located within the revolutionary strategies of Nigugi, which is the logic behind Achebe's position when he claimed that English language, although formerly a European language, has become an asset that must be domesticated. In Achebe's view, the English language must carry the weight of the African experience and must be fully compatible with the African epistemological frame.[33]

The rationale behind Achebe's view is, arguably, an appropriate foundation on which decolonizing philosophy can be anchored; this is because decolonizing is not commensurate with a total rejection of Western knowledge or principles of theorizing but the central emphasis of indigenous views. Like Oyewunmi argues in response to the antinativist argument, embracing the West in a global context is not the issue, as the indigenous person is already locked in embrace with the West; this means that the idea of choice is a displaced metaphor.[34]

---

30 Wali, "Dead End."
31 Ngugi, "Europhonism," 1–11.
32 Ngugi, "Europhonism."
33 Achebe, *Morning*.
34 Oyewunmi, *Invention*.

The main issue is the extent to which the native self must be extricated. Achebe's and Oyewunmi's views, although approaching the issue from several angles, converge at the same juncture and paint the necessary image of what is required, especially since the language of research and its discursive purpose, on a general level, panders to the West. This is seen in its worthlessness to the indigenous world that sees, in the process and aftermath of research, only a regurgitation of what is already known: the West employs it as an instrument of taxonomy and to further the ascension of the Eurocentric gaze.

In light of this, therefore, the disjoint between documented research—as conducted by Eurocentric researchers or their apologists—and observed reality is ensconced by the disparity between the language employed during the process of research and that of the indigenous context. Such form of language inconsistency fuels Oyewunmi Oyeronke's assertion that there exists a gaping lacuna between what is written as researched material and the lived realities of those who are researched.[35]

For the reason stated above, the language of research must be situated with the sociocultural domains of inquiry. Effective qualitative research, for instance, requires dexterity in the ability to elicit appropriate responses from respondents; and the way to do this is to engage participants in the language with which they are most comfortable. Language as a toolbox cannot be overemphasized because not only can it allow disparate cultures to effectively relate to one another, but it is also the catalyst for thought creation, synthesis, and performance. To accentuate the importance of language in this capacity is to draw attention to the impediment that the absence of mutual intelligibility can cause when the means of relation is defective. The language of formulating research questions and to which a respondent must answer is pivotal considering language is an appropriate conduit toward thought formulation.[36]

In an expanding context for the alienating effects of a nondecolonized language, Ngugi in his book *Decolonizing the Mind* relates language to a spiritual force that powers the soul. The implication is that when an indigenous language is extracted from its setting or substituted with an alien one, an essential force of societal continuity and harmony is being eviscerated. This much is true if language is appreciated for its bonding or

---

35 Oyewunmi, "Decolonizing," 9–34.
36 Ngugi, *Decolonizing*.

harmonizing qualities. Deploying a foreign language, especially the language of the colonizer, is to not only remind those being researched of a history of injustice but to evoke distrust, which would defeat the process, outcome, and initiative.

It will be counterproductive, for example, in a focus group with indigenous participants to engage them in an alien language. The strength of a focus group as part of a research design allows for a fluid relationship between researcher and researched. In an informal setting where participants can better navigate the distance between researcher and researched, and the researcher can bridge this distance, language provides avenues toward a more engaging activity that can spur memory and lead to provision of better responses by way of description and narration of experiences. Moreover, by involving more than one participant, a complementary system is created where feelings of solidarity can be cultivated and where memories related to specific issues of the research otherwise forgotten can be triggered by the responses of others. Focus groups as research implements bridge the gap between formal and informal interviewing.[37] To harness the benefits of this design is to connect with the participants at their most basic level of humanity—language.

To be able to effectively accomplish the goal of research in the indigenous context without privileging Eurocentrism demands emphasizing the role of indigenous languages. Indigenous peoples are largely polyglots, some even capable of articulating thoughts in more than one indigenous language. Research that seeks to centralize indigenous methodologies of knowledge production and preservation should be conducted with linguistic diversity of the native sociosphere in focus. This return to indigenous languages does not mean forfeiting of nonnative languages, which might eventually be used in documenting the final print or transcribed versions of the research. But since the actual research is a process of collecting, centralizing the indigenous language(s) shows respect for the native culture and philosophy and presents the researcher as a seeker of knowledge and not an intruder. Indigenous languages are not merely codification systems; they are cultural identities. They deserve to be preserved, promoted, and centralized as entry points into the knowledge dynamics of native cultures.

---

37   Fontana and Frey, "From Structured Questions," 645–72.

In recognition of these cultures, works conducted in indigenous languages (channeling Ngugi's views on employing indigenous languages in codifying African literatures) that reflect African life and epistemologies are considered examples of the process of decolonizing research. Hamza shares this opinion by arguing that decentering or deemphasizing colonial language in interviews with indigenous peoples not only does away with alienation in their own culture—a rehashing of the colonial experience—but unravels the colonial and imperialist practices in research.[38] This way, according to her, conditions are created through which indigenous people's perspectives are maintained, aired, and made crucial to knowledge production.

When language is used in a primary capacity during research, the intersection of the sociopolitical and the cultural aspects of research can depose the hegemonic status of colonial language. Moreover, there is the responsibility of all researchers, especially indigenous ones, to be aware of this intersection and how not to fall prey to institutionalized ways of seeing and researching indigenous peoples that harken back to an era of colonialism. There is a tripartite connection between research as an activity and the way it is executed and the people who are objects of this research.

Decolonizing research methodology through language is not limited to the process of research but to the academic institutions that sponsor this research. Considering that the goal of decolonizing is to challenge and undo the underlying imperialist practices inherent in the disciplines and their research methods, it is essential that procedures that accommodate indigenous realities during the formulations of research ideas, methods, and questions are encouraged. This is required because coloniality as a condition in modern times entails wrestling with various forms of disempowerment on terms set by the hegemonic force itself. First of all, it is often the case that colonial principles of research are products of the level of coloniality operating at the educational level.

Just as Mdimande argues, conditions are not created for promoting the perspectives of indigenous peoples in many indigenous contexts: the formal language of education in Nigeria is a foreign language; aside from the breakdown in thought creation and transfer from the indigenous mind through a foreign language, leading to instances of loss or shift in intended meaning, there is an exclusion of indigenous tongues from the

---

38 Hamza, "Decolonizing," 123–34.

language of discourse with which research as an intellectual and academic endeavor is executed. The neglect of linguistic recognition leads to the absence or subordination of indigenous thought on indigenous matters. This begs the logical query: who is the research for? This is pertinent, considering the act of researching the indigenous context in an alien language creates communicative and translation barriers that hamper data quality.

For this reason, indigenous researchers have often been encouraged to engage in research using indigenous languages, especially in indigenous contexts—but even this has its own issues. Like Hamza argues, it is difficult conceiving a research question, for example, in English, translating it to an indigenous language, and then translating responses back to English for analysis without losing the original meaning.[39] At the very least, by using an indigenous language for codifying research inquiries, not only is one level of challenge eliminated, but the researcher is able to include, anticipate, and make essential indigenous perspectives at the onset of the research planning before fieldwork is carried out.

The challenge of employing indigenous languages as the language of discourse is tied to an after-effect of coloniality, which is an obsession with the use of English; this causes a condition Fanon explained as existing for the colonizer and perpetuating the death of the indigenous language and culture. This reliance on the language reflects Fanon's position on absorbing the culture of the colonizer in a way that sustains conditions of coloniality where the use of English marginalizes other languages, even in contexts wherein they are most appropriate, like research interviews.

Encouraging the use of indigenous languages for research is a product of a broader decolonizing agenda in academia and research centers and generally a nation's policy on language planning. The discouraged use of native languages as instruments of instruction and research, as well as the refusal to accommodate provisions for native languages in academic writing, of which research writing is a subset, also attest to the foregoing. Research designs are structured in ways that maintain the positional hegemony of the West. It therefore seems contradictory if research meant for the indigenous is written in ways that do not make provisions for the linguistic peculiarities and capacities of the indigenous. Understanding the need to embed indigenous perspectives in several aspects of research

---

39 Hamza, "Decolonizing."

designs provokes questions such as who writes, who is the beneficiary of the writing, and in what context is the writing done?

The Oral-Visual Dyad and Conceptual Turn

If there exists a pertinent need to decolonize the language of research to accommodate indigenous perspectives, to shift marginalized epistemologies to the center would also be to demand that the ideas and conceptual frameworks upon which research designs are premised accommodate indigenous epistemic systems. Looking inward places a premium on reconnecting with traditional epistemologies to better actualize the decolonizing process without merely rendering it as anticolonial.

The emphasis on visuality has often put Western epistemologies at odds with those of the non-Western, leading to what is known as the oral-visual dyad. The emphasis on what is seen, transcribed, or on written evidence has led to the marginalization of alternate forms of knowledge production, consequently engendering notions such as the absence of elaborate, complex, or any worthwhile epistemology in many native and oral-bound cultures. The physical body, not limited to the human but any visually perceivable form, is often considered the evidence of a presence in Western epistemology; this has led to the ascendancy of writing as the yardstick for the believability or legitimacy of a culture's claim to civilization and knowledge. Oyewunmi, in her essay "Visualizing the Body: Western Theories and African Subjects," makes reference to the reliance on this sensory detail as the bedrock of the West's philosophy, perception, and construal of phenomena,[40] which embodies the West's understanding of unfamiliar cultures.

In explaining the West's reliance on visuality as a critical mode of understanding, Oyewunmi employs references to the body/gaze and the use of worldview to reinforce her point. In her opinion, the continued presence of the body as a discursive category betrays the essentialism of what is visually expressed in the West; hence, categories like body politic, race, gender, sex, color, and more are discursive notions premised on the ascendancy of visuality in theorizing. The term "worldview" itself is bound up in this undue privileging, which to Oyewunmi is deployed by

---

40 Oyewunmi, *Invention*.

the West to summarize the dynamics of a society's cultural systems.[41] Going by this logic, then, it would be Eurocentric to deploy visuality as a mode of understanding other cultures that privilege other modes of perception. Oyewunmi offers an inclusive alternative: "world sense." This accommodates all types of knowledge-bound spaces.

To decolonize research methodology is to take into account that the written word, document, or scribal evidence of knowledge are not the only portals through which indigenous knowledge and concepts can be accessed, deployed, and used as organizing frames. Emphasis on the written word as logos, what poststructuralist deconstructionist thought argues as logocentrism, is only a manifestation of the modern shift from sound to visual space, with print and electronic culture transferring lasting effects on visual space as the central site for knowledge excavation and codifying. Considering there is an intricate relationship between modernity and imperialism, the privileging of visuality as the basic paradigm of discourse all the more promotes the erasure of non-Western methods of knowledge production from the center.

Returning to orality as a toolbox of knowledge codification and preservation during adoption or framing of research methodology would assist in fully shifting indigenous cultures and epistemes to the center of discourse. Oral lore is a source of cultural data the same way spoken words function as incubators of cultural memory. Oral-based cultures, those Walter Ong consider as reliant on primary orality—orality not diffused with forms of literacy—educate and preserve data through words functioning as mnemonics, through verbal forms, and through oratorical strategies.[42]

Print rose in stature to banish orality as a vehicle of sourcing, interrogating, and advancing indigenous knowledge to the margins of academic discourse. The immediate consequence of this is the dismissal of African philosophy pre-European contact as ill-formed and simplistic at best, and at worst, nonexistent. This relates to a history of advancing notions about the statelessness and "historylessness"[43] of African cultures, an approach that leads to the standardization of all that is Western as the bar against which others must compare. The consequence is simple: questions that

---

41 Oyewunmi, *Invention*.
42 Ong, *Orality*.
43 Oyewunmi, *Invention*.

inform research, operative theories, and concepts that form which methodologies are constructed are derived from the West and have Western focus—or what Oyewunmi calls "Westocentric" focus; a term she uses to accommodate North America in the hegemonic formation.[44] To consciously return the impetus to the subaltern in academia through research in a way where the West is not imaged as the "self" and the inward "self" is seen as the "other" is to privilege indigenous modes of logic.

To do this, indigenous scholars must exhume traditional concepts and epistemes to revitalize the methodologies through which research makes entry into the world of the native. A common challenge put forward against native scholars leaning on Western concepts in interrogating the indigenous reality is their appalling ignorance of their own cultures made apparent by ill-informed analysis of data and operating on supposed universalist principles that are only superimpositions of the West on homegrown but decentered cultural logic. This is the product of the belief that Western ways of existing are universal, and so all that needs to be done is to find African methods of existing on these precepts, a condition Oyewunmi describes as Africans adding their own "burnt bricks" on top of the foundation of thought the West has laid.[45]

The challenge of importing Western precepts and concepts is that they shift attention from homegrown philosophies, all in the bid to establish sameness with Western systems of knowing or bodies of knowledge, forgetting the difference between universals and particulars.[46] Representing the native culture with alien theories, concepts, and operative terms is to have misrepresented the culture in an unacceptable way. A destabilizing divorce is already made when submissions are made absent apposite cultural contexts; this is often the situation when the native concepts meant to establish links between reality and the epistemic constructs that have brought such realities into existence have been pushed aside.

---

44 Oyewunmi, *Invention*.
45 Oyewunmi, *Invention*.
46 Oyewunmi carefully explains that the reason African scholars and researchers often seek relevance within Western frames of identity and reason is because they are unable to approach Western philosophies as universals, thus "putting up Western manifestations of the human condition as the human condition itself." See Oyewunmi, *Invention*, 21.

For instance, it would be remiss of anyone researching the Yoruba art and identity to not consider the concepts of "omoluabi" and "ona" and how they form a solid foundation for stylistic adherence to tradition, or how both aid in the tempering and idealizing of personal identity in a broader social frame. To accommodate these concepts in research questions is to also admit that written sources upheld as the evidence of presence in the West do not hold up as the principal source of evidence in the indigenous context; it is also to integrate oral genres and lore as sources of data in research methodologies. No better argument sums up the reason for native-culture awareness in formulating research design than the fact that between primary oral cultures and cultures deeply affected by writing technologies, there is a huge gap between ways of managing, disseminating, and producing knowledge.[47] Any researcher willing to breach this gap must unearth the ways each culture is appropriate to each research context.

Politics of Research: Insider-Outsider Conundrum

Considering colonialism was never solely about collection, but rearrangement, re-presentation, and redistribution of indigenous reality,[48] it is not enough for a researcher to categorize oneself on either side of the divide as an indigenous or foreign researcher. The approaches to developing apposite and centralizing research rest mainly on how attuned a researcher is to the methods of reasoning inherent in his or her culture and how the researcher is able to design the research methods in a way that those researched and the researchers themselves are accountable to the indigenous space and people. When questions of accountability, ethics, and positionality are thrown into the mix of what is to be considered when addressing the concept of "harm" in relation to indigenous peoples, the question of the insider-outsider researcher becomes all the more pertinent.

Scott Morgenson rightly argues that colonial legacies have set the permissible standards for determining what is harmful to indigenous peoples in a research context.[49] This reveals a fundamental problem because it

---

47 Ong, "Orality."
48 Smith, *Decolonizing*.
49 Morgenson, "Destabilizing," 805–8.

removes accountability on the part of the researcher, especially those considered outsiders—and to some extent insiders who are oblivious to lines they have crossed during research activity, analyses of research data, and documentation of findings. More than this, it also reveals the institutional (academe) posture toward research, especially in the indigenous context.

One of the drawbacks of academe's position on research designs vis-à-vis the indigenous is in how complicated it is to be both the subject and object of research; that is, how ethics protocols make it hard for indigenous scholars to be both an indigenous person and a scholar—you can speak as either one or the other. This means the indigenous person either takes on the persona of the colonizing researcher or the colonized object of research. This owes largely to how Western academics operate from a hegemonic position that, as Whetung and Wakefield put it, "dis-embeds knowledge that is rooted outside of the academy to bring it into the academy by validating some aspects of it as research."[50]

Ultimately, the researcher operating according to Western policies of research is implicated in the colonial machinery of "collecting," even if such a researcher were indigenous, especially since the end product of this process is archived away from the indigenous space and person. Therefore, without carefully considering and painstakingly applying the principles of research with an awareness that dis-embeds colonial legacies, the indigenous scholar would reproduce colonial understandings of respect, responsibility, and relationships and fail to establish accountability beyond the provisions of the academe, which is no provision in the real sense.

It is important to possess adequate spatial awareness of the context of research. Simple notions like respect and how respect is expressed during interviews is crucial. Even during qualitative research, such notions are important. How are indigenous notions of reverence preserved by the researcher? During interactions, what measures have been structured into the research to accommodate interpersonal correspondence? How does the research avoid treating respondents as merely data sources? How have the practices and philosophies of human relations been maintained in the course of research? How are the respondents referred to? Are there ways of addressing certain class and age groups in a specific context?

---

50   Whetung and Wakefield, "Colonial Conventions," 148.

Ethnicity or skin color are not enough to claim belonging as an indigenous researcher. An alien researcher might be more welcomed than a supposed indigenous one if the latter manifests an appropriate understanding of space and context in the process of conducting research, exhibiting ethical research policies according to the mandates of the region being researched, into the space between research and researched community. Differences in education, class, education, and lived-in space, as well as the discourse practices and cultural notions, can determine how a researcher is perceived by his home community.[51]

Ignorance of these peculiarities automatically leads to false assumptions and nonethical engagements during research. It is a rehash of the colonial impulse—the absence of a responsibility toward the legacies and heritage of the Other, which being dis-embedded from its context and retooled to conform with an expectation is reproduced from whatever perspective the researcher or institution chooses, thereby reentrenching themselves in the making of that data. This makes recourse to how existing knowledge forms were considered discoveries by the West, as if those things were previously nonexistent.

Responsibility on the part of the researcher to indigenous cultures should reflect the design of the methodology used: their methodology should be formulated in a way that it takes into consideration the future use and benefits of the research itself to the native setting it is extracting knowledge from. The methodology should include a follow-up—something that is lacking considering how front-ended Eurocentric research is often carried out. Front-ended Eurocentric methodology is supposedly designed to envisage in advance field-specific details and knowledge extraction but lacks design on how to monitor the return of the refined knowledge back into their contexts. The research design itself lacks provisions for external supervisions that would ensure the researcher and the team remain accountable to the community during and after research. A researcher's responsibility to indigenous communities is continuous.[52]

It is the indigenous responsibility to discourage the neocolonial imperative, which is to dis-embed knowledge and control the narrative.[53] The indigenous researcher should have his mode of engagement informed by

---

51 Ndimande, "Decolonizing."
52 Whetung and Wakefield, "Colonial Interventions."
53 Whetung and Wakefield, "Colonial Interventions."

both the formal and native paradigms. Situating the indigenous mode of engagement in the heart of a research methodology is itself a way of shifting the center of power. By framing the research methodology to accommodate the colonized notion of what is ethical and what it means to be responsible to a space, the researcher has devolved power at the very least.

The methodology of choice should reflect careful considerations of interlocking points between the world of academic research and that of colonized peoples. Empathetic understanding acquired through interpersonal actions of either the indigenous scholar or outsider researcher is germane to interpretive methods in research.[54] A researcher extracting data from a community necessarily must be reflective and empathetic in their commitment to the community being researched, especially if the researcher is conscious of not treating indigenous spaces as mere data pools.

Conclusion: First-Order and Second-Order Eurocentrism

To formulate an appropriate conclusion, a return must be made to the genesis of the decolonial enterprise. Based on the essentiality of the need to appropriately decolonize the concepts and philosophies upon which methodological approaches to knowledge in research are perpetuated, a return is necessary to the matter of how the decolonial approach itself is implicated in imperialist propaganda. This is where the irony lies: that the approach to, of, and in the decolonial enterprise is predicated on the use of Western thought and paradigms to validate indigenous knowledge and operative systems. The level at which this is done is what culminates into first-order and second-order Eurocentrism.

Eurocentrism in indigenous discourse seems to be hardly excisable. This die-hard colonial vestige owes to the overbearing and intricate ways indigenous spaces are bound to the dominant West. Donahue and Kaylan succinctly argue that "even ostensibly anti-colonial discourses that seek to rescue 'local cultural originality' from colonial stigmatization or erasure become intelligible only insofar as they re-articulate this local culture in ways that resonate, in harmony or discord, with the prevailing values and categories of the West."[55]

---

54 Mirichina, "Reflexive Ethnography."
55 Donahue and Kaylan, "Introduction," 128.

So, either primarily or secondarily, there is a privileging of Western structures of thought in the formulations of even anticolonial discourses, either as backdrops from which indigenous modes of reasoning emanate, standards against which indigenous models are compared, or discursive strongholds whose foundations must be dismantled. This much is evident in the current temper of nationalist and decolonial approaches. They are more articulations of a struggle against modern forms of colonialism than espousal of indigenous traditions. Although both approaches seem to be one and the same, they differ, especially in philosophy, approach, and consequence, by technical differences. Espousal of indigenous philosophy does not necessarily devolve into an all-out struggle against the West as the enemy that must be done away with; its attention is more inward than outward, campaigning for the centralizing of the native. Struggles against modern imperialist forms are identifiable by their outward and antiestablishment consciousness, which often is performed within the discursive limits set by the West.

The consequence of this performance within the discursive space set by the West results in the privileging of Western thought models and scholars as cardinal points of references, even if the intent is in the dismantling of the spirit and temper that provokes such overdependence. By drawing from or depending on the conceptual approaches of Western thinkers to displace Western methodology from the center of discourse, the researcher would have emphasized the dominant perception that the indigenous space provides the data for analysis, never the theoretical framework. This sort of ironic decolonial work embodies second-order Eurocentrism.

For there to be a radical and progressive decolonizing of research methodology, all traces of first-order Eurocentrism, which is the explicit or implicit privileging of Western concepts in indigenous work, and second-order Eurocentrism that centralizes Western thinkers, should be done away with. While this is not a call for disengagement with the West, as pointed out earlier, conscious steps should be made to separate the "globality" of the West, which makes it indispensable to knowledge, and not necessarily—at least theoretically—in a way other non-Western cultures are not, and its centralized "universality."

Chapter Six

Oral Tradition

Cultural Analysis and Epistemic Value

> These were our bedtime stories. Tales that haunted our parents and made them laugh at the same time. We never understood them until we were fully grown and they became our sole inheritance.
> —Edwidge Danticat, *Krik? Krak!*

> It may be that oral records are preserved in them which are handed down from father to son, as in the case of the better known Royal bards in the Metropolis, such records though imperfect should surely not be under-rated.
> —Samuel Johnson, *History of the Yorubas*

Psychologists and anthropologists assert that what separates humans from animals is humans' ability to communicate knowledge to each other.[1] For most of human existence, information has been transferred primarily through oralities. For billions of people around the world, oral traditions continue to be the primary mode of communication. Oral traditions are a form of creative performance that artistically communicate stories, information, and history. If all civilizations, like Mircea Eliade rightly opined, are governed by some "metaphysical-moral vision,"[2] then oral traditions are what gives them a form and living representation. Owing to their

---

1   Taglialatela et al., "Communicative," 343–48.
2   Eliade, in Falola, *Violence*, 6.

efficacy in the daily living experience and their enduring nature in Africa, oral traditions are (re)produced daily, effortlessly, and for generations.[3]

In this way, some traditions are a few decades old, while others date back more than seven thousand years.[4] There are numerous typologies of these traditions in Africa, as there are thousands of languages and cultures, arguably more than anywhere else in the world. Some of these include the proverbs, tales, riddles, poetries, sayings, and songs of different genres for different purposes such as incantations, the Ifa corpus, stories, and many more. Instructively, all of these are embedded with their own peculiar intricacies both in production and delivery.[5] Therefore, oral traditions are clusters of carefully constructed indigenous knowledge production that speak to the history, sociology, ethnography and other social and scientific forms and interpretations of the society.[6] Accordingly, they collectively represent what one might call a societal archive of persons, places, things, and other physical and metaphysical beings/properties captured in the ontology of the people.[7] All of these are usually made through historical processes and experiences of the culture in sight, bringing to the fore the significance of environmental peculiarity to the expressions, form, and content of the art.

Meanwhile, the oral traditions most venerated in modern academia are those originating from Western classics. These include the *Iliad*, *Odyssey*, and *Beowulf*. The Bible and the Qur'an were also developed from oral traditions, passed down over generations, and then recorded. These examples of Western epics represent the oral tradition favored by Western scholars. While much modern research on oral traditions focuses on these few texts, oral traditions continue to flourish in African societies and outnumber their Western counterparts. Among these are the Sundiata: an Epic of Old Mali, Samba Gueladio and other Peul epics, the Mwindo epic of the Bantu-speaking people of eastern Congo, Mvet epics, and more.

Oral traditions are severely understudied, despite the recent and laudable efforts of projects such as the World Oral Literature Project. The study, preservation, and continuation of oral traditions not only has

---

3   Alagoa, *Oral Tradition*.
4   Henige, "Impossible," 127–234.
5   Biobaku, *Sources*.
6   Vansina, "Oral History," 17.
7   Vansina, "Oral History."

intrinsic value for its preservation of culture and aesthetics but also is key to decolonial research. In this chapter, I will describe some of the patterns of oral traditions in Africa, including their general nature and social context. I will also discuss the issues in recording and representing oral traditions in the context of global neocolonialism. In the process, I will demonstrate the immense importance of oral traditions in African cultures and in the African diaspora and as a tool of epistemic liberation.

Defining Oral Traditions

Since oral traditions are so diverse in their nature and purpose, it is difficult to clearly define their boundaries. For the purposes of this chapter, I will use Jan Vansina's definition of oral traditions as oralities that are transferred through multiple generations.[8] This definition of oralities excludes oral law, except when it is passed down through generations. It also excludes oral history, or interviews that give testimonial evidence of an individual's life. While these can be useful and often poetic, they do not follow the sociological processes in which oral traditions function. In other words, oral traditions give a complex account of the evolution and historical patterns of a society, which is equally complex and dynamic and in an often enigmatic and artistic form. Taken from Barber, "oral text," in some cases, "may even be seen as the only thing that outlasts death and time and testifies to the reality of past achievements."[9] Because of their social functions, oral texts stand out among more quotidian utterances found among the culture that produces them, hence the value embedded in their content are rare in, say, collections of oral history.

More importantly, functioning as a text, these traditions stand as viable resources for historical, anthropological, sociological, archeological, and ethnographical interpretation of the society, since they account for all of these at varying degrees. As Ki-Zerbo puts it, "Oral traditions offer us incidental descriptions of facts and objects, which conjure up the social and physical setting in which life went on."[10] Invariably, they form the marrow of every indigenous knowledge production of a preliterate society.

---

8 Vansina, *Oral Tradition*.
9 Barber, *Anthropology*, 1.
10 Ki-Zerbo, *General History*, 4.

Oral traditions, aside from being instrumental in the making of social realities, are sometimes developed as a critique of these realities. In a way, they are the gatekeepers to the civilizations of preliterate societies. Thus, oral traditions are the popular foundations upon which literary studies, anthropology, sociology, archeology, ethnography, and others that study society and man in their different forms—the social archeologists—are built. Adekoya has asserted that "the entire body of knowledge generated by ordinary people in their quotidian struggle with nature in order to create culture, transcends the age-old division into art and science."[11]

Oral Literature

Oral traditions include but are not equivalent to oral literature.[12] The reason that oral traditions are excluded from literature is often the same reason why African crafts are often snubbed by the Western art world: Eurocentric art labels creative works that are functional in society as primitive.[13] This Eurocentric conception of art has roots in the Enlightenment, and the scholars of this period regarded art as something to be appreciated for their aesthetic value.[14] This framework of art can be summed up in the phrase "art for art's sake." Art critics from the Global South have long critiqued "art for art's sake." In African countries, art may take the form of a painting or sculpture that fits into the Western conception of art. However, more often the art is for more practical use in traditions or everyday life. These works may include baskets with intricate geometric weavings, or masks that represent ancestors and are used in religious ceremonies.[15] While these arts are functional, they also have artistic merit. The functionality of African arts in the societal space is premised on the mode and intent of their production, which is closely linked to their obsession with social cohesion and the dissemination of

---

11 Adekoya, "Problems of Field," 52.
12 Parry and Parry, *Making*.
13 Price, *Primitive Art*.
14 Shiner, *Invention*.
15 Gerdes, "Creative Geometric," 63–82.

knowledge aimed at achieving this.[16] Art therefore, to Africans, is not a mere process of seeing but more essentially of living.[17]

As I continue in my analysis of oral tradition, it will be clear how oral traditions play a functional role in African society. The reason these traditions qualify as oral literature is that literature is separate from literacy.[18] The word "literature" traditionally only described works that were written.[19] Yet, spoken words can hold the same artistic and cultural value as written words. In any case, nothing is written and documented without committing it to memory and thought processing: the warehouse of oral literature. Simply put, all literatures are born out of the same rudiments as oral traditions. Moreover, the textual potency of an art or tradition is not determined by the mode of documentation or transmission but rather how the artistic representation of the theme being addressed is captured.[20] Thus, in his attempt to bring to the fore the potency of Yoruba oral traditions, praise poetry in particular and its qualification as literature, Babalola describes literature as the culmination of integral or intellectual words in a language, intellectual words that translate into poems, *arofo*, *itan* (folktales), *alo* (stories), *iroyin* (news), among others.[21] Oral traditions are artistic, experimenting with diction, figurative language, and mnemonic devices.[22]

They have plots, genres, and archetypes, all of which mirror what is "traditionally" regarded as literature.[23] From the foregoing, it is revealing that ideas exist before conceptualization; or rather, it is the existence of ideas that give rise to attempts at understanding them. Therefore, whether or not African languages have an indigenous word that is the equivalent of the Western term "literature," the idea and its implications are conspicuously found in Africa and were the basis of the people's civilization.

---

16 Forde, *African Worlds*.
17 Akporobaro, *Introduction*.
18 Chadwick, "Distribution," 77–94.
19 Ong, *Orality*.
20 Imbua et al., *History*, 67.
21 Babalola and Alaba, *A Dictionary*, i–v.
22 Finnegan, *Oral Literature*.
23 Na'Allah, *Globalization*.

A Note on Linguistic Diversity

The linguistic diversity of Africa is unmatched, with an estimated two thousand or so independent languages.[24] Zambia, for instance, has seven official languages. The most widely spoken is Bemba, which only about 30 percent of the population uses as a spoken language.[25] Despite the crass ignorance and the stereotypes that African languages are "primitive" or somehow simpler than those of Europe, many African languages have a complexity that matches or exceeds that of European languages. For example, Xhosa has over thirty thousand words available for oral traditions to arrange.[26] The linguistic diversity of Africa facilitates the artistic capabilities of African oralities. Ironically, however, there are major issues with the skepticism they generate outside of Africa. Aside from the fact that Western epistemology leans toward broad classifications and would characterize anything outside these parameters as primitive, the diversity of African languages poses a huge challenge to the promotion of these languages and their art, in the sense of the public reach of such a work and the politics often associated with it.[27] Yet, given the complexity of these languages, there is much to be "lost in translation." Oral traditions translated into English lose some of their cultural meanings. Not only do oral traditions reference deep community histories, values, and archetypes, but the diction of oral traditions represents the African worldview. One example often used is the "nzuri" phenomenon; that is, that the Swahili word "nzuri" means that which is morally good and that which is beautiful. This shows the cultural value that morality and beauty are one and the same.[28] A translation of "nzuri" into the English "beautiful" will not have the same meaning. Other Bantu languages have in common with Swahili the organization of words into noun classes that represent how speakers relate to their world. These classes organize animals, people, living objects, and nonliving objects into separate categories. The flexibility

---

24 *Nations Online*, "Official."
25 Central Statistical Office Zambia.
26 Finnegan, *Oral Literature*.
27 Ngugi, *Decolonising*.
28 Shujaa and Shujaa, "Nzuri Model," 656–58.

of the language allows the storyteller to manipulate words to transcend these categories, a feat that also gets lost in the translation process.[29]

In addition to the uniqueness of African oral traditions, it is important to remember their hybridity as well. Individual cultures in Africa do not exist in a vacuum but in a larger cosmopolitan context. Oral traditions might become hybridized with the mingling of cultures or Westernized in the current age of tourism. The history of Islamic and Christian religious influences throughout the continent mean that African oral traditions may be prayers or have roots in missionary work.[30] The subsequent forced migration of African people throughout the world also means the spread of these traditions. Oral traditions brought over with enslaved people encouraged the hybridization of oralities, which may be remembered down through the generations.[31]

As it will be seen in the course of this study, the linguistic essence of the texts embedded in oral traditions is indispensable in meaning making and accurate interpretations of the traditions. And here lies one of the challenging issues in the collection and usage of oral traditions in recent times: a slight deviation from the original intonation and/or pronunciation of a word could give an entirely different meaning to a non-Western people's tradition. Language has always been a form of identity, or rather, the core indicator of the prowess of a culture.[32] Accordingly, it serves as the repository of the civilizations that beget these traditions.

Two ideas that are often overlooked in the making of human civilizations and in understanding their indigenous knowledge production are symbols and signs. *Symbols* and *signs* are relative terms that many scholars in different fields have the tendency to conflate.[33] The observation and articulation of the two in every human society readily debunks the "no civilization" theory of some Eurocentric writers on cultures outside Europe, particularly Africa. According to Susanne Langer, a sign is "anything that announces the existence or imminence of some event, the presence of a thing or a person, or a change in the state of affairs. There are signs of the weather, signs of danger, signs of future good or evil, signs

---

29   Finnegan, *Oral Literature*.
30   Na'Allah, *Globalization*.
31   Simpson, "Oral Tradition," 9.
32   Dakubu, "Role," 210.
33   Langer, "Language," 21–31.

of what the past has been. In every case a sign is closely bound up with something to be noted or expected in experience."[34] Both man and animal, as creatures with different levels of senses, understand these and react to them accordingly. On the other hand, symbols are basically a human invention conceived from thoughtful art. With seasons and time come signs through which the actions of the people are reflected and animated in the arts.

While signs could be natural and others invented, the whole process of a symbol resides in the human mind where the thoughts are conceived, conjured, expressed, animated, transmitted and received. In the end, like signs, symbols are expected to generate reactions from the receiver, only this time, it leads to another cycle of the same process that produced the symbol in the first place. Primarily, in the preservation and interpretation of these symbols is the language and language usage. Langer explains thus: "The result is a symbolic structure whose meaning is a complex of all their respective meanings, and this kaleidoscope of *ideas* is the typical product of the human brain that we call the 'stream of thought.' The process of transforming all direct experience into imagery or into that supreme mode of symbolic expression, language, has so completely taken possession of the human mind that it is not only a special talent but a dominant, organic need."[35]

Revealingly, the foregoing further shows how seamless the process of knowledge production is carried out in both literate and preliterate societies. The difference here only lies in the mode of transmission and not in the quality of thought and experience that produced them. Through the same process of making these symbolic representations, social and historical facts are established, as they give an air of authenticity to a particular narrative in the sociopolitical evolution of people. To this extent, with the power of language and language usage in the production of arts, such as with oral traditions, the difference between African and European arts can only be a question of value, which is determined by the environment these two styles of art evolve in and represent.

So from the Ifa divination corpus among the Yoruba people currently occupying southwestern Nigeria, to the Kasala praises found among the Luba people of southern part of the present-day Democratic Republic

---

34 Langer, "Language."
35 Langer, "Language."

of Congo, as in literary peculiarities of other cultures in Africa, language usage and the environment can be seen as the core components of the art that produces these symbols, giving them meaning and importance through a careful aesthetical weaving. At the very end of these processes is the formation of the identity of the people in question. For as Page notes in his work:

> Linguistic behavior depends upon seeing language primarily not in its communicative functions but as a vehicle—the major vehicle—through which we make acts of identity, project ourselves upon others, and represent in words our positions in the universes we each create in our minds. The images we cast with language may themselves be sharply focused or more diffuse; they may coincide with those casts by others, or they may not.[36]

This way, the representation of death in the oral traditions of the Akan people, in present-day Ghana, could be similar to that of the Luo in Kenya in so far as they share the same cosmological view about the phenomenon.[37] Nonetheless, their presentation in language usage could differ, with one having the potential of capturing the image more vividly than the other. Barber posits on the performance of oral traditions: "Words are not the only form of representation or expressions. People establish and convey meaning through clothing, dance, music, gesture, and through complex rituals which often defy verbal exegesis."[38] Oral traditions represent a performance-based communication. The storyteller will use intonation of voice, pauses, and motions or gestures to add to the meaning of the story.[39] Before further explaining the nature of oral traditions and storytellers, I will explain the nature of performance in African cultures.

The scope of performance in Africa is incredibly diverse. To begin, the term "theater"—similar to the concept of art—is a Eurocentric English term. African performance traditionally differs from that of Europe by being focused on tradition, religion, and community. This is not to say that the European concept of theater does not exist in Africa. In particular,

---

36 Page, "Acts of Identity."
37 Generically, African cosmological belief interprets death as an agent of life and renewal. Moore, "Imagery," 57–70.
38 Barber, *Anthropology*.
39 Lord, *Epic Singers*.

France invested substantial resources to the creation of African plays in West Africa.[40] Works such as that of Wole Soyinka, the first Black African to receive the Nobel Prize in literature, show examples of localized globalization in African performance. Still, the majority of performances in Africa do not take this mainstream "European theater" form. Instead, they are often functional ceremonies or community-driven events. Oyin Ogunba's works on ritual drama accentuate this fact.

One example is Egungun performances by the Yoruba, which incorporate complex costumes, music, dances, oral traditions, and rituals throughout the year.[41] Another example is the Mende people in Sierra Leone. When Mende women reach maturity, they join the Sande society, which is meant to preserve the responsibilities and traditions of womanhood in the community. The women conduct masquerade performances that represent the Sande guardian spirit through dance, costume, and oral traditions.[42]

A hybrid example of African and Western theater working together is the Koteba National du Mali. This group formed in 1969 and performs Malian, African, and other pieces. They practice the oral traditions of Koteba through chants, dance, and comedies. "Koteba" is the Bamana word for "snail," which reflects a Bamana performance produced in a spiral or cylindrical setup. It also has a deeper meaning, referencing a Bamana tale in which the snail carries the world on its back. In the same way, the Koteba performance is meant to carry the culture of Bamana upon its "back." This is representative of the key role of performance and oral tradition, intangible entities, in Bamana culture.[43] They often modernize or mix in international plays in order to renew interest in traditional pieces and stay relevant in a global context.

In many ways, therefore, performance is to oral traditions what water is to the body. Without performance, oral tradition loses its efficacy. Every nuance matters: the pitch, gesture, rhythm, moves, and those elements beyond; these aspects once connected to the poetic words, give life to the art. Surely, many points would be missing in the absence of a commemorative performance of an African oral tradition. Whether

---

40   Banham, *History.*
41   Adolphsen, "Yoruba Performance."
42   Neuberger Museum of Art, "Helmet Mask."
43   Okagbue, "Koteba (kote-tlon)."

Figure 6.1. Etiyeri, Eégún àgbà (Ancestral Egúngún) from Òkè-Igbó, Ondo State, Nigeria. August 9, 2008. Photograph by Olawole Famule.

in the sense of the Whydah Vodun festival in Benin where the memory and interpretation of the transatlantic slave trade is rebirthed and given meaning,[44] or in the recitation of a song about preparedness among the Abaluyia of Western Kenya,[45] some genres of African oral tradition can hardly be understood without going through the rudimentary process of performance. In another instance, the process of installing a new Ooni of Ife mandates the Ooni-elect to be given a symbolic walk by a chief known as Ejio, in commemoration of the agreement between Oduduwa and the aboriginal faction of the Igbomoku communities, then led by Oranfioye. The Ejio chieftaincy is revered and only reserved for the descendants of Oranfioye in the Ife kingdom in southwestern Nigeria.

In the process, Chief Ejio refers to the event in which his forefather led the likes of Obatala, Oranfe, Obameri, and others representing the original Ife settlement (the Igbomoku). In a walk with Oduduwa as they welcome him (Oduduwa) to the place later known as Ile-Ife, saying: "This is the way in which my father Oranfioye took to meet your father Oduduwa on his royal entry into this city."[46] As apothegmatic as this saying is, for mnemonic purposes, Chief Ejio cannot recite it without performing the action nor could anyone one repeat it arbitrarily. It depends on a particular time and circumstance, with accredited actors who must go through a performance to have meaning and be animated. While it is true that the full meaning of a tradition comes to life through performance, it should also be reckoned that some words lose their original form in the process of blending them into rhythmic patterns. This is more so when such a word is becoming archaic among the people.

Essentially, these examples of African performance give us insight into the nature of oral traditions. Oral traditions represent a literature that incorporates a live audience. The orator chooses a context and audience to tell the story, often with an intended message. It is common for him or her to invite the audience to participate in the story through chanting, commenting, or questions. In this way, the audience shapes the story.[47] This became problematic for researchers who are interested in recording oral traditions, as artificial reenactments of oral traditions often lose

---

44 Sutherland, "Ancestral Slaves," 65.
45 Amutabi, "Role, 191–208.
46 Obayemi, "Phenomenon," 70.
47 Na'Allah, *Globalization, Oral Performance*.

their authenticity. This is particularly the case with oral traditions like poetry and others that are meant for social events other than religious ceremonies.

Some oral traditions are strictly controlled in their presentation. Informing the likelihood of either of the two scenarios is the social function performed by this tradition in the given society. Praise poetry, for instance, is perpetually made and remade within the context of the central message that links the addressee to a particular figure and phenomenon.[48] In the process of presentation, the poet could add to the panegyric of his or her subject and depending on the circumstance, this could well be added to the praise poetry ascribed to such a figure or subject as well. This is only made possible because the traditions are expected to evolve with the subject being praised so as to have a full account of important moments in their lives and character evolution. This way, the traditions are established and reproduced through performance.

The interactivity of the oral tradition also depends on the context and setting. For example, a griot performing a learned oral tradition with singing accompanied by a harp cannot be interrupted. In the same vein, informal examples of oral traditions such as jokes or proverbs can be offered at any time.[49] Informal oral traditions take place through daily interactions. In Tunisia, one researcher noticed the repetition inherent in Biyata, short excerpts about the town's history, which were passed between friends and family on a daily basis.[50] Oral traditions are also used in a personal context to give indirect advice.[51] Respect for and relationships with others are very important in many African cultures. To give advice to a child or friend, a father might modify a popular children's tale. The story might already be familiar to the audience but modified slightly for a unique commentary on the current situation. For example, to explain the merit of hard work to a lazy partner, a man might evoke a story of a grasshopper who did not prepare for winter.

A storyteller may use props such as statues or masks. An example of this is various masks used in Egungun, ritual masquerades that take place among the Yoruba in Nigeria. In these rituals, community members wear

---

48   Barber, *I Could Speak*.
49   Hale, *Griots*.
50   Webber, *Romancing*.
51   Schoeffel, "Communicating."

painted masks and robes to represent well-known ancestors.[52] The elaborate costumes, dances and music are as much a part of the religious tradition as the oral traditions included. The meaning of these traditions and associated masks cannot be understood without the cultural, community, and religious context.

Music also plays an integral role in oral traditions. Musical attributes such as tempo, melody, and instrument selection influence the emotional tone of the oral presentation. This is not limited to drums during festivals or wars but extends to lyrical pieces as well. For example, women may sing a eulogistic oral traditional piece at a funeral that has been passed down for generations. They will typically sing this slowly in a dulcet voice to express their despair from the loss. Women also commonly sing lyrical songs to a new bride before her wedding day.[53] These lyrical and musical oral traditions are not for show or celebration only but to inform the new bride on how to be a good wife and mother.[54] Music also functions as a mnemonic device, aiding in the memorization of oral traditions. The variance in the presentation of these traditions is only a testament to the multiplicity of the genres of oral traditions in Africa. Consequently, as some of these are designed for religious purposes and performed at religious gatherings, others are meant for weddings, circumcisions, naming ceremonies, and burials. Yet, others are used in the daily social relations and expressions of people without the need for special performance.

The Storyteller

Since oral traditions have such an integral role in African societies, they cannot be understood without understanding the role of the storyteller. In the previous section, I talked about African theater; many of these examples did not involve a storyteller but were examples of community performances. In some countries in Africa, anyone can be a storyteller. This is especially true with genres such as proverbs and folktales. A storyteller may be specific yet informal, such as a village elder or religious man. In other cases, the storyteller can be a remarkable figure, having some

---

52 Willis, "Negotiating Gender," 322–36.
53 Finnegan, *Oral Literature*.
54 Willis, "Negotiating Gender."

political power or playing an advisory role to politicians and the rich. In all cases, the storyteller has a rich cultural and personal background that influences their telling of the story.

There are two common misconceptions about how oral traditions are created. The first is that there is a single author of a work of orality, such as the misconception that "Homer" is the sole author of the *Odyssey*. Oral traditions are passed down from generation to generation, so even if there was an original and sole author, their work has been transformed through the generations and across regions and performances. The second misconception is that an entire culture could be the collective author. This is also misleading because the storyteller plays such a critical role in the story. The storyteller, the phrase used here broadly to describe the performer of any oral tradition, may exercise artistic freedom to present their content differently every time. Given the critical role of the storyteller, it is incorrect to state that there is no author, or that a single person is responsible for a long-living oral tradition.[55] These two almost paradoxical misconceptions require that the culture of origin and storyteller must be included in any analysis or representation of oral tradition.

In light of the foregoing, Belinga brilliantly suggests that the first to introduce the framework through which other storytellers perform their art should be regarded as the author of the tradition.[56] While it is true that such individuals could be hard to identify, the logic of this assertion alludes to the fact that all ideas are originated in human experience that is first articulated publicly by an individual. Like the proverbs and sayings, all the traditions and arts comprising various genres of African oral traditions originated from individuals and were propelled by certain circumstances that are continuously re-created in the present. In the process of re-creating such circumstances, an idea could also be re-created for symbolic reference by another actor. Aside from the original author who laid the framework, others can only amplify and re-create a work. The basics of the text and structure are judiciously maintained in the process of presentation, as the storyteller, who is also the author-interpreter, incorporates these basics with his own improvisations meant for the particular event, purpose, circumstance, or subject.

---

55   Finnegan, *Oral Literature*.
56   Belinga quoted in Kesteloot, "African Epic," 208–9.

As I continue on with this chapter, the storyteller will become a keystone of the necessary context given to any oral tradition. For now, I will discuss the diverse roles of the storyteller in African societies.

Most African cultures have some sort of formal storyteller, and in some West African cultures, the storyteller is a formal griot. The griot is a specialist of a respected class whose skills are often passed down throughout their family. The griot spends their life perfecting musical storytelling, able to recite great stories of the past for their community. They often earn their livelihood from royalty or the rich through patronage. Storytellers may also come in the form of freelancers.[57] They might be elders who have collected stories throughout their lifetime, or even have attended a formal poetry school such as that in Rwanda.[58] They are very often village elders or older family members.

The nature of the storyteller changes the context and delivery of the oral tradition. In the case of formal storytellers, orations are held in formal settings such as meetings, ceremonies, or public events. In the case of informal storytellers, the orations are given in the evening hours around a fire or in other causal contexts. The line of distinction between the official storytellers and the unofficial ones could be thin in some cases and even blurred in the face of the communal configuration of the society. In every household, for instance, there usually can be found a storyteller familiar with the traditions of the lineage. Usually a woman, they could function in an official capacity during ceremonies within this lineage alongside others to perform the panegyric of the lineage and make money.[59] Yet, they go on to pass these traditions down to children in the compound in the evenings.

The fundamental differences that identify a formal and informal storyteller are in their training and versatility. A formal storyteller is usually a professional performer familiar with traditions of the people and not a just segment of it, as in the case of the informal one. The storyteller and the performance share the same affinity with the text of presentation. Singers of *Ijala, Eye, Rara,* and *Efe* among the Yoruba people of southwestern Nigeria, for instance, may be accompanied by talking drums, which can themselves be used for performing panegyrics. It can also be

---

57   Hale, *Griots*.
58   Finnegan, *Oral Literature*.
59   Barber, *I Could Speak*.

performed with the Omo Oluwo-Alagbede, the traditional blacksmith's hammer. The Kakaki and the Ekutu flutists, professional drummers and Akigbe (criers), and the buglers operate during the festivals under the influence of their knowledge of *oriki* (praise poetry) in order to make money. On the arrival of visitors, the Kakaki and Ekutu players and the Akigbe, call the awareness of the king to the arrival of the visitors in the palace, via their eulogy.[60] They are all staff of the palace and are situated where they can see every visitor coming in; they combine their efforts in performing the role of a storyteller. With genres come the context in which these traditions are presented.

Accordingly, genres such as jokes or proverbs may be told during the day, but in much of Africa there is a taboo against telling stories or poems during the daytime.[61] Poems, like stories, are invented as traditions of leisure and reflection, of which the former is forbidden during the day so as to discourage laziness: hence, the emphasis on the time in which they could be presented. Context and presentation then become the most significant attribute in the understanding of African oral traditions.

The role of a storyteller, whether formal or informal, can take many forms. It is true that the storyteller can function as an entertainer of sorts. Their performance could be done at weddings, at the end of the day, or at a festival. They are artists and musicians, keepers of the artistic culture of their community. Yet, the storyteller is also a historian, keeping in their mind important facts and stories from the history of the community and passing them down to the next generation.[62] There are cases of rote memorization, where the storyteller might recite exactly that which his or her elders had taught them. This is especially true of leadership succession or family history. The storyteller is often responsible for reciting the history of a noble or single family. In some cases, the noble family may hire their own storyteller as a way to maintain their status.[63] In this way the storyteller can be a genealogist. In the same manner, he or she could also be a professional mourner, as they could be employed to lead others in mourning a noble figure who had just passed on. In this role, their performance reflects on the life of the deceased, the futility of life, the power

---

60 Biobaku, *Sources*, 63–76.
61 Hale, *Griots*.
62 Hale, *Griots*.
63 Eldredge, *Kingdoms*.

of death, afterlife, and prayers for the children of the deceased.[64] Their presence is what melts the coldest heart, as they choose their words and weave them strategically to this emotional effect.

It is also possible that the storyteller's own political opinion or alliance can cause him to alter, either knowingly or unknowingly, his recitation of history. The storytellers' important role as gatekeepers of the community's past reflects their political power. By changing or preserving details of a traditional story, the storyteller maintains an ideology within the recitation that supports the current political regime, for instance, and is then paid handsomely for this act. The storyteller offers a continuous reinterpretation of that history.[65] Furthermore, the storyteller may also play a role as a religious man. This is natural because of the religious nature of African oral traditions, as well as the inseparability of politics from religion in many African communities. African religious views often venerate ancestors and great leaders of the past. The storyteller is able to preserve orations about these ancestors and leaders, influencing the religious inclinations of the community. He is often central to religious traditions and ceremonies.[66]

In the instance of mourning given above, the storyteller, in performing this social function, prays to the spirit of the departed ancestor to protect and guide his/her descendants and the rest of the community in the presentations. Political leaders or ordinary people might consult the storyteller for advice, in light of his possession of wisdom that has been passed down to him. In this case, storytellers may play the role of advisor, as they choose which stories apply to current situations and how.[67] Thus, he plays an active role in the religious and political activities of his community. In giving advice to individuals, the storyteller may also act as a social worker. In cases of spousal abuse or conflict, the storyteller is able to mediate the conflict by providing relevant proverbs or traditional stories.[68]

The political and religious role of the storyteller also gives him the ability to be a spokesman. Since he represents the community's history—and the core of the community's values—he may speak out on important

---

64   Ellis, *Yoruba*, 155–63.
65   Webber, *Romancing*.
66   Hale, *Griots*.
67   Zenani and Scheub, *World*.
68   Zenani and Scheub, *World*.

issues to give advice. He may also be sent by political leaders to other countries to tell of national successes, entertain them, and serve as a diplomat. Since his art inherently incorporates ideology, this may also represent the storyteller's role in warfare, as he can plant the ideological seeds to legitimize a regime.[69] Therefore, what the storyteller gives as the account of an event is not only blurred by the physical angle in which he was positioned during the event (which limits what he could see at the time) but more extensively by his ideological preferences.

All of this speaks to the quality of information to be deduced from such an account, which by this time is no longer in its organic form, having been distorted by countless storytellers' own perspectives and beliefs. However, as in the limitations found in written texts, this does not preclude the validity of the information embedded in them without putting them in a wider context.[70] The great power that the storyteller has in preserving oral traditions gives him the ability to personalize said traditions. Therefore, the storyteller plays a critical and active role in perpetuating any oral tradition.[71] The audience hearing these stories also plays an active role. For starters, the version of the story—or even what story will be told—will depend on the particular audience. For example, in the case of foreigners, abstruse elements of stories may be left out in the telling. In the presence of nobles, crude parts of a story or oral tradition may be omitted.[72]

Since the storyteller has such great influence over oral traditions and their community, the context in which the storyteller exists is critical. This includes the storyteller's language, culture, family, and personal history but also includes the global context. For example, political crisis and poverty may limit the storyteller's abilities or even force him to change his orations. Colonialism, as I will explain later, may have undermined the authority of or changed the roles of a storyteller.[73] The economic context of the storyteller is important because the nature of his or her orations will reflect who is providing for them. Even in countries in Africa with a free market, that market works on different terms compared to those

---

69   Hale, *Griots*.
70   Odey, Nengel and Okpeh, *History Research*.
71   Webber, *Romancing*.
72   Finnegan, *Oral Literature*.
73   Na'Allah, *Globalization*.

in the Western world. Familial ties can influence how much things cost, a factor that can make the presence of the free market relevant.[74] The result is that the storyteller is not free for hire by just any person, even if he is a freelancer. He is more inclined to visit those who are in power or those he has a close relation to. These relations influence the way that oral traditions are handed down and should be included in any outside representation of an oral tradition.

Genres of Oral Traditions

Before going into the specific genres of African oral traditions it is important to recognize the artificiality of categorization. The purpose of genres is to group certain oral traditions together based on their purpose and form for analysis. Because of the immense diversity of the continent, many oral traditions will not fit within one of these categories. The genres exist not to exclude, but to encourage patterns. Therefore, they should be thought of more as ecologies of oralities, or more flexible and interrelated than mutually exclusive.[75] In light of this, it has been argued that these genres should be taken as "an orienting framework for the production and reception of discourse."[76]

This remark made by Barber, however, that genres should not be seen "as a set of morphological features but as a repertoire of skills, disposition and expectations,"[77] begs the question of what morphological features, otherwise referred to as structural properties, consist of if not the repertoire of skills, dispositions, and expectations that characterize and inform literary production. As Barber departs from Propp's view, this could be taken to mean that the morphological features of texts should be understood within the local context of their production as opposed to the universal/cross cultural comparative literary production of another culture. But in the final analysis, the peculiar repertoire of skills, disposition, and expectations of a particular locally produced text become the structural

---

74 Na'Allah, *Globalization*.
75 Foley, "Traditional," 145–53.
76 Briggs and Bauman quoted in Barber, *Anthropology*, 37.
77 Briggs and Bauman quoted in Barber, *Anthropology*, 37.

properties of the text. And of course, in some cases, similarities of this form could be found in other cultures.

Then, the fundamental question to be considered in a comparative categorization exercise is the intent with which the traditions were produced, the purpose they serve in society, and the structure of presentation—and not based strictly on the principles that limit the production of such an art to one civilization or the other. This debate is particularly telling when we consider the position of African epics in world literature.

An extensively studied yet small category of African oral tradition is that of the epic. Epics are defined in Western culture as large narratives that tell a heroic story, often with a consistent linguistic pattern. Such examples are the *Iliad*, the *Odyssey*, and *Beowulf*.[78] Since epics are the most often studied Western oral traditions, they were the first subject of study for oral traditions in Africa. Epics also traditionally come from a place of some historical truth. It is the historical truth supposedly deduced from such works that the contemporary cultures (together referred to as Western culture) that inherited the civilizations that produced these epics, have been building on since the start of their civilizations. Like the epics and the author-interpreter of the epics, the history of the state, to the latter Western historians and intellectuals was, for a long time, the history of nobles, conquest, and warrior-figures.

When society metamorphosed into a different political entity from medieval times, the obsession shifted to political history, so much so that twentieth-century British historians like Trevor-Roper, Alan Barnes, Margery Perham, and others were still scholars of troubadours (i.e., medieval lyric poets and poet-musicians well versed in oral history) in their presentation of historical accounts and philosophy of history. It was only that the process of producing and presenting their own works was different from that of the troubadours; their so-called scientific writings were heavily dotted with national glorification, typically known as feudal epics in African literature.

They were the modern griots. To be sure, these epic traditions have since informed American civilization and others in the West. Epistemically and ontologically, they form the basis upon which the universality of their world is premised. Unlike Africa, these traditions have been the source of inspiration for modern Western inventions and interpretation of

---

78   Lord, *Epic Singers*.

the world. Yet, the Sahel and African forest zones are often known as Africa's "epic belt," with pieces such as "Fulbe and Wolof," "Mande" and "Songhay and Zarma." African narratives are often poetic, detailing historic and heroic figures, but they don't always seem to fit this Western epic mold. Scholars such as Finnegan and Vansina have argued that the definition of epic cannot extend to oralities from Africa because of their shorter lengths and divergence from the form of Western epics. Other scholars argue that it depends on the use of the term "epic" and suggest a wider definition of the genre.[79] Either way, from the West African tale of "Bayajidda" to the annals of Ramesses II, Africa is rich in lengthy narrative stories of heroism passed down through the ages.

In his contribution to this discourse, Adekoya posited that "it used to be said that Black Africa lacked the epic genre. Then researchers went into the field and unearthed "Sundiata: an Epic of Old Mali, The Ozidi Saga, and Emperor Shaka the Great: a Zulu Epic." And he continues, "Who knows what other forms are lying out there waiting to be discovered and to change outsiders erroneous perceptions of Black Africa?"[80] The skepticism of some scholars regarding African epics is not only in relation to their length, or the absence of written forms, but more importantly to the ability of the people to commit this to memory. Epics are different from other folktales. For one, only specialists in the art could function as the author-interpreters, and unlike others, these epics are usually long, in multiple volumes and consist of prose, poems, proverbs, songs, and other complex cultural forms. It is precisely because of the number and complexity of all of these elements that skeptics believe epics cannot be produced and reproduced orally like other African oral traditions and so therefore do not exist. The point often missed here is that since written culture came late to many parts of Africa, the culture of orally transmitting vital information, preserved as texts, had been developed to such a sophisticated degree that an apprentice would go through a formal process of learning. This could take more than seven years. Commenting on the initiation process of an Ifa priest, which is typical of this training across Africa, Abimbola noted that "the method of training of Ifa priests and the mode of transmission of their repertoire represents a startling example of an indigenous African pre-literate academic system. . . .

---

79   Johnson, Hale, and Belcher, *Oral Epics*.
80   Adekoya, "Problems," 51–75.

A better example of the meticulous care usually taken by the pre-literate societies to preserve and disseminate the ingredients of their own culture can hardly be found."[81]

The flexibility of learning and its grounding in the everyday societal course of Africans, created an educational system based on oral transmissions to the extent that no subject of learning could lose its essence in its presentation. Furthermore, the development of a writing culture or sophisticated polity is not a prerequisite for developing epic literature. In other words, epics or the genre of oral traditions found among certain cultures is not in itself a testament to the sophistication of the civilization; rather, they symbolize the consciousness of the people and aspects of their civilization they prioritize in the documentation of their lives for the sake of prosperity. If the Oyo empire, like the kingdoms of Asanti, Bamoun, Kuba, and the Baoule, despite their exploits up until the nineteenth century, could not produce their own *Iliad*s or *Odyssey*s, it is probably because their praise poems, eulogizing such epiclike figures, and other poems meant for religious purposes, served the purpose and function of an epic. In the same manner, others like the Bamileke chiefdoms in present-day Cameroon and Kanem Borno in northern Nigeria, developed chronicles but never produced works of epic proportions. Ironically, less sophisticated cultures like the Fang and the Obamba-Bateke have the Mvet and the Olende epics, respectively.[82]

African epics, like the praise poems and other forms of African oral traditions produced in admiration of a particular figure and/or event, preserve and communicate the social structures, philosophy, culture, cosmologies, ontologies, and other core elements of societies past to their audience in an entertaining manner. In a broad categorization, Mei gave seven typologies of African epics: epics of Central Africa, hunters' traditions and epics; traditions of the Soninke; Sunjata and the traditions of the Manden, Segou, and the Bamana; traditions of the Fula; and emergent traditions.[83] All of these could be summed under the Feudal and Clan typologies of Lilyan.[84]

---

81   Abimbola, *Sixteen*, iii.
82   Kesteloot, "African Epic," 207.
83   Mei, "Distinctive," 150.
84   Kesteloot, "African Epic," 204.

A unique and well-known oral tradition of Africa is the proverb. African proverbs are well-known internationally with phrases such as "It takes a village to raise a child" and "Wisdom does not come overnight." Proverbs function to admonish, advise, criticize, and defend.[85] Since African religious traditions are often informal or hybrid, they do not have a text. Stories and proverbs are how African people communicate morality standards to each other.[86] Short stories or proverbs may even take on a role as legal case studies.[87] They are especially used with regard to teaching life lessons. In some cases when proverbs are used for didactic purposes, they come in reference to some significant historical event along the narrative. This way, they also serve the purpose of preserving and enhancing the historical as well as the social consciousness of the people. When, a Yoruba man says, "*Amuni nje amuni, afinihan nje afinihan, ewo ni 'nle o, ara Ibadan l'ojude Sodeke'?*" ("There is a difference between greeting and insinuation. Why would you say 'Hello, Ibadan man' to someone passing by in front of Sodeke's house?"), for instance, he refers to hypocrisy and betrayal. This has its historical roots in the development that led to the emergence of Abeokuta and the creation of Ibadan in the nineteenth century.

The Yoruba refrain above literally means that show yourself as an enemy, instead of pretending to be a friend. Those familiar with this proverb can easily relate to the amount of poetic injustice and distortions done to it in the translation. These proverbs translated into English often lose their poetic form. Consider, again, the Swahili proverb, "Haraka haraka haina baraka, polepole ndio mwendo." This translates to "fast work is not blessed, slowly is the way." When translated, the phrase loses both its assonance and connotation of words—thereby losing much of its power. It goes without saying that this reality speaks pointedly to the importance of language and language usage noted earlier in the presentation, as well as the preservation of the nature of these traditions.

Next we will broach the complex category of poetry. There are a wide variety of poems and lyrical pieces in African cultures. Poetry may serve a eulogistic or panegyric purpose. It can aid in the pursuit of love or even express grief over a difficult loss. In praise poetry, the orator may

---

85   Na'Allah, *Globalization*.
86   Shujaa and Shujaa, eds., "Oral Traditions, 656–58.
87   Zenani and Scheub, *World*.

sing praises to the rich and their families.[88] Such orations are made to enforce the authority of the rich or those in power. Praise poetry might be tied to politics, in which the orator praises the current government and sings of an enforcing ideology.[89] One example of praise poetry is the Izigbo, a poetry form practiced by the Zulu in South Africa; these poems praise one person—this could be a hero, a leader, or even God or another religious figure.[90] Unlike epics, poetry represents the common form through which African oral traditions are expressed. Poetry and music are the two "soft" means devised by Africans to preserve and communicate their worldview and environment to generations. Because of the leisurely tones found in their presentation, they connote some sort of "soft" mnemonic loops of entextualization in African cultures. Poetry among the Yoruba people of southwestern Nigeria can be separated into a dozen distinct typologies, all serving different social and religious purposes.

Among these include: *Iyere* (the Ifa priest poetry), *Ijala ode* (the style of the hunters' guild), *orin Arungbe* (*Arungbe* song), *esa* (the style of the Egungun of the Labala group), *ewi* (a style peculiar to the Egbado Yoruba), *ege* (a style originally peculiar to the people of Owu who now live in Ibadan and Abeokuta), *Ofo* or *Ogede* (incantation), *Ori Aremo* (lullaby), *rara* (a style practice by the Ibadan and Oyo), *oriki* (praise poetry) and many more.[91] Praise poetry alone can be subcategorized into another dozen classifications, each with their peculiar purpose among the Yoruba people.[92] Knowing when and how to engage with these traditions is even more important than knowing them because, in the case of the wrong application, they lose their meaning and essence.

Praise poems serve many purposes all across Africa, the primary purpose of which is the role they play in the process of initiation and induction of a child or person into a certain societal level. This also serves as the generic value shared by the numerous forms of African oral poetry. A Luba chief or other prominent personality, for instance, is not yet fully formed until a Kasala poem is performed for them. In ceremonies, rituals, festivals, and even daily engagements, poetry is an essential element of

---

88 Finnegan, *Oral Literature*.
89 Hale, *Griots*.
90 Cope, *Izibongo*.
91 Babalola, *Content*, v–xiv.
92 Olatunji, *Features*.

social relations in Africa, and it contains vast stores of information about the innerworkings and configuration of African society from a historical, sociological, anthropological, and ethnographic sense.

Another famous category is the African folktale. Folktales are short narratives without form that circulate by word of mouth. They become popular stories and often have interrelated themes or recurring characters. Nelson Mandela published a selection of Xhosa tales together in a book entitled *Favorite African Folktales*. The fact that such a politically revered individual took the time to publish children's tales attests to their significance to the Xhosa culture. Folktales in Africa often have a moral lesson that emphasizes values such as community, hard work, honesty, and determination. The story might involve archetypes, such as animals or holy figures that enhance the cultural relativity of the tale.[93] For example, in Ghana stories of the spider Ananse are popular.[94] At the telling of each Ananse story, the audience is already familiar with the main character and several recurring ones. Thus, small changes in the story can have meaningful consequences for the repeated archetypes.

Child psychologists have found that folktales can play an integral role in children's lives through moral and socioemotional development,[95] and indeed, it was based on this consciousness that these tales were created and given special hours during the day to communicate moral and life-world lessons to children. Although, like other forms of African lore, they are communicated in the spirit of leisure; they are full of details that inform, enhance, and shape the social aspects of society.

Myths are often intertwined with folklore but take on a more religious perspective. Myths deal with the spiritual realm specifically, including gods, deities, ancestors, and their interactions with humankind. These myths may also be tied to power or political patterns.[96] For example, the Shilluk near the Nile in Sudan believe that Nyikang was the original Shilluk king. Every king after him is said to be a reincarnation of Nyikang's spirit. The king's physical health and length of life are thought to influence the politics, environment, and spiritual well-being of the

---

93 Shujaa and Shujaa, "Nzuri Model."
94 Owusu-Acheampong, "Adventures."
95 Agbenyega, Tamakloe, and Klibthong, "Folklore Epistemology," 112–26.
96 Lord, *Epic Singers*.

community.[97] Myths could also be fictional representations of reality. Cultures, "primitive" or "advanced," at various times invented myths for the same purpose of creating as well as maintaining social cohesion. The potency of myths in human civilization as a whole is a testament to the assertion that humans live through stories, and it is through good stories that cooperation exists, communities are formed, and humans are separated from animals.[98] Hundreds of people agree to live under the command of an authority created through the story of a central figure, often, as in the past, with mythical prowess and sagacity that surpasses the terrestrial world.

These stories can sometimes combine truth and fantasy: from the volcano eruptions that gave birth to stories of gods among men, to the sun and the moon that gave birth to certain kings and warriors, among others that share a boundary with epic tales where the supernatural meets the natural. If there is anything that epitomizes the collective consciousness of man, it is the creation of myths. Even cultures thousands of miles apart have been able to reflect on the same subject of human creation, the purpose of man and the aftermath, all of which are annotated and explored in myths. Although the stories they tell might be fictional, they give sense to human struggle, existence, and purpose according to the cosmological inclination of the culture. Simply put, they are cosmological, philosophical, and ontological interpretations of the human environment in view of the culture where they evolve.[99]

Oral traditions also take the form of historical narratives. These are accounts of news or personal narratives from past family or community members. For example, a man in South Africa retells the story of his grandfather having to relocate to a new farm during apartheid. Yet he says that his grandfather did not see the story as part of a larger historical tale, just a personal hardship. This is, unbeknownst to the one conveying the personal experience, an important historical narrative.[100] This is a narrative that is not necessarily memorized word by word but simply a personal account of the family history. These narratives differ from oral history because they are not firsthand accounts but are handed down

---

97   Evans-Pritchard, *Divine*.
98   Falola, *Cultural Modernity*, 21.
99   Falola and Akinyemi, *Encyclopedia*, 6–8.
100 Schneider and Crowell, *Living*.

through generations. If a historical narrative is then related to the larger cultural or historical patterns, it becomes an ethnography.

Next are traditional religious performances such as the Yoruba tradition of Egungun, which was described earlier. These are done annually, for a specific purpose, and should be carried out in a certain way. Specific oralities are chanted by the crowd or performed by talented individuals to commemorate the occasion. These performances include props such as masks, instruments, and statues, and often also include a dance. Sometimes, even the beat of the drum during a religious ceremony can qualify as orality. Certain rhythms with the drums have a meaning equivalent to a verbal phrase.[101] Fundamentally, Egungun festivals are conducted among the Yoruba people as a form of ancestral worship. The *Egungun*, it is believed, is the returning spirit of an ancestor who has come to visit his children and cleanse the community of evils and calamities. This practice is different in some ways from the one referred to as *oro* (bull-roarer), as they represent different cults in society. Both are regarded as ancestral spirits invoked by the people for cleansing purposes. When invoked, they walk or dance, as in the case of the *Egungun*, through the community, while members of this cult sing and recite the appropriate poems behind them. For the *Egungun*, this is often followed by the poetic form identified above as *esa*; and in the case of *oro*, this is followed by the *orin-Arungbe* form of poetry. However, both are invoked at different times, and while the *Egungun* ritual is performed during the day with the entire community having access, the latter is secretly done in darkness with only the male members of the community participating. In this process, the community accounts for its needs and its beliefs that the ancestral spirit could help fix those needs and issues. Aside from the fact that these traditions display the cosmology of the people and their sociological aspects, they also help enhance their spirituality.

A final category is that of jokes or riddles. These function as entertainment but often also provide ironic social commentary and promote critical thinking skills and explore questions of morality. The function of riddles and jokes, unlike proverbs, is to entertain rather than invite serious moral contemplation. But even then, they enhance the intellectual growth of children, as they feed into their curiosity. One example is the Karanga riddle "my father's little hill which is easily destroyed—porridge." Riddles

---

101 Finnegan, *Oral Literature*.

are an art form in Africa and are distinguishable by their question-answer format.[102] Children's songs and games are also passed down throughout generations. These may include hand-clap games or songs that mothers sing to their children. Children also may jump together while chanting or sing a song while throwing rocks.[103]

This list of African oral traditions is in no way exhaustive but instead a sampler. The functionality of these oral traditions depends on the occasion. Most oral traditions have a social message.[104] African authors that present the narrative oral traditions of their cultures often organize them by occasion or for their functionality. Occasions may include birth, childhood, puberty, marriage, and aging.[105] As previously stated, proverbs and narratives are often used as case studies in terms of the law. The community is familiar with these oral traditions and can use them to measure different cases.[106] Oral traditions can provide legitimization for the government through the recitation of histories, family lineage or praise poetry. In this way, oral traditions can be politically modified as well.[107] In general, oral traditions are used to communicate social and moral standards to the community.

Accuracy of Oral Traditions

Much of the debate in recent academic journals on oral traditions is centered on how "accurate" African oral traditions are. Several scholars have published methodologies to scrutinize oral traditions and discover what, if anything, is "true." Of course, the perceived accuracy of African oral traditions depends on the purpose of the study. For Africans living in their communities, oral traditions are infallible because they represent the community's values and perspectives. Even if the facts might be toyed with over time, every oral tradition is "true" in the sense that it represents the cultural memory of that group. Many scholars are concerned

---

102 Finnegan, *Oral Literature*.
103 Moon, "African Children," 8.
104 Schoeffel, "Communicating."
105 Zenani and Scheub, *World*.
106 Zenani and Scheub, *World*.
107 Eldredge, *Kingdoms*.

primarily with finding facts, ranging from the archaeological and historical to environmental.

The factual accuracy of African oral traditions is a complex matter. The epistemic foundations of African societies have different standards for truth than Western academia. In short, that which is known through religious means, experience, or told by elders is often considered truth.[108] This affects the genesis of oral traditions and their later versions. It is true that some oral traditions were created specifically for the purpose of being passed down through the generations. Others can be gossip, personal narratives, repeated old news, or even spontaneous group chants that are commemorated.[109] In short, the original version of the oral tradition is not necessarily based on facts but is the product of human interactions and motivations. Then comes the question of how faithfully the oral tradition was reproduced over time. Given the imperfection of the human brain, word-by-word repetition throughout multiple generations is virtually impossible.

Each oral genre will greatly reflect how faithfully it is reproduced. For example, a joke or folktale is more likely to be altered over time than a proverb or oration on the succession of kings. Genres that have practical implications, especially those of significant religious or historical value, are more likely to endure faithfully to "version one" throughout time. In many cultures, storytellers are said to have "bad luck" if they do not adhere strictly to the history of their ancestors.[110] These genres that demand accurate reproduction can be transferred across generations surprisingly accurately due to the use of mnemonic devices, pairing with music, or intense repetition.[111] The "accuracy" of oral traditions and their usefulness in reconstructing history might be lost to foreign scholars who miss key symbolic meanings and cultural contexts. This concept will be explained further as I discuss issues regarding the analysis of oral traditions.

It is instructive to clarify here that the accuracy of African oral traditions does not depend on a specific type of scholar interested in studying these arts. If it did, these traditions wouldn't have been the major

---

108 Ellis and Haar, "Religion," 385–401.
109 Vansina, *Oral Tradition*.
110 Vansina, *Oral Tradition*.
111 Johnson, Hale, and Belcher, *Oral Epics*.

preoccupation of British colonial administrators in Africa trained in anthropology and ethnography. These traditions could sometimes present their meanings in plain sight, while others were shrouded in enigmatic forms requiring special skills and extra efforts to piece together their meanings. For instance, in his comparison of the British and the French colonial rules in western Yorubaland, Asiwaju gave some valid notes in his appendix on the reaction of the people in these areas through poetic lines. The example of poetic lines against Ida Alaba, the notorious female Chief de Canton of Ketu in 1911–19; the Gelede song in Ketu against government instruction for all taxpayers in the area to wear plastic tax receipts around the neck, and the Gelede song that shed light on the French conscription policy and its effect on the local populations after World War I, are instances of an African's textual response to their environment, specifically the colonial institution.[112] Clearly, these traditions offer more firsthand information about the evolution of the society from the perspective of the common people than any narrative about the accounts preserved by these traditions.

Nevertheless, this does not ameliorate the flaws of subjectivity from their presentations. It has now become almost trite to acknowledge that the bias and sentimentalism often ascribed to oral traditions are not unique but rather a generic feature of knowledge production that is later written or orally preserved.

Relationship to Slavery and Colonialism

Oral traditions cannot be discussed without describing the massive impact that slavery had on them. The transatlantic slave trade that took place from the late fifteenth century to the early nineteenth century represents the largest forced relocation of any peoples in human history. This slave trade, which included both whites raiding for slaves and Africans selling prisoners as slaves, disrupted the flow of African societies—including oral traditions. It is impossible to say exactly how many stories were lost due to displacement and traumas caused by the trade. However, the aftermath of the slave trade also saw a global expansion of the African oral tradition. As the African diaspora grew around the world, families continued to

---

112 Akinjogbin, *Western Yorubaland*.

pass down oral traditions from their home countries while creating new traditions wherever they ended up. This served to preserve African identities in a new world.[113] Many new oral traditions that memorialized the trauma of the slave trade continued on.[114]

African diasporic oral traditions continue around the world. Some are remnants of the past, taken directly from Africa. Others are new oralities that were created in a hybrid cultural context. Diasporic oral traditions sometimes account for the only portion of their heritage language that those in the diasporas know. As global contexts of racism and colonialism continued to develop, these oral traditions were continuously discredited from being "art" or "literature" in mainstream culture.[115]

The collection of oral traditions that have been recorded by Western scholars began with the efforts of missionaries and colonial administrators in the service of cultural imperialism and political domination. These missionaries and their counterparts in the colonial government would collect oral traditions for the purpose of learning more about the culture and language of the people so as to aid their colonial projects. These early collections of African oral traditions were marred by racism and prejudice. Although extensive work has been done by Western scholars on African oral traditions, the preponderance of African cosmological contexts and interpretations in these traditions perpetuates misunderstandings.[116] The case of oral traditions further shows the resilience of Africans in the face of foreign domination and stigmatization perpetuated by the colonial project. They have survived years of demonization and have been strengthened by the increasing attention paid to these realities by scholars, many of whom are, ironically, products of colonialism.

The academic studies of oral traditions in Africa have increased significantly since the 1950s-era view that this subject was unworthy of study. However, the field of oral traditions continues to exist in the context of neocolonialism. This means that Western scholars, including their ideas and theories, are privileged above those of Africans who inherently understand the subject better. To combat this, the field of oral traditions in Africa should be led by accomplished Africans, and Africans should

---

113 Smart, "African," 16–25.
114 Fergus, "Negotiating Time," 74–85.
115 Webber, *Romancing the Real.*
116 Shohat and Stam, *Unthinking Eurocentrism.*

be encouraged to provide testimony about oral traditions and their personal meaning. Western scholars who study African oral traditions should refrain from words that perpetuate the stereotype of African oral traditions as not "literary" and the associated religious traditions as anything less than religion.

The stigmatization of African oral traditions as lesser literature is one reason these traditions have been chronically understudied. To combat this stereotype and preserve the vibrant cultures in Africa and among the African diaspora, oral traditions must be showcased. Art performances, public libraries, universities, textbooks, and schools should all incorporate African oral traditions into their programming.[117] Later, I will discuss the implications of incorporating African oral tradition into mainstream academia as a tool of decolonial research.

Recording and Translating Oral Traditions

Having discussed the nature of oral traditions as well as their place in the global context of colonialism, the issue of recording oral traditions can be examined. The World Oral Literature Project cites how "globalization and rapid socio-economic change exert complex pressures on smaller communities" as the reasons for the active preservation of world oral traditions.[118] The number of oral traditions that have thus far been recorded are miniscule compared to the wider proliferation of African oral traditions. There are several ways that researchers can record oral traditions. Missionaries would often record oral traditions by writing them down, either directly, through an assistant, or via memory. These recordings were not designed for word-for-word faithfulness. In fact, they are infamous for omitting the context, which I have explained is vital to the understanding of the oral tradition, including the storyteller, cultural setting, audience, and intended meaning.[119] A more faithful recording of oral traditions can be done using a microphone, which method guarantees word-for-word repetition but still leaves out context and much of the physical aspect of the performance. Video recordings offer the most

---

117 Hamilton and Shopes, *Oral History*.
118 *World Oral Literature Project*, "Home."
119 Finnegan, *Oral Literature*.

complete representation of the oral traditions, as they capture the physical performance aspects that disappear from written or audio accounts.

The most comprehensive way to represent a traditional oral performance is to include as much supplemental information as possible. Supplemental documents might take the form of interviews with or personal testimonies of the storyteller, including biographical information, intended meaning, and personal interpretation of the story. Interviews with the audience, or details of the audiences' reactions, are also useful. In analyzing a story, multiple recordings of the performance would be useful to see the commonalities and differences in the oral tradition. A translation done by or with the assistance of a member of the community that the oral performance originates from is essential in order to get as accurate a translation as possible. This translation would go beyond simply word-for-word interpretation, providing the cultural context and linguistic analysis of why certain words are used, as well as their connotations and meanings in African societies.

A danger posed by foreign recordings of oral traditions is the lack of protection against foreign influences. If an oral tradition is performed, for example, for the sole purpose of recording, the audience and context are missing. The storyteller will not perform the oral tradition as he normally does, possibly even adjusting the performance to what he thinks the foreign researcher wants to hear or what they would understand.[120] This is why systemic text linguists draw a line between demonstration and performance. Performance is organic, spontaneous, and uninhibited; demonstration—the kind where the performer's awareness of external influences, presence of foreigners, recordings of any form, etc.—is considered to be a more superficial mode of presentation. Therefore, it is best if the oral tradition recording is done without the presence of foreign researchers and in a naturalistic setting.

The practical issues of recording oral traditions start with a lack of funding for preservation efforts. This limits the number of scholars and physical resources that can be devoted to recording and translating oralities. There are also, as stated before, limitations on knowledgeable and interested researchers and programs. There are also practical issues with foreign researchers partnering with communities. Africans in poor communities are also less willing and able to help foreigners without payment

---

120 Finnegan, *Oral Literature*.

due to their own need to survive. The relationship between Africans and foreign researchers exists within the context of colonialism, leading to an earned distrust of foreign researchers.

There are many ethical dilemmas associated with the recording of oral tradition. First is the question of intellectual property rights. Earlier I described the misconceptions of authorship of oral traditions: first, that only the community can ultimately be the author and second that the storyteller is the author. Neither of these is accurate.[121] Especially inappropriate is for the researcher to take credit for the oral tradition, especially when he or she used a translator. If a book is published and makes money from the oral traditions, it seems unfair to remunerate the author alone. Yet it is often impractical to split the money between an entire community and the author/writer/researcher. The result is that most authors thank the community and the storyteller but retain the authorship and income for themselves. For example, many international authors write about the Ghanaian Ananse, the spider, keeping the profits to themselves. An international scholar cannot claim to have written such a tale yet often wants to be compensated for their authorship and illustrations.[122] The authorship of oral traditions is often a case of legal and ethical complexity.[123]

Translators and researchers must be careful when it comes to the context of the oral traditions. If an oral tradition, for example, contains unwarranted slander—the researcher may be held liable for the damage done in court.[124] This brings into question how the recordings, once taken, should be represented. Western scholars and artists tend to take African art, music, and literature out of context. A Western musician might reproduce a traditional African song in an orchestral setting, or an author might include a folktale in a collection of fairy tales. Artists who choose to represent African art must approach them with a sense of tradition and humility. It is important that they try to adhere to the cultural protocol when reproducing material, even if it is modified. In this way,

---

121 Finnegan, *Oral Literature*.
122 Collins, "Who Owns Ananse," 178.
123 Schneider and Crowell, *Living*.
124 Schneider and Crowell, *Living*.

scholars and artists have the potential to work together to respectfully and thoughtfully represent the oral traditions of Africa.[125]

Meanwhile, the present age characterized by the Internet of Things has huge implications for the recording and preservation of these oral traditions in Africa. Leaving aside the fact that some of these traditions, including their performance, can now be accessed online via platforms like YouTube, Facebook, Instagram, and the rest, research can be conducted with relative ease compared to the past. Telecommunication has seen significant improvement in this part of the world. Emails and social media networks are readily available for researchers to communicate with and use to discuss their works. Additional quick assistance to at least begin a project on African oral traditions, like every other field of research, is scattered on the internet in different databases and platforms.

Critical Analysis of Oral Traditions

Once an oral tradition is recorded and translated with the help of multiple resources, a critical analysis can be conducted. I will not delve too deep into how to go about this analysis, since I have described various components of that analysis throughout this piece. Below, I have included an iceberg model to aid in summarizing the analysis of oral traditions. It is a useful but not exhaustive model that prefers analysis of recordings with plentiful supplemental documentation and context. In this model, the tip of the iceberg represents the words spoken—the orality itself. From written oral traditions alone, no more information can be used in the analysis of the tradition. With video, photography, interviews, and extensive notetaking, the other visible components of the "iceberg"—including the storyteller's performance, music, costumes, physical objects, audience, and setting—can all be accounted for. These are the visible parts of the iceberg because they are the only clues that the outside researcher has to the meaning of the oral tradition.

Below the surface lies the deep and interconnected contexts underlying oral traditions. This includes the storyteller's perspective, intentions, and relationship to the audience. This is counterintuitive to Western scholars who are trained to analyze literature as if the writer of the work in

---

125 Sramek, "Seeking," 212–20.

question had died upon its completion.[126] It also includes the culturally specific meanings and symbols tied the words in the oral tradition, as well as the plot or content itself. Part of this is analyzing both the genre and the formulaic nature of the piece. This may include archetypes or poetic devices made to impact the work's meaning. Or there are those that lie within the religious worldview of the culture performing the oral tradition and are central to the piece. The oral tradition may take place in larger historical, political, and socioeconomic contexts.

Standardized, comprehensive literary analysis theories developed in the West are not likely to grasp the complete meaning of African oral traditions. I will make this point through two popular literary analysis theorists, especially in the fields of "folklore" or oral tradition. The first is Carl Jung, a Swiss psychologist who in the 1950s expanded the Freudian concept of the unconscious into the "collective" unconscious. Western psychology has long been criticized as Eurocentric and individualistic in itself, but Jung held that his theory was cross-cultural. He asserted that cultures used symbols to interact with each other via a collective unconscious. He believed that these symbols could be found in stories as archetypes and that these archetypes could be analyzed to access the deeper meaning of the story.[127]

Levi-Strauss, on the other hand, was a French anthropologist working from the 1960s to 1980s who took a structuralist approach to "folktale" analysis. He argued that myths and folktales revealed binaries, giving insight into how a particular culture sees the world.[128] Both the theories of Jung and Levi-Strauss, as well as many other literary analyses on mythology or "folktales," have been critiqued as complicated and unhelpful in the analysis of Africa's oral traditions. However, scholars do agree that the careful analysis of oral traditions, with the proper contextual information, can give outsiders a valuable insight into African societies.[129] This includes the epics that allow for insight into the military history of the African people,[130] praise poems that aid our imagery of

---

126 Na'Allah, *Globalization*.
127 Jung, *Collected Works*.
128 Lévi-Strauss, "Structural," 428–44.
129 Bekalu and Eggermont, "Aligning HIV/AIDS," 441–50.
130 Shaibu, "Military," 158.

the past through their descriptive prowess,[131] tales that expose us to societal norms,[132] and songs that speak to the social milieu under historical reconstruction.[133]

Indeed, oral traditions, when used for purposes of historical reconstruction, give the people's history back to them in their own words.[134] The challenge for the scholar, like the historian, for instance, is that he or she may not be looking for the terms and conditions of the past in the words of the people concerned; hence, the historian becomes another storyteller.[135] The most important thing for the historian investigating the past using indigenous knowledge production systems of the subject is to uncover the truth of that past. This goes for the anthropologist, too, and others dealing with the reality of a given society. The events, practices, and phenomena of the past are to be adumbrated in something factual, objective, and relatable to anyone presented with the same data.[136] Therefore, written or oral traditions preserved as texts can only be scrutinized through the same process of understanding the author and his or her interest vis-à-vis other related texts on the theme and rationality of claims within the particular social context.

It goes without saying that the efficacy of these traditions in accurately presenting the past and the lifeworld of the people of Africa is paradoxically responsible for one of the reasons they were derided as anything but art. Succinctly put, these traditions are seen as oral artifacts that function as an archeological site. Language, as noted earlier, is the most important factor in the accuracy of these traditions. In some cases, these traditions lose their core message in the process of interpretation. The risk of falling into this trap is palpable when working on texts whose original linguistic form is not necessarily compatible with the evolution of language. Improvisation, extrapolation, and linguistics skills then become important in making meaning out of such a text. All of the above speaks to now-popular knowledge that oral traditions are fertile ground for intellectual

---

131 Alabi, "Voices," 124–46.
132 Houseman, "Toward a Complex," 658–77.
133 Owino, "What Have We," 103–24.
134 Thompson and Bornat, *Voice*.
135 Carr, *What Is History*.
136 Afigbo, "Fact and Myth," 122–23.

exploration. The techniques in extracting the knowledge buried deep within them should be the primary concern of the interested scholar.

Epistemic Disobedience

The system of academia in which the analysis of oral traditions exists is a critical part of the so-called colonial matrix of power, which refers to the global systems that validate and perpetuate colonial patterns of the past into neocolonialism.[137] Crucial to the colonial matrix of power is a validating ideology. The scientific method is the foundation upon which Western academia exists. The system extends beyond this epistemology and includes networks of vocabulary, universities, positions, institutions, and academic journals. These are systems of knowing that are based on Eurocentrism, thus scholars with knowledge that falls outside those Eurocentric boundaries are rejected by mainstream academia.[138]

The solution is epistemic disobedience through academic writing that challenges the boundaries of mainstream academia. Well-known tools of epistemic disobedience are ethnographies, which are personal narratives that relate to the cultural and global context in which the speaker exists. They are qualitative and personal but also generalizable and relatable to larger cultural patterns. Oral traditions can be used in ethnographies in many ways.[139] To start, an oral tradition may be a historical narrative. In this case, ethnography can take the narrative in the form of the oral tradition and then relate it to the larger cultural context. Other oral traditions, such as proverbs or riddles, may serve as smaller components of a larger narrative. Or an oral tradition in the form of a performance or written piece can serve as an ethnography on its own, so long as it is applied to the topic being studied from a cultural perspective.

Another way oral traditions can be used as a tool for epistemic liberation is in teaching pedagogy. In African cultures, oral traditions, because of their central role in African cultures, should be integrated into curricula from preschool to university level. Oral traditions are extremely diverse and range in complexity, making them flexible for relating to different

---

137 Alcoff, "Mignolo's Epistemology," 79.
138 Ndlovu-Gatsheni, "Why Decoloniality," 10–15.
139 Webber, *Romancing the Real*.

age groups and academic levels. Children can study proverbs, folktales, or historical figures; secondary and university students can analyze oral traditions and their implications in the fields of science, language, literature, history, philosophy, and much more. Oral traditions can and should be related to any subject pertaining to Africa or African students. Including oral traditions in education is key to improving the Afrocentric perspective in a Eurocentric system of academia.[140] Especially in fields such as science, oral traditions can make subjects more relatable to students and their families.[141]

Oral traditions are relevant to fields of study far beyond the humanities, even reaching into disciplines such as the health sciences. Oral traditions may preserve indigenous health-care solutions and may also provide critical insight into how cultures view health care or their common health-care practices.[142] The emotional and narrative nature of oral traditions also means that they have healing properties when it comes to trauma and psychological disorders. Some studies show that oral traditions may even be key to health education efforts in Africa in contexts such as family planning, HIV/AIDS prevention, and maternal health care.[143]

The concept of truth as something absolute is a Western invention that is incompatible with the beliefs of many other cultures. An alternative model for knowledge, called the "constellation of knowledge," proposes that the truth can take many forms.[144] For example, there are multiple sides to the same story in history; there are also multiple ways to cure a cold. Using "border-thinking," or critical analysis of when each of these systems of knowledge is useful and appropriate, will be critical moving forward in working against the Eurocentric fields in academia.[145] Oral traditions' central place in African indigenous knowledge puts it in a position to make an invaluable contribution to academia.[146]

---

140 Johnson, "Afro-Ecuadorian," 115–37.
141 Stapleton, "Oral Traditions," 189–98.
142 Banks-Wallace, "Talk That Talk," 410–26.
143 Bekalu and Eggermont, "Aligning HIV/AIDS."
144 de Sousa, "General Introduction," xvii–xxxiii.
145 Mignolo, *Local Histories/Global Designs*.
146 Banks-Wallace, "Talk That Talk."

Oral Tradition and Sociological Analysis

The cross-cultural validity of Western scholars' theories on literature might be questionable, but one thing is certain: oral traditions are useful for sociological analysis. The theory of dynamic homeostasis of culture is that there is a congruence between social organization and tradition. Any change in social organization will be followed by a change in traditions.[147] By this theory, changes in the social structure of African communities would result in alterations in oral traditions. Through dynamic homeostasis, traditions mirror society. With oral traditions, this is more complex as oral traditions are not simply a reflection of society but an integral part of it. Oral traditions not only reflect society but also help to shape it. In light of the functionality of the tales in the everyday living experience of Africans, at least in a traditional setting, their sociological significance could be seen consistently emphasized as the core of their messages. Thus, characters like the tortoise teach children how to behave and educate them about how society works, such as via lessons related to societal conduct and ethics.

From studying the themes and transmission of oral traditions, much can be learned about the African worldview. These are not universally true throughout Africa but adjust individually for the histories and structures of individual communities. Oral traditions demonstrate the African focus on the past. Oralities are often narratives or histories from ancestors or great heroes. They reflect a worldview in which Africans look to the past to determine their future. Proverbs, narratives, and songs often center around themes of doing what's right. This often takes a religious approach and emphasizes the role of the individual within the community. Oral traditions also emphasize relationships; whether the story revolves around relationships or their transmission is done through close friend and family bonds.[148]

Scholars who are studying specific historical themes or events can study oral traditions in order to understand how communities represent the past. This brings forth one of the most important roles of oral traditions: a collective memory.[149] The way that a community remembers its

---

147 Goody and Watt, "Consequences," 304–45.
148 Vansina, *Oral Tradition*.
149 Hamilton and Shopes, *Oral History*.

past is indicative of how it will face its future. Collective memories are representations of a culture's identity and values and are key to understanding African communities.

Relationship of Oral Tradition to Archaeology

Archaeologists who study landforms and past peoples in Africa are often Western and disconnected from indigenous populations. Oral traditions are discredited by Western scholars as "inaccurate" or "unreliable." Some scholars claim that uncovering oral traditions creates "more roadblocks than bridges to archaeologists."[150] Close attention to the oral traditions can give irreplaceable insider information on the history of the land and people. Oral traditions may recount such things as migrations, trade patterns, environmental stressors, cultural marriages, or divorces.[151] In this way, oral traditions could actually act as the maps needed to locate historic sites or extract meaning from these sites and the objects they contain. Jan Vansina created a systematic approach to analyzing oral traditions for historical truth. The fieldworker must make every effort to find all of the accounts and variations on the history he or she is interested in. Then, the samples should be carefully chosen, taking into account any geographical or societal boundaries that may impede or hinder the spread of traditions. Before recording the testimonies, a comprehensive examination of selected locations and information, as well as a previous study of sources, should be conducted.[152] While this is useful, oral traditions should be seen as an act of epistemic disobedience and analyzed through more Afrocentric approaches.[153] These traditions can be used in conjunction with scientific practices such as carbon dating to uncover historical truth.[154] Who says a praise poem or epic cannot assist in ascertaining the extent to which a historical artifact has deteriorated? If they are descriptive and true to historical facts, oral traditions can be fertile ground for cultivating new studies.

---

150 Mason, "Archaeology," 239–66.
151 Clack, Brittain, and Turton, "Oral Histories," 669–89.
152 Vansina, *Oral Tradition*.
153 Jones and Russell, "Archaeology," 267–83.
154 Robbins et al., "Mogapelwa," 13–32.

Let me shed more light on this using the example of the Olduvai Gorge. Much archaeological work has been done in the Olduvai Gorge since the 1900s, with a focus on developmental evidence of early humans. The most well-known part of this research was done by Mary and Lewis Leaky from the 1930s to the 1950s. The site is preserved as an archaeological wonder, and archaeologists continue to study the area today. The blunder that the researchers have made in the past is an inability to collaborate with the local Masaai people.

Interviews have shown that the Masaai see themselves as the first humans in the region and are offended by how their ancestors have been portrayed in past studies. Peaceful relations and vital historical information would be available to the researchers in Olduvai Gorge if they were willing to build relationships with the Masaai. This means carefully listening to their oral traditions that pertain to the area, including their origin stories and the environmental history of Olduvai Gorge. Masaai members could be trained in analysis of the footprints in order to collaborate on scientific discoveries of the area. In turn, foreign archaeologists could study the epistemology of the Masaai to gain a library of unique knowledge about the site. The Masaai have a rich cultural history and vast environmental knowledge of Olduvai Gorge; thus their historic exclusion from research in the area is a loss to the scientific community.[155]

Technology and Oral Traditions

As mentioned previously, the new digital age has brought new possibilities for oral traditions. There are new ideas afoot for storing oral tradition—for example, one lab has tried to create an oral tradition "jukebox." This digital creation plays an oral tradition on demand from a selection, along with related visuals and contextual information. Such innovations increase the possibility of cross-cultural research collaboration, as oral traditions could be open sources available for any Western or African university to study.[156]

More common ways of how oral traditions are affected by technology is through audio or video capture. This has been dubbed "Digi-Orature,"

---

155 Lee et al., "Scientific Facts," 57–83.
156 Schneider, *So They Understand*.

a phenomenon that could help preserve traditions.[157] Recording an oral tradition as a singular performance and storing it is reductionist, removing the variable of storytelling from the tradition. There is also the threat of globalization, as digital orature efforts might kow-tow to the West due to economic pressures. To combat this, it has been suggested that the digital preservation of oral traditions take place at the behest of local leadership.[158] The question, however, would remain the extent to which African leadership is ready to pursue this task.

Oral Tradition in Popular Culture

Oral traditions of Africa have survived for thousands of years and spread across the world with the African diaspora. They have adapted to the new digital age through TV shows such as the East African *Tinga Tinga Tales*, which emphasize African folktales for children through animation. Radio shows, which have high audience ratings in sub-Saharan Africa, also continue oral traditions in a nontraditional manner. An example of this is the broadcast show *Parana* in San, Mali.[159] Novels or Pan-African literature also preserve oral traditions through ethnographic descriptions and biographical information.[160]

African oral traditions also influence American popular culture. Take, for example, the cartoon character Bugs Bunny. The rabbit is known as an archetypal trickster in traditional African folktales. In the same way, Bugs Bunny is always tricking Wile E. Coyote into chasing after him for comedic effect. Another more straightforward example is the *Lion King*, which also uses animal archetypes to tell a larger story, using the scenery of Africa and Swahili words and names such as "Simba," "Rafiki," and "hakuna matata."

From their use in popular culture today, it is apparent that African oral traditions are timeless, resonating with African people, the African diaspora, and beyond. As the digital age progresses and globalization

---

157 Ikyer, "Deep Digital," 196–210.
158 Na'Allah, *Globalization*.
159 Leguy and Mitsch, "Revitalizing," 136–47.
160 Guèye, "Criticism," 86–102.

continues, the role of these traditions in culture will bend with time. The extent to which it will bend remains to seen.

Conclusion

African oral traditions are not only of great intrinsic and artistic value, but they represent the fabric of African societies. They continue to play invaluable roles in fields of research such as archeology, literature, history, sociology, anthropology, and education. Due to threatening forces such as poverty, government censure, and environmental change, projects that document these oral traditions are all the more valuable. Deep cultural meanings of oral traditions and their translation require Africans to take the lead in this initiative. Nonindigenous researchers should continue their work only with close consultation from members of the community. The increased use of technology and globalization will continue to shape the distribution and nature of oral traditions. Moving forward, the efforts of projects such as the World Oral Literature Project should be expanded, especially in recruiting more African universities and scholars. Global academic institutions should move beyond viewing oral traditions as exoticism and understand their value as tools of epistemic disobedience. In this way, oral traditions are relevant to all academic subjects involving Africa or Africans.

Although the earliest documentation and study of oral traditions in Africa as textual forms of understanding the culture, civilization, and peoples of the region was premised on attempts to subjugate these societies for the imperial gains of the West,[161] the use of these traditions as a methodology for studying the peoples of Africa should now be viewed in light of decoloniality. Native texts, as these traditions could otherwise imply, are ingenious ways of preserving and communicating the innermost part of the society. In other words, they offer a rare opportunity to unfettered access and assessment of what ordinarily might not surface through mere historical accounts (i.e., oral history).

---

161 Hiribarren, "A European," 77–98.

Part Two
Agencies and Voices

Chapter Seven

Voices of Decolonization

In probably every form, decolonization efforts have taken place since the twentieth century, both in colonial and postcolonial Africa. The nationalist movements for the liberation of Africa contributed to the political decolonization witnessed in the 1960s across the continent. Thus, one can say that as an idea and practice, decolonization is nothing new. It has long existed as a concept, an idea, a movement, and an integral aspect of African scholarship. Several scholars (myself included) have contributed to academic expressions of decolonization, both as an idea and as a movement, and from differing orientations, perspectives, and different fields of inquiry.

This makes it compelling to review works of leading African scholars of decolonization and aggregate their views, most of which lend narrative support to the epistemologies. This review looks at the leading scholars in different fields, areas, and approaches to decolonization: Walter Rodney on African socioeconomic decolonization; Achille Mbembe on knowledge production; V. Y. Mudimbe on "Otherness;" Mahmood Mamdani's work on Eurocentric epistemology; Molefi Asante's Afrocentrism; Archie Mafeje's scholarship on anticolonial movement; Samir Amin's thoughts on Marxism in Africa, Claude Ake's decolonization discourse on democracy and development; and Ali Mazrui's Africa's "Triple Heritage." Added also is a brief segment on women's voices, as a preface to two substantial chapters that follow. These voices demonstrate the value of inclusivity and epistemic decoloniality. The significance of this chapter and the next is multifaceted. First, they offer a summary of the different fields and voices of decolonization while analyzing leading thoughts in different areas. Second, the extensive study achieved herein makes for a different approach to the subject matter of decolonization and decoloniality and encourages the multidisciplinary study and further research of these twin concepts.

Walter Rodney: Decolonization of African Socioeconomy

Walter Rodney remains a strong force in repudiating Eurocentric narratives around the economic subservience of the African continent. His intellectual engagements are directed toward the unveiling of the impact of European imperialism in the delegitimization of African economic power. When the world is fed wild claims that Africans are inherently incapable of turning their economic misfortune around using their natural and human resources, Walter Rodney refuses to fall victim to this rhetoric as he offers critical evaluation of the African conditions in relation to the colonial and neocolonial domination of the people. Thus, he produces works that basically explain the interconnectedness of imperialism and Africa's purported retrogression. While it is undeniable that the current socioeconomic situation of the African people does not reflect their respective countries' collective resources, this dire situation is due to Western economic exploitation. As such, Rodney rejects the demeaning insinuations that the African condition is tied to the people's own ignorance and inability to look to the future.

Critically, Rodney is less interested in the questions of morality that surround the history of colonialism. Rather, his intellectual attention is fixed on the economics of colonial adventures that ravaged Africa for more than four hundred years. When one considers his classic work, *How Europe Underdeveloped Africa*, one could easily connect the dots between race relations between Europe and Africa and how the continuous exploitation of African resources has led to Africa's underdevelopment. To end the enduring servitude and economic injustice inherent in the Euro-African relationship, Rodney maintains that Africans should be genuinely wary of European philanthropy or parasitic benevolence that seeks to cunningly dispossess Africans of their natural resources. He often notes that the racial agenda that led to the extirpation of Black populations from Africa was exclusively created to undermine the people's growth in favor of European colonialism. To correct the economic anomaly instituted by colonialists, Walter Rodney proposes an economic theory that centers Africans within their own economy.

He views development as an independent phenomenon whose power of influence lies in the freedom to develop and progress at one's own speed. Therefore, when people immediately aggregate African socioeconomic conditions as indexes of nondevelopment or underdevelopment

Figure 7.1. Walter Rodney and other Working People's Alliance members leaving the Ministry of Labour and Society in Guyana in the 1970s. Guyana History.

without considering the efforts of colonizers whose history of racial exploitation of Africans dictated the socioeconomic imbalance, they are being deliberately biased, Rodney alleges. In other words, the sudden economic expansion of the European countries with limited natural resources cannot be disconnected from the activities of exploitation that Europeans embarked on through colonization. Even when it appears that visible threats and domination of European imperialists—enhanced by their use of force and power—have been pushed to extinction, Rodney laments that nowadays more subtle means of exploitation are used by the West. Evidenced by the imposition of suspicious philanthropic institutions like the World Bank (WB) and the International Monetary Fund (IMF), he points to the correlation between the old system and the modern one. In short, Africans continue to face underdevelopment because they fall victim to new forms of oppression.

Rodney's anticolonialist struggle aims to deconstruct the fallacy that colonialism had minimal impact on the outlook of the African people and that a postcolonial age meant the abrogation of such heinous practices. To him, making such claims undermines the virulence of colonialism and trivializes the renewed power structure that saw to the establishment of institutions seeking to completely subjugate Africans. On the question of the socioeconomic viability of slavery, for example, using as an example the knighthood of John Hopkins, Rodney summarizes the correlation between the commodification of African people in the transatlantic environment and the rich economic transformation it sparked in England. After a series of trips, explained Rodney, having ventured into the continent with a ship named the *Jesus*, Hopkins financially profited so much from the slave trade that Queen Elizabeth I honored him with a knighthood.[1] Considering the underlying dangers inherent in colonization, Rodney was intellectually radical to reject proposed aid from the European world. As an alternative, therefore, he suggests Africa should not socioeconomically dependent on Western sources.

Strangely, attaining upward mobility in a developmental index involves active collaborations from different components of socioeconomic and political existence. As such, exposing European exploitative engagements in Africa during the historical antecedents of slavery and thereafter would assist Africans in contextualizing their challenges and then devise the appropriate means of righting these wrongs. In this spirit therefore, Rodney advocates a revolutionary stance in resisting the hegemonic culture that seeks to keep Africa underdeveloped politically and economically. To achieve this, various economic models and theories are required to guide the activities of Africa in the contemporary world. It is in this spirit that he proposed repudiation of Western ways to enhance African economic independence.

Rodney also believes that Africans must adapt Marxist policies for a general displacement of the Eurocentric agenda. Bearing in mind the infinite contributions of Africans to the exponential economic advancement of Europe, the scholar strongly condemns the reliance of Africans on Europeans to boost their stagnant economy, for it is difficult to be genuinely rescued by parties that enhanced one's downfall. Therefore, Rodney laments that the ultimate solution to African problems is the

---

1 Rodney, *How Europe*.

appropriation of Pan-Africanist economic models to African challenges, as every other means would subvert rather than enhance Africans' attempts at meeting extant economic challenges. Using this model for emancipation struggles would mean that progress would be contingent upon Africans deconstructing the mischievous generalization that they are perhaps biologically inferior.

Reliance on Eurocentric models would continue to misdirect Africans, as their conception of development would be colored by imperialist biases. To ensure that Africans do not fall victim to this Eurocentric temptation, Rodney deconstructs the concept of development and underdevelopment in his classic work *How Europe Underdeveloped Africa*. Emphasizing the notion of "underdevelopment," the socialist activist establishes that the purported retrogression of Africans is misunderstood when certain issues that determine progress or otherwise are not factored into comparisons. In fact, he reports that the history of European's swift development cannot be detached from the roles they played in the colonial and slavery expeditions. Consequently, the failure to understand the economic and political agenda that Europeans pursued would impede objective evaluation because it was this very agenda that instituted Western racial prejudices against Africans. Therefore, the master-subordinate relations between Europe and Africa were not predicated on racism especially (by that I mean color difference): the European goal was to dismantle the African economic system so that Africa would always be economically and culturally inferior.

Rodney argues vociferously that rather than avoiding responsibility for the economic deprivations of Africa, Europeans should understand and accept that their individualism, entrenched in a culture of exploitation that set its sights on African resources, was the beginning of African underdevelopment. Before European contact in the fifteenth century, it was common knowledge in Africa that Marxism and communalism would be useful for collective progress as a culture. Africans used their systems and philosophies for their own benefit and to promote whatever belonged to them. Suddenly, industrial slavery was introduced, and this became another marker of history that effectively destroyed the African systems. Knowing the impact of the Europeans in the slave trade, even scholars of Eurocentric and Anglo-American persuasions began to distance imperialist involvement from African economic regression. Rodney, however, refutes the argument that slavery was not alien to Africans prior to the European presence in Africa, as it became obvious that Europeans would use this as a way to escape blame. He therefore establishes a distinction. He differentiates between the two by saying that "slavery as a mode of production was not present in any African society, although some slaves were to be found where the decomposition of communal equality had gone furthest."[2]

In summary, Rodney's voice continues to reverberate widely through his protest literature that assisted in debunking European falsities about so-called African underdevelopment. In his hopes for Africans to attain greater economic and cultural heights, Rodney introduced a Marxist element to apply to the African economic system in order to promote African self-sufficiency and discourage dependency on foreign aid. His influence on African decolonization struggles transcends the economic perspective from which he studied the impact of colonialism on the African people. Accordingly, Rodney was not a scholar who shied away from speaking the truth about European colonialism even if it meant being subjected to threats. European scholars such as J. D. Fage have written texts that downplay the European enslavement of Africans by identifying that there were internal African slavery expeditions before Europeans came to Africa. It was Rodney's analytical prowess that helped dislocate such unsubstantiated conclusions. He was therefore a force to be reckoned with in the struggle for Africa's freedom.

Achille Mbembe: Decolonization of Knowledge

Achille Mbembe is an African scholar that questioned the legitimacy of Western epistemic hegemony and its globalist supremacy, as he considered the philosophy that produced such thinking as repugnant and vain. To him, the one-sided argument that the West holds the exclusive power of imagination and reasoning to dictate global affairs has no validity. Consequently, Mbembe argues for a pluriversalist view of the world in recognition of all other disregarded epistemologies to occupy their deserved position in the scheme of global affairs. Apparently, Eurocentric hegemonic thinking has dominated global intellectualism for a protracted period and its domination of the avenues of global power have helped shape the ways

---

2   Rodney, *How Europe*, 82.

Figure 7.2. Achille Mbembe. Photograph by Heike Huslage-Koch. Creative Commons License CC BY-SA 4.0.

that other races of people, especially Africans, have perceived themselves down through the ages. Africans have been the primary victims of this imbalanced intellectual structure: hence the need for a rethinking.

The reality is that the domain of knowledge systems has been influenced and dominated by Western supremacy, which unconsciously has conditioned African perceptions of themselves and their history. Therefore, the sudden acceptance by Africans that the standard for determining the validity of every knowledge episteme should rest exclusively on the Europeanized models has forced African victims of colonization to accept an inferior status. To continue with this mindset therefore is to continue colonization in different forms. Mbembe challenged this by proposing epistemological decolonization, as this would encourage African reflections on their immediate history and consider when they began internalizing European knowledge models fraught with outright racism and hegemonic intent. Mbembe had noted implicitly that the European arrogance reflected in the philosophy that birthed colonization does not see any alternative non-Eurocentric knowledge production as legitimate.

For example, it is globally understood that the European knowledge model is attributed to science with its capacity for empiricism and due process. Any knowledge production that takes a different approach is considered inferior and barbaric. While it is a sign of an educated mind to accept one's ignorance, even in knowledge systems, it became taboo for the Western supremacist to accept African or other methods of knowledge production. The problem the Eurocentric supremacist had was not an African problem, as the African intellectuals who understand the Afrocentric knowledge systems easily recognize them accordingly. However, acceptance in this case refers to the idea that many Africans who are immersed in Eurocentric values developed psychological resistance to these knowledge systems. African knowledge systems therefore suffered extensive criticism and denigration by Western scholars: these African systems were bullied into silence and met with racial discrimination. The Western knowledge episteme was placed above other knowledge systems, and its destructive exclusion of other systems became the reason for resisting the Western hegemonic agenda. Quijano and Ennis understand this bias when they note that "Europe's hegemony over the new model of global power concentrated all forms of the control of subjectivity, culture, and especially knowledge and the production of knowledge under its hegemony."[3]

The intellectual activism of Mbembe obviously transcends the knowledge or education domain. This is true because he extends his decolonization crusade beyond the evaluation of the epistemic insincerity that made the West arrogate supremacy to themselves and to the detriment of their colonized subjects. For Mbembe, decolonization should be all-encompassing, allowing us to question not only the political totalitarianism of imperialism but also the legacy it left in education, history, culture, and even the economy. The inherent arrogance that drives colonizers to co-opt natural and human resources of Blacks during colonization is the same behavior that is reflected in their thinking that indigenous Africans are devoid of any historical past. This same mindset is behind the Western line of thinking that Africans cannot make sufficient use of their land, for example. Therefore, the overbearing power of the West in many African countries eventually comes with appalling human consequences. Given these conditions, therefore, it became necessary to protest Western hegemony, which Achille Mbembe dedicated himself to.

For Mbembe, tearing down the supremacist legacy of the colonizers begins with the installation of Afrocentrism as the guiding light for the development of the people. In other words, Mbembe calls for the

---

3   Quijano et al., *Coloniality*.

radicalization of African resistance to reflect all aspects of African existence, as that would pave the way for African's true freedom. Independence does not necessarily mean controlling one's political life by shutting out the Western world. Instead, it begins with the application of African values, the patronage of African knowledge systems, and the appropriation of African epistemological ideas, among others. This would therefore reveal the human potential of Africans to contribute to the global knowledge economy. Mbembe's decolonization recognizes all these factors as indispensable in the pursuit of true freedom and the commitment to the development of African countries.

Mbembe argues that the refusal to ensure the reversal of colonial politics and thinking in shaping the new South Africa, for example, would unavoidably lead people to make those errors of inequity that produced the Eurocentric supremacist thinking of colonialism. In essence, the society would become fragmented, which would have devastating consequences on Africa in the long run. Of course, Mbembe noted that the process of emancipation from the vestiges of colonialism would be difficult, but he understands that the failure to embrace the culture of decolonization would only prolong the mental degradation that Africans have suffered, this time not at the hands of an outsider but through their own complicity. To avert this outcome, Mbembe continues to crusade for the eradication of certain outdated and inappropriate monuments to Western culture. This would make Africans appreciate how far they've come and help them understand the roles played by European imperialists in impeding their culture's progress for some time.

All this, however, does not lead to the cancellation of Western perspectives on knowledge and philosophy. In fact, these steps help to place Western ideas within an appropriate context where they could be considered as a credible alternative and not the only option. In other words, decolonization does not equal complete eradication of Western influence. More than anything, Mbembe's decolonization project seeks to detach Africans from the unwholesome reliance on the influence of the West and the institutionalization of Western ideas at the expense of others. To protest this arrangement is to condemn the structures in both the physical and philosophical sense that the culture enthroned. Mbembe argues logically that the process of decolonization starts with the effacement of colonial ideas and values, an approach that would break up the dialectics of supremacy inherent in the colonizers' engagement. He explained that the defacement of the colonial legacy would become a healing process for Blacks who have suffered bitter racial prejudice from the West.

Achille Mbembe laments the infiltration of Western education systems and philosophy, which has lingered longer than predicted in African lives. He believes that the legacy of the education system inherited from the colonizers has not actually reflected African realities and therefore would not produce the results that would fundamentally benefit the African people. This is essentially because African school systems still maintain the colonial philosophy that sought to denigrate the African knowledge production system, at best as a shadow of its European counterparts and at worst as a mere fantasy. In his own words, Mbembe submits that "there is something fundamentally cynical when institutions whose character is profoundly ethno-provincial keep masquerading as replicas of Oxford and Cambridge without demonstrating the same productivity as the original places they are mimicking."[4] First, the African education system was Westernized because it was aimed at producing intellectuals who would downplay their African lifestyle and epistemes to impress European teachers.

In essence, allowing the Eurocentric canon in African schools, to use Mbembe's words, is to accept the monosource of knowledge production proposed by the West and reject the others out of hand. When Africans commit to this, they threaten the existence of their African epistemological difference. To combat this, therefore, Mbembe proposes complete decolonization. In this process, indigenous knowledge must be upheld as a credible replacement for domineering Eurocentrism, for instance. This means that the application of Western knowledge in the construction of African ideas and values would be condemned in the strongest possible terms. Therefore, decolonization for Mbembe begins with the repossession of values and resources that belong to Africa, along with the filtering out of Westernized ideas that have become an everyday part of African lives.

V. Y. Mudimbe: Decolonizing Otherness

V. Y. Mudimbe is the African scholar that shed much light on the question of the identity politics that became one of the core tenets of contemporary discourses in the academic world. African identity, from contact

---

4   Mbembe, "Decolonizing," 29–45.

with the Western world, has been reshaped and structured to suit the narrative of its colonizers. And in this way, Africa's epistemological beginnings and their modes of knowledge generation were detested and concluded to be inferior. To counter this bias requires that scholars conduct extensive research in an attempt to either validate or invalidate these wild claims of superiority made by the European imperialists. Dutifully, Mudimbe was one of the scholars that came to the rescue. Primarily, the notion that European culture should be seen as the benchmark for African ideas and philosophies was critically rejected by Mudimbe as supremacist hegemony.

As a philosopher, Mudimbe is aware that the domain of philosophy in Africa is littered with people (scholars) who are influenced by Western ideas, thereby considering non-European modes and models of knowledge to be inferior. To understand clearly how this supremacism became inculcated in the Western philosophical mind, one needs to understand the place of a few Western philosophers, including but not limited to David Hume, Immanuel Kant, and anthropological thinkers like Claude Levi-Strauss, S. F. Nadel, and Franz Boas. In his *Philosophy of History*, to which the question of African's philosophical capabilities was raised, Georg Wilhelm Friedrich Hegel responded in the negative because of the assumption that Africans are vain, emotional, and lacked the ability to engage in logical thinking. It is important to therefore understand that these scholars—whose intelligence was already colored with premeditated bias—went on to construct identities for Africans in the education system and political ideologies that were to be used to guide their activities. For the obvious reasons, a very discerning observer would, even without familiarity of the substance of educational values imposed on Africans, understand that their processes of learning are shaped to make them an extension of the West: in other words, an inferior white in Black skin.

It was then inevitable that Africans would be confronted with an epistemic struggle that would include them correcting wrongheaded notions already institutionalized by the Europeans, who obviously were irreversibly committed to their desecrating agenda. It was a profitable exercise apparently, evidenced by the bewilderment of Eurocentric audiences when they read about or watch Africans resisting their imposed identity through the production of knowledge that clearly questions Eurocentrism. This means that Africans now have a dual identity: one that was forced on them by the European imperialists and their true African selves. While the former was falsified and deliberately maligned, the latter is facing up to the challenge of authenticity. The reason this is challenging is because the notion of true identity is a dicey question, as Africans have lost a lot in the process of identity transformation that began when a Western identity was foisted upon them. Important African philosophers like Mudimbe concluded that this imposed identity is malicious because of the overwhelming harm it does to the African ontology and therefore calls for the decolonization of the image. We would therefore understand that Africans, even in their quest for identity repossession, are now stuck in the politics of "Otherness" that was started a long time ago.

It is context-worthy to invoke Mudimbe on the introduction of colonialism to Africans:

> Because of the colonializing structure, a dichotomizing system has emerged, and with it a great number of current paradigmatic oppositions have developed: traditional versus modern; oral versus written and printed; agrarian and customary communities versus urban and industrialized civilization; subsistence economies versus highly productive economies. In Africa, a great deal of attention is generally given to the evolution implied and promised by the passage from the former paradigms to the latter.[5]

Within the moral framework of Western thought, Europeans, even despite their differences in perception occasioned by language variation and cultural particularities, considered themselves as the sole acceptable standard for measuring human dignity, progress, and sophistication. Consequently, African values and resources were sacrificed when the West began "civilizing" them. As such, Africans were automatically seen as people without a significant past and unworthy of human dignity or decency. Implicitly, Mudimbe warned that this was the beginning of identity politics, where the Europeans placed themselves on a high pedestal above other cultures. It was because of the understanding and belief that Africans did not evolve intellectually to manage, say, their resources, their environment, their land, and their education that led to either the forceful or diplomatic dismantling of the African legacy in the first place.

Without a doubt, Mudimbe understood these Western imperialist politics and grasped their outcomes. For example, in his classic *The*

---

5   Mudimbe, *Invention*, 17.

Invention of Africa, Mudimbe identifies how the instrumentalization of Eurocentrism has conditioned the views of the West in this way. Therefore, he argued that the West is guilty of the politics of "otherness" because they have chosen to look at the African epistemological beginnings, their ontology, and their political beliefs through a single cultural lens: Eurocentrism, therefore, being the judging of other people's culture and epistemic background through a European lens. African scholars are expected to resist the stereotype institutionalized by this Eurocentrism if they truly are committed to decolonization.

In the spirit of Mudimbe's resistance, when one considers the vitriolic effect of Eurocentrism and also analyzes its destructive influence on African identity, one would perhaps understand why Africa continues to face extensive challenges in the essentialization of the African ontology in the global knowledge economy. It is the concerted efforts of these thinkers that dislodged the misinformed bias that Europeans had and still have. In the late eighteenth century, philosophers such as David Hume made the assertion that Africans were less than human. This he did in the domain of philosophy, corroborating what some other scholars were saying even in the scientific community. As recent as the second half of the twentieth century, another notable scholar by the name of Trevor-Roper denied the integrity of African history, making a wild assertion that Africans did not have a history except for the history of the European presence on the continent. This, then, is to validate a misconception that African history began with slavery and colonialism. This obviously is a deliberate antagonism to the survival and existence of Africans expressed in different biases. Therefore, it was noted in the works of Mudimbe that Eurocentric politics of otherness would always have devastating consequences on the image of Africa, especially when Africans had to rely on Europeans for a true representation of their identity.

The Manichean construction of "us" versus "them," "superior" versus "inferior," "white" versus "Black" in that order would therefore always influence the perception of the superstructure against those considered as occupants of the base of the pyramidal structure. This misconception became the norm in the global knowledge economy before many Africans began to see revolutionary actions from other cultural activists. To combat these structures, therefore, Mudimbe astutely proposed a couple of intellectual frameworks that would be used to challenge the narrative and therefore change the system. Principally, Africa would need to be reinvented. The symbol of reinvention is found in his book title, and the activity of rebirth leans clearly and exclusively on Africans themselves. Given the fact that the African's distorted image could be attributed to deliberate orientalist scheming on the part of Europeans, Mudimbe offers suggestions that the recalibration of this image into something purely African must also be deliberate and must be aimed at combating the apparent misinformation of the West.

Mudimbe demonstrates that Western exploitation of Africans embodied the imbalance of class, as espoused in the philosophy of Karl Marx. In other words, Africans occupied the lower rung of power and were considered a labor force for the production of materials to benefit Western powers. To combat this, therefore, Mudimbe thought that Africans should revert to the Marxist design and envision economic relationships that would factor in the needs of all Africans and not just the privileged elite. He understood that Africans creating any economic distance between and among other Africans would mean the continuation of the us-versus-them dichotomy brought to Africa exclusively by Europeans. Mudimbe thought that if this Marxist system could be implemented, Africans would develop to their own advantage and then live more rewarding political, spiritual, religious, epistemic, and ontological lives. The political arrangement that concentrates power in the hands of the few to the detriment of the masses is a continuation of the Eurocentric philosophy.

Mahmood Mamdani: Decolonization of Eurocentric Epistemology

Academic research can be an important instrument of transformation and has always been the backbone of a thriving society, as it provides the opportunity for self-evaluation and encourages adjustments that meet current necessities. The problem, however, begins when this research does not incorporate indigenous knowledge systems into its processes of inquiry. Such research is bound to alienate the people it should be serving to educate. This is usually when a research project fails to conduct or disseminate information and knowledge that reflect the sociocultural conditions of the people. This is always the case when the research methodology is nonindigenous. When the Western model of education is used, the end product cannot be entirely divorced from Western results.

Meanwhile the struggles of decolonization would be for naught when models and theories developed in the West are continuously applied to the education of Africans in Africa. For one thing, it delegitimizes indigenous knowledge and marginalizes its productions. Since the models of Western education remain in place, it is obvious that African knowledge economy would remain overshadowed even within its native environment. The eventual result therefore would be catastrophic, not only for the African identity alone but also for academic society in general. Most importantly, African schools and scholars would be the puppets of Western education and experts, respectively. It was against this backdrop that the revolutionary intellectualism of Mahmood Mamdani came to the fore. Mamdani is an African scholar whose focus was the outright decolonization of an African knowledge economy that had become an offshoot of its European counterparts from its inception. Mamdani wanted to change the fact that the African education system, in curriculum and practice, continued to resemble Western knowledge epistemology.

A Ugandan with educational experience acquired both in Africa and outside of it, Mamdani has always protested the overbearing influence of the Western education system on the African system and sees it as a corrosive impediment. Despite the fact that African knowledge production should reflect African problems and challenges and therefore propose effective solutions and policies, the immersion of a number of African scholars into the Western knowledge epistemology has been the reason the anticolonial activists usually hit a brick wall in their quests for decolonialization. However, Mamdani is unwavering. Having experienced a number of insults from the government of Uganda during his decolonization revolution, he remains steadfastly committed to Afrocentric education. He was convinced that the true freedom of the African people and the continent lies in exposing and eradicating superficial Eurocentric understandings of Africa. This is why Africans, despite their knowledge base and educational attainments, have not been competing on the same level as their contemporaries in developed countries.

Mamdani made notable contributions to the African knowledge economy and its decolonization. He spearheaded a research team that sought to revolutionize African knowledge systems, as they were implicitly considered an inferior version of Western education. Therefore, the African education system was bound to be decolonized to meet the following ends: projecting an African image from an insider and not an outsider perspective, as this would eradicate the imposed Eurocentric views of Africans that have robbed the continent of its true image and identity; conducting research that would reflect and tackle the challenges that the continent is confronted with and abrogating Western theories used as the pillars of the African education system. Given his dedication of interest and intellectual might to this course, Mamdani found his way into the heart of Makerere University in Uganda to begin the process of decolonization. Accordingly, he was confronted with internal and external pressures from two groups: one group consisted of those brainwashed by the Western education system; the other considered the Afrocentric crusade an unrealistic project.

To reform the African education curriculum was a revolutionary action in a society that does not believe it is heavily influenced by the colonialist ethos. This condition provides an uninviting atmosphere for anyone who would undertake the duty of spearheading the course of decolonization. Mamdani became the most well-known intellectual to undertake the decolonial exercise. Having long served as an educator at the University of Makerere, the intricacies of politics compelled him to travel to Cape Town, South Africa, where they offered him this revolutionary work. Since the atmosphere was already heavily laden with skepticism toward such a movement, he was the target of a number of attacks that almost extinguished his intellectual flame. Having failed to anticipate such antagonism, he was met by an eventual uproar: "The tussle that followed with the Working Group and the Deputy Dean was one for which I was totally unprepared. As it unraveled, it highlighted issues that I think go beyond my personal predicament: the relationship between the defense of academic freedom and the pursuit of academic excellence, administrative decision-making in academic affairs, and the relationship of pedagogy to content."[6] Even though Mamdani met resistance in the process of taking Africa, especially the University of Cape Town, he never faltered through the journey of decolonization. This committed scholar is a disciple of Afrocentric ideologies, which is demonstrated in his fight against major European instruments of colonization still found in the African education system.

Mahmood Mamdani challenged the Western imposition of knowledge on the African people and their postcolonial knowledge systems.

---

6   Mamdani, "African Studies."

He mainly decries the idea that Western cultures and experiences were taught to Africans and have molded the African mind. Without being aware of the inherent danger, even the African intellectual community unconsciously submit to unfair racial politics in the educational system. By doing this, the expansive precolonial African experience was dragged to the intellectual margins, being subjected to undeserved humiliation. As such, unsuspecting Africans introduced to the education system and its curricula become the victims of epistemological division and are compelled to learn things that do not reflect the reality of their immediate environment. And this is what Mamdani staunchly opposed. He designed education curricula that would highlight experiences of Africans in their precolonial environment, what they encountered during the colonial period, and then their contemporary trajectory. This would help them understand African struggles and challenges and as such inspire them to develop solutions that are essentially African.

The reason for this Afrocentrism was obvious. Without understanding the pretexts of colonization, it would be difficult for Africans to understand the connections between the presence of the European imperialists and the long-standing retrogression that characterized Africa after the colonial powers departed. More importantly, it would deny them an appraisal of the consequences of colonialism and would assist the people to interpret accordingly the African identity, as the miscegenation of Africans and Europeans has led to the influx of international migrants who have the potential to change or influence the Black identity, mostly in a negative way. To many scholars, Mamdani's propositions were too combative and reeked of separatism. For example, he claimed that South Africa was geographically African, but the lingering influence of European imperialists, even postindependence, has tarnished the identity of Blackness that country claims to have. Mamdani experienced much resistance and condemnation from various groups who considered him too radical. However, he stood firm for the decolonization of African knowledge economy so that Africans would understand why and how some aspects of history became significant in their journey.

Molefi Asante: Afrocentrism, and the Decolonization of Africana Studies

Professor Molefi Kete Asante of Philadelphia's Temple University has led the way in developing theories of Afrocentricity (which some now refer to as "Africology"). He strives to reframe educational systems in order to place African history and narratives at the center of African curricula. Asante and the Afrocentricity school of thought have made great contributions to the decolonization of Africana studies by working to either undermine or overthrow the suspected supremacy of European epistemologies. To Asante, this is a way to allow for Afrocentric education and perspectives to flourish. However, many curricula continue to rely upon European modes of thinking, including those of African universities. Asante, however, rejects this institutionalized form of white supremacy and instead supports the complete restructuring of curricula to advance Afrocentrism.

Asante's epistemological construction of Afrocentricity revolutionized theories of how one should obtain knowledge. Asante's theory relies upon the centrality of the African experience and advocates that people around the world should evaluate propositions of knowledge concerning Africa through an African lens of understanding, rather than through the accepted, mainstream European lens. By reframing knowledge, Asante asserts that people can become the central actors of their own narratives rather than peripheral figures.[7] Afrocentricity, according to him, is crucial, as it treats Black people as subjects instead of objects. Asante's Afrocentric method requires that each phenomenon or event must be located and analyzed within the context of psychological time and space to obtain a greater understanding of the interrelationships among "science and art, design and execution, creation and maintenance, generation and tradition, and other areas bypassed by theory." While phenomena vary considerably, they are not stagnant. Therefore, to properly contextualize the event, one must understand where he or she stands in relation to the event being studied.

This method is a type of cultural criticism that studies the origins of words to understand the author's perspective. According to Asante, "This allows us to intersect ideas with actions and actions with ideas on

---

7   Chawane, "Development," 78–99.

Figure 7.3. Molefi Asante, 2011. Still photograph from video recording of Asante's presentation at the Multiversity International Conference on Decolonising Our Universities, held in Penang, Malaysia, 27–29 June 2011. TV Multiversity. Creative Commons License CC-BY 3.0. *Source:* https://www.youtube.com/watch?v=S8gZT6Vc9pk.

the basis of what is pejorative and ineffective and what is creative and transformative at the political and economic levels." The purpose of this method is to uncover the holders of power to evaluate how their influence affects experiences within time and space. By utilizing critical contemplation, the true nature of power is established, and it is revealed that this power is "nothing but the projection of a cadre of adventurers" and "the Afrocentric method locates the imaginative structure of a system of economics, bureau of politics, policy of government, expression of cultural form in the attitude, direction, and language of the phenom, be it text, institution, personality, interaction, or event."[8]

---

8   Asante, "Afrocentricity."

Thus, Asante's Afrocentrism seeks to deconstruct the power structures of European epistemology by encouraging the questioning of established norms. For example, Afrocentrism champions reevaluation of norms such as the idea that a democratic nation-state is the best form of governance. While some claim that Afrocentrism is antiwhite, it simply offers an alternative perspective that demonstrates that the European method of thinking is only one of many epistemic options. Asante's Afrocentrism, therefore, rests upon the idea that an African perspective is central for African people and must be adopted to obtain a greater understanding of who they are within a sociohistorical context often dominated by European perspectives.[9]

Moreover, Asante's Afrocentrism is not exclusive; hence, anyone who embraces African ideals—when analyzing African history or culture—can be an Afrocentrist in the name of global solidarity.[10] Instead of espousing epistemic absolutism, Asante favors epistemic relativism. Asante reasons that "all analysis is culturally centered and flows from ideological assumptions."[11] Accordingly, developing the skill of Afrocentric analysis is a task that is available to African and European peoples. However, Asante argues that regardless of the intellectual revelation that culture and ideology shape knowledge, Europeans do not understand the limited scope of their perspective.[12] The limitations caused by a restricted, European epistemology led Asante to form and uphold Afrocentric academic programs.

In 1987, Asante established the first PhD program in African American studies. The formation of this doctoral program at Temple University sparked a resurgence of African and African American studies to provide a platform for the study of Afrocentrism. Asante presided over the first dissertations on African American studies by white, Japanese, and Chinese students, which demonstrates the expansion of the field due to his efforts.[13] However, Asante faced major challenges when building this program. Asante states that when he arrived at Temple, the Black studies department was in noticeable decline.[14]

---

9   Mazama, "Afrocentric Paradigm," 387.
10 Verharen, "Molefi Asante," 224.
11 Asante, *Afrocentric Idea*.
12 Verharen, "Molefi Asante," 225.
13 Turner, "An Oral History," 713.
14 Molefi Asante, "Creation."

By creating a program that would exclusively focus on Africana studies, Asante and his supporters went against the grain of the university as an institution, including its racist hiring policies, its Eurocentric curriculum, and its collusion in continuing societal oppression through selective education. Consequently, opposing this institutionalism meant fighting for ownership of their history and against outside control of African narratives. Besides intellectual and political freedom, Asante was also supporting a culturally relevant education that was meaningful to students. Indeed, the early advocates of Africana studies saw this style of education as a crucial tool in preparing students to advocate for equality, fight against injustice, and protect Black culture.[15] The Temple program, under Asante's tutelage, has now morphed into a Department of Africology, and Asante is back at the helm.

The creation of this PhD program—now an Africology PhD—revolutionized the academic landscape of African studies. This transformation legitimized the field, paved the way for other schools to form similar programs, expanded students' curricular opportunities, and catalyzed academic discussions and research on unexplored topics.[16] Dr. Ama Mazama, the associate professor and director of the graduate programs of the Department of African American Studies at Temple University, claims that Asante's achievement accomplished three major feats. First, creating this program represented a major break from the white supremacy found in academic institutions; Asante's direction and creation of the degree usurped typical power structures where white people dominated the formation and administration of college degrees. Thus, according to Mazama, "The doctorate in African American Studies at Temple was the first time that a new terminal degree was written and proposed entirely by an African intellectual and then accepted and approved by a predominantly white institution."[17]

The program's second major achievement was that it introduced a new paradigm or system for evaluating the African experience. Previously, Africana narratives were understood from a Western historical perspective and analyzed through Eurocentric modes of reasoning and philosophical theories. Asante's program was the first of its kind to truly break from the

---

15 Karenga, "Founding," 576–603.
16 Karenga, "Founding the First PhD."
17 Mazama, "African American," 24–28.

European model and allow Black students to place themselves at the center of their own history, culture, and experience. As a result, this program provided Black students with agency in obtaining knowledge about their identities. Finally, Mazama asserts that the establishment of a doctoral program by Black intellectuals disproves the racist sentiments that educational systems created by whites are superior. Moreover, Afrocentricity enables all people to add their unique perspectives to educational discussions, which expands the scope of the university and its relevance to student life.[18]

As similar programs spread, Asante continued his work by utilizing Afrocentrism to decolonize Africana studies. Asante, in "A Discourse on Black Studies," argues that Africology involves the Afrocentric study of African phenomena, and Africologists must agree upon what to emphasize in their academic work to further understand the African experience. Asante supports Afrocentrism as the way forward, as it upholds critical thinking, the scientific method, humanism, and the agency of Africana peoples everywhere. Due to the theory's critique of the West, Afrocentrism provides a degree of liberation for those who adhere to its principles. Afrocentrism also strips the power from oppressors to institute societal, cultural, and epistemic norms, which effectively decolonizes Africana studies and hands authority back to the people who are central within African narratives. Asante concludes by asserting the benefits of Afrocentricity, including its functions as a critique of social history and as a mechanism for evaluating economic and infrastructural situations.[19]

The push for Afrocentrism also led to the development of Afrocentric schools in the United States. In 1993, there were less than twenty Afrocentric schools, but in 1999, there were around four hundred of them. These schools are largely independent charter institutions. Charter schools are often ideal for Afrocentric education because they allow for curricular freedom while demanding high achievement. Afrocentric charter schools may also be utilized to decrease the achievement gap between Black and white students. Out of a comprehensive literature review, the following description of Afrocentric schools in the United States was constructed:

---

18   Mazama, "African American."
19   Asante, "Discourse."

Afrocentric schools legitimize African knowledge and perspectives.

Afrocentric schools build community and reinforce cultural practices.

Afrocentric schools further the study of indigenous languages.

Afrocentric schools encourage the ideals of community service.

Afrocentric schools contribute to the formation of positive relationships.

Afrocentric schools communicate the importance of agency and self-sufficiency within one's people while respecting the value of others.

Afrocentric schools uphold preserving culture while maintaining critical thinking.[20]

In recent years, Afrocentric schools have become less popular. Currently, there is not enough demand from families, the tuition is too expensive, and bureaucratic red tape makes managing Afrocentric charter schools difficult. For example, Bernida Thompson, founder of Roots Activity Learning Center, had to shut down certain grade levels within her Afrocentric school because there were not enough students. Thompson believes that a reason for this shift is the diversity of school options available to students. When discussing the variety of educational institutions today, Thompson says, "When you haven't had choices all your life and all of a sudden you have eighty-five different choices, you walk away from your culture and heritage."[21] There are also concerns that charter schools promote segregation due to their racial isolation. According to Myron Orfield, the director of the Institute on Metropolitan Opportunity at the University of Minnesota, saying that all-Black schools are "culturally affirming" or "culturally specific" is "the new flavor for rotten segregated schools." Moreover, Afrocentric schools are at risk of being shut down by public charter school boards due to poor performance on standardized testing.[22]

---

20 Murrell, "Chartering," 565–83.
21 Cohen, "Afrocentric."
22 Cohen, "Afrocentric."

A study published in the *Journal of African American Studies* found that there were twenty-seven functioning Afrocentric schools in the United States. Out of the twenty-three that met the study's analytical criteria, 34 percent of the schools met or surpassed basic expectations for standardized testing regarding their state-wide adequate yearly progress (AYP) status. Examples include the Joseph Littles-Nguzo Saba Charter School in Palm Beach, Florida, which has 180 to 200 students from grades K-8; from 2004 to 2011, this school did not meet its AYP. However, some schools did achieve basic requirements. The Woodlawn Community School in Chicago instructs 245 students from preschool to sixth grade in the Kemetic virtues of Ma'at, Nguzo Saba, and the Seven Principles of Kwanza; from 2004 to 2012, the school generally met its AYP standards—the only exception being 2011, when it did not achieve basic standardized scores.

The study emphasizes the rise of school choice in educational discussions, as well as the importance of African American students in this debate. Since charter schools arose due to dissatisfaction with the general public school system, this study recommends further investigation into Afrocentric schools as a place for African American students who are currently disenfranchised by failing school systems. This study concludes by endorsing the development of Afrocentric charter schools so as to gain legitimacy and recognition. By doing this, the study hopes that these schools will become a practical option for African American students currently being underserved by urban public schools.[23]

At the International Conference on Decolonizing Our Universities in 2011, Asante extended Afrocentrism to universities within Africa. Asante says he knows of no true African universities and argues that the quality of university education in Africa is determined by its resemblance to European education: universities in Africa mimic Western education and, in the process, disregard African epistemologies. Asante advocates that universities in Africa must be restructured to save African perspectives and proposes reforming curriculum so as to begin with studies of Egypt and Nubia instead of Greece. He cites the construction of the pyramids (which occurred before the formation of Greece and its civilization) as one of the various reasons African history should be taught before European history. By doing so, Asante suggests that the power of

---

23 Teasley et al., "School Choice," 99–119.

African societies will be established in the minds of students, which will correct current chronological misconceptions and counteract notions of European epistemological supremacy.

Asante also urges that universities should teach ancient African philosophy, which predated Greek philosophy, for many Greek philosophers traveled to Africa to study philosophy. Additionally, Asante argues that a school curriculum is a political instrument, and because current curricula in Africa are bereft of African history, culture, as well as frames of reference, African universities have not been decolonized. Therefore, since he considers many European epistemologies to be arising from ancient African civilizations, Asante recommends that all curricula be reassessed and restructured to effectively communicate the African legacy of systems of knowledge.[24]

Asante's establishment of the first PhD program in African American studies, coupled with the expansion of Afrocentrism, has assisted in decolonizing Africana studies by providing an epistemic perspective that liberates those oppressed by Eurocentric institutions. Asante rails against the Eurocentrism present in so many educational institutions and encourages universities to broaden their curricula to include different modes of thinking.

In an interview with Dr. George Yancy, a professor of philosophy at Duquesne University, Asante proclaimed, "Intellectual space must be shared because all humans have contributed to human civilization. The ancient African philosophers such as Amenhotep, the son of Hapu, Imhotep, Ptahhotep, Amenemhat, Merikare, and Akhenaten lived hundreds, even thousands of years before Socrates, Plato, and Aristotle. Why is it that children do not learn that the African Imhotep built the first pyramid? Our children do not know that Hypatia, Plotinus, and St. Augustine were born in Africa."[25] Asante, therefore, pushes for a broadened education that provides alternative perspectives and, in essence, does not accept Western ideas without critical thought. To achieve this, Asante urges the restructuring of curricula to accurately represent human history and oppose white supremacy in the education system.

There has been a generic critique of the "Africanist Africologists" (Molefi Asante school) concerning their inability to be eclectic and their

---

24 KillahManjaro, "Decolonising."
25 Yancy and Asante, "Molefi Kete Asante."

insistence on being either Eurocentric or Afrocentric with no middle ground. This stance does not play well among many academics and is quite unsustainable in the intellectual world dominated by the Western academy. This was a debate in the early 1980s when the Asante school at Temple was engaged in an all-out war with the Yale school (Henry Louis Gates being the face of Yale, along with Anthony Appiah). At that time, Molefi Asante believed you could not teach African American studies if you were not of African descent. The problem is that without a balance, no school of thought is supreme or all-encompassing. The Milwaukee school (which is the closest disciple of Asante) with its Africology department at UW-Milwaukee, has never advanced beyond the local influence. Students in its Africa Immersion Schools (three middle schools in Milwaukee) failed miserably in academic performance and social adjustment for many reasons, including the marginalization of Western influence in education. The problem is simple to diagnose: ultimately the ideas are Western (the English language), and the source of the funding is Western (the dollar).

Archie Mafeje and the Anticolonial Movement

Archibald Boyce Monwabisi Mafeje, otherwise simply known as Archie Mafeje, should be considered one of the pioneers of the anticolonialist movement in African scholarship. While there are some disagreements about the application of his research methods, Mafeje's scholarship makes it clear that anticolonialism as a distinct philosophy ultimately strives to find a non-European and, more specifically, an African-centered view of the African people and their history. This brief section will examine just how Mafeje argued for an Afrocentric approach through his activism and work but also demonstrate how Mafeje's legacy lives on and how his ideas can serve as the implementation of anticolonialist ideals.

Indeed, Mafeje is considered to be a hero in African scholarship. His influence was profoundly felt by other scholars around him, as well as by scholars who value Afrocentric history in general. In a tribute to Mafeje after his death in 2007 by several of his fellow colleagues, he was praised for his work that managed to reach across all disciplines. Furthermore, he was described as being remarkably combative with his contemporaries who were writing on similar issues. But this combativeness was mainly about passion. Mostly, he ridiculed any contemporary who adhered to Western values in their research because he embodied the anticolonialist spirit. He also constantly encouraged his peers to "resist the intellectual servitude" that defined academia and to find "liberation" in the collective mindset of society.[26] Upon his death, his colleagues found a kernel of wisdom that represents his legacy and keeps his memory alive: "Keep the Mafeje spirit alive by investing ourselves with dedication to the quest for the knowledge we need in order to transform our societies—and the human condition for the better.[27]

Mafeje believed in "ethnographic inquiries," as he thought that the best way to learn about the African people and their history was by gaining firsthand knowledge of them[28]—in other words, not from a colonialist perspective. It is important to emphasize that Mafeje was undoubtedly an anticolonialist theorist, but he also wrote with an Afrocentric focus. He wrote two pieces on Africanity in 2000 and 2001,[29] making a case for the relevance of Africanity connected with ongoing debates of the time. However, his legacy should not be considered just one of Africanity but also of the larger question of methodology.[30] Mafeje's main contributions are, instead, in his Afrocentric beliefs in general, as well as in his belief that "ideographic inquiry" is more valuable than "nomothetic enquiry" in anthropological studies.[31] In other words, researchers should not look at the data through the lens of their own presumptions or preconceived theories. Instead, they should let the data "speak" and bring about theories. This means that if the data contradict researchers' assumptions, the researchers should not bend the data to match said assumptions. This also means that if the data contradict established theories, these established theories should be revisited.[32]

Arguably, Mafeje was a man ahead of his time in that he did not rely on Western thoughts and research to form conclusions about the African

---

26 Olukoshi et al., "Tribute," 395.
27 Olukoshi et al., "Tribute," 396.
28 Sharp, "Mafeje and Langa," 165.
29 See Archie Mafeje's "Africanity: A Combative Ontology," and "Africanity: A Commentary," 14–16.
30 Nyoka, "Mafeje," 5–6.
31 Mafeje, "On the Articulation," 6.
32 Nyoka, "Mafeje," 6.

continent. Instead, he wanted the African continent to be the sole source of information. In this way, he allowed for an approach in the use of language to ebb into the academic consciousness of its African recipients, a language that was not the European white man's. He let the African people speak for themselves so that their stories could no longer be silenced as they had been for generations. Mafeje's respect for the African perspective has paved the way for contemporary scholars like Dr. Olivia U. Rutazibwa to look for African-based stories from African people, stories that will help break the collectively colonized mindset of the world and bring about a true democracy.[33] Mafeje revolutionized the concept of academics by refusing to believe that the standards developed by Western minds were the only ones that could apply to each and every concept.

Although Mafeje disavowed Western methods, he also argued that researchers should not limit themselves to any one standardized research method. They should instead be "authentic interlocutors" in that they should research topics on their own terms[34], thereby forging methods that were likely established with a colonialist mindset. Indeed, one of Mafeje's greatest academic qualities is his advocacy for a discursive method of research: "I preferred to let my work speak for me. . . . This as it may, dispensing with existing epistemologies does not solve methodological problems in the inter-mediate term and the long run."[35] On this point, however, Mafeje received a fair criticism. If he was a believer in African-centered thought, was he not also just as biased as other researchers he criticized? True, his other colleagues may have had a Eurocentric bias, but was he not just as guilty for having an Afrocentric bias? Many have critiqued Mafeje on this point. One such critic, Nabudere, asked: "But in such a case how different is he from the colonial scholar who claims to be 'neutral' and 'objective'?"[36]

Mafeje and other like-minded academics could never quite overcome this cognitive dissonance, even after Mafeje's death. However, Mafeje can be spared from some criticism if one considers how he did not necessarily believe that facts and interpretations were the same. He admitted that "theory-building" must be based on interpretation and not facts

---

33   TEDx Talks, "TEDxFlanders."
34   Nyoka, "Mafeje," 6.
35   Mafeje, *Anthropology*, 55–56.
36   Nabudere, "Archie Mafeje," 3–4.

alone.[37] Mafeje looked at African issues through an Afrocentric lens that was by definition not neutral. After all, he was bold enough to challenge Eurocentric beliefs on Africa's development and to propose models that are arguably more representative of various African experiences.

In Mafeje's defense, no scholar—no matter how well intended he or she may be—can ever be entirely neutral in any given situation. After all, all human beings are products of their experiences and the information to which they are exposed. Perhaps Mafeje himself began to realize this over time as his academic thinking matured. Therefore, Mafeje's academic triumph is not that he somehow defied human nature and remained neutral on all accounts. It is unrealistic to expect any reputable scholar to break this sort of ground. Instead, Mafeje's academic triumph is his boldness to counterattack the vast majority of research that was Eurocentric in its nature. By believing in "authentic interlocution," he essentially rebelled against arbitrary systems of correctness and prized individual autonomy in scholarship.

Mafeje was unique because his academic work was fully aligned with his political views and activism.[38] Mafeje in his early twenties was a political activist during the split by the Non-European Unity Movement (NEUM). NEUM had been led by Isaac Bangani Tabata, who argued after the separation that Africans were capable of being mobilized because of their "land hunger."[39] Mafeje sided with Tabata, and the lessons he gained from his experience can be found in his academic work.[40]

In 1978 Mafeje wrote his first political piece, titled "Soweto and its Aftermath," which was about the student revolts that occurred in Soweto on June 16, 1976. He analyzed the students' strategies, as well as their relationship with the South African urban workers and the South African liberation movement itself.[41] Ultimately he concluded that while the students did achieve some victories, their lack of strategy when it came to the pushback from the establishment led to errors.[42] He stated explicitly that "revolutionary commitment is impossible without a guiding

---

37 Mafeje, *Theory*, 10.
38 Ntsebeza, "What Can We Learn," 923.
39 Drew, "Social Mobilization."
40 Ntsebeza, "What Can We Learn," 925.
41 Mafeje, "Soweto," 17–18.
42 Mafeje, "Leadership," 21.

ideology, a program of demands and a clear policy."[43] This powerful criticism can also be paralleled with his belief that scholarship cannot progress if it adheres to arbitrary standards. It is also worth noting that Mafeje was personally affected by politics because he was forced into self-imposed exile during apartheid in South Africa.[44] It is unlikely that such an experience, lasting for most of his lifetime, would have little to no bearing on his perspectives on colonialism and African scholarship.

In varied ways, activism can be an essential component to living an anticolonial academic vision. By being an activist for democracy and equity, a scholar can become fully aware of how peoples are affected in different spaces and times. Subsequently, a scholar can write more accurately on the true issues at hand. Furthermore, as an activist, a scholar can serve as a living example of anticolonialism at work through the concerted restraint against oppression and injustice in society. Therefore, according to Dr. Achille Mbembe, decolonization and activism work in a mutually beneficial relationship; theories on decolonization can strengthen activists' platforms of democracy and equity, and activism can broaden the reach of decolonization. Additionally, Mbembe asserts that activism toward democracy and equity can be a tool the general public can use to become more interested in and involved in the decolonization vision.[45] Certainly, it is prudent to conclude, at this juncture, that Mafeje helped contribute to these virtues of decolonized activism, and his spirit lives on through modern African scholars who continue to push for a more equal and just society.

Above all, Mafeje is a cornerstone of anticolonialist ideals. This is in spite of the fact that his scholarship has been somewhat obscured by his supposed inconsistency between his self-proclaimed neutrality and an evident African-centered perspective; yet his influence on African scholarship has carried on. Without a doubt, those who knew Mafeje best could not blame him for his research methods, which served their purpose and abundantly shed new light on a continent that had previously been belittled and oversimplified by those who had never truly lived there, including those who, like Conrad, saw Africa as the "heart of darkness." Mafeje was a force of action and a brilliant mind, who has earned

---

43 Mafeje, "Leadership," 23.
44 Devisch et al., *Postcolonial Turn*, 2.
45 Duke Franklin Humanities Institute, "Achille Mbembe."

worldwide renown because of his determination to give Africa its own voice. Undoubtedly, he achieved just that. His ideals have been embodied in many African studies scholars and is the best evidence of anticolonialism in action.

Samir Amin and Marxism

Samir Amin (1931–2018) was the radical voice of modern Marxism, a voice that has resonated far and wide for over forty years. Though his opinions may be considered unpopular by staunch capitalists and globalists, Amin continuously warned of the steep decline of capitalism and the need for socialism. He argued that capitalism has experienced two crises within its lifetime—the second of which is still extant in 2018. He also maintained, contrary to some popular opinion, that capitalism is not expected to recover and that it is the modern manifestation of a vicious, collective imperialism that forces Global South countries into submission

Figure 7.4. Samir Amin in 2012. Still photograph from video recording of Amin speaking at the Subversive Festival in Zagreb. Source, Rosa Luxemburg Foundation. https://www.youtube.com/watch?v=hdQLp0sDh8w. Creative Commons License CC-BY 3.0.

and increases global inequity. This section will briefly examine Amin's life and his accomplishments, as well as what his insights mean for the anticolonial philosophy.

Amin was born in Cairo, Egypt, in 1931. He received his first university degree at Institut d'Etudes Politiques de Paris in 1952, and his PhD from the Sorbonne in 1957 on "the origins of underdevelopment—capitalist accumulation on a world scale." In 1957 he also received a mathematical statistics certificate from L'institut national de la statistique et des etudes economiques. From 1957 to 1960, he was in Egypt and part of a planning agency. By 1960 he had been forced to leave Egypt because of Gamal Abdel Nasser's persecution of Communists. From 1960 to 1963, he was in Mali and part of its Ministry of Planning. By 1966, he was a full-time professor in Paris-Vincennes and Dakar, Senegal. From 1980 until his death, he was the director of the Third World Forum. Furthermore, from 1997 also until his death, he was the chair of the World Forum for Alternatives.[46] In August of 2018, he passed away in Paris, where his body now rests.[47]

Throughout his entire career, Amin emphasized that since capitalism's inception, this economic system was doomed to struggle due to its inherently weak foundations. Even though it has undoubtedly seen prosperous times—particularly from about 1945 to 1975[48]—it has also experienced two major crises: the first being from about 1871 to 1945, and the second being from around the mid-1970s until the present day.[49] According to Amin, the beginning of the end was in the year 1971, when the US dollar was "delinked" from the gold standard, and the average growth rate of the Economic Triad—comprising Europe, Japan, and the United States—fell by half of what it had been between the years 1945 and 1975. Since this time, the average growth rate has continued to decline, and there is no hope for it to return to what it was in the three decades after the Second World War. This means that capitalism can never return to the glory days of expansion and growth. Undoubtedly, this trend is alarming, but some economists have argued that this trend is only discussed because the "center" of capitalism has shifted from the Triad to Brazil, China, and

---

46 John et al., "There is a Structural Crisis."
47 Patnaik et al., "In Memoriam."
48 Global University for Sustainability, "Crisis."
49 John et al., "There is a Structural Crisis."

India. However, Amin, not being one to simply shirk logic for the sake of conformity, completely disagreed with this belief because these countries, known as the "peripheries," still remain suppressed by the Triad. As such, they are not truly experiencing any benefits that capitalism has to offer.[50]

Amin saw capitalism as a dying system because its main beneficiaries—the Triad—have become more violent due to diminishing returns. Because of this pattern, Amin claimed that capitalism had reached a new state of what he called "senile capitalism"—a form of capitalism that is dangerous and destructive, even as it faces imminent death: for "either you kill it, or it kills you."[51] Capitalism in the past has responded to struggles by creating a monopoly. However, the monopoly created in the modern era is not the same as it was before. It is now, in Amin's terms, a "generalized monopoly capitalism" because it is based upon a greater centralization of capital for only a select few.[52]

This centralization of capital is not merely qualitative but quantitative. From 1975 to 1990, the quantitate centralization for the Triad became undeniable, and this trend has continued ever since.[53] As such, generalized monopoly capitalism means more than just controlling territory through colonies; it is now much more invasive and ideological in nature because it involves the influencing of entire economies from afar. Furthermore, capitalism is much more ruthless now because it no longer has to respond to an elite bourgeoisie or other entrepreneurs as it did in the past. As a result, there is no longer a market but rather a monopoly that moves the market entirely on its own. Even the mass media serve as a "clergy" of sorts to this monopoly because the monopoly orders them to repeat the same information to the public, and the media happily comply. The public therefore is deceived into thinking that they are free, when in reality they are actually just consumers glued to their TV sets.[54]

For these reasons, senile capitalism is dangerous and a form of "soft totalitarianism." This capitalism cannot qualify as "hard totalitarianism" because it demands mindless acceptance rather than support of the system. However, Amin qualified, the system can become "hard

---

50 Global University for Sustainability, "Crisis."
51 Global University for Sustainability, "Crisis."
52 Global University for Sustainability, "Crisis."
53 NewsClickin, "Samir Amin."
54 Global University for Sustainability, "Crisis."

totalitarianism" if others resist the ways of the system. The system will attack the people and force them to capitulate. In fact, the system could literally criminalize one's resistance.[55]

There are other ways in which senile capitalism is different from any other form of capitalism. The generalized monopoly strategy for the first time unites the central capitalist nations—the Triad, as well as its allies Canada and Australia—in a sort of collective imperialism. In other words, this 15 percent of the world no longer has its own separate imperialisms—American imperialism, British imperialism, and so on. This 15 percent of the world also no longer has colonies, at least in the Old World sense. Instead, this 15 percent must work together as a unit. However, this imperialism is not at all viable because it leaves the remaining 85 percent of the world "miserable" (with the exception of China), and it must systematically use force in order to make ends meet.[56]

Amin calls for "revolutionary advances" across the world, lest peace and democracy become completely out of reach for all countries. Happily, in Amin's lifetime, he saw individual revolutions of sorts taking place, and he certainly commended them for their recognition of inequities in the world. However, he also criticized such revolutions because they failed to put the capitalist system at the heart of their critique. For these reasons, Amin acknowledged that these revolutions were a good start, but in order for real change to happen, they must not only unify but also establish strategies that retaliate against the capitalist system. Furthermore, Amin argued, national and international organizations should be built in order to make these revolutions a reality. Amin clarified: these organizations cannot be, as Lenin said, of "one class, one party." They should instead respect diversity and diversify the party system. Sadly, this revolutionary form will not come about anytime soon, according to Amin. Yet, when it does, it will cause the monopoly to be on the defensive.[57]

Amin was a modern Marxist nationalist—two concepts that may instinctively cause some confusion because they are on the surface antithetical to what some deem to be progressive. Even worse, nationalism is often wrongly attributed to fascism. However, Amin was not a fascist nationalist. In fact, he was vehemently opposed to fascism, and he

---

55 Global University for Sustainability, "Crisis."
56 Global University for Sustainability, "Crisis."
57 Global University for Sustainability, "Crisis."

claimed that modern capitalism and its supporters were the true revitalization of fascism, particularly because modern capitalism discourages any entity that opposes it.[58] Indeed, Amin argued that many wrongly condemn nationalism because they do not understand exactly what it means: for Amin, it was the philosophy that nations should always act in their own best interest and not be slaves to a system (capitalism) that suppresses their autonomy.[59]

Because Samir Amin was of such a worldview, he was cautiously optimistic about the election of Donald Trump, while much of the Western world was either laughing in disbelief or paralyzed with fear. With Hillary Clinton's defeat, former President Obama's NATO and globalization agenda could be squelched. For Amin, this is a good thing because while NATO and globalization may appear to be unifying, they actually act to "guarantee [the West] . . . domination of the entire planet."[60] In fact, Amin believed that the policies of NATO and the positions of globalization are symptoms of the greater liberal globalization movement, whereby African countries are stripped of their natural resources and South Asia, Latin America, and India are manipulated in different but equally devastating ways.[61]

However, even though the defeat of Hillary Clinton is a positive outcome, according to Amin, he remained only cautiously optimistic because, as of the election of 2016, then-candidate Trump did not necessarily state his opinions outright about capitalism. Furthermore, he was not even close to the ideal candidate in Amin's eyes because he was a billionaire—by definition, someone with plenty of assets and monopolies of his own. Yet the worst part about Trump, in Amin's estimation, was his "false" nationalism, in that Trump appears to criticize globalism but also strives to strengthen Washington so that it can keep its allies subordinate to the United States.[62] Indeed, when President Trump recites his mantra "America first," he does not prize the autonomy of other nations: he undermines them.

---

58   Amin, "Return," 1.
59   Amin, "Election."
60   Amin, "Election."
61   John et al., "There Is a Structural Crisis."
62   Amin, "Election."

Amin said that because of monopoly capitalism's methods and the extensive control benefiting the Triad, one "cannot dissociate capitalism from imperialism."[63] This point is arguably Amin's greatest legacy. His radicalism, though perhaps off-putting to some, holds tremendous truth because of this statement. Amin argued for why Marx was a man ahead of his time who foresaw the fall of capitalism while his contemporaries were reaping its temporary benefits.[64] With this statement, Amin demonstrated why Marxism is "not a dead philosophy"[65] but rather one that proves painfully relatable and desirable in the twenty-first century. Ultimately, this statement showed why Amin was an anti-imperialist: not only for ethical reasons but also for quantitative and economic reasons that cannot be easily ignored.

Through Amin's work, it is clear that imperialism is also not a dead philosophy. It is a living parasitical ideology that evolves over time and seeps into systems that are supposedly virtuous, like capitalism and globalism. Imperialism, considered to be the standard historical system from the seventeenth through twentieth centuries, was also considered virtuous; it is only with time that many have seen that this was not the case. Amin, like Marx, was ahead of his time and saw how this "generalized monopoly capitalism" was just as insidious. His warning to the Third World echoes even after his death: do not be fooled by capitalism; it is imperialism in disguise. Furthermore, as Amin insisted, do not let the death of capitalism be the death of humanity: only through socialism and unification can humanity survive this senile capitalist collapse.

Claude Ake: Decolonization, Democracy, and Development

Claude Ake was one of the most influential voices in the field of African political thought during his life, and his philosophies are still discussed today regarding decolonization, democracy, and development in African states. He had the unique experience of living through both periods of colonial domination and political independence in Africa and throughout his life held a variety of different positions. While his work and

---

63 NewsClickin, "Samir Amin."
64 Global University for Sustainability, "Crisis."
65 Cross et al., "In Tribute," 365–77.

philosophy regarding state building and reconstruction focused mainly on post–Cold War conflicts in Africa, many of his insights and arguments are still relevant today.[66] Claude Ake's critique of the state of postcolonial Africa and his neo-Marxist ideas on how to transform the continent are well worth studying, even twenty years after his death. In this section, I will delve into his understanding of the fundamental issues of African civil society and observe how his philosophy can be applied to modern-day Africa.

Before his untimely death in 1996, Claude Ake was developing the Center for Advanced Social Science in Port Harcourt, Nigeria, and close to resigning his seat on a Shell Oil commission in protest of the hanging of Ken Saro-Wiwa.[67] Much like Saro-Wiwa, Ake's death was tragic and subject to conspiracy in some fringe circles, but his legacy as an activist and political thinker lives on. During his life, he worked to find an alternative path of development and decolonization in Africa and sought out others to support him in his mission.[68]

As African states began to tackle the new challenges of independence during the 1950s and 1960s, Claude Ake began to publish his ideas about how Africa can best develop political stability. His first publication in 1967, *A Theory of Political Integration*, focused mainly on finding order and stability in a time riddled with conflict and corruption, but his philosophy changed significantly as time went on.[69] Ake's work *Social Science as Imperialism* was a vastly different take on the theory of development. According to him, the problem of Western social science, which was the model of governance African states attempted to adopt following independence, was that it instituted capitalist values and structures, which in turn inhibit oppressed people.[70] He argued that oppressed people instead needed a social science committed to self-determination rather than strict order.

It should be noted that Ake defined the "state" as a set of interactions and relationships among social groups organized and maintained by

---

66   Arowosegbe, "State Reconstruction," 651–70.
67   Harris, "Still Relevant," 73–88.
68   Harris, "Still Relevant."
69   Harris, "Still Relevant."
70   Harris, "Still Relevant."

political power.[71] He saw the state in Africa as a capitalist phenomenon and in his work addressed the damages to civil society caused by such a form of state domination. Ake argued that capitalist production allows for a high degree of class domination, where people are reduced to their role as commodity bearers, and the economy is dictated by the market. In such a society, people are coerced into dependence on the market and are subject to the rule of capital. The conflict and chaos between social groups are heightened because of the limited autonomy of the state in Africa, where the struggle for power is viciously competitive.

Ake was particularly critical of the weaknesses in the composition of the state in Africa: flaws that inhibit formal freedom, equality, political representation, and competitive politics. He described in his works how if not fundamentally transformed, African states will never meet the expectations of modern statehood. Ake specifically moves away from building upon a Western foundation and turns to Africa's cultural experiences and historical contexts as the foundation for provincializing notions of power. In his mind, Africa must go beyond the borrowed European conceptions of civil society and focus on the societal relations that are uniquely African.[72] As Africa transitions from a continent of colonial states to one made up of sustainable, sovereign nations, they need to be on a path of development appropriate for their individual challenges and population needs. It is wrong to believe that one mode of production or one political model will work in an African state in the same way it would in the West.

Ake created the Center for Advanced Social Science (CASS) to continue trying to develop and decolonialize social science in Africa. While there, he published a number of monographs centered on the prospects of democracy in the continent. One of the first was *Democratization and Disempowerment in Africa*, in which he argued that due to the push by Western governments and the idea of liberal democracy, Africa is democratizing the disempowerment of everyday people and marginalized groups. Ake described how the conception of democracy as "electoral competition" is an advantage to the wealthy and powerful elite, armed with the resources to exploit politics and disadvantaged people. As he argued, such a society is in need of transformation, where everyone can get involved in grassroots movements and have representation in government.

---

71 Arowosegbe, "State Reconstruction."
72 Arowosegbe, "State Reconstruction."

In his 1993 work, "The Unique Case of African Democracy," Ake says, "In order for African democracy to be relevant and sustainable it will have to be radically different from liberal democracy"[73] and must emphasize political and economic rights for all people. He describes how everyday Africans (at the time of publication) tend not to differentiate one's political democracy from economic well-being, and instead see their political empowerment as an important aspect of economic development. In other words, everyday people do not question the demands of the free market because they believe they are contributing to national development and working toward individual benefits. With regard to African liberal democracy, Ake writes:

> African democracy is unique in that it reflects the socio-cultural realities of Africa. Liberal democracy which pretends to universalism is historically specific. It is a child of industrial civilization, a product of a socially atomized society where production and exchange are already commodified, a society which is essentially a market. It is the product of a society in which interests are so particularized that the very notion of common interest becomes problematic, hence the imperative of democracy.[74]

Ake believed that democracy in Africa must be re-created in the context of present realities and cultural arrangements without sacrificing its core principles and values of equality and representation. For him, this meant a "consocietal arrangement—the use of ethnic groups, nationalities and communities as the constituencies for representation," a decentralized system of government with emphasis on individual and communal rights.[75] Ake understood that achieving democracy is not as simple as copying Western nations: for Africa there should be a system that is uniquely African. Though the continent may not look exactly the same as it did twenty or thirty years ago, the principle remains the same. Democracy should be designed to address the needs and concerns of the population, with resources to support people in all social classes and groups. Only then can true development begin.

---

73 Ake, "Unique Case," 239.
74 Ake, "African Democracy."
75 Ake, "African Democracy."

Much of what Ake discussed in his work is relevant today, as many of the problems of capitalist African states continue. Democracy is meaningless if certain groups of people dominate while marginalized groups lack representation and a voice. Furthermore, African governments cannot pretend to adopt economic and political policies that are clearly unsuited to them, allowing certain populations to thrive while others are forced to submit to the demands of the capital elite. It would be beneficial for African states to acknowledge Ake's ideas on decolonizing social sciences and transforming civil society in order to further develop and protect the rights of all African citizens.

Ali Mazrui and Africa's Triple Heritage

African studies, defined as the study of the infrastructure, institutions, and people of Africa and African origin, arises from a complex history not only pertaining to the imposed social, political, and economic systems

Figure 7.5. Ali Mazrui. Bentley Historical Library, University of Michigan. Creative Commons License CC BY 2.0.

upon the continent but also the challenges of validity and assertion of the entire field of study. This wide field includes the evolving perception of the continent from prospective viewpoints of Africans to those of Islamic migrants and influences, as well as the European agenda and now to those calling for continual decolonization.

African studies, through both past influences and present movements, examines the history and conditions of Africa prior to the arrival of Islamic influences. These views on Africa—ranging from appreciation and recognition of the vast diversity of indigenous groups, languages, practices, and traditions, to the condemnation of the unfamiliar and to the expression of cultures as well as "primitive" infrastructure—exemplify the characteristics of varying dominant narratives of the African continent and the contexts of its people. The religious history of Islam has also linked Africa to its origins in many key instances in the founding and preservation of the Islamic faith.[76] Not only has this impacted the interaction of many Islamic regions, but it has also shifted the defining narrative of African Islam. In the Arabo-Persian narrative,[77] the African nations serve to bring Islam into the mainstream of the region/demographic.[78] However, through the rising Pan-African movements and interpretations of Islam, the African Islamic community is finding it challenging to interact with the global community of Muslims, bound not only through similar beliefs and restrictions but by religious scriptures and discursive practices.[79] The earlier perspective of the unique rigidity of the African culture, as exemplified by the unique characterization of African Islam,[80] is reexamined through the placing of African Islamic culture within the larger framework of the global Islamic tradition.

As Islamic institutions transformed established economic and political organizations within the African state, the collective, large-scale imposition of the European influence guided many successive alterations of the grounded institutions of the African continent. The elevated status of Europeans and their role in developing the history of the continent were responsible for Western ideology that sees the African continent as

---

76   Resse, "Islam in Africa," 17–26.
77   Resse, "Islam in Africa."
78   Resse, "Islam in Africa."
79   Resse, "Islam in Africa."
80   Resse, "Islam in Africa."

one dimensional, and acts of colonial intervention were said to be justified through claims of uncivility, superstition-based practices, and criminalized behaviors and cultural expressions. Through the European lens, a negative image of Africa was created that spread worldwide. It was these practices that contributed to the global oppression of not only Africans but the African diaspora that continues to this day in varying social, political, and economic capacities in many Western and non-Western nations.

In the wake of oppressive regimes, anticolonial activists in the twentieth century worked to guide an African perspective of the African nation and its people. This idea was to appreciate the value of the African identity as well as the unique characteristics that were fundamental to the continent and its people. Independence movements across the continent as well as the ideologies of Pan-Africanism contributed and resulted in the rise of many African and Black scholars[81] who called for a decolonization of the dominating perspective foisted upon them by others. While previous bouts of African studies inquired into the quality of lives of African people, they often sought to establish a championed European perspective of the contribution of others to the African continent. The inherent devaluation of the African people and their culture by previous powers, and ideological impositions such as Social Darwinism,[82] prevented African studies from complete cultural convergence with Western ideals. Though African culture was examined, primarily Egyptian civilization, the borders of African studies with regard to the specificities of the African tradition were never fully defined, and the cultural landscape of the African people was distorted in relation to global history.[83]

In the midst of both the Islamic and European influence on the development of Africa one of the most renowned African scholars emerged. Dr. Ali Mazrui is a scholar of African postcolonial theory, alongside his contribution to the understanding of Islamic politics within Africa. Apart from his own considerable academic achievements, Mazrui has assisted in educating many other scholars through his professorships and his writings regarding the importance of recognizing the influence of external ideologies within African society and developing approaches to these impacts and the future of the African continent. In influencing the structure of

---

81 Allen et al., "African Studies," 60–68.
82 Allen et al., "African Studies."
83 Allen et al., "African Studies.

African studies as well as its proliferation within the university, Mazrui challenges the established positions and practices through new ideas. In championing the decolonization of African education, Mazrui focused on placing the new perspective of an African-centered education within the global context by proposing a more flexible curriculum,[84] as well as developing a valuation for traditional skills.[85] Mazrui's ideologies seem to place him in a paradoxical position of turning "outward" or to external divisions in matters of internal focus.[86]

Mazrui also describes the discrepancy between the perception of Africa and its reality through the lens of paradox. In this way, Mazrui challenges the colonial outlook as well as the apparent contradictions between the diversity, richness, and potential of the continent with the contemporary truth of the state of the African nations.[87] While specifically focusing on these key elements of the condition of the African nation, Mazrui exhibits a confrontational style of both speaking and writing, not only when examining the Western position within African infrastructure but also the presence of the Islamic faith and Islamic practices within the global context. Mazrui's *Cultural Forces in the World of Politics*[88] examines the ideas of Salman Rushdie in his portrayal of the Islamic faith in his controversial work *The Satanic Verses*. Mazrui attacks the divisive nature of Rushdie's work[89] regarding the origins and influence of the Islamic faith. Mazrui also focuses on Islam and its interaction with the West, more specifically the United States.[90] Mazrui's work highlights the similarities between the Western values and those of the Islamic faith, and their eventual divergences as well as their social interaction.[91] Here, he explicitly calls for the reexamination of American democracy as well as the relationship between the Israeli forces and those of Palestinian populations.[92] Mazrui, in this sense, conveys not only his own opinion regarding these matters but also

---

84 Mittelman. "Better Intellectual," 153–70.
85 Mittelman, "Better Intellectual."
86 Mittelman, "Better Intellectual."
87 Conrad, "Review," 186–88.
88 Rothchild, "Review," 145–46.
89 Rothchild, "Review."
90 Mazrui, "Islam."
91 Mazrui, "Islam."
92 Mazrui, "Islam."

allows for his audience and others to begin a proper informed discourse as to the impacts and outcomes of these issues.

Mazrui's attempts at not only shifting the paradigm of African studies but also to alter the discourse regarding the development of Africa is best exhibited in his documentary, *The Africans: A Triple Heritage*. Here, Mazrui highlights a central ideology held by many scholars: that Africa comprises an intersection of three heritages—indigenous, Islamic, and Western.[93] It is through this intersectionality that African nations must work to provide a better future for their people without rejecting any of these heritages but also without forgetting the consequences of this diversity as well. Mazrui's approach through this series ultimately demonstrated his imposition on the postcolonial theory of the continent through pointed links between the African state of mind, quality of life, and future projection as a result of Western and Islamic interaction. Mazrui's series is seen as an eye-opening work through which African values and needs are brought to the center[94] of the global society. Nevertheless, the work has also been criticized for positing extreme negative outcomes of global politics and Western domination, including Mazrui's calculated possibility of a nuclear war.[95] The series has also been criticized for its direct accusations to the colonial powers and underplaying the complacency of the indigenous powers in the face of colonial regimes.

Ali Mazrui's contribution to the field of African studies can be explored from multiple dimensions. Through his writings, he committed to challenging structures presented to the African people as well as those proliferated by the Western standard. For Mazrui, it was important to respect the necessity of introspective action without removing the African power and presence from the globalized world. Mazrui's criticism of the position of Islam within the Western world, as well as its preservation among the global Muslim community, not only showed his commitment to the incorporation of multiple heritages across the African culture but also shored up his stance regarding the importance of global participation and inclusivity.

Mazrui's criticism of governments[96] demonstrated an ideology focused on accountability regarding the interaction between the people

---

93 Adem, "Ali A. Mazrui," 135–52.
94 Adem, "Ali A. Mazrui."
95 Martin, "Ali Mazrui."
96 Copley et al., "In Memoriam."

and the government, as well as between the intellectual development of people and governments to achieve a self-sustaining future for the African continent. However, Mazrui himself did not escape criticism. His "triple heritage" thesis is seen in some academic circles as a biased assessment coming from a man who struggled hard to marry scholarship with personal religious beliefs. He seemed to use his status to promote Islam rather than advance scholarship or objectively embrace the other two African heritages. Thus, to his critics, Mazrui was a great scholar with a personal agenda. His controversial personal life was always as interesting as his public contributions to political debates and scholarship.

Women's Voices

The discussion of the voices of decolonization would be incomplete without recognizing women's voices as well. This is especially important as many scholars do not immediately acknowledge the important work done by many pioneering African feminist writers over the last decades. There has been much groundbreaking decolonial literature that centralizes the struggle by women scholars to make their perspectives a major part of scholarship on Africa. Women's theorizing and writing has long been treated as marginal in relation to the "greats," which of course include only male scholars. It is not that there is a lack of female voices in decolonization scholarship; it is just that men who dominate the knowledgescapes consistently ignore women's voices and frame women's concerns as irrelevant.

Thus, I recommend that we begin from this epistemological starting point and try to reconceptualize the boundaries of decolonialization literature. Then we will find that women have been there all along, under the radar, but working hard alongside the so-called great men that have been promoted and worshipped by the field for so long: men whose works have largely ignored not only women's perspectives but have also overlooked the deeply colonial structure of gender in Africa.

A study of the preceding discussions of Asante, Amin, Mafeje, Ake, and Mazrui shows that many feminist writers did the exact same things that men did: advocate an Afrocentric mode of reasoning, promote the decolonizing of academia, advocate for new African methodologies, protest for social change (writing books on varied subjects that apply these principles), creating institutions (Development Alternatives for Women in a New Era [DAWN], African Women for Research and Development [AAWORD], WORDOC at Ibadan, the African Gender Institute at Cape Town, the journal *Feminist Africa*, the journal *JENDA*, etc.), and so on. Of course, just like the men we study, no single woman author covers all the important bases; they focus on particular subjects/activisms, in particular periods, in particular national/social contexts, and maximize their relevance by not being generalists.

On texts/authors, Chandra Talpade Mohanty, is the first major voice from the South one would think of in relation to feminist decolonization theory, and I reference her two seminal works here. However, she is not African. And before her, African feminists who did comparable but less globalized work included Bolanle Awe, Simi Afonja, Nina Mba, Filomina Steady, Fatou Sow, Zenebeworke Tadesse, Nawal El-Sadaawi, and Christine Achola Pala Okeyo, among others. This first generation was followed by perhaps a more vibrant generation whose works reinscribed African women's theorizing into global narratives: for example, Oyeronke Oyewumi, Filomina Steady (again), Amina Mama, Ayesha Imam, Akosua Adomako Ampofo, Takyiwaah Manuh, Patricia McFadden, and Sylvia Tamale, among others.[97]

---

97 For intellectual stature and depth/breadth of contribution to the decolonization corpus, I would recommend Amina Mama for her pioneering writing on many fronts and for linking women's issues with critical discourses on democracy, development, and the state in an African context struggling with authoritarianism and social conflicts. I would also recommend Oyeronke Oyewumi for profoundly shattering foundational theoretical assumptions of Western and colonial literatures both about women and about society, culture, tradition, and epistemology. I recommend both because they were successful in globalizing their work and in entrenching their specific critical feminist African perspectives in the academy, much in the same way that people like Molefi Asante sought to do. I have seen Oyewumi's work on syllabi/reading lists in Europe, across Africa, the United States, and elsewhere. Amina Mama was instrumental and pivotal to the success of the Cape Town African Gender Institute, institutionalizing some of the ideas she and her fellows had written about for years and making the AGI a hub for all sorts of feminist theorizing by scholars, activists, poets, writers, politicians, and others from across Africa and the world.

Chapter Eight

Voices of Decoloniality

Introduction

The state of the world presently, that is, the genus of relation between the Global North, the Global South, and the much-purported crises of modernity is such that to not decolonize is considered an aberration, a failing of cultural and political implications often extending across generations. One idea in support of this is that the continued insistence on decoloniality and decolonization measures as endless political-cum-cultural projects evince some sort of failure: the failure of victory. Arguably, the failure of victory can be reinterpreted as undervaluing decoloniality as a point of departure and not as a destination point. We need to move beyond this ideological dialectic to see how these projects directly contribute to a world that is transmodern and pluriversal.

Since failing to decolonize is gradually becoming a cultural transgression in the Global South, it is worthwhile to examine the voices recommending decoloniality through critical analysis and insightful discourse. It is likewise imperative to engage decoloniality and its extensively complex ideological possibility, vis-à-vis the hypothesis and conclusions of some of its major forerunners, especially from the myriad of perspectives with which they have broached the subject, developed the field, and added to a cross-fertilization of knowledge. This essentially underscores decoloniality as an emancipating tool for subalternized peoples as well as in studies concerned with the matter of decolonization.

Thinkers and scholars continually (re)visit the theoretical possibilities of decoloniality, ideologically expounding on the corrective dialectics decolonial studies engenders with the view of rethinking, generating, and adapting decoloniality to the ever-changing fabric and structure of the Global South and much of the world in general. These scholarly and timely interventions sustain the remarkable multiplicity of ideas located within the heart of decolonial epistemology and studies while also undergirding the concept and utility of decoloniality as a toolkit for the epistemological survival of the Global South and its thinkers.[1] As a result, the quality/range of thought abounding within the discourses of decoloniality is as homogenous as it is heterogeneous. The ideas are exigent and contiguous; they showcase not only the presence of a paradigmatic use and interactive blend of anticolonial, de-Westernization, and decolonization thoughts on decoloniality but also the relevance and effectiveness of these thoughts in unpacking the essence of postcolonial societies. Also, they speak to the relevance of decolonizing the postcolonial state or the Global South in general.

Working within the political provisions of countercolonial mechanisms and ideologies are two broad (but not exhaustive) schools of ideologies: the epic and the episodic. Both schools attest to the end of colonialism as an epoch of forced European inhabitation, administration, and control of Africa and its people: that is, the end of colonial Africa as a historical phase. Hence, these schools both recognize the conclusion of European direct control and its application of power in managing the diversity of Africa: both human and nonhuman resources. The point of discontinuity, however, rests at the foot of an irreconcilable concept of the type and range of colonialism's impact in Africa after waves of independence. Hence, while the two schools, broadly representing much of what is possible when it comes to countercolonial enterprises in a postcolonial society, agree that colonialism as a palpable period of foreign (European) dominance, exploitation, and flattening of the cultures and history of Africa, they diverge in their recognition of the impact of such incursion on the postcolonial state of previous sites of colonialism.

Four scholars are revisited here but with differing perspectives essential to providing substantive arguments for decoloniality. It is important to mention that it is possible to draw strict lines between the ideas of these scholars spread across multiple nations and operating from different disciplines. This complexity itself shows how interdisciplinary, far-reaching, and equally relevant decoloniality and its logic are to both scholars and nonacademics.

---

[1] Nontyatyambo and Ndlovu-Gatsheni, "Power, Knowledge and Being," 105–34.

Sabelo J. Ndluvo-Gatsheni

Belonging to the epic school is Sabelo J. Ndlovu-Gatsheni, whose archive on decoloniality mirrors and refreshes the argument that the machineries of colonialism are still operational, both in covert and overt forms, in postcolonial nations. Whether direct or indirect, the implementation of colonial apparatuses and logics of control in postcolonial sites are achieved through coloniality, which is the sum total of the consequences of the extensive alterations to African past, present, and future by European imperial control.[2] While not having propounded the term "coloniality," Ndlovu-Gatsheni's intervention in the application and localization of that term to truthfully capture lived realities and experiences in Africa is refreshing and considered to be original, expedient, and relevant.

Ndluvo-Gatsheni's provocative contributions as well as excursions into the treacherous terrain of coloniality to seek its various transmutations and the forces upholding it (or with which it asserts and maintains itself), have made him an important addition to a long list of notable voices on decoloniality. His ability to tease out the faux-advancements in African nations on intellectual (epistemological) and nationalistic fronts as mired in retrogressive politics as well as perpetuating European paradigms of control[3] and imperial designs[4] attest to a scholarship attuned to the shifting nature of postcolonial Euro-American dominance of Africa: the power-plays and subtle inequalities that have drastic long-term consequences. His inquiries on the systematic inequalities preserved by postcolonial structures and practices upheld as nationalistic uncovered them not only as bogus indices of development but as vectors of retrogression.

One important ideology located within the web of ideas Ndlovu-Gatshen works with is "Euro-North American-centric modernity."[5] Europe being the center of modernity and its initial global reach to the corners of the world had allowed the promotion of Eurocentric ideals that failed to recognize the humanity of others.[6] Its insistence on rationality as the benchmark of humanity and civilization (civilized cultures) allowed it to fashion a paradigm of difference that alienated others,

---

2   Ndlovu-Gatsheni, "Global Coloniality," 182–202.
3   Nontyatyambo and Ndlovu-Gatsheni, "Power, Knowledge and Being."
4   Ndlovu-Gatsheni, "World," 80–96.
5   Ndlovu-Gatsheni, "Decoloniality," 485–96.
6   Ndlovu-Gatsheni, "World."

dehumanized non-Europeans, stagnated the natural order and progression of non-European cultures as well as created various staggering levels of epistemicides, genocides, and epistemic violence. Ndlovu-Gatsheni charts a genealogy that recognizes the impetus guiding the integration and centrality of these imperial interventions in non-European centers as shaped by philosophies of European civilization dating as far back as the fifteenth century.[7]

Sabelo's archive of work is particularly enlightening within the ever-increasing discourse of decoloniality and decolonization given his systematic unpacking of the resilient and lasting indices of colonialism in a theoretically postcolonial age. Sabelo's theoretical but sufficiently methodical uncovering of how the West's (Euro-America) takeover of Africa, riding roughshod over the continent's epistemologies, is bound up in coloniality, what he duly conceives of as Euro-North and America-centric modernity, building on the theoretical and discursive directions provided by major thinkers in the field of decoloniality like Boaventura de Sousa Santos, Walter Mignolo, Anibal Quijano, and Nelson Maldanado-Torres.[8] The understanding that these interventions are no longer solely activated within non-European centers of European control but now constitutive of globality and global power frames his submission that Africa resides on the lowest rung of a global power structure.

Given that his archive resonates within a larger pool of intellectualism, Ndlovu-Gatsheni has not only accentuated the ideological fundaments upon which his decolonial work is based but also devoted resources in acknowledging and recognizing these sources as paving the way for his scholarship. His article on ideological postures repudiating global matrices of power and their historical enunciation[9] identifies scholars like Frantz Fanon, Ngugi wa Thiong'o, W. E. B. Du Bois, Aime Cesare, Julius Nyerere, Ali Mazrui, and Marcus Garvey among others as laying the groundwork for decolonial interventions, which not only identifies the structures of oppression normalized in the postcolony but also the way they have been normalized.

---

7   Ndlovu-Gatsheni, "Entrapment," 331–53; Ndlovu-Gatsheni, "Genealogies," 11–38.
8   Ndlovu-Gatsheni, "Entrapment."
9   Ndlovu-Gatsheni, "When Did the Masks," 1–14.

Each of these scholars has recognized the replacement of the direct colonial model with that of a modern economic and/or political intervention that was marketed as a progression initiative. Ndlovu-Gatsheni in his works engages with the ideas posed by these individuals and many more in his research, entangling them in the term "coloniality" as defined by Nelson Maldanado-Torres.[10] The concept of coloniality emerges in the postcolonial society wherein the direct powers of colonialism have been replaced by a normalization of a "racially hierarchised, imperialistic, colonialist, Euro-American-centric, Christian-centric, hetero-normative, patriarchal, violent and modern world."[11] These ideas have not only achieved a global imbalance of power within the political and economic realms but in the epistemologies, linguistics, relationships, and innovative ideas of former colonized individuals and environments. These ideas project the prescribed perspective Africa, its history, and its limitations for its future. The effect of coloniality, as recognized by Ndlovu-Gatsheni, is to steal the history of Africa, its languages, and its knowledge as seen fit by those who exercise their influence under the new power structures.

The range of Ndlovu-Gatsheni's engagement with coloniality and Africa is wide enough to be the subject of many tomes, but for the sake of engagement, the major themes he dealt with can be identified as follows, displaying the range and substance of his thoughts on decoloniality in Africa:

Euro-North American centered modernity

Decoloniality and African futures

Decoloniality and the Badung Spirit (Conference)

Decoloniality as toolkit for African thinkers

Africa as a locus of enunciation and genealogies of coloniality

Matrices of global coloniality

---

10   Ndlovu-Gatsheni, "When Did the Masks."
11   Ndlovu-Gatsheni, "Decoloniality."

Ndlovu-Gatsheni's important ideas about coloniality representing a specific face of modern imperialism are important, as the author names and identifies an almost-amorphous but pervasive force with equally imperialistic designs and functions. The importance of this thinking cannot be overemphasized in a world where the idea of globalization is deployed by the centers of Eurocentric modernity to push a false narrative of inclusivity in the production of knowledge, generation of broad-scale policies, and faux market/economic strategies that favor Euro-American culture.

The narratives of globalization and cosmopolitanism have the perhaps unintended consequence of glossing over the indices of imperialism; they also cloak the retention of the European model of modernity and perpetuation of inequalities fostered by European epidemics of epistemological violence, colonization of futures, demonizing of cultures, theft of knowledge, othering of humanity, and exoticization of humans. The structure of the modern world has shaped Euro-America as the West, which example is then adopted by the Global South, culminating in what Ndlovu-Gatsheni explains as an "asymmetrical and pyramidal constitution of the modern global political and world ordering."[12] Consequently, when Ndlovu-Gatsheni points out the nature of present-day expression of modernity as imperialist and its domestication in Africa as perpetuating the practice and inequalities of colonialism, his articulation of the fossilization of global power in the West evokes his paradigmatic use of Euro-American-centered modernity.

This modernity recognizes two global power shifts or, more precisely, power redistribution that sustains (present-day) modernity: Euro-North and American-centric modernity, that is, Europe and America. Europe, after rising from its own ashes in the seventeenth century, riding the wave Enlightenment provided, articulated a specific expression of modernity based on its own cultural reforms that the world continues to follow. These structural reforms, such as the emergence of the welfare state, rise in democratic governance, the decline of religion, industrial revolution, decline of kinship authority, devotion and reliance on science and logic, individual subjectivity, popular notions of liberty and freedom, rise of the free market, and practice of capitalism were translocated through

---

12   Ndlovu-Gatsheni, "Provisional Notes."

colonialism and other designs of imperialism like neoliberal capitalism into new(ly) discovered) terrains regardless of the levels of cultural incompatibility.

The success of these translocations hinged on the nature of cultural contact initiated by Europe, which was asymmetrical and imperialist, guided by racist and dehumanizing philosophies that Ndlovu-Gatsheni traces all the way back to European cultural philosophy and thought: for example, the place of rationality in defining human subjectivity, Cartesian subjectivism, and the Lacanian void.[13] All of these he argues were deployed to (1) "other" and dehumanize Africans, so as to justify their enslavement and later colonization; (2) maintain the structural and systemic glorification of Europe and all its represents and goad the rest of the world to aspire to European mores; (3) steal African cultural production under the pretense of guarding these artifacts against cultural irrelevance; and (4) destroy cultural expressions they found unappealing. Ndlovu-Gatsheni situates his ideas in a rich context of anti- and decolonial theorizing that teases out the patterns of European cultural and political incursion into non-European spaces.

With these reflections on Euro-modernity, Ndlovu-Gatsheni is able to identify Europe's contribution to the creation of a "racially hierarchized, imperialistic, colonialist, Euro-American-centric, Christian-centric, hetero-normative, patriarchal, violent and modern world."[14] These realities are integral to European modernity but did not fade away with the end of slavery and colonialism, which were Europe's way of conquering non-European sites. What happened was that a global shift of power occurred, from Europe to America, which continues to mask lopsided power relations between the Global North and Global South.[15] This shift retained the European penchant for imperialistic encounters, so much so that even in recessions where Europe's power as the foremost driver of Euro-modernity and modernization makes room for the emergence of other cultures from the Orient and South America, which he identifies as South-South power blocs such as BRICS (Brazil, Russia, Iraq,

---

13 Ndlovu-Gatsheni, "A World."
14 Ndlovu-Gatsheni, "Decoloniality." See also Ndlovu-Gatsheni, "African Futures," 243–55.
15 Ndlovu-Gatsheni, "Decoloniality."

Congo, South Africa),[16] informing "a Sinocentric economic power and de-Westernisation processes,"[17] a true redistribution of power and deimperialization, decolonization, and de-Westernization does not happen.

Ndlovu-Gatsheni not only informs of the inhibitory consequences of such failures and covert power sharing between Europe and America on African futures and much of the Global South, he ingeniously reaffirms Quijano's idea[18] that America's representation as the major site of imperialism perpetuates the European colonial structure of power and imperialist designs that has contributed to a fixed global power structure perpetually in service of the West, thus creating room for global coloniality. In other words, global coloniality exhibits the transition from European colonialism to Western imperialism with the structures and regnant logic engendered by the form integral to the latter, thus demonstrating the constitution of Euro-North American–centered modernity, which not only fosters the creation of a Global South that stands in contrast to a Global North but also suspends the possibilities of postcolonial nations achieving true independent futures.

The importance of Ndlovu-Gatsheni's work to decoloniality is further exemplified in his work studying the imperial paradigms and global colonial matrices of power that sustain inequality in previous sites of colonialism. Global coloniality is sustained on four levels according to Ndlovu-Gatsheni: colonial matrix of power, being, knowledge, and nature. He calls this the "four facets of coloniality," through which it maintains itself in the imaginations and imaginaries of non-Europeans and shows how the ways of knowing, imagining, and producing knowledge are contaminated or locked up in Euro-American knowledge patterns, which reproduces paradigms of control contrived by Europe for empire creation.[19]

Explicating how decoloniality furthers the discourse and narratives of decolonization, Ndlovu-Gatsheni also identifies how the trio of power, being, and knowledge as matrices of global coloniality exploit African people and must include African approaches and uses of decoloniality as epistemic perspectives. While these are terms attributed to decolonial

---

16 Ndlovu-Gatsheni, "Decoloniality."
17 Ndlovu-Gatsheni, "Decoloniality," 181.
18 Quijano, "Coloniality," 168–78.
19 Nontyatyambo and Ndlovu-Gatsheni, "Power, Knowledge and Being."

thinkers like Walter Mignolo, the perspective that Ndlovu-Gatsheni brings is refreshing. His work illuminates how coloniality of power underpins the capitalist and mercantilist global order spearheaded by Europe and North America, and under which Africa and much of the Global South still languish. Operating in recognition of the importance of the colonial matrix of power as a network of relation of exploitation, control, and domination,[20] his work spotlights the failures of independence in African nations often overlooked as a result of the over-glorification of what independence stood for—the complete withdrawal of European influence—and how acknowledging this through understanding what coloniality of power stands for is crucial for any successful attempt at locating the continued presence and designs of control of the West (read Europe and North America).

Ndlovu-Gatsheni also reflects on how the coloniality of being perpetuates the difference that engendered slavery and colonialism, tracing the ideological designs behind it to the European thoughts rooted in Enlightenment that anchored Euro-modernity. His article "Coloniality and African Futures" furthers ideas pursued in his take on decoloniality as a toolkit for Pan-Africanists. In that article, Ndlovu-Gatsheni links the "othering" of non-Europeans under the guise of liberal humanism and anthropocentricism's philosophical emphasis on rationality to the classification of non-Europeans as barbarians needing salvation. This philosophic foundation anchored Euro-modernity and its messianic complex as global solutions to a nonexistent problem; it also created room for the development and application of the paradigm of difference that had initially set Europe as the standard that the world measured itself against, a paradigm now manifesting as part of an imperial design to sustain coloniality.

This particular trajectory of thought and attempt at historicizing coloniality beyond the period of colonialism, that is, in Europe's own philosophic tradition, creates room for a robust understanding of the nature of global imperial designs and the place of coloniality of knowledge in it. Coloniality of knowledge, as characterized by Ndlovu-Gatsheni, "speaks directly to epistemological colonization whereby Euro-American technoscientific knowledge managed to displace, discipline, destroy alternative knowledges it found outside the Euro-American zones (colonies) while at the same time appropriating what it considered useful to global

---

20   Nontyatyambo and Ndlovu-Gatsheni, "Power, Knowledge and Being," 109.

imperial designs."[21] Reliance on the criterion of rationality as set forth by European philosophy and maintained by their epistemic systems galvanized the creation of paradigms that continued the process of "othering" that characterized the era between the sixteenth century and end of the twentieth century, which has continued in subtle but powerful forms in the twenty-first century. It is his articulation of the technologies of subjectivation, whereby Euro-American epistemologies displaced indigenous knowledge and emplaced the Western knowledge forms, that we understand the transition from European modernity to Western modernity and its implications for African knowledge, epistemic systems, and place in a global knowledge network. Coloniality of knowledge attacks modes of knowing, imagining, and knowledge production, which when understood, allows Africans to mount credible resistance that exposes and erodes the influence of global coloniality.

Coloniality of being pools together these norms of subjectivation and reveals the cultural rationale and political uses of European modes of othering, which Nelson-Maldonado-Torres calls the "Imperial Manichean Misanthropic Skepticism."[22] Othering of humans and demonizing their humanity on the basis of European conceptions of humanity paved way for supremacist thinking that birthed slavery, colonialism, and racism. While emphasizing the need for developing a fourth category, coloniality of nature, which he offers important insights into, Ndlovu-Gatsheni enjoins Pan-African thinkers to think along these lines so as to enable imaginaries of the future that are far removed from Euro-American patterns of knowledge production and would relocate to African knowledge systems.

Ndlovu-Gatsheni's connection of possible Afrocentric futures to an understanding of the past fleshes out the relevance of decolonial epistemic perspective in Africa, which provides his locus of enunciation. This is important, because while Africa belongs to that realm of difference created by a global colonial order (North and South distinction), that which Walter Mignolo references as a reality still persisting in the colonial game and operating from its margins, the modes and patterns of utilizing coloniality are different. As Mignolo argues, decoloniality is a political project

---

21 Nontyatyambo and Ndlovu-Gatsheni, "Power, Knowledge and Being," 110.

22 Nontyatyambo and Ndlovu-Gatsheni, "Power, Knowledge and Being," 112.

of delinking and is executed differently from space to space.[23] Hence, in emphasizing Africa as his locus of enunciation, Ndlovu-Gatsheni opens up spaces for tracking the trajectory and connection of decolonial efforts in the past to present perspectives.[24]

However, despite the excellent take on decoloniality in Africa, there is the minor but also apparent issue in Ndlovu-Gatsheni's connection of decoloniality in Africa as an epistemic liberation tool and consciousness to the Badung Conference[25] when there are historical watersheds abound that serve similar purposes, such as the Makerere Conference of 1963 and the dialectical dialogues it generated. In rethinking the relevance of the conference, Ndlovu-Gatsheni argues that the Badung spirit of decolonization encapsulates "a melange of resistance and struggles against colonial encounters, colonialism, and coloniality—going as far back as the time of the Haitian Revolution (1791–1804)."[26] What his conception instructs is that the Badung Conference can be reflected upon in a way that it becomes in Africa a watershed, predating current decolonial perspectives. Consequently, it "gains a broader canvas as a name for the long-standing anti-colonial resistances and decolonial struggles not only against global imperial designs and breaking from Cold War coloniality but also as a terrain of self-invention in opposition to the Northern domination."[27]

Ndlovu-Gatsheni will be duly credited for locating his thinking within existing African perspectives on decolonization. And although his theorizing on the Badung Conference as projecting a decolonial activist spirit that stretches back to the Haitian Revolution provides a rich source of historical grounding for Africa as part of a Global South liberation movement (decolonial), and indeed liberation movements across the Black Atlantic, it does not avoid the unintended error of existing within a reactionary decolonization campaign forced by the epistemic games of the West. To put this differently, his articulation of the problem within this historical frame falls into an antagonist-resistive pattern: what Mignolo[28] identifies as resisting rather than delinking.

---

23 Mignolo, "Coloniality," 39–44.
24 Ndlovu-Gatsheni, "African Decolonization."
25 Ndlovu-Gatsheni, "Mask of Coloniality."
26 Ndlovu-Gatsheni, "Mask of Coloniality," 1.
27 Ndlovu-Gatsheni, "Mask of Coloniality."
28 Mignolo, "Coloniality."

This is not to say the Badung spirit is not useful—it certainly is, and this has been iterated above. It only has the minor consequence of emphasizing how Africa's decolonial attempts connect the continent to a preexisting and broader de-Westernization/anticolonization formation of empire resistance encapsulated in the Global South against Global North paradigm. This foundation of the paradigm is anchored in a carefully calibrated distraction by global coloniality and imperialist designs to keep ex-colonized imaginations and knowledge occupied in an endless process of resistance. Resistance is useful, but so is reexisting, which is the point of the epistemic imperatives of decoloniality. Mignolo explains it as delinking from the Western global order to relink and affirm useful practices, akin to taking steps back to emphasize what needs to be emphasized rather than be caught up in a battle of which is superior or who is being supremacist.

The aim here is to highlight one potential drawback of the larger context that the Badung spirit provides, which is that it expands the political project of decoloniality into the terrains of de-Westernization, decolonization, anticolonialization, anti-Westernization, and even indigeneity and other such nuanced anti-Western perspectives, which it is related to but systematically different from, a point even Ndlovu-Gatsheni makes elsewhere. Essentially, the Badung spirit does not see Africa for itself, but as part of an(other) order of resistance, an order forced into action by modern epistemology, and as such, trapped in a counter-resistive game or practice by global colonial imperialist designs.

Two other issues are also worth mentioning. The first is minor but still important and is to be found in Ndlovu-Gatsehni's highly important and succinctly argued article on a world without "others" and how Europe came to its global dominance. He claims rightly that the idea of Europe is that of "self-definition, expansion, conquest of the world, and definition of 'others' in relation to Europe's self-image."[29] This self-definition paved the way for the alienation of others and development of rationales, such as the emptiness of the world, which led to a series of colonizations and epistemicides. The idea of "empty" as pursed by Ndlovu-Gatsehni provides useful insight on Europe's ascendancy, eventual domination, and "othering" of the rest of the world. But it rests on assumptions or explications that require careful articulations. In one of his explanations, which

---

29   Ndlovu-Gatsheni, "A World," 87.

references existing studies, he reveals that emptiness as a colonial rationale of European understanding of non-European regions as "empty" or "near empty" of people.[30] This statement is made by Blaut, but it is one Ndlovu-Sabelo references, enlisting it in his judgment on the matter. It is not false but only advances one interpretation out of many interpretational consequences of emptiness when it is set against Europe's attempt at empire building. Europe did not blatantly consider non-European sites as empty (or nearly empty) of people but of subhumans who require European salvation. Much of what is known of the world presently is invented, especially since the end of the fifteenth century, and such invention came from a line of thought that considered the world to be "empty": not devoid of people in the sense that they were ultimately absent but that they were lesser beings, which the various cartographies of the world would eventually reveal. It would seem that the phrase "nearly empty of people" hints at this possibility, which has immense importance in uncovering the rationales that supported the messianic complex of Europe, which the various cartographies of the world at different times would reveal.

The other issue is very vital as it connects with the level of success decoloniality is poised to achieve. Common to decolonial studies is the need to proclaim the death of the Global North as sites of epistemologies, which has the consequence of masking the continued usurpation of subaltern epistemologies by the Global North and their continued shifting of global world order to mask the true nature and range of coloniality currently happening. This premature victory has several consequences for decoloniality itself. While the general consensus, one that is also echoed in Ndlovu-Gatsheni's archive, is that the Global North seems to have lost the capacity to learn in noncolonial terms,[31] its ability to extract epistemologies from the South to reintroduce them back into the world makes that claim trivial. The success of the European empire did not come from learning from the world. Its ability to extract and appropriate potential wealth from non-Western sites makes it as potent and dangerous as ever.

---

30   Ndlovu-Gatsheni, "A World," 91.
31   Santos, *Epistemologies*.

Walter D. Mignolo

Walter Mignolo, a Latin-American scholar at Duke University in the United States, is another prominent voice on decoloniality. His contributions to decolonization studies and discourses on decolonization have laid important foundations on how the effect of colonialism in a neocolonial framework can be uncovered and how colonialism itself is to be interpreted as a defining epoch and experience in the history of humanity across cultures. Mignolo's scholarship can be said, at the risk of collapsing a wide and apparently versatile interest into a single frame, to be concerned with the active imprints of colonialism and the logics that sustained its preeminence for as long as it lasted. He is concerned with teasing out the appearances of colonial ideology and the realities they make possible in supposedly postcolonial environments, and he has expressed this interest unequivocally.[32]

Mignolo's works touch on the composition of contemporary coloniality and how it reflects the historical moments or ideologies that created and sustained it, while relating its pervasiveness to the nature of world order. Two things are important to Mignolo's scholarship: its wide focus but direct approach in confronting coloniality. One instructive revelation Mignolo's corpus of work affords the observant reader is that Mignolo exemplifies what he champions in theory: that decoloniality is a political project that can take many forms.[33] Mignolo exhibits how decoloniality can uncover the logic of coloniality, the rhetoric of modernity, and the colonial epistemic difference, which he holds accountable for the maintenance of Western dominance in all spheres of culture and knowledge.

It is possible, although not definitively, to distill Mignolo's contributions to a field he helped define down to five principal concepts: *indigeneity and decoloniality*; *de-linking, border epistemology or epistemic disobedience*; *colonial epistemic difference*; *logic of coloniality and rhetoric of modernity*; and *loci of enunciation*. Engaging these terms as he has deployed them in unraveling the ways coloniality alters epistemology and even cultures of scholarship will afford one a good understanding of Mignolo's position toward coloniality and decoloniality and his style of engagement.

---

32 Mignolo, "Coloniality."
33 Mignolo, "Coloniality."

Mignolo's submissions on the idea and formation of the nation-state provide a useful starting point on the nature and trajectory of his thinking. In his article arguing for the continuity and utility of decoloniality as a philosophy of resisting covert and overt Western control in postcolonial regions, he problematizes the common reception of the nation-state,[34] its origins with regard to European ideological conception and circumscription of rights of man and citizens, and its current uses in narratives of immigrants and nationals. This particular exposé informs and expands on what is known about the extent to which European colonial difference has invaded modern modes of knowing, perceiving, and thinking. The concept of "natives" is derived from European hierachization of humans for the purpose of domination through difference. In reinforcing ideas about persons who were to be protected and those who were expendable, the idea of the "citizen" is birthed: nationals who espoused European fundamentals and to whom these fundamentals are inherent.

Coloniality of knowledge and coloniality of power, indeed Mignolo's CMP (colonial matrix of power) have created narratives, grand fictions that are integral to the cultures of scholarships as well as epistemologies and rhetoric of modernity. As captured by Mignolo, all these as apparatuses of control create compelling narratives that have modern man believe in the ontology proffered in the Euro-North's "universal fictions." They create dichotomies predicated on a colonial epistemology of difference, and the modern world rests on such dichotomies: subject/object, rational/irrational, civilized/uncultured, human/barbarian. Much of the world's racism and anti-immigration sentiments, especially in Euro-America, have their foundations in this. As Mignolo posits, Europeans express these prejudices in feeling that they are "menaced" by foreigners and nonindigenous people.[35] The choice of word here (menace) is apt as well as evocative. It not only carries the weight of the supposedly righteous anger perpetuating xenophobia and other group-driven racist acts/rhetoric but also connects these practices to a European foundation. This threat is the logical aftermath of Europe's shock at the unraveling of the myth of emptiness, which Sabelo had theorized emanated from a place of hypersupremacist and provincial conception of the "Europeanity" and

---

34 Mignolo, "Coloniality."
35 Mignolo, "Prophets," 111–27.

is commonly referred to as the instigating force behind many Europeans' miseducation on the nature of the world beyond its borders.

Given that the "myth of empty" had caused a solipsistic self-imposed view of Europe's place in the world and the consequent rupturing of that myth through expeditions and travel did not temper the pomposity that supported the view; Europeans had simply lapsed into the natural tendency to categorize non-Europeans as "other." This not only failed to conform to the natural order of things but also promoted a general European consensus about Europe's place in the world that pervaded European cultural ideology and spread to other cultures to become a universal narrative of human onto-epistemology.

One of the ways this is done is through cartography. Mignolo's insightful article, "Putting the Americas on the Map: Geography and the Colonization of Space," provided context for the historical significance of mapmaking, its place in race relations, its importance in connection with the "discovery" of America narrative,[36] as well as the maintenance of dichotomies that keep coloniality alive. The history of cartography-driven European attempts at understanding the world reveals various ideological undercurrents that shaped European posture toward non-European communities and influenced the making of different maps that centralized Europe in a vast world. The T-O maps, like Henricus Martellus composed circa 1490, to cite an example, were drawn with an ideological conception of the world and not a geographical one:[37] Christian symbolism (which provided much of the political and sociocultural direction for Europe at the time) was at the heart of this representation of the world as opposed to physical navigation.

This sort of global representation carried on into the fifteenth century, paving the way for the hyper-progression of the ideals that made Europe see itself as the center of the world. Approaching the T-O maps, as Mignolo argues, in this context provides avenues for understanding how they—and indeed (subsequent) maps in general—represented "many ways of conceiving and graphically organizing the world, with no particular significance for members of non-European cultures."[38] Consequently, following Mignolo's arguments across his works, the ways in which the

---

36 Mignolo, "Putting the Americas," 25–63.
37 Mignolo, "Putting the Americas," 25.
38 Mignolo, "Putting the Americas," 26.

logic of imperial difference produced the thinking that othered people based on their locations becomes apparent as rooted in European onto-epistemological foundations. These Eurocentric attitudes were promoted by the structures of modernity and then maintained in coloniality: imperial designs, colonial epistemic difference, dichotomies, rhetoric of modernity, and CMP. All of these Mignolo describes as comprising the dark side of modernity, one of which is the coloniality underpinning the state uses of "nationals versus immigrant" rhetoric and even the idea of the nation-state.

The idea of the nation-state in its sustenance of the philosophical projects that led to it being a modern phenomenon (i.e., Enlightenment, which led to Euro-modernity) unveils the Eurocentrism inherent in it and the workings of colonial epistemic difference. Mignolo's emphasis on the relevance of cartography to America and the meta-narratives (or "fictions" as he puts it) of the discovery of non-European spaces is related to his views on the coloniality inherent in modernity. Apart from cartography being used to inscribe Europe as the center of the world in the minds of Europeans, it also depicted non-Europeans as uncivilized, a narrative that fueled the regnant supremacist philosophies and fictions of civilizing missions in Africa. Overcoming the myth of emptiness thus did not cure Europe of its solipsism but hyped it beyond restraints, so much that the awareness that came from entering other cultures and being aware of the world's diversity only produced an extreme form of European supremacy. In Mignolo's words, "The growing European awareness of a previously unknown part of the earth became a decisive factor in the process of integrating the unknown to the known, which also transformed the configuration of the known."[39] The implication of this is that Europe's self-importance required condescending relations with and othering of non-Europeans. The rhetoric of modernity, which Mignolo repeatedly laments as veiling the dark sides of modernity, is deeply implicated in this history.

Consequently, the darker uses to which the representations of the nation-state as a Euro-modernist project can be put are accentuated in the xenophobic "nationals versus immigrants" xenophobic narrative. The preservation of the interests of Europeans from non-Europeans required making nationalistic distinctions between Europeans and non-Europeans,

---

39 Mignolo, "Putting the Americas," 37.

which meant propping up the nation-state as a construct of Euro-modernity on the premise of this dichotomy, one that persists even today in state-sponsored narratives that privilege nationals over nonnationals, privileging one as an important human being while implying the tertiary status of the others. The perpetuation of these discriminatory nationalistic attitudes is simply the persistence of coloniality in subtler form.

The rhetoric of modernity, which Mignolo itemizes as "salvation, conviviality, freedom, and prosperity,"[40] deemphasizes the dark side of modernity, such as the logic of coloniality-cum-CMP and the realities it produces. Coloniality has the effect of shaping "modes of knowing, sensing and believing."[41] Given that these two things (although more nuanced in human interaction) causatively relate to each other, understanding them in the light of the foregoing helps in highlighting the xenophobic implications behind the idea of nationals and nation-state in state-sponsored programs, as well as their racial connotations, with strong roots traceable to Thomas Paine's *Rights of Man* (1791) and the "lesser" citizens as conceived of in Europe. In problematizing the idea of the nation-state along this line, Mignolo proffers an evaluative reading of the disjuncture between the common but erroneous perception of nation-state in theory and the nation-state in practice by stating that "the nation-state cares (in practice but not in theory) for nationals and not for human beings. Non-nationals are lesser human beings; they are foreigners, immigrants, refugees, and for colonial settlers, indigenous from the land they settled in as second-class nationals."[42] Following Mignolo's line of reasoning, this reality might be oblivious to many because coloniality has a way of hiding the colonial matrix of power that keeps the imperial designs and the imperative of the colonial difference alive.

Although this consciousness can be discerned across his work in the arguments he makes, it is easy to make a connection that provides a solid launching point for engaging and connecting with his body of work, especially because circumscribing this vast corpus is a deep probe of coloniality showing the desire to bring to light its covert workings. This is the issue at hand for Mignolo. It is thus not far-fetched when Mignolo makes a claim

---

40   See Mignolo's "Cosmopolitanism," 111–27; and "Prophets."
41   Mignolo, "Coloniality."
42   Mignolo, "Coloniality," 40.

for decoloniality in contrast to indigeneity as a practical way of achieving visibility for the Global South, even without expressly saying so.

In his chapter on the relevance of decoloniality, Mignolo claims the multiplicity of views decoloniality allows are crucial as a response to coloniality; he calls it a political project that can be inhabited differently, from space to space, which allows for multiple expressions of decoloniality. The shifting nature of the world order, which continually hides the core power of Western imperialism (i.e., CMP), fails in the presence of decoloniality, which is not simply anti-Westernization but a delinking that requires identifying the presence of imperial designs and the ways and modes of thinking, knowing, and seeing they make possible.

Delinking to Mignolo is reexisting, which has the dual advantage of allowing the Global South to define their existence outside of the entrapment of Western modes of resistance while also affirming this existence in relation to the world without isolating itself or being at cross-purposes with it. It is vital that the project of reexisting on the South's own terms, which has been denied ever since slavery, is removed from the antithetical and antagonistic nature of resistance. Mignolo defines it as being "trapped in the rules of the game others created, specifically the narrative and promises of modernity and the necessary implementation of coloniality."[43] It can be as simple as (unknowingly) living for the other, even if in antagonistic ways. Although Mignolo does not say this, one can see how he relates this idea to nativist and indigeneity-centered attempts at decolonization.

For him, indigeneity advocates for one model of reexisting since it is bound by the fact of being indigenous. Indigeneity does not only advocate for a resistive mode of existing but holds out space for one universal mode of it, limitations put to bed by decoloniality, which advocates for a pluriversal mode of reexisting, carving out room for other forms of localism. Indigeneity continues in the universal mode set by Europe in trying to replace Eurocentrism, which Mignolo elsewhere refers to as "Western localism with a global design that became synonymous with universalism," with a specific (subaltern) geopolitically natured/nurtured nativism.[44]

---

43 Mignolo, "Coloniality Is Far from Over."
44 Mignolo, "Cosmopolitanism."

Seeing as decolonial epistemology rejects imposed dichotomies by pushing for a planetary globalism, a term used by Enrique Dussel in advocating rethinking the way the Global South can generate philosophies that remain in analogical dialogues with other global philosophies,[45] it encourages a pluriversal form of globalism/cosmopolitanism, not only based on the universalism of the West but on all global cultures. It is in this context that Mignolo sees the usefulness of decoloniality, pursuing and championing it not as an ethnic or national identification but as a heterogeneous cleavage that has boundaries manifest in its relation to other parallel ethnicities or nationalisms. On this ground, decoloniality differs from indigeneity, and for subaltern groups, it is an open-space political project that can be habituated differently and that connects with individuals outside of the scrutiny or agendas of the state. Mignolo makes sure not to prescribe or champion decoloniality as an advanced and corrective form of indigeneity but also emphasizes the way decoloniality provides subaltern people avenues for reexisting on their own terms.

To do this, however, is to promote a pluriversal globalism that has multiple centers, that is, a product of planetary globalism, which according to Mignolo is the function of border epistemology. Mignolo's idea of border epistemology promotes a disobedient conservativism, which emphasizes the kind of epistemic delinking that engenders "decolonial healing" and "dignified anger," to use Mignolo's words, which are manifested in the ways subaltern societies or the communities of the Global South delink from the North to reexist by relinking with their own desired legacies. In decoloniality's espousal of disobedient conservatism—that is, conserving the previously diminished, disavowed, and demonized customs, expressions, and heritage of non-Western societies by the rhetoric of modernity—is achievable by civil and epistemic disobedience, which not only can be space-specific but also distinguishes the decolonial epistemology from other forms of decolonization.

Through border epistemology, Global Southern societies are not only able to escape the dichotomies created by Euro-modernity and entrenched as natural/integral by the logic of coloniality through CMP and veiled by rhetoric of modernity but are also able to push toward a transmodern society. This kind of society, proposed by Durrell, is created and supported by coloniality and has two entrapping facets:

---

45 Dussel, "Agenda," 3–18.

On the one hand, the dominant rhetoric of modernity and alleged "universal" values and principles that reflect the perspective and the interests of those who, consciously or not, pronounce what "universal" values and principles are (which are culturally relative—principles and values, of democracy, of freedom, of science and technology), and, on the other hand, the opposing forces, which in the name of tradition (e.g. Vedic science) remains within the same logic of the system.[46]

Escaping this facet is the domain of epistemic delinking, which tries to achieve a visibility for epistemologies and retrieval of subjectivities remanded to the margins by the darker side of modernity. Thus, while the good side to this is empowering those legacies modernity has made invisible, Mignolo puts forward border epistemology, which does not seek to supplant Western localism as the universalized global epistemology with particular subaltern nativism (as this will keep alive the antithetical frames fashioned by Euro-modernity) but to reinvest these nativist particulars in the global space by being in dialogue with Western thought and epistemology, sometimes confrontationally, at other times congenially. To cite Mignolo's words on the matter for better clarification, border epistemology in canvassing for reinvesting means also to change the perspective (to change it and not to invert it). Changing but not inverting perspectives brings as a consequence border epistemology, an epistemology of the border from the perspective of what has been denied and the possibility of conceptual delinking. Border epistemology is a powerful one for the simple reason that it is based, on the one hand, on the critical examination of non-Western languages and traditions and, on the other, on the critical examination of Western languages and traditions.[47]

Mignolo believes that through border epistemology a truly global planetary epistemology that comes from transmodernity—which reflects on the radical transformation altering the founding ethos upon which modernity is built—can be derived that places all cultures in a position to thrive.[48] To achieve this requires being cognizant of coloniality and the binaries that keep it alive, the place of the rhetoric of modernity, and the dark sides of modernity as affecting even cultures of scholarship. Mignolo's argument here is that locus of enunciation of decoloniality is

---

46 Mignolo, "Prophets," 120.
47 Mignolo, "Prophets," 124.
48 Mignolo, "Coloniality," 1–10.

implicated in the politics of location.[49] Being conversant with how all these collectively inform the institutions of the modern world and the way they sustain epistemology formation and use allow for a progressive undermining of coloniality in ways that promote the reexisting of the indigenous.

The end game of decoloniality is a transmodern world like Mignolo envisioned, but the assumptions that institute this idea as a worthy goal are problematic in their general assessment of the situation, a general or common supposition, which is apparently required to, among other things, argue for the success of decoloniality: that of the radical transformation of the foundations of modernity in the current sociocultural moment. While this is true to an extent, and while decoloniality helps to stave off the darker sides of modernity, the foundations of modernity, especially in dominant centers, are not being radicalized enough to promote the demise of coloniality.

So, while it is indeed true that some of the founding philosophies of the modern world are in jeopardy judging by their failure to recommend solutions to recurrent world crises and their inability to continue the project of Westernization, the pervasive reach of Euro-North American–centered epistemology, and consequently, modernity across the world has made it that such claims are to be made carefully, especially since the discredited formations that sustained Euro-modernity are still being returned to by the forces of coloniality. Seeing as this is true to an observable extent, and the rise of multiple modernities in localized centers as well as new formations such as BRICS threaten the dominance of Euro-North power (but have not yet succeeded in dismantling it politically, economically, or socioculturally), trans-modernity should be seen as an achievable project in the making having not yet done away with its rival: Euro-North American–centered modernity.

Enrique Dussel

On a general note, it would seem that the work of Dussel provides a glimpse of the ultimate goal of decoloniality, especially as pursued by Ndlovu-Gatsheni and Mignolo. This means, in a sense, Dussel provides a key piece that, in retrospect, would seem to complete the picture—even

---

49 Mignolo, "I Think," 234–45.

if he does not forthrightly say so. Two major concerns of Dussel, which sum up his major contributions as an important voice for the Global South in its decolonization struggle are the philosophy of liberation and transmodernity, concepts that he originated and that he has devoted much of his career to making relevant to both the North and South, but particularly the latter.

Dussel is particularly useful for the bridgehead his work provides, which connected avenues of scholarship that are not easily definable. The philosophy he has worked with over the course of several essays and lectures can be found to work at the foundational level of many decolonial arguments. On this note, it is vital to realize that Dussel performs the work of the philosopher, adhering to his own injunctions and living by principle in providing a solid philosophical basis to work with, signaling possible directions to take, and highlighting the destinations so as to preclude possibilities of straying from this path.

Given the breadth of his philosophy and his ability to condense it into practical and workable theses, it is not hard to find echoes of Dussel in several works employing or engaging with the decolonial option, as Mignolo succinctly puts it. Dussel's transmodern world is the ultimate goal of decoloniality; it evinces a world of multiple modernities, demonstrating the possibility of a global dialogue informed by several epistemologies, representatives of the societies of the Global North and South interacting with one another on an even plane. This world is achievable through the conscious and deliberate movement of societies trapped in the periphery of modernity but moving to the center by reaching inward to affirm legacies rejected by Euro-modernity.

One of the ways this philosophy is achieved, which is cultural and political in its insinuations and connotations, is in the initiation of an interphilosophical global dialogue, which can serve as the epistemological and ontological anchor for the type of world that can be transmodern. The gravity of this proposition is evinced by the type of radicalism it advocates and pursues. A transmodern world itself is a radical departure from the genus of modernity at present, which is Western driven and Western derived. It is a departure from the European derived "I," which as a result of the dominance of colonialism that displaced other cultures became the benchmark for epistemic and philosophical practices.[50] This

---

50 Dussel, "Agenda."

departure from the present obtainable normal—that is, the dominance of Euro-American epistemology and the world order its supports—is lent credence by the palpable need for postcolonial societies to affirm their own cultures but not doing this according to the edicts of Euro-modernity, which persists within and perpetuates the imperial binaries of colonialism. It is also affirmed and energized by the creative possibilities and epistemological potentials of Global South cultures, so as to bring to the altar of global philosophical discourse cultural particulars that can exist on an equal plane with the North without having to negotiate from a disadvantaged position, as Western modernity (Euro–North American) have structured it. According to Dussel, doing this will enable a pluri-verse, "where each culture will be in dialogue with all others from the perspective of a common similarity, enabling each culture to recreate its own analogical 'distinction' and to diffuse itself within a dialogical, reciprocally creative universe."[51]

Dussel's analogical distinction encourages convergences that enable the Global South dialogues required to initiate the process of transmodernity, which he aptly conceptualizes as a horizon opening up gradually and sustained by the gradual erosion of the "assumptions of modernity, capitalism, Eurocentricism, and colonialism."[52] This is a new epoch set apart by its immanently constitutive requirement that humans alter and transform existing ontological and epistemology-driven dispositions toward all aspects of reality, that of the postcolonial societies and of the others.[53] This returns us to the idea of radicalism inherent in Dussel's philosophy, which in contrast to Western modernity, lies in the exteriority, the border, which Mignolo and Dussel define as the periphery of the metropolitan core.[54]

The metropolitan core, to Dussel, is the interiority of Western modernity, within which the logic of coloniality and the imperial designs hiding the power source of the world order resides; it is the realm of the epistemologies that converted European philosophies and local features of modernity into a universal global benchmark. It is also the realm of

---

51 Dussel, "Agenda," 3.
52 Dussel, "Agenda," 17.
53 Dussel, "Agenda."
54 Dussel, "Transmodernity," 1–26.

"destructive consideration,"[55] to use Dussel's own phrase, given its ability to displace and invalidate the legitimacy of other knowledge systems, or banish them to the periphery—its own exteriority.

Exiting the periphery and undoing the hegemony of the West in the process is thus implied in the idea and reality of a transmodern world. Moreover, given that it stems from a self-affirmative process, where delinking from the patterns of existing laid down by Western modernity is analogous to reaffirming the delegitimated indigenous values, mores, and knowledge systems of postcolonial societies, it becomes a political project as far reaching in the transitions it engenders. This is true as it not only undermines the narrative of a Euro-American standard across epistemic and ontologic categories and discourses in the process of self-valorization of negated and devalued cultural forms, legacies, and knowledge systems. It also invokes a critical self-reflection that reaches inward into the heart of indigenous cultures to generate relevant philosophic codes that can engage in symmetrical dialogues with other cultures, doing away with the asymmetric patterns of relation instituted by the West. The possibilities these interphilosophical—and generally speaking cultural—dialogues can bring about is the transmodern world itself.

Dussel, to avoid misunderstanding, points out that the dialogue should emanate from a culture's critical thinkers or cultural innovators who are able to approach parallel cultures, both in the Global North and South, in a nonantagonistic way, especially the North. In this case then, the force—which Dussel calls "creative"—that brings about the possibility of a transmodern world is exterior to Euro-American modernity. To quote Dussel, "This exteriority is not pure negativity. It is the positivity rooted in a tradition distinct from the Modern."[56] What Dussel means here reflects on the arguments Mignolo and Ndlovu-Gatsheni and much of what decoloniality is about: interculturality that fails to fall into patterns set by coloniality and its matrixes. The positivity recognizes, acts on, and exudes its difference from the metropolitan core but yet initiates an engagement with it, this time from an equal footing; this engagement, to use Mignolo's terms, can be sometimes friendly and sometimes confrontational (i.e., civil disobedience). This civil obedience and decolonial anger are revealed in the choice of phrasing Dussel uses: "not purely

---

55   Dussel, "Transmodernity."
56   Dussel, "Transmodernity," 25–26.

negative." The semantic implication of this phrase is that it exists in contrast, that is by difference—a fact of reality caused by coloniality—but chooses to reexist and in relegitimating its own validity in the face of imperial designs approaches this supposedly superior order to engage it as each situation demands.

Understanding Dussel within this frame heightens appreciation for transmodern pluri-versality's call for an intercultural dialogue that does not seek to replace one with the other but emphasizes a mutually symbiotic cultural relation. Thus, the pluriversality a transmodern world proposes is one that affirms and develops the difference, that is the "cultural alterity of postcolonial communities"; it affirms and develops this difference for a general good, since difference presupposes the particularity and peculiarity—revealed and discursively provided after much critical cultural self-introspection by creative cultural innovators—that can be used in generating analogous cultural philosophies, which can then engender a globalism where cultural particularities are universal. This difference is not the colonial epistemic difference that has redefined perceptions of ontologies and epistemologies across the globe as inferior if not nonexistent. Dussel's difference emphasizes peculiarity and particularity; it does not seek to inferiorize these traits as Euro-modernity did.

This transmodern world is, thus, one of the pluriversalities of universalities.[57] It is where postcolonial societies can redevelop their epistemologies and cultures in dialogue with the "best elements of Modernity," which emphasizes the possibility of a North-South dialogue and stresses this dialogue as the way forward. Dussel stresses the place of difference in this, affirming that an undifferentiated globality will only replicate from the exterior the project of Euro-modernity in universalizing the world in its own image.

It is in advocating for a kind of border epistemology—one that comes from a place of internal consistency as opposed to being at odds with oneself—that Dussel argues for a kind of philosophy of liberation. This philosophy comes from the interiority of Europe's exteriority and is not antagonistic as a result, as it comes from a need to relink with indigenous customs and knowledge. Although Dussel does not explicitly make reference to this "interiority of exteriority," Mignolo employs it to shore up his refutation of reading the decolonial option from the borders of

---

57 Dussel, "Transmodernity."

Euro-American modernity as reactionary, the thinking that there is a core to the exteriority where indigenous cultures exist resonates well enough. It is also rather extensively fleshed out in Mignolo's idea in (as well as article on) geopolitics of knowledge and the colonial difference. In fact, in defining a core, the interiority to this exteriority, the wholeness of indigenous knowledge spaces is reaffirmed, while preserving the necessary cross-cultural dialogues that will facilitate a transmodern philosophy. This wholeness allows this philosophy and its epistemologies the authenticity Euro-modernity denied it by framing it as its foil.

The philosophy of liberation is a critical cultural philosophy that has as its aim the generation of new forms of enlightenment that liberates it from the rhetoric of modernity and the colonial matrixes of power.[58] This philosophy must be generated as a result of critical self-reflection by critical culture participants from the Global South, first within individual cultures, paying attention to internal schisms and diehard symbols of Eurocentrism and imperialism, before initiating an intra–Global South philosophical discourse, where, although distinctions are retained, the points of divergence and departures allow for appreciating analogic cultural similarities as a possible basis of creating useful Southern philosophies or "philosophies of the South"[59] that can engage the North to create a true pluriverse. This philosophy will replace the modern philosophy retaining the world order, which is bound up in European history, particularly the Enlightenment, Atlantic trade, as well as science, industrial, and technology revolutions. Returning to a philosophy that can produce true experience and reflect moments of creativity in ecologies of knowledge in the South is validating those epistemic enterprises colonialism invalidated, like mythologies, for instance, and what Boaventura de Sousa Santos[60] calls "commonsense knowledge," which Euro-modernity replaced with science as its foil and a universal mode of knowledge. Quite ironically, Dussel rightly argues that science, like other ethnophilosophies, has rich roots in mythopoesis.[61]

---

58 Dussel, "Transmodernity."
59 Dussel, "Agenda," 11.
60 Santos, "Room," 149–64.
61 See Dussel's "A New Age," 1–22; and "Agenda."

Boaventura de Sousa Santos

It is important to end this chapter with Santos, as he returns us to the foundation of Euro-modernity and the groundwork of the troubles initiated by coloniality in non-European sites of knowledge and experience. Santos's thinking ideally complements what has been discussed here so far, particularly corroborating, extending, and bringing fresh insight from the perspective of sociology and law to the matter of decoloniality, especially as she does not particularly identify her scholarship as decolonial. It is thus these two distinctions that make her a worthy addition here, aside from the breadth of her work and its immense importance to the field.

Like others already engaged, Santos shares a common premise: the crises of modernity. In fact, much more than Mignolo—who shares almost the same emphasis—her emphasis is on the crises of modernity and solutions to these problems that lie elsewhere, beyond the confines of modernity. What is being touted here is not only the failure of the rhetoric of Western modernity as adhering to the Euro-North model, which Santos and Mignolo have taken time to flesh out,[62] but also that of modernity itself in providing solutions to the problems it has engendered. There are many explanations for this. One of them proposed by Ndlovu-Gatsheni and shared by many, including Santos, is that Western modernity has failed through its unchecked imperialist universal campaigns to learn from other epistemologies. In so doing, it failed to learn to criticize its own epistemologies, a form of self-criticism initiated by learning from the other.

Yet, despite this convergence, unlike Dussel (and even Ndlovu-Gatsheni to an extent), Santos sees a problem in generating the required critical theory needed to combat this reality without falling into natural or expected patterns—"that is not reducing reality to what exists."[63] It is not that Santos fails to see the possibility in generating critical theories like Dussel does with the idea of the philosophy of liberation, which requires critical and creative cultural thinkers, or that he diverges from Dussel in their positions—or the implications of their positions—in relation to modern science and the myth/common sense of non-European cultural sites as modes of knowledge making. It is that these theories will need to track variations in reality as possibilities that are yet to be

---

62 Santos, "Oppositional," 121–39.
63 Santos, "Oppositional," 122.

empirically specified. Santos provides several reasons for this seeming difficulty, one of which is the totalizing nature of the knowledge (modern knowledge and science as its epistemic system) provided or provisionally available in addressing these issues.

Here, the logic Santos pursues evokes an existing argument on coloniality of knowledge and the consequences of modes of knowing and seeing, and in relation to Santos, of devising solutions to the crises of critical theory that it makes available. Two reasons are provided, among others, that flesh out Santos's concerns: the insurmountable divide between the "reason that criticizes" trying to assume the position of the 'reason that thinks, constructs, and legitimizes the criticizable."[64] The irreconcilability is in the fact that there is no totalizing knowledge—a fact that would have been visible to modern critical theory had it allowed for its own criticism. Emphasis here is on modern science and its hegemonic expansion through colonialism and the colonial matrix of power. Santos argues that critical knowledge is most effective when originating from a critique of knowledge. This is not the same with modern science, whose epistemology shielded itself from critical self-reflection. Thus, modern critical theory and its subsequent crises arose from such a lapse. It is important to stress here that central to Dussel's philosophy of liberation is the need for critical thinkers from the South to reflect critically inward. This requirement of self-criticism marks the alternative solutions to the modern crises and is central to the argument for solutions that reject Euro-American modern centers and science as its defining knowledge system.

Santos goes on to provide a useful distinction: knowledge-as-regulation and knowledge-as-emancipation.[65] This distinction reveals the nature of knowledge as contributing to order or chaos, depending on to what extent it allows for internal critique, which exposes the interconnectedness of knowledge in ignorance, a facet of modern knowledge hidden by coloniality and as such, according to Santos, unavailable to modern critical theory. With references to knowledge, there is always a point of ignorance and knowledge: with regard to knowledge-as-regulation, its point of ignorance is chaos, while knowledge is its point of order; for knowledge-as-emancipation, the origin of ignorance is colonialism, and knowledge is gained through solidarity. In the inability of modern science

---

64   Santos, "Oppositional," 128.
65   Santos, *Toward*.

to yield itself to self-criticism as a form of knowledge-as-emancipation, extending the lifespan of its own blind spot, its ignorance produces chaos and turns it into a form of knowledge-as-regulation.

In the context of revealing the totalitarian nature of modern science as an epistemic system, Santos's arguments are convincing. An emancipating form of knowledge is that which recognizes the Other as a subject and hence recognizes the epistemological validity in the Other and extends solidarity in the process. Given that this sought-out knowledge is missing in modern critical theory, which has been founded upon the supposed epistemological supremacy of modern science, it would be discovered elsewhere, which is why Santos advocates for oppositional postmodernism: or a postmodern critical theory that defers to the direction of (celebratory) postmodernism.

Perhaps because of the approach to the question of coloniality (or, more specifically, coloniality of knowledge), which is what Santos essentially deals with, some of his submissions contradict some of the arguments for decoloniality. But this is only superficially so. For instance, he recognizes the faux emancipative progress of modern science as knowledge-as-emancipation in liberating mankind but problematizes the claim in view of the subduing of nature and particular groups of people. In marginalizing non-Europeans, modern science creates, for instance, a hierarchy: nature versus human or what is nature (by the very fact of being or close to in its natural form) and what is nurtured as human, that is, civilized and rational. This distinction is not far from what obtains in decoloniality in uncovering the Euro-modern philosophies that led to "othering" of groups of people such as non-Europeans. Hence, the rhetoric of modernity and its false savior complex are marshaled into action in the principle of knowledge-as-emancipation as revealed in the epistemological foundations of modern science. It sought to regulate this inclination toward "nature" by imperially relating to non-Europeans.

Thus, with epistemological recognition, the Other is a producer of knowledge. This seems to be Santos's bone of contention, although intricately defined, and for which he proposes a new critical theory that would rest on knowledge-as-emancipation, one that solidarizes and does not seek to control. This knowledge strives to achieve balance between its actions and consequences.[66] A knowledge that can do this is opposi-

---

66 Santos, "Oppositional."

tional postmodernism, which is not postmodernism as a Euro-American response to the crises in modernity but the natural response of what Santos calls a period of paradigmatic transition: periods of extreme competition between opposing epistemologies.[67] In this period, the paradigm of modernity is undone. This is to abolish the modes of expressing social regulation and social emancipation akin to modernity and the paradigms of knowledge it generated by discrediting and destroying alternative knowledge modes and systems.

Santos's concerns are analogous to those of previous decolonial scholars, as with the implication of the crises of the paradigm of modernity and, by extension, crises of modern science and the modes of knowledge for which it serves as epistemic fundament. His solutions, which reside in pursuing alternative remedies or epistemic solutions, also dovetails with the solutions centrally positioned within decoloniality. He advocates for undoing the consequential influences of modernity, which constrains modes of seeing and knowing and as such of thinking of possibilities beyond what exists—which is what exactly frames his complaint about the inability of modern critical theory to generate solutions or speak to existential possibilities. Santos's advocacy for a utopia as the way forward from the miasma of modern crises is to deploy the imagination "to explore new modes of human possibility and styles of will and to oppose the necessity of what exists on behalf of something radically better that is worth fighting for, and to which humanity is fully entitled."[68] His utopian thinking emphasizes the integrality of those whose nonexistent status is not a natural absence but one induced by the regulatory mode of the paradigm of modernity. His conception of utopia foregrounds what does not exist as a result of the hegemony of modern science and its epistemological dominance.

This utopian thinking provides the fuel for critical, cultural, and philosophical possibilities much in the same way Dussel advocated for a Southern philosophy and philosophies of the South from the exteriority of modernity and Mignolo has argued for a border epistemology, which is exterior to the interior of Western modernity. Santos's solutions are "a new epistemology" and "a new psychology." This new epistemology does not

---

67   Santos, "Three Metaphors," 569–84.
68   Santos, "Three Metaphors," 574.

run contrary to Mignolo and Dussel, especially when viewed as a reaction to the hegemony of the paradigm of modernity and its imperial designs.

In fact, Santos's use of postmodern critical theory, which is provided as a solution, is espoused by him to be both compatible and contradictory to the paradigm of modernity, which evokes the concept of double critique and a transmodern pluriversality.[69] It is on this ground that Santos makes a distinction between the postmodernism he advocates for and the kind he opposes: Santos's is an oppositional postmodernism countering that which is often celebrated and practiced in academia. While this connects with Dussel's rejection of postmodernity as Euro-American response to Euro-American modern crises on the level of appropriate response from the exteriority of Western modernity, it also allows for a conversation between transmodern pluriversality, cosmopolitan localism, pluriversal universalities, and Santos's idea of globalizations as opposed to a single globalization, which he describes as one localism (Western localism) localizing other localisms by being received and perceived as the "global." To sum up his points, he discursively proposes time-space compression: while this allows for multicultural (thus multilocal) flows and interflows that contribute to globalization, it also locks the producers of such currents at the local level.

Given that "the time-space compression identifies the social process by which phenomena sped up and spread out across the globe"[70] and that certain indigenous groups might not be in control of such a process, localism could be subordinate or dominant. In pursuing this power relation and asymmetry, Santos extends the debate on globalization, identifying an imperial South and a nonimperial South: the former is produced by imperial modernity as empire, and the latter is contained within the North. By doing this, he calls attention to the shifting geopolitical realities of power asymmetries wherein the South is both exterior and interior to the North, a kind of internal Third World. In emphasizing the heterogeneity of the periphery, Santos claims the concept of the Third World has become questionable, a claim that is true but not without implications. Even within the North, the so-called internal Third World is exterior to the interiority of the North because to assume the North is not configured so is to deny the hierarchies and layers of asymmetry that

---

69   Santos, "Oppositional."
70   Santos, "Oppositional," 137.

constitute it. It also has implications for the integral parts of societies that are made nonexistent realities by modern science and the epistemologies it serves.

Santos's contributions offer rich insight into how expansive the reaches and ideological currents fueling decoloniality are. His ideas on hegemonic and nonhegemonic globalization recognize the ideological waves of decoloniality, but they also recognize not only the importance of discourses of localization and globalization (or what is now being referred to as "glocalization") but also that globalization is not the problem. Rather, the problem is the hegemonic form in which a particular localism, thus globalized, localizes other localisms, promoting the identification of the globalized localism as the only one possible. A nonhegemonic globalization does not kick against globalization but rather the hegemonic form of globalization. What happens, as succinctly put by Santos, is that "the local becomes global if it manages to deglobalise itself from the set of conditions that has localized it and reglobalises itself in an alternative set of conditions"[71]—or the premises of decoloniality—which he references as having gained increasing momentum in the 1990s.

---

71 Dale, Robertson, and Santos, "Interview," 1–22.

Chapter Nine

Decoloniality

A Critique

Centuries of imperial brutality, decades of colonialism, and eventual coloniality after the attainment of independence have had a profound impact on every aspect of African history. The effects on African social, economic, political, cultural, religious, and even intellectual life have been devastating to say the least. Intellectual colonialism has been perpetuated by the domination and eventual coloniality of the mind. It can be traced to Columbus's 1492 voyage to the Americas and its resultant triangle trade—the transatlantic slave trade carted Africans away by the millions, forcing them to work on foreign plantations for the economic benefit of Europe and North America. The African mind was brutalized and suppressed, and Africa's political, economic, religious, and cultural institutions were similarly devastated. Akinyemi and Amusan have stated: "There is no gainsaying that the experiences of colonialism are enduring and continue to manifest in diverse forms: political, educational, philosophico-epistemological, psycho-cultural, and socio-developmental dimensions. All these have extensive, intensive, formative, de-formative, and severely limiting implications on the lives of the colonized and predictably, many generations after, in their onto-existential locations and outcomes."[1]

The existing political system practiced on the continent is a direct reflection of decades of colonialism. Indigenous institutions, which were democratic in nature, have been replaced with alien ones that engender ethnic politics and authoritarian political culture. The political structure

---

1   Akinyemi and Amusan, "Between the Town," 176.

inherited by newly independent nations was originally rigged to benefit Western colonizers, and it was left mostly unchanged to benefit the elites who replaced those colonizers.

Although African leaders such as Kwame Nkrumah of Ghana and Julius Nyerere of Tanzania identified this problem, there were few efforts to address it other than through political statements. The failure to reform political structures promoted intense ethnic and regional rivalries, damaging national unity and undermining efforts to build nations. This failure has fostered African dependence on former colonial powers and invited their ongoing intervention.[2] Julius Nyerere was an advocate for African development through Africanized solutions to African problems and stated the following:

> It is stupid to rely on money as the major instrument of development when we know only too well that our country is poor. It is equally stupid, and indeed it is even more stupid, for us to imagine that we shall rid ourselves of our poverty through foreign financial assistance rather than our own financial resources.... From now on we shall stand upright and walk forward on our feet rather than look at this problem upside down. Industries will come and money will come, but their foundation is the people and their hard work, especially in agriculture. This is the meaning of self-reliance.[3]

As the maxim goes, talk is cheap. Nyerere's solution was brilliant and Afrocentric, but it lacked a feasible strategy and structural commitment. In the decade after that statement was issued, and in the decades that followed to the present day, the direct opposite has been witnessed politically and economically.

Democracy and popular participation were not promoted during the colonial era, which explains the authoritarian and corrupt nature of centralized political systems in postcolonial Africa. Political party systems ignore the desires of the people and fail to consider the capabilities of "leaders" before they are imposed as candidates for office.[4] It has entrenched a flawed political system that recycles corrupt leaders. The centralization of political power and modernity of capitalism have turned

---

2   Talton, "Challenge."
3   Talton, "Challenge."
4   Bayeh, "Political," 89–93.

political portfolios into an avenue for advancing self-interest. This political consequence of colonialism is evident in Africa today.

The consequences of colonialism are also apparent in Africa's economic reality. The transatlantic slave trade and subsequent colonization of Africa extracted African resources and used them to fuel the industrial revolution in Europe while relegating Africa to the status of a captive market. Even after the end of colonialism, African countries participated in global trade by exporting raw materials and importing finished products. Terms and prices are dictated by the former colonizers, and the African economy remains dependent on Europe.[5] Hahnel has identified two significant ways in which Africa ended up underdeveloped: exploitation through trade and exploitation through investment.[6]

Capitalist countries have dictated the value and prices paid for African exports, which are frequently reduced through market regulations, and they determine the prices that African countries pay for imports. Foreign investments claim lands and mines used to establish banks and multinational firms that keep capital flowing out of Africa, or they take the form of loans to African governments that charge high interest rates or attract imperial takeovers. This last assertion is supported by Guy Scott, former agriculture minister of Zambia:

> It's hard to know how they all got here.... If you go to the market you find Chinese selling cabbages and beansprouts. What is the point in letting them in to do that? There's a lot of Chinese here doing construction. Zambians can do that. The Chinese building firms are undercutting the local firms. Our textile factories can't compete with cheap Chinese imports subsidized by a foreign government. People are saying: "We've had bad people before. The whites were bad, the Indians were worse but the Chinese are worst of all."[7]

Such claims illustrate the continual existence of coloniality as well as the resumption of colonialism, albeit in other forms. China loaned nearly $143 billion to African countries between 2000 and 2017,[8] which dwarfs

---

5   Rodney, *How Europe*.
6   King and Hahnel, "ABCs," 72–74.
7   McGreal, "Thanks China."
8   Bavier, Leng, and Shalal, "China."

the WB's loan to Africa. An interest rate of 17 percent[9] has made Angola ($25b), Ethiopia ($13.5b), Zambia ($7.4b), Republic of Congo ($7.3b), and North Sudan ($6.4billion) into the top five biggest debtors as of 2018.[10] The numbers have increased since then, especially in Nigeria.

China's investments have been described as a "takeover trap," and the activity associated with these loans has been described as "abusive behavior" toward African countries. Such investments empower Africa "infrastructurally," but they control the workforce and either alienate the indigenous population or reduce them to menial or unskilled labor, which resembles nineteenth- and twentieth-century colonialism in Africa.[11] The above quotation[12] also shows how the colonial trend of importing foreign goods not only competes with African indigenous products, it also alienates indigenous Africans, enabling the systematic destruction of the African economy.[13]

The gradual recolonization of Africa is even more glaring in the treatment of indebted countries—financially strategic places in indebted African countries are claimed as collateral to ensure payment. A typical example is found in a statement on Zambia: "Chinese companies are putting pressure on the Zambian Finance Ministry to avert further delayed payments or defaults on their loans. However, Chinese companies are refusing to restructure existing debts and are instead seeking fresh collateral in case of default."[14]

The same report claims that China is looking to liquidate the Konkola Copper mines and "Glencore's Zambian operation Mopani, which may be heading towards a sale, and the country's largest producer, First Quantum Minerals." China's StarTimes retains 60 percent of rights over a digital joint venture with Zambia National Broadcasting Company, TopStar.[15] Copper is 72.6 percent of Zambian exports,[16] making it easy to see China's gradual takeover of the country's economy. Other examples abound in

---

9   Brautigam, "Opinion."
10 Chiwanza, "Top Ten."
11 Dok and Thayer, "Takeover Trap."
12 McGreal, "Thanks China."
13 Dok and Thayer, "Takeover Trap."
14 Smith, "Zambia."
15 Smith, "Zambia."
16 Workman, "Zambia."

Sri Lanka,[17] and a possible agreement for the Port of Mombasa in Kenya could continue China's "debt diplomacy" in Africa.[18]

An agreement between China and Kenya mirrors the forced colonization pacts from European imperialists in the nineteenth century, compelling African countries to surrender their sovereignty: "Neither the borrower (Kenya) nor any of its assets is entitled to any right of immunity on the grounds of sovereignty or otherwise from arbitration, suit, execution or any other legal process with respect to its obligations under this Agreement, as the case may be in any jurisdiction."[19]

China's approach and the implications of clauses that challenge African sovereignty are a reminder of the continent's dependence on "developed" nations. This level of dependency calls into question the potential impact of decoloniality for African studies—some people expect a vast tangle of economic and political problems to be solved by such an undertaking. The belief that solving one problem could solve all of them is rooted in the concept of epistemic decoloniality as an important entry point "because most of the crises that manifest in the society, politics, development, and economy have their foundations in epistemology."[20] Ndlovu-Gatsheni, in particular, supports this idea with a biblical analogy.[21] The reality of Africa's academic situation suggests that this idea must be questioned, and a critical look at the reality of African society counters this position. A full-blown decoloniality of African studies is not the sole means for decolonizing Africa; the inherent problem is the situational coloniality of African political and economic history.

This sentiment is reinforced by dependency theory, stating that "the condition of underdevelopment is precisely the result of the incorporation of the Third World economies into the capitalist world system which is dominated by the West and the North America."[22] In Africa, the survival and growth of one is dependent on the other. The problems of sustained coloniality evident in Africa's economic history cannot be undone by introducing the "epistemological perspective of African studies"—at

---

17 Abi-Habib "How China Got Sri Lanka."
18 Wheeler, "Is Kenya's Mombasa."
19 Okoth, "Kenya."
20 Ndlovu-Gatsheni, "Cognitive Empire," 3.
21 Ndlovu-Gatsheni, "Cognitive Empire," 3.
22 Emeh, "Dependency," 116.

best, it would solve the problem of the "coloniality of knowledge."[23] It is interesting that decolonial scholars see "modernity" and "development" as Eurocentric and evil, because these values are used by the Global North to perpetually discriminate against the subaltern, partition the world, and maintain the colonial matrix of power.[24] One must ask how Ndlovu-Gatsheni's discontinuation approach[25] to modernity and development could help Africa achieve political and economic decoloniality.

The Discontinuation of Modernity and Development

Not only do some decolonial approaches reflexively tag concepts like modernity and development with negative connotations—approaches that have little or no real impact on political and economic institutions in Africa—they also fail to withstand basic criticism. Grofosguel, another decolonial scholar, asks, "How can we overcome the Eurocentric modernity without throwing away the best of modernity as many Third World Fundamentalists do?"[26] Modernization is part of globalization, and although it began with the colonialist voyages of the Middle Ages and their consequent triangular trade, the impact since then has been felt by social, cultural, economic, political, cultural, and religious institutions in Africa and the rest of the world.

The modernizing forces of globalization are characterized by "capitalism, military power, surveillance systems and industrialization."[27] They have intruded into the most personal and private aspects of human life, but every cloud has a silver lining. Returning to Grofosguel's question, should one completely abandon a long-running process to stop its perceived negative impacts when that means losing benefits? Such benefits have included women's liberation from patriarchal constraints, offering more options for marriage, relationships, and participation in the

---

23 Adams, "Decolonizing," 467–74.
24 Ndlovu-Gatsheni, "Genealogies," 13–40.
25 Ndlovu-Gatsheni, "Genealogies."
26 Grosfoguel, "Decolonizing."
27 Bitrus. "Globalizing," 68–83.

workforce; the advent of the internet, which offers new opportunities to Africans; and the spread of industrialization and labor-saving devices.[28]

The Gown and the Town Afrocentric Divide

Akinyemi agrees that the effect of "colonial socio-philosophical" impositions on Africa has been quite significant, extending beyond the realm of epistemology:

> It is not only evident in the pedagogical structure but engrained also into the political structure, hence its perpetuation through conservative reforms since after colonial rule. As such, the Eurocentric conception of education, its content and methods have continued to shape the nature of governance and administrative decision-making on the continent. There is no gainsaying the fact that leadership and decision making plays important roles in the interaction between intellectual capital and development.[29]

Although colonialism's lasting impact has stripped academic and development goals of their indigenous knowledge base, the problem does not stop there—it has impaired the development of socially responsive leaders who can transform the wealth of African intellectualism into development. This disconnect from the indigenous knowledge base has created a gap between "the gown and the town"—a metonym describing academics and the enactors of political and economic policies—preventing academic research and recommendations from being applied for developmental purposes.

Decolonial scholars see the decoloniality of African studies, ultimately perceived as the decoloniality of African society, to be an initial step to achieving the holistic decolonization of African history. This belief, that decolonizing African history should spark the emancipation of African thought from Western-imposed ideologies, faces the stumbling block of Africa's current situation. Realistically, it is Eurocentric thinking that is unfeasible for Africa.

---

28   Bitrus, "Globalizing."
29   Akinyemi and Amusan, "Between the Town."

Kaunda is a decolonial scholar who posits that the subject matter of decolonial discourse should be the decoloniality of the mind, asserting that its emancipation is crucial to the decoloniality of external problems that include foreign-imposed institutions and foreign dependence. In his view, the knowledge that comes from a free mind "gives order, meaning, and pleasure to social, political, economic, aesthetic, and religious norms."[30] Kaunda's process can be summarized as intellectual liberation, which should automatically liberate African studies, with the liberation of Africa as a whole to follow. This is analogous to the oft-referenced "seek ye first the political kingdom and all else shall be added unto you."[31]

Political independence in Africa has not delivered the political freedom, economic prosperity, and societal development promised by African nationalists. The struggle continues more than half a century later. It may be true that "a mind that knows is a mind that is free,"[32] but in reality, a mind that knows and acts is a mind that is free. This is not an attempt to deemphasize the significance of knowledge-first epistemic decolonization, but it acknowledges the missing link to achieving a holistic decoloniality of African history; this is a point frequently overlooked by African scholars who focus on education.

There has been a high level of cooperation between the gown and the town in the Global North (Europeans and North America), especially with issues related to "urban management, traffic control, student accommodation, economic development, inner-city regeneration, internationalization, skills development, social justice, sport and technological innovations."[33] The relationship between gown and town is linked to the benefit that accrues to each of the distinct-but-cooperating parties. The reward of such relationships in Africa was identified by Akinyemi and Amusan; the "gown" (i.e., universities and research institutions) ought to be the innovation hub for their local "town" societies, with political and economic actors making better-informed decisions based on research output from academia.[34] After the adoption of Western education, Africa

---

30   Kaunda, "Denial," 87.
31   Kwame Nkrumah's words to Ghana and Africa during the era of decolonization in Africa.
32   See the University of Ibadan (Nigeria) school anthem.
33   Bank, "Embracing."
34   Akinyemi and Amusan, "Between the Town," 161–87.

recorded great strides in developing Eurocentric research systems and scholarship, boasting millions of researchers, scholars, and graduate students since the end of colonialism.[35] And despite the Eurocentric focus of the scholarship, intellectualism, philosophy, and epistemology, these systems are still relevant to communal and social development.

A historical parallel can be drawn with Thomas Paine's *Common Sense*.[36] His work, which was the all-time best-selling American book (relative to the times and American population) until 2006,[37] persuasively argued in favor of Americans fighting for independence. Paine's clarion call supported an ongoing cause, but change is only possible through action and subject to the whims of policymakers and political leaders. The history of the 1776 American revolution lists Thomas Jefferson, George Washington, James Madison, John Adams, John Jay, Benjamin Franklin, and Alexander Hamilton as primary actors and founding fathers of the revolution that liberated the United States—Paine is fondly remembered for the impact of his work alone.[38] American historian R. B. Morris considers the first seven figures as major players in the American struggle for independence.[39] The fact is, every Thomas Paine who advances ideas requires a George Washington to act on them.

Similar examples can be drawn from African advocates for independence. African nationalist ideologues include Herbert Macaulay, Nnamdi Azikiwe, Ahmadu Bello, and Obafemi Awolowo of Nigeria; Kwame Nkrumah of Ghana; Amilcar Cabral of Cape Verde; Patrice Lumumba of the Democratic Republic of Congo; Jomo Kenyatta of Kenya; Nelson Mandela of South Africa; and Julius Nyerere of Tanzania. These figures not only stirred the spirit of nationalism and fought for the end of colonialism in Africa they also acted in support of their advocacy. A few, like Frantz Fanon, supported decolonization through writing, but Africa's thinkers and actors for decolonization were the abovementioned

---

35 Akinyemi and Amusan, "Between the Town."
36 Thomas Paine's "Common Sense" is widely acclaimed as the first pamphlet to push for American Independence published on January 10, 1776. Thomas Paine, *Common Sense*.
37 Kaye, *Thomas Paine*, 43.
38 See the key personalities in the American War of Independence or its founding fathers.
39 Morris, *Seven*.

nationalist ideologues. They fought in the press and on the ground to implement their desired changes.

It is not as though decolonial scholars take physical action to decolonize African history. But they provide insight into the problem of Africa's reality: the wide gap between the gown and the town presents challenges for the transformation of ideas into action. According to Akinyemi: "The challenge of [the] wide-gap between researchers and policymakers is real in Africa and has become a major issue of concern to scholars as research from Cote d'Ivoire, Kenya, Madagascar, Namibia, Nigeria, Senegal and South Africa shows. In these countries, research activities most of the time end up on the shelves of the institutions where they are conducted."[40]

This statement captures the role that research plays—or more importantly, fails to play—in effective development for African societies. Student research, especially for long essays and other projects, frequently ends up stored or "dumped" in libraries where it remains undisturbed. On paper, the aim is to contribute to the existing body of knowledge. In reality, such work rarely gets published, to say nothing of achieving its primary goal.

The research done by lecturers is largely for their own advancement up the academic ladder. Chukwuemeka et al. corroborate this point with the statement that "researches in many universities in Africa are conducted mostly to earn promotions, thus, most researchers are aspiring and relatively new PhD holders. In fact, once a university lecturer is promoted to the rank of professor, research ends."[41]

Most academic research bears no relevance for industrial applications, prompting industries in Africa to depend on "foreign technical partners for research and development."[42] With research bearing little value for African society, and with the knowledge that such research is motivated by personal goals, then one must ask whether the decolonizing of African studies can fix the problem. If you teach someone to farm productively, they will also need access to farmland and agricultural tools so that they can apply their skills. If epistemic liberation is achieved, how far can it go to effect real change?

---

40   Akinyemi and Amusan, "Between the Town," 176.
41   Chukwuemeka et al., "Research," 49.
42   Chukwuemeka et al., "Research," 49.

Although Africa contains 12.5 percent of the global population, it produced less than 1 percent of the world's research output in 2018.[43] Research is crucial for revolutionizing industries, government, commerce, and educational institutions in Africa for social and economic development, but it is gravely underfunded. Research output in Africa is also less widely adopted than in developed countries.[44] The importance of research cannot be understated for effecting real change and development—effective policies and decisions are not made unconsciously.

Without adequate research and reflection, poorly informed leaders can make disastrous decisions, such as scrapping the post–Unified Tertiary Matriculation Examination (post-UTME) in Nigeria in 2017. It was blamed for corruption and low standards in the education system, and the cut-off was reduced from two hundred (which was already 50 percent of the total obtainable score).[45] Not only did this reduce standards with a new requirement of 180 for admission into universities, but it was also a "calamitous mistake which posed a danger and an irreversible adverse effect on the quality of education in the country."[46]

The consequence of the changed post-UTME policy was apparent at the University of Ibadan, where 328 students—almost 11 percent of the total number of students admitted—were asked to withdraw. Another 115 students were incapable of attending the institutions that had accepted them, changing to "less demanding courses/faculties" due to poor grades. The university blames this outcome on the inability to conduct post-UTME assessments to identify students worthy of admission in the first place.[47] When post-UTME examinations were reinstated the following year, the improved selectivity was evident when only 69 students, out of 3,001 admitted, averaged below 1.0 (representing 2.3 percent).[48] Admission issues are just one of many reasons why Africa experiences stunted development; each step forward is accompanied by several steps backward.

---

43 Charon, Amir, and Schoombee, "Africa."
44 Chukwuemeka et al., "Research."
45 Edeh, "FG."
46 Adeyemi, "Scrapping."
47 Olayinka, "2016/2017."
48 Olayinka, "First Semester 2017/2018."

From a funding perspective, research in Africa suffers the same budgetary allocation tragedies as education. Countries in the African Union agreed to set aside 1 percent of GDP for research and development, but average funding for research on the continent has barely risen from 0.36 percent in 2007 to 0.45 percent of GDP in 2013. Their counterparts in the Western world allocate seven times as much.[49] Madagascar commits 0.01 percent of GDP to research and development, and even though the greatest investment is made by South Africa, which invests 0.82 percent, that still falls short of the 1 percent goal.[50] It has become almost cliché among lecturers in African universities to mention the lack of research funds.

The lack of public funds explains why lecturers in African universities focus time and energy on work that advances personal goals instead of research capable of stimulating socioeconomic development or addressing relevant problems for the continent. In Nigeria, "99.5 percent if not all 100 percent of the university activity and time is devoted to teaching and assessing of students throughout the year, without definite official time designated for doing research."[51] Nigerian universities also spend 98 percent of their research budget on paying salaries and allowances, while the remaining 2 percent is used to maintain services. There is no allocation for research.[52]

The decline of research quantity and quality at Nigerian universities can be traced back to the 1980s. The Nigerian University Commission (NUC) revealed that the productivity of Nigerian researchers was at its best in Africa up to the 1980s, when support for research—including proper research training, the availability of equipment, and excellent library facilities—began to gradually decline. By 1996 research hit an all-time low.[53] National budget allocations to the educational sector and universities in general dropped from an average of 30 percent in the 1960s to 15 percent in the 1970s and 1980s before falling to 3 percent in the 2000s.[54]

---

49   African Union-European Union (AU-EU), *Research*.
50   UNESCO Institute for Statistics, Index Mundi, "Research."
51   Bako, "Universities," 8.
52   Chukwuemeka et al., "Research," 49.
53   Okebukola, *State*.
54   Bako, "Universities," 8.

The NUC has found that more than 70 percent of laboratory equipment and books in Nigerian libraries were purchased between the 1960s and 1980s.[55] The sad state of African research is described by Bako:

> It is clear that the bulk of university-based research has been self-funded by the graduate students, staff-in-training and academic staff, in fact, over 80 percent has been from salaries and parents. Less than ten percent of the university based research is funded externally by foreign bodies, and the same percentage by the university research boards. Another major constraint of Nigerian university research is that it has been increasingly delinked from the productive sectors of the economy, but surprisingly even from the community and polity problems and issues.[56]

Not only is research terribly underfunded, but it is receiving funding from foreign bodies. Decolonial scholars have found that research in Africa, even when it interrelates with the specific details of the subalterns, only extrapolates data. A lack of funding independence would eventually create a situation where "he who pays the piper dictates the tune," nullifying the struggle for decoloniality as funders dictate not only the methodology but also the result of the research to suit their desires. Another problem has been identified by Ndlovu-Gatsheni, one of the foremost modern decolonial scholars:

> Europe and North America remain the centre from which what is considered valid and scientific knowledge cascades and circulates to the rest of the world. In this uneven division of labour, Africa in particular and the Global South in general exist as sites for hunting and gathering of raw data. Europe and North America remain the key sites of professional processing of data for the purposes of formulation of social theories. These theories are voraciously consumed in Africa. What are considered to be prestigious and international peer-reviewed journals that easily earn African scholars recognition and promotion are based in Europe and North America.[57]

Ndlovu-Gatsheni sees the above as "intellectual/academic dependence" triggering a call for "epistemic freedom." Already two decades into the

---

55 Bako, "Universities," 18.
56 Bako, "Universities," 11.
57 Ndlovu-Gatsheni, "Cognitive Empire," 6.

twenty-first century, I see it as the outermost layer of an onion, with many more layers beneath. Corroborating the apparent helplessness of the situation is Ndlovu-Gatsheni's review of Ramon Grofosguel:

> The success of colonialism and coloniality in the domain of knowledge was and is always dependent on winning some of the colonized people and peripherized people to its side to the extent that they then speak and write as though they were located on the racially privileged side of the colonial matrices of power. This confused mentality is nourished by the seductive aspects of coloniality, particularly its time-perfected strategy of always masquerading as a civilizing enterprise while in reality it was a death project.[58]

Ndlovu-Gatsheni is correct about the "confused mentality" created through seduction, but the passage of time has introduced a different method of seduction. The fantasy of Western civilization's superiority can be resolved by epistemic decoloniality, but ongoing trends have seen funding become the new method of seduction that is compelling enough to buy or win (in Ramon Grofosguel's words) African scholars over to the colonial side.

The problem of funding cannot be solved with arguments from decolonial scholars, and this has far-reaching consequences.[59] If you want to fight the system, you must expect the system to fight back. When Africans engaged with Europeans in the twentieth century, they got their political freedom, but they remained economically, culturally, and intellectually dependent. The CMP was sustained by a belief in the superiority of foreign products and academic deference to European centers of learning. Africa has been politically subsumed to the point where the continent can no longer be called independent—what Kwame Nkrumah would later look back on and describe as neocolonialism.

Even if the decolonial goal of epistemic liberation is achieved and the legitimization and standardization of research is no longer confined to Western dictates, a lack of funding still leaves African researchers in search of foreign grants. They would ultimately be subject to the dictates of their sponsors, and the battle would be won while the war was lost. If

---

58 Ndlovu-Gatsheni, "Cognitive Empire," 6–7.
59 See the discussion on the African university as a subject of decoloniality: Ndlovu-Gatsheni, "Cognitive Empire," 6–7.

decoloniality is to achieve sustainable epistemic liberation, it cannot end with the liberation of knowledge.

Decolonizing African Universities and Continuous Setbacks

The initiative to decolonize African university education, promoting the worldviews enshrined in "African realities and experience," can be traced back to the 1960s.[60] It was triggered by the clusters of political independence developing on the continent, which stimulated a call for transformation, Africanizing "existing 'universities in Africa' into 'African universities.'"[61] Ndlovu-Gatsheni states:

> At its deepest level, this struggle entailed formulating a new philosophy of higher education grounded in deep appreciation of African histories, cultures, ideas and inspiration as well as a fundamental redefinition of the role of the university. . . . With specific reference to Africa, the dawn of political independence in the 1960s was accompanied by efforts to create an African developmental university. Such a university was expected to be truly African and to play an active role in nation-building, socio-economic development and promoting African consciousness.[62]

The goal of African universities engendered the birth of more universities in Africa, increasing the number of scholars who embraced the cause, but the same problems remained with the structure and curriculum used for teaching.

There was a transformative change in personnel as scholars including Kenneth Dike and Ade-Ajayi emerged, who "contributed immensely to the Africanization of history as a discipline" and also to the project of nation-building in Africa.[63] However, the same problem exists today that was present fifty years ago. The structure and curriculum identified by Ndlovu-Gatsheni has remained the same: some lecturers still teach with outdated methods, and worse still, outdated facts.

A typical example can be drawn from a story told by graduate students at a Nigerian University's department of history. According to them, a

---

60 Nyamnjoh, "Decolonizing," 1.
61 Ndlovu-Gatsheni, "Cognitive Empire," 9.
62 Ndlovu-Gatsheni, "Cognitive Empire."
63 Falola, *Nationalism,* 224.

professor of history taught from the first year to final exams by reading from lecture notes that he claims to have taken when he was a student. Another lecturer confirmed the use of outdated materials, distributing materials that claimed there were six million people in the world—this despite UN figures establishing that the "global population reached the 7 billion mark" in 2011, [64] estimating it at 7.7 billion around the time the lecturer used the material.[65] This was one of many incorrect statistics presented in the material.

Professor Jonathan Jansen of Stellenbosch University also criticizes attempts to decolonize Africa's academic curriculum, opining that the decolonial movement will have no real impact on the institutional curriculum "because it offers the wrong solution to a real problem."[66] In his speech "The Problem with Decolonization," he states that decolonization has a "rich intellectual ancestry," but his position is that "there was a failure among academics and students to scrutinize concepts as they emerge in society or on university campuses, abrogating their responsibility to think as academics and to be 'suspicious of things that parade as truth.'"[67]

Much has been said about funding, but it is also difficult to ensure that adequate time is allocated for research. Time spent on research is often stolen from classroom time or spare time, which are both in short supply already, and this affects not only the quality of investigative research[68] but also the knowledge imparted to university students. Some lecturers show up for class half-prepared with lecture notes assembled at the last minute, mixing up dates and figures as they attempt to recall information that was hastily memorized. Other professors show up and dictate notes with little explanation before declaring that class time is over. Nigeria could be the case study for the continuing use of practices, data, and systems that are hopelessly outdated in the twenty-first century. A change of practice is especially necessary as part of the efforts that decolonial scholars, such as Ndlovu-Gatsheni and Falola, have recommended for African universities.

The struggle for decolonization has been ongoing since the 1960s, and the scholars cited above are still agitating for reform more than five

---

64 *United Nations*, "World Population Day."
65 United Nations Department of Economic and Social Affairs, *World Population*.
66 Makoni, "Limitations."
67 Makoni, "Limitations."
68 Bako, "Universities," 8–9.

decades later. Falola has identified and presented four significant factors that have been blocking progress, and they are further explained by Ndlovu-Gatsheni. The first factor is the "decline in African economies, which made it impossible for African governments to continue financing higher education."[69] The second factor is tied to the first, the third is a result of the continent's political situation, and the final factor is due to global forces and economic dependence.[70] All four reasons remain relevant to Africa today, constituting the entirety of this chapter's arguments and criticism of decoloniality.

Decolonial scholars in the 1970s began their efforts to create an African university while ignoring Africa's ongoing economic decline[71] (and it is worth noting that Albert Einstein has famously defined insanity as repeating the same actions while expecting different results). Given the difficulty in achieving African history's decoloniality, which has become even more pronounced in the presence of rising corruption, bad leadership, trade dependence, and economic woes—and given that little progress has been made by African decolonial scholars in advancing comprehensive solutions—the decolonizing of African studies and Africa as a whole appears futile. Africa's current political leaders are not the same nationalists who fought and won political freedom, and even they failed to decolonize Africa. Apart from that, Africa's economic situation has worsened, its culture continues to decline, and its acceptance of Eurocentric civilizations is growing. Beyond these problems, academic research faces other obstacles preventing it from contributing to development; these have been described by other scholars.[72]

Conclusion

There is no doubt that research is vastly important for realizing socioeconomic development.[73] However, the fundamental problems that ham-

---

69 Ndlovu-Gatsheni, "Emergence," 51–77.
70 Ndlovu-Gatsheni, "Emergence."
71 Ndlovu-Gatsheni, "Emergence," 67.
72 Chikwe, Ogidi, and Nwachukwu, "Challenges," 44–47. Chukwuemeka et al., "Research," 50.
73 Chukwuemeka et al., "Research," 54.

per research mean that the results of decolonization—legitimizing and incorporating African perspectives—would not be substantial enough to decolonize African history and stimulate economic development like their Western counterparts. The reality is that the Africanization of African studies faces such great obstacles that it seems decolonial scholars did not weigh the costs before embarking on their struggle. The persistent mistakes of the past are more enduring than ever, and Africa continues in a colonized state due to its economy.

The Africanization of African studies faces obstacles from African scholars, not only in failing to adopt an Afrocentric curriculum and restructuring universities and centers of research, but also in the perception that the decoloniality of African studies is a movement led chiefly by African scholars in the diaspora; this may be part of the second problem identified by Falola as leading to the decline of African universities. Conferences are organized from time to time, but what happens when these scholars return to their respective countries and institutions—do they adopt and continue discussions from the conference? One might also infer that there is a problem with the conversion gap between African-based African scholars and African scholars in the diaspora.

The task is not as easy as it seems, which is due to the endemic problem of inadequate funding for education and research. Nigerian universities are especially plagued by yearly industrial actions initiated by teaching and nonteaching staff. Even if the goal of academic decoloniality is achieved, decolonial scholars are ignoring the problem of economic coloniality just as they did in the 1980s. Economic coloniality impedes epistemic decoloniality, but the focus has remained on epistemic decoloniality as a means to achieve other goals, overlooking the fact that a vibrant African economy is necessary to support innovations from African scholars.

Finally, and most importantly, the wide gap between town and gown must be bridged to achieve sufficient development. Decolonial scholars should not seek solutions in isolation; decolonial scholars themselves (chiefly Falola and Ndlovu-Gatsheni) have proven that their work is extremely dependent on appropriate political leadership and economic policies to liberate Africa from Sino-European dependence.

Chapter Ten

Women's Voices on Decolonization

Introduction

Decolonization in the African intellectual context implies the elimination of unnecessary Western-based philosophies and theories that are vestiges of Africa's colonial past. This is an exercise aimed at achieving a more African-rooted scholarship that will effectively reflect the intellectual needs of Africa. The concept of decolonization and the need thereof has stirred much rhetoric among African scholars due to a consistency of Western epistemological frames in supposed African scholarship.

The process of decolonization in the areas of African knowledge production begins with the development of indigenous African principles that will provide a more credible perspective on the African reality, as well as reveal the superimposition of Western philosophies on African intellectual space. This would involve restructuring of the education curriculum to include and reflect homegrown philosophies as well as the publication of various materials that document and advance the cause for decolonization. This strategy has the potential to recondition Africa's thought patterns and for Africa's intellectual growth and a more incisive collective self-awareness.

Several African scholars can be linked to studies on decolonization and, like many other areas of human endeavor, the works of men have continued to be the mainstream in decolonization discourses. Women scholars have been marginalized and their works ghettoized by the men who are at the frontline of African scholarship. However, women have continued to write, hence the presence of several feminine voices in relation to the decolonization of African studies: for example, scholars like Chandra Talpade Mohanty[1], the first major voice from the Global South in feminist decolonization theory. A long list of feminist scholars followed. The works of these female scholars will be interrogated to explore their contributions to the cause of decolonizing African studies.

Women's Contributions to the Decolonization Project

This part of the study will provide insight on the specific contributions of women to the process of decolonizing African studies and eliminating women marginalization in society and scholarship. With the focus on inputs such as advocating for an African mode of reasoning, women's activism for social change, their publication of essays and books on varied subjects, and their creation of women-based institutions for the decolonization of African studies, the following sections will address women's voices in decolonizing African studies.

Advocating for an African Mode of Reasoning

Irrespective of her non-African origin, Chandra Talpade Mohanty's work on decolonization is still relevant to African scholarship since it involves a juxtaposition of the privileged Western feministic ideologies and the flaws of its Third World representation. Therefore, Africa, being located within the politics of Third World nations, would profit from her scholarly theorizing. In her work "Under Western Eyes," she identifies a systemic hegemony at play between the West and Third World feminist scholarship. She criticizes the monolithic construction and representation of

---

1 Before her were African feminists who did comparable but less globalized work, including Bolanle Awe, Simi Afonja, Nina Mba, Filomina Steady, Fatou Sow, Zenebeworke Tadesse, Nawal El-Sadaawi, and Christine Achola Pala Okeyo, among others. This first generation was followed by perhaps a more vibrant and effective generation whose works reinscribed African women's theorizing into global narratives through their work. These ones were Oyeronke Oyewumi, Filomina Steady, Amina Mama, Ayesha Imam, Akosua Adomako Ampofo, Takyiwaah Manu, Patricia McFadden, Sylvia Tamale, among others.

Third World women in cross-cultural Western feminist studies as: "religious (read: not progressive), family-oriented (read: traditional), legally unsophisticated (read: they are still not conscious of their rights), illiterate (read: ignorant), domestic (read: backward), and sometimes revolutionary (read: their country is in a state of war; they must fight!)."[2]

However, this conception of Third World women stands against the image of liberated, progressive, sophisticated Western women in "control of their lives."[3] For her, in Western feminist discourses, women from the Third World are suspended in time and are constantly represented as oppressed while having their economic, legal, and social status judged using Western parameters. With this, Mohanty implies that these discourses do not consider the specificities of these societies; neither do they acknowledge the forms of resistance employed by these women. Therefore, with that ethnocentric consciousness, the concept of underdevelopment and a Third World "difference" through the Western lens is created, hence the more unlikely intercultural alliances become in feminist scholarship.[4] This image of Third World women contributes to the sustenance of the Third World/First World hierarchy. In other words, the creation of a Third World identity sustains and maintains the First World hegemony. Mohanty, however, opines that the sustained monolithic representation of the Third World woman as dependent, unrepentantly subsumed by the structures of patriarchy and perpetually in need of Western help, can only be attributed to a possible disinterest in self representation, which is in turn a manifestation of cultural colonialism. In other words, the responsibility of representation should not be abandoned for the West.

By identifying the flaws of Western feminist ideologies in relation to Third World women, Mohanty draws attention to the cultural hegemony that exists in feminist scholarship, which in turn reinforces a supposed superiority of the West and continues to foster Western cultural imperialism. With this, Mohanty bares the realities of mainstream feminism and in turn advocates for social change from the bottom up. In this context, Third World feminist scholarship constitutes the bottom, having been subject to the social domination of Western scholarship. Therefore, the

---

2   Mohanty, "Under Western Eyes."
3   Mohanty, "Under Western Eyes."
4   Mohanty, "Under Western Eyes."

process of decolonization for the Third World feminist scholar implies an investment in re-creating the image and representation of Third World women with detailed information on the region's historical philosophies and specificities for the benefit of its feminist studies and discourses. However, reflecting the tenacity of historians and literary scholars from the Third World, Mohanty represents the many women who, though marginalized, are equally invested in the cause for scholarly decolonization, activism, and cultural preservation in multidisciplinary and cross-cultural feminist studies.

Therefore, with reference to the need for cultural preservation and consciousness in African scholarship, Amadiume stresses the need for a proper awareness of history by stating the following: "The relevance of historical materialism is the fact that one can look at continuity, reversibility, transitory systems, aggregates, borrowing from systems, actual processes of negotiation and new formations; but, more importantly, one can locate instances of cultural imperialism following foreign invasions."[5]

In other words, an awareness of history provides evidence and resources for cultural continuity as well as changes and adoptions of methodologies and theories inspired by cultural systems. This will, however, equip cultures against foreign imperialism as well as in the identification of such, if and when it occurs. Amadiume's opinion therefore gives perspective to Oyewumi's study of the generalization of the Western conception of gender and the absence thereof in the precolonial Yoruba community. Her work exposes the pervasive yet limited knowledge in Yoruba studies on issues relating to gender as well as the cultural stance of the indigenous communities toward the concept. With that consciousness, Oyewumi's study on the invention of the concept of "women" by Western epistemology as a distinct group of people who share common interests, social positions, and aspirations, explores the misconstrued assumption that the social category of gender has been in existence in Africa from time immemorial.[6]

With a focus on the Oyo people of the Yoruba community, Oyewumi's work asserts that the concept of women as a distinct social category is solely a Western construct and did not exist in the Oyo Yoruba community until its contact with colonial society. In her opinion, the Western

---

5   Amadiume, "Theorizing."
6   Oyewumi, *Invention*.

categorization of gender is based on biology. In other words, the difference between the physical appearances and biological makeup of one individual and another has therefore yielded societal hierarchies between one sex and the other.[7] However, Oyewumi opines that the physical body in Yoruba society prior to Western contact was never a determinant for social relevance, roles, inclusions, and exclusions. It was simply not a basis for hierarchy. Rather, social identity and position were related to people's interactions, hence the concept of seniority irrespective of gender. In other words, the Yoruba society did not assign superiority to one group of people at the expense of the others as a result of physical appearance or biological makeup.

However, with the infusion of Western principles and ideologies of gender into the African society, and the propagation of Universalist theorizations like Oyewumi's observation that gender is often considered "universal and timeless and have been present in every society at all times."[8] Therefore, it implies that gender stratification has been an existing practice all around the world. The concept of gender in the contemporary Yoruba society has been normalized and ingrained in the very fabric of African and Yoruba existence, which therefore makes the conception of a cultural absence of gender ludicrous and gives credence to the following statement by Balibar: "What is certain is that normality cannot be separated from the hierarchization of identities the great hegemonic, rational, political-philosophical mechanisms are precisely what fabricate normality, with the consent of the group concerned."[9]

In other words, the hegemony of the West through colonialism has brought about the normalization of Western principles and ideologies, hence Oyewumi's observation of the inclusion of gender categorizations as a fundamental aspect of the Yoruba culture in contemporary Yoruba studies. However, given Hussein's postulation that a gendered society and culture tends to encourage and reinforce the behavioral expectations of men and women,[10] the internalization of patriarchy and assignment of roles to men and women in Africa based on gender is a reflection of Africa's adoption of the Western ideologies of gender. It therefore shows

---

7   Oyewumi, *Invention*.
8   Oyewumi, *Invention*, xi.
9   Mama, "Challenging," 63–73.
10 Hussein, "Social," 59–87.

the true extent of the erosion of local Yoruba cultural ideologies, especially the domination of Western scholarly ideologies in African studies. Oyewumi's work further accentuates the dangers of cultural ignorance on a people, hence her decision to look into the invention of gender in the lives of the Oyo people of the Yoruba society.

However, as part of the process of decolonizing African studies, Oyewumi specifically states that her work focuses only on the Oyo community and, therefore, her findings should not be generalized. This is not to say that African societies do not share a commonality in their cultural philosophies but rather so as to avoid the dangers of the sort of unfounded generalizations that are the specialty of the West. This, therefore, explains the Universalist conceptions of the subordination of the socially constructed female gender that have permeated global scholarship, paving the way for her marginalization in several areas of society including African scholarship.

Having established women's marginalization as a product of Africans' ignorance of their cultural heritage as well as their internalization of a gendered Western philosophy, Oyewumi's paper on "Gender Epistemologies in Africa," and most specifically the chapter on "Decolonizing the Intellectual and the Custodian: Yoruba Scholarship and Male Dominance," interrogates the blatant normalization of male dominance and the marginalization of women in African scholarship.[11] In the context of dominance, Oyewumi carefully explains that her reference to dominance is not limited to the presence of more men than women in scholarship, even though Bradford recognizes the neglect of women in African historiography,[12] but rather incorporates the privileging of the male concepts in several cultural ideologies of Yoruba scholarship, such as the arrogation of the male persona to the Yoruba concept of Olodumare, which she describes as originally devoid of gender and even humanity.[13] This observation further foregrounds Oyewumi's recognition of gender as a colonial construct and legacy, one that privileges the male gender and has unfortunately been successfully inculcated into the African victims of colonialism, hence the reproduction of sexist notions and attitudes even by the so-called custodians of African-based scholarship. The latter

---

11   Oyewumi, "Decolonizing."
12   Bradford, "Women," 350–70.
13   Oyewumi, "Decolonizing."

statement is most sensitive given that Oyewumi's analysis of the Yoruba oral traditions, system of knowledge (Ifa), culture, and religion bears no traces of gendering. The concept of gender, as argued by Oyewumi, is foreign to Yoruba epistemology.

Therefore, with keen understanding of the operations of gender in society, the need for the institutionalization of gender and feminist studies cannot be overemphasized. However, the study of mainstream feminism has for so long catered to the needs of the average white middle-class woman while going further to universalize white women's experiences.[14] However, in a different study, Oyewumi explores the Eurocentric foundations of the mainstream feminist concept, stating that mainstream feminism is founded on the nuclear family construct of the West. She interrogates the inappropriateness in universalizing Western feminism, of which its tenets clearly emanate from the power relations in the nuclear family without taking into consideration the different family structures in different parts of Africa with a focus on the Yoruba society.[15] For her, what the Euro-American woman experiences in her private home forms the basis for gender research; and gender has therefore become an important universal academic tool for analyzing Yoruba society.

Identifying gender as a social construct, Oyewumi opines that the construction of gender creates the place of a woman and her attendant subordination, which has so far been universalized by the Western cultural ethos.[16] She questions the prominent position of gender in the life of the white woman against other factors like race—which is pertinent to African Americans—and imperialism or colonialism for the African. However, while analyzing the nuclear family as the basis for white feminism, Oyewumi recognizes that society often views the nuclear family as comprising the wife, husband, and her children, without room for outsiders, which therefore explains the inability of white feminism to include other factors like race and class. For her, the question of gender should be thoroughly critiqued, especially when trying to criticize African epistemologies.

In her opinion, the family hierarchy in the Western nuclear family is organized by gender; therefore, the father stands as a patriarch whose authority is derived from his status as the family's provider, while the

---

14 Oyewumi, "Decolonizing."
15 Oyewumi, "Conceptualizing," 1–5.
16 Oyewumi, "Conceptualizing."

mother's subordinate status comes from domesticity and her place as the nurturer. Therefore, the gendered division of labor in the family has certain psychological implications on the children, creating a gendered society.[17] This supports the notion of gender as learned and not innate, which is therefore why West and Zimmerman suggest that "gender is not something we are born with, and not something we possesses, but something we do from observation."[18] In other words the conditionings of the nuclear family continue to replicate gender structures and roles in society.

However, in the Yoruba society as presented by Oyewumi, the family organizations are different and, most importantly, nongendered, mostly because the family roles are defined based on seniority and not gender. Bascom consolidates Oyewumi's opinion by also examining the principle of seniority in his study of the Yoruba people. In his opinion, the kinship terms used in Yoruba families are an indication of the seniority-based ranking systems in the family. In fact, he goes on to state that "seniority is defined in terms of the length of an individual's affiliation either by marriage, or by birth with the patrilocal kinship group whose members are known as children of the house."[19] Therefore, these Western feminist concepts pose many challenges when applied to the realities of the African society and African gender studies. This is particularly because biological designations of sex are the basics for gender distinction and roles that present the man as superior to the woman. These distinctions in cultural conceptions of sex and hierarchy make it difficult to apply Western feminist concepts to African gender studies. To clarify this point, Oyewumi states that "when African realities are interpreted based on these Western claims, what we find are distortions, obfuscations in language and often a total lack of comprehension due to the incommensurability of social categories and institutions. In fact, the two basic categories of woman and gender demand rethinking."[20]

Oyewumi's observation is most likely not unique to the Yoruba community. This is primarily because several studies on other indigenous communities within Africa attest to the flexibility of the concept of gender in their power structures and cultural philosophies. Ifi Amadiume's

---

17   Oyewumi, "Conceptualizing."
18   West and Zimmerman, "Doing Gender," 125–51.
19   Bascom, "Principle," 37–46.
20   Oyewumi, "Conceptualizing," 4.

work "Male Daughters, Female Husbands: Gender and Sex in an African Society" attests to a decentralized power structure among the Igbo women from Nnobi, southeast Nigeria.[21] She further examines the colonial imposition of masculinist ideologies on an otherwise flexible gender system that did not indulge a relationship between gender roles and sex, hence the possibility of female husbands who married wives outside a sexual context to assist in their accumulation of wealth by serving as human resources, as well as the "male daughter" who attained eligibility to acquire power and economic status by assuming the position of a male daughter, and whose sole purpose was to ensure the continuity of the lineage as well.

However, with the subtle conditioning of the European male-centered religions and colonial political structures, not to mention the demonization of the people's indigenous religious systems and cultural practices, the Igbo society gradually shifted to a male-centric system that encouraged the marginalization of women in all areas of society. This unconscious acceptance of domination as the status quo brought about the economic suppression of women as well as the patriarchal monopoly of the political systems.

Consolidating this assumption, Anunuobi opines that the legacy of colonialism and Western imperialism is mostly responsible for the economic dependency and overall subordination of women in Africa. This can be attributed to the structural overhaul the African political and economic systems witnessed during this period. She equally observes that European incursion into Africa led to the strengthening of the patriarchy: in other words, she does not romanticize the woman's position in a precolonial African state, hence her insinuation of certain elements of the patriarchy that were eventually strengthened and sustained with the expansion of the West into Africa.[22] However, Amadiume's exposure of the consequences of internalized sexist orientation and aggressive patriarchy calls for a mental decolonization of African societies from privileged Western-based notions by coming to the awareness of the original place of women in African society.

Also with a focus on decolonizing African knowledge in relation to gender, Yacob-Haliso and Falola "examine contemporary gender relations in

---

21 Amadiume, *Male Daughters*.
22 Anunuobi, "Women," 41–43.

Africa and the diaspora by historical African standards.[23] In other words, they interrogate universal conceptions of gender found in African narratives for inaccuracy, while attempting to rewrite the history of gender in Africa; but, like Oyewumi and Amadiume as well as other studies on African decolonization, Yacob-Haliso and Falola both recognize the pervasiveness and privilege of Western narratives of gender in Africa. These narratives are rather based on a "Conradian view of African history and culture."[24] Therefore, with the allusion to Joseph Conrad and his portrayal of Africa in "Heart of Darkness," both scholars try to convey the one-dimensional representations of African women by dominant narratives as culturally repressed and unsophisticated, hence their attempt at reconstructing these biased notions of African women and gender relations.

Quite ironically, contemporary African attempts to reflect the indigenous African cultural reality end up reproducing colonial values championed by the Western monopoly of African narratives, further illuminating the extent of the alien cultural diffusion among Africans. For instance, in the indigenous attempts at writing African history, Ayesha's work on the presentation of women in historical writing reveals a neglect of women's narratives and an invisibility of women in African historiography. This is on its own a relegation of women to the margins of society and a reinforcement of the sexist values and male privilege in Western cultural ideologies. However, Hunt debunks the notions of omission and silence on women's narratives by stating specifically that "African women, whether as subjects or objects (and to a lesser extent authors) of history, are no longer invisible in African historiography."[25] This therefore poses a question about the type of image and presence women have in present-day historiography.

Mama's work explores the burden of so-called African cultures on the African woman and how men became enforcers of these obvious erroneous oppressive systems posing as African culture.[26] She goes further to examine the impact of colonialism on the distortion of the true African cultural systems in relation to gender, which is more devastating because Western discourses on gender misconstrue these changes as rooted in African culture, and through this erroneous postulating maintain a

---

23 Yacob-Haliso and Falola, "Introduction," 1–15.
24 Yacob-Haliso and Falola, "Introduction."
25 Hunt, "Placing," 359–79.
26 Mama, "Shedding."

backward portrait of Africa. For her, the changes that evidently occurred in Africa's gender relations qualify as the crux of the dramatic changes Africa has experienced so far.[27]

Considering these changes in history, the importance of accurate documentation and research cannot be overemphasized. It is therefore no wonder Yacob-Haliso and Falola dedicate themselves to rewriting historical accounts of gender in Africa and African communities in the diaspora, while also paying attention to the narratives on gender and power structures in different locations across the world. However, with feminism being a part of gender studies and activism, their work equally explores the influence of feminism in focalizing women's studies in academia through their various movements, activisms, and theorizations and attempts to revitalize traditional methodologies, modes, and theories instead of adapting Western theories to African contexts.

Constituting a major part of the African diaspora are African Americans in the United States, a group that constitutes a prominent presence on the chain of the oppressed. Women, on the other hand, take a lower position on this chain of oppression. Patricia Collins notes that African American women in the United States are often denied some privileges and even rights that are easily accessible to the white male population.[28] She attributes Black women's oppression to the history and conditioning of slavery, which have long inadvertently shaped the Black woman's experience in the United States. The disenfranchisement of Black women, the legal biases against them as well as educational segregation, are geared toward maintaining their subordination while enforcing racist and sexist notions as justification for said oppression.

In other words, the conception of white superiority strengthened by stereotypical images of the Black woman is used to justify the oppression at play in society. It is, however, unsurprising given that this work has so far explored and interrogated the play of hegemonic ideologies of Western and male superiority that are part and parcel of colonialism. These ideologies have been internalized by Africans and have continued to maintain a superimposition of Western values and the subordination of the African heritage. Also, applicable to both spaces is the political, economic, and

---

27 Mama, "Shedding."
28 Collins, *Black Feminist*.

ideological modes of oppression that have so far been wielded successfully in exerting the social inequality between nations and races alike.

Collins's work also explores the obscurity of African American women's voices in the intellectual space. By recognizing the impact of women intellectuals like Maria W. Stewart, whose ideas she employs in foregrounding the notions of Black feminist thought, Collins focuses on still-extant oppression and the intellectual efforts aimed at instigating Black women's activism. She also notes that many other African American women intellectuals have been unfairly unnoticed and understudied. This process of obscuring the African American woman's intellect is seen by Collins as a deliberate attempt by the oppressor to keep their knowledge under wraps, hence suppressing the Black woman and further asserting their dominance and maintaining the "pots and kettles" symbols of the Black woman's subordination in society while sustaining its existing inequalities.[29]

Suppressing the intellect of the Black woman through restricting her access to literacy and impeding Black female intellectuals from attaining positions of leadership in social and academic institutions: this constitutes part of the grand scheme of elevating the interests and views of the US white male majority. Collins, however, observes that these calculated attempts at suppressing Black women's agency is not limited to the United States alone but can also be found in Africa, Europe, the Caribbean, and South America. However, these efforts have so far not totally deterred African women from intellectual engagement with the important issues of the day. Therefore, by monopolizing knowledge production, white male elites foster the interests of maintaining white dominance and promoting stereotypical conceptions of Black women.

Collins recognizes the efforts of feminist women's studies in questioning the dominant views of white elites. In her opinion the vanguard of Western feminist studies has also casually overlooked the interests of Black women, treating all women irrespective of race, ethnicity, religion, class, and educational levels as a homogenous group with the same challenges.[30] This has led to criticism of Western feminism as being selective in its views and frameworks while posing as universal thinking. However, this argument is quite similar to the continental African women's concerns on the subject of feminism, hence their domestication of feminism

---

29 Collins, *Black Feminist*, 2.
30 Anunobi, "Women."

to fit the continental demands of women in Africa, therefore giving credence to the following definition of African feminism by Goredema:

> African feminism is a feminist epistemology and a form of rhetoric that has provided arguments, which validates the experiences of women of Africa of African origin against a mainstream feminist discourse. It is a justice that aims to create a discernible difference between women who were colonised and those who were deemed the colonizers, and a social movement that aims to raise a global consciousness which sympathises with African women's histories, present realities and future expectations. African feminism concerns itself not only with the rights of women from Africa but is also inclusive of those living in the diaspora as many of the contributors to the literature have often lived "abroad."[31]

The above definition of African feminism takes into consideration the peculiarities of the African experience—or in this context, African American realities—which will include differences absent in mainstream feminism. Mainstream feminist theory superimposes itself on the realities of "other" women of color across the globe while considering middle-class white women's experiences as universal. With these variant feminisms erupting worldwide, long-subordinated women intellectuals are exhibiting a sense of self-awareness and therefore taking steps to define themselves on their own terms.

However, with a growing list of oppressive techniques aimed at marginalizing African American feminist discourse, these women intellectuals have begun to assert their thoughts on gender inequality and racism. In fact, Collins observes that since the 1970s, African American women intellectuals have participated in discourses on "the masculinist bias in Black social and political thought, the racist bias in feminist theory, and the heterosexist bias in both to be corrected."[32] Almost as expected, given the internalization of sexism at play in society, it is therefore not surprising that Collins points to hostile opposition from the Black male to the early political writings of Black women. However, Collins's work reveals the ideological and political factors at play in the subordination of African women and the suppression of their intellectual ideas, as well as how these women have against all odds continued to make their voices heard in

---

31 Goredema, "African Feminism," 33–41.
32 Collins, *Black Feminist*, 8.

society. Therefore, the African American woman, just like other women of "color" in places across the globe, has to deal with issues of race and sexism in her bid to assert herself in the academy and in the larger society.

Language, as observed by Ngugi, is a system of cultural transmission, and therefore can serve as a tool for cultural hegemony.[33] However, on the continental African space and on issues of cultural imperialism, Oyewumi recognizes the play of the English language in the subtle Anglicization of the Yoruba culture; therefore, she painstakingly unravels the superimposition, misinterpretation, and reconstruction of Yoruba cultural views by the mere translation of the Yoruba oral text into the English language.[34] Her work examines the damage of translation as something that usually materializes in the erosion of values and infusion of the ideologies of the dominant language and its attendant culture on the language undergoing translation.

However, in this context Oyewumi opines that the translation of Yoruba oral texts to English has several implications on the various spheres of the Yoruba belief system such as religion and the Ifa, which is the indigenous Yoruba system of knowledge. This is mainly because Oyewumi observes a wide linguistic chasm between the English language and Yoruba. She carefully delineates the absence of gender in the Yoruba language but identifies the play of gender in the translation and analysis of these cultural texts translated in English, a language she considers a "male privileging language."[35] The tendency for the English language to attribute the male pronouns to figures of supremacy and authority explains the postcolonial maleness of Olodumare and other spiritual beings like Odunmbaku, who is considered the son of Agbonniregun, a divination deity. In other words, Oyewumi's work exposes the role of language in extending colonialism. This ideology therefore gives credence to literary icon Ngugi's refusal to publish in English, his decision stemming from his conception of language as culture. He further opines that "language as culture is the collective memory bank of a people's experience in history. Culture is almost indistinguishable from the language that makes possible

---

33 Ngugi, *Decolonising*.
34 Oyewumi, "Decolonizing."
35 Oyewumi, "Decolonizing," 11.

its genesis, growth, banking articulation and indeed its transmission from one generation to the next."[36]

Therefore, Oyewumi's argument that Western ideals of patriarchy have been infused in Yoruba culture through the English language is justifiable, given the derivative notion of patriarchy at play in the translation of Yoruba oral texts. Her work also interrogates the misinterpretation of personalities like the Esu and Aje by translators using the Christian European outlook in viewing Yoruba religious cosmology. Therefore, being indistinguishable from language, as Ngugi observes, culture finds its expression through the superimposition of the English language on the Yoruba people, thereby shaping the people's outlook via the distorting Western interpretation of their indigenous philosophies.

Foregrounding Collins's claims on the ghettoization of women's studies and ideas, Oyewumi draws on own her personal experiences from her years of scholarship and relationship with male scholars to further expose the ignorance and effusion of sexism—a product of Africa's colonial contact by men who occupy high positions in Yoruba studies. With reference to the inaugural lecture delivered by the Nigerian sociologist Akinsola Akiwowo at the University of Ile Ife in 1980, Oyewumi deduces the pervasive male dominance in Nigerian universities as well as its normalization. This, however, reveals the problems inherent in the following statement cited in Oyewumi and contained in Akiwowo's inaugural speech: "In a male-dominated society, it is a credit to the male staff that the social organizational structure of the Department has not been irreparably shredded by conflicts. It is also a clear evidence of the fine sensibility of our female colleagues that they maintain their own as intellectual equals without fuss."[37]

Therefore, in light of Oyewumi's deductions, Akiwowo betrays the subtle hint that females tend to instigate conflicts; but it also commends men for somehow steering the focus of the department away from conflict and maintaining a cordial relationship with the "volatile" women. In other words, the suggestion is that the men in the department have been instrumental in maintaining an even keel in the department. Therefore, the fact that Akiwowo delivered such a speech publicly without any blowback shows the true extent of the patriarchy at play among intellectuals in

---

36 Ngugi, *Decolonising*, 15.
37 Oyewumi, "Decolonizing."

academia. Also, by recounting her experience at the Harvard conference on Ifa in 2008, Oyewumi reveals the extent of women's marginalization in scholarship and the trivialization of their ideas and theories.

She also examines the blatant disregard for women's studies exemplified at the conference. Firstly, Oyewumi notes that gender-related topics were scheduled toward the end of the conference; then she noted the several rebuttals she received during the presentation of her paper. She posed questions that triggered criticism and even animosity from male scholars. With reference to the study on the relationship between Islam and Yoruba culture, which was prompted by a paper presented on Islamic tradition in Ifa, she questioned the supposed relationship between Islam and Yoruba given that the Yoruba culture was blind to gender and therefore could never have permitted the seclusion and subordination of women that abides in Islam. However, Akiwowo's refusal to further entertain questions on gender by stating that gender had nothing to do with his study was criticized as revealing an inherent disregard for women's and gender issues, which would explain the tension created by Oyewumi's paper on gender and the questions posed by gender studies.[38] Therefore, by not understanding the play of gender in virtually all areas of scholarship, Oyewumi's male critics reveal the true extent of their deliberate ignorance despite the wealth of research and knowledge they have acquired with their years of study. It also poses the question of whether the male scholars in question have been blind to these realities on the basis of the benefits they derive from the colonial introduction of gender into the Yoruba society.

Ironically, the decolonization process necessary to correct the theoretical inadequacies of these male scholars was suggested by one of the men present at the conference. By stating that Oyewumi did not have a firm grasp of the Yoruba language exigencies, and by sarcastically suggesting that she take a course on Yoruba 101, he proffers the solution to the continued Western dominance on the African philosophical space. In other words, referring back to the basics of the Yoruba language and truly understanding it (with the consciousness of the attendant Westernization of the language) would supply much-needed insight into the realities of African and Yoruba heritage and in turn instigate the decolonization of Africa's collective consciousness as well as its scholarship. Therefore, Oyewumi advocates for an African mode of reasoning by exposing the subtle infusions

---

38   Oyewumi, "Decolonizing," 13.

of Westernization using language and concepts unique to the English language and culture. On a different yet related note, her study further advocates for a historical form of feminism, stating that mainstream feminism does not take into account the historical absence of gender in cultures like that of the Yoruba but rather universalizes the conception that women have been oppressed from time immemorial. With this, she advocates for new methodologies in her activism for social change.

Consolidating Oyewumi's conception of women's relegation to the margins of scholarship, Zeleza equally explores the invisibility of women in African narratives, history, and scholarship. In his opinion, there are more published male historians than women, hence the historical invisibility of and trivialization of women in the African historical space specifically. According to Imam et al., these historical works usually revolve around issues of nationalism, Marxism, underdevelopment, and dependency, the final two being part of the Western ploy to disparage Africa.[39] Zeleza similarly observes the absence of women in these works of history while pointing out that their rare appearances were usually clichéd, further validating Mohanty's opinion of the static representation of the African woman, defined usually within the confines of domesticity or saddled with the stereotypical responsibility of wifehood and motherhood. Mohanty's comprehension of this representation stems from the uneven power relations between the Third World and the historically dominant West.

Therefore, with the West enjoying an ideological monopoly on Third World narratives, they continue to present a static portrait of Third World women and their existence.[40] On the other hand, Zeleza's claim of women's invisibility is a product of male domination in African scholarship and around the world. However, by identifying male domination as the root cause of women's invisibility in scholarship, Zeleza does not imply that Western domination and the hijacking of African narratives is nonexistent. Therefore, like Mohanty, Zeleza admits the problems of Western ethnocentrism and male-centrism but also acknowledges the efforts of African women scholars in decolonizing women studies in Africa.

However, the contributions of scholars like Judith Van Allen have gone a long way in correcting inaccurate representations of African women in

---

39 Imam, "Engendering."
40 Mohanty, "Under Western Eyes."

history. Allen focuses on presenting the authorities of precolonial Nigerian women, with the aim of accurately representing the African woman's history and eliminating the stereotypes of them being docile, domestic, and unproductive, which are popular misconceptions of African women perpetuated by male scholars and Western imperialists alike.[41]

Nwando Achebe is a prominent female historian who in her work has unearthed the hidden narratives of influential women in prominent positions and who served as kings during the precolonial and colonial era. These narratives explore the evolution and era of female power in Nigeria that otherwise would have gone unnoticed.[42] In the political scene, works by Nina Mba explore the position and active participation of Nigerian women in politics; her work also explores the influence of Ransome Funmilayo Kuti, who was a prominent activist for women's rights and movements in the colonial era.[43] Ifi Amadiume's work examines African conceptualizations of gender and sex in the society. Her work has contributed to the studies of gender and feminism in African and global scholarship.[44] Bolanle Awe's works focus on highlighting the position of women in the history of Nigeria and Africa in general. These works are therefore responses to the marginalization of women's history; such scholarship has eliminated the previously male-centric representation of African history to include the status and influence of women. These works have also put paid to the harmful clichés that had previously passed for representation of African women by Western imperialists.

Also, Zeleza explores the adoption of oral narratives for women's history as an approach to recovering women's historical realities and eliminating the dominance of male-centered narratives. Oral histories, as observed by Zeleza, are often more efficient in providing useful historical information devoid of the self-serving antics hidden in the pages of the colonial works. By employing oral history as a methodology, Zeleza more efficiently conveys the truths of African history. However, he also states that "feminist and nationalist historians tend to privilege oral methods in their efforts to dismantle deeply entrenched biases and recover the history

---

41   Allen, "Sitting," 165–81.
42   Achebe, *Farmers*; Achebe, *Female*, 1.
43   Mba, *Nigerian*; Johnson-Odim and Mba, *For Women*.
44   Amadiume, "Theorizing."

of long suppressed, exploited, and humiliated groups of people."[45] This therefore qualifies as one of the feminist contributions to the decolonization of African narratives. Zeleza also goes on to point to a recent proliferation of women's history across Africa but still sees it as a ghettoized subject nonetheless.

Also, while exploring the need for indigenous historical research, oral or written, Gloria Chuku's work on the Igbo women in southeastern Nigeria provides a valuable historical resource for the study of precolonial and colonial discourse. Her study on gender also provides the necessary platform for the reconstruction and proper representation of the histories of African society.[46] Therefore, just like most attempts by women scholars at decolonization, especially in relation to the agency of women in African history, Chuku's work deals with issues of gender as well as the flexibility of women's precolonial roles. It also interrogates the effects of the ideological transformations brought about by the Victorian colonial ethos that permeated the African way of life, from the economy to religion and politics.

These colonial transformations led to the internalization of patriarchy and the subordinate role of women in contemporary society.[47] Chuku's study contributes to what was a small body of work from indigenous women scholars at the time of its publication. It focuses on the historical discourse of African women with reference to the flexibility of their precolonial coexistence with men, as well as their attempts at staving off toxic masculinity from their cultural space. Therefore, the study has the potential to significantly change feminist conceptions of the African experience during colonialism as well as the far-reaching effects of the incursion of colonialism on women in African society.

Other scholars like Amina Mama have linked women's issues with critical discourses on democracy, development, and the state in an African context struggling with authoritarianism and social conflicts. Mama's works tend to situate the woman within the postcolonial extremes of patriarchy, which is often manifested through myriad conflicts and militarism. Therefore, in the male-centered events of wars and conflicts in Africa, women are hardly taken into consideration, and their efforts are

---

45 Zeleza, "Gender."
46 Chuku, "Igbo Women."
47 Chuku, "Igbo Women."

rarely recognized. Her work with Margo Okazawa-Rey explores a "feminist perspective to militarism in Africa" as well as the role of colonialism in the incursion of violence and militarism, which is to them a tool of dominance and a capitalist venture.[48]

Their study recognizes the colonizers' utilization of military advantage through the use of fear and coercion, which led to heavy taxation, exploitation, forced labor, and patriarchal rule. In their opinion, the colonial regimes ran a different military system in their colonies compared to the ones in the West. The military system in colonial Africa was hardly there to protect the masses; it was there to fulfill the selfish desires of the Western colonialists in the suppression of antitaxation agitations, quashing protests of the restive masses, and acquiring the indigenous natural resources of the African people.

However, from a feminist perspective Mama and Okazawa-Rey consider the internalization of the militarism and patriarchy as the aftermath of colonialism and therefore a political burden the African society has had to battle with. Mirra tries to define militarism as "a range of values, prestige, actions and thought associated to armies and wars yet transcending true military purposes."[49] In other words, militarism transcends the best interests of the masses by employing the use of force to dominate the structure of society. Therefore, Mama and Okazawa-Rey are of the opinion that a closer look at the operations of militarism in Africa shows that they have done more harm than good; little wonder they begin their work with the following quote from Ake: "The real security need for Africans is not military security but social security, security against poverty, ignorance, anxiety and fear, disease and famine, against arbitrary power and exploitation; security against those things which render democracy improbable in Africa."[50]

From the above excerpt, it is obvious how these scholars feel about military authoritarianism and what they consider to be antidemocratic politics. In their opinion, militarism is another tool for sustaining Western capitalism and fostering violence and terrorism in the African state. While examining the influence of the West on African militarism, however, they cite the assertions of Härtung and Moix in the following excerpt:

---

48 Mama and Okazawa-Rey, "Militarism," 97–123.
49 Mirra, "Countering," 93–98.
50 Ake, *Feasibility*, 147.

> From 1991–1995, the U.S. provided military assistance to 50 countries in Africa, 94% of the nations on the continent. Between 1991-1998, U.S. weapons and training deliveries to Africa totaled more than $227 million. Because many of the recipient countries remain some of the world's poorest, the U.S. government provided around $87 million in foreign military financing loans to cover the costs, increasing the debt burden that is already suffocating the continent. These loans, accrued while corrupt dictators were serving as U.S. clients, have further contributed to the economic hardships of these nations by saddling them with unproductive military debt.[51]

In a nutshell, the above excerpt paints a vivid picture of the burden of militarism and the complicity of the West in further impoverishing and controlling Africa. It also shows how undemocratic militarism plays a role in impeding development and sustaining what Mohanty considers a First and Third World hierarchy in the global sphere. From a feminist perspective, Mama and Okazawa-Rey consider militarism a "gendered and gendering phenomenon,"[52] having explored the consequences of the phenomenon from a political angle; feminists tend to view the situation through the lens of gender and its effects on women. They also examine how the attendant institutionalization of patriarchy and its effects on women has continued. This is usually because some of the measures put in place for the reconstruction of society encourage the marginalization of women, especially since the security and military forces heavily influence postwar policies. In other words, the economic, gender, and political baggage of militarism is believed to hold potency in the nations affected, even after peace had been restored.

With reference to the brutal wars fought in Nigeria, Sierra Leone, and Liberia, Mama and Okazawa-Rey explore women's connection to the military and their economic involvement in the wars, as well as the changes in women's activism and organization between the Nigerian war and the present. However, they opine that most conflicts in Africa are usually rooted in factors like class, ethnicity, race, and various other issues. In their work, they consider the events of the various wars and the gendered experiences of women, which in turn reveal the negative impact of militarism on the status and position of women in the society.

---

51 Mama and Okazawa-Rey, "Militarism," 99.
52 Mama and Okazawa-Rey, "Militarism," 100.

However, their study also claims that the women are hardly taken into consideration before the men indulge in these patriarchal and capitalist expeditions of conflicts and wars. To crown the issue, the contributions of women to this effect are hardly recognized by male-centric academia.

Creation of Women-Based Institutions/Methodologies

The institutionalization of women's studies in Africa tends to promote the visibility of African-based women researchers, as well as assist in producing insightful indigenous knowledge that will tell the stories of African women more accurately. These women's narratives aim at replacing privileged Western conceptions of the African reality, which are usually misrepresented and stationary, while giving women voices in a male-dominated space.[53] In the quest for visibility and proper representation of women, Oladejo affirms the work of Bolanle Awe, a prominent Nigerian historian whose works on women in Nigeria have contributed to putting the African woman on the map. With the help of other women from several other disciplines, she saw to the establishment of the Women's Research and Documentation Centre (WORDOC).[54] This institution was enacted for the sole purpose of displacing the misrepresented narratives of Western scholars. Therefore, WORDOC invested in documentation and library facilities and is also "involved in research and consultancies, education and outreach. The institution was also virile in the publication of occasional papers and compilation of conference proceedings."[55]

Awe equally advocates for new methodologies in the projection of women's voices and views the experience and presence of African women in their societies as an advantage to responding to the social and intellectual needs of the African space. She adopts a biographic approach to the representation of women's realities in Nigeria. Oladepo states that Awe's methodology "spans through biographical writing, historiographical tradition and feminist ideology."[56] She, however, believed the social and economic conditions of African universities to be instrumental to

---

53 Mohanty, "Under Western Eyes."
54 Oladejo, "Female Historians," 30–37.
55 Oladejo, "Female Historians," 32.
56 Oladejo, "Female Historians," 33.

the Western monopoly on African narratives, stating that the problem of access to resources contributes to the scarcity of research by indigenous scholars. Consolidating Awe's claims, Steady identifies the issue of information organization, the trivialization of social science studies, and the massive brain drain in that area as contributory factors to the paucity of research on African narratives and gender in the continent.[57]

Also, Awe examines the marginalization of women's studies and history in tertiary Nigerian institutions as equally responsible for the misrepresentations of women's narratives and Western monopoly.[58] Therefore, in a bid to correct the existing misrepresentations of women in Africa, Awe published "Nigerian Women in Historical Perspective" with emphasis on the status and relevance of the precolonial and colonial Nigerian woman in the different regions of the country. The work projects the contributions of women to the nation's economy and politics, as well as the sociocultural conditions of women at the time. This process provides credence to Zeleza's conception of recovering the lives of women by restoring their real stories to history.[59] The historical relevance of Awe's work cannot be overemphasized, as it provides an indigenous perspective to the study of women in Nigeria's history and also provides the much-needed resource for an understanding of the historical realities of the precolonial Nigerian narrative.

African societies, as earlier observed, have dabbled in conflicts and civil wars emanating from several factors with possible roots in the colonial experience. However, several feminist studies tend to explore the effects of these wars on women as well as the patterns and coping mechanisms they adopt irrespective of country or region. There are also several approaches adopted by women scholars in the exploration of women's experiences in the history of civil wars in Africa. Mama and Okazawa-Rey examine Peterson's postulation of what she considers three economic modes that inevitably surface in times of conflict: coping, criminal, and combat; while the study further explores the play of gender in these modes as observed by Peterson.[60] These modes are formed out of the observation that economic crises are an inevitable part of conflicts. The coping

---

57 Steady, "An Investigative Framework."
58 Awe, "Writing." 211–20.
59 Zeleza, "Gender," 207–32.
60 Mama and Okazawa-Rey, "Militarism."

economy is a prominent aspect of survival during the wars and, not surprisingly, women constitute an active part of the survival and nourishment of the society in times of war. Peterson considers the coping economy as a "feminized aspect of the economy."[61] Therefore, saddled with the domestic responsibility of sustenance before the events of war, the outbreak of conflict tends to aggravate this responsibility, hence the presence of women at the core of any coping economy.

Women are usually responsible for the nurturing of children and elderly people, as well as feeding and providing for the men who are usually fighting in the war. The ability to provide is often hampered when the war disrupts the smooth operations of economic activities like farming and trading. As much as the coping economy is proof of a gendered war economy, it also shows the crucial roles of women in sustaining life during conflict and therefore proves that women's roles during conflicts are just as important as those of soldiers in battle and merit being included in the pages of history textbooks. However, the combat economy is a male-centered domain that is primarily involved in planning and carrying out war activities. This area of the economy is usually nationally and internationally networked. The criminal economy, in Peterson's opinion, is managed by opportunistic self-serving persons who take advantage of the temporary disorder in the state and its attendant economic deregulation to introduce illegitimate businesses like human and sex trafficking, money laundering, and a host of other atrocities facilitated by war.

Therefore, even though women do not feature prominently in the combat economy, this is not to say that women have never been involved in military activities as fighters. Therefore, with or without their involvement in fighting, they are equally affected, and the same goes for the criminal economy where they are victims and perpetrators alike. They are stated by Uchendu to be victims of sex and human trafficking, rape, as well as "voluntary" sex trades with men for the purpose of survival, while some of the women were said to recruit younger women for the purpose of soliciting sex.[62] This situation is specifically detailed by Uchendu to have occurred during the Nigerian civil war; however, the pattern remains the same with each region and the outbreaks of war. Civil wars and

---

61 Mama and Okazawa-Rey, "Militarism," 102.
62 Uchendu, *Women*.

conflict constitute a huge part of Africa's history, and oftentimes human involvements tend to go unrecognized.

Therefore, according to Mama and Okazawa-Rey, the theorization of women and their survival in wars and conflicts tends to scrutinize the gendering of war histories in Africa. However, they state that Peterson's theorization of the coping economy is relevant since it creates a connection between the women's cultural responsibility of nurturing and the economy during wartime. Using Peterson's conceptualizations, Mama and Okazawa-Rey come to the realization that women in the history of African wars are not just participants in the coping economy but have engaged in other activities of combat as fighters, spies, and even commanders. This knowledge, as well as evidence that proves the involvement of some women in violence against civilians, goes on to debunk the theory that women are more peaceful than men. However, they also state that the criminal economy was a male-dominated arena.

Peterson's theorization provides an objective perspective to the realities of the war and women's involvement in war activities in African states, revealing the realities of a gendered economy during wartime as well as an apparent play of male dominance, which is discovered from the objectification of women as sexual commodities. The study further opines that conflicts and wars are averse to any form of development, which in turn affects the society and encourages the marginalization and subjugation of women. However, the active role of women during these periods cannot be overemphasized. Therefore, the study calls for a recognition of the relevance and prominence of women's contributions to African military contexts. The study also tries to define the concept of security from a feminist perspective by observing that the life of the African woman is characterized by several forms of insecurity, which are usually aggravated in the event of conflicts and are hardly better even with the end of conflict. Security to them, therefore, means genuine respect and value for human life irrespective of gender for effective political and economic development in the society.[63]

Furthermore, Steady's study on the investigative framework for gender research in Africa interrogates some of the existent Eurocentric frameworks in the disciplines of social sciences and anthropology that tend to show African society in a negative light. With a closer look at the discipline

---

63 Mama and Okazawa-Rey, "Militarism."

of anthropology, Steady points out three main concepts that encourage the sustenance of racism and colonial domination: "Social Darwinism, structural/functionalism and 'acculturation' theories."[64] These theories have reinforced the idea of Africa as barbaric. The centralization of Western-based notions in the African society is a colonial process that aided in the subjugation of Africa's thought processes and the silencing of its indigenous philosophies. Aside from the field of anthropology, Steady opines that the field of history continues to produce these Eurocentric conceptions by the sustained presentation of Africa as a region devoid of history, culture, or any form of civilization. This also materializes through the counter-imposition of self-serving Western narratives at the expense of worthy testimonies of Africa's contributions to the great civilizations of the world. Steady admits that the fields of social sciences have been designed to entertain colonial and imperialist methodologies and have gone a long way in influencing gender and feminist discourses around the globe, hence the universality of Eurocentric feminist conceptions. For Steady, these methodologies and theories are biased and therefore do not hold a heuristic quality, especially in their application to Africa.[65]

However, she recognizes postmodern and postcolonial studies as relevant to the reexamination of these Eurocentric paradigms through their ability to challenge Western-based philosophies and theories by providing the much-needed historical directives from which studies on gender in Africa can be more productive. In her opinion, as a result of the biases in European models, they cannot effectively interrogate African society, for instance, by viewing social inequality as responsible for the pervasive poverty of women in African countries. For Steady, with the proliferation of feminist studies in the South, the dominance of Western feminists in global feminist discourse is analyzed with emphasis on the Western tendency to categorize all women using Western parameters without considering unique characteristics of race, culture, and sexuality, among other factors. Thus, Steady advocates for African women's customization of feminist discourses to meet the specific requirements of the continent. Some of these requirements are classified into three categories that accentuate the angles from which African women wish to address feminism. Firstly, Nkealah identifies the need to examine feminism from the

64 Steady, "An Investigative Framework."
65 Steady, "An Investigative Framework."

cultural perspectives of Africans, and the need to consider the geography and politics of the African people, as well as to explore the concept using continental epistemologies and philosophies.[66] Therefore with further interrogation on universalized approaches that do not apply to Africa's peculiarities, Steady advocates for redefined approaches to African and women's studies. In order to achieve this, Steady posits that

> African research on gender has to develop methodologies for criticisms and revisionist endeavours as well as methodologies for alternative research ... that will satisfy the basic scientific requirements of validity, reliability and replicability have to be applied. Added to this will be new methods related to language and to indigenous systems of thought so that the framing of gender will be determined within the context of the relationship of language to culture. Crucial to the redefining of an alternative approach to research from an African perspective will be the following: Policy-orientation; critique of donor-driven research; social impact and basic research; viewpoint and value orientation, time orientation, geographical orientation; levels of analysis and an emphasis on culture.[67]

Steady's work therefore exposes the place of globalization in the continued colonization of African studies in relation to women and gender. Her work is relevant because it interrogates the play of Western hegemony in African scholarship and proffers directives and methodologies on creating applicable models for gender criticism in African scholarship.

However, in the application of methodologies and knowledge to issues of gender in African scholarship, Imam shares Steady's hopes in facilitating the production and analysis of knowledge in African studies.[68] Imam et al. try to examine the concept of gender as a necessary tool for analyzing and understanding social sciences. In their opinion, the study of social sciences is male-centered; in other words, the production and preservation of knowledge in that field of study is hardly representative of the entire society but rather is weaved around masculine contexts and politics.[69] The work takes a critical look at social science theories and

---

66 Nkealah, "Conceptualizing" 133–41.
67 Steady, "An Investigative Framework," 5.
68 Imam, "Engendering."
69 Imam, "Engendering."

methodologies and advocates for the adoption and utilization of gender as a tool for research in the social sciences, so as to transcend masculine-centered methodologies to creating a well-rounded analytical tool. However, since masculine domination is a colonial trope, it is no wonder the works of these women scholars are aimed at achieving a healthy equilibrium in scholarship and knowledge production.

Still, on the exploration of suitable methodologies for African scholarship, Bennett's study also examines the intricacies of designing African feminist research methodologies that will cater to the complex needs of the African community. She identifies the biggest challenge for African feminists: the need to create knowledge from African contexts, which would adequately interrogate the complexities of the continent while bringing about the needed transformation. Also, her work also notes the inability of African feminist researchers to differentiate between the framework on which the feminist initiative is based and the methods that will facilitate the creation of new knowledge.[70] In her opinion, this issue leads to the application of inadequate procedures to research projects:

> We find PhD candidates with radical, and feminist, ideas about the need to interrogate sexuality education in schools being required to explore the context through standardized questionnaires, or feminist researchers being asked by donor-driven agendas to submit findings "with recommendations" as though "recommendations" from the author(s) of a research report were likely to be useful (sometimes, they are, of course. But any feminist worth her/his salt knows that only decisions reached collectively, over much time and difficult negotiation, have any genuine hope of addressing complex problems).[71]

Bennett admits that the rigors of their work make it almost impossible for them to conduct research with methodologies suitable for African contexts, but for her this does not mean that feminist research cannot appropriately address issues from an African perspective. With the creation of Association of African Women for Research and Development (AAWORD) and Agency for Accelerated Regional Development (AFARD), Bennett is of the opinion that African feminists have churned out several publications that have adhered to practical methodologies

---

70 Bennett, "Editorial."
71 Bennett, "Researching," 4.

subject to critical appraisal, while taking into consideration the African context in shaping the outcome of the research work.

The place of context and experiences in formulating and applying suitable research methodologies and theoretical frameworks for the analysis of African studies cannot be overemphasized. This, therefore, substantiates Collins's claims that African American women's difficult experiences in relation to the issues of race, class and gender have provided the adequate background and equipment for the social thought and theory aimed at challenging the oppression of Black women in general.[72] These social theories hope to provide survival mechanisms for the oppressed minority of Black women within the United States. They are usually a reflection of women's efforts in combating the issues that affect the free expression and true freedom of the African woman.

Collins identifies "Black feminist thought" as aimed at addressing the collective questions and thoughts of Black women in the United States. Therefore, as a theory for the Black woman crafted from exclusive Black knowledge and experience, it seeks justice for the oppressed in society who often include Black women. African American studies have formed exclusive Black conceptions of social institutions like the family and community, as well as other social concepts like motherhood. Collins advocates the role of the Black woman in constructing definitions of Blackness that challenge the hegemonic images and stereotypes of the dominant white voices. With this, as well as the communal living experiences of the Black community, it is easy to create a deeply Black-centered concept of feminism.

With *Black Feminist Thought*, Collins advocates for the exploration of Black women's ideas, which particularly has to do with engaging in a reanalysis or reinterpretation of works of distinguished Black women thinkers whose ideas have, luckily, been preserved. This often involves a collection of scattered thoughts of these women found in essays or speeches and would go a long way in illuminating these long-obscured Black women. However, she also recognizes the voices of women who are otherwise not seen as intellectuals but equally relevant to the development of Black feminist thought. In her opinion, not all Black women intellectuals are considered educated or academic; however, by citing the valuable contribution of Sojourner Truth's speech at the 1851 women's

---

72   Collins, *Black Feminist*.

convention, she drives home her point. In other words, the relevance and contributions of that speech to women's studies call for a deconstruction of the concept of the intellectual.[73]

Women have therefore continued to make substantive contributions to the decolonization process in African studies. Their intensive research and ideas have begun to generate an exclusively African mode of reasoning in scholarship. Their generation of informed African methodologies calls for an overhaul of the education curriculum to reflect an African-rooted scholarship. However, in relation to studies on gender, there is a close relationship between activism and scholarly research, which gives credence to some institutions aimed at providing a safe place for women to express themselves intellectually while working to carry out the intentions of the institutions. AAWORD is one such organization run by African women aimed at assisting scholarly research intended to promote the socioeconomic and political rights of women on the African continent. It was founded in 1977 by a group of African women identified by Ampofo et al. as "Simi Afonja, Bolanle Awe, Nina Mba, Molara Ogundipe, Filomena Steady, Fatou Sow, N'dri Assie Lumumba, Zenebeworke Tadesse, Christine Obbo, Achola Pala Okeyo, and Nawal El Sadaawi. Those associated with the second phase of research and activism are Amina Mama, Ayesha Imam, Charmaine Pereira, Maria Nzomo, Rudo Gaidzanwa, Patricia MacFadden, and Takyiwaa Manuh."[74]

These women's names are frequently encountered by historical, social, and literary scholars. They have worked on several gender and women's studies research projects in relation to African scholarship, identifying the challenges of scholarship in Africa and the status and place of women on several important issues in society. Their desire to generate accurate research, promote the interests of women, and strengthen gender and women's studies in African scholarship are properly represented in their works with the establishment of a women-centered organization like AAWORD.

However, these interests are not limited to AAWORD; there are several other women's organizations for the promotion of gender and women's studies research in African scholarship. One of these is WORDOC, established in 1986 with Bolanle Awe as the founding chairperson of the

---

73 Collins, *Black Feminist*.
74 Ampofo et al., "Women," 685–714.

center.[75] The organization aims at addressing postcolonial women's challenges with a focus on research on gender and women. The organization takes part in "researches, education, the gathering and dissemination of information and social policy formulation."[76] With funding from organizations like Ford, UNICEF, and the WB, WORDOC conducts various researches on agriculture, the girl child, labor, economy and many other subjects related to relevant social issues. WORDOC also organizes seminars, public lectures and workshops on several issues pertaining to women and the society as well as the publication of materials pertaining to research on women and their local concerns. In networking, WORDOC has established a relationship with other similar organizations run by women scholars. Odejide is of the opinion that the organization is closely linked with DAWN (Development Alternatives for Women of the New Era), particularly with the ambition to promote cultural experiences with women whose experiences and challenges are similar to those of the Nigerian women, especially since the organization is a network of women scholars from the Third World. Also, in the dissemination of information, the organization is said to have a vibrant library and documentation center, which aims to provide otherwise inaccessible resources on women, including books, seminar papers, magazines, newsletters, conference papers, newspapers, journals, and many other information resources.

Also, as an autonomous organization incorporated into the Institute of African Studies in the University of Ibadan, the organization has intellectual and political ambitions that make room for activism on local and international issues and has been outspoken on several political issues pertaining to women. Some of WORDOC's objectives as noted by Odejide include the following:

1. To provide a focus on women's studies and to promote new methodologies for this purpose through coordination of research projects in Nigeria;
2. To provide a basis for policy formulation by encouraging a women's studies network and by promoting understanding of the various roles and concerns of women in Nigeria, Africa and the world at large;
3. To coordinate a documentation centre for use by scholars, researchers, and other interested persons;

---

75   Odejide, "Profile," 100–107.
76   Odejide, "Profile," 4.

4. To seek sources of funding for research work; and
5. To provide a link with other women's research centres within and outside the country.[77]

So far, the organizations explored are only a part of the women-founded organizations for the promotion of women's research and scholarship; there are many other organizations with the same mission. This shows the true extent of women's voices and actions in decolonizing African studies and rescuing women's studies and research from the margins of scholarship.

Conclusion

The theme of decolonization is prominent in many postcolonial discourses and publications in Africa. The proliferation of these publications is proof of their relevance and just how necessary postcolonial dialogues are in African society. However, African scholarship has been male-centered at best; the impressive body of work by pioneering African feminist writers over the last few decades has not got the recognition it deserves as groundbreaking decolonial literature. This exemplifies the struggle of African women scholars for centralization of their perspectives in African scholarship. However, this study has been able to explore the ghettoization of women studies in African scholarship in the continent and in diaspora. It has also examined the current state of women's subordination in society and scholarship as a product of colonial contact. It explores women's publications and their calls for an African mode of reasoning, activism for social change, and their creation of women-based institutions for the promotion of research and studies on women and gender in Africa as their contribution to the decolonization of African studies.

---

77 Odejide, "Profile," 5.

Chapter Eleven

Empowering Marginal Voices

LGBTQ and African Studies

Introduction

The world is changing, and Africa's decolonization has gained momentum in the bid by new "democratic" governments to catch up with the rest of the world in a postcolonial setup. Africa dreams of becoming a developed continent without compromising certain traditional values that should ordinarily be tolerated as a "modern and democratic" continent. While tolerance among different ethnic groups remains balanced but with an unhealthy competition for scarce economic and political resources, one issue on which many African people and governments—regardless of ethnicity, nationality, or history—agree is the distaste for the LGBTQ community, thus earning Africa the rightful reputation of being the most homophobic place in the world.[1]

With the growth of academic scholarship by African scholars on African issues, there is a visible and intentional disinterest in research on the LGBTQ community, despite its undeniable existence in Africa. Only a few scholars have written academic materials for or against the LGBTQ community, while the majority choose to remain silent, which has only ensured a lack of interest in the community's welfare, mental health, and human rights. Thus, this peculiarity makes it even more compelling to include a chapter dedicated to reviewing some issues surrounding the LGBTQ community from the few academic works that give the African perspective on said community.

---

1   Smith, "Why Africa."

In this chapter, several issues related to the LGBTQ community will be discussed to reflect the strength of available materials while also highlighting the gaps in knowledge on human rights, health care, suicidality, feminism, and sexual colonialism.

Human Rights Issues for LGBTQ Community in Africa

Homosexuality should be seen as nothing more than a sexual orientation: something as ordinary as skin color. But to consolidate their power, African leaders often look for issues that exalt their moral or religious superiority and present them as independent from colonial control. As a result, issues surrounding LGBTQ matters have been subjected to a barrage of political, social, economic, religious, and cultural opposition even in countries that have implemented pro-LGBTQ laws.

In most cases, countries that have signed LGBTQ rights into law often lack the political will to fully enforce such dictates. This may be because these laws are often the product of external pressure and are meant to score diplomatic and international favors with certain groups or companies while lacking local popularity among their voters. It is becoming increasingly obvious that powerful religious and political leaders, regardless of affiliation, embody enough anti-LGBTQ sentiment to ensure that pro-LGBTQ laws are rendered inefficient, even in progressive African countries such as South Africa.[2]

However, progress (albeit uneven, slow, and spontaneous) is being made across Africa regarding tolerance for the LGBTQ community, especially among members of Africa's young population who are on the whole more liberal than previous generations. This "newfound" tolerance by Africa's leaders of tomorrow is attributed to increased levels of education, urbanization, and exposure to foreign media. But this tolerance has yet to have a palpable effect on members of the LGBTQ community, as the older generation is still firmly in control of all the state's instruments. This progress for LGBTQ human rights remains hindered by laws in influential African states such as Kenya, Nigeria, and Tanzania, among others, where members of the LGBTQ community are subjected

---

2   Van Klinken and Chitando, *Public Religion*.

to imprisonment and sometimes even the death penalty merely because of their sexual orientation.

According to the Human Rights Watch in a report published in 2019, thirty-two African countries (out of fifty-four) have outlawed homosexuality.[3] However, it may be misleading to believe that the other twenty-two countries are tolerant of nonheteresexual men and women, as some countries have merely opted to remain neutral out of deference to the political and economic powers that may hold their collective future at stake. Africa's homophobic sentiments are still pervasive across the continent, especially among rural dwellers and conservative religious adherents.

There have been academic and humanitarian interests in the perceived attempt at creating a divide between gay rights and human rights. This has led to certain opinions regarding the concept of "common humanity" rooted in the religious (Christian) concept of all humans being created in God's image.[4] It is a simple attempt at proving that regardless of the sexual orientation of the individual, gay people should not be treated as less than human. The argument is that members of the LGBTQ community should not be given any special rights (as in gay rights) but should be treated the same as other members of society. This is in opposition to those in society that do not regard members of the LGBTQ community as human, as well as others who deem any sexuality other than heterosexuality to be a form of moral corruption or pathological disease.

Religious groups in Africa will most likely be the last segment of society to accept LGBTQ realities and yet remains one of the most influential sectors. Religious sentiments usually find their way into social, political, and legal efforts to garner more equality for those members of the LGBTQ community. Thus, accepting LGBTQ individuals as human beings and recognizing their human rights can only be resolved by addressing moral and religious concerns and medical misconstructions, perhaps beginning with academia.[5]

Also, there are indications of how LGBTQ discrimination can be addressed using "international human rights discourses."[6] By their very nature, human rights should be applied equally and universally to

---

3   Van Klinken and Chitando, *Public Religion*.
4   Van Klinken and Chitando, *Public Religion*.
5   Van Klinken and Chitando, *Public Religion*.
6   Tucker, "Geographies," 683–703.

all humans, regardless of their differences. However, there have been instances when efforts were made not to classify members of the LGBTQ community as humans, thus denying them of such fundamental rights. While African governments have rejected international efforts to include LGBTQ groups in the human rights framework, academic research works continue to upend the narrative surrounding the "un-Africanness" of homosexuality (and other sexualities) to sidestep the idea of LGBTQ groups being vestiges of colonialization.[7]

It would be wishful thinking to believe that the human rights approach is succeeding in strong-arming African governments into recognizing LGBTQ rights. Cheney's research in Uganda reflects how a country can seriously promote human rights and still exclude LGBTQ groups.[8] This foregrounds the desire of African governments to be respected in the international community on human rights without allowing "foreign" values such as nonheterosexuality to be smuggled into treaties or human rights charters. These traditional values are the major source of power for the ruling (political and religious) class.

The discourse on human rights and the acceptance of LGBTQ groups without discrimination will be concluded with Devji's compilation of the various elements in the queer rights spectrum. According to this spectrum, the first stage is "Total Marginalization,"[9] which is expected because society will sharply react to anything regarded as a threat to its stability. This stage often involves an outright ban on campaigns displaying queer behavior or identification with queer movements and symbols. Society attempts to hide these "abnormal" behaviors and to prevent LGBTQ groups from gaining much-needed visibility. Following that, LGBTQ groups are likely to reject all forms of repression. The next stage is often characterized by formal and legal restrictions on all forms of queer actions. This stage implies that LGBTQ groups are criminals whose actions deserve punishment. Most African states are stuck in these early stages, with the prominent exception of South Africa.

However, changes are bound to occur that will transition the status of LGBTQ people in Africa from criminals to full-fledged members of society with rights, especially in what are currently the most homophobic

---

7   Tucker, "Reconsidering," 295–305.
8   Cheney, "Locating Neocolonialism," 77–95.
9   Zahrah Devji, "Forging Paths," 343–63.

countries. While countries' intentions for accepting changes to the status quo may be far from noble, the next two stages are preparatory in nature in a few countries. They are attempts at undoing the earlier stages and are described by the International Lesbian, Gay, Trans, and Intersex Association as the primary steps toward full recognition. The third stage is a direct reversal of the second stage with the passing of antidiscrimination laws that protect LGBTQ people from any form of legal prosecution and persecution. The second stage of the preparatory phase (and fourth overall stage) is establishing positive rights that lead to full legal recognition of LGBTQ movements.

The last couple of stages are the consolidation phase. This is characterized by a society gradually consolidating the gains of the preparatory phase. The penultimate stage recognizes "full legal equality" for the LGBTQ community, as all distinctions are nonexistent, and LGBTQ people are fully integrated into society's legal sphere. However, it is the last stage that ensures the permanence of such recognition. It is rightly tagged "cultural integration," which births a new society that fully recognizes queerness as a normal human expression with no negative consequences. The initial five stages have only achieved legal and political recognition, which confers legitimacy on LGBTQ groups that may not be popular with society at large.

Feminism and Queer Theory

Feminism in Africa has always been seen as a subversive movement. While there are many strands of feminism, radical feminism is what looms the largest in the African mind, conjuring up associations with lesbianism, disruptions of the institution of marriage and family, and opposition to certain African traditions. This concept of feminism takes on the social construct of Western evils—an imposition by Western colonial powers, placing it firmly in the same ranks as the LGBTQ community.

The African feminist movement is not without its problems on the continent and has initially made feminist scholars hesitant to include LGBTQ issues in feminist discourses. However, scholars have agreed that, regardless of the form of feminism being professed, the African feminist movement's core issues are to improve the living (and working) conditions of African women and a desire for the acceptance of such issues affecting women globally.[10] However, while this enhances the acceptability of feminism, it does not necessarily lead to acceptance of LGBTQ peoples.

African feminism is a movement against the oppression of women in all spheres of society. Several challenges happen within African feminism, such as widowhood practices, inheritance laws, women's oppression, and genital mutilation, but sexual orientation issues are largely left unconsidered.[11] LGBTQ affairs, according to Pindi, generate controversies in feminist discourse. This is because the nonheterosexual intimacy that characterizes queer relations is considered unacceptable in African cultures.[12] The noninclusion of LGBTQ issues in feminist discourse is not unconnected from the desire for scholars to redefine feminism within the African context. Feminist discourses therefore seek to avoid complications from the perception of LGBTQ groups as a foreign (read: colonial) imposition.

Research has since shown, however, that LGBTQ groups are subjected to attacks that are associated specifically with minority groups, providing grounds for affinity with feminists in redefining man-woman relations and recognizing alternative constructions of sexuality.[13]

G. N. Pindi:
Building a Theoretical Framework for
African Feminist Queer Agenda

Pindi is a critical intercultural and African feminism scholar who has attempted to advocate for a transnational feminist framework built on an interface between African feminism and LGBTQ movements. Pindi complained about the concept of traditional African culture as being static, thus allowing conservative political leaders to continue to refer to a culture that has changed. Instead, she advocates a rethink that constructs the African culture as "dynamic and hybrid."[14] Africans need to accept

---

10   Sophia, *Woman*.
11   Pindi, *Beyond Labels*, 106–12.
12   Pindi, *Beyond Labels*.
13   Currier and Cruz, "Civil Society," 337–60.
14   Pindi, *Beyond Labels*, 106–12.

that cultures change and become a hybrid form of what is known and what is accommodated.

Adopting a two-pronged approach, Pindi presented her case for an intersectional approach to promoting the interests of the LGBTQ community without undermining the core interests of feminists on the African continent and even beyond. These two points involve deconstructing the intersecting oppression of sexuality and promoting a humanistic vision.[15] These two points equally work toward the acceptance of the LGBTQ community.

Pindi believes that African feminism and queer theory are similar in that both seek to deconstruct the social and cultural perceptions of sexuality: both address problems associated with discriminatory views that promote heterosexuality as the norm, which leads to public perceptions of the LGBTQ community as abnormal. Sexual identity has become a central bone of contention as feminism and queer theorists advocate for recognizing that sexual identities are not rigid and should not be assigned.

Pindi reminds feminists that African feminism is a movement against all forms of the systemic manifestation of bias while advocating for an intersectional approach with queer theorists to deconstruct sexual identities. Feminism is often restricted to women's sexual and social liberation, which is heteronormative. Thus, Pindi recommends that such an intersectional approach should allow feminist support of queer theorists to achieve total deconstruction of heteronormativity and liberate African sexual minorities.

There is also the idea of "promoting a humanistic vision"[16] that refers to African feminism's encouragement of the humane treatment of sexual minorities and defending the rights of other oppressed minorities such as Black people, women, and children. Presenting a case for humane treatment of the LGBTQ community, feminists have undertaken the task of deconstructing religious and colonial legacies upon which the prejudicial "nonhuman" tag of the LGBTQ community is based. Feminists have also targeted the weaponization of religion by political and religious leaders who promote the LGBTQ community as less than human and preach queerness as a sign of religious and cultural deviance. Even so, African feminists and queer theorists have decolonized religious homophobia

---

15 Pindi, *Beyond Labels*, 106–12.
16 Pindi, *Beyond Labels*, 106–12.

across the globe to create a narrative that does not offend religious sensitivities. As Sylvia Tamale observes, "Attempts to assert sexual citizenship have spawned social movements on the continent, challenging the dominant sexual discourses and demanding increases sexual autonomy and freedom. These movements have the potential to profoundly shape our understanding of the links between sexualities and religion."[17]

Suicide among the LGBTQ Community

Studies have shown that LGBTQ youth are often lonelier and more depressed than their heterosexual peers.[18] They are more likely to withdraw from themselves and from others. A growing body of evidence also suggests that there is an increased likelihood for a young queer person to inflict self-harm or die by suicide.[19] Yet there has been little effort by the government, international bodies, or even independent researchers to collect data, raise awareness, and set up proactive measures, especially in Africa.[20] Because there is no authoritative data on suicide rates, scholars are advocating for a focus on mental health concerns, suicide ideation, and suicide attempts. This attitude is not unexpected in Africa since the paucity of research efforts on suicidality among LGBTQ people is not surprising considering Africa's homophobic stance. The criminalization of LGBTQ groups in most parts of Africa fuels an intense culture of homophobia on the continent.[21] Thus, queer Africans are ultimately difficult to reach out to (except through gay rights organizations) and difficult to persuade to participate in research.

Although in recent years there have been more positive representations of LGBTQ people in the African media, stigmas associated with the gay community are still pervasive. This leads to the devaluation of queer people, resulting in higher levels of social stress and mood swings, anxiety, and substance abuse among the LGBTQ community.[22] Homophobia in

---

17 Tamale, "Exploring the Contours," 150.
18 Westefeld et al., "Gay, Lesbian, and Bisexual," 71–82.
19 Miranda-Mendizábal et al., "Sexual Orientation," 77–87.
20 Nii-Boye Quarshie, "Self-Harm."
21 Kapya Kaoma, *Christianity*.
22 Meyer, "Prejudice," 674.

the form of discrimination and criminalization continues to create a hostile environment that forces queer people to accept a sexual identity that does not suit them. When the psychological trauma of young LGBTQ people becomes too great, especially if they do not have access to older queer people, they may resort to self-harm, including suicide.

In dealing with mental issues related to the LGBTQ community, there are risks and protective factors that must be identified. An individual's exposure to parental and peer rejection, verbal abuse, depression, and substance abuse increases the likelihood of suicide. However, there are necessary protections that can be put in place for an LGBTQ person to be less prone to taking their own life. These allow for a better handling of risks and obstacles that may present themselves. Some of these protective factors include family connection, peer support, and the presence of LGBTQ support groups.

The Role of Media on the LGBTQ Discourse

Many studies are optimistic about the roles and influence of various media platforms on the quality of political engagements. In the modern world, the media plays a very important role in public affairs. Closed societies go to great lengths to censor the media content being consumed by people, especially if such content is deemed foreign and inimical to government interests. The International Lesbian, Gay, Bisexual, Trans and Intersex Association sees the media as an important tool for advancing the case of queer people and even organizes training for sister organizations[23] on taking advantage of the publicity that various media can offer. Most activists adopt this tool in advancing the LGBTQ case and raising awareness about the existence and plight of the queer community in Africa.

Queer groups have used certain media platforms to portray the "humanness" of gay people in order to counter the religious narrative. As pointed out in this discourse, visibility is a key element in the quest for recognition and will likely increase tolerance among the general population. For this to be achieved, there are two functions that media platforms

---

23 Lusimbo and Oguaghamba, *Pan Africa*, 1–20.

must perform in LGBTQ affairs, as identified by Stephen Winkler,[24] which will result in a positive attitudinal change toward the LGBTQ community.

Media platforms can allow for positive representations of the queer community. An honest presentation of their humanity and progressive ideas about fluid sexuality without the bias of religious or political leaders may give the general public the opportunity to evaluate the existence of the LGBTQ community and become increasingly aware of the misinformation that may have been promoted by homophobic groups. Allowing the LGBTQ community to control the narrative will cause a gradual change in attitudes and reactions to queer people. Also, beyond this, media outlets allow the LGBTQ community to share general information about their plight as humans with the aim being to spur the public to seek more information and even initiate public engagement of queer issues.

However, Winkler identifies the limitations of the ability of media platforms to achieve desired results. Positive attitudinal changes can only be achieved if citizens have access to both mainstream and alternative media outlets that are not heavily censored (or outright banned). The more democratic a society is, the more likely it is that queer content may circulate, thus resulting in higher levels of tolerance, especially when such media outlets are allowed to objectively cover LGBTQ issues. Globalization has resulted in the diffusion of values and norms, and this has largely helped LGBTQ people reach out to others in ways that would not have been possible with traditional media. This is because traditional media platforms in Africa remain firmly within censorious African governments' control.

Sexual Health Needs of LGBTQ Youth: Issues Arising

Health care must be made available to all members of African society, especially the youth. This is largely because young persons are, more than any other age group, vulnerable to various health complications such as sexually transmitted diseases and infections because of lack of maturity or education. Young persons are also reluctant to seek health care for sexually

---

24 Winkler, "Media's Influence," 1–20.

transmitted diseases because of the judgmental attitude from medical practitioners who are of an older generation, thus prompting them to opt for self-care or online solutions.[25] While this situation is unacceptable, it is even worse for LGBTQ youths who have suffered marginalization in an underfunded health-care system.

Stigmatization and marginalization of LGBTQ youths pose extra hindrances to gaining access to better health care because of LGBTQ patients' reluctance to be subjected to inhumane and homophobic treatment. This only serves the purpose of exacerbating the medical risks that may be associated with sexual activity. Due to the insensitivity and ignorance of health-care service providers about LGBTQ groups' unique needs,[26] they are at higher risk of contracting diseases such as HIV/AIDS and STDs.

With Africa being a predominantly homophobic continent, health research on marginalized sexual minority groups' conditions is often almost nonexistent or at best inadequate. Even when these facts are publicized, they rarely influence government decisions because of the open antigay posture and criminalization of LGBTQ groups by most African governments. Thus, LGBTQ people are left to suffer the consequences of a health-care system that is ill-equipped and insensitive to their plight and, worse, denies them access to important programs related to HIV/AIDS, thereby increasing vulnerability.[27] Equally, most in the LGBTQ community are reluctant to seek health-care services for fear of being reported to public authorities and being subject to stigmatization, even in a country like South Africa that constitutionally recognizes gay rights. These are some of the many issues affecting the LGBTQ community in Africa's often unsympathetic legal and sociocultural environment.

While progress is being made on the global front to achieve sexual inclusion, to adapt the heteronormative structure of health-care systems, and to improve the general quality of the health-care industry, LGBTQ access to health-care services in Africa remains limited. This has led to calls from various organizations and scholars for an increase in investment and funding of youth-friendly health-care centers that can address general medical issues experienced by heterosexual youths and the unique sexual health-care needs of LGBTQ persons.

---

25   Alli et al., "Interpersonal," 150–55.
26   Center for Disease Control and Prevention, "Protective."
27   Mkhize, and Maharaj, "Meeting," 1–17.

The case of South Africa is enlightening. As the only African country whose constitution provides equal legal rights for the LGBTQ community, South Africa sets itself apart from the rest of Africa in this way. However, despite constitutional recognition, those in the LGBTQ community in South Africa, as in many countries in Africa, still experience issues such as "stigma, inequality, prejudice, and lack of awareness about LGBTQ health issues."[28] The health-care system in South Africa is unresponsive to the sexual health needs of LGBTQ people as the system is designed in line with its heteronormative construction of sexual identity.

However, this insensitivity to the plight of homosexuals cannot be solely blamed on the individual, the institutional homophobia of health-care service providers, or the lack of knowledge about such peculiarities of LGBTQ sexual health needs. Health-care service providers in South Africa were reportedly concerned about the lack of skills required to deal with the varying sexual identities as medical schools have failed to include LGBTQ health issues in the curriculum,[29] which has resulted in the provision of low-quality health-care services to LGBTQ peoples. For instance, certain members of the LGBTQ community choose to express themselves in ways that are considered to be gender nonconforming. For instance, they might dress in ways that reflect their own recognized sexual identity, but this may not align with sociocultural expectations and may even draw sharp comments from health-care providers and heterosexual patients. Also, such stigmatization may take the form of using cultural and religious terms[30] to condemn their sexual preference.

From the foregoing, healthcare providers' ignorance denies them the chance to build the much-needed interpersonal relationship that will encourage LGBTQ patients to trust them with sensitive information regarding their sexual and general health needs. This sets in motion a chain of events resulting in the prevalence of sexual infections/diseases among LGBTQ people. However, this can be countered with the provision and availability of LGBTQ-friendly professionals in special health-care centers. A professional who has had the training to care for LGBTQ people will need to be properly versed in the appropriate discourse, even if they do not identify as being part of the LGBTQ community themselves.

---

28 Mkhize, and Maharaj, "Meeting."
29 Alex Müller, "Scrambling," 16.
30 Ireland, "A Macro-Level," 47–66.

Access to equal health-care services for LGBTQ patients is important but can only be fully maximized when such services are affordable for LGBTQ groups most likely to be financially disadvantaged. Regardless of their constitutional status, employment opportunities for LGBTQ people are still being withheld, which leads to limitations on LGBTQ people's spending power and ability to access certain health-care services.

Sources of African State Homophobia

However slow or quick the society reacts to or resists contact with foreign elements, the mere interaction is enough to instigate changes. Homophobic laws do not exist in a vacuum but are products of certain underlying assumptions and factors. Africa may remain largely homophobic, but the continent as a whole must come to terms with the fact that LGBTQ people are exactly that: people. All forms of homophobia are already in decline, faster in some places than in others. Sodomy laws are being phased out gradually, and nonheterosexuals are gaining legal and social recognition. These changes are erratic in various countries on the African continent, but such changes are bound to be widespread because of the similarities in the underlying factors causing homophobia in Africa.

Overwhelming evidence suggests that countries with higher levels of secularity are more accepting of nonheterosexuals than religious states because there are fewer religious sensibilities to offend. The very etymology of sodomy laws is rooted in religious texts. The high population of Christian and Muslim adherents on the continent is part of the increased intolerance for homosexuality, as religious leaders remain at the forefront of pressurizing governments to enforce antigay laws in various countries. Thus, it is safe to conclude that homophobia in Africa is driven mostly by religion, among other factors.

Equally, homophobia has proven to be an interesting front for Africans in resisting Western dominance. The negative consequences of globalization and neoliberalism on African countries seeking pathways to become developed have led to an intricate linkage of gay lifestyles to the free-market system's growth. In the rejection of Western control over Africa's destiny, LGBTQ identities have become the perfect scapegoat in that struggle. Ireland posits that African leaders continue to stoke homophobic sentiments among the citizens for selfish political reasons, such as creating unifying grounds for citizens to vent their frustrations stemming from abysmal economic performance and corruption. These regimes consolidate power via nationalism based on creating a common enemy: the LGBTQ community, often thought of by certain regimes as a Western evil designed to make Africa an immoral society.

While the presence of the LGBTQ community in Africa has been stigmatized as a foreign element, it has escaped the attention of those who push the narrative that sodomy laws are colonial inheritances because most of the colonial powers outlawed homosexuality in the past. Although most of these European countries have since moved on to legalize and recognize LGBTQ groups, most African countries have adapted repealed colonial antigay laws to fight a phenomenon that is seen as an unwanted colonial import.

These are some identified causes of state homophobia in Africa that must be comprehensively addressed in order to ensure that LGBTQ groups gain some form of sociocultural acceptance instead of mere tolerance. It will be erroneous to believe that these elements exist independently of each other because most African states are characterized by strong religious leaders, selfish and corrupt political leaders, and bad governance as a whole.

Decolonization and African LGBTQ Movement

Ashley Currier sees feminist and LGBTQ groups as important to the decolonization movement in Africa. These groups emerged as a challenge to the authority of the ruling elites over the direction and focus of the decolonization effort.[31] Feminist theorists have built a national and transnational ideology out of a collection of "national, ethnic, gender and sexual collective identities."[32] They have done this to tackle anticolonial, masculinist efforts heavily reliant on women's subordination and the rejection of queer culture as Western, non-African, and un-Christian.

The increased awareness of the LGBTQ community in Africa has led to African nationalist movements' leaders portraying LGBTQ groups as antagonistic to African traditions and as a foreign element that must be eradicated to fully decolonize Africa. And since the concept of

---

31   Currier, "Decolonizing."
32   Currier, "Decolonizing."

decolonization implies a clean break from colonial history and experience through "destroying" the ideologies and practices associated with colonialism, feminist queer movements have since decried the hypocrisy that characterizes the decolonization effort that seeks to promote the heterosexual subordination of women as merely glorifying and invoking a colonial construction of gender and sexuality.[33] Thus, every decolonization effort that attempts to retain certain foreign heterosexual definitions of sexual identity is stuck in the colonial era and influenced by neocolonial ideology. Currier posits that decolonization implies "thorough change" rather than merely the political or economic liberation that follows. As a result, the African nationalist movement must re-create and promote a purely African narrative of sexual identity without the vestiges of African colonial experience.

Going forward, Currier identifies two major approaches to decolonization efforts in Africa, especially as they relate to sexual colonialism. The first is a selective approach in which political leaders and the elite promote only cultural projects that reinforce their rule based on masculinist and heteronormative national imagery.[34] This is evident in the refusal of several lawmakers to repeal colonial-era antigay laws without recognizing that such laws are part of colonial infrastructures that should be dismantled in the decolonization process. African nationalist movements ought to completely dismantle many colonial inheritances and chart a truly African outlook. The second approach is the transformation of the decolonization narrative to counter nationalist movements, resulting in a move championed by LGBTQ groups to transform heterosexist legal, political, and social institutions inherited from colonial powers, while promoting the rights of all minorities. Legal reform is a key element of the decolonization process.

Workplace Experience of LGBTQ Physicians

In describing health-care issues experienced by LGBTQ people, the focus has always been on their experiences in a heteronormative environment. One of the many issues raised regarding stigmatization of LGBTQ people

---

33 Spurlin, "African Intimacies," 201–4.
34 Currier, "Political Homophobia," 110–29.

in health-care centers is the lack of professionals who can relate to their experiences and build interpersonal relations that will facilitate communication between patient and physician. This is due to improperly trained health-care service providers.

Physicians who are professed members of the LGBTQ community often face the same discrimination as many would for their gender or race. Furthermore, collated data from a questionnaire mailed to 1949 physicians in New Mexico indicate that heterosexual physicians will often not refer patients to an LGBTQ physician colleague, while patients also discriminate.[35] This is the reality of an LGBTQ physician's workplace experience, but this is not surprising. A closer look will reveal that LGBTQ issues are yet to become a regular part of medical school curricula and residency programs, which also means that medical practitioners are more likely to express homophobic sentiments. The closest mention of fluid sexual identities in the survey is a mention of "exotic forms of human sexuality,"[36] which leads to more stigma associated with LGBTQ identities as deviant and abnormal.

Certain consequences befall LGBTQ physicians as reported in the survey. Some of these include denial of promotion and referrals, verbal harassment, and ostracization. These experiences have led to more applicants concealing their sexuality for fear of discrimination[37] from patients. While efforts have been made to include LGBTQ issues in medical education, the body of available knowledge remains inadequate.[38]

Sexual Identity and Sexual Orientation

The concept of sexual orientation refers to an individual's physiological inclination to others as relating to sexual or romantic desires, feelings, and thoughts. The sex or identity to which the recipient of such desires, feelings, or thought belongs determines whether an individual is sexually attracted to persons in the "same-sex, other sex, both sex, or neither

---

35   Ramos et al., "Attitudes," 436–38.
36   Eliason et al., "Lesbian, Gay, Bisexual, and Transgender," 1355–71.
37   Merchant et al., "Disclosure," 786.
38   Eliason et al., "Lesbian, Gay, Bisexual, and Transgender,"

sex."[39] However, the relationship between an individual's sexual identity and sexual orientation cannot always be predicted as one can occur independently of the other even as these sexual categories remain subject to dynamic cultural factors.

Identity is a personal and social definition of an individual's goals, values, beliefs, and life, which play out at different levels of identity formation—individual, collective, and relational.[40] Scholars define sexual identity as comprising the understanding of a person's relationship or attraction to others.[41] The most important part of an individual's sexual identity is the understanding of their attractions as falling into pansexual, asexual, heterosexual, bisexual, or homosexual categories.[42] The formation of sexual identity in a heterosexual will usually not be wrought with the same conflicts experienced by nonheterosexuals.

The development of sexual orientation in human beings is often concluded at the early stages of adulthood in which the individual can identify their sexual attraction toward members of the same or opposite sex (or both sexes).[43] This occurs at the subconscious level of human action as heterosexuals become "fixed," while sexual minorities take on appropriate labels.[44] Emerging adulthood is a phase that involves the transition from adolescence: it is becoming increasingly lengthy due to various socioeconomic changes that characterize an industrialized society. One of these changes relevant to the discourse is the increased tolerance and acceptance of premarital sex. This transitional phase is characterized by identity exploration, feelings of physiological and physical transition, higher levels of self-focus, and negotiation of instability. Such adventures result in flexible commitments to various identity options.

The emerging adulthood phase allows for experiments beyond the traditional norms of the heteronormative society. However, society marks the transition into adulthood with such heteronormative standards such as marriage and childbearing, which may create legal and social barriers for sexual minorities to be regarded as normal adults, and hence,

---

39 Vrangalova and Savin-Williams, "Mostly Heterosexual," 85–101.
40 Waters et al., *Coming*.
41 Vignoles et al., "Introduction," 1–27.
42 Savin-Williams, "Identity," 671–89.
43 Morgan, "Contemporary," 52–66.
44 J. P. Calzo et al., "Retrospective," 1658.

discrimination and marginalization may be in store for individuals who fail to conform.

Positive Effects of Parenting an LGBTQ Child

It is common knowledge that every LGBTQ child is a family member, whatever the composition of such a family, and that sexual identity is not usually inherited from a parent. This has made discourse on parenting quite interesting in the twenty-first century with the perceived growing number of sexual minorities. The development of a child through the various stages is often overseen and dependent on parents and parenting styles. Often, discourses focused on parenting an LGBTQ child only present the negative aspects of such an experience. Parents of LGBTQ children are often likely to develop more social connections, especially with persons connected to or who are members of LGBTQ communities and support groups, which gives room for social integration. It is important to note that heterosexual parents do not usually respond positively to the child's revelation of their sexual identity until they have had the chance to do a cognitive reappraisal of long-held beliefs.

Positive interactions between a parent and child result in increased cognitive flexibility, self-acceptance, open-mindedness, and strong connections. There are even more benefits observed by parents of LGBTQ children in many studies such as Gonzalez, et al.[45] Parenting of LGBTQ children often results in open-mindedness because such parents are exposed and "forced" to adopt new perspectives about the plight of sexual minorities, especially in a society filled with wrongheaded perceptions about the humanity of gay people. For some, it gives a clear and personal understanding and experience of discrimination against minorities and sexual minorities. This results in greater levels of empathy for marginalized people.

Due to the discrimination that LGBTQ children are likely to face (as well as their family's awareness about this), parents of these children are more likely to be nurturing and protective. This performs the dual function of bringing parents closer to their children and drawing other family members closer to each other. Parenting an LGBTQ child raises a sense of

---

45 Gonzalez et al., "Positive," 325–37.

awareness and activism in such a parent who, after dealing with an LGBTQ child's experience, may become attached to promoting the welfare of others who may not have supportive parents or guardians. This newfound activism may also give a new sense of purpose and meaning to their lives.

Benefits of Religious Acceptance of LGBTQ People

The religious institution is an important aspect of so many human lives, regardless of sexual identity or orientation. Organized religions have widespread benefits for their adherents, such as physical and mental health,[46] coping strategies, and emotional and social support.[47] The relationship between the religious institution and LGBTQ community has always been conflicted; religious bodies have been very vocal in condemning LGBTQ persons and promoting homophobic laws while contributing to guilt, ostracization, vigilance, suicidal ideation among members of the LGBTQ community.[48]

Usually, LGBTQ persons may attempt to make concessions to religious restrictiveness by changing or compromising their identity or opting for outright rejection of their faith. While this narrative may illustrate a negative relationship between religion and LGBTQ groups, there is evidence of the benefits of religion on their health and well-being. The reconciliation of an individual's spiritual/religious identity provides a foundation of support and allows for a more wholesome representation of the LGBTQ identity. Affirming faith communities provide LGBTQ people with feelings of love and acceptance, and social integration will probably result in a reduced suicide rate.

The feeling of love and acceptance can enhance the ability of LGBTQ people to cope with discrimination as members of a community that accepts them as they are because, unlike heterosexuals, LGBTQ persons are constantly searching for ways to validate their sexuality.[49] Also, religious support can deepen the sense of purpose among LGBTQ persons as they develop a new understanding of their religion and balance their identities.

---

46 Koenig, "Religion," 1194–1200.
47 Aten et al., *Psychology*.
48 Rosenkrantz et al., "Positive," 127.
49 Murr, "I Became Proud," 349–72.

Conclusion

Africa is, undoubtedly, a very homophobic and traditional society whose traditions have been infused with colonial values and norms that have informed certain difficult changes in African culture(s). The end of colonialism has seen Africans scrambling to reclaim their identity. In traditional African thought, LGBTQ identities are foreign elements that are unwanted vestiges of colonialism. However, this doesn't ring true because a number of different nonheterosexual orientations are present in certain indigenous African groups, and had always been banned by colonial laws, which, ironically, is the same basis upon which African governments are creating antigay laws.

The homophobic stance of African governments results in humanitarian crises brought about by stigmatization, criminalization, societal marginalization, as well as a hostile attitude among the general populace. The sources of such homophobic extremism on the part of African governments can be traced to religious homophobia, political homophobia, and a desire to be seen fighting neocolonial elements. Now, Western powers have stepped in to ensure that African governments treat LGBTQ people humanely, even though such a move's success is still in question. Ireland explains how the possibility of losing foreign aid assistance from international donors and governments is becoming critical to the efforts to get African governments to tone down antigay sentiments and laws.[50] Beyond the ideological difference and cultural intolerance, African governments are reminded of the humanitarian crises that homophobic discrimination can cause on the continent. In South Africa, for example, a large-scale march in Soweto attracted attention to the rampant rape of lesbians in the city, an act offenders claim is their efforts to "correct" the raped women's sexuality. In Uganda, too, violence against persons based on their sexual orientation is prevalent, with a newspaper posting photographs of a hundred Ugandans who were recognized as gays or lesbians, with the caption "hang them."[51]

The legal and sociocultural environment that most LGBTQ people in Africa live in has also affected the quality of health-care services. This

---

50 Ireland, "A Macro-Level."
51 Navanethem Pillay, "Homophobia: The Violence of Intolerance," Africa Renewal, accessed September 29, 2021, https://www.un.org/africarenewal/web-features/homophobia-violence-intolerance.

is because much of African society does not legally recognize LGBTQ people or a health-care system that is unapologetically heteronormative. Between an improperly equipped health-care service provider and a medical workforce predominantly constituted by older generation folks who are judgmental and less tolerant, LGBTQ people are at greater risk of receiving poor health care in general. The mental health status of LGBTQ people remains under threat from various risk factors that enhance suicidal ideation.

Despite some progress, institutional discrimination has yet to be tackled, even among medical school applicants and LGBTQ physicians. Medical schools have yet to properly introduce LGBTQ issues into medical education, while physicians who are openly gay are stigmatized, verbally abused, and discriminated against by patients and administrative boards. This has resulted in new applicants to medical schools who feel they must conceal their sexual identity.

The media's role in the positive presentation and dissemination of information is important enough for para-democratic governments to wield censorship powers against LGBTQ platforms, whether mainstream or alternative. The population's tolerance level and attitude may be positively influenced if LGBTQ content is disseminated widely. It is high time that Africa, Africans, and African studies entertained alternative discourses on sexual identities because the LGBTQ community is deserving of respect, celebration, and human decency.

Part Three
The Disciplines

Chapter Twelve

Decolonizing the African Academy

Introduction

Education is a fundamental tool for developing humans and society, making people aware of their society's culture. Education is a continuous process as long as mechanisms for transmitting cultural values are developed and sustained. As an instrument of socialization, education globally supports the transfer of skills and knowledge at different levels. Human attempts to develop a culture of learning gave birth to organized educational systems and the institutions that serve as knowledge production centers around the world.[1]

The university is the highest institution of learning developed to date. It has historically been responsible for knowledge production, and it has assisted with the development of societies. Under normal circumstances, universities are engine rooms for innovation, driving socioeconomic development. They create knowledge and ideas that propel science and technology. Research plays a vital role in developing new knowledge and the growth of all higher education. A goal of university education, apart from teaching, is to advance, create, and disseminate knowledge through research—universities provide services for the community and a supply of qualified young researchers that assist societies with cultural, social, and economic development. Research promotes the goals of national development.

---

1 This is drawn from the context of the development of European universities. The African experience is quite different, being affected as it was by colonialism.

In Africa, many universities are unable to uphold these responsibilities due to poor infrastructural development, inadequate funding, flagging research interest, flawed education policies, and other factors. The restrictions attached to government support prevent universities from operating independently, free from government control; academic freedom is especially constrained in areas where research results may be critical of government activities. Many African universities have also been applying colonial education policies and using curricula that are unable to address the fundamental problems of development within the context of the continent. These problems have rekindled interest among African scholars reexamining the role of African universities in the development of African societies.

The call for reexamination is not new, but ongoing engagement is necessary to reform African universities, which must address the challenges of development on the continent and continue to decolonize the curricula in appropriate areas. Some African countries have already attempted to reform their university system to solve their specific problems, but most African universities have been left behind in the global competition for knowledge production, research, and development. The call for change has become especially urgent because many universities, after almost fifty years of effort, remain incapable of performing their roles in either research or community development.

The appeal for decolonization is essential. The imposition of colonialism—one of humanity's most destructive forms of international interaction—has impaired the development of African university systems and continued to assert its influence in the years after independence. Eurocentrism, as a concept, was developed to serve the domineering mission of colonial enterprise, and its epistemic challenge elicited discourse on the impact of colonialism in Africa and a methodology for deconstructing it.

The so-called civilizing mission of colonialists portrayed Europeans as idealized humans and the standard for excellence; this mindset has justified and perpetuated colonialism in Africa long after independence. Although its underlying motive was the appropriation of Africa's economic resources, Eurocentrism became the central principle for the social, economic, and political organization of colonized people in accordance with European values. Through colonial enterprise, the concept provided a roadmap for the destruction of indigenous knowledge systems that were replaced by the European, colonial system of education. These activities are evident in the kinds of knowledge and knowledge systems produced and imposed by Europeans, not only through the creation of universities across Africa but also through the development of the curriculum that supports them.

In the book *How Europe Underdeveloped Africa*, Walter Rodney describes colonialism as a one-armed-bandit[2] because of its predatory dynamics. In *Orientalism*, Edward Said describes colonial education as an organized form of imperialism through which colonial authorities indoctrinated students with new subjects while effectively filtering out all traces of local culture that students might bring to their education.[3] This further attests to "the interpretive ideological valorization of Euro-American society as superior, progressive, and universal,"[4] successfully eradicating the relics of indigenous African cultures that were previously treasured in society.

The struggle to liberate Africa is as old as the forces that have besieged it. In Africa, nationalists (Pan-Africanists) and intellectuals have taken various approaches to decolonization even as the powers controlling the continent mutate into more complex forms. African nationalists and intellectuals have weakened the forces of colonialism by dismantling some of their structures and instituting independent political systems and democratic governments. However, the African academics (intellectuals) have been left with the battle to save Africa's soul from the European knowledge system and the destructive curricula that define power relations in Africa's academy.[5] For decades, this task has shaped African intellectualism, particularly in the areas of curriculum development and the reconstruction of methodologies to defeat the idea of Eurocentrism and its colonial academic enterprise.

There is a general awareness of the African educational system's colonial legacy, but this has not translated into a sufficient grasp of the nature and process of transforming African universities. It is also relevant to the question of how the African intelligentsia conceives the concept of transforming universities in the face of the current challenges confronting the

---

2   Rodney, *How Europe*.
3   Said, *Orientalism*, 9.
4   Grosfoguel, "Decolonizing," 199.
5   This is not separating the two. Intellectuals and nationalists have complemented each other in the struggle for Africa's liberation.

educational system. The massive brain drain experienced by Africa over the years suggests that the challenges faced by African universities are inadequate funding, lack of academic freedom, poor infrastructural development, and a substandard commitment to research and development.

Such challenges may exist, but they are not the sole reason for the problems facing the university system in Africa. These crises must be contextualized with the origin and development of African universities and the impact on African universities and indigenous knowledge systems. This assessment of the crisis can evaluate whether postcolonial initiatives can overcome these challenges. Beyond the process of transforming institutions through adequate funding and infrastructural development, there is also the challenge of decolonizing the pedagogy that has entrenched backwardness in research and educational development in Africa—and specifically in universities.

Developing a pedagogy based on Africanist principles, using their conception of humanity, is essential to chart a path for development that can solve Africa's problems. This chapter examines the history of colonial institutional knowledge systems (the universities) established in Africa and their impact on African people and societies. It also examines the purpose behind the creation of the universities, whether that purpose has been realized, what kind of knowledge is produced, and which limitations constrain universities from working to solve problems in Africa. The chapter discusses postcolonial initiatives of African intellectuals in its attempt to decolonize the academy and transform the entire university system into one that can serve Africa's needs while also ensuring that Africa is competitive and effective in the affairs of international development.

Colonialism and the Making of the African Academy

There is a consensus among African scholars that precolonial Africa had already developed its own systematic, organized institutions for higher learning. J. F. Ade Ajayi has shown that the continent had an established system of higher education prior to European occupation and domination. This system, equivalent to a Western university system, produced knowledge for understanding the world, humans in their society, and religion while promoting agriculture, health, literature, and philosophy.[6] In

---

6   Ajayi et al., *African Experience*, 5.

the last two or three centuries BC and AD, Egypt had a community of scholars with an international outlook, implementing the sophisticated Alexandria model along with the monastic system of knowledge production.[7] Famous educational systems in Africa include the Karawiyyinn in Fez (Morocco), in 859 AD; Cairo, in 970; and Sankore, Timbuktu from the twelfth century. Egypt has the oldest institution of higher learning, and it has continued to operate as a university.[8]

Despite the evidence of precolonial universities in Africa, the colonialist overseers mistakenly did not recognize such strides as an essential part of a people's history and civilization. The character of colonial enterprise, in Africa and elsewhere, dismissed the local value systems that had effectively organized existing residents. Or when such systems were recognized, they were often exploited. Colonialism had cocooned itself within the notion that "natives" were not capable of developing systems that could produce useful knowledge, which is why the establishment of universities and university education was different in Europe and Africa.

In Europe, universities emerged out of religious institutions in the Christian faith, particularly the Catholic Church. Growing urbanism and an emerging class of wealthy people eroded the church's control over centers of learning. Wealthy people and politicians, who recognized the relevance of human resources for supporting and developing the economic system that they controlled, took over the business of education. They began to establish schools, some of which came under the control of kings and queens. This process revolutionized higher education in Europe. Africa's experience was different because its European-styled universities emerged out of the vicious, controlling experience of colonialism.

Although Christianity was responsible for the transfer of systematic Western education in Africa, universities did not emerge the same way as in Europe. The education policies of colonial governments allowed churches to organize and implement educational systems with no regard for indigenous culture, namely African languages and socioeconomic and political organization. The reorganization of the colonies and the creation of artificial boundaries dislocated systems of social, economic, or political organization that had previously served the people. The colonial mandate allowed the church to establish schools, referred to as "colleges," which

---

7   Ajayi et al., *African Experience*, 5.
8   Arab Information Center, *Education*, 282.

cleared the way for the emergence of universities and other institutions of higher learning in Africa.

Early colleges were Makerere Government College in Kampala, Uganda; Yaba Higher College in Lagos, Nigeria; Fourah Bay College in Freetown, Sierra Leone; Gordon Memorial College in Khartoum, Sudan; and Princess of Wales School and College in Achimota, Ghana. The Nigerian college offered two-year courses in arts or science; three-year professional courses for teacher training; two-year programs for engineering, agriculture, and surveying; and five-year medical and veterinary courses. At Makerere, skills in various occupations were introduced. In Ghana, the model comprehensive school offered classes for kindergarten through secondary school, and it had a first-year university college affiliation with the University of London. Ghana was serious about the promotion of cultural heritage and languages.[9]

The transformation of these colleges into universities was facilitated through advisory reports from the Elliot Commission and similar projects across Africa. The Elliot Commission toured West Africa, holding meetings and receiving petitions. There was disagreement among members of the commission, but the report culminated in the establishment of universities in the West African region that were affiliated with British universities—these universities were intended to be truly African in their outlook and content. Some have argued that the British ran out of excuses for obstructing educational development in the colonies; the question is, how can local universities affiliated with British institutions be fully African?[10]

In the late 1940s, the continent began witnessing the transformation of colleges into universities and institutions of higher learning. The University of Makerere in Uganda; University College Ibadan, Nigeria; and the University College in the Gold Coast (now known as Ghana), were all created in a process supported by the Phelps-Stoke advisory committee. The committee had recommended that the colleges be affiliated with the University of London and Cambridge University. The emergence of these universities was seen as a development that could usher in a new class of educated elite to champion the cause of Africa's independence and guide the socioeconomic affairs of newly independent

---

9   Effah, "Higher Education, 338–49.
10 Ajayi, *African Experience*, 52.

African nation-states. The universities were financed by the Colonial Development Welfare Fund designed by the British colonial government.

Colonialists had always been motivated to maintain their grip on Africa for as long as possible, making it difficult to accept that universities were established to support the colonized in their struggle for independence. Such institutions were created as a way of building capacity in contemporary international development.[11] Many universities had been established by the 1960s, during the years when influential movements pushed for independence and self-government. However, the education system—and universities in particular—retained the structural dependence and academic models that sustained colonial education in independent Africa. New universities were later established under the same structure.

The situation in French colonies was different. The French colonial policy of assimilation extended to their educational goals. French colonialists sought to educate a small number of the colonized in a way that allowed them to remain firmly committed to the French colonial agenda. French colonialists allowed their subjects enough latitude to study in France without discrimination—Ajayi has posited that the policy was intended to make the colonized feel more comfortable in France than in Africa.[12] As a result, French colonialists established few universities. The Instituts des Hautes Etudes in Dakar, Tananarive, and Abidjan were only just developed in the 1960s, toward the end of the independence movement for French colonies.

Many African scholars from Francophone countries received university education in France. The French education policy, which was an extension of their assimilation policy, not only assimilated a number of Africans, but it also bequeathed a structure of perpetual dependence for many African countries. Today, not only are the education systems of many Francophone African countries built on a French model, but their economies are also tied to the economy and monetary policies of France. France continues to hold 50 percent of the foreign reserves of twelve African countries in its Central Bank, continuing to enrich itself with Africa's wealth many years after independence.[13]

11 Harris, "Building," 7–11.
12 Ajayi, *African Experience*, 39.
13 www.moguldom.com.

The eastern part of Africa had a separate experience. Universities in this region emerged under the influence and control of two colonial powers: Belgium and France. The Democratic Republic of Congo, Rwanda, and Burundi were trusteeship territories administered by the Belgians. It is not clear whether the Vatican entered into an agreement with King Leopold II, but the colonial education policy in these areas was supervised by the Catholic Church, which was mainly concerned with primary education. The church did not establish institutions of higher education in the region. At independence, the people had to request a university, and the Universite Lavonium[14] was established in 1954 by the Catholic Jesuit order. It operated under a structure similar to that of Universite de Louvain Brussels, with various institutes and programs. Examples included the Foundation Medicale de l' Universite de Louvain au Congo (Famulac) in 1926, educating Congolese medical personnel and researchers specializing in tropical medicine, and Centres Agronomiques de l'Universite de Louvain au Congo (Cadulac) in Kisantu in 1932.

In 1971, initiatives from within led to the establishment of Libre du Congo and Universitaire de Luluabourg, which later merged to form Universite Nationale du Zaire (UNAZA). In 1980, UNAZA separated to form three institutions: University of Kinshasa, Kisangani University, and University of Lubumbashi. According to Gondola, "Academic training provided the Congolese with nothing more than a veneer of moral education based on Catholic principles and the technical skills necessary to create lower middle class."[15] Catholic schools were common, promoting the use of French over indigenous languages. Catholic mission schools worked in unison under the authority of King Leopold. Fabian noted that "being involved in education, to the point of having a near monopoly of it, the mission worked indirectly and often directly, for the promotion of private commercial and industrial interest."[16] In 1883, King Leopold wrote to the missionaries in Congo:

---

14 The university receives a lot of funding and support from the colonial government and international donor agencies such as the Rockefeller Foundation and United States Agency for International Development (USAID).
15 Gondola, *History*, 13.
16 Fabian, "Missions," 169.

Your essential role is to facilitate the task of administrators and industrials, which means you will go to interpret the gospel in the way it will be the best to protect your interests in that part of the world. For these things, you have to keep watch on disinteresting our savages from the richness that is plenty in their underground. To avoid that, they get interested in it, and make you murderous competition and dream one day to overthrow you.[17]

The Belgian colonial mission was purely exploitative in the Congo and East African region, with no interest in educational development. Missionary activities were undertaken there solely to consolidate the Belgian colonial enterprise.

It was not within the colonial scheme to educate the colonized. Many colonial powers did not want to increase the metropole's annual expenses from managing the colonies, which would be the consequence of educating Africans. Such education could be dangerous to European interests because it could promote competition between the European colonizers and their subjects. Education provided to Africans in the early stage of European programs did not encourage intellectual development and was strictly for acquiring basic skills and vocational training.

The British Advisory Committee on Education in Tropical Africa was established in response to reports issued by the Phelps-Stokes Commission in 1922. The committee stated that "as resources permit, the door of advancement, through higher education, in Africa must be increasingly opened for those who by character, ability and temperament show themselves fitted to profit by such education."[18] The politics of providing education continued as colonialists contemplated the establishment of universities in Africa. The initiatives were shaped by colonial powers, which meant that universities, at their inception, were not able to adapt to their surroundings and needed to rely on affiliations with European institutions.

The external imposition of these universities took place within a framework that was dictated by Europeans, including European curricula that were shaped by colonizing interests. University graduates had a limited understanding of Africa's socioeconomic realities because they were detached from the sociocultural milieu that could have provided that

---

17   King Leopold II of Belgium to Colonial Missionaries.
18   Ajayi, *African Experience*, 44.

understanding; universities were established not to solve local problems but to serve colonial demands. The affiliation created a false perception that established the metropole as the standard for educational quality. Not only was this an insult to African higher education, but it also created a structure of dependence for knowledge and skills. The knowledge and skills acquired by educated African elites were not applicable to local contexts; graduates returned to their local communities as academics who could read and write about subjects that held little relevance for their villages.[19]

Some good, however, came from this system. Young Africans who studied in Britain became radicalized and socialized in Pan-African movements, criticizing the colonial regimes at home. This forced colonialists to reconsider their decision to educate "natives" in the metropole. An advisory committee headed by James Currie stated that "African thirst for higher education remains unabated; if this is not satisfied at home it can only lead to increasing efflux of undergraduate African students towards universities in Europe and America."[20] Colonialists saw an opportunity to avoid the expense of funding education in their colonies by allowing Africans to "take charge" of their own education. Africans lacked the necessary staff to operate these universities, which meant that the "independence" of universities triggered a recruitment process that ultimately employed large numbers of European educators. This was another opportunity for Europeans to increase the dependency of African universities, having them rely on European institutions for global recognition and European staff for designing their curricula and steering their development.

A university was established in the Cape of Good Hope, South Africa, in 1873. It was named the University of Good Hope and was later referred to as the University of South Africa. The exceptional nature of imperialist domination in South Africa created a unique history of university education in that part of the continent. The apartheid regime made no effort to serve anyone's interests except its own. Systematic segregation and racial inequality permeated every aspect of society and linked one's ability to advance with one's skin color. The South African experience perfected the Euro-American script on worldwide racial discrimination.

---

19 Brown, "British Educational Policy," 365–77.
20 Ajayi, *African Experience*, 49.

Strict laws were passed in South Africa to regulate the conduct of citizens in public spaces, including universities, and to determine which schools were available to South African citizens. By 1948 restrictive apartheid racial bills were incorporated into the colonial education scheme. By 1957 Blacks were allowed to register for college at Fort Hare, but the universities of Witwatersrand, Cape Town (UCT), and Natal operated along vicious racial lines. It was an offense punishable by law for a non-white to teach in white universities. Violators were charged a fine of £100 and they risked six months' imprisonment. Nonwhites could not register to attend these universities without authorization from the minister of Bantu education; whites who registered to attend nonwhite institutions could be punished with similar penalties.[21]

As racial policies perpetuated racially segregated universities, structural defects emerged in the standard of knowledge and orientation for students who were left unaware of their society's socioeconomic realities, warping the nexus between the role of the university and the development agenda of the apartheid state. Throughout the apartheid era in South Africa, the country's major universities aligned their programs with the promotion of the Afrikaans ethnocentric agenda, adopting the Afrikaans language as a medium of instruction. As the movement for decolonizing the African academy strengthened in the 1960s, 1970s, and 1980s, Pretoria, Stellenbosch, and Potchefstroom universities remained committed to the apartheid agenda; they neglected the discourse on decolonizing colonial knowledge that propelled the evolution of the humanities discipline within South Africa and globally.

In a paper titled, "Between the Public Intellectual and the Scholar: Decolonization and Some Independence Initiatives in African Higher Education," Mahmood Mamdani cited Van Oselen in Wolpe and Barends on the existing inequalities in the universities, especially between universities for Blacks and whites:

> Developed legitimately" and "organically" in relation to the core life of the economy, black universities at the periphery were the result of an "artificial" development, through social engineering. Stuart Saunders, a former Vice Chancellor of UCT, elaborated this point of view: "Nurtured by their links to the core political economy, the

---

21 Ashby, *Universities: British*, 346–47.

white universities developed into centres of excellence indexed by high reputation ratings, access to resources, good student outputs and the development of talent or 'value added' reflected in research and publications.[22]

Black universities, according to Altbach, were relegated to the periphery, and white universities became the center:

> Academic centres provide leadership in all aspects of science and scholarship—such as research and teaching, the organizational patterns and directions of universities, and knowledge dissemination. The centres tend to be located in larger and wealthier countries and benefit from the full array of resources—including funding and infrastructures such as libraries and laboratories for research, academic staff with appropriate qualifications, traditions and legislation in support of academic freedom, and an orientation toward high achievement levels on the part of individual professors and students and by the institutions themselves. Typically, these top institutions use one of the major international languages for teaching and research, and they enjoy appropriate support from the state for their work.[23]

Colonial universities in Africa and elsewhere had never been established with the intention of creating higher education that would be relevant to its immediate environment to improve local research and development. Movements for independence in Africa were not a product of careful research conducted by so-called African universities to understand the philosophy and guiding principles of colonialism: they were a response to years of brutal colonial domination. In many ways, socioeconomic and scientific research was absent. Africans were merely meant to learn skills and receive vocational education that had no significant impact on the socioeconomic realities of African societies. This continued in postcolonial university education.

Colonial university education severely contrasted with the sociocultural realities of African societies. Universities did not assume African identities or value systems that were capable of driving change in economies and societies, which set a process of deculturalization in motion that deliberately refused to acknowledge the multicultural nature and

---

22 Mamdani, "Between the Public," 77.
23 Altbach, "Globalization" 63–74.

traditions of African societies. They also displaced traditional African education systems that were the basis for social organization. According to Ali Mazrui, "Western education in Africa conditions a process of psychological de-culturalisation. The educated African became . . . a misfit in his own village . . . when he graduated . . . His parents did not expect him to continue living with them tending cattle or cultivating the land."[24]

The French policy of assimilation did not promote research and development in Africa; it enabled cultural imperialism. The history of university education in colonial Africa was a process that entrenched the Europeanization of education, research, and development. To cite Mazrui again:

> The nature of westernization in Africa has been very different. Far from emphasizing western productive technology and reducing western life-styles and verbal culture, Africa has reversed the Japanese order of emphasis. Among the factors which have facilitated this reversal has been the role of the African university as a vehicle of western culture.[25]

Decolonizing the Academy: Postcolonial Initiatives and Transformations

Although much work remains in the decolonization agenda for higher education in Africa, it is relevant to consider some of the African initiatives to achieve this milestone. At independence, some African countries were modeled along an Afrocentric ideology against the Eurocentric colonial ideology, and such conflicting ideologies dominated intellectual discourse in African university education. Many Pan-Africanists called

---

24 Mazrui, *Political Values*, 16.
25 Mazrui, "Towards Re-Africanizing," 141. According to Mazrui, the Japanese model of modernization involves selectivity to sort out what remains beneficial to Japanese society from the many choices Euro-American civilization offers and discarding those regarded as valueless. In this way, cultural values of Japan can remain useful and relevant in their society's development. The Japanese placed more emphasis on the technical and technological techniques of the West without submitting to Western literary and verbal culture.

for the Africanization of faculties as university education expanded. This is important, but so is the Africanization of curricula and the funding of institutions. There has been a push to incorporate indigenous knowledge, moving away from curricula that originated in colonial times, but much outdated colonial-era theory has been retained from that period. "Africanization" became the mantra in teaching and research. Ironically, the language of the colonizer has remained the language of instruction in African universities. These contradictions complicated the idea of establishing an African university from the very start.

Despite the fact that many initiatives to advance Africans and their system of higher education are routinely sabotaged,[26] Africans have developed the capacity to understand their problems and they have engaged with the forces that undermine their progress. At independence, African intellectuals and nationalists realized the urgent need to decolonize the knowledge systems that had been left to them. This understanding came from an awareness that the colonial knowledge system was dysfunctional, incompatible, and deliberately incapable of dealing with Africa's developmental challenges. This was especially true for the role that African universities needed to play in national development, serving emerging African states.

Decolonization, also called Africanization or Afrocentrism, is an expression of resentment against existing colonial education structures that persist in higher education in Africa. The decolonization of education is not a static knowledge orientation; it is a process that must be continued with a complex knowledge dynamism in devotion to disciplinary and transdisciplinary foundations, remaining constantly alive to problem solving. In other words, knowledge constructions should be approached using its dynamics while remaining cognizant of the construct necessary to advance the general progress of humanity.

To decolonize is to integrate the full scope of knowledge—created in different locales and by different people—into the school system. The idea of decolonization is not new, because Africans have wrestled with

---

26 The structural adjustment of the 1980s was a major example of how Africans were coerced into accepting the Bretton Woods financial institutions and their conditions for reforming the educational system, especially primary education, as against the transformation of higher education in Africa. For details, see Albert, "University Students," 374.

the forces of colonialism in the organization of their social, political, and economic systems. The fight against colonialism created a platform for the production of anticolonial knowledge. This interest is often renewed within the context of emerging themes of socioeconomic and political development on the continent, making it clear that scholarship must continue to be Africanized to benefit the African people. One example is the "Rhodes Must Fall" movement in South Africa.

Africans have resisted colonialism and its educational philosophy for a long time. Prior to the postcolonial debate on decolonizing education, dialogues were held by Africans in the diaspora. Notable African Americans discussed the advancement of an Africanist scholarship and how it could provide support for developing African society. Such debates took place between James Johnson and Edward Blyden but also between W. E. B. Du Bois and Booker T. Washington. The central focus of the discourse around colonial education was how the project of transforming education in Africa could serve the continent's programs for nation building. Cheik Anta Diop made significant efforts with works that included *The African Origins of Civilization: Myth or Reality?* (1974), and *Precolonial Black Africa* (1987). These works depict Africans as the architects of their own history and civilization, in contrast to racialized Eurocentric scholarship.

African universities deepened the debate around decolonizing the colonial knowledge system upon independence. As they attempted to reach

Figure 12.1. #RMF Statue Removal 35. Photograph by Desmond R. Bowles. Used with permission.

consensus on these efforts, they raised many relevant issues—especially for initiatives generated within Africa and the knowledge produced by African universities in connection with earlier discourse from Johnson, Blyden, and Du Bois.[27] Two schools of thought, the Dar-es-Salaam school and the Makerere school, produced knowledge that has continued to inspire ideas of decolonizing the African academy.

The Dar-es-Salaam school, headed by Walter Rodney, saw national development as essential for the total dismantling of imperialism's forces in Africa. On the other hand, Ali Mazrui posited that the authoritarian tendencies of nationalists in power were counterproductive for anticolonial struggles. These discussions are central to understanding the relationship between African society and the university system. Some ideas were promoted through establishment of a magazine known as the *Transition*, which was a platform for African intellectuals and nationalists to publicize their views on national development.

Many Africans contributed to the *Transition*, including Julius Nyerere of Tanzania. The Arusha declaration and other political developments in Tanzania led to a renewal of interest in properly conceptualizing the role of universities in national development. The student demonstration against the compulsory national service that had been introduced by Nyerere's socialist regime was a significant stage in the university's transformation. The demonstration laid the foundation for a review of the university's curriculum at a conference on the "Role of the University in Socialist Tanzania." The conference considered many viewpoints on transforming the university's academic programs, recognizing that their current state did not reflect the wishes of the postcolonial generation in either Tanzania or East Africa.[28]

The 1960s were characterized by intellectual debates and new schools of thought in African universities that broadened the horizon of African historiography and developed models for studying colonial misconduct. The intellectual ferment of that time established new universities across the continent and formed academic societies and academic journals to produce and promote African knowledge produced by African scholars. This knowledge was not only relevant to the development of Africanist historiography but was also significant for defining an Africanist

---

27   See Ajayi, *African Experience*, 20.
28   Kimambo, "Establishment," 77.

conception of humanity that was separate from the Europeanist conceptions of humanity and history in general. The Ibadan school produced theses that criticized missionary activity for supporting and developing the colonial enterprise in Africa, and its counterparts in Dar-es-Salaam advanced different strands of dependency theory and models for building Africa's academy. These initiatives popularized Africa's past and transformed African academia into an enterprise that could produce knowledge that was relevant for the continent's socioeconomic realities.

One of the most important contributions from African intellectuals was the *UNESCO General History of Africa* (1965–1993) and the *Cambridge History of Africa* (1974–1986). These important exercises in knowledge production, undertaken by Africans, contributed to the preservation of African history and the development of historiography with an Africanist perspective.[29] These compendiums were the catalyst for additional contributions from intellectuals across the continent. Historical archaeologists and scholars in adjoining fields of inquiry used the material as evidence to support the development of African knowledge production.

The 1967 establishment of the Association of African Universities (AAU) was another important initiative to promote Africanist research and development. This association includes more than 340 members from 46 countries. This platform is for "research, reflection, consultation, debates, co-operation and collaboration on issues pertaining to higher education."[30] It has built a substantial network of African intellectuals across all five subregions of the continent. It has a unique capacity to convene policymakers and institutional leaders to discuss issues of higher education, as demonstrated by the World Trade Organization (WTO) and General Agreements on Trade in Service (GTS) workshop in 2004. Its academic staff exchange program aims to promote academic synergy among African intellectuals for cross-fertilization of ideas in various institutions of higher education.[31]

The establishment of Pan-African University was another giant stride in decolonization education in Africa. The university was founded in

---

29 For more on the UNESCO project, see Barbosa, "African Perspective," 400–422.
30 www.aau.com.
31 http://www.aau.com.

2008 by the African Union to raise the quality of higher education on the continent. The African Union felt that higher education standards on the continent had dropped significantly, especially in the 1980s and 1990s, creating a need for Africans to attain the "vision to generate a home-grown solution to African challenges in accordance with the philosophy of NEPAD which is aimed at Africa's participation in the global knowledge economy."[32]

Six objectives were set for Pan-African University:

1. Develop continent-wide and world-class graduate and postgraduate programs in science, technology, innovation, humanities, social sciences, and governance;
2. Stimulate collaborative, internationally competitive, cutting-edge fundamental- and development-oriented research in areas having a direct bearing on Africa's technical, economic, and social development;
3. Enhance the mobility of students, lecturers, researchers and administrative staff at African universities to improve teaching, leadership, and collaborative research;
4. Contribute to the capacity building of present and future African Union stakeholders;
5. Enhance the attractiveness of African higher education and research institutions for developing and retaining young African talent, attracting the best intellectual capital from across the globe, including the African Diaspora;
6. Invigorate dynamic and productive partnerships with public and private sectors.[33]

The university is guided by the following principles:

1. Excellence and international partnerships in academic and research activities;
2. Academic freedom, autonomy, quality assurance, and accountability;
3. Strengthening the capacity of existing African institutions;
4. Encouraging intra-African mobility of students and academic and research staff;

---

32 http://www.africa-union.org.
33 http://www.africa-union.org.

5. Offering an innovative continental framework to the African Diaspora for contributing to the development of higher education and research in Africa;
6. Promoting inter-disciplinary and multidisciplinary research programs integrated into development policy at continental and national levels;
7. Enhancing and optimizing the use of information and communications technologies for pedagogy, research, and management;
8. Promoting innovation through technology incubation and patenting to ensure that value is added.[34]

Other African intellectuals across the continent have made independent efforts to decolonize education, which is demonstrated by the many research papers distributed through journals, seminars, conferences, workshops, and other publication platforms found across university campuses in Africa. These important contributions have assisted with the production of knowledge by Africans and the development of an Africanist narrative on the history of the African academy and the need to expand it by any means.

Progress has been made, but challenges continue to emerge and undermine this process in many ways; dynamics of change and continuity have emerged from attempts to decolonize higher education and knowledge production in general. Some of these challenges are internal, such as the commitment of universities to deliver on their mandate or the need for governments to demonstrate the political will to support higher education in Africa. External challenges include the internationalization[35] of higher education and the development of information and communication

---

34 http://www.africa-union.org.
35 For details on internationalization see Altbach, "Globalization and the University," 227–47. Internationalization of the university entails an unequal relationship in the production of knowledge between universities of the Global North and those in the Global South. While those in the North have advanced to become the "center," those in the South receive whatever comes from the North as part of the "periphery." This gap in knowledge production between North (center) and South (periphery) becomes even more pronounced with the emergence of information and communication technology in the North. At the moment, Africa is still battling to adapt to systems of information and communication technologies to increase capacity in knowledge production. The internationalization of knowledge not only improved the enterprise of knowledge

technology that promotes a knowledge economy. Higher education in Africa has needed to transform its curricula so that it can meet these international demands while remaining relevant for Africa and the rest of the world. Africans have demonstrated the ability to address these challenges as they surface, but more is required to address the effects of internationalization—otherwise known as globalization—on the African academy.

Contemporary Challenges

Although the decolonization of education is tied to African development, African governments and higher education institutions have not managed to improve the higher education system in a systematic way. The frenzy of activity that accompanied independence would suggest that a significant portion of Africa's education systems should be decolonized by now, but the work of decolonization is an ongoing process. Despite the early promise of Africa's independence, very little has been achieved since.

African universities have succeeded in Africanizing personnel, including in South Africa, which secured freedom from apartheid in the 1990s. However, many universities retain colonial curricula and pedagogical structures and epistemologies that have no significant impact on Africa's existential problems. Scholars have argued that part of the frustration of decolonizing Africa's educational institutions comes from a lack of funding and schools' vulnerability to market forces. Intellectuals are exposed to the effects of supply and demand, which requires them to promote their work and focus on marketable research, restricting the enterprise of knowledge production to market spaces. Skills are no longer applied for national development, as had been the case in the 1960s and 1970s.[36] Mamdani explains:

---

production, but it has unified the global system of knowledge production in favor of—and according to the dictates of—the North.

36   This is the experience of many intellectuals who offer consultancy services in order to eke out a living. Many African intellectuals have become tools in the hands of international nongovernmental organizations. Some of their projects might undermine the development of Africa, but they may unknowingly contribute to such enterprises because they need to make a living. There was a synergy between universities and national development

Unlike in the 1960s and 1970s, the public intellectual of the early 21st century cannot be presumed to be a progressive intellectual; in this era, the "public" is no longer just the "people," it also includes the government, and the donor and the financial institutions on which governments increasingly depend. The new type of public intellectual is recruited and funded by these organizations to do constant monitoring of public institutions, both from within and from the outside, in the name of "accountability".[37]

Among African intellectuals, the rise of consultancy services has reduced the interest in and commitment to higher education. Many seek out employers capable of recognizing and rewarding their skills, while poor job opportunities have created a mass migration of intellectuals from Africa heading for developed countries (or "brain drain," which has been previously discussed). In their new environments, these people contribute to the development of higher education elsewhere through the production of knowledge that is changing the world today. African governments should focus on higher education and on retaining the continent's best minds, putting them to work solving local problems.

Authoritarian regimes in Africa also pose challenges to the work of decolonizing education, preventing African intellectuals from engaging in healthy debate on national development. Academic freedom in Africa has been a major problem: many scholars face incarceration for criticizing draconian governments, regulations concerning higher education, or failures to protect the rights of citizens. Two lecturers were recently dismissed in Nigeria because they were critical of government policies.[38] This censorship has prevented teachers from carrying out their responsibilities and has slowed commitments to research and development. It implies that any research findings that do not support government policy—or findings that oppose government policy—are likely to be discarded.

A university's importance can be judged by whether its research and knowledge-building capacity are rooted in the African environment.

---

    policies at independence—the development of higher education was emphasized before the years of structural adjustment, when governments began to neglect higher education on the recommendation of Bretton Woods institutions.
37 Mamdani, "Between the Public," 80.
38 Binniyat, "Product."

Universities are only useful for eradicating poverty when they research the problems of Africa; they must be reformed to construct a foundation of research and knowledge that can solve Africa's main problems. African universities constantly struggle to fund research. In Nigeria, the Academic Staff Union of Universities (ASUU) has fought to improve funding for research and for other resources that can strengthen the role of universities in national development. The government's inability or unwillingness to meet these demands has resulted in prolonged industrial actions that affect academic calendars and block students from pursuing higher education.

Research output is extremely low at many African universities when compared with their counterparts worldwide, partly due to a lack of experienced research faculty. Other reasons for the reduced output include a heavy teaching load for the faculty members who remain and a lack of resources, such as library facilities, technology infrastructure, and well-equipped laboratories. These have all contributed to the low quality and quantity of research activities from African universities. It is difficult to deny the questionable quality and relevance of research performed at most African universities.

A common refrain among university lecturers concerns the need to either "publish or perish." A massive number of papers are published for self-promotion and not to advance national development.[39] In some places, research does not receive funding from local donor agencies that could promote programs for a national development agenda. Instead, research is externally funded by organizations pursuing topics that are not relevant for national or even regional development.

Research results from major studies at most African universities are often stored in libraries and not applied through government programs. Calls have been made at every opportunity to rethink how the government engages with higher education, especially when producing or using the knowledge generated by universities. Universities should be able to streamline their curricula in support of national development programs, and the government must apply university research in pursuit of development goals.

Student enrollment in higher education has increased in Africa, but this has not been matched by an increase in public funding. Public spending

---

39   Nyamnjoh, "From Publish," 331–55. See also Teferra, "Funding."

per student has declined drastically over the years, signaling a worsening quality of education. The increasing number of students in African higher education requires more faculty recruitment and additional infrastructure to meet their growing needs.[40] Some public institutions have begun charging tuition fees, which could lead public higher education to be operated as a private enterprise—another excuse for governments to reduce funding for higher education. When there is no synergy between government and higher education, the ability to create and maintain vital infrastructure suffers.

Graduates across the continent face challenges finding employment. African countries have been unable to build successful economies since independence, and some national economies were stronger at the time of independence than they are now. The economies of most African states are a shambles; they cannot fully employ the large numbers of graduates regularly churned out by universities. Some universities in Africa are using curricula that fail to meet the needs of employers. Some efforts have been made to correct this; universities in Nigeria have introduced entrepreneurship development in their general studies courses to help students find roles in the economy after graduation. However, most graduates are not employable.

Higher education in Africa is still battling the challenges of incorporating information and communications technology (ICT) into the curriculum. Some institutions only cover the theories involved; adequate ICT infrastructure does not exist to provide practical experience for the growing number of students in universities. Globally, ICT has become an essential tool in the production and improvement of knowledge in many fields of study. African universities must employ ICT to equip their graduates for participation in a global economy, allowing them to compete with the rest of the world.

The globalization of knowledge is also a challenge to the decolonization agenda in Africa. Globalization is characterized by the destruction of state independence and the rise of powerful nonstate actors that are determined to profit from the system at the expense of the weak. Its increasing influence is linked with the further commodification of the knowledge system. The globalization of knowledge has strengthened relationships between neocolonial forces, capitalism, and multinational corporations

---

40 For details, see Mohamedbhai, "Massification."

that place profits above the needs of society. The dynamics of globalization in higher education are rapidly changing relations in African universities and their relevance to African society, eroding indigenous knowledge systems and mechanisms for producing knowledge.

Rhodes Must Fall: The Academy in a Decolonial Age

Decolonization is not a new phenomenon in Africa's struggle to liberate itself from the shackles of colonialism and neocolonial ventures. The call to decolonize Africa's academy is often reinvigorated by changing dynamics between African institutions of higher education and political developments that occur within the state. Opposition to colonial structures was strengthened in 2015 by student protests in South Africa, culminating in the Rhodes Must Fall movement. Students demanded that the statue of Cecil Rhodes[41] be removed from the University of Cape Town as part of efforts to purge the campus of physically and psychologically oppressive colonial structures.[42] To Achille Mbembe, "There is something profoundly wrong when, for instance, syllabuses designed to meet the needs of colonialism and Apartheid should continue well into the liberation era. There is something not only wrong, but profoundly demeaning, when we are asked to bow in deference before the statues of those who did not consider us as human and who deployed every single mean in their power to remind us of our supposed worthlessness."[43] To Mbembe, "The movement has revealed numerous lines of fracture within South African society and has brought back on the agenda the question of the de-racialization of this country's institutions and public culture."[44] The Rhodes Must Fall movement not only reinforced the call for decolonization but also challenged the foundations of the African academy,

---

41 Born in 1853, the one-time British imperialist Cecil John Rhodes was a principal figure in the late nineteenth century, when Africa fell victim to the scramble for European expansionist imperial activities. Rhodes made a fortune in the southern African states, where he established the British South African Company (BSC). His discriminatory policy against Blacks is cited as the foundation of apartheid South Africa.
42 Mamdani, "Between the Public," 1.
43 Mbembe, "Decolonizing," 29–45.
44 Mbembe, "Decolonizing."

especially between decolonization and the crisis of adaptation in South Africa[45] and in Africa as a whole. At the center of the crisis is Africa's ability to define what should be considered decolonization in today's changing world and how the African academy can adapt to these changes while remaining relevant in the global economy of knowledge production.

If the survival of the African Academy is significant for the development of scholarship in Africa, then what should be the strategy for survival? The African academy must work to dismantle the colonial architecture in its educational system, and it must include relevant lessons in developing a sustainable knowledge system.

The African academy can adapt by broadening its transformational efforts, moving beyond a mere Africanization of personnel to embrace fully Africanized curricula. The removal of the Rhodes statue is significant—part of the struggle to reject colonial architecture that symbolizes dominance and oppression—but it is not enough. Knowledge production is global, even though the globalization of knowledge in Africa is largely perceived as a Euro-American affair. The African academy must oppose this perception and recognize other participants involved in the international work of knowledge production, including Asia. This can improve Africa's bargaining power, making African knowledge relevant and redirecting global focus to include the type of knowledge produced in Africa. In a decolonial age, the academy must reconsider its concept of Africanization to include the focused use of available personnel, without discrimination, to advance Africa's knowledge system. Mamdani states that

> the political understanding of decolonization has moved from one limited to political independence, independence from external domination, to a broader transformation of institutions, especially those critical to the reproduction of racial and ethnic subjectivities legally enforced under colonialism. The economic understanding has also broadened from one of local ownership over local resources to the transformation of both internal and external institutions that sustain unequal colonial-type economic relations. The epistemological di-

---

45 South Africa has a complex history of colonial domination. As a colonial settler state, higher education is torn between generating curricula that work for the indigenous South Africans and what should work for the "settlers." This crisis is part of the conflict that continues to dominate academic debates in Africa.

mension of decolonization has focused on the categories with which we make, unmake and remake, and thereby apprehend, the world. It is intimately tied to our notions of what is human, what is particular and what is universal.[46]

When decolonization goes beyond merely claiming institutions and liberating them from foreign control, transforming them to serve their intended purpose, this may not necessarily mean Africanizing the staff; but it may involve changing the entire orientation of the productive framework for the common good of all (humanity).[47] Africa must be able to accommodate intellectuals from other parts of the world, but the focus of African curricula for higher education must first be tilted toward Africa's national and international goals. We have seen this in the Euro-American homogenization of the global system of knowledge production, adapted to serve their national and international agendas.

The African academy can adapt by promoting Africa-based research that solves African problems. African governments must participate in this process with clear-cut definitions of their national development programs, in all spheres, including education development planning. This cannot be achieved without the sincere participation of government and a commitment to funding socioeconomic research that will enhance the development of human and material resources. African research networks should be established with the goal of merging resources to produce better outcomes. These efforts can connect the functions of the academy with the progress of African people.

The African academy must adapt to changing dynamics in the political economy of knowledge production. Information and communications technology has simplified the production, distribution, and consumption of knowledge. African governments must commit to providing the resources that higher education needs to thrive—universities require adequate funding and technology to ensure the safety of knowledge production. African academies must improve regional synergies and relationships with other parts of the world to improve their content, standards,

---

46 Mamdani, "Between the Public."
47 This is what Paulo Freire refers to as "being human." To be humanistic is for the oppressed to liberate themselves and to liberate the oppressors as well. For details, see Freire, *Pedagogy*.

and acceptance. However, collaboration should be approached carefully to avoid reinforcing the dynamics of dependence. Currently, "African academic knowledge systems, like our economies, suffer from limited regional integration and high levels of external dependency."[48] Zeleza adds, "That is a challenge we must overcome if our higher education systems are to contribute to integrated, inclusive, and innovative sustainable development."[49] Addressing this challenge will encourage publications that are genuinely focused on national development instead of personal promotion within the academic ranks.

Activities such as debates, seminars, conferences, and workshops should be encouraged among African scholars as they have been in the past. Serious issues of national, regional, and international importance should be part of deliberations that provide focus for national development. Research findings should be taken seriously and used to promote African national development programs.

This brings us to the question of how students choose research topics. Universities and faculty must guide students to select topics that are relevant for national development issues. African research must be functional and focused on solving African problems. African science and technology studies must answer questions about national space programs, nuclear enrichment programs, and other techniques and products that are emerging in information sciences, communications, biotechnology, space science and aeronautics, and medicine. Science and technology are essential for a country's development in the modern era. Although African countries are deficient in these fields, African universities and research institutes can rise to the challenge.

Universities in Africa can become more flexible by shedding the excess baggage carried from the colonial era and by reequipping themselves with more efficient resources.[50] Universities of agriculture can address the continent's problems with food security instead of leaving it to multinational research institutes such as the International Institute of Tropical Agriculture and noncommercial Euro-American research agencies. African universities with expertise in geology and mining should meet the challenges of extracting and applying Africa's mineral resources instead of

---

48 Zeleza, "Decolonization."
49 Zeleza, "Decolonization."
50 Sawyerr, "Issues."

leaving the work to Chinese, American, and European interests. Africa's medical and pharmaceutical faculties, departments, and indigenous companies must work together to treat diseases such as malaria, leprosy, tuberculosis, and other ailments usually left to giant international companies and their corporate donors. National research institutes must be promoted and protected so that they can carry out relevant research for improving government development programs. National and regional research regulatory bodies should be established, enabling Africa to control what is released for international consumption. Several agencies across Africa are currently conducting research, but their results and relevance are not connected with the development of the continent—at best, they are only relevant to Euro-American interests there.

The Academy and Indigenous Knowledge Systems

It is clear that the African Academy has suffered from the erosion of African indigenous knowledge systems and the imposition of a Western curriculum for colonial education of the kind that has dominated developmental methods and models in the contemporary African academy. Indigenous knowledge systems find expression within both formal and informal education systems, developing within a specific geographical region or associated with a particular group of people. In Africa, indigenous knowledge is a form of learning in African precolonial societies where knowledge, skills, attitudes, and values are transferred to children through oral instruction and practical activities.

African indigenous knowledge systems place emphasis on practical learning through observation, participation, and application of the learned skills. Skills such as pottery, blacksmithing, carving, cloth making, building, canoe making, food production, food preservation, food processing, and home management were shared with children in local communities. Training was freely available to all citizens because it consisted of basic skills, knowledge, and attitudes that empowered individuals to function effectively, which is beneficial in the context of the environment. The skills and values were relevant to the socioeconomic activity of every individual.

Globally, indigenous knowledge systems originate from indigenous people. The development of disciplines such as medicine or veterinary medicine is discovered through a complex process of interaction between people and their environment. This process develops indigenous knowledge so it can adapt in a gradually changing environment over many generations. The inclusion of indigenous knowledge within curricula, instructional materials, and other learning resources has the same educational effects found in other systems, such as in Western education.

Western knowledge has a strong foundation in African higher education because Africa promotes Western culture in many spheres, more than any other territory colonized by the West. This could pose a challenge to the inclusion of indigenous knowledge systems in higher education—Africa must work to ensure that it does not mortgage the future of its own education to other cultures of the world. It is important to understand relevant alternatives while advancing the decolonization of Western education, identifying how the academy can integrate indigenous knowledge into its higher education while remaining relevant to Africa and the global economy of knowledge production.

The developers of African education curricula must capture aspects of African culture and civilization in the syllabi of higher education. African music and dance should find legitimate expression in the development of African arts and entertainment. This work can harness the potential of Africa's diverse ethnic groups, especially within the specific cultural environments where universities are located.

Knowledge is broad, and scholarship should not be limited to a sole source of knowledge production or a single epistemic model. However, African universities have promoted Western culture, languages, theories, perspectives, and literature to the extent that not much attention is given to other civilizations, such as Asia.[51] The African academy should examine Asian civilization side by side with African civilization, studying its methods of knowledge production to identify approaches that could also support the African academy.[52] Language is one of the major instruments in preserving and transmitting European knowledge; the development and use of African languages can support a similar process of preservation and transmission for ideas specific to Africa. As a criterion for admission, candidates seeking higher education in African universities should have some knowledge of an indigenous language.

---

51 Mazrui, "Towards Re-Africanizing," 3–4.
52 Mazrui, "Towards Re-Africanizing."

In the field of medicine, African institutions of higher education should establish departments or other academic units for herbal medicine, which has been demonstrated by Ahmadu Bello University, Zaria, in Nigeria. Universities should be encouraged to collect local species of plants and animals as part of a larger effort to develop a comprehensive botanical and zoological catalogue. The impact of climate change can be measured as it affects these species, and strategies could be devised to manage a healthy ecosystem.

Despite the value and potential of indigenous knowledge, educators need to examine the implications that its inclusion would have on the pedagogy of the African knowledge system along with its sustainability in current classroom situations. In an African context, learning can take place in multiple spaces. The multiethnic nature of African society can also make it difficult to incorporate indigenous knowledge into formal Western education models. However, the debate around the integration of indigenous education and knowledge with traditional modes of schooling continues the process of cultural negotiation and renegotiation. Africa's academy and educational development programs are already part of an ongoing negotiation to ensure that they address Africa's problems.

The Western educational system's limitations in addressing Africa's problems make it necessary to incorporate indigenous knowledge systems, although the process of integration must be gradual. Skills such as pottery should find expression in establishing and improving the educational curriculum in departments of fine arts and ceramic production. Local blacksmithing knowledge should be incorporated into departments of mechanical or mechatronics engineering. Other disciplines could benefit from knowledge of carving, cloth making (textile and industrial design), building canoes (marine and water resources engineering), food production, food preservation, and food processing (nutrition and dietetics). When education serves the needs of the people, it serves the needs of the nation.

Africa's knowledge system must be transformed to meet the socioeconomic needs of its people. Education in Africa should be as practical as possible, and its successful application is the key to Africa's development. Educational curricula will continue to change in order to meet the needs of businesses and industries. Africa must build a strong economy, which depends on its educational system's ability to provide an economy-sustaining workforce.

Conclusion

This chapter has examined decolonization and its relevance for the development of the African academy, discussing efforts to decolonize education across the continent. To date, these efforts have not lived up to the ambitious 1960s efforts to decolonize the academy. Areas that saw initial success were soon marred by adverse economic and political developments, which had local and international implications for decolonization efforts in the African academy—decolonization of the African academy is only possible when African leaders are genuinely interested in taking part in such a process. The chapter has also discussed the current economy of knowledge production, in which internationalized knowledge can be counterproductive for African decolonization efforts. Within the international system of globalizing knowledge, there is an opportunity for Africa to ensure that its system of knowledge production remains relevant.

This chapter noted that the decolonization of the African academy must incorporate other knowledge systems from around the world—Western knowledge systems have been followed by Africans for a long time. Asian systems, especially those from China and Korea, and Islamic systems should be examined alongside the African system of education, incorporating components that will support the African knowledge system. The development of the African academy must continue to rely on genuine research reflecting the socioeconomic realities of Africa. Linking the academy and the society at large will make the academy's role more prominent in the development of African society.

Chapter Thirteen

Decolonizing Knowledge through Language

Introduction

In 1884 and 1885, in Berlin at a roundtable that mostly hosted representatives of countries in Europe, Africa was sliced into portions and distributed between the then-European superpowers. The English, French, Portuguese, Belgians, and Dutch all had their share of the continent. This area of colonial discourse has received a lot of attention in and outside of academia. However, that is not the focus here. One of the effects of the forceful invasion and eventual colonization that took place in Africa after the Berlin Conference was the adoption, willingly or otherwise, of colonizer languages by the colonized. Although prior to the colonial influx some parts of Africa had been saturated by Christian missionaries, these areas were consequently introduced to Western forms of education. The menace and misfortune associated with the knowledge system—and educational sector as a whole—of postcolonial Africa finds its advent in the colonial era.

Whereas African nationalists achieved freedom from the claws of colonialism in the twentieth century, the continent has remained colonized psychologically. Franz Fanon has opined that through dependency on foreign languages, Africans are subjected to the ways of the colonizers through their consciousness. It therefore appears that Africa has only been able to win the physical battle against its colonizers, while still being bound mentally to colonial systems. The introduction of English, French, Portuguese, and other foreign languages into the African knowledge space has stripped Africans of their true identity and heritage, according to many scholars.

The experience of Ngugi wa Thiong'o[1], as documented in his seminal work *Decolonising the Mind*, is perhaps an appropriate example here. Ngugi notes that he and other children within his Gikuyu circle in Kenya had been exposed to a form of education where they were taught in the Gikuyu language in the earliest stage of learning. The stories they were told by adults were told in Gikuyu, the local language, which conveyed the experiences and sensibilities of the Gikuyu people. He goes on to establish that the first time he went to a school in the Western sense of the word, he was still taught in his local language of Gikuyu. Note that at this time, Europeans had started trading in Africa, and his immediate community was not left out. However, in 1952, the language of teaching changed for him and others to English, as this marked a time when district education boards began to be chaired by Englishmen.[2] This justifies the notion earlier established about the enforcement of the English language in formal education being occasioned by the activities of colonial masters. Ngugi wa Thiong'o's experience, like many other African children of the precolonial era, is one of mental burden and discomfort, which of course is the consequence of the introduction of the English language.

It will appear that many of these African children struggled with using the English language as a medium of instruction in school. Sadly, this is still the case with many African learners to date, so much so that the average contemporary African parents would rather their children be educated in a school where a colonial language is used over another school where an indigenous language is the dominant language of instruction. At this point, it no longer matters if such children would do better if taught in their mother tongue, despite many research works that support this point. This chapter therefore attempts to bring to light the many-sided issues that relate to language in Africa, particularly pointing to the obvious fact, as Fanon submitted, that Africa will continue to be a stooge of her colonial masters if the languages used for official transactions are not decolonized. That is, it is imperative for African policymakers to decolonize the knowledge space of the continent by adopting an endogenous language for the business side of things rather than its continual general usage.

---

1   Ngugi, *Decolonizing*.
2   Ngugi, *Decolonizing*, 11.

Meanwhile, commendable efforts have been made to establish the place of indigenous languages in Africa, both in academia and corridors of power. Some of these efforts are considered here, and instances are pooled from randomly selected countries in Africa covering the West, East, South, and North of Africa. The argument below shows the peculiarity in the different countries selected from the different regions in Africa. These peculiarities are informed by historical antecedents, religion, political activities, and happenings in the international arena.

Makerere and the Language Problem in Africa

We begin by tracing this discourse to the epochal conference of 1962 that was hosted at Makerere University in Kampala, Uganda. Among other reasons, this conference opened up a formal conversation around the question of language in Africa, albeit with a focus on the language of African literature. The Makerere conference, whose theme was "African Writers of English Expression," was a gathering of African intellectuals with a focus on African writers who wrote in English, just as the name suggests. Meanwhile, as Ngugi[3] asserts, the conference had, by its theme and makeup, left out some prominent African writers just because they wrote in their local languages. An example was D. O. Fagunwa of Nigeria, who wrote in his native language of Yoruba. By implication, the conference and its organizers were hinting that English is a superior language—an unfortunate blow for African indigenous languages—and that anyone of repute in Anglophone Africa must be able to communicate in English despite this language being a colonial relic to many African people.

Consequently, at the conference, Obi Wali questioned the rationale behind the use of the English language to capture African experiences and sensibilities. For Wali, it was an aberration. Ngugi wa Thiong'o, who was then a student at Makerere University, had been invited to the conference for publishing a particular scholarly work in English; he would later expand on Wali's idea in *Decolonising the Mind*. Wali, Ngugi wa Thiong'o, and others had been influenced by the relativist theory of language as properly espoused in the Sapir-Whorf hypothesis. This theory is based on the fact that there is a correlation between a man's culture

---

3   Ngugi, *Decolonizing*, 11.

and his language. In other words, a man's language affects his worldview. Therefore, for the relativist, language cannot be taken at its face value and that knowledge is people specific. This belief leads Whorf to posit: "From this fact proceeds what I have called the 'linguistic relativity principle,' which means, in informal terms, that users of markedly different grammars are pointed by their grammars towards different types of observations and different evaluations of externally similar acts of observation, and hence are not equivalent as observers but must arrive at somewhat different views of the world."[4]

To understand the meaning of any word in any language, one must have an understanding of that language and its cultural context. By inference, therefore, to choose to learn a language or express thoughts in a language is reflective of the fact that such a person is willing to learn the culture or has some understanding of the culture of the language.

It will appear that the relativist's viewpoint—in this case, Wali, Ngugi, and other believers—is that to write in the language of the colonizer is to glorify the already troubling effects of colonialism on the colonized. For them, to write in the language of the colonizer is to continue to relegate African languages to a subordinate role. Again, to quote Ngugi, "Language carries culture, and culture carries, particularly through orature and literature, the entire body of values by which we come to perceive ourselves and our place in the world."[5] Therefore, continuing to embrace the colonizer's language is also to continue to embrace colonial culture while African cultures and heritage suffer neglect due to the abandonment of African indigenous languages. Catherine Miller also argues along these lines when she succinctly states that "language is not only a means of communication, but more importantly it is the essence of the culture of the people, the symbol of their cultural survival and community."[6]

The intricacy of the question of language in African literature is further complicated by Achebe's view. He disagrees with Ngugi on the choice of language for an African writer. Achebe and other notable literary giants like Ezekiel Mphahlele and Gerald Moore hold the opinion that colonial languages have been given to Africans and the least Africans can do with them is transfer the burden of their native languages to the colonizer's

---

4   Whorf, "Linguistics," 282.
5   Ngugi, *Decolonizing the Mind*, 16.
6   Miller, "Linguistic," 3.

languages. Achebe asserts that it is the responsibility of African writers to rework the language colonial masters have given them to suit their own indigenous purpose. Achebe focuses on the merits of colonization, which, according to him, is uniting small communities within Africa and making them a larger political unit and also gifting them a common language for communication—a language that is capable of connecting them (the African man/woman) to a wider audience. Perhaps Achebe is right. For just as he posits, it would have been impossible for the world to read or learn about the Igbo ways, philosophy, and culture at large if he himself had chosen to write in his mother tongue.

The Nigerian writer-activist Ken Saro-Wiwa also supported Achebe's view from the standpoint of one from a society where the local language is a minority language in Nigeria.[7] As explained by Saro-Wiwa, it would have been impossible for him as a student to communicate with students from other regions of the country without the English language. Furthermore, he, like Achebe, chose to write in the English language but encourages others who so desire to write in their indigenous languages.

Consequently, there are people who argue for the use of foreign languages in Africa, using the multilingual nature of the continent as the reasoning behind this. This set of people asserts, and rightly so, that Africa is a diverse continent, home to a sizeable number of languages. For this school of thought, the colonizer's languages serve as the string that binds a heterogeneous African continent together. Hence, most countries in Africa, especially sub-Saharan Africa, when faced with such a diverse pool of languages, simply surrender to the use of foreign languages.[8] This is argued in more detail below.

However, one of the counterarguments of Ngugi is that the language of the colonizer slowly erodes Africans' true selves:[9] "The bullet was the means of the physical subjugation. Language was the means of the spiritual subjugation."[10] In other words, adhering to the colonizers' language as the medium of knowledge dissemination denies Africans their true identity. There is a gradual shift—alienation—from their own culture toward the colonizer's culture—acculturation. Such Africans, though

---

7   Saro-Wiwa, "Language," 153–57.
8   Dellal, "On the Decolonization," 5–17.
9   Ngugi, *Decolonizing*, 9.
10 Ngugi, *Decolonizing*, 9.

free from the physical bonds that came with colonization, are still bound to the colonial masters by means of language at the expense of their culture and identity. The Africans would then find out that they neither fit into the culture of their colonizer, which they pine for by learning the colonizer's language, nor do they have their own culture or identity anymore. It therefore becomes important for African indigenous languages to be deployed as tools against this kind of mental and psychological imperialism.

Moreover, for Ngugi, linguistic heterogeneity in Africa is not a disadvantage. He believes that indigenous African languages are a legitimate, unique component of a common worldview heritage. Hence the assertion, "A world of many languages should be like a field of flowers of different [colors]. There is no flower which becomes more of a flower on the account of its [color] or its shape. All such flowers express their common "floralness" in their diverse (colors) and shapes . . . [Therefore], all our languages should join in the demand for a new international, economic, and, cultural order."[11]

The above quote shows how African multilingualism is being misunderstood. Countries like Mongolia, Japan, Finland, Norway, Sweden, Denmark, and Italy are linguistically diverse,[12] and they have been able to resolve their language issues for the most part. Some of these countries have an indigenous language as the official language, while almost all adopt the use of a mother tongue at the start of formal education for children.[13]

Multilingualism and the Question of Universal Acceptance of African Languages

There is no doubting the fact that the biggest arguments against appropriating African indigenous languages for knowledge dissemination, especially at the national level, are multilingualism and the question of the relevance of these languages at the global level. It is not enough for Africans to attempt to topple colonial languages in their territory with indigenous languages. It is also important to understand the political and

---

11 Ngugi, *Decolonizing*, 9.
12 Brock-Utne, "Language."
13 Brock-Utne, "Language."

economic dynamics that surround the use of the colonizer's language. This is by no means suggesting that prominent use of foreign languages is the best route for Africa.

Let us not forget that Africa is one of the most diverse continents on the planet with regard to language and culture. There are over two thousand languages spoken; however, the really complicated aspect is the fact that some African countries are home to hundreds of speakers of said languages. In Nigeria alone, there are four hundred to five hundred native languages in active use. In Ghana, another West African country, about eighty native languages are in use. In the southern part of Africa, South Africa to be specific, there are at least thirty-five languages spoken by natives, while Kenya, in East Africa, boasts about sixty-eight native languages. As the list goes on, it is important to note as well that there are some other countries in Africa, as in Somalia, where the Somali-speaking natives are united by only one language. This section proceeds to draw attention to the obvious challenge of multilingualism, which is the reality in most countries in Africa, especially in sub-Saharan Africa. Like Dellal rightly points out, "The problem of dependency on the colonial language resides also in the complexity of the sociolinguistic spectrum made up of a multitude of languages spoken by the same people of the same country."[14]

It therefore becomes a herculean task for most African nations to settle for one or more indigenous languages as the official language(s). To do this, especially in countries where there are many languages spoken, would mean the marginalization of minority languages. This then brings up the question of democratization, as preferring a language over another not only profiles languages based on importance but also puts the seemingly less important language(s) at risk of disuse and eventual endangerment. Again, the conglomeration of communities into nations without proper consideration for the compatibility of these communities based on their differences by the colonial masters leaves most postcolonial African countries to face such a quagmire as this. More so, according to Dellal, colonial languages have already ensured the erosion or extinction of local African languages.[15] He further states that "in some parts of Africa where there have been no locally written languages—literally

---

14 Dellal, "On the Decolonization," 9.
15 Dellal, "On the Decolonization," 6.

the majority of sub-Saharan countries, to my knowledge—the endeavour towards empowering autochthonous population, has been tantamount to systematic replacement of these languages by the colonising ones."[16]

The next assumption, beyond the dilemma of Africa's policymakers in settling for the use of indigenous languages as the medium of knowledge dissemination, is the relevance of such language(s) among the comity of nations. Without emotional attachments, colonial languages, though imposed on Africans as the medium of communication, have become tools with which Africans can have a dialogue with the rest of the world. The colonial languages have become the languages of trade, commerce, and technology, which therefore suggests that the failure to be fluent in French or English is national and individual self-sabotage. Just like the world under the leadership of the Greek and Roman empires either spoke or aspired to speak Greek or Latin respectively, so do most people and nations aspire to speak the English and French languages in the present age because these are the languages of power. Obviously, the United States, which is the country with the biggest economy in the world at the moment, has English as its official language. Hence, any form of political, economic, and technological relations with the country will likely be transacted in English, as in the United Kingdom, another economic powerhouse.

Therefore, it could be argued that most African countries are not just holding on to the English language, for example, as a relic of the colonial era but wielding it as a tool for political, economic, and technological gains. Who would blame them? Clearly, to be globally relevant is to speak the languages that control the world's economy and commerce.

Place of the Mother Tongue in Decolonizing Knowledge in Africa

As sound, and sometimes tenable, as some of the arguments around the choice of foreign languages as the medium of knowledge and official uses are, it is imperative to consider the other side of the coin. It would be short-sighted to write off the multilingual nature of Africa as a source of chaos. Rather, the diversity in African culture and language

---

16 Dellal, "On the Decolonization," 6.

should be seen as an advantage. As already seen above, Ngugi attests to this. Consequently, notable research works have been done on the possible benefits, if there are any, of adopting indigenous African languages to teach in class, particularly elementary classes and especially learners for whom these languages happen to be their mother tongue. The argument is that because learners are raised with their mother tongue, which in most cases for an African child is an indigenous language spoken by the people of his or her community, it becomes easier for them to learn in class when taught with the same language. This position is in tandem with UNESCO's submission in 1953, which states:

> It is axiomatic that the best medium for teaching a child is his mother tongue. Psychologically, it is the system of meaningful signs that in his mind works automatically for expression and understanding. Sociologically, it is a means of identification among the members of the community to which he belongs. Educationally, he learns more quickly through it than through an unfamiliar linguistic medium.[17]

This, then, brings up the vital place of mother tongues and indigenous languages in the dissemination of knowledge in Africa. In his discussion paper of 2002, "Language, Democracy and Education in Africa," Brock-Utne explains how in his observation of classes taught in Kiswahili in Tanzania, he noticed an active participation of learners and their engagement with what they were being taught. He further establishes that not only were the students eager to learn, but teachers were also bustling with life and enthusiasm. This was a research experiment he undertook between the years 1987 and 1992.[18] According to Brock-Utne, teaching a specially designed subject at the primary level in Kiswahili had been an initiative under the then president of Tanzania, and it was meant to be a commendable attempt to revolutionize the Tanzanian educational system. Brock-Utne notes that he had also observed the same set of students that were taught a subject in Kiswahili being taught another subject in a foreign language: English. The difference in both the teachers' attitudes to teaching and students' attitudes to learning were too notable to be ignored. In his words, "The teachers were struggling with English, their vivacity and enthusiasm were gone. When I talked to the teachers about

---

17   UNESCO, "Use of Vernacular."
18   Brock-Utne, "Language."

the changes that I had observed, they admitted that the use of English as the medium of instruction was a great barrier to them."[19]

Brock-Utne's observation relates to other empirical findings in Tanzania, one of which is recorded by Kithaka wa Mberia.[20] Mberia unravels the connectedness of productive learning with the use of the mother tongue as the medium of instruction in education. The 2007 research, as recorded by Mberia, compared the attitude of students in Tanzania who were taught in Kiswahili with those being taught in English or by code switching. The experiment showed that students who were taught in their mother tongue performed better than those who were not. Amazingly, this experiment, which was done with secondary school students, had the same teacher instruct both in the mother tongue and a foreign language. The only difference, apparently, was the medium of communication.

Furthermore, there was an experiment in Niger where there was a similar reaction from both students and teachers.[21] The experiment began in 1973, and its aim was to accommodate five different indigenous mother tongue languages in Niger for the first three years of learning and for the learners to transition to learning in French in the fourth year while they still learned the mother tongue in subsequent years.[22] As was the case in Tanzania above, the bilingual class, which was the class for experimentation, was more interactive and engaging than the other classes where learners were taught in a foreign language. The Niger experiment also showed, according to Mberia, that teaching students in their mother tongue does not make them perform worse than those who were taught in French.[23] Contrary to the popular notion that those taught in local or indigenous languages will perform poorly compared to their counterparts taught in a foreign language, the Niger language project proves that African languages are not inferior to foreign languages, especially when used as the medium of instruction in education.

At different times, countries like Kenya, Nigeria, Ethiopia, Uganda, and Zambia have also experimented with the use of local languages as

---

19 Brock-Utne, "Language."
20 Mberia, "Place," 53.
21 Alidou et al., "Optimizing."
22 Alidou et al., "Optimizing."
23 Mberia, "Place."

the language of learning, especially at the primary level of schooling. The same is true of South Africa, where "during the eight-year period that the mother tongue was phased in and maintained as the primary language of learning, the matriculation results of Black students steadily improved, reaching their zenith in 1976."[24] One thing remains consistent in all the experimental studies: learners do not become less intelligent when taught in an indigenous language. What is more astounding is that in some of the experiments, learners who were taught in an indigenous language outdid those who were taught in a foreign language. In other words, indigenous languages have the capacity to convey knowledge at the formal level of education in Africa. Bekisizwe S. Ndimande, echoing Hamza,[25] posits that "conducting research in indigenous languages can be framed as a "decolonizing" method."[26]

Consequently, it is imperative for African policymakers and intellectuals to take a cursory look at the recurring proposal from different quarters to engage indigenous languages in teaching because there are strong arguments for the interconnectedness between better educational performance and the language of education on one hand, and the holistic development of Africa and African languages on the other. The first part, which is the performance of learners, is clear from some of the cited experiments above. The second part, which has to do with the development of Africa, will now be discussed and juxtaposed with some attendant problems militating against upward social mobility of African indigenous languages.

At present, most postcolonial African countries still have foreign languages as their official language of instruction both in education and in other vital sectors. In Nigeria, for instance, less than 10 percent of the population are proficient in their use of the English language.[27] Emmanuel Sibomana supplies further information on the wide gulf that exists between the minority who speak the foreign languages being used as the official language in some other African countries vis-a-vis the actual population in these countries:

> In Namibia, only 1% of the population spoke English in 2000 while this language was an official language and a medium of instruction

---

24 Brock-Utne, "Language," 16.
25 Hamza, "Decolonizing," 123–34.
26 Ndimande, "Unraveling," 386.
27 Ifechelobi and Ifechelobi, "Beyond Barriers," 208–16.

in many schools in this country (Brock-Utne, 2000a). Surprisingly, "there are [then] daily newspapers and an abundance of magazines, but hardly any newspaper or magazines are published in Namibian languages" (Brock-Utne, 2000a, p. 208) [. . .] In 2000, less than 5% of the population had some knowledge of English in Tanzania (Brock-Utne, 2000a). In addition to the limited number of people who are able to use English in African countries, the quality of English that many Africans have access to is not good as is the case in South Africa (Foley, 2002), Tanzania (Brock-Utne, 2000a) and Rwanda.[28]

By implication, many Africans are denied the privilege of vital information. How can they stay informed in a language they can neither speak nor understand? Hence, they are either not involved in decision making or ill-informed about the events around them. Consequently, the country suffers. In other words, "If the great majority of the population does not have access to the tools of self and national development, there are few possibilities for these people to contribute to their countries' development."[29] It therefore becomes a necessity that the people acquire formal education through the language they are already familiar with; a language that carries the depth of their being—their mother tongue. It is with such language that the majority of Africans can access health, political, and even economic information, thereby leading to an unprecedented development in the continent. Africa can then finally claim to be free from the shackles of colonization of the mind.

Unfortunately, most people in the elite political class in Africa, desperate to retain power in the hands of a few, are vehemently opposed to the adoption of mother tongues for teaching and indigenous language for official purposes. Dellal adds, on a similar note, that the elites who seemingly fought to eject colonialists and fronted the agenda for a national culture and language are guilty of patronizing schools where indigenous languages are not used.[30] Taoufik Jaafari writes specifically of the brainwashed elites in Morocco who, having been assimilated into the upper class of society and allowed into French-established schools, rejected any idea of adopting Moroccan indigenous language, despite its popularity in educational use.[31] This is because succumbing to the language of the

---

28 Sibomana, "Postcolonial," 47.
29 Sibomana, "Postcolonial," 44.
30 Dellal, "On the Decolonization," 10.
31 Jaafari, "Language."

masses will blur the line that separates the poor and the elite. Advancing this argument, Prah maintains that the knowledge required to develop Africa lies in educating the masses in science and technology and doing this in their own language.[32]

Beyond the self-sabotage of the political and elite class against the masses, there is the inexcusable intrusion of foreign bodies and organizations in the educational and language affairs of Africa. Perhaps it is safe to say that international bodies are also content with maintaining cultural stasis in Africa because the policies of these bodies promote foreign languages over indigenous ones. These bodies, which are also usually establishments from former colonial countries, operate under the guise of "development aide to Africa" to strengthen the use of their languages in postcolonial Africa. This is evident in a British Council annual report that "admitted that although the British government no longer had the economic and military power to impose its will in other parts of the world, British influence endured through 'the insatiable demand for the English language.'"[33] This means that although Africa lives under the illusion of being democratic, her leaders and, by extension, the people, are still at the beck and call of colonial masters.

Brock-Utne discusses the donor influence in Africa further by focusing on instances of donations that came with conditions related to mandatory use of foreign languages. Citing the case of the Central African Republic, the country was to be granted a loan by the WB on the condition that textbooks would be imported from France and Canada. The irony therein is in the fact that this project was aimed at improving elementary education in the country. Similarly, in the case of Uganda, the language-in-education policy had stated that learners be taught in their mother tongue at the early stage of schooling. Ironically, the American consulting firm that was a part of the project insisted on the use of English as the language of learning materials.[34] The firm's approach and the teaching materials it supplied was directly opposite of the government of Uganda's policy on elementary education.

A similar situation can be found in Tanzania, where British support of the country and her educational sector had been to promote the use of the

---

32 Brock-Utne, "Language," 7.
33 Brock-Utne, "Language," 15.
34 Brock-Utne, "Language," 34.

English language. Under a program called the English Language Teaching Support Project (ELTSP), the British council has continually imposed its will on the people of Tanzania by ensuring that teachers are trained with materials written in the English language.[35] Interestingly, teaching students with English-language books yielded no positive results. Hence, Tanzanian writers were saddled with the responsibility of writing learning materials. Not only did the Tanzanian economy not benefit from this latter project—as local publishers were excluded from the process of production—it was as much a failure as any other project that prioritized the teaching of African students in a colonial language. There was no doubt that the primary problem of this project was the language of communication. There was also the case of the Seychelles, in which a French agency had promised to support the Institute for Democracy based on the condition that French will be used as medium of communication. The head of the institute, according to Brock-Utne, rejected such a preposterous offer from the French agency.[36]

While in a few instances parents show support for the use of the mother tongue as language of education in Africa, in most other cases, they do not want to associate their wards with schools where the vernacular is the language of education. With a mindset that Emmanuel Sibomana describes as accepting the "ideological and discursive constructs" built around colonial languages, parents, teachers, and even students have placed these languages on a superior plane that leads to the view that their indigenous languages as less significant.[37] This perceived superiority of colonial languages means that people who can speak these languages have better opportunities in life. The shameful situation is aptly summarized in the words of a Namibian learner: "If you know English well, you are considered educated. If you just know Namibian languages, even though you may know several of them and speak them well, you are considered dumb and uneducated."[38] There is another similar comment attributed to Taoufik Jaafari in Morocco, who stated: "Why should I learn a language which would only help me one day if ever I traveled to see one of my remaining relatives in my parents' village in the Souss region? I

---

35 Brock-Utne, "Language," 35.
36 Brock-Utne, "Language," 18.
37 Sibomana, "Postcolonial," 39.
38 Sibomana, "Postcolonial," 39.

would rather learn a foreign useful language instead."[39] For these learners and many others, the goal is therefore to be proficient in the English language, disregarding indigenous languages; it no longer matters that learning is more expedient in these indigenous languages. It also doesn't seem to matter that these African languages are being endangered.

Adenowo advances this argument when he echoes the voices of other scholars who have traced preference for colonial languages to the postcolonial elite class who merely want to retain their privileges. Hence, to achieve any form of prominence in postcolonial Africa, one only needs to be well versed in colonial languages, with little or no emphasis on competence and skill sets. It is not surprising that neither students nor their parents will give any consideration to indigenous languages, as most students see little value in learning African languages. Similar views were expressed by high school students learning Kiswahili in Kenya, as found in 2005 research by Mohochi. Most participants in this study, for instance, held that they see "very little to be gained in future, especially in the job market, by studying Kiswahili."[40]

Highlighted above are some of the challenges that stand in the way of mother tongue being the language of education in many African countries. Struggling to continue the use of indigenous languages at even the basest level of education, most African countries have not been able to consider the use of such languages at higher levels of learning. Knowledge production in these languages—academic papers, science and technology, literature—has therefore been alarmingly low.

The Pidgin Option

Since the political and intellectual elites in postcolonial Africa have chosen to follow the path of the colonial masters by imposing the use of foreign languages on a people who largely do not speak these languages, Ngugi posits that the common person in Africa, rather than succumb to the pressure of submitting to these languages or transferring their history and culture to a foreign language, has attempted to demystify these foreign

---

39   Interview, 2018.
40   Ademowo, "Indigenous," 41.

languages.[41] Peasants in Africa have Africanized foreign languages with no regard for their ancestral homes. Frankly, unlike popular African intellectuals-cum-writers like Achebe and Senghor, the common people do not feel compelled to stay true to the colonial master's language. Consequently, they have developed a totally different language for themselves, borrowing from a pool of options that have been placed before them.

According to Ifechelobi and Ifechelobi, the interaction of two groups of people who do not speak the same language will eventually produce a whole new language.[42] They note that the new language is a combination of the two different languages of these two sets of people. This comes about through sheer necessity and the need for a medium of communication. They further assert that this new language can either be a temporary medium or something more permanent.[43] On the characteristic of pidgin languages, "A Pidgin language takes its lexifiers/vocabulary from the superstrate language and the grammar and phonology from the substrate languages."[44]

A case in point is the Nigerian Pidgin, which is a product of the interaction between the English language and Nigerian languages, where English is the superstrate language, and Nigerian languages are the substrate. Nigerian Pidgin has expanded and now seems widely accepted.

One major factor responsible for the continued relevance of Pidgin English is urbanization. By the time colonial masters handed over power to Africans, some city centers had been well developed, while some other places were still very rural. Urbanization led to the birth of developed cities in African countries.[45] The developed city centers promised a better lifestyle for those who came from the countryside. This pattern can still be found in Africa many years after colonialism; some areas have enjoyed more attention and therefore more development than others. For instance, Lagos, Nigeria; Accra, Ghana; Free Town, Sierra Leone; Monrovia, Liberia; and Georgetown, Gambia, are all West African cities that continue to witness an influx of people—young men and women mostly—who are in search of better opportunities. More often than not,

---

41 Ngugi, *Decolonizing*, 23.
42 Ifechelobi and Ifechelobi, "Beyond Barriers," 208.
43 Ifechelobi and Ifechelobi, "Beyond Barriers."
44 Ifechelobi and Ifechelobi, "Beyond Barriers."
45 Mowarin and Tonukari, "Pidgin," 145–53.

this set of people comes from the rural areas of the country and are usually from different and diverse ethnic orientations. Meeting up in city centers, these people are left with no choice but to communicate with pidgin or creole—languages that unify all the ethnic groups. Therefore, West African Pidgin English keeps growing in scope as more people embrace it as the lingua franca.

While there is Nigerian Pidgin, Ghanaian Pidgin, and Cameroonian Pidgin (also called Kamtok),[46] there is also Krio, spoken in Sierra Leone, and many other language forms that are derivatives of the interaction between indigenous African languages and European languages. Interestingly, the different pidgins and creoles have become widely used and accepted languages in most African communities, as discussed above. Hence, the average African might be exposed to his or her mother tongue as a first language and pidgin or creole as a second language. In fact, in some instances like the Niger Delta people of Nigeria, Pidgin English is fast becoming the first language and being converted to a creole language. It is based on this fact that Ifechelobi and Ifechelobi argue that Nigerian Pidgin has become the lingua franca of the country.

For them, a language is not the lingua franca because policymakers designate it as such but because it is widely used by the people. They assert, like others, that the English language is used by a minority in Nigeria, whereas the Nigerian Pidgin is used by many more people. They further argue that the Nigerian Pidgin should be adopted as the national language for the country based on the following facts: first, its geographical spread, which implies that it is spoken by a lot of people from diverse ethnic backgrounds in the country; and second, the fact that the language originated, was sustained, and is being expanded in Nigeria.[47] Rather than continue to allow the three main languages in Nigeria—Hausa, Igbo, and Yoruba—to play second fiddle behind the English language, or falling into the trap of marginalizing minority languages, Ifechelobi and Ifechelobi are convinced that Nigerian Pidgin can be a true and unifying national language.

Ofulue's research on the state of pidgin in Africa has a wider coverage than that of Ifechelobi and Ifechelobi. Her research accommodates not just Nigerian Pidgin but also Cameroonian and Ghanaian Pidgins. She

---

46 Ofulue, "Nigerian Pidgin," 2.
47 Ifechelobi and Ifechelobi, "Beyond Barriers," 215.

notes that there are noticeable similarities between the Nigerian variety of pidgin and that which is spoken in Cameroon. Also, that the Ghanaian variety has depended heavily on Nigerian Pidgin over the years. There is no doubt that West African Pidgin English (WAPE), an umbrella name she uses for all the three varieties, came to being as a result of contact of the people living in the West Africa region with Europeans in the fifteenth century. However, there is also no doubt about the fact that WAPE bears the burden of African identity and experiences.

Though Africans were forced to develop a language that enhanced communication between them and Europeans, they have also settled for this same language to bridge the gap created by multiculturalism and multilingualism. In other words, pidgin, especially in West Africa, is still around because it is still being deployed for the purpose of communication. Ofulue's research shows the level of pidgin acceptability and use in each of the three West African countries in her study. Nigerian Pidgin, according to her, enjoys the most popularity of the three, both in the formal and informal sector. Although she also notes that the use of Nigerian Pidgin English is wider and stronger in the southern part of the country, it is also used by many people in the northern part. By comparison, Mowarin and Tonukari add that Nigerian Pidgin English has more speakers than Krio, albeit Krio is more developed.[48] Unlike the case of Ghana, where Ghanaian Pidgin is used mainly by educated young males on one hand, and those without Western education on the other, Nigerian and Cameroonian Pidgins are the lingua franca of choice for most people in these countries, with the numbers favoring the Nigerian Pidgin above Cameroonian Pidgin. Ofulue's research also shows that Nigerian Pidgin and Cameroonian Pidgin are generally believed to be appropriate as the national languages in their respective countries. Ghanaian Pidgin, however, has not received the same acceptability as Cameroonian Pidgin.

In Nigeria, Ghana, and Cameroon, however, there is the resentment toward embracing Pidgin English as the medium of instruction in education. The people of West Africa have stigmatized Pidgin English based on its association with common people in society. This is based on the general belief that Pidgin English is for those who cannot adequately express their thoughts in the English language. Hence, most elite and educated

---

48   Mowarin and Tonukari, "Pidgin," 145–53.

Africans do not want to associate with Pidgin English,[49] except perhaps at an informal level. Judging by the factors that necessitated the development and use of pidgin, however, we can say that the use of pidgin by postcolonial Africans has nothing to do with level of education. Pidgin English was born out of the need for communication between two people of different languages—Europeans and Africans—and should be regarded as such. If anything, as already stated, it should be a language to promote unity in a multilingual setting. Moreover, Ifechelobi and Ifechelobi make an attempt to differentiate between Nigerian Pidgin English and broken English. While the former was necessitated by the contact of Nigerians with Europeans, the latter is an attempt by half-educated Nigerians to use the English language, which ends up being futile as a result of poor mastery. Indeed, "Nigerian Pidgin has a unique linguistic structure and identity and like every other language, it is dynamic and has evolved over time. Broken English is a pejorative label used by native speakers of English to describe the often-hysterical violations of the basic rules of Standard English."[50]

While a case for Ghanaian Pidgin and even Cameroonian Pidgin might be weak, Nigerian Pidgin has proven to be adequately equipped to attain the status of a national language—and perhaps official language—in Nigeria and West Africa as a whole, as some will argue. Although Nigerian Pidgin does not yet meet all the criteria stipulated by Osaji on the characteristics a national language should exhibit, a sincere attempt to build a case for upgrading Nigerian Pidgin would agree that it is the best option available. These characteristics, as enumerated by Ugwu,[51] include:

1. Population of speakers, with age, occupation and class distribution;
2. Location: geographical, political and social boundaries;
3. Present status: any evidence of change in status e.g. decline, increase, age shift, geographical extension, etc.;
4. Literature: oral and written tradition; use in educational institutions and in political, religious, and other organizations; mass media using language, such as newspapers, radio, television etc.;

---

49   Ugwu, "Pidgin-Creole," 84.
50   Ifechelobi and Ifechelobi, "Beyond Barriers," 212.
51   Ugwu, "Pidgin-Creole," 83.

5. History of any specialized use of the language including education, history of social and religious pressure groups, and history of any relation with other languages of the area concerned;
6. Economic strength: method of finance—state, private or national; staff recruitment and training facilities; availability of teaching materials, foreign aid, and technical assistance requirements;
7. Administrative, commercial and mass media requirements in terms of cost for changing languages;
8. Adult education facilities and literacy campaigns.

Frankly, Nigerian Pidgin already addresses the problem of a unifying language for a multilingual country like Nigeria and would serve the same purpose if extended to other West African countries. As already shown above, it is the pidgin with the highest number of speakers in West Africa. This is coupled with the fact that it is easily acquired and already being spoken by a mixed demography. Furthermore, many literary works have been authored using Nigerian Pidgin, and there is hope of more to come. There is no doubt that the language has served as a vehicle for many economic activities within the country, while also attempting to bridge the communication gap with natives of the country and other countries for economic purposes.

Ofulue agrees that Pidgin English needs to be standardized based on some of the criteria above to achieve the desired upward social mobility.[52] She postulates that a written language is more highly valued than an unwritten one. Although Nigerian Pidgin has enjoyed a dimension of use in writing in the Nigerian literary space, as already stated, there is more to be done. Standardizing the language will ensure consistency in writing, spelling, and language use. Yet standardization will not be an easy task. Ofulue, citing Sebba, highlights the four major problems that would make the task of standardization much harder: "low status; their similarity with their lexifiers (which causes them to be perceived as inferior); their variable nature; and the adoption of a model/variety for their standardization."[53] Regardless, Nigerian Pidgin, with necessary concerted efforts, can be made to fit both national and official purposes in West African countries.

---

52 Ofulue, "Nigerian Pidgin," 30.
53 Ofulue, "Nigerian Pidgin," 31.

Language Policy in Africa: Nigeria, Tanzania, South Africa

The language policy of any nation assigns responsibilities to the language(s) available for use. This responsibility primarily lies with political leaders, and language policies are made through considerations of language use for the purpose of economic well-being, education, and the ability to unify the people. While in multilingual nations like South Africa, Nigeria, and Kenya, some languages receive more recognition than others, it is the responsibility of policymakers to ensure equal privileges for languages in a nation. Language policies are therefore reviewed from time to time to accommodate the communication needs of a people and to foster unity and development. As already argued above, language plays an important role in the development of any people.

Nigeria, with its diverse population and linguistic heritage, has chosen to stick to the English language as its official language as stipulated in that country's language policy.[54] What this implies is that the English language is the language used in governance, media, business, and other strategic interactions within the federation. The policy also confers the privilege of a national language on the three main languages in the country—Hausa, Igbo, and Yoruba. While indigenous languages that are languages of the immediate community are meant to be used as the medium of instruction for the first three years of schooling for a Nigerian child, the less importance placed on minority languages and absence of laws that enforce the use of indigenous languages in the first three years of learning puts these minority languages in danger of extinction.

South Africa's language policy is a unique case in Africa. There is no discussing the country's language policy without taking into consideration the apartheid experience. The majority Blacks in South Africa were not only oppressed physically and socially, but their languages were also subjected to oppression. In early 1925, the Dutch ruling class had imposed the use of Afrikaans as an official language in South Africa. Meanwhile, it is important to state that Afrikaans is not an indigenous language but a by-product of an interaction between the Dutch language and indigenous languages. Consequently, the British took over from the Dutch, and English became the leading South African language.

---

54   Ofulue, "Nigerian Pidgin," 12.

In 1953, the Bantu Education Act was passed. The purpose of the act, at the superficial level, appeared to promote the use of indigenous languages as education was administered at the regional level, and the mother tongue was stipulated to be the language of education. This was superficial, however, because the aim of those who conceived the act—white supremacists—was not to elevate indigenous languages but rather to extend the gulf of difference that existed between the Blacks and the whites in the country. Consequently, Black South Africans were further segregated from the few but powerful whites.

Rachel Hazeltine notes that the abolition of apartheid in South Africa ushered in a new era for the nation as the dividing lines between races in the country began to fade. According to her, the status quo changed after apartheid but not completely.[55] The government allowed primary school students to be taught in their mother tongue for the first ten years of schooling and to switch to either Afrikaans or English after the ten years. However, despite the good intentions of the new inclusive government, a language conundrum had already come about. Hazeltine submits that as early as the fourth year in school, learners usually opt for the English language or Afrikaans rather than continue with their indigenous language as the medium of education.[56] The other challenge to the use of mother tongue, evident also in almost every other country in Africa, is the shortage of educational materials in indigenous languages, especially in core subject areas like the sciences and mathematics.[57]

Still, in furtherance of elevating the status of indigenous languages, the 1996 South African constitution recognized and included eleven indigenous languages as the official languages of the country. These are Zulu, Xhosa, Afrikaans, Sepedi, English, Setswana, Sesotho, Xitsonga, Swati, Tshivenda, and Ndebele, in the order of how widely spoken they are.[58] Although this is a move that has been commended as endearing and inclusive, some argue that the number of official languages should be reduced to just four. As it stands, however, the eleven languages do not cover all the linguistic needs of the country, as some other languages like Xri are already endangered.

---

55 Hazeltine, "Language," 27.
56 Hazeltine, "Language."
57 Hazeltine, "Language," 28.
58 Hazeltine, "Language," 26.

Aside from the languages endangered by their exclusion from the constitution, every indigenous language in South Africa holds an inferior position relative to Afrikaans and English. The prestige that has been placed on both languages and resources deployed to English and Afrikaans-centered schools during the apartheid era are still relevant in postapartheid South Africa. According to Brock-Utne, "Despite the progressive language policy, languages other than Afrikaans and English seem almost completely absent from practical planning. The spaces opened for them in the constitution and in such important documents as the Langtag Report remain largely vacant."[59] Parents have no trust in non-English/Afrikaans schools since these languages have come to be associated with opportunities for better living.

It will appear, by consensus from most scholars, that Tanzania seems to be the only African country that has fared better in the area of language policy and planning. Yet the prominence of Swahili in Tanzania is not without its own challenges with the English language. However, to understand the modest success Tanzania has had with its language policy, it is important to view the country from a historical perspective. Prior to the arrival of the British in Tanzania, formerly known as Tanganyika, the people of this region had had contact with the Germans who had conceded Swahili as the official language of administration within their colony. This singular action gave prominence to Swahili, not just in Tanganyika, but in most parts of the eastern region of Africa. Swahili became the language of education, religion, politics, and much more. However, when the British came into the region, in order to have full control of the people and their way of life, they also imposed the English language on Tanzanians.

Meanwhile, Swahili not only gained prominence in Tanzania historically—it became part of the heritage of the East African people. While West Africa might hope to agree on the use of one of its varieties of pidgin as a unifying language, East Africa already has Swahili unifying all the countries in the region. What's more, Swahili is arguably the African language with the highest number of speakers. Trade exchanges and other international relationships are therefore made easy for the people of the eastern region of the continent. This has also made the choice of a national language easy for some countries in this region, as evident in Tanzania and Kenya, with Swahili as the national language of both countries.

---

59 Brock-Utne, "Language," 12.

In the early 1950s, Tanzanian nationalists, of whom Julius Nyerere was a prominent figure, agitated for the freedom of the people from the British. Among other strategies, the Tanganyika African National Union (TANU) deployed the use of Swahili to rally the natives against their colonial masters. This was a strategy that worked well for the nationalists. By 1961, Tanzania attained independence, and Julius Nyerere assumed the post of the first president of the independent country. Nyerere's administration continued using Swahili. Meanwhile, it became imperative to review the use of language in the country as the British had established English as a superior language during the colonial era. The subsequent actions and inactions of the government of Nyerere and other governments contributed to the modest successes with the language policy in Tanzania, some of which are worth noting.

As highlighted by Mari Yogi, Nyerere and the vice president made it clear in 1962 that the use of English will not be tolerated in governance. The guiding principle for the importance placed on Swahili in this era in Tanzanian history is spelled out in the government's blueprint on education:

> But even if this suggestion were based on provable fact, it could not be allowed to over-ride the need for change in the direction of educational integration with our national life. For the majority of our people the thing that matters is that they should be able to read and write fluently in Swahili, that they have an ability to do arithmetic, and that they should know something of the history, values, and working of their country and their government, and that they should acquire the skills necessary to earn their living. Things like health, science, geography and the beginning of English are also important, especially so that the people who wish may be able to learn more by themselves in later life. But most important of all is that our primary school graduates should be able to fit into, and to serve, the communities from which they come.[60]

In 1967, Kiswahili became the language of primary school education. That was the year Swahili was made the official language, and National Swahili Council was established.[61] The aim was that by 1973 Kiswahili

---

60 Kassim, "National Language," 79.
61 Yogi, "Kiswahili," 78.

would be incorporated as the language of instruction in the initial two years of secondary school education. Furthermore, the Presidential Commission of Education, set up by the Nyerere administration, proposed in January 1982 that all secondary schools in Tanzania should have adopted the use of Kiswahili for teaching by 1985, followed by tertiary institutions in 1992. As grand as the scheme was, it would be scrapped by the government of the day. Eleuthera Sa notes that it was unclear why the government refused to go further on the proposed policy but suggests it must have been partly due to fears of political unrest if there was a switch from English to Swahili. Another possible reason, according to Sa, is the economic implications of running Tanzania's secondary school education in Swahili.[62] The assumption of the Office of the President by Jakaya Kikwete revisited the country's issue of restoring the dignity of Swahili, but his new policy on education was properly carried out by the administration of John Magufili. This policy stated that every Tanzanian child will have access to free and compulsory basic education for the first ten years of schooling. During this time, which consists of six years of primary education and four years of secondary education, the language of education will be Swahili.

Indigenizing the Foreign: The Peculiar Case of North Africa

North Africa is often seen as somewhat unique and distant from the rest of Africa in literature, economy, education, and many other sectors. A reason for this is partly due to skin color and the region's proximity to the Middle East. The proximity of North Africa to the Middle East leads to both regions sharing a lot of similarities, including the issue of language as a tool for decolonization. Perhaps apart from countries like Tanzania in East Africa, North Africa is another region of the continent where measurable success has been recorded in decolonization through language, thanks to Arabization.

The peculiar history of North Africa is one that has relegated most of its ancient cultural and linguistic heritage to the background, granting prominence to Islam and Arabic. While a few minority local and indigenous languages in the region have barely survived, Arabic has flourished

---

62 Sa, "Language."

and has been embraced by many in the region. Yet this is a deviation from what was initially the case in North Africa. Speaking generally, Catherine Miller explains that

> historical studies indicate that for centuries Muslim states were able to accommodate different linguistic communities and that multilingualism was widespread. This is partly due to the fact that following the fall of the Abbassid Caliphate, many members of the Muslim ruling elites throughout the Muslim Empire were from non-Arab ethnic backgrounds. Moreover Empires tend to be multilingual while contemporary Nation-States tend to become monolingual (Baggioni, 1997) following the model of the 19th century European nationalism.[63]

In the ancient Arab world, of which North African countries were a part, distinctions of class and social status never came about through language. Therefore, it was possible for an elite and a commoner to speak the same language in the ancient Arab world. As Miller further notes, identity was not based on language or an attachment to kinship, rather, the true Arab was the Bedouin Arab.[64] This is evident in the era of the Ottoman Empire of 1299 to 1923,[65] which accommodated as many languages as possible. Miller posits that "at the written level, Osmanli, Arabic, Greek, Armenian, Judeo-Spanish, Serbian, Bulgarian and Slavic were used by different communities, each one with its own script."[66] This also shows that local languages were allowed to thrive in the region, although they were not the language of administration.

In the nineteenth and twentieth centuries, there was a wave of European colonization of North Africa and the Arab world at large, especially by the Turkish and French. This would set a new tone for language use in the region. Just as in other African regions, there was a major nationalistic movement in North Africa. According to Suleiman:

> The early impulses of Arab Nationalism were influenced by the success of the Balkan nations in achieving their independence from Ottoman

---

63 Miller, "Linguistic," 2.
64 Miller, "Linguistic," 3.
65 Or, "Language," 3.
66 Miller, "Linguistic," 6.

rule in the 19th century. The important and unifying role of language as a symbol of national identity in the struggle of these nations for independence was not lost on the Arabic-speaking elite in their efforts to promote the interest of their people whether within or outside the Ottoman Empire. However, the major impetus in the development of the Arab Nationalist i.e. at the beginning of the 20th century came from the aggressive policy of Turkification adopted by the Young Turks after their arrival to power in 1908.[67]

The nationalists did not only seek physical freedom but also pursued liberty in cognitive space by calling for the replacement of colonial languages with Arabic. This was what led to the Arabization of North Africa. Another major reason for Arabization is the connection between Islam and Arabic; if the religion spreads, so does the language. Mohand Tilmatine agrees that the spread of Islam was associated with the spread of Arabic in North Africa.[68] Consequently, according to Abdulaziz Lodhi's 1993 research, Arabic is spoken as the official language of seven African countries.[69]

Therefore, "Arabization refers to a broad array of language policies designed to strengthen the status of Arabic and reverse language shift initially caused by colonialism and later by globalization."[70] Coupled with the need to shed every trace of colonialism, Arabization also helped in securing linguistic and cultural unification of the North African region.[71] Arabization, however, came with its attendant problems: a major one being the marginalization of other languages in North Africa. As already noted, Arabization aimed to unify the people linguistically, and this meant settling for one variety of the Arabic language amidst many available ones. This led to the adoption of classical Arabic, which is regarded as prestigious. Classical Arabic is also reserved for special functions like Islamic sermons and creative and academic writings.[72] It should also be noted that by the time prominence was given to the Arabic language, class distinction along the lines of language had begun to be apparent in

---

67 Suleiman, "Nationalism," 6.
68 Tilmatine, "Arabization."
69 Lodhi, "Language," 80.
70 Or, "Language," 3.
71 Jaafari, "Language," 131.
72 Jaafari, "Language," 131.

North Africa. Consequently, classical Arabic was simplified to modern standard Arabic (MSA), which is now adopted as the official language in most North African countries.

The adoption of MSA is what necessitates the marginalization of other forms of Arabic in North Africa. This is a language situation that is often referred to as diglossia:

> DIGLOSSIA is a relatively stable language situation in which, in addition to the primary dialects of the language (which may include a standard or regional standards), there is a very divergent, highly codified (often grammatically more complex) superposed variety, the vehicle of a large and respected body of written literature, either of an earlier period or in another speech community, which is learned largely by formal education and is used for most written and formal spoken purposes but is not used by any sector of the community for ordinary conversation.[73]

The highly codified and respected form of Arabic, as labeled above, is the modern standard Arabic. Local Arabic dialects, just like other local languages that serve as mother tongue languages in Africa, have met with rejection from natives. These local dialects are regarded as inferior, hence natives have a negative attitude toward this language. This negative attitude is not directed at local Arabic dialects alone but toward other indigenous languages as well. Taking the case of Morocco as an example, Taoufik Jaafari states that "Moroccans hold negative attitudes towards their mother tongues (Darija and Tamazight) because of the low status that these languages have in the linguistic market."[74] The Moroccan Arabic dialect is also referred to as "Darija." This remains the status quo despite the statistics that show that 89.42 percent of Moroccans communicate with the local Arabic dialect,[75] and 60 percent of the Moroccan population are Berbers,[76] who have their indigenous Berber language. It shows that though fewer people, by comparison, use the Modern Standard Arabic, it has been imposed on the people.

---

73 Ferguson, "Diglossia," 325.
74 Jaafari, "Language," 128.
75 Jaafari, "Language," 128.
76 Miller, "Linguistic," 2.

Consequently, North African countries have ratified the use of Arabic as the official language of the country. In essence, for most of these countries, Arabic is the language of education mostly at the primary and high school levels. Arabic continues to enjoy this level of esteem and usage as political leaders, intellectuals, and even academics throw their weight behind the adoption of the language for official purposes.[77]

Despite the efforts put into Arabization, foreign languages are still a "threat" to the Arab world and North Africa in particular. Interestingly, North African countries that speak French due to colonization are being influenced more by the English language than French. In this regard, it is important to note that the effort to decolonize the knowledge space in postcolonial Africa through language has a somewhat peculiar twist in North Africa in comparison with most other parts of the continent explored in the earlier parts of this chapter. As already discussed, Arabization was embraced in virtually all North African countries, yet it became apparent that Arabic was not a competitive language in the global scheme of things. In Morocco, while Arabic has been adopted as the language in education at the primary and high school levels, the university level was never Arabized.[78] Moreover, as contained in the 2015–2030 Strategic Vision document of Morocco, students would be exposed to both the French and English languages at their elementary level of schooling.[79]

Further, Taoufik Jaafari convincingly argues that international languages, and especially the English language, are becoming more relevant and recognized in Morocco. Both French and Spanish, which are colonial languages, are being relegated to the background in favor of the English language. Interestingly, the French prime minister in 2018 had publicly uttered the following: "Mastering English well is better for securing and controlling your future. Every student at the end of their high school or at the latest at the end of their bachelor's degree will have reached a high score in one of the English international tests like IELTS, TOEFL, or TOEIC, funded by the state."[80] It therefore shows that though people in North Africa have chosen to embrace Arabic and accept it as their

---

77 Jaafari, "Language."
78 Jaafari, "Language."
79 Jaafari, "Language."
80 Jaafari, "Language," 135.

own,[81] they are not blind to the advantages that come with knowing an international language like English. Unlike other countries in Africa discussed above, however, the choice of an international language is deliberate in North African countries and its uses are limited to spheres like the university level of education.

While one might posit that North Africa lives the self-illusion of being physically and mentally free from the shackles of colonialism because of the policy of Arabization, an objective view of the region portrays that the region battles with other issues of similar magnitude to enslavement by language. Mohand Tilmatine asserts that Arabic is as much of an imperial language as French and English. However, "Arabic's dominance is legitimized by two fundamental pillars: religion, which has used Arabic as the sacred language of the Qur'an for centuries and then nationalism which decreed that 'Arabic' was a unique national language at the birth of the North African nation-states."[82]

On the other hand, there is the resentment from the North African Berber community, who make up a substantial percentage of the region's population. Due to years of neglect and domination by Arabic language activists from the Berber stock of North Africa have embarked on series of campaigns over the years to ensure their language is included in notable books about North Africa. Speaking about a particular sect of Berber activists in Algeria, Mohand Tilmatine said that the Kabylians "have intensified their efforts to slow down if not to halt the Arabisation campaigns."[83] Similarly, in Morocco, efforts of Amazigh activists were crowned when in 2011, their indigenous language of Tamazight was constitutionally recognized as an official language alongside Arabic.

Conclusion

The evidence above speaks to the quagmire in which Africa finds herself regarding language and language policies on the continent. Multilingualism and multiculturalism have been seen by many as one of the continent's biggest challenges. Blaming multiculturalism is

---

81 Tilmatine, "Arabization," 12.
82 Tilmatine, "Arabization," 12.
83 Tilmatine, "Arabization," 13.

short-sighted because there are many other countries worldwide with a multilingual and multicultural heritage, yet they excel linguistically, economically, and politically.

It is also easy to blame the problems of language policy in Africa on the influence of colonial languages. But as argued in the instances of Tanzania, Kenya, and North Africa, it is not impossible to reject the colonizers' language. There is no doubt that languages like French and English have an international appeal, and those who can communicate in these languages will be at an advantage. However, the African culture and identity should not be sacrificed on the altar of global appeal. Instead, other African countries should adopt the approach of Tanzania and North Africa, where indigenous languages are prioritized as the official language while also making room for other foreign languages in their educational system.

It will appear that the main challenge here is not the different policies among African countries but an inability to follow these policies to the letter. For instance, the constitution of Nigeria explicitly states that a child should receive education in his/her mother tongue for the first six years of learning, but this is only applicable on paper and not in practice. Governments, parents, and even learners in Africa have little interest in being educated in their mother tongue or appropriation of indigenous languages for knowledge dissemination.

Finally, it is important to state that countries like China, Russia, and Japan are excelling in many areas without the unnecessary intrusion of any foreign language. While these countries understand the international status of some foreign languages like English and make room for them as appropriate, it is never at the expense of indigenous languages as it is in Africa. For instance, English is the second official language in countries like Sweden and Denmark. Therefore, for real progress to take place in Africa, in using indigenous languages or indigenized languages, the example of West African Pidgins and Arabic should be followed. A fundamental aspect of this progress is restoring the connection between the African child and his environment, which can be facilitated by the use of their mother tongue as the language-in-education.

Chapter Fourteen

Decolonizing African Literature

Introduction

This chapter examines the decolonization project in African literature and languages. Contributions to the decolonization project in Africa since the end of colonialism has seen a lot of tremendous work being done. It is, therefore, necessary to state that the intellectual space in postcolonial Africa has faced some necessary scrutiny in which intellectuals have helped to examine how colonialism has an ineradicable effect on Africans. The effects are physical and mental. This chapter is dedicated to examining the ongoing decolonial project. In other words, the decolonializing project is not only a project set up to scrutinize the effects of colonialism on our political structures but also a project to indeed help Africans rediscover their true identities. One of the main tasks of decolonization is not to compulsorily return Africans to a precolonial state. However, it is an attempt to help Africans understand what it is like to be African. This project cannot be achieved without taking on relevant topics in intellectual spaces. The pertinence of the chapter is based on the evaluation of the efforts so far in asking a critical question: is true decolonization of African literature and languages possible?

Colonialism in Africa is often seen as a period that violated fundamental human rights of Africans as a whole. If anything, it was a period in which colonialists invaded the culture, geography, and humanity of Africans. There is no way for such an invasion to not have layered effects on the people that have been overrun in such a callous manner. It is sometimes argued that colonialism was motivated by European economic and political desires. Whatever the case, their greed changed the history of Africa as a continent and led to many years marked by the subjugation of the African people. Many commentators have argued that the effects of colonialism are more negative than positive. However, colonialism, despite its myriad detrimental effects, has certain positives as well. One thing cannot be denied: colonialism halted the development of African systems, and this had a profound effect on the African people.

In the postcolonial era, the systems and modernity colonials brought to Africa have become an essential and indelible aspect of African lives, which has invariably made it difficult for Africans to operate the systems they had in place had before the era of colonialism. The African way of life was forever changed: the colonialists may have left the continent physically, but they left behind the vestiges of their systems and cultures that are now exalted above genuine African systems and cultures. Ultimately, this became a point of contention for early African nationalists and intellectuals. The problem can be summarized as the fear that Africans have neglected the true African self for the identities of their oppressors.

Decolonization as a project has been extended to all aspects of African lives. As you will see in the chapters that follow, there has been decolonization of history, education, literature, sociopolitical systems, among others. Decolonization, therefore, is a project that liberates Africans from the shackles of continuous colonialism. Despite independence, African countries maintained the European systems they inherited: the mode of governance, the education system, the thinking and so on were all modeled on those of the Europeans. By decolonizing, there can be a reinvigoration of the African self through delimiting the influence of colonialism on sociopolitical and epistemological systems.

African languages and literature, among many other aspects of African cultures, have been negatively impacted by colonialism; they have been neglected and undervalued because they are regarded as inferior and are often marginalized. Decolonization in African literature and languages is to ensure a true liberation from the systemic imposition of European languages and literature on Africans.

Since the end of colonialism, however, there have been numerous critical works on decolonization. Many have taken different approaches into providing decolonial projects that can fill the indigenous knowledge gaps created by colonialism. However, the central theme of these approaches is to repudiate the Eurocentric characterization of African epistemological paradigms as inferior and illogical. If one is to truly decolonize African literature, one will have to reestablish the rationale that African literature and languages do not need to be modeled after their European counterparts. However, these decolonization projects seem to be paradoxical and antithetical because in decolonizing, the tools of decolonization are often the tools supplied by the colonizer.

This chapter cannot achieve its aims without first considering colonialism itself. Etymologically, there can be no decolonization without colonization. Colonization in this work shall be established as a mental and physical exercise. It is pertinent to note that colonialism is binary, therefore, it has its good and bad aspects, although the focus has mainly been on how it has stolen the soul of Africa. Although saying aspects of colonialism are "good" may be stretching things, there are some positives.

Decolonization as we know it is a project that has been ongoing since the 1950s. It is necessary in this work to give a somewhat historical trajectory of decolonization in Africa. By doing this, the political and intellectual nature and efforts of decolonization are brought to light. Decolonization is both a sociopolitical and intellectual project. It is easy to forget the political aspect of decolonization because the most popular and recent efforts of decolonization are mainly intellectual and academic. However, even the intellectual is intrinsically linked to the political. This chapter will delve into the decolonization of African literature and languages. Whether oral or written literature, language is the vehicle of literature. This, therefore, explains why decolonizing literature and languages have been inextricably linked. That is, language leaves impressions on literature, and literature, in turn, affects language; if language and literature are inseparable, then the decolonization of one means the decolonization of the other. This chapter aims to consider the possibility of true decolonization and the idea of decolonization in an ever-growing globalized world.

Characterizing Colonialism

The nature of colonialism is not hard to determine nor to define. Colonialism as a concept and phenomenon is exploitative and largely racist. In context, the idea of colonialism anywhere in the world is motivated by the need to dominate and exploit. Colonialism was motivated by the European need for economic expansion and dominance over the people of Africa. This made Ocheni and Nwankwo posit the following:

The colonization of Africa by European powers was necessitated by several factors. Notable, among the factors was the emergence of the industrial revolution which brought about a rapid change in the socio-economic transformation and technology of the European countries. The industrial revolution led to increase in production. The progress in the industry went faster than the progress in agriculture. It was becoming increasingly hard or difficult for the agriculture to satisfy the demand for raw materials required in the industries. There was therefore, the need for the European powers, for example, the British to go outside the country to look for additional raw materials. Furthermore, as a result of the decline in agricultural production, there was the problem of how to produce enough or adequate food to feed the fast-growing urban population. In other words, the rural areas in Britain for example, were finding it increasingly difficult to produce enough food to feed the increasing urban population. Similarly, there was also need for market, not only for the production of raw materials but for food to sustain the increasing population.[1]

Colonialism is historical as it is ideological. It is a historical process informed by the ideology of territorial and economic exploitation of the original habitants of a place. It is important to reiterate that the goals of colonialism as stated by Aime Césaire were neither for evangelization nor philanthropy.[2] There is often an interchangeable use of colonialism and coloniality. However, the two are distinct as Maldonado-Torres clearly states:

> Coloniality is different from colonialism. Colonialism denotes a political and economic relation in which the sovereignty of a nation or a people rests on the power of another nation, which makes such nation an empire. Coloniality, instead, refers to long-standing patterns of power that emerged as a result of colonialism, but that define culture, labour, intersubjective relations, and knowledge production well beyond the strict limits of colonial administrations. Thus coloniality survives colonialism. It is maintained alive in books, in the criteria for academic performance, in cultural patterns, in common sense, in the self-image of people, in aspirations of self, and so many other aspects of our modern experience. In a way, as modern subjects we breathe coloniality all the time and every day.[3]

---

1 Ocheni and Nwankwo, "Analysis," 47.
2 Césaire and Pinkham, *Discourse*.
3 Maldonado-Torres, "On the Coloniality," 243.

Colonialism is the need to displace the systems of the locals being colonized. Subsequently, the aim is not only to dominate the people but to also point out to them that their systems and systems of belief are not modern enough. This is why most anthropologists, philosophers and historians have always used a Eurocentric microscope to evaluate African systems and beliefs. There is consciousness before, during, and after colonialism to undermine whatever is truly African. Take for instance, Hugh Trevor-Roper's scathing remarks that there is no such thing as African history but only history of Europeans in Africa.[4] To discard the history of a people is to erase their culture and their personhood. This is just one of the many examples of the rationale behind the domineering ideology of Europeans in Africa. In a sense, the intentional misconceptions of Africa and its people were propagated to cast an air of European superiority to help colonialists ensure that their systems, history, religion, and modernity were accepted as universal paradigms. Colonialism not only spread domination but also the imperialism of history.

The Eurocentric notion of Africa and what it entailed before European contact characterizes colonialism as a ludicrous agenda. The foundations of colonialism were not laid through missionary work. It started with the scholarly works of great minds who saw Africa as nothing but a land of savages. There seems to be a conscious consensus reached by racist intellectuals before, during, and after colonialism that Africans had no objective consciousness of their own before European contact. G. W. F. Hegel opined that Africa "the land of childhood, which lying beyond the day of self-conscious history, is enveloped in the dark mantle of Night."[5] This sort of notion and erroneous assessment of colonialism was one of the most important blocks in the foundation of colonialist agenda. By claiming that Africa was enveloped in darkness, Hegel suggests that the darkness in which Africa is enveloped clouds the rationality of its people.

Hegel went further into analyzing religion in Africa. First, he claimed that the souls of Africans are, in their natural form, unrefined. Therefore, the behaviors of Africans are expected to be irrational and illogical. Then he claimed that African religions are based on sorcery and fetishism. In a stroke, Hegel had dismissed African religions and rationality. With

---

4   Trevor-Roper, "Past and Present," 3–17.
5   Hegel, *Philosophy*, 91.

mythmaking like this, any racist colonialist can find a way to build a system using these kinds of sentiments to justify domination of another people.

Hegel provides a political analysis also. He believed that Africans lacked political institutions because they had not yet realized their being and could not participate in any objective political institution formulated by universal law. The point made here is that Hegel's assessment is a fair representation of what colonizers thought about Africans, which made it easier to dismantle African political institutions. Their political and economic institutions were displaced because they were seen as insufficient. Jay Ciaffa believes that

> colonialism in Africa was supported by a broad range of popular and scholarly literature which highlighted fundamental differences between Europeans and Africans, and which reinforced ideas of European superiority. One of the most notorious examples of this literature was the work of the French anthropologist Lucien Levy-Bruhl. In a series of works bearing titles such as The Primitive Mentality and The Mental Functions of Inferior Civilizations, Levy-Bruhl distinguished between two fundamentally different mentalities: the mentality of the civilized European and that of the primitive non-European. According to Levy-Bruhl, the civilized mentality is regulated by reason, and interacts with the world through carefully organized conceptual schemes. In contrast, the primitive mentality is "hardly capable of abstract thought," and is regulated by the forces of myth and superstition (see Levy-Bruhl 1995, 54ff.). The racism expressed in Levy-Bruhl's work under the guise of scientific objectivity was echoed not only in popular European writings, but in remarks of esteemed philosophers, such as Hume, Kant, and Hegel. Although this discourse fulfilled several functions in the context of European culture, for our purposes its most important function was the role it played in the European understanding of colonialism. The images of the civilized European and the primitive African helped sustain the idea that colonialism was a fundamentally benevolent enterprise—that is, an enterprise in which Europeans were attempting to bring civilization to the "dark continent." In short, European domination, exploitation, and cultural devastation were rationalized under the guise of a so called "civilizing mission."[6]

---

6   Ciaffa, "Tradition," 124.

These notions as presented in Hegel and other scholars' works were, in a way, the bedrock of the theoretical framework of colonialism. These sentiments essentially furnished the idea of domination that characterized colonial conquest.

Furthermore, the European systems then began to be seen as absolute, and Europeans assumed the role of "God." In establishing the idea of African religions, systems, and cultures being enveloped in darkness, they goaded Africans into believing that Europeans are indeed superior in skin pigmentation, institution, and rationality. This summed up why Europeans proposed a single-minded modernity. In order to further ingrain colonialism and racial supremacy, they claimed that Africans were living in an age of "darkness," and only modern European systems were the way out. However, again, the idea of modernity in this context is Eurocentric. When subjected to scrutiny, the idea of modernity was the principal reason Africans abandoned their traditional systems and values. It is important to clarify the idea of modernity.

According to J. O. Fashola, modernity is "used in relation to the present period in history and as description of the latest and most advanced equipment and techniques available at every point in history."[7] Succinctly, modernity is a process of history by which each society evolves over time in order to cope with new cultural phenomena. However, modernity in a sense "consists only of the imposition of European models onto other societies, which either imitate them or reject them outright: such societies being deemed incapable a priori of fashioning their own creative responses. and fourth, where they reject European modernity, they do so on the basis of wholly different (and, by definition, Irrational) cultural Traditions."[8]

Modernity as defined by Washbrook captures the idea expressed earlier on how Europeans have imposed their idea of modernity on other societies. This is in the same manner in which Frantz Fanon claimed that colonialism is not mere domination of a people but an attempt to look at a people's past to distort, disfigure, and destroy it.[9] However, in Adeshina Afolayan's "Is Modernity Single and Unilateral? Òlàjú and the

---

7 Fashola, "Modernization," 188.
8 Washbrook, "Global," 299.
9 Fanon, *Wretched*.

Multilateral Modernity," he argued that there is a multilateral understanding of modernity. He asserts that

> the fact of confrontations between different cultures necessarily raises the issue of the creative responses available to the receiving culture. This suggests, I suspect, that modernity grows as a gradual process within the continual illuminatory boundary of the constant enlightenment that contact and confrontation bring. Enlightenment happens to societies in constant contact with other societies and at different rates. Modernity is a process borne out of creative adaptability that leads to the multilateral manufacture of cultural possibilities and institutions. Thus, multilateralism is to modernity what hybridity is to colonialism. and we can add that it is within its multilateral framework that modernity achieves its phenomenal status.[10]

The position held by Afolayan is that the interaction between cultures leads to each culture responding to new changes in different ways. However, rather than adhering to the European historical particularism portrayed as universalism, this is only seen as an episodic encounter because there are several modernities. Encounters between cultures, no matter how basic, produce results. Colonialists posited a dependency notion that Africa as a continent would not have survived without the European encounter. Unfortunately, to achieve the European ideal of modernity, Africans had to abandon their traditional ways of life, since the antithesis of "traditional" in the myopic Eurocentric view is "modern." Europeans, however, failed to acknowledge that other societies had their own form of modernity. The Eurocentric disregard for African ideas of modernity was so well presented that Africans began to neglect their past and traditions.

Despite all this, it is hypocritical of scholars to claim that colonialism had no positive impact on Africa. There are myriads of positive outcomes, such as the "scientific" writing system, education system, and health care. In Nigeria for example, Fashola writes that

> prior to the amalgamation of the country, the numerous ethnic nations had different modes of rulership, the most popular one which is the kingship system otherwise known as monarchy. Post-colonial era in Nigeria strived to entrench the western democratic system which is

---

10 Afolayan, "Is Modernity," 100.

presently undergoing stages of development in the country. Education in the country today has moved from the non-formal to the formal system which incorporates virtually western modes of thought. The benefit of this is that it affords the people enablement to interact with fast globalising world.[11]

Encounters between cultures are reformative. The reformation can then turn out to be good or bad. And the adoption of Western modes of thought as mentioned by Fashola can either then be a curse or a blessing. Many are left to wonder what Africans would have made of their own systems if they had not encountered Europeans.

Whatever the case may be, colonialism has left a profound mark on the history of Africa. One aspect of the aftermath of colonialism is Africans' willingness to revisit the past and bring to the forefront African systems before their European encounter. For some, colonialism has left scars on the people of Africa because years of colonialism not only affect physical attributes but also mental aspects. The mental side is often described as the intellectual impact of colonialism, something Fashola called "mode of thoughts." According to Toyin Falola, colonialism, which started as an economic expansion of European powers and historical process, became an issue of superior-inferior relations. This was meant to happen as the relationship between "subjects" (the colonized) and power (the colonizer) is practiced as a binary between slaves and masters. Therefore, there is an intellectual struggle that led to intellectual discourses and projects being modeled in the European image.[12]

Succinctly, colonialism in Africa is a grand episodic moment in the history of Africa that cannot be erased. Colonialism is characterized by domination, exploitation, epistemological tyranny, political subjugation, and an erroneous particularist notion of modernity. It is not out of place to think that European modernity exported its darker side to the rest of the world. There is a sense of corroboration in Fred Dallmyr's work "Return to the Source: African Identity (After Cabral)." He lucidly explains that

> European colonialism, including its Portuguese variety, always coupled exploitation with a missionary goal: the spreading of a (suppos-

---

11   Fashola, "Modernization," 192.
12   Falola, *Nationalism*.

edly) superior culture to the rest of the world. Even where wholesale conversion proved unfeasible, administrators sought to assimilate at least certain elite sections of society—while branding remaining indigenous life forms as hopelessly backward or obsolete. To this extent, colonialism subscribed to an imperialist version of the 'Enlightenment project' by extolling the virtues of Western-style universalism at the expense of local or traditional modes of thought and practice.[13]

These characterizations of colonialism linger on the socioeconomic, sociopolitical, and epistemological systems in Africa. The effect of colonialism on Africa cannot be underestimated. Whether good or bad, it brought major changes into Africa. These changes have been managed by nationalists and intellectuals since the end of colonialism. In general, they have tried to grapple with the grip colonialism had on them. Colonialism forced Africans to reject the old order of things: African cultures, languages, and systems are now taking a mere supporting role in the affairs of their own homeland. Colonialism has shaped postcolonial discourses and rightly so. The hubris of Europeans during and after colonialism has called for the end of a colonialism that continues even years after colonialists left Africa. In retrospect, colonialism and its effects still generate important debates in intellectual and sociopolitical institutions.

What Is This Thing Called Decolonization?

According to Rianna Oelofsen:

> Decolonization is the change that colonised countries go through when they become politically independent from their former colonisers. However, decolonization is not merely a matter of political independence. Structures of government and other institutions, the way in which a country is economically organised, as well as the way in which former colonial subjects were encouraged to think, are often still determined by the former colonial powers in post-colonial countries, as a result of the economic and cultural power the former colonisers wield. To claim that the colonial project stops having an impact on the newly decolonised country and its citizens, is to misunderstand how deeply the colonial project affected these countries and their citizens. In order

---

13   Dallmyr, "Return," 2.

to overcome the legacy of colonialism, it is necessary to also decolonise the intellectual landscape of the country in question, and, ultimately, decolonise the mind of the formerly colonised.[14]

The decolonization project started with colonial masters leaving their colonized countries. However, despite the nonphysical presence of colonial rule, there is still an entangled relationship between former colonies and their colonizers. The relations are due to the fact that these African countries have adopted the political, economic, and intellectual structures of their colonizers.

Decolonization, as much as it affects a people, can have a very subjective definition. In fact, it may be difficult to pin it down conceptually. For Smith and Jeppesen, "Decolonization resists easy definition or periodization. Like the process itself, writing the history of decolonization in Africa remains fraught and contested. In its shallowest and narrowest form, decolonization refers to the transfer of sovereignty from the colonizer to the colonized."[15]

Another perspective on decolonization is that it "aspires to break with monologic modernity."[16] Colonialism brought monologic modernity to Africa in which modernity is viewed as a European entity. Decolonization is a conscious effort by the formerly colonized to repudiate such a notion. As Maldonado-Torres contends,

> Decolonization is an idea that is probably as old as colonization itself. But it only becomes a project in the twentieth century. That is what Du Bois suggested when he stated that the problem of the twentieth-century is the problem of the colour-line. The idea was not that the colour-line was unique to the twentieth century, but that critical and violent confrontations with it were unavoidable then. With decolonization I do not have in mind simply the end of formal colonial relations, as it happened throughout the Americas in the late eighteenth and the nineteenth centuries. I am instead referring to a confrontation with the racial, gender, and sexual hierarchies that were put in place or strengthened by European modernity as it colonized and enslaved populations through the planet. In short, with decolonization I am thinking of oppositions to the coloniality of power, knowledge, and

---

14 Oelofsen, "Decolonization," 131.
15 Smith and Jeppesen, *Britain*, 2.
16 Maldonado-Torres, "On the Coloniality," 261.

being! It may be more consistent to refer to it as 'decoloniality', as Chela Sandoval and Catherine Walsh suggest.[17]

Decolonization has multiple perspectives, as decolonial authors examine the past in relation to the present, Africa in relation to Europe, and the African "personality" in relation to others. Phyllis Taoua believes that "since decolonization, there has been a gradual but steady evolution in the formation of identities away from a colonialist epistemology. The system of symbolic Othering that used to be organized by the outmoded colonizer–colonized binary has given way to a new set of oppositional identities that are decidedly more dynamic in nature."[18]

Decolonization as conceptualized so far indicates the separation from every colonial experience, epistemology, and political structure. It is a method of jettisoning colonialism and neocolonialism.

In going about implementing the decolonial project, there are several schools of thought. The first notable trend in decolonization is the nationalist-ideological movement. In the early 1940s, a lot of freedom fighters began returning to Africa from the West. Nationalists like Kwame Nkrumah, Julius Nyerere, Kenneth Kaunda, Leopold Senghor, and others adhered to the spirit of nationalism, which is "is the expression of national feeling; the expression of a radically changed form of consciousness".[19] According to Anthony Smith, it is "an ideological movement for attaining and maintaining autonomy, unity and identity on behalf of a population deemed by some of its members to constitute an actual or potential nation."[20]

It can also be construed as the birth of self-consciousness that is paradoxically brought about by Western education. According to Falola, "Missionary education produced new elite, different in its mode of thinking and skills from the indigenous and Islamic intelligentsia. Bookbinding, printing, carpentry, and smithing were some of the new skills associated with this elite. To some extent, a new 'industrial class' was also being created."[21] Consequently, the missionary education metamor-

---

17   Maldonado-Torres, "On the Coloniality."
18   Taoua, "Postcolonial," 211.
19   Anderson, *Imagined*, 142.
20   Smith, *National Identity*, 173.
21   Falola, *Nationalism*, 23.

Figure 14.1. Toyin Falola. Photograph by Koltron11. Creative Commons License CC BY-SA 3.0.

phosized many Africans into nationalists who were grounded in Western knowledge and later used this to their advantage in demanding their own liberation. Nationalism produced new leaders who demanded the freedom of their people and an end to colonialism.

With nationalism comes the ideological notion of the elevation of nationhood and the sense of community that are integral aspects of Africa's past. African nationalists became self-conscious in the 1940s of the idea that "sustaining Western colonialism was seriously undermining, if not destroying, the African social infrastructure based on traditional humanistic values."[22] Some of these nationalists came up with their own ideologies largely influenced by Marxism. For Nkrumah it was philosophical consciencism, and for Nyerere, it was African socialism. For the two, there was a romanticization of Africa's past and an explicit ambition to revisit the African past for suitable values to help push aside colonial political and economic structures.[23] For Senghor, it is adherence to the idea of negritude, a philosophy that is "a reaction against colonial machinations."[24] While Nkrumah and Nyerere favored reaching into Africa's past through African values and systems, Senghor believes that racialization is the way forward. Despite the failures of the nationalists and their ideologies, the notion of nationalism was to decolonize the African socioeconomic and political structures.

The other important trend is the intellectual and psychological school of thought in decolonization. The movement of this school started with the notion that the mind, which is the seat of reason and intellect, was also colonized. Colonialism to the adherents of this school suggests that the phenomenological and psychological traumas suffered by the colonized affected their psychological state enough to adjust to the idea of European superiority. Consequently, the epistemological paradigms imposed by Europeans were retained and maintained as the universal paradigm. One of the proponents of this school is Frantz Fanon. His works generally situated colonialism as oppression of the mind. To truly rid oneself of colonialism, oppression of the mind must be overcome.[25]

For intellectual context, one of the prominent moves for intellectual decolonization is Kwasi Wiredu's conceptual decolonization. For Wiredu,

> Colonialism has caused a wide-spread involuntary intermixing of Western and African intellectual categories in the thinking of contemporary Africans. Common sense alone dictates that we Africans of the immediate post-independence era should try to unravel the conceptual entanglements. We should then be in a position to view our own philosophic inheritance in its true lineaments. . . . To define conceptual decolonization is easy enough. It is the elimination from our thought of modes of conceptualization that came to us through

---

22   Bell, *Understanding*, 36.
23   See Nkrumah, *Towards;* and Nyerere, Freedom.
24   Oguejiofor, "Negritude," 86.
25   Fanon and Markmann, *Black Skin*.

colonization and remain in our thinking owing to inertia rather than to our own reflective choices.[26]

Wiredu clearly elucidates that decolonization in this form is the repudiation and rejection of Western intellectual imposition. The epistemological systems of African countries have been greatly influenced by colonialism. In the cases where they cannot be influenced, they are replaced with Western epistemologies. The call for conceptual decolonization was an attempt to separate the wheat from the chaff.

Decolonizing the Mind: The Politics of Language in African Literature by Ngugi wa Thiong'o is a popular work in the African decolonial project. While language is cultural, the author has framed the language problem in Africa as a mental and intellectual issue. He went through a period of not writing in a colonial language. What is common among all the forms of decolonization is cultural revivalism. Cultural revivalism is a critical response to how European writers talk about African culture and identity that dominated colonial and postcolonial debates.[27] In sum, decolonization, like colonialism, is a historical process. It is nearly impossible to repudiate the impact of colonialism on African experience; thus, decolonization will always be an ever-present project and concern.

Traditional African Literature

According to Dauda and Falola,

> Literature is an essential aspect of human life, interaction, and scholarship; it is not an art that happens in a vacuum. Writers have tried to use literature to mirror the reality of life. Arthur Schopenhauer carefully analyzed how literature deals with noble matters, especially the riddle of our existence and the psychological flux of society and the human heart, ultimately declaring that literature should carry a message that can be used as a tool for the discernment of some deep moral truth. An author is born into a social reality, grows up in it, and reflects it in his or her storytelling.[28]

---

26   Wiredu, "Conceptual Decolonization," 54–56.
27   Ciaffa, "Tradition," 121–45.
28   Dauda and Falola, *Wole Soyinka*, 135.

For Eileen Julien, the expression "African literature" means poetry, plays, and novels written by Africans in English and French, and perhaps Portuguese.[29] According to Chiwenzu, Jemie, and Madubuike, "Works done for African audiences, by Africans, and in African Languages, whether these works are oral or written, constitute the historically indubitable core of African literature."[30]

African literature transcends the works written in the colonial masters' languages. The oral component of life is included in African conception of literature. African oral literature is a crucial part of African existence because its body of knowledge is fully manifested in the way we speak. However, outside of the African continent, oral literature is mostly unknown, unrecognized, or disregarded. Prior to colonization, African literature was firmly rooted in culture. It was an excellent socialization tool for passing on society's core values from one generation to the next. But there is a common misconception that African literature is only about the stories of tortoises and other animals because of books like Chinua Achebe's *The Drum*[31] and Gerald McDermott's *Anansi the Spider: A Tale from the Ashanti*.[32] This is not true in any sense because African literature is much more than that.[33]

African literature served social, religious, economic, and political purposes prior to colonialization and European education. Traditional works were essentially rooted in orality. Orality was the basis or foundation of African intellectual systems. This is not to deny the absence of the writing form in Africa. But whatever writing form they used during the precolonial era was mostly in symbolic form. Emphatically, "African orature is culturally idiosyncratic and does not conform to the Western style of speech-making. The underlying understandings, assumptions, expectations, and symbolic meanings are drawn from the African belief system and tradition."[34]

Many people erroneously believe that African literature began at the moment of contact with the Western writing system. This is similar to

---

29 Julien, "African Literature," 295.
30 Chinweizu and Madubuike, *Toward*, 11–12.
31 Achebe, *Drum*.
32 McDermott, *Anansi the Spider*.
33 Dauda and Falola, *Wole Soyinka: Literature, Activism*.
34 Knowles-Borishade, "Paradigm," 489.

Paulin Hountondji's parochial view that philosophy "begins at the precise moment of transcription."[35] Contrary to this notion put forward by scholars like Hountondji, S. A. Babalola, in his work *The Content and Form of Yoruba Ijala*, he argued that his aim is to "help correct the erroneous idea given in many journal articles on African Literature that its beginning coincides with the introduction of literacy to African communities."[36]

Traditional African literature is made up of griot performances, folktales, folklores, and other oral performances. According to Kwasi Wiredu,

> An oral tradition is a transmission of thought over generations by the spoken word and techniques of communication other than writing. Under this definition, such items as poems, lyrics, proverbs, and maxims, of course, qualify as elements of our oral traditions. So too do drum texts and art motifs. But languages do have embedded in their syntax and semantics various notions about reality and human experience. Through these, our habits of speech influence our habits of writing. And so we cannot regard written traditions as altogether independent of orality.[37]

The last line from Wiredu suggests that orality is the foundation of the written form of African literature. The power of orality in African literature links the traditional phase of African literature with the modern phase of African literature.

Modern African Literature

From the adjective ("modern") ascribed to this era of literature, one begins to see the change in approach and style. "Modern" in this context is also the understanding of modern as a process of change over a long period. Since the colonial phase, according to Eileen Julien,

> African literature has changed tremendously . . . because of several important developments: the ever-increasing numbers of women writers, greater awareness of written and oral production in national languages

---

35 Hountondji, *African Philosophy,* 103.
36 Babalola, *Content,* v.
37 Wiredu, "An Oral Philosophy," 8.

(such as Yoruba, Poular, and Zulu), and greater critical attention to factors such as the politics of publishing and African literature's multiple audiences. These developments coincide with and have, in fact, helped produce a general shift in literary sensibility away from literature as pure text, the dominant paradigm for many years, to literature as an act between parties located within historical, socioeconomic, and other contexts. Fiction, plays, and poetry by women from around the continent have been singularly important because they "complicate" the meaning of works by their literary forefathers, bringing those works into sharper relief, forcing us to see their limits as well as their merits.[38]

The change and development of African literature can be traced to colonialism. Modern African literature arose as a result of colonialism's imposition of Western educational systems on Africans. So, works by African writers were critical of colonial rule and oftentimes juxtaposed old cultures with new ones.

Furthermore, it is pertinent to reiterate that what became modern African literature was born out of two or more civilizations: the writing systems and languages of the West along with the shared experience and identity of the past. In early postcolonial intellectualism, there seems to be a debate on the dichotomy between the oral and the written form of intellectual engagements. The oral form belonged to the precolonial era and the written form to the colonial and postcolonial eras. However, despite the new reality of colonialism and its effects, the prowess of oral literature in Africa cannot be denied or underestimated. To further this argument, Johnathan Peters's position can help:

> African literature includes the epic tradition kept alive by the griots, traditional bards who recounted the history of their clans as well as of heroic figures in their region . . . oral literatures of West Africa have for the most part been defined from culture to culture, though a handful of studies treat folklore in general and oral traditions in particular as a national or regional phenomenon. Scholars tend to consider the oral tradition separately from the written body of creative literature, even though the latter has been informed to a great degree by the traditional cultures of which the writers are inheritors.[39]

---

38 Julien, "African Literature," 295.
39 Peters, "English-Language," 9.

The distinctive attribute to be noted between the era of traditional African literature and modern African literature is the variance in languages. While traditional African literature used the linguistic tools of its language, modern African literature uses mainly foreign languages in this way. African authors writing in foreign languages dates back to the 1950s with works from Tutuola, Achebe, and others. Owomoyela lucidly explicates that "modern African literatures are a product of the encounter between African and European cultures. Their development has been significantly influenced by the nature of that encounter, and later by colonial expediency and the exigencies of decolonization. An understanding of the linguistic anomaly that is a feature of those literatures thus necessitates an archaeological probing of those events."[40]

Owomoyela understands that the interaction of cultures brings about the birth of new ideas and realities. One of these new realities is modern African literature. Modern African literature is a fusion of African and European cultures. At the beginning of African publishing in the 1950s, Africans who wrote did so with a wonderful grasp of the culture of their people. Most importantly, they took into account the importance of orality in the lives of their people. This is seen clearly in Amos Tutuola's *The Palm-Wine Drinkard*.[41]

Language Problem in Africa

Since the struggle for African independence, Africans who are revivalists argued for the resuscitation of African languages. Since the beginning of colonialism, African languages have been pushed aside. European languages like English, French, Portuguese, and German became the languages of instruction. So, it is well established and undeniable that "historical conditions such as colonialism, economic and political dependency, contribute to the fact of the international weakness of regional languages."[42] According to Alamin Mazrui: "The process of colonial education had the effect of marginalizing African languages in favour of Euro-languages, thus creating a linguistic configuration that served to legitimize and reproduce the unequal division of power and resources

---

40 Owomoyela, *History*, 348.
41 Tutuola, *Palm-Wine*.
42 Rettová, "Role," 129.

between the speakers of Euro-languages and the speakers of African languages. The overwhelming majority of post-colonial African governments thus inherited educational systems with imperial languages as the predominant media of instruction."[43] As Africans began to seek self-governance, they sought ways to rid themselves of the influence of colonial policy on their culture and language.

It is important to note that intercultural semblance has led scholars to argue that African cultures are homogenous. Africa before colonialism was characterized by pluralism, flexibility, and multiple identities. All these were bound by rigidities of invented tradition. Traditions were culturally and sociopolitically created, while culture is heuristic and shapes decision making. Cultural traits are subject to historical processes, and conceptually, historical events have an impact on cultural behaviors and traits. Cultural traits are transmitted from generation to generation. The impact of these traits and cultural impacts is persistent throughout history. This is the same with African cultures as it is with any culture worldwide. As stated, the historical events of each culture in Africa are different and unique to the people of each culture. Therefore, the idea of an "African language" is not tenable: rather, Africa is a multilingual society. It is from this premise that one is able to deduce the language debates in Africa that have called for a one-language system (one language as the mode of instruction in Africa, and a language that is used in schools, homes, markets, and other places).

The biggest concern of intellectuals is not the adoption of European languages. It is rather the rejection of African languages. African languages are construed as primitive even in their homeland. This is because, according to Kishani,

> The colonial Western world was out to teach us European languages and civilize us for colonial purposes. We became almost passive pupils, neglecting our own linguistic resources, overlooking them as a basis for rethinking our colonial situation, and never asking ourselves whether our own languages—which we often spoke furtively in and out of colonial discourses—could, in the short or long term, become the accepted languages of learning in Africa. Moreover, we forgot the value of our strength as students who are just as important in a learning situation as the teachers are.[44]

---

43   Mazrui, "English," 40.
44   Kishani, "On the Interface," 29.

Language, according to Ngugi, serves two aspects: "One aspect is its role as an agent that enables us to communicate with one another in our struggle to find the means for survival. The other is its role as a carrier of the history and the culture built into the process of that communication over time."[45]

Language is used for communication as well as for the preservation of culture. Unfortunately for Africans, the adopted European languages fulfilled the communicative role in Africa and concurrently discarded the histories and cultures of Africans. The result of this is that with the neglect of African languages comes the neglect of precolonial African history and intellectual systems that define the continent's being. The language problem in Africa cannot, however, be solved by agreeing to adopt a single African language because, as previously mentioned, African cultures and languages are heterogeneous. By adopting one language, we erase the history and cultural identity of the other. Then we are guilty of whatever we accuse European languages of. True linguistic liberation is to let each language continue to exist side by side with European languages.

The Task of Decolonizing African Languages and Literatures

There is an urgent purpose underlying decolonization of African literatures and languages. The significance of seeing it as a joint task is that the decolonization of African languages is linked with decolonization of African literature. That is, decolonization of African languages and literature are like two sides of the same coin. The argument in the foregoing section centered on the adoption of European languages. One of the most critical voices on this adoption is Ngugi wa Thiong'o. One of the most common ways in which Africans have maintained the colonial experience and retained neocolonialism is by forbidding children from speaking their mother tongue, an act that children were humiliated, beaten, and fined for. New African parents now take pride in the fact that their wards cannot speak traditional African languages. Ngugi believes that with this kind of policy, a child beaten and humiliated will "by extension hate the values carried by that language and also dislike or look down upon the people who created [that] language,"[46] and with this "the rubber stamp

---

45 Ngugi, *Moving*, 30.
46 Ngugi, "Commitment," 20.

that certifies the neo-colonial mind as being truly made in Europe."[47] The call for decolonization by Ngugi is motivated by the need to stop taking intellectual and linguistic dictations from colonial and neocolonial authority. He states that

> imperialism in its colonial and neo-colonial phases continuously press-ganging the African hand to the plough to turn the soil over, and putting blinkers on him to make him view the path ahead only as determined for him by the master armed with Bible and sword. In other words, imperialism continues to control the economy, politics and cultures of Africa. But on the other, and pitted against it, are the ceaseless struggles of African people to liberate their economy, politics and culture from that Euro-American-based stranglehold to usher a new era of true communal self-regulation and self-determination. It is an ever-continuing struggle to seize back their creative initiative in history through a real control of all the means of communal self-definition in time and space. The choice of language and the use to which language is put is central to a people's definition of themselves in relation to their natural and social environment, indeed in relation to the entire universe.[48]

In this manner, the language of self-determination and struggle for Africans is their indigenous language. It is the mechanism by which you understand your cultural past and experience, and thereby understand the universe. Ngugi bitterly remarked that

> Unfortunately, writers who should have been mapping paths out of that linguistic encirclement of their continent also came to be defined and to define themselves in terms of the languages of imperialist imposition. Even at their most radical and pro-African in their sentiments and articulation of problems they still took it as axiomatic that the renaissance of African cultures lay in the languages of Europe.[49]

This may be viewed as harsh criticism of his writer colleagues, but according to Ngugi:

> If in these essays I criticise the Afro-European (or Eurafrican) choice

---

47 Ngugi, "Freeing," 168.
48 Ngugi, *Decolonising,* 4.
49 Ngugi, *Decolonizing,* 5.

of our linguistic praxis, it is not to take away from the talent and the genius of those who have written in English, French, or Portuguese. On the contrary I am lamenting a neo-colonial situation which has meant the European bourgeoisie once again stealing our talents and geniuses as they have stolen our economies.[50]

For Rafal Smolen, Ngugi's "statements on the role of African writers creating in colonial languages are radical, vituperative, or just extremely sour."[51] Ngugi's point is clear, and his frustrations understandable. The manner in which they have been delivered may be vituperative, but one should take the message seriously and not the tone in which it is delivered.

Undoubtedly, the Ngugi stance is that to repudiate colonial attitudes and decolonize African culture, native African languages must come to the fore and play a dominant role in African society. At the same time, writers have significant roles to play if this is to be achieved. When it comes to decolonization, Ngugi is considered a radical in calling for the abolition of the English department because it is a constant reminder of the colonial experience and imperial imposition. The need for teaching and writing in African languages is understood as a move or call to disclaim and reject the superiority of the intellectual capacity of European languages over African languages.

In relation to Ngugi and the call for writing in African languages with the new world order, it is very possible to write in other people's languages and still effectively display your cultural heritage and philosophy to the world. Chinua Achebe is a great example of such a writer. We must remember that colonialism is also an African experience. We cannot decolonize by just throwing the colonial languages away. We can, however, reflect on how the European language has been internalized. After all, "most African Writers write out of an African experience and out of commitment to an African destiny."[52] Achebe also warns, "Let no one be fooled by the fact that we may write in English, for we intend to do unheard of things with it."[53] He further clarified in *There Was a Country: A Personal History of Biafra* that

---

50 Ngugi, *Decolonising*, 12.
51 Smoleń, "Language," 140.
52 Achebe, *Morning*, 9.
53 Achebe, *Morning*.

to help create a unique and authentic African literary tradition would mean some of us would decide to use the coloniser's tools: his language, altered sufficiently to bear the weight of an African creative aesthetic, infused with elements of the African literary tradition. I borrowed proverbs from our culture and history, colloquialisms and African expressive language from the ancient griots, the worldviews, perspectives, and customs from my Igbo tradition and cosmology, and the sensibilities of everyday people.[54]

Achebe's idea is that the English language is the best means of interacting and connecting with a large percentage of Africans and widely sharing African history and predictions of its future. This was the attitude common with modern African writers: to attach their identity to an indigenous paradigm but write in a language that is known the world over. In this sense of decolonization, Achebe hopes to achieve decolonialization by narrating stories that are infused with the traditional customs of African people. African languages are brought to the fore in translation and translinguistic approaches, which helps Africans to easily comprehend their ideas in familiar language. With this, Africans can reminisce on the nature of their own language and take what they need from it, rather than solely relying on European languages. And this is best accomplished by first addressing the African public in a global language like English.

One of the most well-known works in the decolonization of African literature is Chinweizu, Onwuchekwa Jemie, and Ihechukwu Madubuike's *Towards Decolonization of African Literature*. For the trio,

> The cultural task in hand is to end all foreign domination of African culture, to systematically destroy all encrustations of colonial and slave mentality, to clear the bushes and stake out new foundations for a liberated African modernity. This is a process that must take place in all spheres of African life, in government, industry, family and social life, education, city planning, architecture, arts, entertainments, etc.[55]

These authors help put into perspective the earlier clarification on forms and ways in which decolonization can take place. Decolonization is not

---

54   Achebe, *There Was a Country*, 55.
55   Chinweizu and Madubuike, *Toward*.

only the eradication of colonial rule but also the repudiation of the colonial attitude, which still exists despite the end of colonialism.

What this trio of authors understands is the importance of orature. As aforementioned, oral literature abhors the true self and identity of Africans. According to them,

> African orature is important to this enterprise of decolonizing African literature, for the important reason that it is the incontestable reservoir of the values, sensibilities, esthetics, and achievements of traditional African thought and imagination our plastic arts. Thus, it must serve as the ultimate foundation, guidepost, and point of departure for a modern liberated African literature.[56]

Just like the cultural revivalism explicated earlier, by digging into the well of African orature one reaches into the original African identity and intellectual system before colonialism. The subscription to the idea of sophistication of African orature is a reasonable one. It directly antagonizes Eurocentric criticism of African literature and languages that are not written and seen as illogical, primitive, and invalid. The Eurocentric notion is based on the over-glorification of the writing tradition. Writing is at the heart of Eurocentric discourse, and it is a tool used by Europeans to discredit the African past. Mazama asserts that writing is so glorified that "any event taking place prior to or independently of the use of writing by a particular group is dismissed as prehistorical."[57] By elevating the importance of African orature, our pasts and languages are revisited and placed above European systems and imposed imperialist languages. With this, decolonization will help writers and intellectuals set their own rules and keep the unique attributes of their cultures, and language is one of the tools to aid in this process. The colonial mentality is to discredit anything that is truly African.

From the foregoing we can discern the problem the trio have with Wole Soyinka. Soyinka is simply one of the most difficult writers anyone can choose to read. His writing can be cultlike, in the sense that one may need a thorough initiation to understand some of it. Some of his critics believe that "Soyinka is not in fact attempting to say anything to anyone. Rather, he is out to demonstrate that he is able to manipulate the English

---

56 Jemie and Madubuike, *Toward*, 2.
57 Mazama, "Eurocentric," 6.

language far better than the owners of the language . . . and to also demonstrate his cleverness."[58] Chinweizu et al. do not just have a language problem with him but also a problem with his imagery. They first accused Soyinka of using obscure language in his poems and also the importation of foreign imagery to project an African experience. Chinweizu and others try to point out the Euromodernist hold on African writers that influenced Soyinka to use obscure English language to deviate from the simple nature of traditional African literature founded in orature.

The point behind this is that African oral literature thrives on its simplicity. Now the idea of Chinweizu and his colleagues becomes evident: if modern African literature is built on African oral literature, languages of modern African literature become easy to access for readers. This, in turn, helps to revitalize the lost pride in African language and literature. However, in Soyinka's defense, he has always insisted that he is a child of two civilizations: the African civilization, which he was born into, and Western civilization, which he has experienced through language and culture.[59] Again, there lies the recurring question of decolonization. Is true decolonization possible?

Conclusion

The decolonial project as we know it is still an ongoing process. Like Soyinka, Africans are children of two civilizations. When two cultures come in contact with one another, the influence they have on each other cannot be easily discarded. However, the agonizing aspect of this encounter is the forceful imperialist imposition of Euro-Western systems on Africans. The systems have affected them in countless ways. Their social lives, political systems, and intellectual systems are forever marked by the colonial experience. So, logically, it is only fair for Africans to try and alienate themselves from colonial identities and reclaim their cultural past. African languages and literature among intellectual and cultural structures have been subjected to decolonization. There are calls for rejection of European languages as means of instruction at home, schools, offices, markets, and so on due to the effect of colonialism and how it

---

58　Omotoso, *Achebe or Soyinka*, 4.
59　Omotoso, *Achebe or Soyinka*.

has affected the nature of our languages and their treatments. This has taken a toll on the minds of many Africans in seeing African languages as primitive. They treat their own languages with disdain and take European tongues as accepted linguistic paradigms. Therefore, African minds became places where colonial principles are still deep-seated. Necessarily, a need for mental, intellectual, and linguistic decolonization is required.

This work has taken up the task of explicating the implications of colonialism and the eradication of mental and linguistic domination. The common ground among decolonialists and forms of decolonization examined in this work suggest that we return to the African values and belief systems of our traditional past. This may, however, be an over-romanticization of Africa's past before the colonial encounter. The dilemma is this: Can we truly return to an African past before colonialism? And further, can we return to the way African literature and languages were before colonialism? This is nearly impossible. But it will be misleading to think that by saying "return," we mean canceling the years of colonialism and going back to precolonial conditions. Rather, the notion is to debunk Eurocentric notions about African languages and literature.

The project is to ensure that African traditional literature and indigenous languages are used in dismantling colonial presuppositions that still have a grip on African minds. Total decolonization may not be possible, but it is an ongoing process. It will continue to stand against domination, and in this case, the domination of African languages and literature by European literature and languages.

Chapter Fifteen

Identity and the African Feminist Writer

Introduction

The decolonization of knowledge can be grounded in "difference," defined by race, gender, class, ethnicity, religion, and much more. In this chapter, the focus is on "identity" in relation to the work of African women about women. The African feminist writer has a unique identity; her work differs from feminist works written by non-Africans. This chapter aims at evaluating the circumstances culminating in the uniqueness and relevance of African feminist writers.

These feminist writers take a different path from Western gender epistemologies by grounding their work in rich, heterogenous, and dynamic local contexts; by foregrounding the shifting conceptions of feminist ideologies in Africa; by bridging modern and traditional practices that give women agency; and by providing bold platforms for these processes in their creative works. African feminist writers participate in the unending task of decolonizing knowledge about African women, gender, society, and nations.

The chapter will also explore the development of feminism in Africa, as well as the different conceptualizations of feminism by African scholars and critics. This will provide insight into the new discourse in feminist and gender studies in Africa. The chapter will look at selected feminist works to examine the ideological basis of each and how they express feminist ideals. It will also further explore the relevance of these African feminist writers in relation to African women and culture, while examining the writer's responsibilities in ideological reformation and illumination of women's struggles.

The African feminist writer is a product of both traditional and modern influences and therefore relevant to the present society. The chapter also posits the feminist writer and her works as revealing nonhomogeneity in the various conceptions of feminism. With no consensus among the writers, the resulting ambiguity surrounding the concept of feminism in Africa is also considered. Human society is in a process of constant change; it is still rapidly evolving to a state of large-scale industrialization not to mention technological and ideological advancements, hence the steadiness of pervasive transformations in the several agencies that control the affairs of society. Aside from the tangible changes of material inventions, these transformations are often characterized by alterations in cultural ideologies, attitudes, and norms. African society has undergone major sociocultural adjustments in the course of its interaction with other cultures worldwide. Some of these changes can be characterized as invasive, while some others are just necessary responses to the demands of the contemporary African state. In light of that consciousness, feminism as a movement in Africa and beyond can be credited to the changes in perception of women's issues in recent times and the need to liberate the modern woman from the adverse effects of patriarchy.[1]

The origin of feminism in the West as a term and movement is multifarious. Many scholars claim that the movement started long before its prominence in the twentieth century. For Peter Barry, the "'women's movement' of the 1960s was not, of course, the start of feminism."[2] The use of "feminism" dates as far back as the eighteenth century. The word *feminisme*, which is the French equivalent of "feminism," was adopted in the early 1890s to describe the emancipation of women. Hubertine Auclert, an advocate for women's suffrage, is considered to be the "first self-proclaimed 'feminist'" in France, who used the word to describe herself and her associates in her periodical *la Citoyenne*. In 1894–95, the word *feminist* began to be used in Great Britain, and by the late 1890s it was being bandied about in the United States.[3] The movement first sought women's right to vote, to own property, and have equal job

---

[1] It should be noted that some feminist writers argue that "patriarchy" is also a Western construct and cannot be said to mean the same thing in the African context and thus should not be constructed as the oppositional value to women's emancipation.

[2] Barry, *Beginning*, 84.

[3] Chaka, "Defining Feminism," 119–57.

opportunities. Currently, feminism has come to mean different things for different people. This multiplicity of meanings will be explored subsequently in this work, but the basic principle of the earliest movement of feminism is equal rights and opportunities for men and women.

The representation of women in literary works spurred the publication of books that focused on the unequal treatment of women at the time. According to Barry, *The Second Sex* published by the French existentialist Simone de Beauvoir (1949), talks about women's experiences through history and has a prominent section on the portrayal of women in the novels of D. H. Lawrence.[4] The women's movement of the 1960s, which still has a profound effect on contemporary feminist literary criticism, took into consideration the portrayal of women in literary works while examining the relevance of such portrayals to the woman's perception of self and its direct effect on the movement. Literature is often considered an effective means of social conditioning and thus a tool for cultural reorientation. Therefore, this implies the valuable position of feminist writers in the movement for the redefinition of women in society.

In African society, feminism is often considered an offshoot of Western civilization, a speculation that survived possibly as a result of the interconnectedness of modern society and the recent trend of globalization. In other words, most African counterarguments are usually based on the foreignness of the concept. This notion, therefore, explains the controversial nature of the feminist ideology in African society. So many anti-feminist opinions in Africa are usually based on the idea that feminism is an imported foreign concept and, therefore, anathema to African culture. This argument is usually presented with the intention to validate the operations of patriarchy in society. There is little doubt that the word *feminism* has its origins in the West; the practice of opposing patriarchy is, however, not entirely a Western ideological invention.

Development of African Feminism

The African feminist movement has its beginnings in the precolonial women's activities and organizations that were geared toward addressing issues that affected women in the various spheres of their existence.

---

4   Barry, *Beginning Theory*, 84.

As described by Wanyande, these movements survived into the colonial period while the resultant nationalist movements carved a niche for women's organizing within the movement for independence.[5] These organizations were safe havens for women to identify their goals at the time and devise means through their activities and engagements to explore and advance opportunities and rights for women in a male-dominated society.

There have been specific practices by these women's movements identified within Africa to represent earlier attempts by women to protest issues that were not in their best interest. For example, in the colonial Nigerian society, as related by the historian Judith Van Allen, the southeastern women of Nigeria engaged in a cultural practice known as "sitting on a man."[6] This practice involved a form of ritualized dancing and singing in which the lyrics of the song contained the women's grievances against the man in question. These angry visits by the women often took an aggressive turn where the women would deface the man's house or bang on the walls with their mortars and pestles while questioning the man's masculinity. This is an earlier form of feminine assertion, a way of exerting control over some of the injustices against women at the time. These organized activities reveal the colonial-era Nigerian women's need for liberation and checks on misogynist behavior.

Other forms of activities, as stated by Sylvia Tamale, were geared toward protecting women's livelihoods.[7] This explains the women's trade unions, formed to protect the interests of working women, which meant a considerable amount of financial autonomy for women. These protests and movements grew exponentially during the various struggles for independence in many parts of Africa. For Medie, these women's organizations ranged from grassroots women's groups without written statements to properly coordinated professional petitions to NGOs.[8]

Other examples of women's activities abound in various parts of Africa. The southwestern women of Nigeria, according to Sinmi Akin-Aina, formed three different organizations aimed at improving the welfare of women and protesting against unfair taxation policies.[9] These organi-

---

5   Wanyande, "Mass Media-State," 54–75.
6   Allan, "Sitting," 165–81.
7   Tamale, "Point of Order," 8–15.
8   Medie, "Women," 1–4.
9   Akin-Aina, "Beyond," 2.

zations included the Lagos Market Women's Association, the Nigerian Women's Party, and the Abeokuta Women's Union. The Aba women's riot in Nigeria, as recorded by Mba, was a political protest against the British attempt to tax the women, not to mention their other grievances against the corruption within the native courts, leading to the death of fifty women and injuries to many others.[10] Steady states that the Sierra Leonean women led a protest against the increase in food prices as a result of the monopolization of food distribution by Lebanese traders.[11]

The activities of these women's movements were initial practices of feminine assertion, which further explicates the need for women's movements and feminism in African society. Women's importance to socioeconomic and political developments in society cannot be overemphasized. Therefore, feminism is not entirely a foreign concept. Political agitation has been a natural reaction of African women to unpalatable social issues, especially their involvements in anticolonial struggles. However, being a more formal and radicalized aspect of women's movements, feminism is, therefore, necessary for the political, economic, and social evolution of the modern-day African woman.

The Journey So Far

The aforementioned organizations and their activities precede the present-day feminist movements; however, they are considered foundational to the development of feminism in Africa today. The increasing involvement and access of women and girls to education on the continent is an indication of the progress of feminist protest. Josephine Ahikire accounts for these changes as follows: "The 1990s opened a wave of rapid change, with women's movements across the African continent registering gains in various fields; including governance, health, education and domestic relations. In several countries across the continent women's scholarship and activism has made inroads, for example, into constitution-making processes and broadening the public agenda, making the gender question a remarkably public issue."[12]

---

10   Mba, *Nigerian Women*.
11   Steady, *Women*.
12   Ahikire, "African Feminism," 9.

In the 1990s African scholarship also experienced a surge of feminist discourse and activism. The ideological concerns of feminism have permeated academia and have led to a much more dignified and intellectual approach to the movement. Mama Amina affirms this claim by arguing that the 1990s experienced an influx of indigenous women scholars of gender studies, and even though their studies revolved around Western ideological concerns, it was still a step toward the development of African feminist studies within the continent.[13] African research on feminism now tries to explore Africa's cultural and historical realities to come up with theoretical frameworks on the African woman, and pressure is put on African universities to contribute to gender and African studies.

Also, several organizations with the sole purpose of advancing the feminist movement in Africa have been established over the years. Kenya's Maendeleo Ya Wanawake has been described by Aina as a survivor of the women's movement during the colonial era and remained so for many years.[14] Initiated in 1952, the movement continues to tackle issues of gender disparity in Africa, while campaigning for women's rights in social and political contexts. It has also focused on the inclusion and mobilization of women in rural areas. The title of the organization simply translates in Kiswahili to "women's progress." The organization takes into account the cultural specificity of the African continent and enjoys a vast membership in Kenya and around the globe.[15] However, this organization and many others have sprung up and continue to advance the course of the African woman in terms of social and political development in the continent.

The political, cultural, and economic spheres of the society have also felt a notable impact from the feminist movement, which must be the reason why Ahikire is of the opinion that "[p]erhaps more than any other social struggles, feminist engagement has been able to lodge a claim within the global political and development discourse."[16] The percentage of women in politics has also improved tremendously in many African nations, while women's involvement in the law-making arms of government has brought about the implementation of women-friendly policies

---

13   Mama, *Women Studies*.
14   Akin-Aina, "Beyond."
15   Ahikire, "African."
16   Ahikire, "African Feminism," 9.

in African society. These policies, which have gained presence and legitimacy in government and policymaking bodies, address violence against women as well as some mundane cultural practices that promote sexism and infringe on the rights and free expression of women. For instance, Ahikire states that

> the African Union (AU) policy discourse indicates the efficacy of feminist activism. Instruments such as the African Union (AU) Protocol on the Rights of Women in Africa—which includes a commitment to 50:50 gender parity in politics—point to the influence of feminism on this continental body. The AU Protocol addresses a range of things, among these: the elimination of discrimination against women's rights to dignity and security of the person, secure livelihoods, health and reproductive rights, social security and protection by the state.[17]

These milestones in women's liberation notwithstanding, the patriarchy is still alive and well. The continued presence of patriarchal systems has given rise to feminist writers with multiple approaches against mainstream male-dominated society within the continent.[18]

However, irrespective of these growing reforms and political protests by women in Africa, UNDP's 2016 reports show that the issue of gender disparity in education is still a problem in central African nations, with women attending educational institutions for a period of 2.5 years as opposed to 4.5 years for men. The eastern African region has attendance averages of about 3.6 years for women and 5.1 years for men, while in the Western region it ranges from 6.2 years for the women to 6.9 for the men. However, in view of these attendance rates in Africa, there are still large gender differences in higher education attendance by African women.[19]

These factors tend to affect the employability rates of women in Africa. According to UNDP statistics, these rates have risen to about 61 percent. However, these jobs are neither productive nor well paying. According to the report, due to the inequalities in their educational level, professional

---

17 Ahikire, "African Feminism," 11.
18 Tripp, "Women," 233–55.
19 Stiftung, *Feminism in Africa,* 1–15.

qualifications and skills, women are more likely to be found in "vulnerable jobs without social protection."[20]

The election of women and their participation in public office has experienced remarkable progress in recent times. According to a UNDP (2017) report, about sixteen African countries have exceeded the "30 percent mark of representation in national parliaments established at the Beijing World Conference." These countries are within the southern and eastern parts of Africa. This inclusive opportunity for women in those areas has brought about significant changes to the movement for gender equality in Africa.[21]

However, this does not invalidate the claim that the presence of women in government has brought about some positive change. It rather reports that in spite of their inclusion, the western and central regions of Africa are documented as having a high rate of discriminatory practices against women. This is, therefore, blamed on the political structures in place to check the woman's ability to influence local and national policies in their favor. The report goes further to state that "African countries have adopted international and regional legal frameworks on human rights, but there is a significant gap between intent and action."[22]

This information implicates the roles of traditional African law systems in impeding the implementation of new legal frameworks. Acts like child marriage and physical and sexual violence protected by traditional legal systems tend to affect the health and human rights of these women, leading to maternal mortality and the general unproductivity of these women. According to a 2015 UNDP report, the rate of early marriages is at the highest in central Africa with a whopping 41.5 percent, followed by West Africa with 38.4 percent, East Africa 34.7 percent, and southern Africa with 9.9 percent.[23]

There have been significant improvements in awareness of women's issues across the continent but also problems of implementation regarding legal concepts initiated by the feminist movement in these regions. In spite of these ideological advancements and awareness levels, feminism is

---

20 Stiftung, *Feminism in Africa*, 1–15.
21 Stiftung, *Feminism in Africa*, 3.
22 Stiftung, *Feminism in Africa*, 5.
23 Stiftung, *Feminism in Africa*, 5.

still being stigmatized and misinterpreted in the African continent and, unfortunately, even among Africa's literary elites.

Feminism and the Identity of African Women Writers

Skepticism toward feminism in Africa is one of the factors contributing to the challenges of the African woman writer. Feminism has for many years garnered much controversy in Africa, thereby affecting its acceptance among African women writers. According to Chielozona Eze, "for many Africans, feminism is a curse word . . . and an outright rejection of Africanness."[24] The African feminist writer has been berated for being antimale, antireligious, and un-African. She is seen as applying principles that attack the very foundations of patriarchy embedded in the values of African culture, leading to the detachment of so many African women writers even though their works express feminist ideas.

For Nkealah, the subject of feminism is treated cautiously by African women writers, such that "even the most vocal of current African women writers prefer to approach the subject of feminism with an evasiveness that bespeaks detachment."[25] Some of these writers include the pioneer woman writer Flora Nwapa, who denied her feminist identity by arguing that she was accused of being a feminist just because she wrote about women. Arndt is of the opinion that Nwapa did not want to touch feminism because she saw it as unfair prejudice toward men.[26] The latter would go on to retract her previous denial by fully adopting the feminist stance and encouraging others to do so. Zaynab Alkali equally rejects the feminist identity and views it as an "interference to women's writing."[27] Buchi Emecheta also goes through this stage of rejection, but in her case she does it more subtly by calling herself a feminist with a small "f."[28] So many factors are therefore responsible for this self-contradiction among African women writers. We can regard this as self-contradiction because to espouse the ideologies of a particular concept means that one is dedicated

---

24 Eze, "Feminist Empathy," 310–26.
25 Nkealah, "Conceptualizing," 133–41.
26 Arndt, "Perspectives," 31–44.
27 Arndt, "Perspectives," 31–44.
28 Arndt, "Perspectives," 31.

to that particular school of thought. Therefore, rejecting the label that comes with embracing the concept of feminism simply expresses an inherent fear of societal perception and a resultant backlash. So many factors, some of which will be discussed below, are responsible for the reluctance of these women writers to identify with the "feminist" tag.

The African woman writer has, over the years, experienced the problem of under-representation on the African literary scene. According to Jeanie Forte, writing, like many other human endeavors, has been dominated by men.[29] Therefore, for a long time, women's writing depended on public and male approval, which means that to identify as feminist is to fully oppose the patriarchal systems, as well as challenge the male dominance on the literary scene. In that consciousness, Yovanka Paquette Perdigao asserts that Nwapa's first novel with its antipatriarchal expression, upon publication, received brutal criticism from critics. For her, "many considered Nwapa's writing weak and the story unauthentic (Perhaps an indication of sexism in literary circles)."[30]

Religious factors have contributed to the reluctance of African women writers to embrace the feminist identity. Religion is a fundamental aspect of African society. The popular religious practices in Africa place the woman as subordinate to the man and has led women to believe that any ideology negating that is a pure rebellious act against God.[31] Susan Swart consolidates this assumption by stating that "the belief that men are superior to the woman characterises all religions in the world including, Islam, Judaism and Christianity."[32] The sacredness and unquestionable position of religion in African society makes it difficult for religious African women writers to accept the feminist label, especially given that feminists are hoping to address the marginalization of women via religious doctrines and injunctions. In African society, this feminist agenda is usually thought to be against the teachings of God. This gives credence to Nkealah's opinion that "reconstructing the mindset of a person or group is one of the most demanding of all processes of enlightenment."[33] With that in mind, African society and its perception of feminism is marked

---

29 Forte, "Realism," 115–27.
30 Perdiagao, "Flora Nwapa," 2017.
31 Obaji and Swart, "Religion," 114.
32 Swart, "Beyond the Veil."
33 Nkealah, "Conceptualizing," 135.

by the inability to see that religion is a channel through which patriarchy and oppression of women find expression.

The traditional African system assigns secondary roles to women and conditions them to consider themselves second-class citizens compared to men. This takes place via cultural practices of polygamy and the centrality of motherhood and caregiving at the expense of personal development. Other measures like genital mutilation—which restricts women's sexual experiences—the rituals women have to perform to cleanse themselves from menstrual impurity, the overemphasis on female chastity, and many other practices are cultural indicators of women's secondary place in African society.[34] However, some radical forms of feminist ideology propagate sexual freedoms for women. Feminism also offers ambition as an alternative to motherhood, and these choices are at odds with African traditional values and seen as an attempt to encourage promiscuity and disrupt normalcy in conservative African society.

The aspect of feminism that has to do with sexuality—like the lesbian feminist movement, which according to Elise Chenier is a "dominant ideology among politicised lesbians in the 1970s and 80s based on the premise that lesbianism and feminism were inextricably linked"—has also contributed to the reluctance in accepting the "feminist" label.[35] This is mainly because the issue of nonnormative sexualities has long been viewed as un-African; Daniel Hrdy states that "homosexuality is not part of the traditional societies in Africa."[36] Therefore, this subtle connection between issues of sexuality and the feminist movement is one of the main reasons feminism is perceived as un-African.

Even though most of these writers did not identify as feminists due to the factors explored above, their works contributed immensely to the cause of women's emancipation in Africa and encouraged many other women to lend their voices to issues that affect women through their works. This is exactly what Ogundipe-Leslie means when she stated that "feminists have posited that the woman writer has two major responsibilities; first to tell about being a woman; secondly, to describe reality from a woman's point of view, a woman's perspective."[37] This spearheaded the

---

34   Pui-Lan, "Mercy Amba Oduyoye," 7–22.
35   Chenier, *Lesbian*.
36   Hrdy, "Cultural Practices," 1109–19.
37   Ogundipe-Leslie, "Female," 5–13.

movement of feminism on the African literary scene and led to retractions from women writers who previously could not identify as feminists nor with the bold emergence of African feminist writers.

However, considering the peculiarities of the African continent, its cultures and realities, these feminist writers and critics have conceptualized variations on feminist concepts that aim to maintain Africa's uniqueness while distancing themselves from Western cultural ideologies that contradict the African value system. This, therefore, gives credence to Ogundipe-Leslie's statement that "African feminism is not a cry for any one kind of sexual orientation and I am not homophobic or heterosexist. Sexual practice in Africa tends to be private and considered private."[38] Ogundipe's opinion could be a denial of the realities of the African situation. However, she goes further to prove that African feminism is selective when it comes to espousal of mainstream feminism in relation to the African cultural space.

The conceptualization and ideological divorce of African feminism from mainstream Western feminism to fit the continental space has not eliminated the negativity that the feminist label attracts. However, there have been multiple efforts at theorizing African feminism, creating non-homogenous feminist models, which have further complicated the concept and broadened the discourse in literary scholarship. A look into the different feminisms in Africa will shed light on the present-day movement for the liberation of women. It will further explore the discourses and opinions surrounding the subject matter and the different identities the various forms of feminism provide to its adherents.

African Feminism(s)

African feminism is a customized form of feminist ideology that provides room for several theoretical discourses that specifically try to explore African women's experiences as distinct from mainstream Western feminism. Western-style feminism tends to generalize women's challenges and realities and does not consider the peculiarities of the African woman's past, present, and future. There are consistent areas of continuity between both ideologies and places of departure, the latter being credited to the

---

38 Ogundipe-Leslie, *Re-Creating*, 219.

different forms of socialization and experiences both groups might have undergone. African women scholars condemn Western feminism for its exclusion of men from the theoretical discourse and its categorization of African women as "women of color." For the majority of the proponents of African feminism, this implies that the theory subsumes continental African women within the racial constructs of the West, thereby applying "white privilege" and "colored otherness" to the African context where race is not centralized at the expense of African cultural specificity. The question of sexual identity, which is an intrinsic aspect of Western feminism, is carefully repressed in African feminist theories. For the African feminist, as described by Nkealah, sex and sexuality are personal, private matters in Africa.[39]

Also, African feminism is not limited to just the experiences of the women living within the continent; Ogunyemi's "Womanism" tends to include the experiences of African women also living in the diaspora.[40] This inclusion is necessary, since the many contributors to African feminist literature are often tagged as Africans in the diaspora, while the dialogues and debates take place within the continent. However, the recent theorizing by African scholars is a direct response to the exclusivity of Western feminism to the ideological needs of the continental African woman. Nkealah groups the aims of these conceptualized African feminist models into three parts. These theories aim to address feminism from (1) an African cultural perspective; (2) the African political and geographical location; and finally, (3) from an indigenous philosophical and ideological standpoint.[41] Aina is of the opinion that African feminism also shares similarities with its Western counterpart along with the ideological tug-of-war that seems to exist between the two forms.[42]

In light of this departure from mainstream feminism with the aim of addressing and validating African women's peculiarities, African feminism lacks an indigenous homogeneity. For Susan Arndt, debates on gender, sex, and the controversies of cultural imperialism have led to an understanding of the complexities inherent in feminism, thereby offsetting different perspectives for different African women scholars, hence the need

---

39 Nkealah, "(West) African Feminisms," 61–74.
40 Goredema, "African Feminism," 33–41.
41 Nkealah, "(West) African Feminisms," 62.
42 Nkealah, "(West) African Feminisms," 62.

to explore the different extant African feminisms.[43] Obioma fully consolidates the previous claims by stating the following:

> It will be more accurate to argue not in the context of a monolith (African feminism) but rather in the context of a pluralism (African feminisms) that captures the fluidity and dynamism of the different cultural imperatives, historical forces, and localized realities conditioning women's activism/movements in Africa ... the inscription of feminisms ... underscores the heterogeneity of African feminist thinking and engagement as manifested in strategies and approaches that are sometimes complementary and supportive, and sometimes competing and adversarial.[44]

African feminism's pluralism is a reflection of the many perspectives that African feminists have on the subject. Aina views African feminism as comprising the various processes of self-definition and redefinition available to African women, which view tends to resist the many misinterpretations and distortions by Western global feminism.[45] Several variants of African feminism describe the diversity and uniqueness of women of African heritage. "Womanism" is a variant of feminism that was conceptualized in the 1980s by African American Alice Walker alongside the Nigerian feminist and writer Chikwenye Ogunyemi's concept of "womanism." Ogunyemi's womanism was later modified to "African womanism," taking a more indigenous African approach against the former globalist feminist outlook.

Ogunyemi's modification is clearly a result of the distinctive atmospheres that birthed both concepts. However, Rhonda Wilbon and Gaynell Marie Simpson are of the opinion that a critical examination of both concepts will reveal a diversity as well as a commonality that binds women of African ancestry.[46] Clenora Hudson-Weems also came up with a version of Africana womanism.[47] These theories of African feminism all have to do with addressing the challenges of the African woman within or outside the continent; their aim is to inspire Black women to speak

---

43 Arndt, "Perspectives."
44 Nnaemeka, "Introduction," 5.
45 Aina, "Beyond," 66.
46 Wells-Gibon and Simpson, "Transitioning," 87–105.
47 Nkealah, "(West) African Feminisms."

up. However, this commonality does not erase the regional differences that distinguish each of these alternative concepts of feminism. The issues of race and sexuality are central to the discourse of the African American concepts but are more or less on the periphery of continental African reality. Therefore, for the purpose of exploring the identity of the African feminist writer, this study will stick to the continental African variants propounded by African women.

Aside from Ogunyemi's "African womanism," African women critics, particularly from West Africa, have developed other theoretical models of feminism including: Molara Ogundipe-Leslie's "Stiwanism" ("Stiwan" simply being the acronym for "social transformations including women in Africa"); Catherine Obianuju Acholonu's "motherism"; Obioma Nnaemeka's "Nego-feminism"; Akachi Adimora-Ezeigbo's "snail-sense feminism"[48]; and lastly, "femalism" by Chioma Opara.[49]

These concepts are products of the differing perspectives of West African literary scholars and critics regarding global feminism and the African necessity. These scholars are primarily Nigerians. However, the scope of their feminist discourse is not restricted to the Nigerian cultural space; it draws deeply from a wealth of Africa's cultural philosophy and literature to create fitting concepts that will adequately respond to African women's challenges. However, just like every other theory in history, these African feminist models are not entirely without flaws.

Ogunyemi's African womanism "believes in the freedom and independence of women like feminism, but unlike mainstream feminism, it advocates for a meaningful relationship between men and women and would wait patiently for men to change their sexist stance."[50] Mary Kolawole defines African feminism as "the totality of feminine self-expression, self-retrieval and self-assertion in positive cultural ways."[51] As a fitting African feminist theory, it aims at eliminating patriarchal systems and the marginalization of women by looking inward. Kolawole's definition goes further to validate Frank's assertion that feminism as a concept is individualistic and opposed the communalistic lifestyle of the African people.[52]

---

48 Arndt, "Perspectives."
49 Nkealah, "(West) African Feminisms."
50 Hadjitheodorou, "Women Speak," 13.
51 Kolawole, *Womanism*, 24.
52 Frank, "Feminist," 34–48.

Specifically, Ogunyemi's version of feminism seeks a peaceful and meaningful coexistence between men and women, but its reference to the attitude of "waiting" implies that African women will expect the men and patriarchal system as a whole to decide to liberate women. Therefore, for the African woman to get the change she seeks requires a challenge to the traditional systems fueling the patriarchy in African society.

"Stiwanism" is regarded by Ogundipe-Leslie as "feminism in the African context."[53] In other words, it is feminism solely propounded for the continental African woman with little or no regard for the African woman in the diaspora. Its primary ideology is based on bringing about the social transformations of the continental African woman with the inclusion of men. It also has to do with eliminating gender injustice and bringing about social transformations. It strives for the inclusion of women in the agenda for global social transformation while encouraging equal partnership with men in the fight against injustice against women. "Stiwanism" hopes to build a harmonious African society, and unlike "womanism," it solely addresses continental women issues.

Catherine Obianuju Acholonu's "motherism," on the other hand, has its theoretical basis in the concept of motherhood in Africa. This implies that it views motherhood as an appropriate framework for understanding the experiences of African women. The theory distances itself from the view of motherhood as put forth by the Western theoretical feminist framework, noting that the African woman cannot be divorced from the concept of motherhood. It also embarks on a cultural and psychological comparison of the changes that occurred in Africa as a result of Africa's contact with Western culture.[54] Acholonu strongly believes that it is the African woman's responsibility to nurture society: she romanticizes the position of the rural African woman by describing her as the life source of society; therefore, she holds the physical and spiritual position of nurturer and provider. However, the theory alienates the urban African woman from the role of social and economic development.[55] The theory, in harmony with "Stiwanism," seeks the collective responsibility of both men and women in the reorientation of society and women.

---

53 Ogundipe-Leslie, *Re-Creating*.
54 Alkali et al., "Dwelling," 237–53.
55 Acholonu, *Motherism*.

Nego-feminism, as first put forth by Obioma Nnaemeka, is another African version of feminist theory but with a more globalized outlook that underscores the idea of negotiation between every individual irrespective of class, race, gender, and status. The theory is based on the idea of peace and tolerance in society. The theory draws deeply from the indigenous African principles of peace and negotiation, which are expressed through the proverbs explored in her text. The proverbs enunciate the ancient African predilection for balance and the give-and-take principle. Nnaemeka affirms that

> Nego-feminism is the feminism of negotiation; second, nego-feminism stands for "no ego" feminism. In the foundation of shared values in many African cultures are the principles of negotiation, give and take, compromise, and balance. Here, negotiation has the double meaning of "give and take/exchange" and "cope with successfully/go around." African feminism (or feminism as I have seen it practiced in Africa) challenges through negotiations and compromise. It knows when, where, and how to detonate patriarchal land mines; it also knows when, where, and how to go around patriarchal land mines. In other words, it knows when, where, and how to negotiate with or negotiate around patriarchy in different contexts.[56]

The theory, based in African culture, presents its faith in cultural philosophy to produce an appropriate feminist model that will advance the cause of women and society in general. Describing nego-feminism as a "no ego" feminism is Nnaemeka's way of insinuating that the global feminist movement is ego-based, especially given the fact that the popular belief is that it is an antimale movement. In other words, for a certain group of people to believe that they can efficiently exist without the other is proof of egocentrism, which nego-feminism detests.

Akachi Adimora Ezeigbo's "snail-sense feminism" and Nnaemeka's "nego-feminism" share similar ideas about the inclusion of men, complementarity, and collaboration in the quest for social development. Nkealah is of the opinion that the theory was specifically created for West African women.[57] She uses the analogy of the snail to describe the strategies of the African woman in a patriarchal society. Like the snail, the woman moves

---

56 Nnaemeka, "Negofeminism," 357–85.
57 Nkealah, "(West) African Feminisms."

around with caution, sensibility, sensitivity to danger, a tolerance for sexism, and flexibility to the demands of society. She works hand-in-hand with nonsexist men and is diplomatic in her dealings with patriarchs. The theory does not encourage violent resistance but rather a conciliatory approach to women's dealings with men. This implies a restiveness on the part of women and connotes an appeal to African women to adjust and address the operations of patriarchy in African society.

"Femalism," just like the other variants explored, is a continental African woman's theoretical framework. It centralizes the woman's body in its feminist discourse and presents the African woman as a representation of the African nation. This connection projects the female as merely symbolic without personal opinions. Propounded by Chioma Opara, she describes it as "a hue of African feminism, is a softer tone than liberal feminism and highly polarized from radical feminism."[58] These African variants of feminism have tried to explore the ideological necessities of African women, but the heterogenous nature of the African woman's reality makes them inadequate for the needs and experiences of all African women. However, they share a uniformity in their rejection of a Western-based feminism, and their principles—hinging on indigenous philosophies—show the desire of the African woman scholar to create appropriate theories that will incorporate and respond to the specific cultural needs of the African woman and create an identity that will best represent the African experience.

Classification of African Feminist Writers and Their Works

This section discusses how the versions of African feminism discussed above are depicted in the literary works of prominent African feminist writers. The element of nonhomogeneity in the versions of African feminism explored calls for a classification of African feminist writers with regard to the tenets of these alternative conceptions of feminism. So many African women writers use women as central characters and most of the time as an embodiment of the ideological agenda of their works. However, not every woman writer who writes about women can be called a feminist, let alone be classified under a specific African feminist ideology. This

---

58   Opara, "On the African Concept," 189–200.

critical exposition intends to categorize African feminist writers in light of the various feminist ideologies earlier explored. This will provide a fresh perspective on the identity of the African feminist writer.

The identity of the African feminist writer is determined by several parameters, among which is whether their work is situated at the center of the discourse. Arndt developed three major classificatory paradigms for the literary works of African feminist writers. These paradigms include: reformist, transformative, and radical African-feminist literature.[59] Using these paradigms, this exercise will also classify the works of select West African authors like Flora Nwapa's *Efuru* (1966), Buchi Emecheta's *Joys of Motherhood*, Chimamanda Adichie's *Purple Hibiscus* (2006), Mariama Ba's *So Long a Letter*, and Calixthe Beyala's *The Sun Hath Looked Upon Me* (1987), and *Your Name Shall Be Tanga* (1988).

Arndt describes these labels as the "major currents of African feminist literature."[60] "Reformist African feminist literatures" criticize institutionalized norms and social conventions that try to subjugate African women while encouraging a mutually beneficial relationship between men and women. She sketches a clearer picture with this take: "Reformist African-feminist writers want to negotiate with the patriarchal society to gain new scope for women, but accept the fundamental patriarchal orientation of their society as a given fact. In these texts, alternatives to what is criticised are always discussed. It is assumed that the society is capable of reform; in keeping with this logic, the texts usually have a conciliatory 'happy end.'"[61]

In other words, with this approach the writer's aim is to reform the ideological agencies that encourage patriarchy to thrive in the African society. This is done without necessarily antagonizing men as a group of female oppressors but rather as individuals. These works tend to proffer alternatives to the operations of existing gender inequality. They tend to expose the operations of patriarchy and emphasize how women navigate their roles in such male-dominated environments. They apportion blame to both genders and do not indict men for the imbalance in gender relations in society. Flora Nwapa's *Efuru* belongs to this category and will be extensively examined.

---

59 Arndt, "Perspectives."
60 Arndt, "Perspectives," 31.
61 Arndt, "Perspectives."

Transformative feminist literatures, on the other hand, criticize patriarchal agencies in society and also view men as responsible for the adverse effects of patriarchy. Those considered a part of the patriarchy are presented as the chief perpetrators of the crimes against women. However, these critiques of men do not fail to question the existing social structures that inhibit women while also trying to transform the society by launching a negotiation between men and women. Men in transformative feminist texts are not just regarded as perpetrators but also as "products of patriarchal patterns of thought."[62] Arndt puts it succinctly by stating the following:

> In transformative African-feminist literature, men are criticised much more sharply and more complexly than in reformist literature. Though, as a rule, the demands which are directed at men are more fundamental and extensive than those made in reformist literature, transformative texts start off by assuming men's capability to transform. However, to a much lesser extent than in reformist literature is this capability suggested by having a man change his way of thinking and behaviour radically in the course of the plot. Much more often it is symbolised by the fact that the man, who embodies the behaviour to be criticised and overcome, is contrasted with one or more positive counterparts.[63]

These transformative feminist texts, as further described by Arndt, also present contrasting male characters to the ones criticized. These characters are often too idealistic, in contrast with the current realities of the African society. The transformative ideology addresses the place of women as contributors to the operations of patriarchy while also considering them as transformable.[64]

The reformist and transformative currents of African feminist literature still create a space for men within their fight for equality. Both currents believe men to be capable of reform and transformation respectively. On the other hand, radical African feminist texts consider men an irredeemable lot who do nothing but perpetuate sexism, immorality, uncivility, violence, and other vices. Arndt expands this notion by stating that "men

---

62 Arndt, "Perspectives," 34.
63 Arndt, "Perspectives," 34.
64 Arndt, "Perspectives," 34.

characters are, 'by nature' or because of their socialisation, hopelessly sexist and usually deeply immoral. Men characters who depart from this pattern are rarely found—and those who do are powerless. This powerlessness is symbolised either by their premature death or by their inability to realise their positive ambitions."[65] These texts also encourage sisterhood between the characters in the texts and imply that a closer bond between women is the only source of hope.

Flora Nwapa's *Efuru*, published in 1966, is considered to be among the first books to set the tone for the women's literary revolution in the African continent.[66] *Efuru*, according to Yovanka Paquete's review, is said to have defied the "traditional portrayal of women as passive."[67] Nwapa had initially put out a claim saying that just because she wrote about women did not mean that she was a feminist. Even though the writer did not associate with the label of "feminist" because it contradicted the principles of the African culture and appeared to be anti-male, it does not eliminate the fact that her work embodies the tenets of the reformist feminist musings explored in Arndt's publication and Nnaemeka's nego-feminism.

Nnaemeka asserts that in Nwapa's speech at a conference in Nigeria, she retracts her statement against feminism by stating that

> years back, when I go on my tours to America and Europe, I'm usually asked, Are you a feminist? I deny that I am a feminist. . . . But they say, all your works, everything is about feminism. And I say, No, I am not a feminist. Buchi Emecheta is another one that said: I'm a feminist with a small f (whatever Buchi means). Having heard Obioma on Monday, having heard Ama [Ata Aidoo] today, I think that I will go out and say that I am a feminist with a big f because Obioma said on Monday that feminism is about possibilities; there are possibilities, there are choices. Let us not be afraid to say that we are feminists . . . Globally, we need one another.[68]

The reformist feminist writer, as described by Arndt, presents characters that tolerate the patriarchy and try to negotiate with the patriarchal

---

65 Arndt, "Perspectives," 34.
66 Nadaswaran, "Legacy," 146–50.
67 Perdiagao, "Flora Nwapa," 1.
68 Nnaemeka, "Feminism," 80–113.

systems in their immediate environment.[69] Nwapa's Efuru embodies this major feature of reformist feminism. In the text, Efuru is presented as smart, kind, and financially independent, which is the ideological agenda of most feminist writers: to encourage the growth and independence of women in African societies. In the text, Efuru elopes with Adizua, the man she loves, even without him paying her bride price. She does not settle for an arranged marriage but insists on marrying for love. However, as the plot progresses, Efuru insists that Adizua pays her bride price; with this, she navigates her environment by negotiating with the cultural agencies of the patriarchy. In choosing the conditions of her marriage, she does not disregard the place of the bride price and does not see it as a way of commodifying the woman like the mainstream feminist ideals warn against.

Efuru understands how the patriarchy operates, and her approach to bringing change is not rebellious. She does not fight the system but rather finds a way around it. Eventually, when her second husband Gilbert decides to take another wife because of Efuru's inability to bear children, she does not rebel against him but accepts his decision with the understanding that he needs a child, and it was only customary for him to do so. For her, "Only a bad woman would like to be married alone to her husband."[70] She tries to change the worldview of women through her successes in business and her devotion to other people's needs and those of society.

In Adichie's *Purple Hibiscus*, the tolerance for the patriarchy is evident through the lifestyle of the protagonist Kambili and her mother Beatrice. Kambili is portrayed as reticent, a quality that can be attributed to her father's domination and tyranny over his family. At most she is submissive to her father's cruelty and does not think that there is another way to deal with her father except to obey him. Her conditioning in the family and what she had grown to observe has made her the shy and timid character the reader meets. Her inability to resist the cruel operation of patriarchy in her home is courtesy of her mother's equal negligence and inability to fight. As a reformist text, the writer paints a vivid albeit harsh portrait of domestic violence in the nuclear family where the man is the breadwinner and therefore the head of the family. The writer does not

---

69 Arndt, "Perspectives."
70 Nwapa, *Efuru*, 57.

condemn the position of the man but rather condemns how he wields his position as a weapon of human subjugation.

However, as a reformist text, the men in Adichie's *Purple Hibiscus* and Nwapa's *Efuru* are not criticized as a group but rather as individuals with tendencies toward fallibility. Even though Efuru's husbands abandon her due to childlessness, which is mostly as a result of an existing system that offers men freedom to have many partners and yet prohibits the woman from having such choice, Nwapa uses Efuru's relationship with other men in the text to express that the shortcomings of one or two men do not automatically translate to a collective cruelty in all men. This is exemplified using Nwashike Ogene—Efuru's father—who is presented as caring and genuinely concerned about his daughter's welfare. Furthermore, Dr. Uzaru is a male medical doctor from Onitsha in the text who is portrayed as competent and caring.

Many of the other male characters in *Purple Hibiscus* are presented as decent and even victims of the system. Jaja, who is Kambili's brother, also experiences his own fair share of physical abuse from his father. He doesn't follow in his father's footsteps but rather decides to protect his family after his father's death. This he does by taking the blame for his father's murder to protect his mother, who had dropped daily doses of poison in his tea until the day he died. Father Amadi is also a male Catholic priest who is not considered just another evil man but is rather an individual with genuine love and respect for humans. Pa Nnukwu, who is their grandfather, is also portrayed as kind and decent. Abandoned by his son and deprived of the privilege of getting to know his grandchildren, he genuinely prays for the peace and prosperity of his son. Therefore, as a reformist feminist text, *Purple Hibiscus* aims at portraying a patriarchal society that produces both vicious and decent men in society, giving credence to Arndt's idea that contrasting male characters "tend to be capable of rethinking and overcoming their reprehensible behavior."[71] Using the text as an agent for reform, Adichie calls for the inclusion of men in the fight against female oppression.

Also, like most feminist texts,[72] Flora Nwapa's *Efuru* promotes the ideology of sisterhood as a place of succor and hope. This is portrayed through the friendship and loyalty between the protagonist Efuru and her

---

71   Arndt, "Perspectives," 33.
72   See feminist texts like: Adichie, *Purple Hibiscus*; Sefi Atta, *Everything*.

mother-in-law's elder sister Ajanupu, whom she runs to for help in troubling times. The text also provides an antiradical account of women's relationships in African society by presenting women as accomplices to the adverse effects of patriarchy, using the character of Nkoyeni who happens to be Efuru's rival and antagonist. Furthermore, the relationship between Beatrice and Ifeoma in *Purple Hibiscus* is Adichie's way of encouraging friendships and sisterhood between women in African society.

Efuru respects the provisions of culture; in fact, her only attempt at deviance is eloping with Adizua. She agrees to the act of circumcision, seeing it as a cultural necessity and not an attempt to repress her sexuality. That act notwithstanding, she leaves her marriage because of her husband's adultery. She also refuses to farm with her husband but makes her own choice: "I am not cut out for farm work I'm going to trade."[73] The image of a woman presented here is one who understands her position in society and is a hard worker and not dependent on men for survival. This bears a similarity to the character of Ifeoma in Adichie's *Purple Hibiscus*. Gloria Fwangyil describes her as "bold, hardworking, economically independent, strong and assertive."[74] This definition is most accurate given that she is singlehandedly raising her children after the death of her husband and does not bend to her brother's conditions for offering help. She steps in to bury her father when her brother refuses to bury a "heathen," and she never gives in to the threats of her in-laws.

Using this text, Adichie might be categorized as a feminist writer who belongs to the adherents of Ogundipe-Leslie's "Stiwanism" offshoot of feminist thought. She calls for the social transformation of women in Africa by encouraging financial independence and boldness. The fact that Beatrice has no other place to go leads to her continued stay in the marriage and her eventual involvement in the murder of her husband. Independence for women means having the ability to exit an abusive marriage, which in turn reduces the criminal act of murder from either the abuser or the abused.

Also, in Nwapa's *Efuru*, motherism is mildly introduced when Efuru questions the essence of womanhood without children by interrogating the place of the woman-deity, Uhamiri. In her words, "She is happy, she was wealthy, she was beautiful. She gave women, beauty and wealth but

---

73 Nwapa, *Efuru*, 32.
74 Fwangyil, "A Reformist-Feminist," 261–67.

she had no child. She had never experienced the joy of motherhood. why then did women worship her?"[75] Nwapa might be accused of using the deity as a symbol of womanhood, one that does not hinge on the definition of motherhood. Efuru does not see her happiness as dependent on a man, hence her acceptance to abandon the quest for marriage and serve the sea goddess. Ossai, Efuru's mother in-law, also confirms this notion when she says, "Efuru's patience couldn't be tried . . . life for her meant living it fully, she did not want to merely exist, she wanted to live and use the world to her advantage."[76]

From this text, one can easily categorize Nwapa as a nego-feminist through her presentation of the ideals of patience, negotiation, and tolerance, given that the character is expected to adhere to the set rules put in place by the patriarchy, while reforming the society she lives in. Using her text, Nwapa encourages the African woman to employ negotiation, to lay aside her ego and fight within the confines of societal structures. She also endorses an involvement in the cultures and traditions of a society. Also, she advocates for women's independence by creating a financially independent character who lends money to men and whose happiness is not defined by the presence of men in her life. Her reference to a female deity whom the major character ends up serving implies that women are made for bigger tasks than just birthing children, and in her words "there are possibilities, there are choices. Let us not be afraid to say that we are feminists. . . ."[77]

Buchi Emecheta's *Joys of Motherhood* and Mariama Ba's *So Long a Letter* presents aspects of transformative feminism. Transformative feminism views men as a social group, while their demonstration of patriarchal behavior is "criticized more sharply."[78] This form of feminist criticism is more aggressive than the reformist approach but not as aggressive as radical African feminism. These two works deal with the adverse effects of patriarchy in examining the life of a woman in a society rife with dominant patriarchal structures. The central characters of the texts, Nnuego and Ramatoulaye, suffer at the hands of men through their tumultuous marriages. By exposing the challenges experienced by both women in

---

75 Nwapa, *Efuru*, 441.
76 Nwapa, *Efuru*, 78.
77 Arndt, "Perspectives," 31.
78 Arndt, "Perspectives," 33.

their respective texts, Emecheta and Ba examine the sociocultural experiences of African woman. Their works criticize the patriarchal systems put in place by religion and culture to successfully dominate female expression in society.

In Emecheta's *Joys of Motherhood*, the idea of phallic superiority is explored. Nnuego's first husband Amatokwu physically assaults her, disregards her, and then reduces her to the position of a servant. Her husband then goes on to blame her for their inability to have a child. In the excerpt below, Amatokwu sees his semen as precious male seeds unworthy of waste and would go further to brandish his maleness by picking a new wife to have the sons that Nnuego is unable to provide:

> I am a busy man; I have no time to waste my precious seed on a woman who is infertile. I have to raise children for my line. If you really want to know, you do not appeal to me anymore. You are so dry and jumpy. When a man comes to a woman he wants to be cooled, not scratched by a nervy female who is all bones . . . but now if you cannot produce sons, at least, you can help harvest yams.[79]

Ramatoulaye in Ba's *So Long a Letter* experiences the harsh psychological effects of polygamy. Her husband Modou Fall abandons her after thirty years to marry her daughter's friend. In this text, Modou Fall represents a segment of the male social group who are willing participants in the oppression and subjugation of women. Ba, in *So Long a Letter,* writes:

> The mirasse commanded by the Koran requires that a dead person be stripped of his most intimate secrets; thus is exposed to others what was carefully concealed. These exposures crudely explain a man's life. With consternation, I measure the extent of Modou's betrayal. His abandonment of his first family (myself and my children) was the outcome of the choice of a new wife. He rejected us. He mapped out his future without taking our existence into account.[80]

The position of polygamy and the trauma it presents is carefully examined as an instrument of women's oppression and male hegemony in both texts. Polygamy, as defined by Koktevd Gaard, is a nonmonogamous

---

79   Emecheta, *Joys*, 32.
80   Ba, *So Long a Letter*, 9.

marriage; in other words, it includes more than one partner.[81] However, polygamy manifests itself in two different forms, according to Obonye Jonas: "polyandry" refers to an arrangement where a woman is married to more than one husband; while in a polygamous arrangement a man has more than one wife.[82] Anderson affirms that polygamy is more prevalent in West African nations.[83] Diverse factors are considered to be responsible for the prominence of polygamy in Africa. In some parts of the continent, polygamy can be a social, economic, and religious choice. So many women in polygamous marriages have different experiences that are largely framed by allowances made in the particular society.

Ogundipe-Leslie identifies structures like "polygamy, gender asymmetry, religion and patriarchy"[84] as the foundations for the subjugation of women in society. According to Boserup, polygamy in Africa, which includes Nigeria and Senegal (where both narratives are set), is an age-old practice that has coexisted with the ancient system of agriculture where women are married into farm work. She is equally of the opinion that these women often have no right to property and are mostly treated like property themselves; they are usually given in exchange for material goods and used as cheap labor to expand their husband's wealth.[85]

The subordination of women to men cannot be overemphasized in both texts. Therefore, Emecheta and Ba both expose the hegemonic influences of patriarchy and its operation in African society. Emecheta's Nnuego is twice introduced to polygamy where she questions the essence of being childless, leading to her exit from her first marriage and her attempted suicide after the death of her first child in her second marriage. She is unable to divorce womanhood from motherhood; for her, a woman is not whole without the presence of children, particularly sons for her husband. In the text, the place of a female child is traditionally secondary to a male child. However, Ba's *So Long a Letter* contradicts Nnuego's belief that the true essence of womanhood and possibly marital security emanates from birthing many children. This is seen in the writer's portrayal of

---

81 Gaard, *Polygamy*.
82 Obonye, "Practice," 142–49.
83 Anderson, "Perspectives," 99.
84 Ogundipe-Leslie, "African Literature," 307–22.
85 Boserup, *Women's Role*.

the character of Ramatoulaye, who is abandoned by her husband of thirty years after the birth of twelve children.

Men in these texts are just products of the existing patriarchal system that permits the ownership of more than one wife. In other words, these men have been socially acculturated to see polygamy as the norm and therefore keep reproducing and fostering the practice of polygamy. These men are accomplices and enforcers of these horrible injunctions of patriarchy and are, therefore, seen as a social group of people existing to subdue women. They are portrayed as selfish and without respect for the place of women in society. In Ba's *So Long a Letter*, the characters of Mwado and Modou Fall fit into the category of men who are intent on subjugating their wives by bringing in a younger wife, while waving around their masculinity and leaning on religious injunctions for defense. In Emecheta's *Joys of Motherhood*, the character Amatokwu and even Obi Umunna—Nnuego's grandfather who is bent on having a son, even it means denying his daughter the opportunity to marry—equally represents the social group of men who use women as sources of self-aggrandizement.

That scenario notwithstanding, in transformative feminist texts, a balanced view of society is presented. Women are portrayed as reproducing gender relationships that also discriminate against women.[86] In this case, Emecheta's character Adaku Nnuego's eventual cowife proffers a new perspective from which to view Nnuego. In the text, Nnuego exhibits jealousy toward Adaku, which further contributes to the former's oppression in her marriage to Nnaife. She refuses to consider Adaku an ally in the fight against male oppression but rather as an opponent in a fight for male attention, thereby enforcing male superiority and further enslaving both of them.

> To Nnuego's eyes, Adaku was enviably attractive, young looking and comfortably plump with the kind of roundness that really suited a woman. The woman radiated peace and satisfaction . . . Nnu ego felt that she could be bowing to this perfect creature—she who had once been acclaimed the most beautiful woman ever since . . . jealously, fear and anger Nnu Ego in turns. She hated this type of woman, who would flatter a man, depend on him. . . . Now there was a threat.[87]

---

86 Arndt, "Perspectives."
87 Emecheta, *Joys*, 118.

However, in the case of Ramatoulaye, Binetou's mother, the "lady in-law" who supports her young daughter's marriage to Modou at the expense of Ramatoulaye and her children facilitates the thriving of the patriarchy and encourages discrimination against women.

These texts also proffer a contrast between the behaviors that encourage the oppressive mechanisms of patriarchy and those actions that frustrate these oppressive measures.[88] This exposition places the characters of Nnuego/Ramatoulaye and Adaku/Aissatou/Ona as contrasting personalities that expose the psychological effects of patriarchy against the resilience that transformative feminism endorses. Nnuego's irrational desire for children is self-destructive behavior, criticized by Emecheta as a desire that places the woman at the mercy of patriarchal ideologies that only recognize a woman's identity as it relates to motherhood. Throughout the text, Nnuego is seen searching endlessly for a child—she buys into the belief that a woman without a child for her husband has failed. Therefore, when the protagonist bears these children, she devotes her entire life to their service. With this notion, Nnuego sacrifices any ambition to be financially successful because it will impede her ultimate role as a mother: "She had reminded herself of the old saying that money and children don't go together. If you spend all your time making money and getting rich, the gods wouldn't give you children; if you wanted children, you had to forget money and be content to be poor."[89]

This mindset, however, places Nnuego outside the ideology of transformative feminists. With that hindsight, Emecheta tries to draw African women's attention to these ideologies that tend to suppress the expression of a woman's abilities and impede her psychological and financial independence. However, Adaku's industriousness and financial independence serve as a suitable contrast to the previous ideology that Nnuego buys into. Both women can be viewed as "two personalities that exist on opposite poles."[90] Adaku can be viewed as a woman who wears the sociological effects of the urban and rural environments admirably. Although she is from the same rural environment as Nnuego, Adaku adapts quickly to the demands of Lagos and soon becomes financially independent, while Nnuego is held back by the traditional ideals of subservience,

---

88   Arndt, "Perspectives."
89   Emecheta, *Joys*, 80.
90   Holmes, "Limited Woman," 38.

motherhood, and dependence. In the text, both women's reactions to changes in environment are reflected from Nnuego's musings:

> This woman knows a thing or two, she thought. So independent in her way of thinking. Was it because Adaku came from a low family where people were not tied to pleasing the rest of their members, as she Nnu Ego had to please her titled father Agbadi all the time? She sighed and remarked aloud, "you are right. The trouble with me is that I find it difficult to change."[91]

This excerpt subtly insinuates the role of Nnuego's upbringing in her lack of survival skills in the Lagos metropolis, and the author obviously advocates for flexibility and resilience for women's liberation in the text. Using the character of Ona, Nnuego's mother, Emecheta creates a character that neither desires to please society nor keen on becoming any man's wife. She accepts the position of a "male-woman" and takes her pick among the men. She is a person more interested in living a life not dictated by others. Before her death, she instructs Nnuego's father to give their daughter an opportunity to make her lot in life: "See that however much you love our daughter Nnuego you allow her to have a life of her own, a husband if she wants one. Allow her to be a woman."[92]

From the excerpt, it is clear that Ona does not equate womanhood and motherhood but rather exhibits an individuality that the author hopes African women will emulate. Therefore, the eventual death of the protagonist on the roadside without the children or husband beside her (after years of hard work nurturing them) implies that contrary to popular traditional belief, motherhood does not culminate in success, happiness, and self-fulfillment. With this, Emecheta intends to transform this misguided perception of women in hopes that they will invest in themselves as individuals.

Ramatoulaye, on the other hand, is as dutiful as Nnuego; she is subservient to and tolerant of her burdensome sisters-in-law, as opposed to Aissatou who is portrayed as more assertive. Aissatou is conscious of her perception of self, hence she leads her life with individual pride by clearly rejecting and fighting oppressive measures put in place by society to subjugate women. In light of this notion, Aissatou disassociates herself from

---

91   Emecheta, *Joys*, 127.
92   Emecheta, *Joys*, 28.

in-laws who are traditionally permitted to dominate her matrimonial home. This is quite unlike Ramatoulaye, who endures and encourages this behavior. Aissatou eventually takes a radical decision of divorcing her husband, on account of his polygamy, and raising her four children by herself in the United States. She urges her friend Ramatoulaye to do the same and goes as far as getting her a car to allow her more mobility. On the other hand, Ramatoulaye does not consider divorce an option but continues to languish in a polygamous marriage where she and her children are deserted by her husband:

> I tolerated his sister, who too often would desert their own homes to encumber my own. They allowed themselves to be fed and petted. They would look on without reacting as their children romped around on my chairs. . . . His mother would stop by again and again while on her outings, always flanked by different friends, just to show off her son's social success . . . I would receive her with all the respect due to a queen . . . you Aissatou, you forsook your family-in-law, tightly shut in with their hurt dignity.[93]

Ba's opinion on polygamy is made clear in her text. She explores the negative effects of polygamy and its effects on women and children, which eventually affects the society at large. She encourages fruitful female relationships like the one that exists between Aissatou and Ramatoulaye in the text. While implying the place of sisterhood in alleviating the struggles and pains of patriarchy, both texts primarily aim at "transforming and advancing the female character towards organization and personhood."[94] Emecheta believes that women constitute a greater portion of the oppressed in society; they are mostly underprivileged and victims of all the worst effects of patriarchy. Therefore, she assumes the responsibility of championing the cause of women in African society.[95] Ba subtly changes the narrative of women as underprivileged and helpless using the character of Aissatou, who rejects the cruel polygamous scenario and finds success working in the Senegalese embassy in the United States.

Interestingly, Emecheta identifies as a womanist. Nadaswaran affirms this claim by noting that "Buchi Emecheta states that her

---

93   Ba, *So Long*, 19–20.
94   Nadaswaran, "Legacy," 146.
95   Mohammed, "Maternal Oppression," 462–70.

kind of women's liberation is an African sort of women's rights called womanism."[96] Ogunyemi's African womanism deals with African peculiarities and the play of patriarchy in the metamorphosis of a woman and her arrival at a sense of self and womanhood and how these peculiar experiences are grounded in African society and culture. Mariama Ba might equally be categorized as a womanist, due to her portrayal of characters who reach an understanding of selfhood while using the context of African society to explain how patriarchy works in her home country of Senegal.

Emecheta basically shied away from mainstream feminism to identify with a specifically African feminism mostly because she believed it was an antimale movement. However, her womanist ideologies, which are based on the collective responsibility of both men and women to bring about change in the society, find expression in *Joys of Motherhood* through the male characters like Agbadi Nnuego's father, who is willing to stand by her daughter in any decision she makes to boycott the society's construct of marriage. "Don't worry daughter, if you find life unbearable, you can always come here to live."[97] The text also addresses specific African female experiences by exploring their life in rural and urban areas of Africa, which is basically the intention of womanism.

Cameroonian author Calixthe Beyala's *The Sun Hath Looked upon Me* (1987) was originally written in French as *C'est le Soleil qui m'a Brule* and translated to English by Marjolijn de Jager. The text has been described by Ogunyemi as "lunatic writing."[98] This alludes more to the form than the content. It takes a radical African feminist approach to explore the horrors of an African woman in a "greasy, dirty, neglected, sloppy shantytown . . . the fronts of the houses resemble wrinkled old ladies and the old ladies look like old, rusty tin cans, all of them gnawed at by life, mummified in their endless wait for life."[99]

The text chronicles the experiences of Ateba Leocadie who lives in a squalid neighborhood where women commodify themselves as a source of livelihood. Ateba's mother, who abandoned her as a child, as well as her aunt and grandmother, were well-known prostitutes. Beyala creates an air

---

96 Nadaswaran, "Legacy," 146.
97 Emecheta, *Joys*, 11.
98 Arndt, "African Gender," 709–26.
99 Beyala, *Sun*, 2.

of hopelessness surrounding Ateba, who has known nothing but squalor and poverty. Ateba comes to an awareness of her femininity and its implications in the world they live in. She has no other choice but to toe the same line as her ancestors. Jean Zepp is a stereotypical representation of the radical African feminist writer's conception of men as hopelessly sexist and immoral. In several instances, Zepp is seen engaging in battery and sexual abuse. Zepp does not hold the town's women in very high regard but rather sees himself as superior to women by virtue of his phallus and physical strength.

Phallic superiority, as earlier explored, plays out in this text as well. Zepp weaponizes his male genitalia for the violent domination of women. His penis becomes to him a tool of dominance. In one of the many instances, he is seen sexually abusing Ateba as a form of punishment for walking into his room: "He grabs her by her hair. He forces her down low, forces her to crouch with her head into his manly smells, her mouth against his penis."[100] In this scenario, the character brandishes his superior strength with the sole aim of humiliating and validating his misguided conception of superiority and in his own defense says: "Since time again, woman has prostrated herself before man. It's no accident that God created her from the rib of man"[101] and that "God has sculptured woman on her knee at the feet of man."[102]

The portrayal of all the men in the text is mostly similar to that of Zepp. With the same twisted sense of superiority, a policeman overpowers Ateba during a raid of their shanty and forces her to an abandoned area where he rapes her. Ateba has many such horrid experiences. The sexual depravity seen in this text through the vivid portrayal of incessant rape cases as well as the brutality of the men are the writer's attempts at condemning patriarchy in Africa.

Beyala's texts are largely eccentric, and her portrayal of male characters is unrelentingly critical, as they are portrayed as violent perpetrators of sexual abuse and pedophilia. The males as described by Wunmi Olayinka have "over-bloated egos" and would do anything to resist any challenge to their authority by the women they consider inconsequential,[103] hence

---

100 Beyala, *Sun*, 24.
101 Beyala, *Sun*, 84.
102 Beyala, *Sun*, 118.
103 Olayinka, "Oppressor."

their use of sociocultural agency aimed at shackling women through motherhood and marriage. She also uses her language and style to accentuate the hopelessness of women in societies dominated by men like Jean Zepp. The text focuses on these horrible experiences with vivid imagery, exposing an intense cruelty and morbidity in society. Olayinka corroborates this assumption in the following: "In Beyala's feminist quest, the affective and physical decline of children, women and men sentenced to a miserable ghetto life imprisoned by customary laws and their impediments are themes that fill in her works and are worthy of sympathy.... Men equally need some positive intervention given the scenes of incessant rape and social injustice meted out to women and children by men."[104]

Just like every other feminist-centered work, Ateba eventually seeks the end of male oppression, which she considers the reason for women's suffering—an epiphany she comes to after her friend dies from a crude abortion. It is therefore clear that in this radical African-feminist text, men are indeed not portrayed as friends let alone allies in the struggle for the elimination of patriarchy.

Most of the other tenets of radical African feminist thought play out in Beyala's *Tu t'appelleras Tanga*. The protagonist Tanga is forced into prostitution by her parents; she is also impregnated by her father, who is supposed to be an ally. However, Tanga hopes to eventually find love in the arms of a man and escape the cruelty she has grown used to. Tanga's hopes are continually dashed by the men she meets, all of whom are cruel and incapable of love. She is constantly raped and beaten, while all the men exhibit the same pattern of male domination except Mala, who is disabled and soon dies. Tanga joins a gang of petty thieves after the death of Mala in hopes of eliminating the effects of poverty, but she is caught and dies in prison.

The text ends on a note of pessimism on the plight of women in a patriarchal society. It also explores the impact of poverty and prostitution on the most destitute women in Africa. Beyala touches on pedophilia and many other debased atrocities as the implications of a male-dominated society. Her critical attitude toward the patriarchy as expressed through her works ostensibly explores the horrors women face without the advantage of wealth and privilege. Through these provocative contents,

---

104 Olayinka, "Oppressor," 151.

she draws the attention of society to the experiences of underprivileged African women at the hands of vicious men.

According to Arndt, Beyala describes her "critical examination of gender relations as feminitude, an allusion to Negritude."[105] However, the exposition of the interplay of gender in society with the aim of securing freedom for the oppressed gender is most likely the fundamental duty of the feminist writer. Therefore, this work will distinguish Beyala as a feminist writer of African origin who examine the adverse impact of the patriarchy through a distinctly African lens. However, using the parameters provided by Sarah Arndt, the works of Calixthe Beyala would easily qualify as radical. However, she does not qualify as radical within the bounds of African feminism examined earlier in this chapter, mainly because her work could easily be judged as antimale. Her work also sees the woman's plight as hopeless and clearly does not advocate for a dialogue between both sexes.

African Feminist Writers as Bridges

Understanding the literal meaning of the word "bridge" is the first step toward identifying its role in African feminist writing, as well as its presence in the above subheading. A bridge has been defined by *Merriam Webster* dictionary as "a time, place or means of connection or transition." Therefore, in the context of this critical appraisal, the African feminist writer will first be analyzed as a link between the African cultural philosophies and mandates that give the African woman agency and the modern writing culture. In other words, this section will identify the African feminist writer as self-reflexively feminist in African cultural practices.

Several scholarly works on the African woman and feminism have their focus on African traditional practices that oppress women. Such examples, as cited by Adebiyi-Adelabu Kazeem, include Chioma Opara, Taiwo Oladele, Chikwenye Ogunyemi, and many others.[106] These works carry an extensive analysis of issues related to women's oppression by African cultural practices. However, that does not mean all African cultural practices are oppressive to women; some of the African oral traditions, politics,

---

105 Arndt, "Perspectives," 40.
106 Adebiyi-Adelabu, "From Subversive," 48–62.

and creative expressions have been known to give the African woman agency. The advent of written culture and modernization in Africa has placed the African feminist writer as an embodiment of these practices that promote women's self-sufficiency. In other words, the African feminist writer is herself reflexive of such favorable cultural practices. Through her written works, the African feminist writer helps to channel these agencies.

The African feminist writers discussed here champion the responsibility of educating and acquainting readers with certain ideological and physical realities of African society. She is a compendium of knowledge regarding sociological issues that affect women's lives. Through her documentation of knowledge, she occupies the position of the modern-day griot whose duty it is to possess and transmit a compact knowledge of her past and present cultural, historical, and religious realities. Therefore, she serves as the middle ground between the African woman of the past who was actively involved in the activities of her oral tradition and the modern African feminist who continues these responsibilities in the modern form of writing. According to Nnaemeka, "Studies of the content and form of African oral tradition reveal the centrality of women as subjects."[107] It speaks to the visibility and active participation of women in ancient African communities and the woman's position in the imparting of knowledge, cultural values, and morals in the society as well as her role in the transmission of oral literature. Nnaemeka further surmises her invaluable position by stating the following: "In African oral tradition, women were very visible not only as performers but as producers of knowledge, especially in view of oral literature's didactic relevance, moral(izing) imperatives and pedagogical foundations. Researchers in the field of African oral tradition have documented the active participation of women, at professional and nonprofessional levels, in the crafting, preservation, and transmission of most forms of oral literature."[108]

From the excerpt above, the traditional African woman is regarded as a producer of knowledge, and just like the modern-day African feminist writer, she conceptualized ideologies based on her cultural philosophies and applied it in her teaching. The modern-day African feminist writer

---

107 Nnaemeka, *From Orality*, 138.
108 Nnaemeka, *From Orality*, 138.

uses her capacity as a writer to affect standing societal ideologies and actions that undermine the woman's position in society.

In oral African literature, the African woman played (and still plays) a principal role in the art of storytelling. Nnaemeka also documents that women played vital roles in oral poetry performances. She cites the example of the *oriki*, the panegyric poetry among the Yoruba in western Nigeria and the imaginative stories of Aoua Keita, a woman from Bamana-bom of French Equatorial Africa who led the movement for independence.[109] Ruth Finnegan, in her studies on the Impango and Akan dirges of southern Ghana, asserts that all the women of Akan were traditionally competent in the performance of the dirge.[110] This agency can be seen in the modern-day African feminist writer, who is effectively responsible for the imaginative work of modern poetry, prose, and drama. Through these creative works, the African feminist writer merges the creative heritage of her cultural ancestors with the stylistic formats of modern-day literature, as well as the relevant themes of her time to sensitize the public on issues that affect women and society.

Wendpanga Eric Segueda records a number of women in times past involved in physical fights and wars for the protection and preservation of their homes, kingdoms, and cultural heritage. According to him, these women include:

> Llinga who fought the Portuguese in 1640 in Congo. Nehanda led the MaShona nation of Zimbabwe between 1862 and 1898. Taytu Betul (1850-1918) was an Ethiopian Empress who reigned and personally led troops to establish the modern capital of Addis Ababa. Yaa Asantewaa (1850-1921), Ghana Queen, led her army in continuous battles against the British until her capture. The Hausa warrior Queen Amina extended her nation's boundaries to the Atlantic coast and personally led her army of 20,000 soldiers from 1536 to 157.[111]

The African feminist writer might not be involved in these remarkable acts of brawn and bravery, but she is not exempted from honorable fights for the development, growth, and progress of the African woman and society. Through the works of feminist writers like Chimamanda Adichie,

---

109 Nnaemeka, *From Orality.*
110 Finnegan, *Oral Literature.*
111 Segueda, "Imported," 1–20.

Sefi Atta, Buchi Emecheta, Lola Shoneyin, to mention a few, factors militating against state and women's development, like rape, battery, corruption, patriarchy, and many more are contentiously discussed. The African feminist writer goes beyond the pages of her works to involve herself in activism and movements that advocate for policies that positively affect the growth of the woman and her society.

As an embodiment of creativity itself, the African feminist writer is a reflection of the ancient African woman, known for painting, weaving, sculpting, dancing, and singing. In the spirit of these African women of bygone days, creativity was kept alive. For Soul Shava, basket weaving—a meticulous and creative art that combines the use of plant-based fiber materials like reeds, grasses, sedges, and palms to create intricate woven patterns from natural objects—is predominately the domain of women. Pottery making and the creation of beads and jewelry were also crafts dominated by women.[112] However, given this long history of activities and involvement of African women, the African feminist writer, in her skillful and meticulous creation of believable characters and the bringing to life of historical realities and the cultural heritage of her people, is a totality of the female creative self. This is why she bridges the gap between the type of creativity found in ancient tradition and that of the current civilization. However, the creative art of writing further presents the African feminist writer as a platform for the illumination of the sociocultural experiences of the modern-day African woman.

The African Feminist Writer as a Platform

In this section, African feminist writing will be examined as a platform for the exposure of both covert and overt sociocultural realities of the African woman in society. The act of reflecting the society in which she lives is a major mimetic device used by these writers to inform, educate, and propagate opinions that will bring about changes in society that will ameliorate the plight of the African woman. This notion acknowledges Albrecht's hypothesis that "literature reflects the society . . . and that literature influences or shapes the society."[113] In other words, the

---

112 Shava, "African," 11–16.
113 Albrecht, "Relationship," 1.

works of these writers is an attempt to realistically capture the day-to-day experiences of African women.

Endemic to twenty-first-century African society is a rampant patriarchal ruling class empowered by culture, religion, and government. Feminist writers have taken up the responsibility of educating the public, through their fictional and nonfictional works, on how the patriarchy is allowed to thrive in society. Validating this notion on the feminist writer's responsibility, Gordimer opines that "[r]esponsibility is what awaits outside the Eden of creativity."[114] Therefore, the place of the writer in enlightening society on the implications of patriarchy and the need for more women's movements cannot be overemphasized.

Lloyd Brown affirms that the portrayal of women's struggles has been a major characteristic of African literature; in his words, the woman has been "highly visible as subject and symbol in African literature."[115] This portrayal, though inadequate, does not eliminate the role of these writers in drawing attention to the plight of women in society. However, the feminist writer will provide deeper insight into the situation of women in African society. Her perspective is unique, more personal, and extremely useful in the advancement of the female cause. The works of African feminist writers like Nawal El Sadaawi are mostly fictional narratives that draw deeply from personal experiences and explore the implications of cultural and religious constructs that endorse patriarchy. For Nkealah, El Sadaawi is an internationally recognized feminist writer and activist whose publications reflect the oppressive actions of the patriarchy in Egypt.[116] She concerns herself with how the woman navigates her role in a male-dominated society, therefore validating Eldred Jones's assertion that the African writer "must see around him bad politics, bad religion, the misleading of the ordinary people and he is bound to write about all this if he writes about his environment . . . I think the writer must write about what happens around him."[117]

In this context, the African feminist writer must identify the political structures that discourage women from expressing themselves; she must identify religious doctrines that trivialize the place of women in society

---

114 Gordimer, "Essential."
115 Brown, "African," 493–501.
116 Nkealah, "Conceptualizing," 138.
117 Jones, "Three Nigerian," 127–31.

and ideologies that sanction the subjugation of women in Africa. El Sadaawi recognizes the woman's position in bringing to light these female realities, hence her radical portrayal of the plight of the Muslim woman in Egypt. In her works, she addresses relevant issues like genital mutilation of young girls, child marriage, and the domestication of women for the prime purpose of marriage. She exposes the religious injunctions of Islam that have been wielded by adherents of patriarchy with the aim of silencing women, politically, economically, socially, and sexually. In her work, *A Daughter of Isis*, she sums up the plight of Muslim women by stating the following: "For in this class patriarchal world of ours, a mother's name is of no consequence, a woman is without worth, on earth or in the heavens. In paradise a man is promised seventy-two virgins for his sexual pleasure, but the woman is promised no one except her husband, that is if he has the time for her, and not so busy with the virgins that would surround him."[118]

Through El Sadaawi's work, and that of a host of other feminist writers, the disheartening situation of women in Egypt becomes a global affair. In reflecting their society, the African feminist writer is preserving the realities of her era for posterity. Just like the African writer has used his or her works to preserve the folklore of the African people, the African feminist writer uses her works to chronicle the struggles of the African woman in her era. She transmits the struggles of feminists for future generations. Writers like Flora Nwapa, Buchi Emecheta, Mariama Ba, Nadine Gordimer, Ama Ata Aidoo, and Zukiswa Wanner stand in as bridges between the women's movement of the precolonial and colonial era and the contemporary era of feminism. Their works all share a cautious approach toward issues of women and society.

Much more contemporary writers like Chimamanda Adichie have also helped move women from the periphery of African writings to a place of relevance to the struggle for women's freedoms. In her novel *Purple Hibiscus*, Adichie analyzes and documents violence against women in Africa. She explores the idea of religious fanaticism as a contributory factor to subjugation and the silencing of women in Africa. Therefore, constructs like organized religion become difficult barriers that the African feminist must contend with; she also exposes the male oppressors who hide under the guise of piety to oppress women. Adichie's *Purple Hibiscus*

---

118 Sadaawi, *Daughter*, 3.

reveals forms of physical and psychological abuse in some "perfect homes" ruled by pious husbands and fathers. Through Kambili, the readers are privy to the intimate thoughts of the female child in such homes while viewing the rest of the family through her narrative voice.

The text addresses the implications of silence on the part of women. According to Hewett, "Eugene maneuvers his political standing at the public and his Christian ideology onto his family and thus subjecting the family to a sphere of silence."[119] The writer draws attention to the silence imposed on an entire family as a result of the father's violent controlling activities. On one occasion, Eugene scalds his children's legs for staying in the same house as their grandfather, his father, whom he considers a heathen because he refused to convert to Catholicism. Beatrice is constantly beaten by her husband Eugene, leading to several miscarriages and a silent resentment toward him.

The details of this cruelty are saddening and almost unbelievable. However, it is clearly informed by the social realities of African society and finds its impetus in Ngugi's observation that "literature does not grow or develop in a vacuum; it is given impetus, shape, direction and even area of concern by social and economic forces in a particular society."[120] It imitates the society the feminist writer finds herself in, drawing from women's real experiences; she brings to the fore the horror of violence and the implication of women's silence in the face of such horror.

Adichie's *Americanna*[121] takes a more postmodern ideological stance. Through the character Ifemelu, the author tries to redefine the woman against the subservient, dutiful, bashful, and sexually repressed traditional wife. The new woman is more sexually adventurous, less dependent, more audacious, more ambitious, assertive and on equal footing with the men. According to Agatha Kozak, the sexual revolution engineered a change in women's roles in society and has "freed women from archaic roles of passive, asexual, domestic slaves and dependent on men and devoid of civil rights."[122] Adichie uses her work to acquaint the average African woman

---

119 Hewett, "Coming," 73–97.
120 Ngugi, *Homecoming*.
121 Adichie is vastly different from the feminist writers previously analyzed because of the generation gap between her and the other aforementioned writers.
122 Kozak, "Postmodern Changes," 73–79.

with ongoing developments in gender relations and the new identity of the woman in a postmodern environment. Her ideologies of resilience, boldness, and self-sufficiency are embodied by the protagonist Ifemelu, who is not hemmed in by the constructs of religion or culture but possesses a mindset that transcends such limitations.

Adichie's other literary works deal with issues of sexuality as well as migration, which differentiates her from the first wave of feminist writers who were more cautious in their approach toward such issues. However, Adichie's works tend to be inclusive of all the relevant social issues in contemporary Africa and how they affect women.

Conclusion

Feminism in Africa is a product of the ideological changes the society experiences in the course of its existence. Feminist writings are representations of women's realities in a male-dominated society and have been received with much skepticism in Africa and accompanied by controversies that tend to distort its messages and discourage prospective adherents. Nevertheless, African feminism has come a long way from nameless women's movements and agitations to the point of literary acceptance and indigenous feminist models that cater to the cultural specificities of the African continent.

This chapter has explored how the African feminist writer uses her work to espouse her beliefs of equal political, social, and economic rights for both sexes through analysis of literary texts by select African feminist writers. Through these texts, these African feminist writers serve as the middle ground between the agencies available to African women in the distant past and the modern African woman. They also use their work to draw attention to the experiences of the African woman within the patriarchy. Today's African feminist writers take on a huge responsibility in documenting for posterity the ongoing transformations of the African woman and African society: a historian who paints vivid pictures through words. The progress of feminism in Africa cannot be understated, and the need for more feminist writers and activists cannot be overemphasized.

Chapter Sixteen

Decolonizing African Aesthetics

Introduction

Creative expressions are not a new phenomenon in the African space: they did not come with colonization, Westernization, or globalization. Africans have always been known for their creative endeavors before colonialism and before the intense globalization we have witnessed in the twenty-first century. If anything, the barbaric enslavement of Africans and the imposition of European authority gave brutish colonizers access to African arts and other creative expressions. In his popular book on decolonization, *How Europe Underdeveloped Africa*,[1] Walter Rodney discusses some of the negative impacts of colonialism on African creative spaces by establishing the depth of creativity found in Africa prior to colonialism. With some exaggeration, he describes an "uncontaminated African society"[2] prior to the colonization of the continent. The African fine arts, according to him, stand tall as some of the most beautiful creations in the history of mankind.[3] As a matter of fact, the ancient arts of Egypt, Sudan, and Ethiopia are considered to be remarkable achievements equal or surpassing those of the rest of the world.

It is interesting to note that it was in Africa that the Europeans came into contact with a superior brand of red leather, which Rodney notes was being dyed by the Hausa and Mandinka people of Nigeria and Mali.

---

1 Rodney, *How Europe*.
2 Rodney, *How Europe*, 53.
3 Rodney, *How Europe*, 54.

The superior quality of clothing that the Portuguese came in contact with in Africa made them send word back home (thereby directing the attention of Portugal to the African people). In his own words, Rodney states: "[W]ell into the present century, local cottons from the Guinea coast were stronger than Manchester cottons."[4] It is a distortion of history and a deliberate negative representation of Africa to situate its postcolonial creative expressions primarily in a Western context. Though these artistic expressions may not be classified into categories befitting Western works, they cannot and should not be relegated to obscurity. African culture possessed "a host of performance activities, ranging from ritual to play, from sporting activities such as wrestling, boxing and hunting to masking, dancing, singing and acrobatic displays";[5] these existed before and in spite of colonialism. Moreover, African fashions have inspired Western fashion. The contribution of the continent to Western fashion and style cannot be understated, as evident in the words of Agyeman: "Africa's influence on Western visual culture is evident but often unmentioned or conveyed as an afterthought. When the 'tellers' of our story of creativity continuously fail to embody our voice, something is lost; this has been emblematic of the story of African Art and African fashion on the world stage."[6]

Okagbue further argues that the decision not to compartmentalize African performances as Europeans have done must have been deliberate as a recognition and appreciation of the interconnectedness of the different components of African performances.[7] Okagbue is right. It is extremely common, for instance, to find elements of songs, oral poetry, and other art forms in larger performances resembling stage plays. A genre is rarely exclusive to a single performance; for example, poetry recitations can come in the middle of storytelling and vice versa. This rare trait is also evident in the performers themselves. Leeuw corroborates this idea by stating that "oral literature contains always at the same time elements of drama: the story-telling performance is a total happening, a total theater in several ways: in the first place because the narrator is often also a poet, a singer, a musician and an actor."[8] In the Yoruba movie *Agogo Eewo*, one

---

4   Rodney, *How Europe*, 66.
5   Okagbue, *African Theatres*, 1.
6   Agyeman, "Africa's Design."
7   Okagbue, *African Theatres*, 2.
8   Leeuw, "Origin."

of the texts that will be analyzed later in this chapter, Tunde Kelani is able to replicate this description above with the aid of visual technology: film. In one film, we find the fusion of proverbs, tongue-twisters, African (Yoruba) fashion, and in fact a totality of Yoruba culture, enmeshed with corrupt practices and political decadence to tell a true Nigerian story.

While this is not to imply that there are no specialists in different African performances, each member of the precolonial African community is capable of functioning in one form of performance or the other. Married women can be good storytellers or specialists in the recitation of a particular type of poetry. Young men can be wrestlers and young women professional dancers. Yet, old men can also be singers. Without a doubt, music is part of African lives from birth to death, which is why Bebey notes that "[t]he bond between language and music is so intimate that it is actually possible to tune an instrument so that the music it produces is linguistically comprehensible."[9]

The Eurocentric approach to African performances and creative expressions of the precolonial and colonial periods in Africa stems from the infiltration and domination of the African education systems and knowledge spaces by the West. Even when European and African scholars of African performance like Ruth Finnegan, Ulli Beier, Michael Echeruo, and James Amankulor would study African art forms, they did so from a Western perspective, especially when it came to classifications and groupings.[10] This chapter, by highlighting specific artistic endeavors, argues that African artists are successfully decolonizing this space; through sheer will and creative input they debunk the idea that African creative expressions are dependent on the West.

Decolonizing Knowledge through African Music

Singing in one's own native African language or hearing music sung in one's own native African language allows for Africans to reclaim a sense of identity and culture in a postcolonial world.[11] Musicians with African roots are well aware of this fact, and they have successfully promoted

---

9   Bebey, "Music," 119.
10 Okagbue, *African Theatres*, 4–5.
11 Carter-Ényì and Carter-Ényì, "Decolonizing," 58.

their own cultural values and political messages by taking advantage of the booming African music industry since the mid-twentieth century.[12] According to Ngugi wa Thiong'o, contemporary African musicians have ingeniously rewritten traditional African songs and successfully composed fresh new songs in African languages by relating the music to urban life. These musicians have also "pushed the [African] languages to new limits, renewing and reinvigorating them by coining new words and new expressions."[13]

It should come as no surprise that singing in African languages and hearing music in African languages promote confidence and pride in one's own African heritage because African language and music are so intertwined. For instance, Niger-Congo languages are inherently musical in quality because they are "tone languages." This means that someone who sings in Niger-Congo languages produces contours that naturally occur in spoken Niger-Congo languages: more specifically, the pitch of the melody replicates the pitch of the spoken language.[14] Additionally, among the almost one thousand sub-Saharan African ethnolinguistic cultures, ordinary exchanges typically involve song. If someone tells a story or a joke, they often produce a melody to emphasize their points. Ultimately, African music and language are so interrelated that separating an African melody from the African words risks completely spoiling the music itself as a whole.[15] According to Agawu: "Without language, there would be no song; without song, African music would not exist."[16] Bebey reiterates the notion by affirming that "music [. . .] grows out of the intonations and rhythmic onomatopoeias of speech."[17]

African musicians who understood the power of the relationship between their culture's music and language consciously came up with a music marketing method that would help attract a wide commercial audience. These musicians wanted to send a message about what it is like to be Black in a postcolonial society, and they wanted to communicate that they—as well as others like them—have a voice in a world still rife with

---

12 Carter-Ényì and Carter-Ényì, "Decolonizing," 58–59.
13 Ngugi, *Decolonizing*," 58.
14 Rycroft, "Zulu," 79–85, and Carter-Ényì, "Hooked," 267–90.
15 Carter-Ényì and Carter-Ényì, "Decolonizing," 62.
16 Agawu, *African*, 113.
17 Bebey, "Music," 121.

racism and oppression. Consequently, these musicians would do three things in the music they produced: set an agenda, prime the audience, and frame the message they wanted to communicate.[18] The musicians would first set an agenda by establishing the unique message they wanted to convey. They would then take this message to audience members by priming them to look out for particular "memory traces" in the song that make it more accessible or memorable.[19] They could also prime the audience by developing a program that would help audience members follow the music's melody and words. Much like programs for classical music concerts, these programs usually contained an introduction or description of what the song means. This particular form of priming would also help provide a framework for audience members because it would explicitly convey the context in which the song should be understood.[20]

One powerful example of an African musician who used this strategy was Miriam Makeba, also known as Mama Africa. Makeba was born in South Africa in 1932 and lived under a stringent apartheid government for most of her life. In the midst of this oppressive regime, Makeba almost exclusively sang songs in African languages like Zulu, Xhosa, and Swahili. Initially, Makeba did this because she had no other choice. Afrikaners forbade Black South Africans from singing in English in order to limit the British people's influence from the prior colonial rule that ended in 1934. However, even when Makeba could sing in English in the United States, she found that singing in her native languages was always her preference.

Ultimately, what started as an apartheid rule evolved into Makeba's way of helping herself and others decolonize their minds.[21] Makeba sang songs in African languages (mostly Xhosa) that were infused with cultural significance to a variety of audience members: Black and white Americans, Xhosas, Black and white South Africans, and Europeans. She also consciously dressed and styled her hair according to Xhosa traditions. In doing these things, she made it clear that she had a very well-established agenda, as other African musicians did: to encourage other Africans to be proud of their race and heritage, even with racism and

---

18 Scheufele, "Agenda-Setting," 297–316.
19 Scheufele, ""Agenda-Setting," 299–300.
20 Carter-Ényì and Carter-Ényì, "Decolonizing," 58–59.
21 Carter-Ényì and Carter-Ényì, "Decolonizing," 58–59.

oppression abounding.[22] Makeba also primed her audience and put her agenda into a framework by personally introducing her audience to the background of a song before performing it. For instance, before performing "Qongqothwane" (called "The Click Song" in English), she would inform the audience that the song is native to her hometown of Johannesburg, where people would sing it to a young bride before her wedding day.[23] Over time, however, Makeba's introduction became much more political and activist-conscious:

> This next song . . . it's a Xhosa wedding song. Everywhere we go people often ask me "how do you make that [clicking] noise?" It used to offend me because it isn't a noise, it's my language. But I came to understand that they didn't understand that Xhosa is my language, it's a written language. . . . Now, I'm sure everyone here knows that we in South Africa are still colonized. The colonizers of my country call this song "a click song" simply because they find it rather difficult saying "Qongqothwane."[24]

By reclaiming African music and language, Makeba effectively spread awareness about apartheid, race relations, and identity. According to Carter-Ényì and Carter-Ényì, though Makeba's performance introductions were brief, they were not detrimental to her popularity: her method of providing short historical contexts generated curiosity and incentivized her audiences to educate themselves on the topics she addressed.[25] Makeba became a popular musician because her genuineness and fight for identity resonated with African people. Makeba fundamentally understood that African language has power because it allows for an oppressed African voice to be expressed. She knew that this expression must remain available to Africans so that they can unite and feel galvanized to make change. Happily, Makeba's work helped inspire other influential African artists after her, such as Ònyékà (Igbo of Nigeria), Angélique Kidjo (Yoruba of Benin), Yvonne Chaka Chaka (Xhosa of South Africa), Oumou Sangaré (Mandinka of Mali), and

---

22 Carter-Ényì and Carter-Ényì, "Decolonizing," 63.
23 Carter-Ényì and Carter-Ényì, "Decolonizing," 61.
24 Dutch TV Studios.
25 Carter-Ényì and Carter-Ényì, "Decolonizing," 63.

Chiwoniso Maraire (Shona of Zimbabwe), Àsá (Yoruba of Nigeria), and Eno Williams (Ibibio Sound Machine).[26]

This chapter will take a further look at some of the artists influenced by Makeba to show how they successfully employ African culture in their music and as a way to free it from colonial influence. Although it is necessary to remark that colonialism, while changing much of Africa, also inevitably impacted the musical inclinations of the continent. Hence, when people like Makeba championed a purely African music, it became a landmark event. Eric Charry delves into the history of rap in Africa, for instance. He establishes the 1990s as being the decade that Africans broke ties with the "foreign" elements that came with rap music and hip hop. Charry explains that

> the sequence throughout the decade and into the 1990s was simple and widespread: direct, imitation, substituting their own English language lyrics, and localizing it by rapping in African languages (or at least letting go of the American accents about issues of relevance to their communities). It was not until the early and mid-1990s that African genres had emerged as rappers, deejays, and producers began to localize the music.[27]

Positive Black Soul, a collective of the earliest rappers both in Senegal and Africa at large, make music influenced by African culture. For these African artists the case was one of selection rather than designation; the group not only has an affinity for the language but chooses to showcase the beauty of African culture. Like Awadi submits in a 2008 interview with the *Guardian*, his aim is to portray his culture and African identity to a global audience, and it is through the kora that he attempts to do this.[28] Introducing African elements to their music therefore comes from a place of prideful attachment to their roots, despite heavy exposure to other dominant cultures.

Hence, it becomes obvious that the tone that has been set in the African music industry, in which African languages and music are rightly intertwined, did not end with the era of apartheid (in South Africa) and the fight against colonialism (in other parts of Africa). Rather, African

---

26   Carter-Ényì and Carter-Ényì, "Decolonizing," 64.
27   Charry, "Capsule," 29.
28   Gendre, "Hip-Hop."

artists who have been influenced by pioneering singers like Makeba have continued to appropriate African languages in their music. The notable artists embrace this technique to portray the decadence that has become synonymous with their communities—a continuation on the path of African artists before them. It should be noted that this is one major point of departure with Western colonial influence.

With the acknowledgment of the Western roots of some artists, many African artists have successfully denounced corrupt African political structures as well as condemned discrimination based on color, physiology, social status, and sex. In doing so, African artists uniquely extend the core purpose of performance to include moral and ideological principles, which is not a common phenomenon in the European artistic sphere. For Europe and the wider West, art is often done for its own sake. While for Africans, art is often propaganda and has a host of other cultural uses. The ingenious creative mindset of the artist and the innate musicality found in these African languages has enhanced a style of music that is African flavored, yet globally relevant.

The common forms of music found in Africa today—like rap, Afrobeat, reggae—are arguably not indigenous to Africa. Rather, they were either directly imported, much like rap, or they developed with time and Africans' interactions with different peoples and cultures. This kind of interaction birthed music genres like Apala, Afrobeat, Chimurenga, to mention a few. It is imperative to state that though there are many genres of music in Africa today, they are all connected. These styles both portray the reality of the artists' immediate community and deliberately attempt to showcase African culture above all others. This chapter is not an attempt at classifying African music but to draw practical examples from an array of musical forms that have been experimented with in Africa and by Africans in a bid to demonstrate the ways in which these types of music help decolonize creative space in Africa.

Among many other African artists influenced by Makeba and their famous works that defy Western convention, Chiwoniso Maraire's musical output is worth noting. The singer was born in the United States into a musical family. In spite of Chiwoniso's exposure and interaction with foreign cultures, her music breaks away from stereotypes associated with her place of birth. The influence of African culture on her music is profound, especially with her use of the musical instrument, the mbira—an indigenous instrument that has become synonymous with Chiwoniso's music. Her heavy reliance on the mbira, it should be noted, is a daring act on two fronts: first is the fact that in traditional Zimbabwe, the musical instrument is predominantly played by men in the community, and the second is her uncommon ability to fuse African and Western styles of music.

Note that Zimbabwean music, of which the mbira is an integral part, had suffered a long period of colonization and oppression, much like the people of Zimbabwe themselves. According to Mark, "As Zimbabweans fought a revolutionary war against colonial Rhodesia, traditional music was repressed as a sign of resilience, but before this it was also repressed as anti-colonial, criminal, uncivilized, sinful and pagan."[29] Vuyogo[30] echoes this by reiterating the role of African music as a weapon of opposition against the colonialists and their agenda. This became the impetus for Chiwoniso's infusion of African elements in her music, supporting Vuyogo's further submission that mbira music was instrumental in the fight for independence in Zimbabwe. This struggle was carried over to the postindependent Zimbabwe era.

It is impossible to speak of Chiwonso's music without reference to her father, Dumisani Maraire, a master of the mbira himself. Dumisani had been taken under the wing of Robert Kauffman, a missionary to Zimbabwe who took interest in his musical talent. On returning to the United States, Kauffman invited Dumisani over as a resident artist. This marks the beginning of his sojourn in the Western world and as Lindroth[31] rightly expatiates, the efforts of Dumisani with mbira music in the United States were instrumental in spreading this style music in North America. It was only natural that Chiwoniso would have been attracted to the mbira, just as she could have been irredeemably influenced by the Western world. Chiwoniso manages to balance both, not without noticeable favoritism toward her indigenous culture, however.

The acoustic sound of the mbira in Chiwoniso's songs is unmistakable, even when the listener has no clue what the instrument is. In the instances of songs like "Zvichapera," "Rebel Woman," "Yekufara" and many others, the mbira is either the introductory sound that welcomes a listener into the world of her music or an interlude that entertains the

---

29   Mark, "Sole," 162.
30   http://vuyogo.de/chiwoniso/.
31   Lindroth, "Zimbabwean."

listener. The uniqueness of Chiwoniso's music lies in her ability to dexterously blend the mbira with Western musical instruments. In "Yekufara" for instance, she starts the song with mbira instrumentals and smoothly glides into an interplay of other Western instruments. The song, as an example for others, signifies an equal melding of two cultures—African and Western. Chiwoniso, with this creative blend, challenges the world to accept the uniqueness of African elements in the music. As she rightly notes in a live performance, the mbira holds the significant place of being an instrument that has both entertainment and spiritual purposes, one never conflicting with the other.

Beyond the use of mbira, Chiwoniso's music is well grounded in her indigenous language. As a matter of fact, some of her songs are in the Shona indigenous language, while some are a mix of Shona and the English language. The place of the Shona people in Zimbabwe is strategic. According to Jarus,[32] the role of Shona ancestors in ancient Zimbabwe cannot be underestimated. He notes that they helped in building the great empire of Zimbabwe that thrived from the eleventh to the fifteenth centuries.

Chiwoniso brings the ancient Zimbabwean spirit into her song when she sings in the language of the Shona people. She transports the essence of her people into the minds of her listeners. In actual fact, Vuyogo points to this reality in Chiwoniso's music when he comments on her debut appearance on an album she recorded with her parents as a young girl of ten. Of the song titled "Tichazomuona" (We shall see you) he adds that the song is rooted in both the ancient Shona culture and Christianity.[33] Another vivid instance of taking her listeners into the spiritual world is evident in a lullaby she sang for her two daughters after her husband's death and shortly before her own death. The lullaby is rooted in the Shona culture, heavily accented with emotions. It not only expresses Chiwoniso's affection for her children while trying to sing them to sleep, but it also provides the perfect vehicle through which to lay bare her grieving emotions; in this manner, the mother (Chiwoniso in this case) not only comforts her children but also herself. Again, this is instructive, as one would recall that Chiwoniso had spent a good part of her youth in

---

32   Jarus, "Shona."
33   http://vuyogo.de/chiwoniso/.

the United States. This is, however, not unique to Chiwoniso, as it is evident in other African artists who have embraced a pro-African approach to their music.

Another popular African artist who brought an African musical instrument into the global limelight is the Malian Ballake Sissoko. Sissoko is credited for playing the kora, a traditional instrument of the *jelis* (called "griots" in French) in Mali. The jelis serve as the custodians of history and tradition in Mali. They are storytellers who also use music to tell their tales. For Sissoko playing the kora is something that comes from his father. As a matter of fact, for Sissoko, it goes further: kora is a traditional instrument played by most griots in Mali. Sissoko appropriates his traditional role as a griot and his knowledge of the kora to promote African culture, not just to his local African community but diffusing this knowledge to other parts of the world.

Yvonne Chaka Chaka is another African singer of South African origin who uses her indigenous language to express her opinions. Like others, Chaka Chaka's use of the indigenous language is a deliberate deviation from the colonial influence of the English language, although some of her songs are sung in English. Perhaps what could be regarded as her most popular song, "Umqombothi" ("African Beer"), was the opening tune in the movie *Hotel Rwanda*. The melodious rhythm of Chaka Chaka becomes the soundtrack to the gruesome events of the Rwandan genocide, some of which are depicted in the film. This remains an event etched in the memories of Africans, and the gentle melodies of "Umqombothi" are a soothing antidote to the hard realities the movie depicts. Chaka Chaka has dedicated her music career and life as a whole to championing the cause of deprived and underrepresented Africans. In fact, she served as a goodwill ambassador for UNICEF. It is obvious that Chaka Chaka is not just interested in music but in the African cause as well.

Asa is a more contemporary African artist in terms of age. The Paris-born Nigerian singer, just like Chiwoniso, was immersed in a foreign culture from a very young age, but this does not detract from her appreciation and understanding of the beauty of African culture. Unlike Chiwoniso, Asa's preferred instrument is the guitar, but her songs are also heavily accented by her native Yoruba language. Even though it may seem impossible for nonnative speakers to grasp the messages of the indigenous language in the music of these artists, their conveyed spirit of "Africanness" is not lost on any listener. These are not just artists in the sense of entertaining their audience and listeners; they also perform the role of philosopher, moral judge, and of course, upholder of culture. Functioning in these capacities makes it imperative for them to tap the available wealth of African cultures. There is no doubt that a foreign language like English or French only limits the extent of the artist's ability to communicate his or her intent in the art.

In "Eye Adaba," for instance, a track on her debut album, Asa speaks of the importance of morning in Yoruba. The song has few words, but one who understands the Yoruba language could decipher how important morning is: a time of the day or of one's life that heralds good fortune. Morning is expected to give one an opportunity for a clean slate by erasing whatever jinx the previous day brought. Asa's "Eye Adaba" is both an understanding of the sacredness of morning and a prayer. The morning for the Yoruba sets the agenda for the day and so should not be taken for granted: it is this sacrosanct message that she hopes to pass on by delivering the song in Yoruba. In another song on the same album, titled "Awe," she utilizes satire to describe an imaginary man who has chosen to be irresponsible by impregnating a woman and absconding. The Yoruba language is laced with sarcastic expressions, and Asa does not fail to capitalize on this in questioning this "awe" (man). It would appear she is dishing out a warning to this irresponsible person, as he might be heading toward his own doom. Toward the end of the song, she notes: "Abor'o la' so fun omoluabi, to ba denu re a d'o didi," which roughly translates as: "You need not tell a responsible man everything before he gets the picture of the message you are trying to pass across."

Asa's style in "Awe" is not uncommon in the Yoruba culture where songs are used to correct a wrong and scold erring people. It is safe to say her warning in this song is to every man who prefers to cross boundaries of decency in society. In another song, Asa expounds on the concept of communality and togetherness in African culture, particularly as found among the Yoruba. In the song "Eyo," Asa discusses in simple terms the idea behind Ubuntu philosophy. Archbishop Desmond Tutu of South Africa, in explaining the essence of Ubuntu philosophy and its role in African belief and system of living states that

> Africans have this thing called UBUNTU ... the essence of being human. It is part of the gift that Africans will give the world. It embraces hospitality, caring about others, willing to go the extra mile for the sake of others. We believe a person is person through another

person. That my humanity is caught up, bound up and inextricable in yours. When I dehumanise you I inexorably dehumanise myself. The solitary individual is a contradiction in terms and, therefore, you seek to work for the common good because your humanity comes into its own community, in belonging.[34]

It is in this light that one can understand the message Asa attempts to share in "Eyo" when she says:

Going home
Going home
Where this road goes I already know
Where everybody cares for one another
and they take you as their sister

This is a portrait of someone who is hitherto starved of the love and togetherness that is shared by her own people. She craves to be "where everyone cares for one another." There is no doubt the present abode of the singer is a place where everyone is lonely; people do not care about their neighbors. The present abode of the singer is where everyone is expected to mind their business and never meddle in other people's lives except when invited. This is an aberration in the African context, especially before the culture was diluted by Western ways. In Africa, a member of a community can never be independent of that community. In the specific Yoruba nation that Asa sings about in "Eyo," the child of a neighbor is cared for like their own, which is why Asa would say "and they take you as their sister."

While Asa speaks of what to some extent is now happening in Africa, it can also be regarded as a call to Africans to return to how things used to be. The words of the song can be interpreted as a revolt and an attempt to lead a group of rebels who are no longer comfortable with the Western style. It is a call to people who wish to go back to how things used to be, which is the love of being united and living as a community.

The African musical world has witnessed a proliferation of many artists who project their African identity through their music, fashion sense, and way of life in general. A lot of the more contemporary African artists may seem to have created a new style of music that suits their African

---

34 Nabudere, "Ubuntu," 5.

audience; a style that appears more Western than African in orientation. Yet there is no doubt that an authentic African flavor permeates a lot of this music. For one, most of these musicians were born and bred on African soil. Hence, they find it convenient to look within for their musical content. This is why it is a common practice to hear indigenous words or expressions in contemporary African music. Actually, it is common for these artists to refer to their music and style as Afrobeat—confirming the assertion that African artists have come up with a new form of music that is independent of their colonizer's music.

Postcolonial African Fashion: The Hub of Creative Expression

Clothing serves purposes that go beyond covering the body. Clothes are also regarded as fashion items. Perani and Wolff, as quoted in Akinbileje, assert that "beyond basic role in shelter and protection, cloth and dress have overlapping mediating functions including (1) measurement of self and personal worth; (2) indicator of occupation; (3) measurement of social value; (4) standard of economic value; (5) definition and negotiation of political power; (6) religious signifier and repository of supernatural powers; (7) indicator of culture and change."[35]

The above therefore suggests that Africans do not approach dress with a carefree attitude. Instead, there is a deliberate thought process that goes into how Africans dress themselves. In the Yoruba culture, for instance, there is the saying of "irini si, ni'seni lojo," which could be roughly translated as one who is addressed according to the way he or she is clothed. The expression carries a meaning far deeper than how one is dressed, however. It encapsulates the whole idea of fashion, since physical appearance is not limited to clothes but also involves things like shoes, jewelry, and other accessories worn to complement beauty, including tattoos and body piercings. Also, as noted above, dress signifies social status in traditional African societies. Akinbileje makes a case for *kente* in Ghana and *aso oke* in Nigeria. According to her, *kente* was an attire exclusively reserved for kings and people of royal status in Ashanti Ghana. The cloth is made of gold patterns and coral beads: all of this is to suggest the wealth of the person wearing the *kente*. Similar scenario applies to aso oke and the

---

35 Akinbileje, "Symbolic," 627.

Yoruba people of Western Nigerian where the *aso oke* is the exclusive fashion of royalty. In fact, "It was recorded that the Olubadan of Ibadan (a prominent Yoruba king) at a particular time banned his chiefs from wearing aso oke."[36] Therefore for an African, fashion is a serious business.

Like every other creative industry in Africa, the African fashion industry is highly diverse. In other words, African fashion has been influenced by other global fashions to create a unique form of dress. To therefore talk about a pure African fashion, one would need to go as far back as the precolonial period. Rovine opines that "fashion, thus, offers a rich field for analysis of visual culture that is fueled by its practitioners' reach across cultural divides, revealing networks of direct and indirect interactions, undergirded by histories of colonial and postcolonial power asymmetries."[37]

Rovine[38] explains the multifaceted nature of African fashion. The history of colonialism on the continent has no doubt altered the course of African history, including fashion. The power play that was established by the colonialists was extended by African leaders who took over after them. Also, with colonialism came rapid industrialization and urbanization. All of these factors profoundly affected African fashion.

Colonialism brought with it a dichotomy in dress, apart from the social stratification necessitated by the imbalance of wealth distribution. By arrangement, men in African societies were integrated into the colonial system sooner than the women. This consequently led to the need for men to dress in the colonial style. Men were employed by the colonial system—both the educated and uneducated—and so were required to dress in a certain way: they wore suits and trousers, neckties, and other Western sartorial items. This does not suggest in any way that men totally abandoned traditional dress. Conversely, women continued to dress in the traditional style, a stereotype that was carried into the colonial period. Women were regarded as custodians of culture, and so for a woman to be dressed in the colonial style was often regarded as a form of deviancy. Luttmann puts this into proper perspective: "When they [women] started, however, to follow European fashion styles around the time of independence, they were subjected to harsh public criticism. Western

---

36 Akinbileje, "Symbolic," 628.
37 Rovine, "Style Migrations," 34.
38 Rovine, "Style Migrations," 34–42.

dress was considered amoral or in contradiction to local traditions and their sense of decency and womanhood."[39]

Things changed with time. By the time of independence, and postindependence, African women had triggered another level of fashion. As it were, it was not a complete departure from purist African fashion, but it was not a complete adoption of Western style. Luttmann puts it this way:

> This new fashion phenomenon is grounded in a devotion to fashion and in the fashionalization of older African dress styles. It has led to innovative creations in terms of cloth design, the composition of different materials, the mixing of styles, the revival of old manual techniques and the borrowing of imported materials and ideas. These fashion styles represent much more than being mere consumable goods, they have to be seen as a new form of material cultural expression that turned away from the Western model yet did not go backwards to formal tradition. Instead they have articulated a particular understanding of modernity, modern city life, femininity and African identity. [40]

It is therefore not uncommon to attribute the present buoyancy of African fashion to the efforts of African women keeping it alive, despite the daunting presence of Western fashion and style. African women went on to champion the fashion boom that kicked off in Africa in the 1980s. They took elements of the old (African tradition) and merged it with the seemingly new (Western style) to birth a new form of fashion.

However, the preservation of African fashion was not the sole responsibility of African women. The wave of African nationalists of the twentieth century was another factor that helped spark a renaissance of African fashion. By the time African nationalists rose to fight for their freedom, they engaged with traditions that had hitherto been neglected in African culture—from language to clothing. Again, Luttmann notes that "culture was seen as an effective means of countering political domination and of regaining self-assurance. Sartorial expressions of nationalist feeling were prominently displayed and led to a kind of stylistic synthetization and uniformization. The ethnic differentiation formerly expressed by specific local styles was to be replaced by easily readable uniform signs."[41]

---

39 Luttmann, "Fashion," 65.
40 Luttmann, "Fashion," 51.
41 Luttmann, "Fashion," 54.

Hence, African style became a unifying factor for nationalists, both of homogenous and heterogeneous cultures. It was common for nationalists to set aside their differences in a bid to unite against the colonizers and Western culture as a whole. Africa became home to colorful and fashionable styles, which were also exported outside the continent. Unfortunately, initial discourses on visual art, of which fashion is an integral part, deliberately marginalized African art. The narrative was always about the influence of Western art on Africa, with little to no mention of Africa's contribution to global art. Worse still, while Pablo Picasso's outstanding work, *Les Demoiselles d'Avignon* (1907), had been inspired by his expedition in Africa, the Western narrative has it that the great artist had "discovered" African art.[42] Meanwhile, Picasso himself admitted being inspired by African art. The kind of "African moment" that influenced the landmark Picasso work Agyeman believes was experienced in fashion, too, when he comments that "fashion has also had many 'African moments,'" including in 1968 when *Harper's Bazaar* described Algerian-born Yves Saint Laurent's groundbreaking collection as "a fantasy of primitive genius."[43] John Galliano's 1997 debut couture collection at Dior, featuring a series of reinterpreted Maasai warrior costumes, and Jean Paul Gaultier's Spring 2005 couture and Autumn/Winter 2010/2011 couture collections were all heavily African-inspired."[44]

Chronicling the development of fashion in Africa, Jennings[45] asserts that the increase in the use of African fabrics and fashion items to portray African identity during and after independence had a ripple effect in the African diaspora, especially in the United States where civil rights movements were on the rise. These combined factors led to a crop of African designers who brought African fashion to global attention. Among them was Shade Thomas-Fahm, a Nigerian designer who pioneered new trends in African fashion in the 1960s. Jennings comments that "the pre-tied gele, turning iro and buba into a zip-up wrapper skirt and adapting a man's agbada into a woman's embroidered boubou were all her [Fahm's] fashion firsts."[46] There was Pathé Ouédraogo of Burkina Faso

---

42 Agyeman, "Africa's Design.
43 Jennings, *New African Fashion,* 12.
44 Agyeman, "Africa's Design," 2.
45 Jennings, *New African Fashion.*
46 Jennings, *New African Fashion,* 11.

in 1977, Chris Seydou (1949–1994) of Mali, Tetteh Adzedu of Ghana who reigned in the 1980s, Seidnally Sidhamed of Niger, Oumou Sy of Senegal, and Errol Arendz and Marianne Fassler from South Africa, to mention a few. One thing the names listed above had in common was their ability to transform African fashion from what looked obsolete to something appealing to the postcolonial eyes. They transformed everyday African fashion trends by mixing them with some Western styles, heralding a new era for African fashion.

There can be no comprehensive analysis of African fashion without mentioning Yves Saint Laurent. He was born in 1936, in Oran, Algeria, and was perhaps the best-known fashion designer with roots in Africa. Yves Saint Laurent acknowledged that the inspiration for his designs came from the African continent and especially from his experiences as a child there. According to Jennings, "His designs repeatedly drew on the continent. His landmark Spring/ Summer 1967 African collection featured a series of revealing shift dresses made from raffia, wooden beads and shells (a look re-imagined by Dolce & Gabbana in 2005 and by Gucci in 2011). *Harper's Bazaar* described it at the time as 'a fantasy of primitive genius—shells and jungle jewellery clustered to cover the bosom and hips, latticed to bare the midriff.'"[47]

Aside from the notable contribution of Laurent to global fashion by projecting what is African, he has inspired other African fashion designers who also have gotten worldwide attention from their African-inspired work. Perhaps one could argue that Yves Saint Laurent is to African fashion what Mariam Makeba is to African music. Duro Olowu and Alber Elbaz are some of the names that were influenced by Yves Saint Laurent's designs of African heritage. From there, fashion designers from Africa with international exposure have begun to experiment with African elements in their designs. The FIFA World Cup in 2010 hosted in South Africa had no small role in promoting African culture, especially in the area of fashion. Jennings asserts that in the same year, "Issey Miyake, Marc Jacobs, Kenzo, Gucci, Dries Van Noten and Eley Kishimoto all examined traditional textiles, in part due to the interest in Africa piqued by the 2010 FIFA World Cup in South Africa. Sports brands also followed suit with African-influenced lines. Puma collaborated with Nigerian American

---

47 Jennings, *New African Fashion*, 12.

artist Kehinde Wiley, who used African fabrics as a backdrop to his portraits of football stars and as the basis of the prints in the collection."[48]

An appreciation and incorporation of Blackness was not limited to dresses and fashion accessories in the twentieth century, there was also a wave of accommodating Black models. Jennings claims "Paco Rabanne and Yves Saint Laurent were among the first designers to use models of colour in the 1960s."[49] As African fashion artists continued to excel on the global scene, more African models could also share their beauty with the world. Today, there are a countless number of Black women in global fashion. The major "fashion weeks" worldwide continue to play host to African designers and their works, as well as African and Black models at large.

It should be stated that African fashion at its primitive stage was not just about dressing up. Studies have suggested that Africa was home to some of the earliest tattoos in the world. Some accounts submit that these earliest tattoos were amulets used to strengthen pregnant women in ancient Egypt and some parts now regarded as North Africa. However, there is also the school of thought that believes that tattoos were used as beauty enhancers by prostitutes in ancient Egypt. What is clear here is the fact that Africans were not introduced to tattoos by the West. Moreover, among the Yoruba people of West Africa, it was commonplace for people to have inscriptions on their bodies, some as protection from devilish wiles while some were simply to keep vital information like dates of birth or names given at birth. The kind of tattoo that found its way into Africa from the West, and particularly the United States, is associated with rebellion and deviance. These days, tattoos are regarded as fashion statements by many people all over the world.

African Films and the Question of Decolonization

The lingering arguments on the language of African literature and what makes a work of literature African can be applied to films as well. As a matter of fact, many have argued about the criteria that determine a specifically "African" film. This dilemma in identification necessitated these cogent questions raised by Sanogo:

---

48 Jennings, *New African Fashion*, 13.
49 Jennings, *New African Fashion*, 15.

The debates that rage in African cinema and media encompass the fields of the theoretical, the historiographic, and the critical, and indeed include the question of the articulation of the cultural, the political, and the economic. Chief among them (this is a nonexhaustive compendium) is arguably the question of the identity of the object (What, to paraphrase Stuart Hall, are the "cinema" and the "media" in African cinema and media? What is the "African" in African cinema and media?) These questions lead to the problem of naming: How should the object be referred to? African film/cinema studies? Media studies? Screen studies? Moving-image studies? Screen media studies?[50]

The subsequent analysis points to certain elements in randomly selected films in Africa, not as a contribution to the debate on identification but as a necessary effort to show how African filmmakers have carved a unique identity for Africa and Africans. These creators have asserted an identity through ingenious creativity, an accommodation of both African traditional beliefs and Western culture, as well as their insistent portrayal of the socioeconomic and political realities of Africans.

As previously established, performance was not introduced into Africa by white colonialists. Judging from a postcolonial perspective, it seems appropriate to state that African films today draw from both African indigenous culture and Western culture. It is a general consensus that acting is a reflection of life, and African film on the whole has not failed to reflect its immediate environment.

The advancement of technology and the fact that the first film was made in the West ensured that the best movies would be produced there for a long time to come. As a result, discourse on African films is still traced back to the West. The first set of movies that were shown in Africa were brought by white colonial masters. The intent of white colonialists lay in their selfish desire to manipulate Africa and Africans for the development of their countries and culture. The earliest movies shown in Africa showcased Western culture and its supposed superiority over African indigenous cultures. Moreover, these movies were exclusively available to an audience of white colonists.

According to Botha, "in colonial Africa, film markets were developed only for the entertainment of the colonists. These films which originated

---

50   Sanogo, "In Focus," 114.

mainly from Europe and the USA merely reflected the values and realities of the colonisers."[51] This view is similar to an earlier assertion by Malkmus and Armes who opined that "the roots of their mythical portrait lay in the falsification of reality, whereby the colonizer was 'a technician, a man of progress, from a superior culture and civilization, while the native was a primitive, incapable of technical progress or of mastering his passions."[52]

Meanwhile, in chronicling the development of the cinematic experience in Africa, Ansah[53] referenced the role films played on Africans who agreed to fight in World War II for the British army and its culmination into nationalist protests and eventual independence in places like Ghana. Like Botha and Malkmus and Armes, Ansah notes that the Ghanaian film industry was established to educate and acculturate Ghanaians to the ways of the West. According to Ansah, "in 1937, a British Major, L.A. Notcutt, was commissioned by the Colonial Government to produce series of films to 'civilize Africa.' This marked the beginning of the launching of Colonial Film Units in various parts of Africa, including the Gold Coast. The immediate objective, according to the film historian Jean Rouch, was to use films to get Africans to participate in World War Two."[54]

The films produced by Notcutt and his team were specifically to portray how noble it would be for Africans to join the British in the war against the Germans. With visual art being a strong tool in shaping opinion, a lot of African men (specifically in Ghana in this case) were convinced to fight in World War II. Unfortunately, however, what they were promised before the war was different from the postwar reality they faced. Sadly, Ansah notes, as African war returnees suffered the shame of disappointment from their colonial masters, the documentaries being produced at the time also glorified whites as the heroes of wars at the expense of the hard labor of African soldiers. This led to a protest and the resultant unjust killing of some ex-service men in Ghana. According to Ansah, and corroborated by Kukolova,[55] a similar event of ex-service men complaining about being badly treated by the colonial government and

---

51   Botha, "African Cinema," 4.
52   Malkmus and Armes, *Arab*, 16.
53   Ansah, "Ghanaian Cinema."
54   Ansah, "Ghanaian Cinema," 5.
55   Kukolova, "Rethinking."

their execution had occurred in the French-speaking colony of Senegal, which event was made into a movie by Ousmane Sembene.

One important concept concerning films during the colonial era is that they carried obvious messages about white culture and its superiority with no room for any expression of Africanness. Beyond the movies made to influence the opinion of young men who joined the British army in World War II, subsequent movies seen on the continent were pro-white, including the ones that were made in Africa. Malkmus and Armes, speaking about the experience in North Africa, submitted this: "In addition to the falsity of the myths and the inauthenticity of the life depicted, there was a virtual absence of Arab players on the screen: all substantial roles were played by Europeans, so that the Arabs themselves were reduced to mere silhouettes, essentially a part of the landscape."[56]

Hence, Africa was merely a playground for Western filmmakers; a backdrop for expressing their creativity and ideas. The African people and their culture were never deemed worthy of being depicted in these films. Furthermore, in the movies where African people and culture are represented, these depictions are done in a demeaning manner. By the time independence came for most African countries, little had changed in the indigenous film industries of these countries, as they lacked the financial and infrastructural wherewithal to actualize their own stories. In French-speaking countries, Botha says it took the influence of "African film students and Frenchmen such as the film producer Jean Rouch and the film historian Georges Sadoul in the 1960s to influence the French government's policy with regard to involvement with indigenous African film production."[57] The involvement of the French government in video productions in French-speaking African countries placed them ahead of other parts of the continent when it came to film production. Prior to this time, states Andrade-Watkins, "not a single feature film was made by an African prior to independence, yet by 1975 over 185 shorts and features had been produced with the technical and financial assistance of the Film Bureau. As a result, eighty percent of all black African films were being made by francophone Africans."[58]

---

56 Malkmus and Armes, *Arab*, 17.
57 Botha, "African Cinema," 5.
58 Andrade-Watkins, "Film Production," 26.

Organizations and bodies in France would later become involved in supporting and funding the film industry in these Francophone countries. These relentless efforts led to the eventual establishment of Francophone Africa's first film school, located in Ouagadougou, Burkina Faso, the Institut Africain d'Education Cinematographique (INAFEC).[59] There were other film establishments in the region thereafter. However, the influence of the Western world in the affairs of African films at the time is not negligible as distribution remained the sole function of France and the West for French-speaking African movies for many years.

From these developments, French-speaking African countries became a hub where true African films thrived. African movies began to tell African stories and with African people. Movies of African film makers like Sembène began to receive better attention and acclaim from Africans than those by foreigners, despite the difference in quality and execution. To put it in perspective like Manthia Diawara, echoed by Tcheuyap:

> Why are we still drawn to films like Borom Sarret and La Noire de . . . and less interested in Afrique sur Seine (1957, by Paulin Soumanou Vieyra), which is made in the language of classical cinema and stars a professional actress like Marpesa Dawn? Why are Sembène's images of Africa considered richer and more authentic than those of his countryman Vieyra, who seems to have mastered film language? The same question could be asked when comparing Sembène's earlier films to Jean Rouch's Moi un noir (1958) and Les Maîtres fous (1955). Why are Sembène's considered more authentically African than Rouch's films, which were also shot in Africa and, in other respects, upheld as groundbreaking in visual anthropology and the French New Wave?[60]

One of the many challenges this crop of African filmmakers had to deal with was to change the negative representation of Africa by nonnatives who had earlier seen themselves as custodians of African culture. As opined by Botha, whites who told the African story through the filmic experience did so from a biased perspective: "In her study of nearly 300 feature films about Africa, Fuller (1993) concluded that these predominantly American and European films present stereotypical diametric images of African people as primitive savages or elite, educated, and

---

59 Botha, "African Cinema," 5.
60 Tcheuyap, "African Cinema," 11.

English; the landscape as either gloriously lush or blatantly barren; and animals as 'cute' or 'life-threatening.'"[61]

This distorted representation of African identity needed to be corrected, not just by denouncing popular false representations but by using the same medium of film to accurately portray African culture and identity. This was a challenge even after independence. The African filmmakers at the time were trained by the Europeans to work in Eurocentric styles. Hence, even when African auteurs had genuine African stories to tell, their Western education would always be in evidence. This poses a problem for scholars who attempt to examine African identities as portrayed in feature films.

The needed revolution in the African film community, however, did not come until the early 1990s, according to McCall. He notes that this was the period of transition from celluloid to digital. According to McCall, entrepreneurs from Nigeria and Ghana seized this opportunity to cater to Africans who had always hungered for movies that reflected African realities and experiences. It would appear the digital revolution allowed African filmmakers to produce films at a lower cost than in the celluloid age. This new movement was in no way attached to the Western world, either for funding or for support. Hence, they enjoyed a greater level of liberty to tell the kind of story that would appeal to African audiences.

This revolution resulted in the phenomenon today referred to as Nollywood. Although used to describe Nigerian movie scene, McCall opines that "its spectacular popularity and its unprecedented ability to reach remote and non-elite audiences, is the most radical development to date in the history of African media."[62] He further states that the uniqueness of Nollywood is in the fact that it is not dependent on foreign sponsors, and this allows it to accommodate "a spectrum of cultural views—Christian, Muslim, traditional and folkloric—the industry appears to remain immune to exploitation by Nigeria's notoriously powerful kleptocrats. Instead, every time a corrupt governor or lascivious clergyman is exposed, the scandal is dramatized and folklorized as a Nollywood drama—enhanced with showy special effects. While Nigerian publishers and editors may risk assassination if they publish criticism of

---

61   Botha, "African Cinema," 4.
62   McCall, "Pan-Africanism," 5.

their leaders, Nollywood boldly continues to generate popular discourse on the corrupt government gaudily dressed up as entertainment."[63]

The assertion above not only suggests independence from Western influence, and of course a decolonization of the space, it also shows that the industry is not attached to the country's political structure, which could influence its objectivity to peoples' issues. This independence in Nigeria and other African movie industries has therefore allowed them to explore a form of creativity that can accommodate both indigenous African culture and Western culture. It is vital to state that globalization and the interaction of world cultures, including Western culture, have rubbed off on present-day African films. This in no way is separated from a dependence on past colonial masters.

The thematic engagement of Nollywood movies is drawn from the social, economic, political, and religious realities of the people of Nigeria and their interactions outside the country. This endears viewers who over the years have remained faithful to these filmmakers. Passchier[64] traces the emergence of the Yoruba subsidiary of Nollywood to the efforts of the traveling theater of the ancient Yoruba empires as well as the tradition of Yoruba masquerading and other rituals. Over time, this has morphed into different forms. Passchier opines that "the first Yoruba traveling theatre foray into film was Ajani Ogun, directed by Ola Balogun in 1977. The protagonist is a hunter and symbolically resembles an incarnation of the Yoruba immortal, Ogun. Yoruba films, including Ajani Ogun were shot on exclusive 35mm celluloid in the seventies."[65] Since the revolution in African movie industry that happened in Nigeria, the industry at the continental level has incorporated African history and her oral traditions, which include myths, proverbs, along with the intentional use of indigenous languages.

For the sake of analysis, the chapter will spotlight a few movies with African sensibilities directed by contemporary African filmmakers. The aim of this is to showcase how these filmmakers have, through sheer creativity and dynamism, visually represented revolt against colonial intruders, protecting what is left of the African identity.

---

63 McCall, "Pan-Africanism."
64 Passchier, "Lessons."
65 Passchier, "Lessons," 24.

Unlike the booming movie industries in Nigeria, Ghana, Egypt, and South Africa, most other African countries have not been able to generate the kind of creative results achieved in the above countries. However, it is impossible to overlook the modest but important efforts from them. In 2003, the first movie to come out of the Central African Republic was released and as expected portrays the psychological damage almost every African country still suffers from years of colonialism. The movie *Le silence de la forêt* witnesses the return of its protagonist to his home country, the Central African Republic, and specifically to the BaAka, the so-called pygmies. The use of the term "pygmy" in the subtitle has been seen as derogatory. This is unfortunately a common phenomenon as far as the relationship between the colonialists and their subject is concerned.

The thematic preoccupation of the movie is a common trope in early postindependence African movies. This is because the colonial period had sponsored some African students to study in Western schools: the aim was more to control such young men and women for procolonial purposes rather than to acculturate them and give them an edge in life. These students would come to an understanding of the true intentions of the colonizers; some of these students come back to Africa armed with this new knowledge to fight colonialism and its remnants. The character Gonaba fits into this frame, and like many others, he goes back to effect change, as he was unhappy with the backwardness of the people. Alas, Gonaba is caught in the web of similar injustices perpetuated by colonial masters; he has no tolerance for his people. By juxtaposing the attitude of colonialists against natives of Central Africa Republic and that of a member of the community but with Western ideas that go against his own native people's beliefs, the filmmakers, through the natives, debunk the idea that what is Western is superior to indigenous African ways. Gonaba had come with the intention of "developing" his people and exposing them to Western education. As we will find out, however, the people are content with being hunters and so do not lend an ear to what Gonaba says.

Alongside the dramatic interplay between the protagonist and other characters who play the role of African natives, there is a deliberate projecting of African identity by the filmmakers. One should not be quick to forget that the movie was released in 2003, by which time most African countries had been thoroughly urbanized. Despite this reality, the film is garnished with the Aka creation myth, which deals with the spirit world and the forest. Its significance to the larger narrative is not lost on the viewer, as Gonaba's only child, Kali, is fatally wounded in the forest while on the journey of his initiation ritual with other men. This sort of initiation ritual is a necessary rite in typical African settings. As a matter of fact, it is impossible to successfully transit from one stage in life to another without these rites. Right from birth, a child—male or female—undergoes a rite of initiation. At the point of death, proper burial rites are performed to ensure a smooth transition into the world of the ancestors for those who have lived nobly on earth. In *Death and the King's Horseman*, Wole Soyinka portrays the initiation process of a dead king in the ancient Oyo kingdom passing from this world to the one beyond. This is to emphasize the importance of initiation to an African. Unfortunately for Kali, the process is cut short by an attack from an elephant in the forest. This attack will eventually lead to his death.

The Boy Who Harnessed the Wind, another African film that was made in the twenty-first century and in fact more recently than *Le silence de la forêt* does not narrate the African story in the same pattern as the latter but focuses on the travails of the protagonist and the frustrations he encounters on the journey to acquiring Western education. This movie simply ponders the nature of an average African child, one that is courageous and optimistic. This visual narrative accommodates the multifaceted challenges facing an average African who lives in a rural area. In this movie, this African is represented by William and his family. The young boy, who has a flair for the scientific, is forced to stay away from school as a result of the hardship meted out to him and other people in the community by the unavoidable agency of nature in the form of drought but also human agency in form of the corrupt public officeholders in Malawi who are more interested in profits than in the well-being of their people.

The movie, released in 2019, is the true story of a boy from Malawi. By telling this African story from the perspective of the protagonist, the movie takes a different turn than *Le silence de la forêt*. The goal here is not a comparative analysis but an attempt to showcase another instance of an African film that portrays an African identity through this creative medium. By mixing the indigenous language of Malawians, the filmmaker maintains a suspended state of disbelief in his viewers and suggests that this is a true story. Coupled with the language is the agrarian life of the rural dwellers portrayed in the movie.

Interestingly, while the people are content with being farmers, only expecting minimal help from their government—a favorable infrastructural policy—they are burdened with high taxes from an indifferent government. Despite this hardship, the young boy William devises an ingenious way to harness the wind—the only resource at their disposal for free—to generate water that could irrigate the land and soften it for farming. William's breakthrough marked a turnaround for his people, and it highlighted a new phase both for him and his community.

The thematic trope of corrupt African leaders is not a new phenomenon in African movies and in fact is a common occurrence. Rather sadly, it has become synonymous with the African identity, so much so that to paint an African leader otherwise would take a lot of genuine effort by the filmmakers to achieve believability. The African filmmaker has assumed the role of the conscience of his or her society, a burden also placed on a writer of African literature. Hence, it is the responsibility of an African filmmaker not just to entertain his or her audience; they are also tasked with exposing and condemning the ills of society. By combining the traditional elements with this task, African filmmakers are exhibiting a superior level of creativity.

The legendary Tunde Kelani's *Agogo Eewo* is a masterpiece that satirizes the ills of society without losing touch with Yoruba indigenous culture. Arguably the most prominent crusade for African culture in the medium of film, Tunde Kelani manages to marry the indigenous with twenty-first-century realities and concerns in a typical African society. The physical setting of the film is largely modern, attesting to the advancements that have been witnessed in some African communities, even on a local scale. This semiurban setting is, however, rife with rural African elements. For instance, the first scene of the movie features the sound of a traditional drum and the image of a dancer. The introductory theatrics might be regarded as prelude; a discerning ear can decipher the message of the drummer. This is common in the traditional setting of the Yoruba people. Drums are not just used for entertainment or aesthetic purposes; they are also used to communicate in code. For instance, drummers are permanent staff in the palace of some kings in Yoruba land, as is evident in *Agogo Eewo*. They sometimes use the traditional drum of bata to praise-sing to the king who is regarded as the most exalted citizen of the community.

As the film unfolds, the viewer meets with the character of an old sage in the community. Again, this is typical of African culture. Africans believe in the wisdom of elders; this is wisdom accrued over time from past experiences. Hence, it is only proper for the younger ones to humble themselves to learn at the feet of sages like the one in *Agogo Eewo*. The sage also serves as a visionary in the narrative; he has witnessed governance in other communities in Yorubaland. And with the benefit of this rare insight, he comes to the conclusion that governance in Jogbo, the fictional town in the narrative, demands more than in other places. From time to time, the sage is more of a social commentator and observer of the direction of things in Jogbo. Every appearance of the sage hints at a possible turn of the narrative, albeit with proverbs, allegories, and idioms. This leaves the viewer guessing as to the actual meaning of what the sage says. Consequently, the sage also fits the role of a storyteller in the traditional African sense.

Meanwhile, at the beginning of the movie there is a replica of the old "tales by moonlight" setting that is known within African indigenous societies whereby an elder in the household (usually a woman) leads the children, within the household and in the neighborhood, on a journey of fictional stories told to them. The children sit still listening and allowing themselves to be lost in the tales. Their function is replicated in the movie by an orchestra that responds to the singing call of the storyteller.

The place of African traditional religion is not lost on the viewer. Despite the predominance of Christianity and Islam in the society portrayed in *Agogo Eewo*, Tunde Kelani makes obvious the place of African traditional religion in the movie. Moreover, it is often agreed that Africans are notoriously religious, and so it will be out of place to have a narrative that does not project that sacred religious life.

The tension between traditional ways and Western style is exemplified in Arese, another important character and a contender for the throne of Jogbo kingdom. The viewer is, however, made to understand that Western ways can complement tradition, as Arese decides to forgo his right to contend for the throne temporarily in order to get a college education. Arese's disposition is such that his acquisition of Western education can make him a better man and indeed a better leader of his people when he eventually becomes the king. His spiritual guardian, the chief priest of Jogbo, could not agree less with him as he states this intent. This establishes the obvious fact that some Western ways have become a permanent part of the African man. However, the African man can consider this new culture and decide how it can be of benefit to him while he strives to preserve what is left of his own culture and style.

Tunde Kelani himself is able to balance the two sides of the divide in the movie. This complementary role is also exemplified in a scene where the old sage engages the writing services of one of the young boys in his household. This action shows the important place of Western education but is also a code representing the present state of things in Jogbo: the indeterminate nature of the community, which is necessitated by the recent ascension of a new king to the Jogbo throne. Again, at the inauguration of the new king, Adebosipo, there is the presence of a newsman, an icon of the Western style of journalism.

The movie does not fail to project what is left of Yoruba indigenous fashion. Firstly, all officials are clad in the traditional Yoruba *aso oke* attire. As discussed earlier in this chapter, *aso oke* used to be the exclusive raiment of royals and men of means in Yoruba traditional society. As evident in the movie, *aso oke* and damask materials are worn by the king himself and his chiefs. Apart from this, the women are distinct in their headgear. In one of the scenes where the king and his queen commune on the dining table, Queen Lape informs her husband of her dealings in superior fabrics worn by monarchs and chiefs in Yoruba land. According to her, doing this is a way of further promoting the Yoruba culture. Furthermore, Tunde Kelani does not miss a chance to educate his viewers on the significance of headgear for traditional Yoruba women. He seizes this opportunity in a scene that features an elderly woman who sees a young girl within the household with her headgear tied to the back. The elderly one calls the younger girl to a conference and educates her on the symbolic meaning of headwear for women of various ages. She notes that a young girl's headgear should face front, as people in her age represent the future of a society. Married ladies should tie theirs to the side, as they are the reigning ones. Older women tie theirs to the back to so as to represent the past. It should be noted that all three categories of women are necessary parts of the Yoruba African society.

The allusions in *Agogo Eewo* to the Nigerian state come in the words of Olaiya, who says that "in particular, the essence is to explore the leadership process and composition in Jogbo, an eloquent metaphor for Nigeria's presidentialism with the attendant crisis of resource-money misappropriation and leadership crisis."[66] Indeed, Nigeria, like many other African countries since independence have been neck-deep in corrupt

---

66   Olaiya, "Narrative."

practices. The misappropriations of public funds and resources by African leaders have placed the continent in a backward position among other nations of the world. As Kelani espouses in *Agogo Eewo*, the challenge of African countries is not lack of resources but its misappropriation by selfish entities.

Conclusion

African artists have successfully broken the hold of colonization in the artistic space. The Nigerian film industry, judging by the number of films produced annually, is regarded as the second largest in the world. Most of these films are deeply rooted in African culture and beliefs. While contemporary African artists find ways to emulate trendy Western styles, they have mixed these with indigenous cultures and have birthed something new. Africans now rap in their indigenous languages to the delight of their audiences. Angelique Kidjo and Asa are examples of Africans who have embraced African dress and language in their music and have enjoyed an impressive level of recognition on the global music scene.

Examples of a few Africans who are making the continent proud without abandoning their African identity have been highlighted above. With the artistic successes achieved in the African creative space, there is no doubting that Africa is capable of great achievements simply by projecting its identity and staying true to its own people and culture.

Chapter Seventeen

Decolonizing African History

Introduction

Decolonizing, as the term implies, is a process of breaking away from and ultimately a reversal of the psychological and physical effects of colonial hegemony. In this case, it concerns the break from and reversal of the effects of European colonial hegemony over Africa's political, economic, and cultural processes. With the 1960s juridical-political "independence" of African territories as part of its first fruits, decolonization is ongoing in pursuance of total liberation and self-determination. Decolonizing African history as an intellectual activity provided the foundation upon which all arguments for the decolonization of Africa were made.[1]

Simply put, decolonizing African history is the act of liberating African knowledge systems. It is concerned with the deconstruction of colonialist Eurocentric traditions that have cast Africa as a "dark continent" without any coherent history. By such a rationale, Africa is said to be incapable of having flourishing cultures except with the influence of the mythical Hermitic and Caucasoid outsiders as posited in the Hermitic hypothesis. As a counteraction, decolonizing African history involves the recognition of marginalized peoples or groups as agents of their own histories and experience. It emphasizes the study of African history from an African point of view and its dissemination using an Africanized curriculum, pedagogical structures, and epistemologies.

---

1   Mignolo, *Darker Side.*

The decolonization of Africa, which encompasses the struggle for liberation, self-determination, equality, and dignity of the African, can be traced to centuries of relations between Europe and Africa dating back to 1500. This relationship was a by-product of a chain of events set off in Europe. The struggle for supremacy among European countries necessitated an expansion of political and economic influence into the New World to exploit its resources, and it redirected European interests toward Africa and the trade in human cargo. This in turn led to the dual outcome of both the creation of a diasporic African community and socioeconomic interactions that left Africa devastated. Constructed by Europeans, world racial placements had the Caucasoid stock naturally placed at the zenith in a classification of races based on skin tones starting from the lightest at the top, signifying the most superior, and leading down to the darkest at the bottom representing the most inferior, with other hues in-between marking the levels of degradation.[2]

The culmination of the period of the transatlantic slave trade (1600–1900) saw a reorganization of European interests in Africa into physical (colonial) conquest and domination. This period was to build on earlier perceived notions of "Black" as bad or, at best, good enough only for exploitation. It was a period ushered in by genocide (putting down local resistance), followed by the subjugation of African peoples, their indigenous knowledge and cultures, and the replacement of local systems with alien colonial systems in a bid to create docile minds. This was perpetrated through the colonial reconstruction of African history. It produced colonial African libraries that distorted the African past intentionally as a colonial policy to foster the master narrative, or unintentionally as a product of a faulty and biased worldview built on Eurocentric assumptions that fail to consider African realities.

With Western education, ironically, came the questioning of racial and discriminatory practices by whites against Black people. Some early beneficiaries of missionary education at home in Africa and other educated Black people in the diaspora initiated a movement for the emancipation of Africa and equality with other races by making the argument that Africans had contributed to world development just as much as anyone else. Whereas some fought on the nationalist stage of the liberation movement, seeking an end to colonial domination on the continent,

---

2   Falola and Agbo, "Prospects."

others (especially those in the African diaspora) took a global approach to end racial discrimination and uphold the rights of all Black people worldwide. In pursuance of this agenda, the principle of Pan-Africanism was developed as a rallying call to all Black people.

After euphoria of the 1960s surrounding the national "liberation" of African territories, the question of tackling and unseating the lasting legacies of colonialism arose. These were the products of European colonial strategies and "coloniality" (a continuation of colonial-like relations after the dismantling of direct colonialism),[3] which continue to undermine Africa's development. To achieve this, it has been suggested by different scholars with Africanist outlooks—such as K. O. Dike, Joseph Ki-Zerbo, Thandika Mkandawire, Mahmood Mamdani, Adebayo Olukoshi, and Toyin Falola, among others—that Africa needs to look within and adopt a different (multidisciplinary) approach that draws inspiration from its own culture, history, and creative imaginations in the development of ideas for proffering solutions to Africa's developmental questions. In addition, African intellectuals must apply indigenous theories and methodologies in their analyses. Chiefly, Africa as a whole should adopt non-European ways of knowing and learning in challenging principles and practices that sustain the status quo (a distorted African image). This is what the decolonization of African history is mainly about: setting the record straight where African history is concerned and unleashing the vast potential of Africa that had been formerly suppressed.

Chapter Statement

Over six decades after the liberation of African territories from direct European political control and over two and a half decades since the last one became independent, Africa seems to have given in to strategically ensured and enduring colonial legacies.[4] The national liberation

---

3   Ndlovu-Gatsheni, "Revisiting."
4   It is pertinent to state here that not all Africans in the position to do so pursued the dissolution of continued European political and economic hegemony in Africa. While some did, actively and openly, others secretly worked with European powers to protect their interests and ensure control over economic and political resources.

era admonition by then nationalist Pan-Africanist Kwame Nkrumah, to "seek ye first the political kingdom," did not result in the materialization of the second concluding part of that popular biblical reference: "and every other thing shall be added unto you." Attempts to cash in on the achievements of political independence and bring this success to bear on other spheres of colonial sociocultural and economic hegemony lost momentum as the independence euphoria died down. This was not, however, without the active interference of the Global North in instigating and or exacerbating preexisting tensions and disruptive tendencies in furtherance of its postcolonial neocolonial ambitions in Africa. This is not an attempt to absolve Africans of all responsibility but to point to the relative ease by which earlier colonial divisive strategies made it possible to derail the African decolonization process: the same colonial strategies that decolonizing African history promises to uproot and discard.

This discourse is geared toward presenting an essence of the decolonization of African history: its origins and nature, justification, processes, objectives, and anticipated outcomes. This is especially true in the face of enduring colonial legacies rooted in colonialist strategies that insist on keeping Africa within the confines of Euro-North American political and economic ambitions.

Origin and Nature of the Decolonization of African History

There was a sudden and dramatic change in the enduring and intricate relationship between Africa and Western Europe that had lasted about three centuries (from the 1500s to the 1880s) by the last quarter of the nineteenth century. This change was brought on by imperialist expansionist ambitions that saw a greater influx of Europeans—Portuguese, Dutch, Spanish, British, French, Germans, and Italians—into Africa in a quest for supremacy and to satisfy their political and economic appetites. These colonizers-to-be were to become unwitting progenitors of decolonization.

The decolonization of African history had its origins in, as Amadou M. M'bow put it, "the numerous myths and prejudices that concealed the real history of Africa from the world at large."[5] This was achieved by way of denial, dismissal, misinterpretation, and distortion of Africa's historical

---

5   Ki-Zerbo ed., *UNESCO*, xvii.

antecedents. All these resulted from the European colonialists' attempts to historicize Africans as weak and ineffectual while pursuing their selfish economic and political goals. The process began with the activities of travelers, adventurers, racist traders, geographers, and colonial administrators who were mostly "trained anthropologists." This colonial riffraff, on their various voyages of discovery and trade, purposely distorted and ridiculed to varying degrees the history of Africa as well as its unique cultural attributes related to language, education, literature, and the agency of its people. This was done in an attempt to project that class of colonialists as the vanguards of a "civilizing mission" in the "dark continent" of Africa.[6]

The strategy was used to create a favorable atmosphere for implanting colonial structure. It cut off Africans from their historical and cultural roots in a bid to destroy their self-esteem, identity, patriotism, and their human rights. It was against such a backdrop that certain Western-educated elites in Africa—Nnamdi Azikiwe, Leopold Senghor, Kwame Nkrumah, Mokugwo Okoye, and Casely Hayford, among others—embarked on what has been described as the "historiography of self-assertion." This was followed by the intervention of professional and academic historians both from within and without Africa—Basil Davidson, Adu Boahen, Joseph Ki-Zerbo, Jean Suaret, Kenneth Onwuka Dike, Alione Diop, and Bethwell Ogot—who provided new African historiography, the "historiography of decolonization," to effectively counteract and contain the increasing threat of colonial propagandists and racist jingoists to African dignity, identity, worldview, and self-perception.

In just over a century after its conception,[7] the idea of decolonizing African history has produced an intellectual revolution in the study of Africa; promoted the legacy of an African Renaissance as articulated by the renowned Senegalese scholar, Cheikh Anta Diop; and inspired other

---

6   Awortu, "African Intellectual," 140.
7   The important contributions of Leo Frobenius, Arturo Labriola, and Maurice Delafosse to rendering objective African historical accounts, as early as the first decades of the twentieth century, bestows upon them the status of pioneers in the decolonization idea. It has also been argued that Herodotus's work *Euterpe* on 450 BC Egypt is one of the "major forces from antiquity to forcefully deal with African historiography" with its "unbiased reportage on the nature of Egyptian civilization."

avenues for the pursuance of African liberation such the Pan-African movement. It started with the insistence on the fact of the existence of a glorious and sophisticated African past worth studying—an academic discipline in its merit worthy of historians within university departments and by African graduate students in European universities.[8] It has since seen to the emergence and study of independent African historiography (African historiography separated from colonial official historiography) and provided a basis for political independence as well as an avenue for a wide range of African initiatives such as Pan-Africanism, African Humanism, Ethiopianism, Negritude, and the Black Consciousness Movement (BCM), among others.

The decolonization of African history as earlier hinted provides the basis upon which decolonization in every other sense finds a foothold. It supplied the historical consciousness and knowledge of self-worth required in making a stand. K. O. Dike describes it thus: "True political development can only take place on a basis of profound self-knowledge so long as the African is regarded as a man without culture and a history; doubts concerning his ability to govern himself will find credence."[9]

If African society can be proven to be equal in stature to other major societies around the globe, then there is no reason why it should not be in charge of its fortunes. This argument formed a substantial basis for nationalist claims to independence. However, political independence as was observed in 1960 was just one step in the right direction toward the complete liberation of Africa. Because complete freedom from European control would mean the absence of any signs of cultural and political dominance. And was that the case after achieving political independence in the 1960s? Of course not.

At the end of their physical political occupation, European institutions and structures continued to linger in Africa for decades—and in some cases still do. Decolonization is not just academic but also consists of practical projects to further development and autonomy. The progress of the decolonization of African history has been interrupted by challenges stemming from the rise of a capitalist world economic system that involved the forceful incorporation "of Africa into the evolving nexus of

---

8 Awortu, "African Intellectual," 141.
9 Alagoa, "Of Days," 146.

Figure 17.1. Oil portrait of Kenneth Onwuka Dike as a young man, January 1940. Robert Sivell. Creative Commons License CC BY-SA 3.0.

a structurally asymmetrical world system with its shifting orders."[10] The unbalanced economic and attendant social relations that exist in current world systems are structured by Euro–North American interests to fit their exploitation agendas. These interests have been known to spare no expense—they will resort to war, coups, and other politically destabilizing acts—in defending any status quo tipped in their favor.

In some quarters it has been argued that the decolonization process was doomed from the onset. This point of view posits that the vanguards of the movement were already compromised, having been "hand-picked" and "white-washed" by a brief stay in the mother country. They are said to have returned branded with the principles of Western culture and their mouths "full with high-sounding phrases and grand gluttonous words

---

10   Ndlovu-Gatsheni, "Revisiting."

that stuck to the teeth."[11] And the "walking talking lies," as they were referred to, were left to lead such important tasks of nationalism and self-determination. One cannot be too quick to ignore such claims given the that early African Western-educated elite were not fully opposed to colonial modernity, steeped as they were in the Christian faith and Victorian ideas of liberalism.

In Africa, these unbalanced economic relations have placed Africa at the mercy of European and North American–controlled world economic agencies such as the IMF and the WB. These agencies have capitalized on the sorry state of African economic affairs, which are not unconnected to the activities of the Global North in Africa, to force the continent into debt agreements that have afforded them the authority to dictate economic measures in Africa. Structural adjustment programs represent a policy of austerity. These measures compel the African government to cut funding to key sectors such as education.

When the state skimps on education funding, scholars become less committed to the pursuit of research goals. This happens at the expense and "detriment of essential research and sustained scholarship, exposing education to rigid state control and as a result subjecting it to the whims and caprices of the political establishment and the authoritarian propensities of African states and governments."[12] With most of the support for the decolonization of African history traditionally coming from academia, this indirect interference can be construed as imperialism in the postglobalization form of backlash.

Other factors holding back the process of decolonizing African history range from a lack of political support, insufficient will, lack of sustained commitment by African scholars beyond rhetoric, and dwindling awareness of the general populace. In the area of dwindling awareness, the limiting of the study of history generally as a discipline in African schools and confining it to particular faculties is partly responsible. And it is an outcome of this honorable discipline being increasingly considered outdated and not lucrative enough to be worthy of scholarly endeavor, especially with the attendant expenses involved. Lastly is the number of Africans excluded by the lack of conventional education opportunities, which in turn limits their access to necessary orientation material. This

---

11   Ndlovu-Gatsheni and Chambati, *Coloniality*, 248.
12   Nyamnjoh, "Decolonizing."

highlights another point of address: the use of African languages in the communication of African ideas.

Notwithstanding the challenges, the achievement of the passage of African history to formal academic acceptance marks a fundamental attitudinal change from an Africa with no history to an Africa with a robust history. This commendable foundation and subsequent strides are the result of relentless efforts of both the pioneer class of the field and subsequent generations who have kept Africanist ideals alive. However, there are still more milestones left to reach in order to get to the ultimate goal of equal recognition in social, political, and economic relations between Africa and the Global North.

Justifications for Decolonizing African History

According to Ndlovu-Gatsheni and Chambati:

> One of the most powerful myths of the twentieth century was the notion that the elimination of colonial administrations amounted to the decolonization of the world. This led to the myth of a "postcolonial" world. The heterogeneous and multiple global structures put in place over a period of 450 years did not evaporate with the juridical-political decolonization of the periphery over the past 50 years. We continue to live under the same "colonial power matrix." With juridical political decolonization we moved from a period of "global colonialism" to the current period of "global coloniality."[13]

In twenty-first-century Africa, there is little doubt of the existence of colonial-like relations between Africa, the "developing," and the "developed" world, which have adamantly withstood African attempts at liberation. One must ask: is the goal of decolonizing African history so lofty as to be a mere pipe dream? The hope that one day Africans would stand with pride in their identity, having rid themselves and their histories of debilitating colonial conceptions: Is that still within reach? What is the alternative? Can Africa and Africans afford to live with the global stigma of a "backward" and "victimized" people?

---

13   Ndlovu-Gatsheni and Chambati, *Coloniality*, 4.

Decolonizing African history is the only sensible response to the malicious colonial slandering of an entire continent. The decision by the Global North to launch both mental and physical assaults on the African people was informed by an inordinate quest to take from Africa its wealth and thus its global status. In the course of the events that brought Africa under European colonial subjugation, the very humanity of every African was put on trial by Europe when it called into question his or her cognitive capacities. Under a purely European judge and jury in the form of a prevalent European "scholarly" consensus at the time, which dictated most of Europe's (and indeed the world's) perception of peoples and their agencies, Africa stood no chance. It was condemned as a "dark continent," one bereft of any coherent history.

This perception later became crystallized through the production of Eurocentric literature by then prominent European "thinkers"—both in the biological and social sciences fields—to disseminate this falsehood of a historically insignificant Africa as historical knowledge. Such a poor image of the African continent held much sway between 1885 and 1945, when most of its territories were under colonial domination in a period that became known as the era of "colonial historiography."

The concept of colonial historiography is based on the conclusion that Africa and indeed the Black man were not evolutionarily advanced enough and lacked cognitive skills, as was demonstrated in the absence of the development of an indigenous system of writing. Therefore, using that racist logic, any existing African history must be the history of Europeans in Africa: a "part of the historical progress and development of Western Europe and an appendix of the national history of the metropolis."[14] Thus, African historiography was tied to the official colonial historiography, with prejudices and Eurocentric assumptions disseminated with a certain arrogance. This was the status quo during the colonial period when African historiography as a vehicle for decolonization was developed to correct these distortions and set the pace for further achievements along that trajectory. As E. O. Uya put it, the task was to "rescue African history from the monumental distortions and falsehoods of Euro-American scholars who not only denied our historical heritage but also excluded us, by and large, from having played a significant role in their European drama of exploration, conquest, colonization, and administration of the

---

14 Ogot, *UNESCO*, 71.

continent. The pioneering works of this generation set new challenging directions for African historical studies in content and methodology."[15]

Therefore, it cannot be gainsaid that decolonizing African history is as relevant an agenda for the emancipation of Africa now as it was then. Given this fact, Africa is yet to rid itself of some of the lasting impressions of the colonial era, especially as these still feature in the makeup of African sociocultural and economic practices redressed as globalization goals.

Aspects/Periods in the Decolonizing African History

There are essentially three phases to the process of decolonization of African history. The first phase, resisting colonialism (1880–1914),[16] was purely armed resistance. The second, beginning in the 1950s, was a combination of intellectual and armed struggle. It was more demonstrative and showed that Africa had a past that can be written and recorded, with African history becoming an academic discipline in its own right.[17] The third phase is the postindependent phase, which began in the 1970s after the independence euphoria had passed, the "decade of development" had failed to produce tangible outcomes, and neocolonialism was becoming a reality. This was blamed on the fact that "the development programs were based on the presuppositions of neoliberal economics and external models."[18]

Incidentally, the period after the end of World War II (1945) coincided with the coming of age of Africans educated in the Western tradition. Notable pioneer writers— such as Samuel Ajayi Crowther, James Beale Horton, Nathaniel S. King, Sir Samuel Lewis, Christian F. Cole, James Johnson, Henry Johnson, and Henry Carr—were equipped with the enlightenment that often comes with education. Having had firsthand experience with European society (and in some cases studying it), they were not only demystified by the ordinariness of the so-called superior race, which battled similar societal maladies as Africans, but also began to question the legitimacy of their claim of superiority and rule over Africa.

---

15   Uya, "Trends."
16   Ross, "African Resistance," 89–96.
17   Ogot, *UNESCO*, 71.
18   Ogot, *UNESCO*, 72.

One such individual, Kenneth Onwuka Dike, otherwise known as K. O. Dike, a product of Fourah Bay College Sierra Leone and the University of London, came to play instrumental roles in the decolonization of African history.

Dike's efforts in proving that indeed Africa's past was neither inexistent nor lost were pivotal to challenging colonial historiographical assertions of an unhistorical Africa and solidifying the foundations for decolonizing African history. His doctoral thesis "Trade and Politics in the Niger Delta 1830–1885," which he produced using then unconventional research methods, marked a watershed in the study and perception of African history, setting in motion the development of various historical decolonization processes.[19] Dike's pathfinding achievements in those early decolonization years are critically important in presenting a hierarchy of the processes of decolonizing African history.

Affirming the African Personality and Capabilities

The activities of Prof. Dike, dubbed the "prime mover of the new African history and historiography,"[20] in no small way contributed to the decolonizing of African history. By successfully choosing a subject on Nigerian groups in relation to European merchants, he was able to demonstrate that to objectively interrogate and comment on the nature of Africa's past, the observer (researcher) must take into account its ecology and avoid unrealistic hypotheses. Hence, owing to the unique ecology of Africa, the "wheel" cannot be a yardstick in measuring development in

---

19 Samuel Johnson's *History of the Yoruba* is one other (earlier) history of an African civilization written by an African scholar using oral traditions. Influential as it was, it did not play the revolutionary role of winning recognition for indigenous African sources as ideal for the reconstruction of African history over the prevailing dogmatic belief of the period. This might not be unconnected to the completion of the first manuscripts (1897)—a period when British colonial interests could not afford a social awakening demonstrated by its convenient misplacement by British publishers. Others in East Africa, like Sir Apolo Kawa and S. A. Kiwanuka, wrote the history of the Buganda people of Uganda.

20 Dike, educated at the Fourah Bay College, Sierra Leone, is still considered one of the founding fathers of African historiography.

the area, nor can its absence be considered proof of the backwardness and incapability of man in tropical Africa.

In further attempts to redeem Africa's image from the yoke of various fallacious Eurocentric theories that presented the continent in different derogatory shades like: "the dark continent," "barbarous tribes," and "the white man's burden," Dike investigated an African region with a history of economic relations with the West. In this research (his seminal work), *Trade and Politics in the Niger Delta 1830–1885*, he demonstrated that in the political and economic relations between Great Britain and the Niger Delta in the nineteenth century, both parties traded as equals. This exposed explorers, missionaries, and administrators, the hitherto harbingers of civilization, as agents of European domination and exploitation. It also had the dual effects of recasting Africa's image in a better light and spurring on the fight for dignity, humanity, and self-rule.

The wide circulation and regard that Dike's *Trade and Politics in the Niger Delta* enjoyed, especially with its publication by Oxford University Press, encouraged other African scholars both abroad and on the continent to research African history and even histories of other cultures different from their own. This also helped to dispel the notion of an ahistorical Africa: Dike showed that, in fact, Africa had a robust past. This recognition also led to African history being increasingly accepted as an academic discipline in Western scholarly institutions: soon came the advent of Schools of Oriental Studies (SOAS) in major European universities in Berlin, London, and Vienna—and by 1984 in Asia, Australia, and America. These were in African sociocultural, ethnohistorical, and religious history fields.[21]

Oral Tradition

The next step was to confront a major European objection to African history: the almost total absence of written records in African societies. With statements like "history begins when men begin to write" and "without writing and so without history"[22] from then eminent English writers, the

---

21 Awortu, "African Intellectual," 144.
22 These statements are credited to English writers N. P. Newton and Perham, respectively.

task was to debunk this erroneous view that Africa's past is the concern of archaeologists and anthropologists and not historians.

Oral traditions (i.e., the methods of systematic collection and progressive application of historical information transferred by word of mouth from one generation to another) and other indigenous African sources were used by Dike in his doctoral dissertation to convincingly demonstrate that "African historiography was as respectable as the European perspectives of other spheres of history."[23] The importance of oral traditions for the reconstruction of African history was therefore established by demonstrating that although these traditions were not written down or preserved inside tangible structures like modern archives, they have been preserved in rituals and reenactment ceremonies and have survived. This success also "revealed the crucial place occupied by oral, non-written sources, thereby establishing an acceptable and a valid methodology which became the central thrust and issue in the revolution of African historiography in the twentieth century."[24]

Another aspect of the importance of oral traditions was the respite from an overreliance on and the inadequacies of written sources that were external in origin and orientation. Given the historical monopoly and political and cultural outlook of European historians of the time, which left them predisposed to prejudicial conceptions and interpretation of Africa's past, there was a need for multiple approaches to its interrogation. Oral traditions enabled the historians to add to the resource base of writing. These also informed the need for a multi/interdisciplinary approach to historical study.

Interdisciplinary and Multidisciplinary Approaches

The main character of decolonization has always been intellectual, although with practical political and socioeconomic applications. This is because the very existence of decolonization is in response to

---

23 Awortu, "African Intellectual," 142.
24 It is pertinent to point out here that K. O. Dike's insistence on the use of oral traditions came about partly as a result of restrictions placed by the colonial government on classified public documents as part of the fifty-year rule.

the revisionism of a gang of intellectuals who represented an imperialist dogma that held sway in Europe from the fifteenth century onward. These intellectuals were commissioned to preach the gospel of the superiority and inferiority of peoples (races) with dubious scientific theories and hypotheses to support their claims and provide moral justification for the murder and plunder of civilizations.

This was taken a step further with the establishment of institutions and agencies that developed literature, curricula, and syllabi to perpetuate falsehoods as territorial histories. Therefore, the environment for rallying anticolonial sentiment (decolonization) was inadvertently localized at the institutions for learning and indoctrination: schools.

The inclusion of multidisciplinary as well as interdisciplinary techniques in the methodology of African historiography is essential. The very nature of the historical study is all-encompassing. Historical study cuts across every aspect of human activity. Therefore, to obtain a balanced picture of a historical phenomenon, the historian has to interrogate every available source concerned with its formation or run the risk of arriving at unrealistic conclusions. As in the case of history and linguistics, a historian who does not understand the language of the source is bound to misrepresent the facts. This applies to other disciplines such as economics, botany, archaeology, anthropology, and sociology, to mention a few. However, the historian no longer needs be versed in these fields (though some basic knowledge is advised) to apply their respective techniques where necessary, as professional interdisciplinary consultations are now available.

K. O. Dike is credited with the position of being the first to apply a multidisciplinary approach to African historiography, laying the foundation for interdisciplinary studies. He is said to have been the first to apply two separate disciplines to explaining a historical period: the nineteenth-century European (British) political and economic power play in the Niger Delta of present-day Nigeria. This he achieved by combining economics and history in developing an analytical methodology—a systematic way of studying and explaining socioeconomic behavior over some time—fundamentally creating a new branch of history known as "economic history."[25]

In attempts to further open up access to Africa's past, additional avenues for collecting, storing, and accessing sources were established. These

---

25 Awortu, "African Intellectual," 143.

institutes were established to merge ideas from government officials, the public, and academic institutions. The earliest of these institutions was the Institute of African Studies set up at the University of Ibadan, Nigeria, in 1962. Others were the Nigerian Institute for International Affairs, the Department of Antiquities, and the National Archives.

What this means for decolonizing African history is the availability of additional avenues by which Africa's historical past can be reconstructed in as objective a manner as possible without losing key defining aspects. It also means more ways of deconstructing previously held misconceptions about Africa's past. The interdisciplinary method of research is now presented as conventional in many African universities. It has been improved upon by successive generations of historians after its inception. The social sciences in this context have become an important complementary discipline in the development of African historiography.

Institutions and Departments for Decolonizing African History

The National Archives

In Nigeria, the National Archives has been an invaluable repository of information on colonial Nigeria. This institution has been able to locate, collect, and preserve valuable and previously restricted colonial government documents that have aided a more comprehensive knowledge of the internal intricacies of colonial administration. This has also helped to provide better-founded perspectives and chronology to fill gaps usually mired in speculation. As a national symbol, the National Archives represent tangible evidence of a period in Nigerian as well as African history when the fortunes of its people were in the hands of foreign elements, and Africa's interests were not their chief concern. This serves as a constant reminder of how far Africa has come but how far there is still to go to eradicate the last vestiges of the debilitating colonial system.

National and International Research Schemes

African countries developed national and regional research schemes and also set up international research partnerships that produced journals such as the *Journal of African History*, *International Journal of African and Asian*

Studies; *Journal of Historical Society of Nigeria* (JHSN); *Transactions of the Historical Society of Ghana, Africa*; and *Afrika Zamani, d'histoire Africaine* in francophone West Africa. More recent times have seen the advent of Council for the Development of Social Science Research in Africa (CODESRIA), The Africa Humanities Program (AHP), and International Higher Education and Strategic Projects (IHESP) program. These bodies have worked together over the years to provide grants and platforms for researchers to explore their areas of interest, producing large volumes of research material on a broad spectrum of African areas and topics.

Universities/Colleges

The contributory role of institutions of higher learning (as centers of knowledge production) in the decolonization of African history has been the subject of intense debates from the 1970s to the twenty-first century, especially with the relatively recent independence of southern African states like Zimbabwe and Namibia. South Africa is still in the process of decolonizing/Africanizing its university personnel in recognition of the importance of this step to making the African university/college an ideal instrument for the formation and dissemination of African epistemology. This process, although new to that region of Africa, is not a new phenomenon on the continent.

There were others like the University Colleges of Ibadan, Nigeria, and the Gold Coast (present-day Ghana), both set up in 1948 in West Africa. These had similar preoccupations on the eve of (and a few decades into) the postindependence years, preoccupations that converged on one particular point: decolonization to facilitate increased Africanization of university education in Africa. They also represent the first set of African knowledge producers who "mounted pressure on Western epistemologies through mimicry, counter-factualization of dominant discourses and other means."[26]

Postindependence governments immediately identified education as a priority in building infrastructure by equipping citizens with knowledge in medicine, economics, science, and engineering. Also identified were the importance of postcolonial stories of Africa; its histories, philosophy, literature, arts, and cultural traditions told through the eyes of

---

26 Ndlovu-Gatsheni and Chambati, *Coloniality*, 55.

its indigenous scholars and thinkers. To facilitate this drive, the governments in sub-Saharan Africa invested between 10 to 25 percent of their spending on education, with about a quarter of that amount reserved for universities and colleges.[27]

The University College Ibadan, and especially its history department, was reputable in Africa and around the world for promoting African historiography. With about four professors, the department used its resources to spread its methodology to other parts of Nigeria and Africa in what later came to be known as the "Ibadan school" of thought. The University College Ibadan History Department, under the leadership of Dike, also established professional bodies like the Historical Society of Nigeria (HSN), which introduced the Tarikha[28] and has produced journals of international repute. Such professional historical bodies have formed associations with their counterparts in other African countries, like the decades-old relationship between the Historical Society of Nigeria and the *Transactions of the Historical Society of Ghana*. It served to inspire similar cooperation in other parts of Africa.

The decolonization of universities in Africa through the "promotion of perspectives grounded in African realities and experiences,"[29] has been identified as a prerequisite for the decolonization of African history. However, in Africa, this has hardly gone beyond the Africanization of university personnel. Even so, just because an individual is or appears to be African cannot guarantee that they would be critical of colonial intellectual traditions in their research and teaching.[30] Moreover, relevant aspects such as curricula, pedagogical structures, and epistemologies have remained external to local cultures and institutions. As a result of the existing rigid academic structures and practices, African universities do not turn out knowledge sensitive to African social problems and neither do they encourage critical mindedness. What we have are "Western-oriented institutions located within the African continent producing Westernized graduates who are alienated from the African society and its African values."[31]

---

27 D'Souza, "African History."
28 *Tarikh* is Arabic for "date," "chronology," and "era." Purportedly it was also used in Persian and Turkic languages.
29 Nyamnjoh, "Decolonizing," 3.
30 Nyamnjoh, "Decolonizing," 3.
31 Ndlovu-Gatsheni and Chambati, *Coloniality*, 32.

The gains recorded by immediate postcolonial governments through their education- funding policies also produced the "golden age" of African higher education in the 1960s and 1970s. The challenges of subsequent decades—economic shocks, military and authoritarian regimes, and the debt crisis that brought in the IMF and WB loans and austerity measures—have all taken huge tolls on the tertiary education institutions of many countries on the continent.

The latest identified challenges to decolonizing African universities vis-à-vis African history are lack of funding and marketization of universities, lack of sustained commitment by scholars beyond mere rhetoric, and rigid state control. Funding cuts have resulted in underachievement because researchers are placed "at the mercy of market forces and are therefore pushed to resort to moonlighting to make ends meet, to the detriment of fundamental research and sustained scholarship."[32] If we are being honest, even the most committed would be discouraged by these kinds of challenges, even though there are occasions where some scholars, against the odds, stay the course at great personal expense.

Any attempt at transforming African universities into uncompromisingly inclusive institutions by embracing African epistemology would not only require adequate funding but will also mean "looking beyond the academy in its current configuration for inspiration."[33] It would involve drawing inspiration from personal stories and creative imaginations and a conscious attempt at convivial scholarship:

> Convivial scholarship recognizes the deep power of collective imagination and the importance of interconnections and nuanced complexities. It questions assumptions of prior locations and bounded ideas of power and all other forms of relationships that shape and are shaped by the socio-cultural, political, and economic circumstances of social actors. It is a scholarship that sees the local in the global and the global in the local by bringing them into informed conversations, conscious of the hierarchies and power relations at play at both the micro and macro levels of being and becoming. Convivial scholarship is a scholarship that neither dismisses contested and contrary perspectives a priori nor throws the baby out with the bathwater. It is critical scholarship of recognition and reconciliation, scholarship that has no permanent friends, enemies, or alliances beyond the rigorous and committed

---

32 Nyamnjoh, "Decolonizing," 1.
33 Nyamnjoh, "Decolonizing," 1.

quest for truth in its complexity and nuance, in communion with the natural and supernatural environments that make a balanced existence possible.[34]

Such "convivial" scholarship, as a change from the limiting, reactionary intellectual preoccupations of anticolonial literature, is a step toward the existence of wholesome accounts of African history from whence scholarly inspiration can be drawn to meet present needs. There is no doubt that there exists a correlation between a fully decolonized African university and the existence of robust, globally competitive knowledge-producing institutions that are sacrosanct to Africa's emergence at the global stage.

Antiquities Departments

Another institution that holds timeless relevance for decolonizing African history in all its forms are governmental departments of antiquities. These provide insight into the content and workings of preliterate African societies through their handling of African artistic expression over the years. Departments of antiquities generally trade in works of fine art, which represent the oldest surviving records of human presence, especially in West Africa, serving as an important source for the reconstruction of history. These departments have proven to be of invaluable importance in proving the existence of a culturally rich African past.

African Epistemology

A staunch supporter of a multidisciplinary approach to African studies is Dr. Bala Usman of the Department of History, Ahmadu Bello University Zaria. In his critique of Heinrich Barth's well-regarded travel narratives, Usman drew attention to the latter's emphasis on the genetic and physical characteristics of the individuals he was researching. This, Usman said, was the product of the dominant traditions of nineteenth-century Europe that formed the historian's outlook. To him, the historian as a product of his society is not immune to the influences that society exerts on the individual and cannot be completely divorced from his or her education and life experiences that are most likely to influence his perception and writing.

---

34   Nyamnjoh, "Decolonizing," 25.

The nature of research and available body of academic knowledge from the sixteenth century to at least the first decade of the twentieth century were informed by and relevant to the experience of Europeans and the European continent. As the globally dominant force of that century disseminating its culture and (scholarly) traditions around its imperial possessions, European thought came to dominate global academic conceptions, theories, and methodologies of the study of world phenomena in that period. This meant that the histories of peoples around these areas of European influence were studied through the prism of European prejudice. This situation resulted in the application of perceptions and analytic processes that hardly represented the reality of the subject matter (in this case Africa), which lasted until the eve of colonialism, when active steps were taken to correct it by developing an African epistemology.

African epistemology is the idea of the existence of an Africanized theory of knowledge that includes an African conception of knowledge, the means of gaining knowledge, criteria for the assessment of the validity of knowledge, purpose for the pursuit of knowledge, and the role of knowledge in human existence. The independence of African studies is contingent upon the existence of African epistemology, which would provide it with the African character (methodology) necessary for navigating the nuances of Africa's cultures and civilizations as well as identifying research areas relevant to its development.

To write African history as opposed to a European history of Africa is to think African. This is not about deliberately compromising on objectivity but rather the ability to see truly African perspectives and not those of an outsider. Yes, some level of detachment is required between the researcher and the object of inquiry but not so much that the researcher becomes unaware of key defining characteristics. An African epistemology is about setting a standard for writing histories that reflect true African realities. Without an African epistemology, African studies would be compelled to force its historical findings into predetermined models that do not lend themselves to perpetuation of historical fact.

Historical Consciousness

A popular saying among undergraduate university students in Africa is derived from a quote that reads, "Those who do not learn from the past are doomed to repeat it." This is especially true for Nigerians, who have been accused by their kin of being too eager to leave the past behind. What is a man without his memories? What is medical efficiency without medical history? Historical consciousness is about knowing and having the knowledge of self: not in isolation but as a collective in the grand scheme of things. It is being acutely aware of how the world operates as a prerequisite for navigating the murkiness that is global competing interests. Historical consciousness is to be alive to the world around you and to have a finger on its pulse.

Historical consciousness is the substance of continental (at a broader level) and nationalistic sentiments. It is the source of patriotic dispositions, a key element in decolonizing African history. For without intimate knowledge of Africa and its people, the process of decolonization cannot effectively take place. The critical place of historical consciousness in Africa's development has been demonstrated in the course of the revolutionary evolution of its history, especially in the second half of the twentieth century. It gave momentum to the intellectual and political resistance against colonialism in all its ramifications in that period. Its importance also extended to the political organization of emergent Africa, providing African leaders and peoples with the self-confidence required to move their states forward. This produced in the political elites a better sense of organization and governance, seeing to the funding of projects of historical and cultural value.

However, a few decades after political independence, a keen historical consciousness was not enough to withstand the long aftereffects of the colonial regime's creation of arbitrary boundaries that characterized their "divide and rule" policy. These and the socioeconomic challenges stemming from the neocolonial nature of global relations—in favor of the Global North—have generated more friction in sociocultural relations in Africa.

The increasing tendency of African leaders to divert critical public funds for private use, serve foreign interests as a means of ensuring personal wealth, and undemocratically clinging to power for as long as possible has also betrayed the existence and influence of historical consciousness. This situation is not unconnected with the growing disappearance of history as an academic discipline in African schools. And where the teaching of history does take place, the society and especially its leadership seem to underestimate its value of history as a vehicle of enlightenment and reconstruction. This can also be viewed as a deliberate attempt by the African leadership to avoid accountability by discouraging the culture of record-keeping for future references. In this scenario, Pan-Africanism as a pro-Africa ideal plays a key role in the reawakening of the historical consciousness of people of African descent toward the unification of efforts in achieving complete liberation.

The Objective of Decolonizing African History

As previously illustrated, the singular objective of decolonization is engaging with colonialism in all periods of its existence and at all levels. The emphasis here on "African history" is to highlight the intellectual approach to reversing the psychological effects of colonial indoctrination on the African psyche. This intellectual revolution is identified as having led other expressions of anticolonial activity beginning in the 1950s, from economic and political movements to African Renaissance principles such as Pan-Africanism and Negritude.

Africa's intellectual uprising, promising though it was at the onset, eventually lost momentum owing in no small way to its failure to redefine and restructure Africa's web of connections to Europe and America. That decolonization is still a very significant topic in Africa's intellectual discourse on finding the right path to socioeconomic and political advancement points to one thing: political independence did not translate into the evaporation of centuries of global colonial structures put in place by Euro-American agents of imperialism.

The general objective of decolonizing African history is to liberate African knowledge, as well as adopt and adapt traditional African ways of knowing and knowledge production. It involves creating an indigenous knowledge-based system that is in tune with the African realities and can carve out independent models to resolve Africa's overdependence on the "developed world" for political, economic, sociocultural, and innovative leadership. The objectives of decolonizing African history are united in a singular goal. However, for a comprehensive analysis, this would be split into individual points of assessment. Therefore, the individual objectives would be: knowledge production, African liberation and freedom, and African development. These are broadly categorized objectives at the center of the "postcolonial neo-colonized world" which was never completely actualized beyond "some emancipatory pretensions."[35]

---

35 Ndlovu-Gatsheni, "Decolonizing," 4.

Knowledge Production

This subsection is concerned with the decolonizing of Africa's knowledge production and dissemination systems. It involves the recognition and application of thought patterns that originate and are grounded in African reality. The restoration to prominence of ancient sources of African history such as the Afro-Christian library; Kebra Negaste; Afro-Islamic Ajami Library; *Ta'rīkh al-Sūdān*; *Ta'rīkh al-Fattāsh*; *Kano Chronicle*; *Gonja Chronicle*; *Kilwa Chronicle*; and the griot library (oral traditions) in the conception and reconstruction of African history.

Epistemologically, it involves theorizing on African problems and issues as a way of producing knowledge by African intellectuals for academic uses in Africa by Africans. Part of this process is to disengage from the traditional reliance on Western models of thought[36] that reduce African intellectuals to mere "hunters and gatherers" and "native informants" who collect raw empirical data on Africa that then get processed in the West into theories and concepts for consumption in Africa.[37] The decolonization of Africa's educational institutions means, crucially, transforming them into ideal producers of African thought.

African Liberation and Freedom

This involves social organization through social coherence. The intent is to identify, discontinue, or replace enduring colonial legacies that have either remained in their original forms or operating under the guise of neocolonial neoliberalism (e.g., globalization) in expropriating Africa's wealth. In this respect, the agenda is to achieve self-determination, create nation-states that are ostensibly sovereign, initiate economic development advantageous to all Africans, and install democracy, human rights, and human dignity that were initially denied under colonialism.

To achieve the above-listed agenda (both formal and informal, local and in the diaspora), agencies for the unification of African efforts toward liberation would be brought together by the identification of a common

---

36 Such models are founded on Euro-American epistemological fundamentalism that repudiates the existence of knowledge from non-Western regions of the world.

37 Ndlovu-Gatsheni and Chambati, *Coloniality*.

destiny to collaborate with national governments. To lead this process, continental African bodies such as the African Union (AU), New Partnership for African Development (NEPAD), and New International Economic Order (NIECO), plus intercontinental associations such as a reformed Pan-African movement and the BCM will assume center stage. The idea will be to have a well-oiled system that unites Africa through intercontinental, regional, and international collaborations.

African Development

African development here means escaping global neocolonial traps, which are also known as the "colonial matrix of power." This system is complete with "social-economic, cultural, ideological, aesthetic, and epistemological contours combined to reduce, silence, dominate, oppress, exploit, and overshadow the non-Western world."[38] The conscious attempt to break free from the dictates of greed-fueled Western world powers and their lopsided economic policies would involve Africa distancing itself from IMF and WB interventions (loans) and banking integration arrangements and putting more emphasis on intracontinental dependencies and collaborations.

The collaborations at the intercontinental stage would involve regions of the Global South, which share similar colonial heritage and neocolonial pressures with Africa, such as Latin America. The regional and international levels involve both brushing up on preexisting regional integrated economic formations such as Economic Community of West African States (ECOWAS), the Arab Maghreb Union (AMU), Community of Sahel-Saharan States (CEN-SAD), the Common Market for Eastern and Southern Africa (COMESA), the East African Community (EAC), the Economic Community of Central African States (ECCAS), Intergovernmental Authority for Development (IGAD), and Southern African Development Community (SADC,) and forming new alliances as the need arises. However, this time perhaps this can be done with an emphasis on complementary partnerships, which stands to improve social relations and economic prospects. Such regional African interdependency keeps the wealth within Africa and out of the hands of neocolonial outsiders.

---

38 Ndlovu-Gatsheni and Chambati, *Coloniality*, 5.

Anticipated Outcomes of Decolonizing African History

The extent of entanglement and the "entrapment" of issues of African identity formation, economic development, state-building, knowledge production, and democratization "within the colonial matrices of modern global power"[39] have driven some to the conclusion that full decolonization can only be a myth. From this perspective, African liberation peaked in the era of "juridical-political independence" beginning in the 1950s, culminating with the fall of apartheid in 1994. To these conveniently "pragmatic" views, one might point out that myths are only myths until proven otherwise.

The expectations of those who refuse to lose faith in decolonization are that if some strategic repositioning of Africa's creative and productive energies can be achieved, then just enough space can be cleared to turn the narrative around. This task is incredibly daunting, especially given that the existing Euro-American-dominated racial, hierarchical, hegemonic, capitalist global socioeconomic system exists in its current form to ensure that the status quo stands. That notwithstanding, the continuous onslaught of capitalist greed has made resistance an instinct as much as a duty and necessity.

The intellectual gains of decolonizing African history, especially by Africanizing the university system, are expected to encourage research relevant to improving African realities and provide the epistemological basis for re-creating a true African identity and consciousness, one devoid of the influences of imperialist, neocolonial distortions. This identity should embolden Africans to act in their own collective interests and not as slaves to the West. Decolonizing African history should, therefore, mark the emancipation of African thought from Western-dictated patterns, providing African academics and scholars with the chance to follow their own avenues of research.

Decolonization should help properly historicize Africa as contributing to human civilization and development, thus rescuing the African image from centuries-old slander and negative Euro-American labels and extolling indigenous African methodologies by demonstrating their efficacies as sufficient analytical tools for the interrogation of past and present African realities. It should also substitute both Western and Eastern socioeconomic and political dependencies with intracontinental regional cooperation and

---

39 Ndlovu-Gatsheni and Chambati, *Coloniality*.

strengthened African intuitions. Decolonization should, overall, guarantee Africa's freedom from neocolonial socioeconomic manipulation and set her on a self-determined path to self-realization and prosperity.

Conclusion

The importance of decolonizing African history is reenforced by the extent to which the continent suffers from the multidimensional socioeconomic onslaught from the "developed" world. This is evident in the outcome of an earlier decolonization attempt truncated by neoliberal imperialism, which insisted on the readoption of colonial hegemonic structures rebranded as globalization that has reduced Africa to a theater of conflict.

Now African affairs seem to resemble 1885 all over again. World powers are once again staking their claims through socioeconomic influences under the guise of modernity and democratization. Furthermore, modern African knowledge production systems remain hijacked by the same Euro-American imperialist epistemology and methodology that informed them; These and other issues that revolve around economic dependency and liberation suggest decolonizing Africa as a viable approach to workable and enduring solutions.

As it is, however, the most widespread focus of African scholarly endeavor—epitomized by the available volumes of work—is on almost five centuries of interaction with Europe, which when compared to the five thousand years of conventional history does not cover an adequate period nor the most defining aspect of the continent's evolution. The unbalanced African preoccupation with the West points to the neglect of other important aspects of its being that can provide that elusive, alternative route to independent development. Therefore, as important an agenda as decolonizing African history is, it must not be carried out strictly as a way to unseat Euro-American hegemony.

Chapter Eighteen

Decolonizing African Religion

Many Africans who have partaken of Western education have been de-Africanized in one way or another. The linguistic component of their education played a part in this process; language is neither neutral nor innocent in how it configures minds. A few Africans passing through Western education systems have used their cultural legacies as guides to scrutinize the knowledge that was presented to them. The rest developed a foreign mindset and discarded their inherited values, including religion. They became alienated from indigenous practices and philosophies, removed from the ideas and systems that sustained their people for thousands of years before European missionaries and colonizers arrived. In extreme cases, the de-Africanized graduates of Western institutions collaborated in the disruption of African religious practices, assisting with the destruction of valuable artifacts that had immense social and spiritual worth to African communities.

Adherence to African traditional religion (ATR) began its decline from the time of colonial contact, competing for attention with external religions and cultures. It became difficult for the custodians of these African religious practices to preserve their legacies unless they were willing to completely withdraw from society. Despite allegations from foreign actors, these practices did not fall out of favor because they were inferior or were inherently evil—instead, their support was eroded by colonizers and missionaries who had gained the social, economic, and political power necessary to dislocate ATR either by force or deceit. It is no secret that Africans were generally condemned for worshiping idols and making ritual offerings to inanimate objects, but it is less obvious that such narratives were deliberately weaponized and used in a war for cultural supremacy over Africa and its religious beliefs.

Although it would eventually be revealed that Christian and Islamic religions engaged in the same practices that were condemned in African traditional religion, these Abrahamic faiths distorted aspects of ATR to suit their provincial agenda. The obvious desecration of ATR practices became a potent tool for de-Africanizing Africans. These new converts were willing to perpetuate the attacks against ATR to advance the goals of non-African religions. African traditional religion had allowed precolonial Africans to organize society, maintain peace, encourage political order, support the economy, and instill moral values. The Africans who had converted to the various Abrahamic religions were ignorant of these benefits, and they became accessories to the destruction of African religion and the values it represented in precolonial times. Other converts engaged in mudslinging, fighting for the cause of their erstwhile colonial or missionary lords. African religion deserves decolonization for its capacity to enable resistance and emancipate Africans.

Delegitimizing Colonial Demonization of ATR

Language can shape the human mind and the perception of life. Missionaries, who employed different languages and different mindsets, interpreted African traditional practices in ways that suited their agenda and compelled converts to loathe their traditional heritage. European missionaries had not only been groomed with a different language than the one spoken in African religions, but they were also dedicated to subjugating African ideals and practices, thus aiding the expansion of Western influence.

Within this context, we can understand why European imperialists found it useful to demonize ATR. In conditioning the minds of individuals, it was white superiority in the area of language that dictated the missionaries' interpretation of ATR and their biased generalizations. Europeans summarily dismissed ATR as inferior, concluding that its custodians were incapable of developing informed ideas about the nature of God.

Based on this orientation, missionaries labeled African acts of worship as demonic, characterizing ATR places of worship as evil abodes where spiritual beings were invoked for sinister reasons. Those who served as mediators between ATR and the people were taunted as agents of evil who were solely interested in leading people astray—away from the Christian kingdom of God. The Christian God was upheld as the supreme cosmic power—one that the West tried to foist upon the nonwhite world. This project gained support from African converts who advanced the interests of the West after being programmed with the language of the colonizers. African religious systems were subject to baseless accusations and derided for being uncouth. Although Europeans initially asserted that African religion was inherently evil, comparative research has established that African traditional religion and Western religion share similar values, beliefs, and mores.

It is important to dispel the misinformation that was deliberately spread to undermine African traditional religion. The first step in getting accurate information about ATR is to understand the people's language; this allows researchers to familiarize themselves with religious practices without prejudgment. The reversal of the old order begins by understanding the thought process of Africans, recognizing the forces that shaped their thinking and compelled them to design their religious beliefs in ways that have remained unchanged since the beginning of their existence.

Europeans closely link the ability to understand God with the form and methods recognized by the Abrahamic faiths. Although, as previously stated, the African conceptualization of God was derided as deviant and thought to be inferior by the West, the African concept of God must form the background for the delegitimization of Eurocentric demonization. Understanding the concept of God from the perspective of Africans allows us to decolonize African religion.

God, especially in the Yoruba worldview, is an exalted being distant from human activity. However, this being is actively involved in maintaining order in the universe. In contrast to the missionary understanding that God maintains a personal relationship with each individual, Africans refuse to share similar information about God because of their interpretation of the world around them; this is especially true for the Yoruba people of Nigeria. As suggested in the *Encyclopedia of African Religion*, the Yoruba people have some nominal opinions about God that differ from Western knowledge, which is represented in the names they have given to God.[1] The name "Olodumare" means "the Owner of inexhaustible pot"—a metaphor for the spherical shape of the universe. Other names are Olorun, the owner of heaven, and Oluwa.

---

1   Asante and Mazama, *Encyclopedia*.

These manifestations have influenced the religious practices that Western observers dismissed as animism. Taking an exalted position that is unaffected by emotions, opinion, and human sentiment, the Yoruba people are convinced that their God established a pantheon of gods to carry out day-to-day activities that determine the direction of people on earth. Their physical understanding of the world includes the living and the dead; the former are scientifically accepted as "matter" because they occupy a space, and the latter are not perceived by human sight.

Using this knowledge system, the Yoruba people designed a religious structure that encouraged the veneration of gods and ancestors who are believed to inhabit the world's spiritual realm. This idea is considered mutually intelligible among Africans, according to research work carried out by Pew Research Center's Forum on Religion and Public Life.[2] The missionaries, who lacked a similar background, allowed their biases to associate animism, demons, and other demeaning traits to these locally accepted indexes of worship.

The arrogance of the imperialists and Christian missionaries led to the objective evaluation of African religion as a secondary concern; a fair assessment of African traditional religion would make it harder to reshape African minds in ways that suited their agenda. Instead, the missionaries flaunted their progress in technology and education to convince Africans that Western religion was superior. Indigenous belief systems were comparatively less advanced in these areas, which gave the missionaries an advantage. During this period, many Africans decided to abandon African ways and aligned themselves with the Western world, adding their voices to the others criticizing their heritage.

The colonialist crusade saw itself bringing civilization to Africans, changing their environment and their approach to governance and to life in general. This project disguised its inherent attitude of supremacy with a veneer of altruism—a mission to help people advance assumes that they are primitive, unthinking, and backward. These labels of inferiority allowed Europeans to dislodge not only the political and social systems of Africans but also their religious institutions as well. African religion, like African history, was not preserved in writing. The Abrahamic religions were documented in books, and this difference was used to delegitimize African religion. Missionaries claimed that any religion based in

---

2   Lugo, "Tolerance," 33.

orality must have been created by individuals seeking to control people for parochial gain.

Differences between the conceptual understanding of God in the West and among the African people became another reason to dismiss African beliefs. Among Africans, there are variations in their concept of God. Kwasi Wiredu provides an insightful description of the Akan people of Ghana, who believe in the existence of a supreme being who controls affairs from above. Identified by different names, they accept that God did not create the universe from a void, which contradicts the belief of the missionaries. To believe that God created the universe from nothing, as the Christian God is said to have done, is to exclude the existence of God from a spatial setting that explains nothingness.[3]

The majority of religious Africans do not require any particular physical location for the veneration and the worship of God: this was another source of derision from the missionaries. It is ironic that Christian adherents believe in an all-powerful intelligence, yet they believe that this supreme cosmic being can be restricted within four walls for worship. The African belief does not require fixed physical infrastructure for the worship of God, which supports the idea of omnipresence. Again, it is noteworthy that missionaries condemned African religion for the types of contradictions that were present in their own beliefs.

The African understanding of God seemed to be homogeneous; its minor variations did not justify demonization. People adapted their beliefs through their interpretations of life, but Africans were reviled by the colonialists as pagans, animists, and idol worshipers. This sentiment led to African religion being abandoned by those who should have defended it; its philosophical and ideological approaches suffered a similar fate.

African religion's sacred worship centers are recognized by Africans of all creeds, regardless of their distance from the object of worship. The sacredness of ATR transcends the spatial setting dedicated to worshipping the deities understood as Orisha (or "the exempted"). Africans, including the Yoruba people, associate sacredness with worship and centers of worship, extending this association to places within their community. The sacred nature of their religion can be invoked to deter people from

---

3   Wiredu, "Toward," 30.

encroaching on specific areas. Social, political, or spiritual motives can bestow special protections on ecological materials or landscape features.

The ignorance of Western missionaries led them to claim ownership of sacred areas as part of their hostile attempts to prove the impotency of African spiritual powers. Such sacred places and objects included forests, landscape features, rivers, and oceans that were meant to be protected from human encroachment. These fragile habitats were easily "conquered" by missionaries, which proved the African assertion that those spaces required protection. The invaders saw their occupation of these spaces as a demonstration of their own power, reinforcing their unsubstantiated beliefs that African gods were ineffective. The converts who failed to employ logic or curiosity accepted these claims at face value.

Allegations of demonic activity among Africans and ATR were similarly unfounded. Some deities that had attracted communal worship were wrongly criticized. Osun, the goddess of the river, is associated with aquatic life, feminine affection, and protection. This deity's exalted position was meant to serve purposes outside of religious observances. The sacred aspect associated with the goddess discouraged members of society from disrespecting feminine creatures. This protection was extended to more than just the devotees of Osun, applying to every female in a particular area, especially mothers. The relationship between ATR and morality had associated many social ideas with different symbols that are not immediately understood by outsiders. Christianity and Islam were incapable of maintaining these social concepts, which explains the rapid decline of moral values in many African societies. The influence of ATR was intricate and developed over many years, but the superficial understanding of the West constructed unfounded narratives to justify their predatory, imperialist agenda in African communities.

In the African belief system, forests are reserved for medical and scientific purposes; the narrative of sacredness allows custodians to guide and protect their development. European missionaries, in their unyielding quest to shape African minds and perpetuate colonial expansionism, declared war on these nature reservations and herbal products that were used by Africans to advance their medical knowledge. The Yoruba people have an axiomatic expression, *t'ení bé igi ló jù, igi á rú 'wé*, which translates as "the tree cutter has done his worst, the tree would blossom again." This saying is an expression of the community's disapproval of ecological violence: all things being equal, it suggests, nature will reassert its role in the grand scheme of things. When missionaries realized that such plants were protected from destruction, they hastily concluded that it must be due to the paganism of the supposedly primitive African religion.

Abrahamic religions have compounded the challenges faced by ATR, adding to its ongoing struggles, but they are incapable of inspiring the behavior encouraged by indigenous religious practices. Even those who did not worship the deities of ATR recognized the importance of sacred areas and practices valued by their societies. Western religion brought a philosophy of individualism that created conflict in the minds of converted Africans. Research by Luis Lugo confirmed that many converts still seek the assistance of ATR experts, especially when confronted with overwhelming challenges.[4] African leadership, even in the face of this undeniable reality, remains indifferent to the indiscriminate felling of trees and subtle deforestation undertaken by Christians and Muslims whose extremism hastens the destruction of the African environment. The scant protection offered by the remains of ATR structures provides herbal medicine that cures and prevents all types of diseases.

Intersectional Realities of ATR

African traditional religion extends into other aspects of African living—consider its influence in social and political activity. African people see no separation between religious, moral, and political structures. Weakness in any of them would be reflected in the others, leading to malfunction. Social codes that are developed from ATR are linked with taboos that require communal adherence, maintaining society without requiring extreme measures, even when those principles are violated. In cases of social breakdown or failure of laws due to civil unrest, ATR provides different methods for restoring and maintaining order. The importance of religious roles held by women can be seen as an attempt to readjust the perception of the female gender and rehabilitate their relationship with society. A family's name is considered sacred, and its reputation must be protected.

Virtually all families in the Yoruba world, and in traditional African societies at large, have unique deities with which they identify; they strive

---

4   Lugo, "Tolerance."

to uphold the reputation of that deity and their own lineage. Even members of the family who are not actively involved in venerating these deities are still bound to pay their respects; their conscious or unconscious acceptance of these deities determines how they relate to them and how they interact socially with others guided by their religion's codes. In other words, they are compelled to observe societal norms to protect the family reputation. Moral values are upheld by the society's belief in these deities, which steer them away from evil. Precolonial Africans who were exposed to this method accepted the patterns of internal organicity in ATR as effective. It is reinforced by the belief that every member of society is as one, and their gods are the forces that strengthen their social bonds; there is a level of respect for the values introduced by these religious systems.

The intervention of the spirit that manifests in Egungun worship—a system that is popular among the Yoruba and Igbo people of Nigeria, with the people of Benin, and in some other African countries—is an intersection between ATR, society, and individuals. Egungun are invoked during the annual celebrations to intervene when social codes are violated in ways that threaten the fabric of society, acting as mediators in disputes between families or other groups. These Egungun are exalted as supernatural creatures whose spiritual essence should be honored and revered, making it difficult to ignore the custodians of these religious practices. They wield substantial power and influence while upholding peace in society.

To understand this admiration for the Egungun, we must look closely at the African perception of these figures. The majority of African religion systems accept the triadic existence of the living, the dead, and the unborn as a universal fact, recognizing the Egungun figures as incorporeal elders—people who once inhabited their environment alongside them. The understanding that this eventual state of being is inescapable, and the idea that one must venerate ancestors who remain as spirits to guide the living, leads to the celebration of these figures as a sign of respect. When people flout social codes, punishment is meted out during the observance of these festivals unless the situation is dire enough to require their immediate intervention.

The colonialists lacked the linguistic and cultural experience to understand these interactions. The average missionary saw these different scenarios as disjointed, describing the Africans who engaged in these practices as incoherent and lacking logic. They considered it absurd to rely on supernatural forces to intervene in social affairs—according to their beliefs, special institutions could uphold social codes that were respected by everyone. Apart from the historical failure of the missionaries' systems, crime escalated after the introduction of Western systems for social control. The fact that these crimes were rarely committed when the people had been guided by the social codes embedded in ATR, during the precolonial era, demonstrates how Western methods of control are unsuitable for African societies.

Missionaries imposed their own prejudices on African religion, ridiculing and belittling African beliefs in ways that made them unintelligible for future generations, preventing them from using the values of ATR to maintain society. European imperialists had the power to determine what constituted education and how it was transmitted to colonized Africans, which meant that the exposure to Western religions and the philosophy of individualism negated available African structures and systems from time immemorial.

Missionaries were ignorant of the connection between medical sciences and African traditional religion. Colonizers from the West had difficulty reconciling a group's religion with its medical systems because their religious epistemology separated physical health from spirituality. The compulsion to dismiss anything connected with ATR, recognizing that its survival would work against the business of colonization, led missionaries to demonize and drive people away from related subjects. An ATR diviner is qualified to oversee healing processes because their initiation includes education about herbs, leaves, and natural materials that can be applied to heal different ailments. A mind that is unwilling to accept a relationship between medicinal processes and the invocation of unseen forces automatically becomes antagonistic.

It was expected that traditional African religion was expected to encounter contempt from the colonizers. Not only had their linguistic and cultural inadequacy made it difficult for them to understand the connectivity of ATR components, but they were also bent on delegitimizing African institutions that could thwart their colonial ambitions. Christian indoctrination had programmed Africans to accept Western ways and had a devastating impact on their perception of their true African identity. Medical centers were erected to combat African spirituality and healing processes, demonizing African ways by challenging alleged inadequacies in the African medical systems, and it became an effective methodology.

The technological advancements of Europeans, which had been achieved shortly before they began their expansionist crusade, were exploited by European imperialists to support a campaign of mudslinging against African spirituality. They argued that African methods were unreliable based on their manipulation of unknown forces.

Attempts to undermine African medical processes required an alternative to existing African healing systems. Hospitals were established by the colonialists and their active collaborators, the missionaries, to demonstrate the validity of their claims and display the superiority of their thinking. Political attacks claimed that Western philosophies and methods of government were superior to those found in Africa, and missionaries reinforced the idea that African spirituality was evil. This display of supremacy across multiple fronts included projects like Christian churches and hospitals.

Missionaries disparaged African healing methods as magical thinking, even when they did not completely understand the processes involved. Converts who were taught to value Western approaches as improvements over African processes took on the duty of demonizing and desecrating African systems, especially religion. They saw their acts as patriotism because the colonial government had introduced an administrative system that was an alternative to African governance, similar to the way that Christian spirituality was an alternative to African religious practices that had been dismissed as primitive and crude. The ATR was colonized by colonialists and their accomplices, ensuring that African traditional religion would be subjected to ridicule.

One could speculate that missionaries created African hospitals not from an interest in charity—Africans were considered subhuman and unworthy of mercy—but for predatory exploitation. The predominant reason was to delegitimize African healing processes, disparaging their methods as unscientific. They understood that such labels would disparage African models that did not follow Western methods. Those educated with the language and philosophy of the West, failing to see the underlying condescension in this attitude, became admirers of new medical systems. They developed a hatred of African systems after learning of a credible alternative. A few individuals understood the usefulness of variety and the beauty of varying alternatives, but ATR lost many adherents during this period to either Christianity or Islam. The people's suspicion of ATR was reinforced by messages of doom shared in Christian places of worship, declaring that adherents to ATR would face the wrath of the Christian God.

As the healing components of ATR were called into question, it had a chilling effect on the religion and its practitioners. Many ATR adherents became reluctant to identify with their spiritual identity as ATR became synonymous with primitivity, backwardness, and barbarism. New converts to Western religions believed that they had been ushered into new lives while failing to recognize that they were merely using an alien culture's vehicle on their journey to spirituality; they also actively derided people associated with ATR. Such groups would demonstrate loyalty to European religions by threatening the existence of ATR through malicious campaigns. Hordes of sympathizers hopped on the bandwagon and consigned ATR to irrelevance. The colonialists and their missionary accomplices were disinterested in ATR and dismissed its contributions to collective scholarship and the knowledge economy at the intersection of spirituality and healing in Africa. They began to describe healing products associated with ATR as magic, charms, juju, and other disparaging names in an aggressive attempt to eradicate such indigenous methods. None of these allegations were true, and the missionaries knew as much from their own history of applying ATR methods within their own religious practices.

The first action of decolonization must be strong and deliberate, dispelling ATR's negative associations from the minds of Africans. Fortunately, decolonization does not require the offensive tactics applied by the colonizers who degraded and suppressed ATR. Instead, we can show how and why the ATR healing system was a match for the "scientific" knowledge of the West. The efficacy of these healing methods and processes have never been in doubt in Africa or by Africans; large numbers of Africans still apply ATR healing methods into the twenty-first century.[5] Research has shown that a majority of practitioners consider ATR methods to be homogeneous and efficacious, which is why they turn to ATR for emergency assistance. We must deconstruct the narratological fallacies of the West regarding African traditional religion and its approach to healing, allowing people to integrate this knowledge system into their collective existence. Important questions should be asked about how precolonial

---

5   Lugo, "Tolerance," 4.

Africans conducted their lives and managed their health prior to the ascension of colonialists.

During the precolonial era, for thousands of years Africans managed to stem the spread of diseases, conquer illnesses, and heal the sick. Did these people achieve such outcomes through blind luck? When we understand that their success rested on a foundation of dedication and commitment to medical research, we also understand why a Western approach was no more scientific than their own. The demonization of ATR and its healing systems is only justifiable when the definition of "science" is restricted to processes employed solely by the West. Methods employed by ATR deserve a place in modern science for their contextual applicability to Africans beyond that which has been described as science by the West. The fact that people view these approaches as a credible alternative to Western medicine confirms this assertion.[6] What the West disparaged as magic was the manifestation of spiritual essence sustained by the invocation of unseen forces and facilitated by herbs and other ingredients. UNESCO itself has recently recognized the ATR healing system as valid.

A dismissal of the African healing system as juju or charms is an admission of ignorance, denying its logic and showing a lack of understanding of how the components work. The West has a right to assert this position, of course. However, an attempt to impose their own systems over those they do not understand is an act of white supremacy. This has been challenged as a form of paternalism that should be resisted. The African approach can be recognized as scientific and effective without validation from the Western world. Its mutual intelligibility among the people is enough encouragement for it to continue making an impact in the lives of African people.

For example, in April 2020 in Madagascar, the discovery of "Covid-Organics (CVO)," a herbal infusion made from artemisia (a bright-green fernlike plant) is said to combat the symptoms of coronavirus: this is more proof of the legitimate healing skills of precolonial Africans. Potential remedies must not be abandoned due to false narratives circulated by colonialists and neocolonial apologists. The logical and empirical processes applied by precolonial Africans were condemned by missionaries and colonial powers because they did not follow Western methods. Contrary to Western assumptions that the healing systems and methods

---

6   Falola, *African Spirituality*.

of ATR were unscientific, the African concepts of magic, juju, and other systems can be codified in a language that is understood in modern terms. This could have a massive global impact and establish its importance.

Universalizing and Nationalizing ATR

An American researcher, Frances Henry, undertook a study on Orisha religion in Trinidad in 1956 as a young doctoral student. Her experiences as a firsthand observer of the religion, in addition to her professional engagement with religious tenets, drew informed scholarly conclusions about African religion in the diaspora. Henry's interrogation of the Orisha religion reveals the transformational process of the worship in the transatlantic environment.

The Yoruba Orisha religion was originally labeled crude, primitive, and pristine, but it evolved into an acceptable religion through unimaginable transformations that established it as respectable in a new country. When Henry moved to Trinidad in 1956, her zeal for acquiring information about the religion redefined her understanding and perception of the Orisha African religion. The reality that she personally experienced was different from the general narratives circulated by colonialists and their cronies.[7] Apart from an opportunity to study ATR functioning alongside other religions—shown through interactions and engagement with practitioners discussing the spiritual, social, and intellectual power of the faith—the work also dispelled the dismissive narratives that had been promoted against it.

After arriving in Port of Spain, Henry had difficulty researching Shango, a worship system that originated among the Yoruba people in what is now Nigeria. She approached a number of Trinidadians who denied having any knowledge of Shango, its worshipers, or the related religious philosophies. The facial expressions of respondents suggested that they were afraid to be identified with such beliefs because of the stigma attached to them. Her suspicion was confirmed when she met adherents of other faiths, especially Christian leaders, who pointedly responded that "they had vaguely heard that some misguided and ignorant people did

---

7   Henry, *Reclaiming*.

still believe in 'that sort of African belief' but, of course, no one of any respectability."[8]

General misconceptions about ATR had spread through the transatlantic environment, made worse through transmission from people who lacked the requisite knowledge of the phenomenon. The decolonization of African religion is necessary because its success would liberate the colonized from their unjust confinement at home and abroad. The period from 1956 to the present day in Trinidad, Brazil, Cuba, and other South American countries exemplifies the power of ATR when it is properly understood.

Henry's research is interesting in light of the government's shift from indifference in 1956 to celebration of ATR in modern times. A transformation of its religious practices mandated the government to recognize ATR after the decolonization of minds that were set against the practice. Knowledge, attitudes, and perceptions of ATR have been shaped by narratives of antagonism that were orchestrated by colonialists, missionaries, and their cronies. People like Henry, who conducted extensive qualitative research, understood that that the accusations of demonic activity associated with ATR had been specifically designed by Westerners to discourage people from practicing the religion; such accusations had nothing to do with the true sense of the faith.

The success of ATR in the transatlantic world is linked with the elimination of Christological biases that affected the spread of the religion in the colonial period—even in Africa. The transformation of African religion is linked to its rebirth from unwholesome narratives already in circulation, spread by its various antagonists. For example, Yoruba Orisha religion should be restored to its original status before the distortions perpetrated by the European missionaries and their allies. Pressure had led to some aspects of ATR seeping into new religions as a bid to accommodate Western influence while ensuring that the religion did not disappear completely. However, such evolution defies the originality and respectability of the religion in its initial state. Even in the twenty-first century, there are efforts to shed aspects of the religion that are primordially animistic.

African religion must not be interpreted from the viewpoint of its antagonists—Western imperialists, Christians, and Muslims—but from the perspective of Africans alone. The intelligibility of African religion is

---

8 Henry, *Reclaiming*.

exclusively reserved for its adherents, who should be responsible for its interpretation as well as its practice. Around the time of Henry's research in Trinidad, despite the insignificant status and stigmatized identity of Orisha believers in South America, practitioners remained steadfast in observing the religion by following the tenets recognized at its ancestral beginning. Various components of African religion must be extensively developed and eventually mobilized to claim the status of an international identity, compelling civilizations of the world to acknowledge them. This would serve multiple purposes; not only would it redeem the African identity that had suffered desecration at the hands of its colonial detractors, it would also secure overdue recognition for African culture and dispel many false notions about it.

Components of ATR, such as its medicinal aspects, spiritual essence, sociology, and other aspects must be engaged intellectually with a view to improving their global reception. These efforts would legitimize their methods as an alternative to the empirical system of science currently accepted by the global knowledge economy. African religion cannot always be comprehended by distant observers. Their skepticism notwithstanding, ATR has been a potent instrument employed by Africans for thousands of years before their collision with Western hegemony.

Contemporary African scholars and practitioners of ATR must exchange information useful for reshaping the identity of African religion and its successful integration into global society. Decolonization will help show the world that African healing methods have been effective for ages. These efforts would become grounds for extending the religion beyond the shores of the continent.

There are lessons to be learned from African religion's transition in Trinidad—shifting from a minor religious practice to the mainstream— because nationalizing ATR is essential for its international growth. Before this step occurs, we must understand religion's importance in shaping African societies. The colonial powers were the sole reason for the nation-state systems inherited by Africans in the modern era. Before their arrival, ATR was predominantly influential in political and social organizations within African societies. Diviners were consulted during the selection process for political leaders, and leadership credentials were evaluated in the spiritual realm before a candidate could be endorsed. During colonial times, these processes were marred by imposition and condescension, but they had previously been fair and transparent—every member of society felt like they were part of the process. Traditional African political systems could not accommodate the electoral processes introduced by the West. Indigenous systems were useful and important for Africans, but they interfered with the Western encroachment on African societies. Because these systems did not allow Western interests to influence leaders who held power, they were an impediment to the consuming totalitarianism of the colonizers.

Indigenous political systems were criticized for being insensitive to human equality and only capable of representing the elite few. The European imperialists' unyielding fixation on the people holding positions of power in Africa prevented them from understanding why the process guided by ATR had survived for ages. Diviners were chastised and ridiculed, allowing Europeans to introduce their own system in support of their goals. The introduction of this system severely compromised African leadership. The ritual processes that had led to productive leadership were subverted and replaced by ineffective leaders who kow-towed to colonial powers. As the trend continued, African leadership was weakened and left unable to pursue the social and economic advancements achieved by previous generations. By painting African processes as illegitimate and uncouth, the West had once again cast aspersions on ATR. Traditional systems that were effectively providing fundamental knowledge about the past, present, and the future ended up delegitimized and ineffectual.

The restrictions placed on the selection process for African leaders have contributed to the unusual situation in Africa today. Leadership sets the course for society and enables its collective progress. The traditional African method of selecting leaders came with an accountability that is missing from modern selection processes; in selection processes imposed by the West, leaders have become more individualistic. When unexpected crises emerged in precolonial African societies, leaders were willing to make personal sacrifices. Unlike the system inherited from the colonizers, leaders held positions that were not intrinsically distant from their followers.

As ATR was besmirched and relegated to the background, the values associated with that system were abandoned. African societies experienced an explosion of immoral activity. The habit of propitiating the spirit, to prevent society from plunging into anomie, was criticized and discarded. The same moral corrosion that affected African leaders spread to all aspects of African life during the postcolonial era.

Although colonization has officially ended, its vestiges have lingered for decades. Contemporary Africans must reject the psychological and social colonization that drives them to deny the effectiveness of ATR. The colonialist decision to supplant ATR and drive it underground must be reversed, and ATR must be recognized as useful in social and political affairs. Silencing the influence of ATR in social, political, and cultural life was beneficial for imperialists, not Africans. Decisions to dismiss ATR must be dropped to ensure Africa's future development. Ideas and values introduced by Western powers were only helpful for achieving the objectives of the colonialists. This newfound understanding would allow Africans to appreciate their precolonial legacy, chiefly their religion, as capable of morally reshaping society.

The majority of African leaders patronize ATR, especially when seeking political office, and they only hide their involvement because they are ensnared in neocolonial captivity. Many countries in South America have recognized ATR and have provided support, allowing it to flourish and influence political activities. Africans at home, especially political leaders, should also incorporate ATR philosophies and ideas into their social and political systems, setting their collective or communal affairs on an upward trajectory. It begins with a recognition of ATR as a state religion, deserving of respect and celebration alongside the European and Arabic religions that were pushed into the mainstream in many African countries. This will assist in changing perceptions of the religion and dispelling the negative associations that were made by its many detractors. Nationalizing ATR would bring social respect and encourage people to publicly associate with it.

Contemporary African leaders have a poor sense of purpose. They belittle their inherited religion merely because the Europeans who once colonized them described that religion as illegitimate. There is no scientific evidence for an established connection between ATR and the escalation of evil, but politicians have accepted such narratives pushed by globalist imperialists. Many Africans still appreciate and avail themselves of benefits through the devotees and custodians of ATR, as can be seen in the research carried out by Lugo and his group.[9] Self-denial is an unnecessary moral position for leaders, reflecting a political decision. Even if African leaders have reservations compelling them to act in contravention

---

9   Henry, *Reclaiming*.

of African moral values and beliefs, the exponential growth of ATR outside the continent should be enough reason to accommodate the religion and actively begin the process of nationalization. When the entrenched values of ATR are widely accepted and practiced openly, it will reengineer the people in an entirely African way.

ATR and the African Academy

Scholars have proposed the integration of African traditional religion and its knowledge system into the general African education system. Many of their points are valid, and components of the ATR knowledge system can effectively be incorporated into existing study systems. Inadequate knowledge, which was created by the colonizers' disinformation campaign waged against African religion, is the chief reason behind the castigation of ATR. Africa has maintained its trajectory in the postcolonial environment because it lacks understanding. The ancestral religion of Africans is not inferior to the Western religions of the postcolonial world. Western religions have proven incapable of upholding the moral structures of the African people, which can be seen in the exponential increase of crimes and violence previously absent from African society: the reversal of this situation, accommodating the legacy of ATR as influences on our social and political trajectories, would encourage greater adherence to African morals in daily life.

Components of ATR should be studied because of their direct impact on collective morale. The sacredness of the religion must be researched by a network of experts who can make scientifically informed decisions. The line between African social ethics and the conceptual understanding of sacredness is blurred because one is used to achieve the other. Western imperialists filter African engagement through arrogant logic that is held up as a universal standard for measuring values, but beyond that superficial lens Africans see a strong link between the sanctity of ancestral or cosmological affairs and manifestations of that thinking in social and physical existence. Colonialists denied the possibility of such connectivity based on their ignorance of the ways that Africans perceived ideas and natural phenomena. Appropriate education about social and spiritual events is necessary to correct erroneous notions and assumptions spread by colonialists and their apologists. This requires large-scale efforts that can only be achieved through educational institutions.

We must dispel the false perceptions that led Western audiences to formulate incorrect opinions about ATR and the Africans who have patronized it for centuries. African religion maintains that sacredness is meant to influence certain social behaviors and discourage others because Africans are linguistically wired to accept this. They generally revere ideas that are socially accepted as sacred, avoiding activities that might conflict with established social codes. The specific concepts considered sacred can vary between people, ethnic identities, and geographical locations. Some groups might consider it taboo to kill and consume specific game animals while others might consume those animals voraciously. The justification for something to become either taboo or sacred can be connected to a long history. However, these activities only have limited historical traceability, and those who practice them in the present day may instead associate them with taboos that are detached from their origins. Those who do not uphold the taboos, such as the colonizers, can easily mischaracterize them as paganism or primitive in attempts to undermine African religion.

In the context of scholarship, associating some animals with sacredness or taboos was part of a wildlife management plan based on the necessity of managing a healthy ecosystem. European society would eventually learn through science that the preservation of biological diversity holds a fundamental position in the maintenance of ecological stability. Biodiversity can also ensure good air quality, linking the health of humans, animals, and plants. The African understanding of this simple truth led to social systems that applied a sacred status to people, places, and animals. But these justifications are difficult to discern sometimes, which explains why observers from the West were confused about African perceptions and systems of social living: their hasty conclusions saw Africans as superstitious and vain. Outside observers believed that the African approach to metaphysical existence was unconventional. The associations of sacredness made in connection with elderhood, ancestorhood, dead people, motherhood, and fatherhood, encourages people to act in ways that ensure the collective peace and progress of society.

The ATR medicine system should also be studied. Although various cultural activists have successfully established African studies as a discipline in African universities, this must be expanded to high schools or secondary schools on the continent. Africans should receive background knowledge about medicine as understood by Africans and apply said knowledge for social and economic advancement. This is important for many reasons, including the fact different regions often develop specialized knowledge for treating prevalent local illnesses. One such example is malaria, which is predominantly encountered in Africa. It is logical that Africans should dedicate a team of medical researchers, with sound knowledge of medicine as believed and practiced by the people, to offer important solutions to public health challenges. Relying on Western medical knowledge will only prolong Africa's colonial confinement.

These efforts begin with the decolonization of African education systems, especially the segments conducting medical research, to incorporate recognized experts in ATR medicine, allowing for the cross-fertilization of ideas and exchange of information to advance African knowledge. Some African diseases such as Lassa fever, polio, and yellow fever may go unrecognized in the Western world, which threatens to wreak untold havoc on Africa's population. For example, Western science rejects the idea that people can be psychically traumatized by spiritual pain. However, the phenomenon is accepted in Africa. It is difficult to seek remedies for these kinds of afflictions in an academic society that already stigmatizes the African approach to medical healing. Apart from the fact that there will never be Western solutions to these afflictions, such as "spiritual attacks" and demonic possessions, problematizing them only prolongs their harmful effects on individuals and societies at large. The existence of such ailments is undeniable, but the reluctance to consult people with relevant knowledge poses an additional burden to those who suffer from these issues, moving African society backward. Expanded, informative research should be conducted by engaging the services of experts from the ATR community and forging joint solutions.

The medical knowledge contained within ATR can offer benefits merely through public recognition. Africans who are made aware of the ways that their traditions can advance medicine and human welfare already have the tools to make a positive impact on society. African medical science is available and accessible to everyone. Medical professionals within the global community work in a system that is optimized for economic and financial growth and restricted by patented technologies, but the system in Africa is socially, politically, and economically communal. People who conduct research understand that their intellectual accomplishments are public goods that should be shared to benefit everyone. Findings are widely distributed, ensuring that individuals can respond to emergency situations with immediate action, even in African homes. However, the destructive relationships of colonization have changed this thinking—Africans are currently forced to conceal medical breakthroughs in such areas as sexuality and mental illness for fear of criticisms.

The government does not recognize the medical component of ATR as being worthy of engagement. The communal authorship recognized in the precolonial period has been individualized, making it difficult to share knowledge publicly. The government has censured this knowledge system, even though it is not a threat to the people or the environment. The government's motivations are driven by the economic necessity created by the Western world's private health-care systems. Many Africans waited in vain for validation from the World Health Organization (WHO) for a rumored COVID-19 cure because African researchers were behind the breakthrough. But the African medical system may never get global respect without resisting the economic temptation and imposition of Western-style systems. Allowing medical institutions to incorporate African knowledge and medical systems into their academic curriculum would enable the decolonization of Western medicine, which has enjoyed undeserved patronage at the expense of its African counterpart.

The African divination system is another knowledge system from ATR that may need to be incorporated into African academia. Every form of human expression has unique methods of knowing, which are applied as reliable systems for making discoveries about the environment. There have been many African discoveries, including in astrology, herbal medicine, and general medical knowledge. The knowledge of environmental matters is sometimes attributed to prehuman understanding. To invalidate this claim is to dislodge scientific arguments that validate aspects of metaphysical existence. If we use modern science as our guide and concede that some aspects of existence go beyond physical manifestations, we cannot deny that these materials could expand our knowledge. It would be misleading and crude to assume that efforts to validate African epistemological and ontological independence is due to connections between the author and the community. The work of decolonization makes it necessary to create this awareness.

Jimi Adesina has explained that there are various ways to arrive at knowledge, including "sensing," "reasoning," "inspiration," and "serendipity."[10] This confirms that knowledge is unique to individuals; it may not be universalized. Knowledge derived through sensing could lead to serendipity where information around events is gathered by accident. However, reasoning can also direct people to knowledge. The difference is that some findings are derived from inspiration, which is where the integration of the ATR knowledge system becomes necessary, logical, and helpful. The Ifa divination system has allowed its religious adherents to acquire knowledge of phenomena beyond their intellectual limits. Denying this method of knowledge acquisition has not only impaired the growth of global scholarship but also destabilized methods and approaches that have been denied appropriate environments for testing and inquiry.

Testing precedes condemnation. Before one can dismiss African knowledge systems—such as those explained and offered by the Yoruba divination system—they must be given an opportunity to prove that their alternative information can benefit humanity. This opportunity should be provided by integrating the divination component of ATR into the African school system. Economic assistance should be provided for scholars to conduct research, and avenues should be provided to exchange knowledge and information, expanding the horizon of inquiry. Additional means of acquiring information, offered by ATR, would further expand global knowledge. However, confining this knowledge within the boundaries of Western science would impair the growth of African knowledge systems, especially as established by ATR or its components. African education must be decolonized to accommodate this spectrum of knowledge.

The African knowledge economy can be expanded by exploring the sociological import of practices attached to ATR, such as the belief in ancestral existence and the veneration of the spirit realm's occupants. This epistemic understanding enables an African mindset that believes in sacrifice as a passage to renewal—part of humanity's cyclical journey. When the spiritual realm is appeased by the sacrifice, the activity changes their life. However, the study of ATR should analyze this concept more thoroughly. There are social and moral reasons for encouraging sacrifice in African traditional religion that have become homogeneous among the people. Science has not established an empirical link between the contributions of ancestors in the spiritual realm and manifestations in

---

10 Adesina, "Sociology," 91–114.

the physical world, but this does not invalidate its effects. Sacrifices are offered to create peace and occasionally to settle internal conflicts.

The concept of sacrifice should be incorporated into the African education curriculum within the context of conflict resolution; interethnic, intergeographical, and interclass war could be addressed by collective thinking about sacrifices and the philosophy they espouse, which can be invoked to broker peace. Shared experiences and materials in family groups and social settings could invoke mutual compassion. Beyond this, sacrifice should be taught in the context of leadership. The times, days, and seasons of ATR designated for rituals or sacrifices encourage a collective engagement in sober reflection and an evaluation of society's development. When society appears to be headed in undesirable directions, ATR usually proposes rituals and sacrificial offerings that appease spiritual figures and request their intervention. The European misunderstanding of these rituals and their motives was the primary reason why ATR was delegitimized as crude and animist. However, their sociological importance deserves to be examined more closely.

Africans believe in "inspirational" sources of knowledge, and elements of rituals attempt to instigate spiritual motivation for the revelation of ideas or phenomena. Insights into power relations, political systems, and social philosophy can be derived through an African examination of ATR rituals. Africans conduct rituals to provoke revelations that provide greater knowledge of metaphysics, nature, and their environment. Research into rituals and the accompanying theories could engender a knowledge system to advance African progress. Which situations require it, what conditions qualify for rituals and sacrifices, and what social or spiritual connections do rituals offer for individuals and society? Answering these questions would assist in decolonizing African traditional religion, allowing it to occupy its rightful place in African activities.

Decolonizing ATR as a Tool to Fight Western Imperialism and Cultural Hegemony

ATR suffered excessive stigmatization at the hands of Christianity and its Islamic counterpart. These forces used various denigrating narratives to push African religion out of social and epistemic relevance. Abrahamic faiths took an active role in the expropriation of ATR values and mores, which was a deliberate attempt to weaken its influence on the African people.

Colonialists, who did not understand the social and spiritual essence of African traditional religion, disparaged ATR as too crude to be responsible for societal advancements. They offered religious alternatives that were incapable of making social or spiritual contributions that could sustain the development of the African people. The real decline in the moral and philosophical standards of Africans is connected to the religions that they practice. It is not that other religions are inherently weak or morally delinquent, but they are incapable of shouldering the ideological responsibilities that ATR had previously managed.

How can ATR fight imperialist and cultural hegemony? It is not a straightforward answer; the activity of decolonization itself requires time and dedication. The methods identified above would work together to combat Western hegemony, but the values of ATR must also be contradistinguished from missionary religions on the basis of their moral values and general ideological leanings. African cosmological understanding and interpretation must take a more prominent place in the lives of the African people. For example, ATR condemns morally reprehensible behavior in the strongest possible terms, clearly spelling out its consequences. These values must be introduced to Africans at the start of their education so that they understand the negative effects of poor decisions in adulthood. Every society inculcates social values into their youngest minds at an early age. The values embedded in ATR would be a useful social integration tool for coming generations, demonstrating the value of African morals and mores.

Education is important because those who absorb ideas will keenly defend them after being convinced of their validity. This method was applied by colonialists to mold the minds of Africans, many of whom eventually defended the imperialists and their religious inclinations. The consequences of this approach are not easily identified, but they can be seen in the consistently divisive politics of Africa. Religious values are currently used as a means of division, but ATR united people regardless of their denominational differences. This is absent from the religions imposed on Africans by colonizers. For such religions, African minds are a spiritual battleground where an unending battle is waged to recruit people into rival religious practices. This creates a binary mindset where people harbor dislike for those who believe differently, leading to social struggles that divide Africans on religious grounds. The religious fragmentation of the continent can only be fought with the promotion of an African religion that preaches tolerance, creating peace and possibilities for social development. Instead of being met with suppression, ATR should be politically recognized to become a tool for social integration.

The positive values expounded by ATR are evident in the social behaviors such as child-rearing, marriage, and respect for elders that are identified as norms by the religion's adherents. The inviolability of these norms is strengthened by social tranquility that was ubiquitous in the precolonial environment. ATR does not encourage the wars and violence spread by colonialists and their missionaries. Leaders in the precolonial African world, who were guided by the ethics of ATR, usually understood their obligations to their subjects, carrying out their statutory duties for the general benefit of society. The missionaries incorrectly believed that ATR only prided itself in animistic behavior and was just an impediment to the projects and sinister objectives of European expansionists. A public campaign should arise to keep ATR from being subjected to undeserved humiliation and dispel these wrongheaded notions, allowing African religion to resume its constructive social role in African life.

ATR is not separate from traditional social life, which should compel anyone who has condemned the social functions of ATR to reevaluate their perspective. Social practices identified by the religion as condemnable are frowned upon in social settings. When some Africans say that motherhood should be respected due to women's overall importance in society, this philosophy is reflected in the ways that they were treated in the precolonial African world. Among the Yoruba Orisha religion, some aspects of Ifa expressly condemn stealing or other immoral conduct, which is incorporated into the social psychology of the people. They immediately reject any behavior related to stealing because it may tarnish their family image or good name. Some individuals might perform immoral actions, but they would be condemned in strong terms. African religion, in whatever form, must be used as cultural project to combat Western hegemony.

Essentializing the ATR Worship System

In the current African system, a revolution for ATR requires an atmosphere in which it can thrive; important factors must be considered if the decolonization agenda is to achieve its goals. ATR is often discussed as a singular entity, but it has various denominations. Among Yoruba people who worship Orisha, the denominations of worship are as diverse as the number of identifiable gods. There are Shango worshipers, Osun worshipers, Ogun adherents, and others. The essentialization of such worship would not be a problem if African nation-state systems were made or structured around homogeneous identities, where everyone in society believed and identified with similar religious philosophies. However, the current configuration of nations and national perspectives has created a disharmony that is difficult to reconcile. Practically speaking, it is difficult to integrate these bodies of religious worship into current political systems.

This leads to the argument put forward by Henry, about the question of authenticity that affects the process of essentialization. Orisha religion, as practiced in Trinidad, can become a subject of debate when diasporic versions are developed from existing religious structures. This can be traced to the understanding that when a culture travels beyond its geographic boundaries, it risks becoming domesticated. Different aspects of ATR worship have experienced transformation that separates them from the original practices found in Africa; African religion is exposed to syncretism because of its flexibility, among other characteristics. Henry asserts that "the process of syncretism is largely in scholarly disrepute today, and has been rejected as part of the hegemonic controlling processes of slavery and neo-colonialism. A religion must, according to this view, rid itself of the imposed, syncretic, inauthentic elements in its ritual and belief system."[11] A failure to essentialize ATR—even from its native continent—has become an impediment to its decolonization process.

There is an urgent need to structure ATR in such a way that its religious belief and practices have a universal persuasion. This necessary step requires finding a common ground on accepted methods for their religion, especially for global outreach. This would ease the process of essentialization because strategies of worship would have been formed in ways that allow adherents to easily identify with the religion, regardless of their location. When ATR worship is essentialized, the Africans who practice it would receive recognition that allows them to conduct their activities without fear of oppression.

Recognition of the ATR worship system comes with a validation of its engagements and an opportunity to rewrite its history, casting off the inaccurate associations applied by colonialists and missionaries. To

---

11   Henry, *Reclaiming*, 109.

accomplish this, the worship of Shango on the continent of Africa, for instance, must be in consonance with diasporic practices, and the Akan belief systems in Ghana should share characteristics that make them mutually intelligible across the world. Providing these tools to ATR practitioners would fast-track the process of decolonizing their religion and rebuilding its images.

Conclusion

Decolonization is important for all aspects of African life. This is necessary to ensure that people move forward collectively, but it is also important for reclaiming their dispossessed identity. That identity has been eroded through the persistent efforts of colonizers who were interested in exploiting Africans and who spread misleading narratives to support their agenda. The deeply entrenched system of colonization has continued its work into the present day—this can be seen in the way Africans attempt to make meaning out of legacies inherited from their colonizers.

Considerable effort has been made to turn African lives around, but there has been little to show for the struggle to ensure collective progress, except in situations where Africans have resorted to decolonization. Even when they fail to change their political, social, and economic trajectories, contemporary Africans become enmeshed in internal struggles that make it harder to realize their full potential. Their failure to move forward is connected to the fact that they have lost touch with the religious philosophies that had previously functioned as both a spiritual guide and an ideological foundation.

It is important to decolonize African traditional religion by ending the demonization of ATR, which occurred because colonizers promoted the erroneous assumption that ATR is inherently evil—a baseless claim reeking of racism and promoting white supremacist ideology. Most of the allegations made by colonialists and their apologists smacked of hypocrisy and concerned the condemning of spiritual matters that already existed within their own religions.

If African traditional religion were as demonic and destructive as its detractors claimed, would it have endured for thousands of years before the incursion of the West? In Trinidad in 1956, Frances Henry set out to investigate the Orisha religion, which no one at the time would publicly associate with: now it is widely accepted in South American society. Individuals embraced it at an exponential rate in the diaspora. An examination of ATR as it is practiced shows that it is the opposite of what colonizers claimed.

The effort spent campaigning against ATR unwittingly reveals the intersectional capacity of ATR for managing African affairs—this attribute may have provoked loathing from the West. ATR can formulate stronger social philosophies to manage social lives effectively, and its transcendence from spiritual usefulness to social philosophy remains another reason why it must be appropriately decolonized. Reverence for ATR has primed people to accept its teachings, encouraging them to uphold religious rules that prevent society from collapsing into anomie. Externally imposed religions emphasize the individual, but ATR encourages a sense of community and compels people to meet their responsibilities and uphold social contracts.

Chapter Nineteen

Decolonizing African Philosophy

Introduction

To decolonize African philosophy is to address its controversies and to identify which arguments continue to reflect Eurocentric presumptions. The question of whether an African philosophy exists has persisted in scholarship for decades, and this cynicism was not created in a vacuum—it is connected to many factors, including the philosophical distance between the traditional African conception of philosophy and Western philosophies that are imposed as "standard" philosophical conceptions. For example, Mawere and Mubaya have noted that Western philosophies mainly originate from individual thought processes, in contrast to the communal origins of African philosophy.[1]

African philosophy's communal origins are attributed to the folklore of the African people. Universalist scholars of philosophy, like Hountondji, refute the idea that these works can be considered philosophy, but such an approach has been presented by ethno-philosophers including Mbiti, Senghor, Kagame, and Tempels.[2] To them, African philosophy is laid bare in religious beliefs, myths, proverbs, and the entirety of the people's folkloric forms. Ethno-philosophers consider African philosophy to be an indigenous African product, uncorrupted by Western ideas.

For scholars like Wiredu, it is not a question of whether there is an African philosophy or if Africa is capable of philosophical thinking; it

---

1 Mawere and Mubaya, *African Philosophy.*
2 Bodunrin, "Question," 161–79.

is instead about what this African philosophy is, what it comprises, and how best to engage it.[3] These scholars and a substantial number of others belong to a school of African ethno-philosophers who believe that African philosophy is analysis of and reflection on African social realities and conceptual systems, in addition to the modern resources of knowledge from contemporary philosophers. To them, traditional African thought is worth engaging because it possesses resources that pique philosophical interest.

This school holds that engagements and investigations should be conducted by trained philosophers in collaboration with persons grounded in the people's belief systems and traditions.[4] With that understanding, Wiredu explains that African philosophies do not "emanate from a void but from the brains of individual thinkers. Thus, the existence of philosophy in our traditional culture is a given."[5] He does not entirely negate the position of ethno-philosophers—he states that within these folkloric forms lie fragments of African philosophy but not a compact description of African philosophy.

Universalist philosophers predominantly oppose the sentiments of ethno-philosophers. Universalists hold that there are no specific African truths, just universal truths, meaning that philosophy should refer to the same concepts regardless of culture or geography. However, the methodology and approach of philosophy might be subject to cultural biases and the realities of the society in which the philosophy originates and operates. Philosophers like Bodunrin, Hountundji, Oruka, and Hallen belong to this school of thought. For Oruka and Hallen, ethno-philosophy is a debased form of philosophy; they do not consider descriptive accounts and presentation of "myths, folklores and folk-wisdom" as philosophy in the strict sense of the word.[6] In addition to this sustained controversy over what constitutes African philosophy, other factors have cast doubt on the existence of African philosophy.

Outside African philosophical circles, the Western prejudice against orality questions the existence of African philosophy and exemplifies the ideological distance between traditional Africa and the Global North

---

3   Wiredu, "Conceptual," 53–64.
4   Gbadegesin, *African Philosophy*.
5   Wiredu, "Conceptual Decolonization," 53.
6   Bodunrin, "Question,"

regarding philosophical conceptions. This brings to mind Hountondji's Universalist conceptualization of philosophy within the context of written texts. In his work, *African Philosophy*, he states that "by African philosophy [he] means a set of texts, specifically the set of texts written by Africans and described as philosophical by their authors themselves."[7] This stance seems to disregard orality's place in literary and philosophical expressions, which has been identified by other scholars who include Gbadegesin and Imbo. In a rejoinder essay that samples reviews from critics, Hountondji states,

> Some years ago, in reply to this triple criticism, I pointed out the polemical thrust of the incriminating sentence. Though it had the formal structure of a definition, this prefatory declaration was not meant as a definition. It should be read as counter assertion that was far more important for what it rejected than for its positive content. It aimed at establishing, against the dominant ethnological conception, this very simple equation: African philosophy equals African philosophical literature. That is, the whole of philosophical texts produced by Africans.[8]

Bodunrin concurs that writing is not necessarily a prerequisite for the definition of philosophy. Using an illustration of Oruka's conception of philosophic sagacity, which is the process of critically engaging individual philosophies from nonphilosophers, Bodunrin drives home the idea that literacy and writing are not required for individuals to philosophize.[9]

Most Universalist philosophers belong to the same school of thought, but there are subtle differences in their universal notions of philosophy. For example, Bodunrin and Hountondji disagree on whether writing is a key component of philosophy. Going by Universalist assumptions, philosophy primarily involves a systematic cross-examination of belief systems and worldviews—even if these activities were undocumented, they must have taken place in Africa. Going by the premise of what philosophy is known to be, it is unwise to conclude that a lack of written records proves that Africa is devoid of philosophical thought. Such an approach reinforces the hegemony of written texts over oral narratives, while the

---

7   Hountondji, *African Philosophy*, 1.
8   Hountondji, "Que peut," 2–28.
9   Bodunrin, "Question."

position of Universalist scholars like Hountondji, accepting writing as the only standard for philosophy,[10] fuels ongoing debates about the existence of African philosophy.

Western bias against non-Western epistemologies and knowledge systems also calls into question the existence of African philosophy. This condescending attitude stems from the disparity of worldviews in Africa and the West. European worldviews are influenced by Cartesian philosophy, which is derived from Rene Descartes's phrase "I think therefore I am" (cogito ergo sum). Cartesian philosophy is the bedrock of modern European philosophy, giving rise to a European or Western solipsist view of life, finding impetus in the "Cartesian subject." This subject is a "rational being endowed with rationality and scientific knowledge to overcome all obstacles facing humanity. Here was born the 'Imperial Being' who defined himself as the center of the world as 'He' occupied the place of God."[11]

The Western definition of humanity and the self is derived from this assumption of rationality and superior knowledge, which also distinguishes humans from other species. This perpetuated the "paradigm of difference"[12] that categorizes Africans outside this class of humanity. Ramose corroborates this notion with his opinion that the West considers its knowledge systems to be the ultimate model for deciding what constitutes philosophy. It is as though they consider themselves to be the producers of all worthwhile knowledge and "holders of the truth."[13]

Given that most contemporary African philosophers were trained in Western institutions, one must assume that their exploration of philosophy in Africa could be premised on Western philosophy. In my opinion, it is necessary to conduct an overview of scholarly conceptualizations and controversies regarding African philosophy. The following section will explore the intellectual opinions of Kwasi Wiredu, Paulin Hountondji, Bodunrin, Oruka, and others considered to be seasoned scholars of African philosophy, taking the pulse of philosophy in contemporary Africa before proceeding on a journey of decoloniality.

---

10 Imbo, *Introduction*.
11 Ndlovu-Gatsheni, "World," 80–96.
12 Ndlovu-Gatsheni, "World," 85.
13 Ramose, "Discourses."

Defining/Decolonizing African Philosophy

Defining African philosophy is more challenging than it seems—Mawere and Tubaya have said that the question of what constitutes African philosophy will "boggle minds for many more years to come."[14] To them, it is hardly a question that can be easily answered, and it cannot be addressed in a single scholarly appraisal. Irrespective of such a venture's complexity, this section will examine various attempts to define and conceptualize African philosophy, extracting a working definition and identifying its distinct features to aid the mission of decoloniality.

For Wiredu, there is no question that African philosophy exists. He opines that there are extant fragments of African philosophy in folkloric practices; it is not philosophy but philosophic resources that abound within the culture and oral traditions of African people. He is also of the opinion that African philosophy continues to grow in its current form. There is an ongoing search for the ideal conception of African philosophy, and there exists no designated African philosophy as ethno-philosophers presume. Instead, there is an ongoing process to create an African philosophy fit for the twenty-first century, which implies that African philosophy is in fact currently unfit for this century.[15]

A careful appraisal of Wiredu's work reveals that "unfit" philosophy refers to the philosophical suggestions of ethno-philosophers whose conceptualization of African philosophy is anchored on fossilized notions of pristine indigenous cultural practices and oral literature. Wiredu suggests a system of syncretism in the process of carving out a contemporary African philosophy. For him, "a basic imperative of that process is the need to work out a synthesis of insights from our traditional philosophies with any we can get from modern resources of knowledge and reflection."[16] This implies a critical appraisal of Western philosophic thought, contemporary African experiences, and traditional resources of knowledge. Because philosophy as a field of study is moored to rationality

---

14 Mawere and Mubaya, *African Philosophy.*
15 In some circles, an alternative reading has been that ethno-philosophy was not founded on the critical method of philosophizing; hence it could not be regarded as African philosophy.
16 Wiredu, "Conceptual Decolonization," 54.

and critical inquiry,[17] Wiredu discourages disproportionate reflection on either of these knowledge resources.

Imbo categorizes Wiredu as a philosopher whose scholarship takes on a Universalist approach,[18] in direct opposition to the particularist approaches of ethno-philosophers that engage African philosophy as entirely separate from Western philosophy. For him, any workable African philosophy fit for modern life will include Western and traditional/indigenous elements, and even components from the East. This gives credence to Appiah's statement that "for Wiredu, there are no African truths, only truths—some of them about Africa."[19]

Wiredu rejects the distinctiveness of African philosophy proposed by ethno-philosophers—he expects every philosophy to be assessed for its intrinsic philosophic quality. This approach is similar to Soyinka's concept of "tigritude," which is derived from the analogy of a tiger's self-assurance and the attendant global recognition of its "tigerness." Soyinka presented the analogy in response to the ideology of Negritude, which overindulges in its description of Africa and Africans. Just like Wiredu, Soyinka holds a Universalist view of literature—he states that his expectations regarding poetry is an "intrinsic poetic quality," instead of an essentialist romanticization of African culture packaged as poetry. Wiredu expresses the same sentiments in the context of philosophy:

> It is of importance to try to understand how each mode of thought, and especially the traditional, functions in the total context of its society. Since African societies are among the closest approximations in the modern world to societies in the pre-scientific stage of development, the interest which anthropologists have shown in African thought is largely understandable. However, instead of seeing the basic non-scientific characteristics of African traditional thought as typifying traditional thought in general, Western anthropologists and others besides have mistakenly tended to take them as defining a peculiarly African way of thinking, with unfortunate effects.[20]

---

17 Wiredu, "Conceptual Decolonization," 54.
18 Imbo, *Introduction*.
19 Appiah, *In My Father's House*, 104. The quote is also linked to a different argument on the idea of truth in logic. I fully accept the argument that we have to differentiate between Wiredu's ideas of truth in logic and epistemology from his debate on whether African philosophy exists or not.
20 Wiredu, *Philosophy*, 39.

Scholars with universal notions of philosophy find this ethno-philosophic approach to be reductionist and nonprogressive. (Wiredu conceptually refers to it as anachronistic.) These approaches champion the cause of remolding the present in the image of the past, and Imbo states that such approaches to decolonization wage war against intellectual innovation and sociocultural growth and development.[21] He also suggests that the goal should be good African philosophy, not merely African philosophy.

There is a distinction between what African philosophy is and what it should be. To get it to where it should be, Wiredu embarks on the journey of conceptual decolonization—sifting through African thought conceptualization processes that came to as a result of its historical encounter with colonialism. These processes have remained in place because Africans as a whole have refused to actively reflect on them.

Other Universalist philosophers described by Imbo, such as Bodurin, Hountondji, and Oruka, share similar ideologies that are premised on their disregard for the postulations of ethno-philosophers. They dismiss mere descriptive accounts of African folkloric forms. For Hountondji, who is described by Imbo as the "fiercest critic of ethno-philosophy,"[22] philosophy is not some "unthinking, spontaneous, collective system of thought"[23] specific to past, present, and future Africans. This is invariably how he describes ethno-philosophy.

Hountondji, like Wiredu, does not dismiss or deny the existence of philosophy. And he does not accept that philosophy can have a geographical or cultural application and meaning. To him, the universal meaning of the word "philosophy" should be preserved, premised on specificity to content, not geography; the meaning of the word "philosophy" should not change once the adjective "African" has been applied. His own view "is that this universality must be preserved—not because philosophy must necessarily develop the same themes or even ask the same questions from one country or continent to another, but because these differences of content are meaningful precisely and only as differences of content, which, as such, refer back to the essential unity of a single discipline, of a single style of inquiry."[24]

---

21 Imbo, *Introduction*.
22 Imbo, *Introduction*, 29.
23 Hountondji, *African Philosophy*.
24 Hountondji, *African Philosophy*, 56.

Hountondji advocates for the methodological appraisal of African philosophic resource materials to negate the ossified conceptions of African philosophy that confine it to a geographic definition. In his opinion, this view of philosophy promotes colonial and neocolonial conceptions of African primitiveness and clannish dispositions, playing into the European stereotypes of Africa that encourage narratives of Africa's difference and separateness.

Hountondji asserts that a methodological, systematic approach to the conception of African philosophy expands the narrow horizon of philosophical approaches derived from ethno-philosophy. He refers to his approach as a form of demythologization, and "the purpose of this 'demythologizing' of the idea of Africa and African philosophy is simply to free our faculty for theorizing from all the intellectual impediments and prejudices which have so far prevented it from getting off the ground."[25] This implies that ethno-philosophical conceptions of African philosophy are a reactionary philosophy countering European notions of Africa. Imbo summarizes this conception in the statement that "most of the early discussion in the field [of philosophy] has thus been of a justificatory nature and has aimed primarily at laying the foundation and defining the parameters. Naturally, then, African philosophy appears to the newcomer to take a defensive posture."[26] This philosophical approach is aimed at essentializing Africa by engaging its seeming uniqueness to score points in an imaginary Western debate.

The crux of Hountondji's argument is the need for a deconstruction of Western and traditional systems of thought to develop systematic and methodological inquiries that generate applicable conceptualizations of contemporary African philosophy. Bodurin joins other Universalist philosophers in questioning the segregation of African philosophy—to him, these distinctions are derived from different understandings of what constitutes philosophy. It comes from a monolithic conception of philosophy that he sees as erroneous; a people's philosophy is neither defined by the content of their tradition nor their geographical location. The history of human knowledge and intellectuality is laden with the borrowing and sharing of concepts between groups, nations, and races. Knowledge seldom belongs a specific group of people.

---

25   Hountondji, *African Philosophy*, 66.
26   Imbo, *Introduction*.

For Bodurin, any definition or conceptualization of African philosophy must consider the existential realities of contemporary Africa, because contact with the West has impacted traditional African life. He explores traditional ideologies that governed lives in the age of pre-Western contact to illustrate how those ideologies are inapplicable in contemporary Africa. Bodurin accuses ethno-philosophers and African political philosophers of romanticizing the African past. Not everything about autochthonous Africa was "glorious," which is why he sees a need for philosophical conceptualization and methodological application relevant to contemporary Africa. Like other Universalist philosophers, he admits to the existence of "complex, and in some sense rational and logical conceptual systems in Africa,"[27] but he also opines that not every rational conceptualization is philosophy. Bodurin references the complex, rational, and logical systems involved in the study of mathematics and science, which he clearly does not consider to be philosophy.

Bodurin argues for a thorough interrogation of African society and its thought systems for adequate reconstruction; there is hardly any modern system that can operate effectively by retaining its "pristine" thought systems. In his opinion, when one divorces these nationalistic and cultural biases from such "philosophies," they can lend knowledge and information to cultural and political theories—but to be considered legitimate philosophy these works and ideologies need "more rigour and more systematization."[28]

Greek philosophy was born out of systematic inquisition and criticism of popular beliefs and customs. The systematic ability to critique, question, and argue can produce real philosophical thoughts. Bodurin's thought process reveals that he believes in a stable, systematic approach to the philosophical process itself. In this system, every philosophical thesis should be able to argue its case satisfactorily, showing its own strengths and the weaknesses of other theories while explaining their relevance to specific areas of problem solving. A philosophical thesis should also be subject to revision, willing to yield to change and adjustments when in the presence of a superior argument. In light of these philosophical principles, Bodurin and other critics of ethno-philosophy argue that

---

27 Bodunrin, "Question," 170.
28 Bodunrin, "Question," 167.

ethno-philosophers have a "theological dogmatism" in their opinion of African philosophy. He states thus:

> The pity is that ethno-philosophers usually fall in love so much with the thought system they seek to expound that they become dogmatic in the veneration of the culture to which the thought system belongs. They hardly see why others may refuse totally to share their esteem for the system they describe. They do not raise philosophical issues about the system (because for them no problems arise once we 'understand' the system); therefore they do not attempt to give a philosophical justification of the belief system or of issues that arise in it. It is for these reasons that we find their works philosophically unsatisfactory; it is not because we consider the material on which they have worked unworthy of the philosopher's attention, or their work unscholarly.[29]

In the excerpt above, Bodurin is lenient in his criticism of "ethno-philosophy." Scholars like Hountondji openly describe the work of ethno-philosophers as debased or pseudo-philosophy. Bodurin accuses them of "theological dogmatism" while falling victim to his own accusations. I do not dispute the dogmatism of ethno-philosophers, but a close study of Universalist philosophers reveals their own unresolved assumptions about philosophy. Many of these assumptions are derived from Western conceptions of philosophy that masquerade as universal before being imposed on ethno-philosophers. Bodurin's notion of philosophical Universalism is unwavering, and his presupposition of philosophy comes from the Western notion of philosophy: a methodical and rational reflection on the fundamental realities of human experience and existence, out of which theories and concepts are created to interpret society.

Deleuze and Guattari consider philosophy to be an "art of forming, inventing, and fabricating concepts," although Universalist philosophers assert that this is a simplistic definition. In their description of the philosopher, Deleuze and Guattari explain the place of rigor and rationality in the process of concept creation: "The philosopher is expert in concepts and in the lack of them. He knows which of them are not viable, which are arbitrary or inconsistent, which ones do not hold up for an instant. On the other hand, heal so knows which are well formed and attest to a

---

29   Bodunrin, "Question," 172.

creation."[30] This notion of philosophy and philosophers mirrors the argument and stance of Universalist philosophers.

Deleuze and Guattari expand their idea by noting that the creations of philosophers, in the form of concepts, are not thrust upon philosophers. Concepts are not ready-made, and "they must be invented, fabricated, or rather created and would be nothing without their creator's signature."[31] This ideology strengthens the individuality of Universalist arguments, providing perspective for their criticism of the ethno-philosophic adoption of communal ideologies and concepts as philosophy. This justifies arguments for a wary approach to African ethno-philosophical notions and ideologies, given that most of their ideas of philosophy are ready-made. Nietzsche, cited in Deleuze and Guattari, strengthens these Universalist arguments by stating that "philosophers must no longer accept concepts as a gift, nor merely purify and polish them, but first make and create them, present them and make them convincing. Hitherto one has generally trusted one's concepts as if they were a wonderful dowry from some sort of wonderland."[32]

This gives us insight on the antagonism toward ethno-philosophy—it is seen as a gift of which one should be wary. Deleuze and Guattari enjoin philosophers to distrust concepts that were not self-created. In other words, authentic philosophical concepts should emerge after reflecting upon philosophical resources. The African philosopher should not accept philosophical concepts from the West without reflection, because these preexisting philosophies are invariably "gifts." Neither should indigenous, preexisting cultural philosophies be readily accepted. By Nietzsche's Western standards, they are to create their own philosophies.[33]

Other rhetoric against ethno-philosophy gains its impetus from the unanimity of its sources and the ethno-philosophers' romanticization of African communality. Hallen's opposition to this conception of philosophy stems from the communality and anonymity of these "philosophies." To him, they imply that individual Africans are incapable of independent thought—they suggest that Africa can only produce a communal outlook

---

30   Deleuze and Guattari, *What Is Philosophy*, 3.
31   Deleuze and Guattari, *What Is Philosophy*, 3.
32   Deleuze an Guattari, *What Is Philosophy*, 5.
33   It is noteworthy that Nietzsche's approach grew from existentialism, and some scholars have argued that his methodology is not based on logic.

like Bantu or Akan philosophy and incapable of producing philosophers like Socrates or Kant. The irony of the situation is embedded in this idea: if producing equivalents of individual Western philosophies and philosophers is the only legitimate philosophy, then there is a need for a decolonial approach in the study and research of African philosophy. Hallen is clearly dancing to the tune of Western prejudice against philosophies of the Global South.

Dussel considers all philosophies as ethno-philosophy: "Their origin comes from a certain ontological ingenuousness which considers their own world (their cultural totality assumed as a complete grasp of the meaning of human existence) as the center around which the rest of humanity revolved."[34] In other words, all questions of humanity that birth philosophy revolve around cultural and indigenous occurrences for the people from which that philosophy emanates. However, Europe has peddled the predominant philosophy of the Global North as universal, which strengthens the need to explore and decolonize these so-called universal notions and approaches to philosophical scholarship in the hope of creating an authentic, contemporary African philosophy.

In his essay "Agenda for a South-South Philosophical Dialogue," Dussel negotiates a philosophical dialogue between philosophers of the Global North and South after advocating for an intraphilosophical dialogue among philosophers of the Global South.[35] This suggestion is derived from philosophies of the Global South that have been relegated to the periphery. Dussel proposes this meeting to recognize the existence of these Southern philosophies, which to him are "grounded in the traditions that they have cultivated in the regional philosophies for which they have emerged."[36] Dussel sees the antagonism against the communal nature of these philosophies as a Euro-colonial tactic to denigrate the philosophies of the Global South. By his logic, African Universalist philosophers have been hoodwinked by the intended hegemony of Western conceptual thought, leading them to overtly support Western narratives that denigrate philosophies from the Global South. These African Universalists are actively modeling a conception of philosophy from hegemonic narratives, bowing to the imposition of Western thought processes.

---

34 Dussel, "Agenda," 3–18.
35 Dussel, "Agenda."
36 Dussel, "Agenda," 5.

Hallen's argument substantiates his claims by stating that sources of philosophy are in the African past, a time of pristine African thought processes found in "parables, proverbs, poetry, songs, and myths – oral literature generally."[37] As expected, these philosophical materials are not presented systematically or discursively but are eventually subjected to the analytical and critical skills of academic philosophers and scholars reproducing them as the systematic philosophy of the African people. These philosophical products often appear to be timeless, becoming fossilized traditional truths divorced from rigorous argumentation, constantly imposing ancient views on a fast-changing African society. There is merit in Hallen's examination of ethno-philosophy, but his opinions are not strong enough to dismiss ethno-philosophy as African philosophy.

Dussel argues that humanity has posed ontological questions at each point of development, inquiring about society, the environment, and natural phenomena with minor questions, such as what makes the ground firm, and astronomical questions regarding the composition of the universe. This fundamental curiosity, and the questions it poses, is seen by Dussel as the core universal problem; it is a problem specific to humanity regardless of geography or location. However, the response to these core problems enables various perspectives on rational narratives.[38] Rationality, which remains the crux of the criticism against African "ethno-philosophy," refers to supportive reasons for the assertions made from questioning the world around us. These assertions interpret the phenomena that were initially questioned, and the process of backing up an assertive stance with reason is a rational act. In different human societies, the production of myths is the first rational response to some of these universal core problems. In response to criticism of ethno-philosophy, most of which is based on the notion that it lacks rationality, Dussel notes that "myths are symbolic narratives that are not irrational and that do not refer exclusively to singular phenomena."[39]

Like many philosophers, Dussel agrees that the creation of myths is part of the foundational process of current philosophies. However, he challenges the common notion of a transition from a time of mythos (irrationality) to logos (rationality). For Dussel, this notion is one of the

---

37 Hallen, *Short History*, 75.
38 Dussel, "New Age," 1–22.
39 Dussel, "New Age," 4.

founding arguments that sustains the hegemony of Western philosophy, evolving into the prioritization of science and the relegation of subaltern philosophies that are prevalently mythos. Although this argument has provided the basis for most arguments against ethno-philosophy, Dussel specifically states that the notion of mythology's irrationality is incorrectly applied to disqualify it as philosophy: "They are both [mythos and logos] rational. Each of the narratives at issues has a certain degree of rationality, but their specific character varies."[40] In other words, ethno-philosophical arguments derived from African oral literature and mythology should not be dismissed as nonphilosophy. This lends credence to the claims from Mawere and Tubaya that philosophy is not homogenous, making it impossible for a single conceptualization to exhaust it completely.[41]

It can be inferred that the controversies of philosophical conceptualizations and the Eurocentric undertones of the opinions, criticism, and notions put forward by notable African philosophers are linked with their intensive training in Western institutions with Western philosophical theories and arguments. It is imperative to decolonize these philosophical approaches and generate applicable working philosophies and philosophical traditions for the current African reality. Many of the approaches to African philosophy suggested by Universalist African philosophers—who claim to take a neutral or universal stance in their philosophical scholarship—are rebranding Western philosophical approaches as universal, while so-called ethno-philosophers remain stuck in reactionary positions opposing the hegemony of Western philosophies. Both extremes must be reconciled to create traditions that fit the demands of contemporary Africa and her philosophical scholarship.

Mignolo's decolonial tactic champions a decentering and delinking from the West's faux universalisms, to reexist while relinking with legacies of local histories and culture and existing on one's own terms. It advocates a form of epistemic disobedience, choosing to disobey the rules and methodologies of Western epistemologies to accommodate formerly diminished subaltern narratives. This decolonial process is long and gradual, given the West's many years of entanglement with subaltern regions. For Mignolo, there cannot be one decolonial master plan; the process of decoloniality is not a monolithic venture. If it is, it will be "far too

---

40   Dussel, "A New Age," 4.
41   Mawere and Mubaya, *African Philosophy*.

modern, too Eurocentric, too provincial, too limited and still too universal. Decolonialty operates on pluriversality of truth not universality of truth."[42] When this is applied to the discourse of decolonizing African philosophy, it is evident that both schools are guilty of embracing a decolonial master plan.

For African "ethno-philosophers," a master plan resists Western or modernist philosophical traditions instead of reexisting in the process championed by decoloniality. Mignolo opines that the first step of decoloniality is to delink, and the second is to strive toward reexistence. In philosophical scholarship, reexistence is the process of figuring out how to write one's own narratives and philosophies, standing on one's own two feet instead of consciously buying into Western narratives of universality. It is emphatically not a rejection of non-African philosophical traditions; it is an advocacy for a philosophical dialogue between the Global South and the Global North—but this time, not from the absence of self-knowledge.

Dussel traces a blueprint of what philosophical study should entail in subaltern regions. First, he advocates for a Southern-centric philosophical dialogue to address philosophical issues in Africa, Latin America, Asia, and Eastern Europe while creating a teaching and learning foundation, based on multiple philosophical traditions, for future philosophers in these regions. This suggests a pluriversal approach to philosophy with multiple centers. It mirrors Mignolo's cosmopolitan localism, which captures the coexistence of many worlds with diverse histories connected by their experience of colonialism, or a world without a hegemonic center. In learning philosophy, it can be described with this excerpt:

> It is in this way that Arab philosophy for example could incorporate the hermeneutics of European philosophy develop and apply them in order to discover new interpretation of the Koran that will possible a new, much needed Arab political philosophy or Arab feminism. It will be the fruit of Arab philosophical tradition, updated through interphilosophical dialogue (not only with Europe, but equally with Latin America, India, China, [Africa] etc), oriented towards a pluriversal global philosophy.[43]

---

42   Mignolo, "Coloniality," 38–45.
43   Dussel, "A New Age," 18.

This system, suggested by Dussel, exposes scholars not just to their own indigenous and Western philosophical traditions, but to those of others formerly on the periphery. In this way, the philosophies of the formerly ignored could be developed.[44] Having reconciled the extremes of both schools of thought, the definition of philosophy within circles of African philosophical scholarship will be determined by the textual resources available to students and scholars. To generate decolonized, contemporary African philosophical traditions, this study endorses Mignolo's suggestion to delink from the West and relink with the legacies of indigenous cultures, affirming a nonsubversive philosophical tradition. Such a tradition would privilege neither Western philosophical traditions masquerading as universal nor autochthonous indigenous cultures that are out of place with contemporary reality. The result is contemporary African philosophy that engages a pluriversal world.[45]

By that definition, African philosophy is a philosophy emanating from traditional African thought and accommodating multiple philosophical arguments from around the world, in reference to their relevance to contemporary African needs. The philosophical materials generated by this approach would take African reality into consideration while reflecting the traditional thought of the people along with a nonsubversive sampling of relevant philosophical ideologies for African society, which would be African philosophy.

Language of African Philosophy

Debate exists over which language is appropriate for the writing, teaching, and learning of African philosophy; it is an age-old dilemma. Language is integral to the discourse of decoloniality. Its ability to be more than just

---

44 Dussel, "A New Age," 18.
45 Some scholars have argued that this suggestion does not fit into contemporary definitions of African philosophy; it is a pluriversal philosophy of global reflection. My response is that this may be what Africa needs, given that the continent does not exist in a vacuum. This work champions the positioning of African philosophy amidst global interactions and dialogues. Contemporary African society, in its various spheres, is intricately linked with the rest of the world—its philosophies should reflect this intricate interaction without discounting indigenous knowledge or the decolonization of received ideas.

a means of communication, to function as a vehicle of cultural transmission, and its ontological suggestiveness often conditions how we perceive reality. This raises the following questions: in what language should contemporary African philosophy be written and studied? The work of traditional African philosophy was performed in the indigenous languages of traditional African philosophers.

Kimmerle acknowledges that Western languages drew the attention of international philosophical groups, allowing them to recognize the presence and existence of African philosophy and Africa's distinct thought process.[46] On the other hand, Imbo considers African philosophers using Western languages to be repressive.[47] Kimmerle also recognizes the role of Western languages in responding to questions about the existence of African philosophy, but he notes that much of African thought is rooted in African languages. Other scholars, like Kunene, opine that Western languages do not possess the linguistic capacity to express African philosophical thought and reality.[48] Owomoyela, in his essentialist perception of African philosophy, considers the cultivation of distinct African ways of speaking to be a way to preserve and assert an African identity and expression.[49] Imbo assumes that there is need for Africa to revert to the use of the African languages, which birthed African philosophy, for the sake of authenticity in African philosophizing.

For such scholars, African philosophy can only be African if it is done in African languages. Their stance is corroborated by Ngugi's perception of language as a reflection of a people's identity. His opinion of colonial enslavement through the imposition of language is established in the following excerpt:

> For colonialism this involved two aspects of the same process: the destruction or the deliberate undervaluing of a people's culture, their art, dances, religions, history, geography, education, orature and literature, and the conscious elevation of the language of the coloniser. The domination of a people's language by the language of the colonising nations was crucial to the domination of the mental universe of the colonised.[50]

---

46 Kimmerle, "Afrikanische," 47–74.
47 Imbo, *An Introduction*.
48 Kunene, "Problems," 27–44.
49 Owomoyela, "Language," 83–94.
50 Ngugi, *Decolonising*, 16.

For Imbo, an effective way to eliminate contention about the existence of African philosophy, while simultaneously enriching contemporary African philosophizing, is to revive the use of African languages to promote free cultural expression and production.[51] It is an idea supported by Okara, who claims to be constantly groping for English words that can express deep African thoughts.[52]

Imbo goes further, noting that language provides agency and voice for people to convey thoughts, ideologies, and conceptions in appropriate terms, eliminating any lingering doubts about the existence of indigenous philosophical conceptions. Regarding the adoption of Western languages for African philosophical conception, Imbo states:

> Languages totally removed from their environment, languages that distort the African historical struggles, languages that stifle the creative impulses. . . . Continued debate in these languages only serves to perpetuate the imbalance of power. A return to the African languages is needed to counteract the Eurocentric cultural philosophy that is located and rooted in the Western metropolis. African languages must be enlisted in the struggle for cultural freedoms, the struggle to regain sight of the centrality of language for self-identity.[53]

While there are elements of truth in Imbo's observations, the debate has moved beyond discussion of whether African philosophy exists and whether language perpetuates the stagnation of cultural creativity.

Skepticism toward African philosophy has been addressed by African philosophers such as Wiredu, who specifically identifies the presence of traditional African philosophy in oral tradition. The idea that using non-African languages can hinder Africa's cultural and creative expressions has been countered by demonstrations from scholars, including Chinua Achebe, who have been able to craft effective creative and cultural expression without yielding to the allegedly smothering tendencies of non-African languages. Current polemics concerning the use of language should focus on a specific language's effectuality for adequately carrying the weight of indigenous thought. As Oyewumi observes, Africa is intricately entangled with the West, and the choice of language cannot be restricted solely to indigenous languages.

---

51   Imbo, *Introduction*.
52   Okara, "African Speech," 15–16.
53   Imbo, *Introduction*, 101.

To achieve a truly decolonized philosophy, pluriversality and multiculturalism have become the metric of decoloniality and societal evolution, measured against the de-Westernization and indigenization that is championed by African essentialist thinkers.[54] Achebe is not opposed to writing African literature in indigenous languages; he uses the English language not because he considers it superior but because he recognizes the reality of modern Africa and the possibility of reaching a wider audience through the language. By domesticating the English language and lending it an African spirit, he enhances his authentic African expression.

The 1962 Makerere conference, "A Conference of African Writers of English Expression," laid the foundation for the disagreements about language in African literary scholarship. Obi Wali, in his article "Dead End of African Literature," opined that "until these writers and their Western midwives accept the fact that any true African literature must be written in African languages, they would be merely pursuing a dead end, which can only lead to sterility, un-creativity and frustration."[55] Wali joined Ngugi in advocating for the absolute use of indigenous language in writing African literature.

Following the debates of the Makerere conference, Achebe responded to the opinions of scholars like Wali who clearly opposed using Western languages to write African literature: he considered the English language to be an inevitable vestige of colonialism. In recognition of that reality, Achebe adopted the use of the English language.[56] It may have been

---

54 Mignolo, "Coloniality," 41.
55 Wali, "Dead End," 13–16.
56 The adoption of indigenous languages has been a long and contentious debate. Some have argued that the use of English language in writing literature, history, African philosophy, and poetry is a demonstration to correct European assumptions that Africans had no original history or ideas. African writers also needed acknowledgment and approval from European teachers and mentors to advance their careers and commercial ventures in a global network—there is an inherent conflict of interest for elites who profit from their use of language. This chapter's illustration is intended to deter essentialist arguments that champion indigeneity as the most appropriate decolonial approach. The use of the English language was not particularly reactionary, as some continue to argue, but it was a more practical approach for writers in a multilingual country and for a continent as big as Africa. See the chapter on decolonizing language.

acquired through the unfortunate circumstances of colonialism, but it has come to serve as the national language of his fellow Nigerians. Achebe intended to apply the English language in ways that expertly accommodated the nuances and peculiarities of the African thought process—a domestication of the English language that kept his thoughts in direct contact with his ancestral home. In his words, the African writer "should aim at fashioning out an English which is at once universal and able to carry his peculiar experience."[57] African philosophy should not be limited by the use of language; a series of conversations could explore the possibility of developing ideas on African philosophy of language to understand what this would look like.

There are grave implications for using a colonizer's language, including the language's ability to carry its "own philosophical suggestiveness,"[58] or the learner's unconscious naturalization of thought processes that are specific to the original speakers; it may leave learners unaware of neocolonial properties embedded in the language. Wiredu advocates for philosophers to approach philosophical thoughts in their own native languages, even if they express their findings in Western languages, which may describe Achebe's authentic expressive writing ability. However, Wiredu considers this proposition challenging—how can one know in which language one is thinking?

The exclusive study of philosophy in a foreign language makes the idea of thinking in one's own vernacular more daunting. African philosophers like Kwasi Wiredu, Olusegun Oladipo, Anthony Kwame Appiah, V. Y. Mudimbe, D. A. Masolo, Segun Gbadegesin, Kwame Gyekye, Peter Bodunrin, Godwin Sogolo, Paulin Hountondji, C. S. Momoh, and many others were trained in Western institutions, grounded in Western philosophical theories and arguments. Those who followed were equally grounded in Western philosophies because African departments of philosophy were based on the Western philosophical syllabus, using its texts and canons.

The undeniable entanglement between Western philosophical thinking and African philosophical thought is no surprise, even when excluding the pervasive use of Western languages in these philosophical ventures. However, Wiredu is certain that language does not exert an irreversibly

---

57   Achebe, "African Writer," 27–30.
58   Wiredu, "Conceptual Decolonization," 56.

deterministic influence over philosophical thought processes. He believes that philosophers and philosophical researchers can be made aware of the suggestive power of foreign languages, allowing them to resist such influences. He does not discourage writing in foreign languages; he opposes thinking in them. Wiredu champions a reflexive and critical approach to philosophical thinking. In my opinion, this is the foundational principle for every decolonial exercise.

Recognizing the place of thought—and acknowledging the ability to step away from the web of one language to think in another—champions the notion that any language can be the language for writing African philosophy. This does not dismiss the fears of language's ontological suggestiveness but instead recognizes those fears while awakening the philosopher's consciousness and identifying the need for a reflexive approach in philosophical musings.

African or indigenous languages that carry the pulse of indigenous philosophies should be deployed in the thought processes of academic philosophizing, which will aid authentic philosophical reflection. It is imperative to possess a proficiency and an in-depth understanding of the linguistic and cultural peculiarities of the language of the society from which philosophy emerges. However, contemporary African decolonial reality is characterized by the navigation of multiculturalism and pluriversality, shunning particularist notions that are limiting and atavistic. Research and teaching of African philosophy require multilingual policies. The study and writing of African philosophy should not be confined to indigenous African languages, despite the assertions of some African essentialist scholars. It should engage other languages for broader accessibility, amplifying African philosophical publications and enabling Africa's participation in global philosophical discourses.

African Philosophical Curriculum

This study has navigated the controversial waters of African philosophy to suggest contemporary decolonial approaches for reforming the research, learning, and teaching of African philosophy. Although essentialist thinkers champion a concept of de-Westernization or indigenization seeking to overthrow Western hegemonic influences in African knowledge creation, it is a confrontational reaction to colonialism and its vestiges. Planetary pluriversality is necessary to pursue contemporary decoloniality alongside a nonsubversive approach to knowledge production in subaltern regions, of which Africa is a member, acknowledging a transmodern world where cultures are in equal dialogue with one another. In this context, pluriversality refers to the (co)existence of multiple ontologies and philosophies, critiquing the European claim to universality. It proffers multiple alternatives to negate Euro-modern conceptions of philosophy that masquerade as universal, deconstructing the Euro-modern one-world notion and providing insight to the existence of multiple worlds.

Within the context of adopting decoloniality and its pluriversal approach in decolonizing the African philosophical curriculum, this study acknowledges the hegemonic, imperial imprints of Western philosophical expression existent in curriculums of African philosophy. The traditional accentuation of African knowledge systems is necessary to counter notions of Western superiority, but there is also a need to step away from the defensive essentialist posture of most African scholarship—this wider-angle view can help identify and adopt applicable decolonial strategies in light of the experiential realities of contemporary Africa. To battle the presence of subversive knowledge systems in African philosophy, and to topple the hegemony of on Western universalism in the curriculum and discipline of African philosophy, effort should be made to create curriculums that endorse and encourage a pluriversal approach in the conceptual research, teaching, and institutional expressions of African philosophy. There are now courses on contemporary African philosophies and comparative philosophy, and space remains for a more intensive investment in a decolonial approach.

This implies the creation of a philosophical curriculum that is in deep conversation with itself and the philosophical traditions of the rest of the world. However, this conversation operates from a mindset of equality instead of the subversive history of Euro-modern philosophies. Dialogue and communication are the search for wisdom that is the essence of philosophy; it is not surprising that a decolonial approach of pluriversality calls for communication with other philosophical traditions. Euro-modern philosophies were not and are not only asymmetric in their dialogic pretensions but also hegemonic in their base perceptions of philosophy. Dialogue often involves deliberation, reflection, and examination that opens the philosopher to new ideas and perspectives that enrich philosophical scholarship.

In practical terms, such dialogue should take the approach of the modern Arab philosopher Mahomed Abed Yabri documented by Dussel. Yabri evaluates the philosophy of his Arab cultural tradition, rejecting certain traditions while also rejecting the Eurocentric philosophical tradition that denies the existence of an Arab philosophy. He goes further to

> employ his linguistic skills in Arabic as a native speaker and undertakes original research in the philosophic traditions of the great thinkers of the "Eastern" schools (of Egypt, Baghdad, and towards the East, under the influence of Avicenna) and of the "Western" schools (of the caliphate of Cordoba, including the Berber regions of Fez) that pivot the contributions of 'Ibn Rushd. . . . At the second stage, [he] undertakes a critique of his own philosophical tradition by employing the resources of Arab philosophy itself, but also drawing from some of the achievements of modern hermeneutics (which he studied in Paris).[59]

Dussel states that this dialogue enables Yabri to learn "new historical elements in his own tradition."[60] By Yabri's third and final stage, he had built upon his discoveries to assemble new philosophical creations based on his own indigenous traditions, supported and nourished by the traditions of other regions he had been in communion with. Dussel emphasizes the place of critical philosophers from each philosophical tradition as participants in this dialogue. The aim is to generate critical theories that will be relevant to contemporary African realities instead of involving persons who merely regurgitate traditional philosophies of little relevance for contemporary Africa. African philosophy must not be restricted to a segment commonly known as "traditional philosophies."

Comparative philosophy, as it is now being taught, is one of the many ingredients necessary for a decolonized contemporary African philosophy. This present study champions the in-depth understanding and study of African linguistic and cultural expression with reference to specific locations, and it also engages the philosophical traditions of "othered" regions and Western traditions. African philosophical curriculums should include studies in African linguistics, depending on the region, and select philosophical research from Eastern and Western philosophical traditions.

---

59 Dussel, "New Age," 18.
60 Dussel, "New Age," 18.

In the process of decolonizing African philosophical tradition, effort should be made to Africanize the curriculum for disciplines of philosophy in African tertiary institutions. This means magnifying voices from Africa that have otherwise been silenced and marginalized for decades at these institutions. The structure and content of any educational curriculum frames the orientation and questions of its students. Although this notion of Africanizing the curriculum may seem like an extension of narrow-minded essentialist arguments that reduce African philosophy to territorial defense and historical contestations,[61] the concept corroborates Coetzee's opinion that to achieve an authentic African philosophizing—which is invariably a decolonized African philosophy—African scholars should work toward "the inclusion of that which was deliberately ignored and omitted."[62]

There is no dispute over the philosophical hegemony of the Global North and the deliberate disregard or nonrecognition of philosophical traditions among Africans and others from the Global South. An Africanized curriculum for the discipline of African philosophy is clearly an investment in those alienated, trivialized, and neglected aspects of African philosophical tradition. Africanizing the curriculum of African philosophy is like a systematic investigative project to retrieve Africa's philosophical history and the truth of African philosophy. This project will replicate the efforts of historical philosophers who aim to

> rectify the historical prejudices of negation, indifference, severance, and oblivion that have plagued African philosophy in the hands of European devil's advocates and their African accomplices. African historical investigations in philosophy go beyond defence, confrontations, and corrections. They are also authentic projects and exercises in genuine scientific construction of African philosophy concerning diverse matters of its identity and difference, problem and project, its objectives, discoveries, development, achievements and defects or failures.[63]

It is also a process of localizing the global discourses of decoloniality in the continent, agreeing with Dussel's notion of holding dialogues within

---

61 Chimakonam, "Can the Philosophy," 513–22.
62 Coetzee and Roux, *African Philosophy*, 7.
63 Coetzee and Roux, *African Philosophy*, 6.

before venturing out.[64] Janz observes that philosophy should have "contingent but not arbitrary" interest in the geography from which it emanates, so as to attend to the situation of its environment.[65] This resonates with my opinion that self-perusal is relevant for the generation of carefully thought-out African philosophical traditions that are effective for contemporary existence and scholarship. An internal philosophical appraisal is necessary alongside pluriversal dialogues to address specific, local challenges in African society.

That being said, curricula for African philosophical studies should accommodate courses that expose students to the diversity of African "truths" and realities, including courses that enable them carry out the investigative and retrieval missions of historical philosophers as described by Coetzee. This is primarily to alleviate students' disproportionate consumption of hegemonic Western philosophical narratives, which mostly denigrate African philosophical traditions and universalize Western traditions. Foundational courses should espouse traditional African philosophies and usher students into broader discourses and dialogues with other philosophical traditions, aiding the healthy, balanced philosophical development of the students involved. Training in basic African courses is required because there is no magic wand to change the Eurocentric minds of the young; it is what they know.

Students who are better equipped to engage in unbiased critical appraisal of both indigenous and foreign philosophical traditions are likely to carve out functional contemporary philosophies that are relevant for present-day Africa. This mirrors Wiredu's opinion, which considers Africa's entanglement with the West. For him, contemporary philosophers should engage in a critical reconstruction without deliberately disregarding the philosophical and scientific resources that are a testament to Africa's Western encounters. He discourages over-valuing that which comes from either Africa or the West because not all that comes from Africa is "profound and sound."[66] Even the best description of what is considered African philosophy may still be incapable of helping Africa deal with modern realities.

---

64 Dussel, "Agenda."
65 Janz, *Philosophy*.
66 Wiredu, "Conceptual Decolonization."

For Wiredu, integrating traditional African philosophical thought processes alongside other non-Western ones is the only way to devise a philosophy fit for contemporary African realities. In the context of creating a contemporary philosophical curriculum for Africa, and in light of Wiredu's opinions, I suggest that the curriculum should eliminate extremes. It should favor neither Western nor African philosophical subjects, which are the approaches most likely to produce narrow-minded, essentialist scholars. Decolonizing African philosophy does not mean the elimination of other philosophical modes of inquiry from elsewhere in the world.

The Discipline of African Philosophy: A Question of Relevance

The demands of a constantly changing society have led to a reassessment of educational priorities.[67] In recent times, priority has been determined by relevance, and relevance is linked with tangible output and productivity—many nations in the world are reordering education with this understanding of relevance. Given the developing status of Africa, disciplines like philosophy that lack physical or tangible output have borne the brunt of this reprioritization. Sogolo states that "the greatest difficulty that faces the philosopher, apart from that of defining the very discipline he practises, is the task of showing the relevance of his profession. It is a common problem that faces virtually all the literary disciplines."[68]

This difficulty is primarily the result of the constant economic challenges and intermittent global economic recessions facing developing countries. If they were given the opportunity, most institutions across the continent might strip education to that which they consider essential. The growth of scientific advancements, medical breakthroughs, and demand in digital technologies around the world have made science and technology into essential disciplines in tertiary education. However, disciplines like philosophy should not be considered luxuries suited only for developing nations. Knowledge can be tangible and intangible, intrinsic and extrinsic, and in all its forms it must be evaluated in relation to how societies evolve. In light of this circumstance, the discipline of philosophy

---

67 Miller and Macdonald, "Role," 11–18.
68 Sogolo, "Philosophy," 97–114.

can prove its relevance to African society. The question now is this: of what relevance is the discipline of African philosophy for contemporary African society and its developmental agenda?

Colonialism imposed a dozen spokespersons on Africa who defined the people's truths and experiences, denied the existence of their history and culture, and trivialized their philosophies. Substantiating this assertion is Hegel's claim that Africa "is no historical part of the World; it has no movement or development to exhibit ... Africa is the Unhistorical, Undeveloped Spirit, still involved in the conditions of mere nature, and which had to be presented here only as on the threshold of the World's History."[69]

African philosophy was once questioned with claims similar to this Hegelian notion. Other controversies over what constitutes African philosophy have controlled discourse to the point where Sogolo considers such debates to be the entirety of African philosophy. However, there remains the question of what African society stands to gain from the discipline of African philosophy and how it contributes to national development and governance.

With the end of colonialism came independence, nationalist movements, and ideologies seeking to reaffirm African heritage, remedy the wrongs of historical prejudices, and stop the demonization of (or indifference toward) Africa's people, culture, and society. Nationalist consciousness brought about the de-Westernization of African history and society, making room for the questioning of hegemonic Western narratives that eventually led to the recognition of and research into African philosophy. African philosophy has provided appropriately indigenous answers to questions of African life and society, unveiling the unique heritage of the African people. It is defining African experiences and providing contextual meanings to problems that plague Africa.

Coetzee described decolonization as a crucial catalyst that allowed for expression of unique African experiences and worldviews.[70] Philosophical research has given insight into the authentic African identity. It is gradually unshackling Africa's scholarship, decentering solipsistic and hegemonic Western narratives and eliminating the silence that has long echoed in the area of African history and scholarship. Through philosophical

---

69   Hegel, *Philosophy*, 99.
70   See his introduction in Coetzee and Roux, *The African Philosophy*.

research, the African sense of pride and a near uncompromised knowledge of self has been restored.

The relevance of this discipline cannot be overemphasized, especially given the primal human need to ask questions; humans have been on a constant search for answers to their unending questions about the world. As society evolves, new questions surface in need of answers, and philosophy is there as a field of study to provide rational tools that aid the deliberation and assessment of human activities. It provides reflective tools and thoughts about the organization of people's religious, social, political, judicial, psychological, and historical experiences. As a discipline in academia, African philosophy expresses the principles of logic and reason to understand the realities of the world while answering fundamental questions. It also serves as an outlet for the existential journey of humanity, particularly the African people. It provides a platform for honing problem-solving and analytical skills, critical thinking, and the careful reasoning that is essential to national debates, social analysis, and other forms of societal development.

These are also crucial skills for legal and judicial affairs; it is little wonder that law students are required to take philosophy courses. It plays a concrete role in the policymaking process of many African states. The confused policies of most societies on the continent show an urgent need for the direct influence of homegrown philosophy. Philosophers and their activities should not be confined to the narrow walls of academia. Instead, they must become actively involved in political and policymaking arenas to enrich the continent's sociopolitical scene through their wealth of philosophical knowledge.

Philosophy has had direct and indirect impacts on the social and political affairs of human society.[71] However, African philosophy can have a more direct impact on African society by taking a more applied approach. African society is currently steeped in sociopolitical, moral, and developmental crises that are functions of a struggle to express Western modernity in African society, and there is an urgent need for applied African philosophy in several spheres. Although the core of African philosophy is to generate theories with reference to fundamental truths, these theories must now be applied constructively to society.

---

71   Miller and Macdonald, "Role."

Disciplines in tertiary institutions should craft effective approaches and tactics grounded in philosophy to deal with the social, political, and moral issues of contemporary Africa. This can be achieved by a constant reevaluation of existing methodologies applied by societal institutions and by the creation of methodologies, principles, and approaches to catalyze change based on the people's values. To achieve this, the discipline of philosophy must work closely with other disciplines in academia. An interdisciplinary philosophical scholarship is the key to maintaining relevance and value in African society.

Conclusion

This chapter has interrogated the myriad of conceptions of African philosophy, identifying deficiencies in the ways that different schools of thought perceive the constitution and definition of African philosophy. Despite the multiple voices in African philosophy, there has yet to be a unanimous conception of African philosophy's composition or how it can best work for Africa. This chapter follows the ideologies of various schools of thought to identify extremist notions as to what African philosophy is and is not, revealing the reductionist and atavistic nature of ethno-philosophers' arguments and the continued influence and dominance of Western thought among allegedly Universalist or professional philosophers. It engages in a decolonial exercise referencing these arguments, and in response to the question of what should constitute contemporary African philosophical tradition, it suggests a pluriversal and multicultural approach to the issues of language, content, focus, and the entire morphology of contemporary African philosophy.[72]

---

72   For a recent volume, see Afolayan and Falola, *Palgrave*.

Chapter Twenty

African Futurism

Introduction

In the course of the history of African liberation struggles, there have been some celebrated periods of cohesion and achievement, others characterized by chaos, with heated contestations in between. Having recovered from the euphoria of the era of politico-juridical liberation—a process that was expedited by an almost immediate realization of the limitations of political independence—difficulties represented by the failure to consolidate on the "independence" achievement and deliver on the promise of socioeconomic freedom and progress set the tone for further political and intellectual contention. This saw a number of suggested approaches for the rearticulation of the ideal path to inclusive African liberation—one that includes people of African descent everywhere in a joint (Pan-African) global movement for a prosperous future.

From the ongoing neocolonial, postcolonial/postmodern, neoliberal and futurist discourse on the right approach to achieving inclusive African emancipation, there appears to be a consensus on the importance of an (independent) African identity and episteme as a basis for achieving economic and cultural liberation. This notion is popular among Africanist scholars who feel an African identity would provide cohesion, while an African episteme will deliver solutions to African problems by ensuring that the thought that produces the formulae for resolving Africa's sociocultural and economic challenges is grounded in African reality. Thus, the solutions proffered would be relevant to African needs and in charting the right course to the desired future for peoples of African descent. This has also marked a perceptible shift in intellectual discourse on Africa, from its reactionary preoccupations of the independence era to a focus on reimagining ideas for reinvention of the African identity and redirecting the African developmental trajectory away from subjective tendencies in what is now known as "futurism," that is, African Futurism.[1]

Futurism

The concept of futurism owes its existence to an artistic trend started by the Italian poet Filippo Marinetti in Italy in 1909.[2] Driven by technological obsessions, it stood against traditional forms of being and advocated modern, dynamic expressions. Its essence was to depict in art the vitality of the modern world. Futurists can also be those whose preoccupations lie in futurology; it concerns the endeavor to methodically investigate forecasts about the future and how they can be derived from the present. Their preoccupation is futurist thinking— "imagining, envisioning, projecting and/or predicting what has not been realized yet."[3]

As opposed to futurism, this twentieth-century artistic movement that advances the divulsion of the future from the past, African Futurism sets itself against the linear progression of time and accentuates the significance of the past to the present and the present to the past. Hence, the domineering composition of the future through Eurocentric epistemologies is fragmented and destabilized. In doing so, it seeks to reimagine the

---

[1] I am aware of the emerging mixture and the various definitions of African Futurism, African futurism, African-Afrofuturism, Afrofuturism 3.0, and post-African Futurism. In this chapter, I deploy African Futurism (as two words, uppercased, unhyphenated) to make a distinction from the alternatives. In my deployment of African Futurism, the core of the argument revolves around the concept of African (home and abroad) futuristic thoughts. Here a distinction is made between African Futurism and Afrofuturism. The popular argument is that Afrofuturism, though a part of African futurist thought as captured in African Futurism, is diaspora-rooted and focused. and this is becoming more evident in the lessening of feelings of brotherhood between young Black people on the continent and elsewhere. Therefore, African Futurism should be the embodiment of African Futurist thought, be it in the diaspora (as with Afrofuturism) or in Africa as African Futurism (a united front).

[2] Barness et al., *20th-Century*, 45.

[3] TTI TriMetrix HD, "Futuristic Thinking."

African past, present, and future as an attempt at decoloniality that discovers, empowers, and utilizes Afrocentric onto-epistemologies to actualize a preferable future for the people of African descent.

Central to this agenda of actualizing the best possible future for peoples of African descent is the application of "traditional" (indigenous) instruments of articulation and cohesion such as Afro-spirituality, myths, folklores, and indigenous techno-scientific innovations, deployed in their capacity to actualize future possibilities. As past indices and as agents of future actualization, these traditional forms hold the key to numerous positive outcomes.

African Futurism and Afrofuturism

African Futurism is an advanced stage of African decolonization. Its discourse is centered on the severance of ties with (debilitating) Euro-American legacies, historical contexts, enlightenment reasoning with its totalizing control, its ontology (which destroys otherness by homogenizing it), and its logocentrism (white mythology). It is the proposition of an Africanness—an African identity derived from and rooted geographically and culturally on the African continent. African Futurism as an intellectual and artistic movement also combines Afrofuturism in its efforts at Black (African) liberation.

A term coined in 1993 by Mark Dery, Afrofuturism expresses the (central) ideas and trepidations of the African diaspora through a culture of technology and science fiction.[4] This involves subverting stereotypes and exposing racist conventions, such as engaging American culture via (artistic) critique. Encompassing a shared interest in envisioning Black futures that stem from Afrodiasporic experiences, it covers the African diaspora (media and art) response to racial categorizations and conclusions as well as its attendant inequalities.

As twentieth-century conceptions of the future of peoples of African descent, African Futurism and Afrofuturism might share similar aspirations in their origins, but they have not always had a unified approach to achieving this shared ambition. Evidence in the description of each concept points to their divergence. African Futurism as a vision of the future

---

4 Yaszek, "Afrofuturism," 41–60.

is focused on and mostly written by Black scholars concerned with the future of Africa. They focused on new possibilities instead of "what could have been."[5] Afrofuturism, on the other hand, has at its center African American themes and concerns. It rallies around shared Afrodiasporic experiences, and its "default centre" is not the African continent.

African Futurism is parallel to Afrofuturism in the way Blacks (both on the continent and in the diaspora) are connected by ancestry, spirit, history, and future. The dissimilarity arises in African Futurism's direct roots in African culture, history, mythology, and perspective, which contrasts with Afrofuturism's focus on Western experiences. This difference in Afrodiasporic reactions to Black discrimination can be appreciated when viewed from the diaspora's distinctive experiences such as the prevailing racial socioeconomic relations in the West. Kwame A. Appiah explains this disparity in racial experiences as follows:

> What race meant to the new Africans affectively, however, was not, on the whole, what it meant to educated blacks in the New World. For many African-Americans, raised in a segregated American society and exposed to the crudest forms of discrimination, the social intercourse with white people was painful and uneasy. Many of the Africans, on the other hand (my father among them), took back to their homes European wives and warm memories of European friends; few of them, even from the "settler" cultures of East and southern Africa, seem to have been committed to ideas of racial separation or doctrines of racial hatred. Since they came from cultures where black people were in the majority and where lives continued to be largely controlled by indigenous moral and cognitive conceptions, they had no reason to believe that they were inferior to white people and they had, correspondingly, less reason to resent them.[6]

This, however, is not suggesting that Africans on the continent did not identify with African American political aspirations, as the civil rights movement did much to expose American racial injustices to the world. Also, the refusal of the West to take action in South Africa and Rhodesia (Zimbabwe) was viewed as deep-rooted anti-Black racism. It explains "Afro" reactions to white domination as an outcome of the degree of

---

5   Union College, "African-Futurist Deji Olukotun to Give Inaugural Selley Memorial Lecture March.
6   Appiah, *In My Father's House*, 6–7.

exposure to it, which in turn informs the nature of the approach to resistance and why the West, as the immediate theater of expression of this racial onslaught, has been the primary center of focus for Afrofuturism.

The major dissimilarity between Black futuristic conceptions (African Futurism and Afrofuturism) also demonstrates the growing rift in the unity of Black purpose (between Africans on the continent and the Black diaspora community) toward the desired future. The distance in geographical location and socioeconomic experiences, as well as Black diasporic impressions of Africa influenced by a Western capitalist–informed outlook, has led to a philosophical rift between Africans everywhere, on the continent and in the diaspora. This is especially true with younger generations' indifference toward the era of Black historical struggles while enjoying the comforts won by said struggles.

The understanding here is that African Futurism transcends continental ramifications to include diaspora (artistic) expressions such as Afrofuturism and that, given the uniqueness in the experience of both expressions, there exist points of divergence that can be harmonized by an overriding sentiment found in, for example, Pan-Africanism. This sentiment should, however, be founded on morally and ethically sound principles that also possess attributes of inclusion, adhesion, cohesion, and inspiration.

Negritude, Pan-Africanism, and the Origins of African Futurist Thought

The struggle for the future by peoples of African descent can be argued to be as old as conflict on the continent. However, the struggle for liberation, equality, and self-determination from Euro-American domination can be linked to the relationship between Europe and Africa going back to the fifteenth century.[7] This association forced Africa to the lowest levels in social classification and economic entitlement, with Europe at the top. The quest to change this trajectory of Africa's future development led to the contestation of European racial superiority and other discriminatory ideas used to justify the oppression of African peoples. Africans educated in the West were at the forefront of this liberation agenda.

---

7   Falola and Agbo, "Prospects."

The rise of the African intellectual anti-imperialist struggle, which cumulated in Africa's politico-juridical independence, beginning in the late 1950s, owes its origin largely to the Black consciousness movement Negritude from the 1930s. Negritude, which was primarily developed by Francophone intellectuals, authors, and politicians of the African diaspora, condemned colonialism and called for the creation of a Pan-African sense of self among individuals of African ancestry globally.[8] It was an advocate for pride in the African (Black) nature, the assertion of one's self and identity, and the disavowal of French assimilatory ideas as a medium for resistance.

Negritude at its inception might not have envisaged the possibility of the political independence of French African colonies from France. However, its call for the recognition, expression, and celebration of African traditional customs and ideas is echoed in futurist conceptions for the reconstitution and enthronement of an African identity. And it is this African identity that will be pivotal in building a free and prosperous future for peoples of African descent. Leopold Sedar Senghor, a part originator and major proponent of the Negritude movement, demonstrates support for the recovery of traditional African episteme when he said the following: "To ground an effective revolution, our revolution, we had to rid ourselves of our borrowed clothes—those clothes of assimilation—and affirm our own identity, which is our Negritude."[9]

The Anglophone African diaspora from British colonial African dominions took up the activist mantle and pushed for the unification of Black efforts toward the recognition of their humanity and rights under a Pan-African banner. On the continent, returning Western-educated intellectuals-cum-politicians and nationalist-activists joined in the movement calling for an end to colonialism and independence for Africa at the Fourth Pan-African Congress, which was held in Manchester in 1945.

Pan-Africanism, as a call for the coming together of peoples of African descent based on a shared race and destiny, became the rallying point of Black efforts toward gaining their freedoms. This meant the recognition of Black rights to equality, humanity, and self-determination. These ideas are not divorced from that of the Trinidadian barrister Henry Sylvester

---

8   Revkat, "[Fuusm-1] Sat. 11/28 Daily Meditation Offering."
9   Senghor, *Rapport*.

Williams's 1900 African diaspora organization. Nonetheless, unique to its time, it was reorganized to meet the challenges of the period (after 1945).

The Pan-Africanist successes of the anticolonial and civil rights movement era (the 1960s) represent the best example of the importance of a unified African front both on the continent and in diaspora to pulling down both material and theoretical structures otherwise hindering a desired Afrocentric future. However, given the changing currents in world socioeconomic relations, the gap in the sense of common destiny between Africans on the continent and those in the diaspora keeps growing. A twenty-first-century assessment of the 1990s African renaissance and its Pan-Africanist elements reveals an inability to bridge this gap and harmonize Black efforts toward a future of equality, self-determination, dignity, and prosperity.

African Futurism must identify, accommodate, and be ready to lend its firm geographical roots to providing the ideal basis for various Black expressions of freedom to anchor their agenda. In this scenario, the Pan-Africanist principle of Black unity, liberation, and self-determinism will have to be organized around more than a mutual racial classification that is "grounded in bad biological—and worse ethical—ideas, inherited from the increasingly racialized thought of nineteenth-century Europe and America."[10] Pan-Africanism has been argued to have "matured into a humanist and developmentalist discourse opposed to race as an organizing principle of society and the world."[11] However, just like Negritude, Pan-Africanism has struggled to identify a suitable replacement, one that inspires unity of purpose through shared aspirations stemming from a shared identity.

Therefore, in strengthening the Pan-African sentiment to command the attention, respect, support, and commitment of peoples of African descent around the world, there is a need to tone down, if not eliminate completely, its emphasis on race-shared biological traits as a basis for adhesion and cohesion. Such biological differences are the basis upon which an essential social instrument of segregation and coercion is founded. It has had the effect of painting the Pan-African movement as having a racial/racist ideology (i.e., "pan-African racism"). Nazi Germany

---

10   Appiah, *In My Father's House*.
11   Ndlovu-Gatsheni, "Revisiting."

and the Holocaust are examples of the dangers of adopting shared biological similarities (race) as the basis for ideological and political activism.

Other Approaches in the Articulation of an African Future

History is a procession of events, sometimes with traceable and active interconnections. "Within the context of a 'postcolonial neo-colonized world'" argues Ndlovu-Gatsheni, such issues as "identity formation, nationalism, decolonization, nation-building, liberal democracy, epistemology and economic development form a single part of a complex discursive structure whose genealogy is traceable to the underside of modernity and so cannot be treated separately if a clear and broader picture of the African postcolonial present is to be understood."[12] But the function of African Futurism is not just a mere recounting of the African past in its relation to the present and possible future outcomes. African Futurism seeks to reassess the past and present of Africa using more objective African theories: objective not in the sense that suggests Africa's ownership of the truth but in their relevance as products of the same reality they seek to explain and develop.

In the colonial and postcolonial academy, African twentieth-century thought has been characterized by four traditions: the imperialist/Eurocentric tradition; the nationalist tradition; the radical traditions including Marxist, feminist, and environmental approaches; and the "post" tradition—postcolonialism and postmodernism of the neocolonial period.[13] These approaches beginning from the nationalist tradition, though their methodologies are different, are all attempts at navigating the African neocolonial reality and forming the basis for a prosperous African future.

The contemplation of an African future with a focus on self-determinism toward a free and prosperous existence for peoples of African descent has taken several forms in the above-identified periods. Beginning with anticolonial sentiments, the movement for the future of Africa assumed the form of Negritude, Pan-Africanism, and other intellectual discourses such as neocolonialism, postcolonialism, postmodernism, neoliberalism,

---

12 Ndlovu-Gatsheni, *Coloniality*.
13 Zeleza, "Past," 7.

and African Futurism. On the continent, African intellectuals and political activists rallied around these sentiments like Negritude and Pan-Africanism to achieve the political independence of African territories. And in the Black (African) diaspora there were Black liberation movements like the civil rights movement in the United States in the 1960s. Subsequently, with the attainment of political independence came neocolonialism and the clamor for that elusive economic independence, which was identified as a key component in consolidating on political independence and delivering a prosperous future for Africa. This period marked the use of the "posts"—postcolonialism and postmodernism—as tools for the articulation of Africa's future in this era of neocolonialism.

Neocolonialism, as Kwame Nkrumah aptly describes it, is a contest between positive and negative action. For example, in the colonial situation, negative action outweighed positive action, and neocolonialism "is a guise adopted by negative action to give the impression that it has been overcome by positive action. Neo-colonialism is negative action playing possum."[14] This was the situation that ushered in "independence" and necessitated an adjustment from the anticolonial/independence mindset to the "coloniality of power; coloniality of knowledge; and coloniality of being."[15]

The postcolonial and postmodernism approaches to the study of Africa are both representative of scholarly attempts at thinking differently about Africa. This is in reaction to the conclusions that the old Enlightenment, modernist, and nationalist ideas about Africa have failed the continent. In a period where such ideas as the "African identity," as colonially constituted, are being deconstructed as myths, postcolonialism and postmodernism have been presented as "a new kind of thinking capable of mobilizing enough creative energy to fuel the reconstruction of Africa."[16] This is true especially in the face of the growing neocolonial Euro-American African relations.

However, historians have had a different and complicated relationship with the "posts," marked by advocacy, ambivalence, and hostility.[17] As Paul Tiyambe Zeleza further explains it:

---

14 Nkrumah, *Consciencism,* 100.
15 Ndlovu-Gatsheni, *Coloniality,* 7.
16 Kenzo and Mabiala, "Thinking," 323.
17 Zeleza, "Past," 13.

To the antagonists the "posts" were dismissed as the latest in a long line of disempowering theories and discourses, coming at a time when Africans who had long been silenced had begun to act as the subjects rather than objects of history. They were suspicious of the globalization ambitions of the 'post' theorizing and cultural critique, and its deflationary discourse of Africa that seem to glibly dismiss African difference and world-significance by trying to absorb it into the West's self-indulgent modernity with what Kwaku Korang calls its monocentricism, monolingualism, monologism, and monovision. On the other hand, the accommodationists with their cosmopolitan internationalism sought to Africanise the 'posts' to find an African habitation for them, based on the conviction that Africa is inescapably immersed in the West's material and cultural economy and assimilated into its cognitive and discursive hegemony, thanks to imperial-colonial intervention.[18]

Of the two neocolonial paradigms, the role of postmodernism as another foreign episteme in this new thinking about Africa has generated extensive controversy. Postcolonialism is the awareness that created the "body of writing that attempts to shift the dominant ways in which the relations between Western and non-Western peoples and their worlds are viewed . . . it means looking from the other side of the photograph."[19] It is the preferred discourse among African scholars who dismiss postmodernism as a Western imperialist strategy to disempower Africans and for being too "illusory." This view is derived from the perception that postcolonialism is more concerned with pressing economic, political, and cultural inequalities, while the suspicion of postmodernism is exacerbated by the notion of its existence as an outcome and logical posteriority of modernism—which is itself a product of European Enlightenment, another derivative of European culture.

Postcolonialism, as a historical term, merely suggests the period after colonialism. This same argument can also be made for postmodernism, which itself marks a departure from the era of modernism. However, the change in the conception of postcolonialism to mean the "discursive practice that takes colonialism and its aftermath as its subject matter,"[20] closes

---

18 Zeleza, "Past," 14.
19 Young, *Postcolonialsm*, 2.
20 Kenzo and Mabiala, "Thinking," 325.

the gap in its affinity with postmodernism as an approach for the articulation of Africa's present and especially its future. In other words, the view of these concepts not as mere historical (periodic) demarcations, but as a direct consequence of colonialism and modernity, and also their mutual challenge of the imperial/Enlightenment epistemic order that argues for their similarity. Perhaps the most distinctive characteristic of postmodernism is in the closeness of its origins to Enlightenment reasoning, even if it has been argued to have pre-European African expressions.[21]

Proponents of a complete rejection of either adoption or adaptation of foreign approaches in rethinking Africa cite subjectivity and other totalizing and assimilatory tendencies as the basis for their objection. They dismissed postmodernism as "a typically Western malaise, which breeds angst and despair instead of aiding political action and resistance."[22] Others with a more liberal view, who favor a liberal African episteme, have referred to postcoloniality as the product of "a comprador intelligentsia of a relatively small, Western-style, Western-trained, group of writers who mediate the trade in cultural commodities of world capitalism at the periphery."[23] In all, both approaches' critique of the Universalist pretensions of Enlightenment reason is faulted for their inevitable return to a First World language with universalist epistemological pretensions instead of dispersal into local vernaculars.

These ongoing arguments representing the postcolonial and/or postmodern approach have refused to acknowledge their points of convergence. There have been suggestions that finding some usefulness in foreign epistemologies is the way forward, given how both Western and non-Western perspectives have interacted over time to create trajectories that cannot be completely divorced from each other. Therefore, the pragmatic approach would be to acknowledge that

> the truth is the property of no culture and "we should take the truths we need from wherever we find them" with one caveat, that "for the truth to become the basis of national policy and more widely, of national life, they must be believed and whether or not whatever new

---

21 Kenzo and Mabiala, "Thinking," 328.
22 Kenzo and Mabiala, "Thinking," 324.
23 Attributed to Kwame Anthony Appiah, cited in Xavier, *Migrant Text*, 62.

truths we take from the West will be believed depends in large measure on how we are able to manage the relations between our conceptual heritage and the ideas that rush at us from worlds elsewhere.[24]

The question of either towing a strict, uncompromising epistemological line or a more liberal one raises the issue of degree. To what degree should the African epistemology, in an attempt to accommodate other time-honored alien perspectives, do so without compromising its essence and purpose? This question is made pertinent by the fact that this African episteme would not be operating in a space bereft of knowledge and cannot possibly ignore all that does not originate from its processes. So, the only chance of continued relevance is for African epistemology to further its ability to assess, compare, adapt, adopt, and discard where and when necessary.

Another individual who shares this view is Pastor Mensa Otabil, a "promoter of Africanness" who heads one of Ghana's largest Pentecostal churches. In Pastor Mensa's view, what Africa needs is a "cultural understanding adjustment." He posits that Africa is in the mess it is in largely because it has held on to "antiquated, unusable and unworkable traditions." In his words:

> The whole issue of being African and being modern, we haven't seriously confronted that. When we define other people, we don't define them by their past, we define them by their current status. But anytime Africa is defined it always goes back to the past, deep deep deep ancient. We Africans have defined ourselves that way. When we talk about our culture it is almost always something very very past, remote. The old Pan Africanist movement idolized everything African, reclaimed our Africanness, to restore dignity. But we modernized with the world and kept this African bit behind and anytime we want to be African we have to come back to the past. We can't move with it. That is the contradiction. and it hinders our development agenda. Africa's underdevelopment is not because we cannot develop, but we are afraid to develop. Because development is Western and we will feel like we are moving away from our being, our Africanness. Because those who defined it for us, defined it only in the past of the ancestors. That is the challenge we are facing. There has to be a conscious effort to determine what we are moving with and what we are leaving behind.

---

24   Appiah, *In My Father's House*, 5.

But most of our intellectuals were schooled in the old thinking of preservation of our Africanness. You hardly hear anybody articulating any view of modernity. The intellectuals who must lead the debate are all stuck in the past.[25]

The cultural identity issue appears to be at the center of Africa's past, present, and future. Given its history, especially the colonial episode that had (and is still having) far-reaching consequences on the nature of its present composition (in all its contradictions), Africa has tried unsuccessfully to find common ground. This is what indigenous thinking for indigenous purposes hopes to correct in this plan for the African future.

Epistemology, Identity, and African Futurism

What does it mean to be African? This is one question that has long generated debates among Africa's academics and also with their European and American counterparts. At the core of these conversations were seminal works by philosophers, politicians, and creative writers from Africa and in the diaspora that formed the debates on African identity.

The African identity predicament has been singled out as a major hindrance to African cohesion. It has been identified as a critical means to forging an inclusive path to the desired future for peoples of African descent. The question of the right sociocultural basis upon which to anchor an African identity led to discussions on the suitability of instruments like shared biological and sociocultural substance such as physiological characteristics, language, beliefs, and history. Africa is as diverse in these attributes as it is in its ecology and social interactions, especially interactions with foreign cultures. This leaves shared historical origins and experiences, which are also not without complexities.

To suggest a more appropriate basis that can serve to constitute an inclusive African identity for peoples of African descent everywhere is also to suggest that the preexisting models are defective in one critical aspect or another. Hence, the task is to seek an African identity that has been divested of its exclusivist, derogatory, and oppressive tendencies, one that is highly adaptable and does not infringe on the rights of others

---

25 Witte, "Buy the Future," 72.

to achieve set goals. To achieve this aim, it becomes necessary to assess the preexisting basis of the African identity as a product of Western cultural hegemonic thought and its attendant African reactions. This is all on the premise that an ideal African identity, one that inspires pride in Africanness, is a crucial component in rallying Black agencies to contribute to the ideal African future.

Race

Commenting on the subject of the "illusion race," Kwame A. Appiah draws attention to the centrality of the idea of the "Negro" as an African identity in the nineteenth-century writings of Alexander Crummell, who is often regarded as the father of African nationalism,[26] Wilmot Blyden, and later W. E. B. Du Bois. He thus posits that the notion that the "Negro" is grounded in bad biological and ethical ideas inherited from the racialized thoughts of nineteenth-century Europe and America. These diasporic initiators of the Pan-Africanist discourse, he alleges, developed a nationalism rooted in nineteenth-century theories of race. This might also explain why the earlier forms of "Black consciousness" movements like Negritude had racial undertones in their ideologies.

Race as a scientific biological and an anthropological construct has been argued to be inadequate even when applied to sociohistorical criteria of identification,[27] and at best, retrogressive as a conception of identity. Race in all "racist" social conceptions serves as an exclusivist tool, and attempts at reconciling such tendencies amount to claims of "antiracist racism." Looking at the racial composition of Africa, it becomes clear that one racial stock would not be sufficient to describe the entire continent. There are indeed some who would take exception to be referred to as Black, such as those from Mauritania, Algeria, Egypt, Sudan, Tunisia, and Libya. There are also others who are African in the same sense as their dark-skinned counterparts but are not considered "Black" (like white South Africans, for instance). This stresses the question of the ideals around which peoples of African descent can rally in working toward a future that guarantees their freedoms and well-being.

---

26   Appiah, *In My Father's House*, 3.
27   Appiah, *In My Father's House*, 29.

Common Language

On the impracticality of language as a means of uniting African peoples together under a single identity, the dominant multilingual composition of traditional African societies and their different colonial experiences have made it more difficult to find an indigenous language that transcends ethnic divisions. For this purpose, the class that inherited the colonial state decided on continuing with the languages of their ex-colonizers both as a matter of expediency and as a sign of their elite status. Even so, these languages (English, French, Arabic, and Portuguese) have been mastered by a select few and are hardly ever the first language in any African society, except for Arabic, which is, however, still limited in its coverage. It is the decision to adapt modern African literature to European languages that further emphasizes the need for an African epistemology as a means to cultural emancipation, which identifies linguistics as one important component.

That single issue of the absence of a common language symbolizes the complexities involved in Africa acting as a unified global entity. It also presupposes that for any strategy (identity) developed to harmonize African efforts toward a prosperous future to be effective, it has to either appeal to all of Africa's diversities or inspire them enough to leave their traditional cultural allegiances behind and embrace the newly agreed upon commonalities and other substitutes.

Belief System

The importance of belief systems in the organization and cohesion of African societies can hardly be overstated. This is demonstrated in the diversity of practices spread around the continent. As another major influence of African art, culture, and philosophy, belief systems depend on environment and inform the nature of societal norms and value systems, as well as social interaction, juridical proceedings, health, hygiene, diets, and cures. Belief systems are a known tool for social cohesion, especially among African societies without centralized systems of leadership such as cultural-linguistic groups united by their belief in a common deity, like the Igbos of Nigeria.

The unsuitability of belief systems as a basis for an African identity and unity is evident in the disparity in spiritual beliefs across Africa's regions and the growing influence of foreign Abrahamic religions, which come with alien cultural and material ontology. It has brought about more discord than harmony among adherents in Africa and has become one of the chief sources of conflict. Neither the limited scope and practice of African traditional belief systems nor the alien ontological and confrontational tendencies of imported belief systems will secure a prosperous African future.

Historical Origins/Experiences

There is already an African identity, and being African has a discernible meaning. The issue here is that "the bases through which so far it has largely been theorized—race, a common historical experience, a shared metaphysics—presuppose falsehoods too serious for us to ignore."[28] To be African has been generally taken to mean being Black, native to Africa, or sharing an ancestry with indigenous Africans. From this perception of who an African is, race is undermined, and the notion of "nationality" is obvious only at the level of the continent. This definition also links diasporic Africans through their ancestry, qualifies both Black natives and the white descendants of Boer settlers and other Middle Eastern elements as Africans, all in their rights as natives. Moreover, if we are to believe the recent anthropological claims that place the earliest records of man in the Horn of Africa, then we must also consider that technically we could claim that everyone is African by ancestry.

The very perception of the people who occupy the geographical location now known as Africa is as recent as the renewed European voyages to the region in the 1500s. Before that time, Africa has meant different things to different foreigners who encountered it: such as in the examples of Sudan, Maghreb, Bilad-al-Sudan, Egypt, Ethiopia, and the land of the Moors. Even the term "Africa," credited to the Romans, only referred to a portion of the continent west of Egypt. To the Africans themselves before colonialism, they were Yoruba, Akan, Asante, Hausa, Fulani, Imazighen, Zulu, Khoi, San, Afrikaners, and others. And the difference in their colonial experience has also contributed to shaping the diversities. There is indeed a need for a rethinking of what it means to be African, not just in the sense of ownership but more along the lines of identity and allegiance.

---

28 Appiah, *In My Father's House*, 174.

An African Episteme

The call for an African epistemology is predicated on the need to break away from Euro-American cultural hegemony as the last constitutive element of Western domination. It involves checking the coloniality of power, which "articulates continuities of colonial mentalities, psychologies and worldviews into the so-called 'postcolonial era' and highlights the social hierarchical relationships of exploitation and domination between Westerners and Africans that has its roots in centuries of European colonial expansion but currently continuing through cultural, social and political power relations."[29]

African futurist thought envisions an Africa that has successfully divorced itself from the debilitating vestiges of the colonial/modernist and postcolonial/neocolonial configurations. This is why an African epistemology is suggested as a means of redirecting African formative processes of development away from Western subjective epistemologies. This African epistemology would, therefore, adopt Afrocentric approaches to knowledge production through Afro-ontology (an African perception of reality).

An African epistemology is believed to also contribute to the search for an African identity untouched by Western epistemologies. This would emphasize how Africa sees itself, drawing from both precolonial traditional experiences and more recent ones. In other words, Africans have to rid themselves of the falsehoods of race, ethnicity, and nation, based on which their identity has hitherto been theorized.[30] This suggests that the ideal identity for the unification of Africans would be one devoid of racial, tribal, and national interpretations. Africanized thinking must be the driving force behind peoples of African descent to work together toward a desired future. Therefore, the core importance of this African episteme is in its capacity to reimagine the African past, present, and future as an attempt at decoloniality that discovers, empowers, and utilizes Afrocentric onto-epistemologies to actualize a preferable future for the people of African descent.

---

29 Ndlovu-Gatsheni, *Coloniality*, 8.
30 Kenzo and Mabiala, "Thinking," 332.

Knowledge Economy and Its Relevance to African Development

Before exploring the concept of the knowledge economy and the relevance it might hold for African development, it is necessary to present a description of the nature and level of said development. This is to better appreciate the complementarities of knowledge-driven innovations in the various sectors that contribute to African development: and by development we mean the creation of wealth that at both individual and societal levels is vital for achieving an improved quality of life.

African Development

In the global historical stages of development—preindustrial (agrarian), industrial, and postindustrial—Africa still vacillates between the former two stages. The postindustrial stage in Africa as a whole is still in its infancy. The largest percentage of Africa's labor force,[31] those between the ages of fifteen and sixty-four years, is engaged in unmechanized agricultural production and other extractive activities. The products from this labor are either consumed for subsistence or exported as raw materials. This system has kept Africa largely unindustrialized and dependent on imported industrial goods and services. Without achieving a fully industrialized status, one in which Africa can harness the full potential of its natural endowments (land and minerals), it would be difficult for Africa as a whole to transition into the postindustrial stage of economic development where human resource development and contributions take center stage. This is because the various stages of economic development have remained interactive and complimentary, not relics of some distant agrarian past.

Africa's history of European colonialism, as well as the ensuing problems of decolonization, which became worse with the Cold War, triggered economic and social instability that Africa has not fully recovered from. Africa's huge debt-servicing expenditure and the austerity measures demanded by international funding institutions like the IMF and the WB, have led to funding cuts in key sectors like education, infrastructure, and health: sectors that should ordinarily be contributing to Africa's development. This combined with massive corruption levels—aided by

---

31 OECD/FAO, "Agriculture," 60.

Western banks—has starved Africa of the resources to develop its human capital. Therefore, Africa is left with a young, largely undeveloped and unproductive population.

Africa's development levels, however disparate, are conclusively relatively poor. Every year both Western and continental banking institutions, national governments, consultants, and private sector entities roll out projected growth figures and other economic growth indexes to show that Africa is either growing slowly, quickly, or falling behind. However, there always appears to be a contradiction. African countries can have the fastest growing economies over many years but still end up with the poorest populations. African economic pundits blame economic disruptions for this phenomenon. Political instability, they say, disrupts economic activities, and policy instability results in capital flight, which in turn affects investment and employment and stalls development. Their political counterparts, on the other hand, blame the corruption and ineptitude of those at the helm of affairs. There is no disputing that these factors exert some influence on African development, but they are immediate symptoms of deeper-rooted issues.

An economic historical analysis would reveal continued dependence as one of the chief causes of Africa's developmental predicament.[32] Africa's dependence on Western economic models, production direction, and industrial products—which has perpetuated a consumerist attitude—has kept it undeveloped, in the sense of its inability to produce enough to fulfill the needs of its own people. This dependence is encapsulated in a broader Western cultural hegemonic hold on Africa, mainly by a relationship known commonly among Africanist intellectuals as coloniality.

Knowledge Economy

A knowledge economy is one that uses knowledge to create goods and services. It stands in contrast to "an agricultural economy where land is the key resource. In an industrial economy, natural resources, such as coal and iron ore, and labor are the main resources. A knowledge economy is

---

32 Other challenges have set Africa back in its drive for development that might not be easily traced to Africa's dependence on foreign systems but are in one way or another linked. Such challenges include poverty, illiteracy, starvation and malnutrition, unemployment, and devastating diseases like HIV and AIDS.

one in which knowledge is the key resource."[33] The knowledge economy is also considered the most recent stage in global economic reorganization, such as the transition of the world economy from the preindustrial agrarian age (before 1760) to the age of knowledge economy (the late 1900s to 2000s), and its focus on the technology and human capital sectors. However, this marked change from unskilled labor-driven economies to skilled innovation-driven ones does not mean the end of physical production; however, it provides the opportunity to operate with reduced emphasis on limited, cost-intensive factors of production such as land and menial labor with the application of Information and Communications Technology (ICT).

The use of internet technologies shapes the knowledge economy. In a knowledge economy, the labor force is normally computer literate, trained to handle data and different processing systems. According to Kolo, "This race is currently led by four regions, called knowledge engines, namely, the European Union, East Asia, India and the United States. However, China, Brazil, and others are making quiet strides as contenders."[34] However, Africa has been unable to join this race due to a number of complications, which Kolo argues can be resolved "through the adoption of modern knowledge systems and tools."[35] On the other hand, Simplica A. Asongu and John Kuada[36] advise caution in the application of said foreign models. To them, adoption of these technological knowledge systems should be carried out only in adaptation to local realities, cultures, and epistemologies.

In 2007 the WB outlined four dimensions of a knowledge economy in what is known as the WB's Knowledge Economy Index (KEI). These four dimensions are "economic incentives and the institutional regime, education and human resources, the innovation system, and ICT."[37] The first, economic incentive and institutional regime, consists of tariff and non-tariff barriers, regulatory quality, and rule of law. The second category is education and human resources, which includes adult literacy rates, secondary school, and tertiary institution enrollment. The third component is the innovation system, which covers payments and receipt of royalties

---

33   Houghton and Sheehan, "A Primer."
34   Kolo, "Knowledge," 27.
35   Kolo, "Knowledge."
36   Asongu and Kuada, "Building Knowledge," 5.
37   Asongu, "Comparative."

and licencing fees, as well as patents awarded by the United States Patent and Trademark Office, and scientific and technical journal articles. The fourth is information and communication technology, which includes fixed telephones and mobile and internet users. This is evaluated by the number of telephones per 100 people, computers per 1,000 people, and internet users per 10,000 people.[38]

This index is useful for understanding Africa. First, it can determine the extent of Africa's transformation into a knowledge-based economy by gauging the continent's performances in these aforementioned technological areas of the knowledge economy. Secondly, it reveals the importance of knowledge economy as a tool for Africa's development through its emphasis on the development of known economic growth drivers like education and training and information infrastructure. Anyone with some experience in Africa knows that even where such institutions and laws have been put in place to protect, for example, patent rights, enforcement and compliance are nearly always very minimal: perhaps because this is not the "African way."

For this assessment, we take a look at the expression of two of the four WB dimensions of a knowledge economy in Africa in an attempt to determine the impact of their growth or decline on African development. This, in turn, would clarify the matter of their relevance to Africa's development. These two are education and ICT.

Education

Education in Africa, at all levels, has suffered all the ills that plague the continent as a whole. Education has suffered from, for example, military intervention, brain drain, and limited funding. Economically, financial access has adversely affected lifelong learning—the combined knowledge gained by an individual in three levels of education, namely primary, secondary, and tertiary education. This is true especially at the primary education level, which has been identified as critical for "socio-economic development where economies are at early stages of development."[39] Culturally, there are two issues. Firstly, Western models and standards continue to dominate African education, and this has had the effect of equipping African graduates with explicit ideas against the required tacit

---

38 Abeer Abdelkhalek, "Impact of Knowledge Economy."
39 Asongu and Kuada, "Building," 4.

knowledge. Secondly is the culture of exclusion of young girls in education, which is exacerbated by financial limitations and has resulted in increasing disparity in enrollment between boys and girls.

The cumulative effect of the above on education in Africa results in the worrying percentage of out-of-school children, as well as graduates equipped with knowledge that has little application in their immediate environment (much less enough to compete equally on the global stage). As of 2015, UNESCO put the number of children enrolled in primary schools in sub-Saharan Africa at 57 percent,[40] which means over sixty million children of primary school age are out of school. As for the higher (secondary and tertiary) levels of education, quality and equity of education have been beset by underlying issues such as high dropout rates, grades being repeated, poor infrastructure and supplies, limited access to education in rural and remote areas, and stigmas for marginalized groups. Together, these conditions have left education in Africa in dire straits.

Africa needs the Information Technology Advisory Group's (ITAG) 1999 education recommendation for New Zealand to join the global knowledge economy race. It states:

> Education needs help to understand what business needs. Without the assistance from a business, teachers and schools will continue to design and implement coursework that does not prepare students for the real world of work. We need to look at our human resource as part of a 'knowledge supply chain'. The education system must support lifelong learning. Population trends make it imperative that both young people and people of working age are encouraged and supported to engage in lifelong learning.[41]

The preceding quote describes the situation of higher education in Africa, and in Nigeria especially. An education system that produces graduates trained in professional fields with no way to apply these skills in Africa does not tally with Africa's immediate developmental needs.

Information and Communication Technology

The proliferation of information and communication as mentioned earlier is measured by the number of telephones per one hundred people,

---

40   UNESCO, *Regional Overview.*
41   Kolo, "Knowledge," 46.

and that goes for computer and internet users, too. In the case of Africa, the progress recorded in this sector was a result of the proliferation of mobile phone technology. Africa has recorded growth of up to 66 percent in a single year (2005), with the numbers of mobile phone subscribers increasing from 10 to 647 million from 2000–2011.[42] In Nigeria, there was an annual compound annual growth rate of 150 percent during 2002–2004. It is important to note that this exponential growth has not been replicated in computer and internet access, the other more innovative aspects of ICT usage.

The New Partnership for Economy and Development (NEPAD), an initiative of the African Union (AU), led the agenda by African governments to kickstart ICT development in the region. The NEPAD e-Africa Commission (now NEPAD e-Africa Programme) is

> tasked with developing policies, strategies and projects at the continental level for the development of information and communication technology (ICT) throughout Africa. . . . Another key project of the e-Africa programme is the NEPAD e-Schools Initiative. The initiative aims to harness ICT technology to improve the quality of teaching and learning in African primary and secondary schools in order to equip young Africans with the knowledge and skills that will enable them to participate confidently and effectively in the global information society and knowledge economy.[43]

This initiative worked together with foreign governments like the United States and the LELAND Initiative to connect twenty African countries and Canada in the Acacia Project in 1997 and bring the mobile network to Africa.[44]

The growth in mobile phone usage in Africa facilitated the ease and expanded the scope of economic transactions in what is known as "network trade." This network trade signifies a deeper connection to the global economy and the borderless world. There is no doubt that mobile phone technology, through network service provision opportunities, online transactions, and repair and assemblage services, was responsible for some socioeconomic developments in the continent. However, when looking at the distinction between the information society and knowledge economy,

---

42   Carmody, "Knowledge," 24–39.
43   Jean-Malbuisson, *Africa Internet*.
44   Jean-Malbuisson, *Africa Internet*, 6.

where the former represents information availability and flow, and the latter represents capacity to transform information into innovative ideas, it becomes clear that more needs to be done to put Africa on the right track.

Furthermore, Africa's role in this globalized ICT interconnectedness remains one of consumerism. The increase in demand for mobile phones in Africa has not resulted in the wider establishment of mobile communications industries on the continent. Africa's role has been that of supplier of key raw materials used in cellular technology, but there are only a few cellular assemblage plants across Africa. This is largely due to Africa's infrastructural deficiencies that leave the continent unable to meet growing demands for ICT hardware and unable to fully benefit from new socioeconomic opportunities.

Therefore, as much as the application of ICT mobile technology has enhanced communication and facilitated business, without the relevant infrastructure in place, Africa cannot adequately partake of the benefits that accrue. This combined with the direction of Africa's ICT development—its focus on information flow and not utilization in innovation—has it at a disadvantage. Hence, in the development of a knowledge economy, Africa has not done enough to integrate ICT into its educational activities. A good indicator of Africa's inadequate implementation of ICT is the 2020 COVID-19 pandemic, which necessitated a ban on large gatherings and the closure of schools. This meant that since there were nothing but inadequate web-based solutions available, education activities ground almost to a complete halt.

Education and information communication technology are two key aspects to developing a knowledge economy. Judging by the performances of these sectors in Africa, such as the enrollment, quantitative, and qualitative inadequacies in education activities and the incomprehensive application of ICT, it becomes clear that Africa is not delivering a passable knowledge economy. Without such an economy, Africa cannot compete in an increasingly globalized system of information capitalism. So in developing the infrastructure for a knowledge economy, Africa will be setting up a sturdy foundation for a much-needed productive industrial capacity. This is important because African countries cannot continue to rely solely on commodity exports. It is a position suitably illustrated in the UN Millennium Project that

> without basic infrastructure and human capital, countries are condemned to export a narrow range of low-margin primary commodities

based on natural (physical) endowments, rather than a diversified set of exports based on technology, skills, and capital investments. In such circumstances, globalisation can have significant adverse effects—including brain drain, environmental degradation, capital flight, and terms-of-trade declines—rather than bring benefits through increased foreign direct investment inflows and technological advances.[45]

This case in point also buttresses the need for Africa to not only grow its industrial activity but to also tap into the growing application of technology as a means of effecting the industrial transformation the continent needs to thrive on a global scale.

Africa and the Fourth Industrial Revolution

The fourth industrial revolution is the era that will follow agrarian revolution, the industrial revolution, and the digital revolution. Technology has historically fast-tracked human development. Ironworking and consequently the farming implements crafted from this process brought an end to more than fifty millennia of hunting and gathering and ushered in the agrarian revolution. This revolution in agriculture saw unprecedented population growth, urbanization, the development of knowledge, and eventually mechanization. Another two centuries later, the slave trade, colonization, and the two world wars: then still later the digital revolution came. This revolution was in information and communication, and it brought the world together into one huge marketplace. Today, the world is set at the threshold of another revolution, one that would further blur its physical, digital, and biological boundaries.

According to Sintia Radu, "The Fourth Industrial Revolution is characterized by a fusion of the digital, biological and physical worlds, where artificial intelligence, cloud computing, robotics, 3D printing, the 'internet of things,' and advanced wireless technologies see increased development worldwide."[46] Additionally, Jean Nsengimana states that "Africa has essentially missed the opportunities of the second and third industrial revolutions. The continent is home to 16.3 per cent of humanity but with less 1 percent of the world's billion-dollar companies and only about

---

45 Kolo, "Knowledge," 46.
46 Radu, "Africa Braces for the Fourth Industrial Revolution."

4 per cent of global GDP. Africa cannot afford to miss the possibilities of the 4th Industrial Revolution."[47]

For Africa to benefit from this imminent revolution, the consensus is that Africa has to unite. It is established that Africa is plagued by a plethora of socioeconomic challenges, among which are poverty, illiteracy, corruption, infrastructure deficiencies, and bad government policies, making it ill-prepared to prosper in the fourth industrial revolution. Though some African countries like Kenya are doing better than others in terms of ICT and other technological advancements, no single country can go it alone. Moreover, this type of revolution is not isolated; it is about interconnectedness, data collection, analysis, comparisons, and application, and its success depends on the extent of its reach. Imagine a mobile telephone network (MTN) limited to South Africa alone?

Looking at it from the angle of infrastructure, Africa requires more investment. For an example, around 45 percent of the population have access to electricity, and as the Angolan former minister of finance Armando Manuel aptly put it, "You can't develop in the darkness and you can't go to the Moon when you have constraints to go to the next corner."[48] Hence, the call for unity of purpose to bridge the gaps. Increased regional integration has been identified as the way to go. According to Jeffrey Sachs et al.,

> The fifteen of the forty-nine countries in sub-Saharan Africa that are landlocked have little chance to develop unless they have ready access to the coast with efficient, low-cost infrastructure. Moreover, from a global perspective, the African countries taken individually are very small markets.[49]

Also:

> Regional integration is essential for Africa. It will raise the interest of potential foreign investors by increasing the scope of the market. It is also important in achieving scale economies in infrastructure networks, such as electricity grids, large-scale electricity generation, road transport, railroads, and telecommunications—and in eliciting increased

---

47   Nsengimana, "How Africa Wins."
48   Radu, "Africa Braces."
49   Jeffrey Sachs et al., "Ending Africa's Poverty Trap," 117–240.

R&D on problems specific to Africa's ecology but extending beyond any single country (public health, energy systems, agriculture.[50]

The idea, therefore, is for the whole of Africa to be connected both physically and digitally. This would help harness all the potentials in the different regions together, working to give Africa the platform it needs to launch into this borderless, "internet of things," interconnected world and carve its niche.

For Africa to take an effective part in this new industrial revolution, it must make technology a top priority and invest more in developing the right knowledge economy according to the KEI. This should be done as quickly as possible, keeping in mind that "we are living in a 'connected world' and those who are not connected are relegated. Every job of the future will include a digital component and Africa's workforce needs to be prepared accordingly."[51]

Conclusion

Dubbed the "cradle of humankind" and the "origin of human civilizations," Africa has for millennia been the theater of expression for human ambitions and its conflicting interests, both from within and without the continent. From within, civilizations have risen at different periods with expansionist ambitions to expand territorial domains and spread cultural influence. From without, Africa has been included in the imperial ambitions of cultures and civilizations of the Middle East, Europe, North America, and Asia. However, the most persistent of these ambitions to conquer, control, or exert influence over Africa and its wealth has come from the northern hemisphere, especially Europe and North America.

Western imperialist ambitions facilitated by its superior technological innovation saw to growing European activity around the African coast beginning in the 1500s. This grew into a full-blown Euro-American trade in slaves which lasted about four centuries until around 1860. Conditions prompted by demands of industrialization led eventually to the end of slavery and the commencement of the colonial domination of most of

---

50 McCord et al., "Understanding African Poverty."
51 Nsengimana, "How Africa Wins."

the continent, marking the beginning of the spread of European cultural influence in the area. At the turn of the twentieth century, anticolonial sentiments began to surface in the writings of African American diaspora clergy and intellectuals such as Alexander Crummell and Edward Blyden. These spoke to the humanity of the "Negro race," the unity "inherent" in that identity, and the possibilities it held for the African future.

These ideas of racial unity were later adopted by other African diasporic activists who sought the recognition of the rights and humanity of peoples of African descent in Black emancipation movements such as Negritude and later Pan-Africanism. These movements grew into full-fledged demands for independence after 1945, especially with the involvement of nationalists and political activists on the continent. With political independence came the quest for decolonization, in recognition of the African neocolonial situation and the possible effects of continued Euro-American cultural hegemony on an African future.

The independent decolonization discourse on securing the African future from neocolonial ambitions and delivering on the promise of freedom and prosperity took on theoretical approaches such as postcolonialism, postmodernism, Pan-Africanism, neoliberalism, African Futurism, and Afrofuturism. These have become the avenues through which African intellectuals and philosophers articulate an ideal African future where peoples of African descent enjoy inalienable rights like equality, humanity, socioeconomic freedom, and prosperity.

In discussing the approach to an ideal African future, African thinkers have had to contend with "neocoloniality" and the question of African survival in an increasingly globalized world with recent and ongoing developments such as the switch from commodity to knowledge economies and the imminent fourth industrial revolution. For Africa to survive and realize an ideal future, Africans must first think for themselves and always be ready to adapt to whatever the future brings.

Bibliography

Abdi, Ali A. "Decolonizing Educational and Social Development Platforms in Africa." *African and Asian Studies* 12 (2013): 64–82.

Abi-Habib, Maria. "How China Got Sri Lanka to Cough Up a Port." *New York Times*, June 25, 2018. https://www.nytimes.com/2018/06/25/world/asia/china-sri-lanka-port.html.

Abimbola, Wande. *Sixteen Great Poems of Ifa*. Vol. 3. Paris: UNESCO, 1975.

Acharya, Amitav. "Dialogue and Discovery: In Search of International Relations Theories beyond the West." *Millennium: Journal of International Studies* 39, no. 3 (2011): 619–37.

Achebe, Chinua. "The African Writer and the English Language." *Transition* 18 (1965): 27–30.

———. "An Image of Africa: Racism in Conrad's 'Heart of Darkness.'" *Massachusetts Review* 18 (1977).

———. *Morning Yet on Creation Day*. London: Heinemann, 1975.

———. *The Drum*. Nairobi: Heinemann, 1988.

———. *There Was a Country: A Personal History of Biafra*. London: Penguin, 2012.

Achebe, Nwando. *Farmers, Traders, Warriors, and Kings: Female Power and Authority in Northern Igboland, 1900–1960*. New Hampshire: Heinemann, 2005.

———. *The Female King of Colonial Nigeria: Ahebi Ugabe*. Bloomington: Indiana University Press, 2011.

Acholonu, Catherine O. *Motherism: The Afrocentric Alternative to Feminism*. Owerri: Afa, 1995.

Adams, Glenn. "Decolonizing Methods: African Studies and Qualitative Research." *Journal of Social and Personal Relationships* 31, no. 4 (2014): 467–74.

Adams, William, and Martin Mulligan, eds. *Decolonizing Nature: Strategies for Conservation in a Postcolonial Era*. London: Earthscan, 2003.

Adebiyi-Adelabu, Kazeem. "From Subversive Othering to Uthopian Imagining: Gendered Vision and Revision in Vincent Egbuson's Womandela." *International Journal of Arts and Humanities* 6, no. 2 (2017): 48–62.

Adekoya, Segun. "Problems of Field Research in Nigerian Folklore." In *Current Perspectives on African Folklore: A Festschrift for Professor Dandatti Abdulkadir*, edited by Abubakar Rasheed and Sani Abba Aliyu. Zaria: Ahmadu Bello University Press, 2013.

Adem, Seifudein. "Ali A. Mazrui, the Postcolonial Theorist." *African Studies Review* 57, no. 1 (2014): 135–52.

Ademowo, Adeyemi Johnson. "Teaching Science and Technology: The Employment of Indigenous African Languages." *The Journal of Pan-African Studies* 3, no. 9 (2010): 50–63.

Adesina, Jimi. "Sociology and Yoruba Studies: Epistemic Invention or Doing Sociology in Vernacular." *African Sociological Review* (2002): 91–114.

Adeyemi, Muyiwa. "Scrapping of Post–UTME A Calamitous Mistake, Says Afe Babalola." *Guardian*, June 4, 2016. https://guardian.ng/news/scrapping-of-post-utme-a-calamitous-mistake-says-afe-babalola/.

Adichie, Chimamanda N. *Americanah*. New York: Alfred A. Knopf, 2013.

———. *Purple Hibiscus*. Lagos: Kachifo, 2006.

Adolphsen, Paul. "Yoruba Performance." The Image. Accessed August 5, 2019. https://yorubaperformance.weebly.com/the-image.html.

Advancing Justice. "It's About Time You Took an Asian American Studies Class." Medium.com, October 7, 2015. https://medium.com/advancing-justice-aajc/it-s-about-time-you-took-an-asian-american-studies-class-4c83d6e3f29.

Afigbo, A. E. "Fact and Myth in Nigerian Historiography." *Nigeria Magazine*, no. 122–123 (1977): 81–98.

Afolayan, Adeshina. "Is Modernity Single and Universal? Òlàjú and the Multilateral Modernity," *Yoruba Studies Review* 1, no. 1 (2016): 85–104.

Afolayan, Adeshina, Olajumoke Yacob-Haliso, and Toyin Falola, eds. *Pentecostalism and Politics in Africa*. New York: Palgrave Macmillan, 2018.

———, and Toyin Falola, eds. *The Palgrave Handbook of African Philosophy*. New York: Palgrave-Macmillan, 2018.

African Psychologies. "Decolonizing Knowledge, by Dr. Shose Kessi." YouTube video, 30:51. Posted August 30, 2017. https://www.youtube.com/watch?v=ammCLylRjfQ.

African Union–European Union (AU–EU). Research and Innovation Relations Factsheet. Addis Ababa: African Union, n.d. https://ec.europa.eu/research/iscp/pdf/policy/eu-africa_research_innovation_relations_factsheet_en.pdf.

Agawu, Kofi. *The African Imagination in Music*. New York: Oxford University Press, 2016.

Agbenyega, Joseph, Deborah Tamakloe, and Sunanta Klibthong. "Folklore Epistemology: How Does Traditional Folklore Contribute to Children's Thinking and Concept Development?" *International Journal of Early Years Education* 25, no. 2 (2017): 112–126.

Agogo Eewo. Directed by Tunde Kelani. Lagos: Mainframe Film & Television Productions, 2012.

Agyeman, Adwoa A. "Africa's Design Industry: From Creative Pursuits to the Business of Fashion." https://process.arts.ac.uk/sites/default/files/fp_adwoa_agyeman.pdf.

Ahikire, Josephine. "African Feminism in Context: Reflections on the Legitimation Battles, Victories and Reversals." *Feminist Africa* 19 (2014): 7–23.

Aiken, Maxwell, and Wei Lu. "Historical Instances of Innovative Accounting Practices in the Chinese Dynasties and Beyond." *Accounting Historians Journal* 20, no. 2 (1993): 163–86.

Ajayi, J. F., Lameck K. H. Goma, and G. Ampah Johnson. *The African Experience with Higher Education.* Accra: Association of African Universities, 1996.

Ake, Claude. *The Feasibility of Democracy in Nigeria.* Dakar: CODESRIA, 2000.

———. "The Unique Case of African Democracy." *International Affairs* 69, no. 2 (1993): 239–244.

Akin-Aina, Sinmi. "Beyond an Epistemology of Bread, Butter, Culture and Power: Mapping the African Feminist Movement." *Nokoko* 2 (2011): 65–89.

Akinbileje, Thessy Yemisi. "Symbolic Values of Clothing and Textiles Art in Traditional and Contemporary Africa." *International Journal of Development and Sustainability* 3, no. 4 (2014): 626–41.

Akinjogbin, I. A. *Western Yorubaland Under European Rule 1889–1945: A Comparative Analysis of French and British Colonialism.* London: Longman, 1976.

Akinyemi, T. E., and L. Amusan. "Between the Town and the Gown: Challenges of Research–Development Transition in Africa." *Journal of Gender, Information and Development in Africa* (JGIDA) 7 (2018): 161–87.

Akporobaro, F. B. O. *Introduction to African Oral Literature.* Lagos: Princeton, 2005.

Alabi, S. Aliyu. "Voices After the Maxim Gun: Intellectual and Literary Opposition to Colonial Rule in Northern Nigeria." In *Resurgent Nigeria: Issues in Nigerian Intellectual History: A Festschrift in Honour of Dahiru Yahya*, edited by Sa'idu Babura Ahmad and Ibrahim Khaleel Abdussalam, 124–46. Ibadan: Ibadan University Press, 2011.

Alagoa, E. J., ed. *Of Days, Bread and Mushrooms: The Historian as a Hero.* Port Harcourt: Port Harcourt University Press, 1998.

———. *Oral Tradition and Oral History in Africa and the Diaspora: Theory and Practice.* Lagos: Centre for Black and African Arts and Civilization, 1990.

Albert, Isaac. "University Students in the Politics of Structural Adjustment in Nigeria." In *Between Liberalization and Oppression: The Politics of Structural Adjustment in Africa,* edited by Thandika Mkwandawire and Olukoshi Adebayo, 374. Dakar: CODESRIA, 1995.

Albrecht, Milton C. "The Relationship of Literature and Society." *American Journal of Sociology* 59, no. 5 (1954): 425–36.

Alcoff, Linda. "Mignolo's Epistemology of Coloniality." *New Centennial Review* 7, no. 3 (2007): 79–101.

Alexander, Neville. "English Unassailable but Unattainable: The Dilemma of Language Policy in South African Education." *PRAESA Occasional Papers, Cape Town* 3 (2000).

Alkali, Mohammed, Rosli Talif, Wan Yahaya, and Jariah Jan. "Dwelling or Duelling in Possibilities: How Irrelevant Are African Feminisms." *Journal of Language Studies* 13, no. 3 (2013): 237–53.

Allen, Walter, and Shani O'Neal. "African Studies." In *Encyclopedia of Sociology*, 60–68. 2nd ed. New York: Macmillan Reference USA, 2001.

Alli, Farzana, Pranitha Maharaj, and Mohammed Vawda. "Interpersonal Relations Between Healthcare Workers and Young Clients: Barriers to Accessing Sexual and Reproductive Healthcare." *Journal of Community Health* 38, no. 1 (2013): 150–55.

Altbach, Philip. "Globalization and the University: Myth and Realities in an Unequal World." *Journal of Educational Planning and Administration* 17, no. 2 (2003): 227–47.

Amadiume, Ifi. *Male Daughters, Female Husbands: Gender and Sex in an African Society*. London: Zed, 1987.

———. "Theorizing Matriarchy in Africa: Kinship Ideologies and Systems in Africa and Europe." In *African Gender Studies. A Reader*, edited by Oyeronke Oyewumi. New York: Palgrave Macmillan, 2005.

Amady, Dieng. "Samir Amin." *Development and Change* 38, no. 6 (2007): 1149–59.

American Chemical Society. "What Are the Greenhouse Gas Changes since the Industrial Revolution?" American Chemical Society, n.d. https://www.acs.org/content/ac/enclimatescience/greenhousegases/industrialrevolution.html.

Ampofo, Adomako, and Signe Arnfred, eds. *African Feminist Politics of Knowledge: Tensions, Challenges, Possibilities*. Uppsala: Nordic Africa Institute, 2010.

Ampofo, Adomako, Josephine Beoku–Betts, Wairimu Njambi, and Mary Osirim. "Women's and Gender Studies in English-Speaking Sub-Saharan Africa: A Review of Research in the Social Sciences." *Gender and Society* 18, no. 6 (2004): 685–714.

Amutabi, Maurice. "The Role of Traditional Music in the Writing of Cultural History: The Case of the Abaluyia of Western Kenya." In *Africanizing Knowledge: African Studies Across the Disciplines*, edited by Toyin Falola and Christian Jennings, 191–208. New Brunswick and London: Transaction, 2002.

Anderson, Benedict. *Imagined Communities: Reflections on the Origin and Spread of Nationalism*. London: Verso, 1991.

Anderson, C. M. "The Perspectives of Polygamy as an Adaptive Response to Poverty and Oppression in Apartheid South Africa." *Cross Cultural Research*, no. 39 (2000): 99–112.

Andrade-Watkins, Claire. "Film Production in Francophone Africa 1961 to 1977: Ousmane Sembene—An Exception." *A Journal of African and Afro–American Studies* 11, no. 5 (1993).

Ansah, Kwaw. "Ghanaian Cinema: A Historical Appraisal." In *African Film: Looking Back and Looking Forward*, edited by Foluke Ogunleye. Newcastle: Cambridge Publishing Scholars, 2014.

Anunobi, Fredoline. "Women and Development in Africa: From Marginalization to Gender Inequality." *African Social Science Review* 2, no. 1 (2002): 41–43.

Anzaldúa, Gloria. *Borderlands: The New Mestiza = La Frontera*. San Francisco: Spinsters/Aunt Lute, 1987.

Appiah, Anthony, K. *The Ethics of Identity*. Princeton, NJ: Princeton University Press, 2005.

———. *In My Father's House: Africa in the Philosophy of Culture*. New York: Oxford University Press, 1992.

Arab Information Center. *Education in the Arab State*. New York: Arab Information Center, 1966.

Arias, Arturo. "Violence and Coloniality in Latin America." *Eurocentrism, Racism and Knowledge*. Berlin: Springer, 2014.

Aristotle. *Posterior Analytics*. Translated by Jonathan Barnes. Oxford: Clarendon, 1994.

Arndt, S. "Perspectives on African Feminism: Defining and Classifying African-Feminist Literatures." *Agenda: Empowering Women for Gender Equity* 54 (2002): 31–44.

Arowosegbe, Jeremiah. "African Studies and the Bias of Eurocentricism." *Social Dynamics* 40, no. 2 (2014): 308–21.

———. "State Reconstruction in Africa: The Relevance of Claude Ake's Political Thought." *International Affairs* 87, no. 3 (2011): 651–70.

Asante, Molefi, and Ama Mazam. *Encyclopedia of African Religion*. London: SAGE, 2009.

Ashby, Eric. *Universities: British, Indian, African: A Study in the Ecology of Higher Education*, edited by Mary Anderson, 346–347. Cambridge, MA: Harvard University Press, 1966.

Asongu, Simplice A. "The Comparative Economics of Knowledge Economy in Africa: Policy Benchmarks, Syndromes, and Implications." *Journal of Knowledge Economy* 8, no. 2 (2017): 596–637.

Asongu, Simplice A., and John Kuada. "Building Knowledge Economies in Africa: An Introduction." *European Xtra mile Centre of African Studies (ECSAS) Working Paper WP/20/002* (2020). https://ssrn.com/abstract=3522820.

Aten, Jamie, Kari O'Grady, and Everett Worthington Jr., eds. *The Psychology of Religion and Spirituality for Clinicians: Using Research in your Practice*. New York: Routledge, 2013.

Austin, Algernon. "Barack Obama and the Ironies of Afrocentrism." *Civilisations* 58, no. 1 (2009): 113–128.

Awad, Germine. "Psych of Racism (Whitley Ch 1, Martinez), Updated 9-1-15." PowerPoint. University of Texas, Austin. Fall 2019.

Awe, Bolanle. "Writing Women into History: The Nigerian Experience." In *Writing Women's History: International Perspectives*, edited by Karen Offen, Ruth Pearson, and Jane Rendall, 211–20. Bloomington: Indiana University Press, 1991.

Awortu, Beatrice. "African Intellectual Revolution in the 20th Century: A Review of Kenneth Onwuka Dike's Contributions to African History." *International Journal of African and Asian Studies* 13 (2015).

Ba, Mariama. *So Long a Letter*. Ibadan: Heinemann, 1989.

Babalola, Adeboye, and Olugboyega Alaba. *A Dictionary of Yoruba Personal Names.* Lagos: West African Books, 2008.

Babalola, Solomon. *The Content and Form of Yoruba Ijala.* Oxford: Clarendon, 1966.

Bacon, Francis. *Novum Organum Scientiarum.* Cambridge: Cambridge University Press, 2000.

Bako, S. "Universities, Research and Development in Nigeria: Time for a Paradigmatic Shift." Proceedings of the 11th General Assembly of CODESRIA, on Rethinking African Development: Beyond Impasse, Towards Alternatives, 2005.

Banham, Martin, ed. *A History of Theatre in Africa.* New York: Cambridge University Press, 2004.

Bank, Leslie. "Embracing the Town and Gown Revolution." *University World News*, January 25, 2019. https://www.universityworldnews.com/post.php?story=20190125082942333.

Banks-Wallace, JoAnne. "Talk that Talk: Storytelling and Analysis Rooted in African American Oral Tradition." *Qualitative Health Research* 12, no. 3 (2002): 410–26.

Barber, Karen. *The Anthropology of Texts, Persons and Publics: Oral and Written Culture in Africa and Beyond.* New York: Cambridge University Press, 2007.

———. *I Could Speak Until Tomorrow: Oriki, Women and the Past in A Yoruba Town.* London: Edinburgh University Press, 1991.

Barbosa, Muryatan. "The African Perspective in the General History of Africa." (UNESCO): Universidade Federal do ABC (UFABC)–Santo André (SP). https://orcid.org/0000-0002-6307-8847.

Barness, Rachel. *The 20th Century Art Book.* London: Phaidon, 2001.

Barry, Peter. *Beginning Theory: Introduction to Literary and Cultural Theory.* Oxford: Oxford University Press, 2017.

Bascom, William. "The Principle of Seniority in the Social Structure of the Yoruba." *American Anthropology* 44, no. 1 (1942).

Bathiany, Sebastian, Vasilis Dakos, Marten Scheffer, and Timothy Lenton. "Climate Models Predict Increasing Temperature Variability in Poor Countries." *Science Advances* 4, no. 5 (2018).

Batten, Thomas. *Africa, Past and Present.* London: Oxford University Press, 1943.

Bavier, Joe, Cheng Leng, and Andrea Shalal. "China in the Driver's Seat Amid Calls for Africa Debt Relief." Reuters, April 13, 2020. https://www.reuters.com/article/us-health-coronavirus-africa-china-analy/china-in-the-drivers-seat-amid-calls-for-africa-debt-relief-idUSKCN21V0CS.

Bayeh, E. "The Political and Economic Legacy of Colonialism in the Post-Independence African States." *International Journal in Commerce, IT & Social Sciences* 2, no. 2 (2015): 89–93.

Bebey, Francis. "The Music." In *African Music: The People's Art.* New York: Lawrence Hills, 1975.

Beeson, Jeffrey. "U.S. Celebrates the 40th Anniversary of Black Studies Programs." University of Missouri News Bureau, February 3, 2009. https://munews.missouri.edu/news-releases/2009/02.03.09.brunsma.black.studies.anniversary.php.

Bekalu, Mesfin Awoke, and Steven Eggermont. "Aligning HIV/AIDS Communication with the Oral Tradition of Africans: A Theory-Based Content Analysis of Songs' Potential in Prevention Efforts." *Health Communication* 30, no. 5 (2015): 441–50.

Bell, Richard. *Understanding African Philosophy: A Cross–Cultural Approach to Classical and Contemporary Issues.* New York: Routledge, 2002.

Bendix, Aria. "The US Was Once a Leader for Healthcare and Education—Now it Ranks 27th in the World." *Business Insider*, September 27, 2018. https://www.businessinsider.com/us–ranks–27th–for–healthcare–and–education–2018–9.

Bennett, Jane. "Editorial: Researching for Life: Paradigms and Power." *Feminist Africa* 11 (2008): 1–12.

Bennett, Janet M., ed. "Communicating Across Cultures with People from Africa." In *The SAGE Encyclopedia of Intercultural Competence*. London: SAGE, 2015.

Betts, Raymond. "Decolonization: A Brief History of the Word." In *Beyond Empire and Nation: The Decolonization of African and Asian Societies, 1930s–1970s*, edited by Els Bogaerts and Remco Raben, 23–37. Leiden: Brill, 2012.

Beyala, Calixthe. *Tu Rappelleras Tanga*. Portsmouth, NH: Heinemann, 1988.

———. *The Sun Hath Looked Upon Me*. Portsmouth, NH: Heinemann, 1996.

Bhambra, Gurminder. "Postcolonial and Decolonial Dialogues." *Postcolonial Studies* 17, no. 2 (2014): 115–21.

Binniyat, Luka. "Produce Anti–Govt Lecturer. *Vanguard*, January 27, 2016. https://www.vanguardngr.com/2016/01/police–write–kasu–vc–to–produce–anti–government–lecturer–as–group–kicks/.

Biobaku, Saburi. *Sources of Yoruba History*. Ibadan: Ibadan University Press, 1987.

Bishop, Andrew. "Chatting About 'Nature' with Henry David Thoreau and William Cronon." *Concord Saunterer* 25 (2017): 146–48.

Bitrus, I. S. "Globalizing Impact of Modernity in Africa." *Journal of Globalization Studies* 8, no. 2 (2017): 68–83.

Bodunrin, Peter. O. "The Question of African Philosophy." *Philosophy* 56, no. 216 (1981): 161–79.

Bongani Nyoka. "Archie Mafeje: A Note on the Three Clusters of His Work." *Transformation: Critical Perspectives on Southern Africa* 97 (2018): 111–23.

Boserup, E. *Women's Role in Economic Development*. London: George Allen and Unwin, 1970.

Botha, Martin P. "African Cinema: A Historical, Theoretical and Analytical Exploration." *Communication: South African Journal for Communication Theory and Research* 20, no. 1 (1994): 2–8.

Bourne, J. M. *History at the Universities: A Comparative and Analytical Guide to First Degree Courses in History in United Kingdom Universities*. London: Historical Association, 1985.

Bowersock, Warren, and Martin Bernal. "Black Athena: The Fabrication of Ancient Greece." *Journal of Interdisciplinary History* 19, no. 3 (1989).

The Boy Who Harnessed the Wind. Directed by Chiwetel Ejiofor. United Kingdom and Malawi: Netflix, 2019.

Bradford, Helen. "Women, Gender and Colonialism: Rethinking the History of the British Cape Colony and Its Frontier Zones, 1806–70." *Journal of African History* 37 (1996): 335–70.

Brautigam, Deborah. "Opinion: Is China the World's Loan Shark?" *New York Times*, April 26, 2019. https://www.nytimes.com/2019/04/26/opinion/china-belt-road-initiative.html.

Brennan, Timothy. "Antonio Gramsci and Postcolonial Theory: 'Southernism'." *Diaspora: A Journal of Transnational Studies* 10, no. 2 (2001): 143–87.

Brown, Austin Channing. *I'm Still Here: Black Dignity in a World Made for Whiteness*. New York: Convergent, 2018.

Brown, Godfrey. "British Educational Policy in West and Central Africa." *Journal of Modern African Studies* 2, no. 3 (1964): 365–77.

Bryant, Susan. "The Beauty Ideal: The Effects of European Standards of Beauty on Black Women." *Columbia Social Work Review* 4 (2013): 80–91.

Bunting, Ian. "The Higher Education Landscape under Apartheid." In *Transformation in Higher Education: Global Pressures and Local Realities in South Africa*, edited by Nico Cloete, Peter Maassen, Richard Fehnel, Teboho Moja, Helene Perold, and Trish Gibbon, 2–3. Dordrecht: Kluwer Academic, 2004.

Bunyi, Grace W. "Language Classroom Practices in Kenya." *Decolonisation, Globalisation: Language in Education Policy and Practice* (2005): 133–154.

Caldwell, Cleopatra Howard, Marc A. Zimmerman, Debra Hilkene Bernat, Robert M. Sellers, and Paul C. Notaro. "Racial Identity, Maternal Support, and Psychological Distress Among African American Adolescents." *Child Development* 73 (2002): 1322–36.

Calzo, J. P. et al. "Retrospective Recall of Sexual Orientation Identity Development among Gay, Lesbian, and Bisexual Adults." *Developmental Psychology* 47, no. 6 (2011): 1658.

Carmody, Padraig. "A Knowledge Economy or an Information Society in Africa, Thintegration and Mobile Phone Revolution." *Information Technology for Development* 19, no. 1 (2013): 24–39.

Carr, E. H. *What is History*, edited by R.W. Davies. 2nd ed. New York: Penguin, 1987.

Carroll, Karanja. "An Introduction to African–Centered Sociology: Worldview, Epistemology, and Social Theory." *Critical Sociology* 40, no. 2 (2014): 257–70.

Carroll, Karanja, and DeReef Jamison. "African–Centered Psychology, Education and the Liberation of African Minds: Notes on the Psycho–Cultural Justification for Reparations." *Race, Gender & Class* 18, no. 1/2 (2011): 52–72.

Carter–Ényì, Aaron. "Hooked on Sol–Fa: The Do–Re–Mi Heuristic for Yoruba Speech Tones." *Africa* 88, no. 2 (2018): 267–90.

Carter–Ényì, Aaron, and Quintina Carter–Ényì. "Decolonizing the Mind Through Song." *Performance Research: A Journal of Performing Arts* 24, no. 1 (2019): 58–65.

Center for Disease Control and Prevention, "Protective Factors for LGBT Youth." Center for Disease Control and Prevention, December 20, 2019, https://www.cdc.gov/healthyyouth/disparities/lgbtprotectivefactors.htm.

Central Statistical Office, Zambia. "Census Data from Zambia." https://web.archive.org/web/20120121010214/http://www.zamstats.gov.zm/census.php.

Ces, Alice. "Boaventura de Sousa Santos—Epistemologies of the South. ALICE Interview 5/9." YouTube video, 6:32. September 27, 2012. https://www.youtube.com/watch?v=HN3wkcfkM78.

Césaire, Aime. *Discourse on Colonialism*. New York: Monthly Review, 1955.

Chabal, Patrick. *The End of Conceit: Western Rationality After Postcolonialism*. London and New York: Zed, 2012.

Chadwick, Nora K. "The Distribution of Oral Literature in the Old World." *Journal of the Royal Anthropological Institute of Great Britain and Ireland* 69, no. 1 (1939): 77–94.

Charry, Eric. "A Capsule History of African Rap." *Hip Hop Africa: New African Music in a Globalizing World*. Bloomington: Indiana University Press, 2012.

Chawane, Midas. "The Development of Afrocentricity: A Historical Survey." *Yesterday and Today* 16 (2016): 78–99.

Cheney, Kristen. "Locating Neocolonialism, 'Tradition,' and Human Rights in Uganda's 'Gay Death Penalty.'" *African Studies Review* 55, no. 2 (2012): 77–95.

Chenier, Elise. "Lesbian Feminism." GLBTQ Inc, 2004. http://www.glbtq.Inc.

Chikwe, C. K., R. C. Ogidi, and K. Nwachukwu. "Challenges of Research and Human Capital Development in Nigeria." *Journal of Education and Practice* 28, no. 6 (2015): 44–47.

Chilisa, Bagele. *Indigenous Research Methodologies*. Thousand Oaks: SAGE, 2012.

Chimakonam, Jonathan O. "Can the Philosophy Curriculum be Africanised? An Examination of the Prospects and Challenges of Some Models of Africanisation." *South African Journal of Philosophy* 35, no. 4 (2016): 513–22.

Chitakure, John. *African Traditional Religion Encounters Christianity: The Resilience of a Demonized Religion*. Eugene: Pickwick, 2017.

Chiwanza, T. H. "The Top Ten African Countries with the Largest Chinese Debt." *African Exponent*, October 2, 2018. https://www.africanexponent.com/post/9183-here-are-the-top-ten-countries-in-africa-bearing-the-largest-chinese-debt.

Chrisomalis, Stephen. "The Egyptian Origin of the Greek Alphabetic Numerals." *Antiquity* 77, no. 297 (2003): 485–96.

Chuku, Gloria. "Igbo Women and Economic Transformations in South Eastern Nigeria, 1900–1960." In *African Studies, History, Politics, Economy and Culture*, edited by Molefi Asante. London: Routledge, 2015.

Chukwuemeka, E. E., Okey R. Oji, C. Okafor, and F. Onwuchekwa. "Research and Development in Africa: Addressing the Elephantine Problems." *Kuwait Chapter of Arabian Journal of Business and Management Review* 4, no. 4 (2014): 1–12.

Ciaffa, Jay. "Tradition and Modernity in Postcolonial African Philosophy." *Humanitas* XXI, no. 1–2 (2008): 121–45.
Clack, Timothy, Marcus Brittain, and David Turton. "Oral Histories and the Impact of Archaeological Fieldwork in Contact Encounters: Meeting Socrates on the Omo." *Journal of the Royal Anthropological Institute* 23, no. 4 (2017): 669–89.
Clifford, James. *The Predicament of Culture: Twentieth Century Ethnography, Literature, and Art.* Cambridge, MA: Harvard University Press, 1986.
Coetzee, Peter Hendrix, and Abraham Pieter Jacob Roux, eds. *The African Philosophy Reader.* New York: Routledge, 2004.
Cohen, Rachel. "The Afrocentric Education Crisis." *American Prospect*, September 2, 2016. http://prospect.org/article/afrocentric–education–crisis.
College Board. *AP World History: Modern, Course and Exam Description Effective Fall 2019.* New York: College Board, 2020. https://apcentral.collegeboard.org/pdf/ap–world–history–course–and–exam–description–0.pdf?course=ap–world–history–modern.
College of Ethnic Studies. "Brief Program Overview." University Updates. https://ethnicstudies.sfsu.edu/depts1.
Collins, Patricia. *Black Feminist Thought, Knowledge, Consciousness and the Politics of Empowerment.* 2nd ed. New York: Routledge, 2000.
———. *Black Sexual Politics: African Americans, Gender, and the New Racism.* New York: Routledge, 2004.
Collins, Stephen. "Who Owns Ananse? The Tangled Web of Folklore and Copyright in Ghana." *Journal of African Cultural Studies* 30, no. 2 (2018): 178–91.
Conrad, Jane. "Review of 'The African Condition: A Political Diagnosis by Ali Mazrui.'" *Canadian Journal of African Studies/Revue Canadienne Des Études Africaines* 16, no. 1 (1982): 186–88.
Cope, Trevor. *Izibongo: Zulu Praise Poetry.* Oxford: Clarendon, 1968.
Copley, Amy, and Mwangi Kimenyi. "In Memoriam: Intellectual Ali Mazrui (1933–2014)." Brookings, July 29, 2016. https://www.brookings.edu/blog/africa–in–focus/2014/10/15/in–memoriam–intellectual–ali–mazrui–1933–2014/.
Cornwall, Andrea. *Readings in Gender in Africa.* Bloomington: Indiana University Press, 2005.
Costadi, Mo. "Snapshots Explore Einstein's Unusual Brain." *Nature*, November 16, 2012. https://www.nature.com/news/snapshots–explore–einstein–s–unusual–brain–1.11836.
Cross, Hannah, and Leo Zeilig. "In Tribute to Our Comrade Samir Amin, 1931–2018." *Review of*
African Political Economy 45, no. 157 (2018): 365–77.
Currier, Ashley. "Decolonizing the Law: LGBT Organizing in Namibia and South Africa." *Special Issue Social Movements/Legal Possibilities.* Bingley: Emerald Group, 2011.

———. "Political Homophobia in Post-Colonial Namibia." *Gender & Society* 24, no. 1 (2010): 110–29.
Currier, Ashley and Cruz, Joelle. "Civil Society and Sexual Struggles in Africa." *The Handbook of Civil Society in Africa*. Springer: New York, 2014.
Dale, Roger, Susan Robertson, and Bonaventura de Sousa Santos. "Interview with Bonaventura de Sousa Santo." *Globalization, Sciences and Education* 2, no. 2 (2004): 1–22.
Dakubu, Mary Esther Kropp. "The Role of Language in Forging New Identities: Countering a Heritage of Servitude." In *The Politics of Heritage in Africa: Economies, Histories, and Infrastructure,* edited by Derek R. Peterson, Kodzo Gavua, and Ciraj Rassool. New York and London: International African Institute & Cambridge University Press, 2015.
Dallmyr, Fred. "Return to the Source: African Identity (After Cabral)." *Theoria: A Journal of Social and Political Theory,* no. 88 (1996): 1–23.
Dauda, Bola and Toyin Falola. *Wole Soyinka: Literature, Activism, and African Transformation.* New York: Bloomsbury Academic, 2021.
Davidson, Basil. *The African Awakening.* London: J. Cape, 1956.
De Leeuw, Mineke Schipper. "Origin and Forms of Drama in the African Context." https://openaccess.leidenuniv.nl/bitstream/handle/1887/7769/05_090_048.pdf?sequence=1.
Deleuze, Gilles, and Felix Guattari. *What Is Philosophy?* Translated by Hugh Tomlinson and Graham Burchell. New York: Columbia University Press, 1991.
De Sousa, Santos, ed. "General Introduction: Reinventing Social Emancipation: Toward New Manifestos." *Democratizing Democracy: Beyond the Liberal Democratic Canon.* London: Verso, 2005.
De Witte, Marlene. "Buy the Future: Charismatic Pentecostalism and African Liberation in a Neoliberal World." In *Pentecostalism and Politics in Africa,* edited by Adeshina Afolayan, Olajumoke Yacob-Haliso, and Toyin Falola. New York: Palgrave Macmillan, 2018.
Department of Education of South Africa. *Report of the Ministerial Committee on Transformation and Social Cohesion and the Elimination of Discrimination in Public Higher Education Institutions*: 2008 Final Report. Pretoria: Department of Education, 2008.
Desai, Karishma, and Brenda Nyandiko Sanya. "Towards Decolonial Praxis: Reconfiguring the Human and the Curriculum." *Gender and Education* 28, no. 6 (2016): 710–24.
Descartes, Rene, and Laurence Lafleur. *Meditations on First Philosophy*. Indianapolis: Bobbs-Merrill, 1960.
Desilver, Drew. "US Students' Academic Achievement Still Lags that of Their Peers in Many Other Countries." Pew Research Center. February 15, 2017. https://www.pewresearch.org/fact-tank/2017/02/15/u-s-students-internationally-math-science/.

Devisch, Rene, and Francis Nyamnjoh, eds. *The Postcolonial Turn: Re-imagining Anthropology and Africa*. Bamenda: Langaa RPCIG, 2011.

Devji, Zahrah. "Forging Paths for the African Queer: Is There an 'African' Mechanism for Realizing LGBTIQ Rights?" *Journal of African Law* 60, no. 3 (2016): 343–63.

Dike, K. Onwuka. *Trade and Politics in the Niger Delta, 1830–1885*. New York: ACLS, 2008.

Dok, Akol Nyok Akol, and Bradley A. Thayer. "Takeover Trap: Why Imperialist China is Invading Africa." The National Interest, July 10, 2019. https://nationalinterest.org/feature/takeover-trap-why-imperialist-china-invading-africa-66421.

Donahue, Amy, and Rohan Kaylan. "Introduction: On the Imperative, Challenges, and Prospects of Decolonizing Comparative Methodologies." *Comparative and Continental Philosophy* 7, no. 2 (2015): 124–37.

Dormido, Hannah. "These Countries Are the Most at Risk from a Water Crisis." Bloomberg, August 6, 2019. https://www.bloomberg.com/graphics/2019-countries-facing-water-crisis/.

Drayton, Richard, and David Motadel. "Discussion: The Futures of Global History." *Journal of Global History* 13, no. 1 (2018): 1–21.

Drew, Allison. "Social Mobilization and Racial Capitalism in South Africa, 1928–1960." PhD diss., University of California, Los Angeles, 1991.

Du Bois, W. E. B. *Africa, Its Geography, People and Products*. Kan: Haldeman-Julius, 1930.

———. *Africa: Its Place in Modern History*. Kan: Haldeman-Julius, 1930.

Duermeijer, Charon, Mohamed Amir, and Lucia Schoombe. "Africa Generates Less Than 1% of the World's Research; Data Analytics Can Change That." Elsevier, March 22, 2018. https://www.elsevier.com/connect/africa-generates-less-than-1-of-the-worlds-research-data-analytics-can-change-that#:~:text=Africa%20generates%20less%20than%201,data%20analytics%20can%20change%20that&text=Stories%20keeping%20journal%20authors%20in,industry%20developments%2C%20support%20and%20training, 2018.

Duke Franklin Humanities Institute. "Achille Mbembe: Future Knowledges and the Dilemmas of Decolonization." YouTube video, 1:05:32. September 20, 2017. https://www.youtube.com/watch?v=Qa5NUW7aQAI.

Dussel, Enrique. "Agenda for a South–South Philosophical Dialogue." *Human Architecture: Journal of the Sociology of Self-Knowledge* 11, no. 1 (2013): 3–18.

———. "A New Age in the History of Philosophy: The World Dialogue Between Philosophical Traditions." *Journal of Philosophy and Religion* 9, no. 1 (2008): 1–22.

———. "Transmodernity and Interculturality: An Interpretation from the Perspective of Philosophy of Liberation." *Poligrafi 11*, no. 41–42 (2006): 1–26.

Dutch TV Studios. "Decolonizing the Mind Through Song." September 1979. https://youtu.be/2Mwh9z58iAU.

Dutt-Ballerstadt, Reshmi. "Academic Prioritization of Killing the Liberal Arts?" *Inside Higher* Ed., March 1, 2019. https://www.insidehighered.com/advice/2019/03/01/shrinking–liberal–arts–programs–raise–alarm–bells–among–faculty.

Edeh, Harrison. "FG Scraps Corruption–Riddled Post UTME, Adopts 180 Cut-Off Mark." Business Day Nigeria, June 3, 2016. https://businessday.ng/exclusives/article/fg-scraps–corruption–riddled–post–utme–adopts–180–cut–off–mark/.

Effah, Paul. "Higher Education in Ghana." In *African Higher Education*, edited by Damtew Teferra and Philip Altbach, 338–349. Bloomington: Indiana University Press, 2003.

El Sadaawi, Nadal. *A Daughter of Isis. The Early Life of Nadal El, Sadaawi*. London: Zed, 1999.

Elder, Brent, and Kenneth Odoyo. "Multiple Methodologies: Using Community-Based Participatory Research and Decolonizing Methodologies in Kenya." *International Journal of Qualitative Studies in Education* 31, no. 4 (2018): 293–311.

Eldredge, Elizabeth. *Kingdoms and Chiefdoms of Southeastern Africa: Oral Traditions and History, 1400–1830*. Rochester: Boydell & Brewer, 2015.

Eliason, Michael, Suzanne Dibble, and Patricia Robertson. "Lesbian, Gay, Bisexual, and Transgender (LGBT) Physicians' Experiences in the Workplace." *Journal of Homosexuality* 58, no. 10 (2011): 1355–71.

Elliot, Kennedy. "Where Carbon Emissions are Greatest." *Washington Post*, March 31, 2015. https://www.washingtonpost.com/graphics/international.

Ellis, A. B. *The Yoruba Speaking Peoples of the Slave Coast of West Africa: Their Religion, Manners, Customs, Laws, Language, etc.* Lagos: Pilgrims, 1974.

Ellis, Stephen, and Gerrie ter Haar. "Religion and Politics: Taking African Epistemologies Seriously." *The Journal of Modern African Studies* 45, no. 3 (2007): 385–401.

Emeagwali, Gloria, and George J. Sefa Dei, eds. *Introduction in African Indigenous Knowledge and the Disciplines*. Rotterdam: Sense, 2014.

Emecheta, Buchi. *Joys of Motherhood*. London: Allison & Busby, 1979.

Emeh, I. E. J. "Dependency Theory and Africa's Underdevelopment: A Paradigm Shift from Pseudo–Intellectualism: The Nigerian Perspective." *International Journal of African and Asian Studies* 1, no. 1 (2013): 116–28.

Erim, Erim. "New Trends in African Historical Writing: An Assessment." *The Multi–Disciplinary Approach to African History Essays in Honour of Ebiegberi Joe Alagoa*, edited by Nkparom Ejituwu. Port Harcourt: University of Port Harcourt Press, 1997.

Escobar, Natalie. "How 50 Years of Latino Studies Shaped History Education." *Atlantic*, September 7, 2018. https://www.theatlantic.com/education/archive/2018/09/how–50–years–of–latino–studies–shaped–history–education/569623/.

Evans-Pritchard, Evan. *The Divine Kingship of the Shilluk of the Nilotic Sudan*. Cambridge: Cambridge University Press, 1948; repr. 2014.

Eze, Chielozona. "Feminist Empathy: Unsettling African Cultural Norms in The Secret Lives of Baba Segi's Wives." *Journal of African Studies* 74, no. 3 (2015): 310–26.

Fabian, Johannes. "Missions and the Colonization of African Languages: Developments in the Former Belgian Congo." *Canadian Journal of African Studies* 17, no. 2 (1983): 165–87.

Falola, Toyin. "African Studies in the Twentieth Century." In *The Multi-Disciplinary Approach to African History Essays in Honour of Ebiegberi Joe Alagoa*, edited by Nkparom Ejituwu. Port Harcourt: University of Port Harcourt Press, 1997.

———. *African Spirituality, Politics and Knowledge Systems: Sacred Words and Holy Realms*. London: Bloomsbury, 2022.

———. *Cultural Modernity in a Colonized World: The Writings of Chief Isaac Oluwole Delano*. Austin: Pan-African University Press, 2020.

———. *Nationalism and African Intellectuals*. Rochester: University of Rochester Press, 2001.

———. *Violence in Nigeria: The Crisis of Religious Politics and Secular Ideologies*. Rochester: University of Rochester Press, 1998.

Falola, Toyin, and Akintunde Akinyemi. *Encyclopedia of the Yoruba*. Bloomington and Indianapolis: Indiana University Press, 2016.

Falola, Toyin, and Chukwuemeka Agbo. "The Prospects and Challenges of Pan-Africanism." *Oxford Research Encyclopedia of Politics*. Oxford: Oxford University Press. https://oxfordre.com/politics/view/10.1093/acrefore/9780190228637.001.0001/acrefore–9780190228637718.

Fanon, Frantz. *Black Skin, White Masks*. Translated by Charles Markmann. New York: Grove, 1997.

Fanon, Frantz, Jean-Paul Sartre, and Constance Farrington. Vol. 36 of *The Wretched of the Earth*. New York: Grove, 1963.

Fanon, Frantz, Richard Philcox, Jean-Paul Sartre, and Homi K. Bhabha. *The Wretched of the Earth*. Cape Town: Kwela, 2017.

Fardon, Richard, and Graham Furniss, eds. *African Languages, Development and the State*. London and New York: Routledge, 2003.

Fashola, Joseph. "Modernisation and African Cultures." In *Humanism, Existential Predicaments & Africa. Essays in Honour of Olusegun Oladipo*, edited by Offor Francis and Ademowo, 186–198. A. J. Ibadan: Hope, 2014.

Fergus, Claudius. "Negotiating Time, Space, and Spirit: A Case Study of Oral Tradition and the Construction of Lineage Identity in West Africa." *Research in African Literatures* 40, no. 1 (2009): 74–85.

Finnegan, Ruth. *Oral Literature in Africa*. Cambridge: Open Book, 2012; repr. 2014.

Flikschuh, Katrin. "The Idea of Philosophical Fieldwork: Global Justice, Moral Ignorance, and Intellectual Attitudes." *The Journal of Political Philosophy* 22 (2014): 1–26.

Foley, John Miles. "The Traditional Oral Audience." *Balkan Studies* 18 (1977): 145–53.

Fontana, Andrea, and James Frey. "From Structured Questions to Negotiated Text." In *Handbook of Qualitative Research*, edited by Norman Denzin and Yvonna Lincoln, 645–72. Los Angeles: SAGE, 2000.

Forde, Daryll, ed. *African Worlds Studies in the Cosmological Ideas and Social Values of Africa Peoples*. London: Oxford University Press, 1963.

Forte, Jean. "Realism, Narrative and the Feminist Playwright: A Problem of Reception." *Modern Drama* (1989): 115–27.

Frances, Henry. *Reclaiming African Religions in Trinidad: The Socio-Political Legitimation of the Orisha and Spiritual Baptist Faiths*. Kingston: University of the West Indies Press, 2003.

Frank, Katherine. "Feminist Criticism and the African Novel." *African Literature Today*, no. 14 (1984): 34–48.

Franzki, Hannah. "Eurocentrism." InterAmerican Wiki, n.d. https://www.uni-bielefeld.de/(en)/cias/wiki/e_Eurocentrism.html.

Freire, Paulo. *Pedagogy of the Oppressed*. New York: Bloomsbury Academic, 2018.

Friedrich, Johannes, Mengpin Ge, and Andrew Pickens. "This Interactive Chart Explains World's Top 10 Emitters, and How They've Changed." World Resources Institute, April 11, 2017. https://www.wri.org/blog/2017/04/interactive-chart-explains-worlds-top-10-emitters-and-how-theyve-changed.

Fwangyil, Gloria Ada. "A Reformist-Feminist Approach to Chimamanda Ngozi Adichie's Purple Hibiscus." *African Research Review* 5, no. 3 (2011): 261–67.

Gaard, Koktevd. *Polygamy: A Cross-Cultural Analysis*. New York: New York University Press, 2008.

Galván, Ruth. "Collective Memory of Violence of the Female Brown Body: A Decolonial Feminist Public Pedagogy Engagement with the Feminicides." *Pedagogy, Culture & Society* 24, no. 3 (2016): 343–57.

García, Romeo. "Decoloniality and the Humanities: Possibilities and Predicaments." *Journal of Hispanic Higher Education* 19, no. 3 (2018): 303–17.

Garfield, Jay. *Empty Words: Buddhist Philosophy and Cross-Cultural Interpretation*. Oxford: Oxford University Press, 2001.

Garuba, Harry. "What Is an African Curriculum?" *Mail & Guardian*, April 17, 2015. https://mg.co.za/article/2015-04-17-what-is-an-african-curriculum/.

Gbadegesin, Segun. *African Philosophy: Traditional Yoruba Philosophy and Contemporary African Realities*. New York: Peter Lang, 1991.

Gerdes, Paulus. "Creative Geometric Thought and Endogenous Knowledge Production: Example of Experimentation and Invention Among Tonga Women in Southeast Mozambique." In *African Indigenous Knowledge and the Disciplines*, edited by Gloria Emeagwali and George Sefa Dei, 63–82. Rotterdam: Sense, 2014.

Gettier, Edmund. "Is Justified True Belief Knowledge?" *Analysis* 23, no. 6 (1963): 121–23.

Glăveanu, Vlad, and Zayda Sierra. "Creativity and Epistemologies of the South." *Culture & Psychology* 21, no. 3 (2015): 340–58.

Global University for Sustainability. "Crisis of Senile Capitalism—Interview with Samir Amin 20180506." YouTube video, 1:04:23. August 24, 2018. https://www.youtube.com/watch?v=q5gMaAPagwQ.

Gondola, Didier. *The History of Congo*. Westport: Greenwood, 2002.

Gonzalez, Kirsten et al. "The Positive Aspects of Being the Parent of an LGBTQ Child." *Family Process* 52, no. 2 (2013): 325–37.

Goody, Jack, and Ian Watt. "The Consequences of Literacy." *Comparative Studies in Society and History* 5 (1963): 304–45.

Gordimer, Nadine. "The Essential Gesture: Writers and Responsibility." *The Tanner Lectures on Human Values*, University of Michigan, Ann Arbor, Michigan, October 12, 1984.

Gordon, Lewis. "Disciplinary Decadence and the Decolonization of Knowledge." *Africa Development / Afrique et Développement* 39, no. 1 (2014): 81–92.

Goredema, Ruvimbo. "African Feminism: The African Woman's Struggle for Identity." *African Yearbook of Rhetoric* 1, no. 1 (2010): 33–41.

Gould, Jay. *The Mismeasure of Man*. New York: W. W. Norton & Company, 1996.

Grosfoguel, Ramón. "Decolonizing Post–Colonial Studies and Paradigms of Political–Economy: Transmodernity, Decolonial Thinking, and Global Coloniality." *Transmodernity: Journal of Peripheral Cultural Production of the Luso-Hispanic World* 1, no. 1 (2011).

———. "The Epistemic Decolonial Turn: Beyond Political–Economy Paradigms." *Cultural Studies* 21, no. 2–3 (2007): 211–23.

Guèye, Médoune. "Criticism, Écriture, and Orality in the African Novel: Oral Discourse in Aminata Sow Fall's Work." *Research in African Literatures* 45, no. 2 (2014): 86–102.

Guilherme, Manuela, and Gunther Dietz. "Interview to Boaventura de Sousa Santos." *Arts & Humanities in Higher Education* 16, no. 1 (2017): 17–27.

Haas, Angela. "Race, Rhetoric, and Technology: A Case Study of Decolonial Technical Communication Theory, Methodology, and Pedagogy." *Journal of Business and Technical Communication* 26, no. 3 (2012): 277–310.

Hadjitheodorou Francisca. "Women Speak: The Creative Transformation of Women in African Literature." MA thesis, University of Pretoria, 1999.

Hale, Sondra. "Edward Said—Accidental Feminist: Orientalism and the Legacy of Edward Said." *Amerasia Journal* 31, no. 1 (2005): 1–70.

Hale, Thomas. *Griots and Griottes: Masters of Words and Music*. Bloomington: Indiana University Press, 1998.

Hall, Christine Iijima. "Beauty Is in the Soul of the Beholder: Psychological Implications of Beauty and African American Women." *Cultural Diversity and Mental Health* 1, no. 2 (1995): 125–37.

Hall, Ronald. "Black America's 'Bleaching Syndrome'." The Conversation, February 2, 2018. Accessed September 27, 2021, https://theconversation.com/black-americas-bleaching-syndrome-82200.

Hallen, Barry. *A Short History of African Philosophy*. Bloomington: Indiana University Press, 2009.

Hamilton, Paula, and Linda Shopes. *Oral History and Public Memories*. Philadelphia: Temple University Press, 2008; repr. 2009.

Hamza, Haoua. "Decolonizing Research on Gender Disparity in Education in Niger: Complex of Language, Culture, and Homecoming." In *Decolonizing Research in Cross-Cultural Contexts: Critical Personal Narratives*, edited by Kagendo Mutua and Beth Swadener, 123–34. Albany: SUNY Press, 2004.

Hansen, Davis. "In Defense of Liberal Arts." CBS News, reprinted from *National Review*, December 16, 2010. https://www.cbsnews.com/news/in-defense-of-liberal-arts/.

Harris, Eva. "Building Scientific Capacity in Developing Countries." *EMBO Reports* 5, no. 1 (2004): 7–11.

Harris, Kelly. "Still Relevant: Claude Ake's Challenge to Mainstream Discourse on African Politics and Development." *Journal of Third World Studies* 22, no. 2 (2005): 73–88.

Hegel, Friedrich. *The Philosophy of History*. Translated by John Sibree. New York: Dover, 1956.

Heleta, Savo. "Decolonisation of Higher Education: Dismantling Epistemic Violence and
Eurocentrism in South Africa." *Transformation in Higher Education* 1, no. 1 (2016): 1–8.

Henige, David. "Impossible to Disprove Yet Impossible to Believe: The Unforgiving Epistemology of Deep-Time Oral Tradition." *History in Africa* 36 (2009): 127–234.

Hewett, H. "Coming of Age: Chimamanda Ngozi Adichie and the Voice of the Third Generation." *English in Africa* 10 (2015): 73–97.

Hidalgo-Capitán, Antonio, and Ana Patricia Cubillo-Guevara. "Deconstruction and Genealogy of Latin American Good Living (Buen Vivir) the (Triune) Good Living." *International Development Policy Revue Internationale De Politique De Développement* 9, no. 9 (2017/2018): 23–50.

Higgs, Philip. "Towards an Indigenous African Educational Discourse: A Philosophical Reflection." *International Review of Education* 54, no. 3–4 (2008): 445–458.

Hiribarren, Vincent. "A European and African Joint–Venture: Writing a Seamless History of Borno (1902–1960)." *History in Africa* 40 (2013): 77–98.

Holcomb-McCoy, Cheryl, and Cheryl Moore-Thomas. "Empowering African-American Adolescent Females." *Professional School Counseling* 5, no. 1 (2001): 19–27.

Holmes, Kristin. "A Limited Woman: Character in Question in Buchi Emecheta's Novel *The Joys of Motherhood*." Thesis, University of North Carolina, 2007.

Horsthemke, Kai. "Indigenous Knowledge: Conceptions and Misconceptions." *Journal of Education* 32 (2004): 1–15.

Horwitz, Josh. "Dear Steve King: Here Are Some Things Not Invented by White People." Quartz, July 19, 2016. https://qz.com/735731/dear-steve-king-here-are-some-things-not-invented-by-white-people-in-the-us-or-europe/.
Houghton, John, and Peter Sheehan. "A Primer on The Knowledge Economy." Paper, the National Innovation Summit, Canberra, Melbourne, Australia, February 9–11, 2000.
Hountondji, Paulin. *African Philosophy: Myth and Reality*. Bloomington: Indiana University Press, 1983.
———. "Que peut la philosophie?" Présence Africaine 119 (1981): 47–71. Translated as "What Philosophy Can Do." *Quest: Philosophical Discussions* 1, no. 2 (1987): 2–28.
Houseman, Michael. "Toward a Complex Model of Parenthood: Two African Tale." *American Ethnologist* 15, no. 4 (1988): 658–77.
Hrdy, Daniel B. "Cultural Practices Contributing to the Transmission of Human Immunodeficiency Virus in Africa." *Review of Infectious Diseases*, no. 11 (1987): 1109–19.
Hughes, Arnold. "The Appeal of Marxism to Africans." *Journal of Communist Studies* 8 (1992).
Hugill, Peter, and James Blaut. "The Colonizers Model of the World: Geographical Diffusionism and Eurocentric History." *Geographical Review* 85, no. 2 (1995): 259–61.
Hunt, Nancy. "Placing African Women's History and Locating Gender." *Social History* 14, no. 3 (1989): 359–79.
Hussein, Jeylan. "The Social and Ethno–cultural Construction of Masculinity and Femininity in African Proverbs." *African Study Monograph* 26, no. 2 (2005): 59–87.
Hutchings, Kimberly. "Dialogue Between Whom? The Role of the West/Non–West Distinction in Promoting Global Dialogue in IR." *Millennium* 39, no. 3 (2011): 639–647.
Ikyer, Godwin. "Deep Digital Poetry: Interrogating Tiv Oral Poetry within Postmodernity." *Tydskrif Vir Letterkunde* 54, no. 1 (2017): 196–210.
Ilo, Isaiah. "Language in Modern African Drama." *Comparative Literature and Culture* 8, no. 4 (2006): 1–9.
Imam, Ayesha, Amina Mama, and Fatou Sow, eds. *Engendering African Social Sciences*. Dakar: CODESRIA, 1997.
Imbo, Samuel Oluoch. *An Introduction to African Philosophy*. Lanham, MD: Rowman and Littlefield, 1998.
Imbua, David L., Otoabasi Akpan, I. R. Amadi, and Yakubu A. Ochefu, eds. *History, Culture, Diasporas and Nation Building: The Collected Works of Okon Edet Uya*. Bethesda: Arbi, 2012.
Index Mundi. "Research and Development Expenditure (% of GDP) – Africa." Index Mundi, n.d. https://www.indexmundi.com/facts/indicators/GB.XPD.RSDV.GD.ZS/map/africa.

Ingram, James. "Universalism in History." *Radical Cosmopolitics* (2013): 23–62.
Ireland, Patrick. "A Macro–Level Analysis of the Scope, Causes, and Consequences of Homophobia in Africa." *African Studies Review* (2013): 47–66.
Iseke, Judy, and Bekisizwe Ndimande. "Negotiating Indigenous Language Narratives from Canada and South Africa: A Comparative Approach." *International Multilingual Research Journal* 8 (2014): 141–166.
Jackson, Howard, and Etienne Ze Amvela. *Words, Meaning and Vocabulary: An Introduction to Modern English Lexicology*. London: Continuum, 2000.
Janz, Bruce B. *Philosophy in an African Place*. Lanham, MD: Lexington, 2009.
Jarus, Owen. "Shona People: History & Culture." *Live Science*, February 28, 2017. https://www.livescience.com/58039-shona-people.
Jean-Malbuisson, Galerie. *Africa Internet History: Highlights*. Geneva: Internet Society, n.d. https://www.internetsociety.org/wp–content/uploads/2017/09/history_internet_africa.pdf.
Jegede, Olutoyin. "Women, Power and Subversion in Orature: A Palace Performance in Yorubaland, Nigeria." *Journal of Gender Studies* 15, no. 3 (2006): 253–66.
Jennings, Hellen. *New African Fashion*. Munich, London, and New York: Prestel, 2011.
Jipson, John, and P. M. Jitheesh. "There Is a Structural Crisis of Capitalism." MR Online, May 5, 2018. https://mronline.org/2018/05/05/there-is-a-structural-crisis-of-capitalism/.
Jolley, Dorothy R. "'Ubuntu': A Person is a Person Through Other Persons." Unpublished manuscript, 2010.
Jones, Eldred. "Three Nigerian Novels." *Journal of Commonwealth Literature* 2, no. 1 (1967): 127–31.
Johnson, Ethan. "Afro-Ecuadorian Educational Movement: Racial Oppression, Its Origins and Oral Tradition." *Journal of Pan African Studies* 7, no. 4 (2014): 115–37.
Johnson, John, Thomas Hale, and Stephen Belcher, eds. *Oral Epics from Africa: Vibrant Voices from a Vast Continent*. Bloomington: Indiana University Press, 1997.
Johnson, Samuel, *The History of the Yorubas*. Lagos: CSS, 2009.
Johnson-Odim, Cheryl, and Nina Mba. *For Women and the Nation: Funmilayo Ransome-Kuti of Nigeria*. Chicago: University of Illinois Press, 1997.
Jones, Siân, and Lynette Russell. "Archaeology, Memory and Oral Tradition: An Introduction." *International Journal of Historical Archaeology* 16, no. 2 (2012): 267–83.
Julien, Eileen. "African Literature." In *Africa*, edited by Phyllis Martin and Patrick O'Meara, 295–312. Bloomington: Indiana University Press, 1995.
Jung, Carl Gustav. Vol. 2 of *Collected Works of CG Jung*, edited by Gerhard Adler and Richard Hull. Princeton, NJ: Princeton University Press, 2014.
Jung, Jordan. "Seeking Common Ground Through Oral Tradition." *Biblical Theology Bulletin* 43, no. 4 (2013): 212–20.

Kalichman, Seth, Leickness Simbayi, Sean Jooste, Yoesrie Toefy, Demetria Cain, Chauncey Cherry, and Ashraf Kagee. "Development of a Brief Scale to Measure AIDS-Related Stigma in South Africa." *AIDS and Behavior* 9, no. 2 (2005): 135–43.

Kaoma, Kapya. *Christianity, Globalization, and Protective Homophobia*. Cham: Palgrave Macmillan, 2018.

Karam, Azza. *Women, Islamisms and the State: Contemporary Feminisms in Egypt*. London: Macmillan, 1998.

Kaunda, Chammah. "The Denial of African Agency: A Decolonial Theological Turn." *Black Theology* 13, no. 1 (2015): 73–92.

Kaya, Hassan O., and Yonah N. Seleti. "African Indigenous Knowledge Systems and Relevance of Higher Education in South Africa." *International Education Journal: Comparative Perspectives* 12, no. 1 (2013): 30–44.

Kaye, Harvey J. *Thomas Paine and the Promise of America*. New York: Farrar, Straus and Giroux, 2013.

Keikelame, Mpoe Johannah, and Leslie Swartz. "Decolonising Research Methodologies: Lessons from a Qualitative Research Project." Cape Town, South Africa / *Global Health Action* 12, no. 1 (2019): 1–7.

Kelley, Robin. "A Poetics of Anticolonialism." In *Discourse on Colonialism*, edited by Aimé Césaire. New York: Monthly Review, 2000.

Kenzo, Robert, and Justin Mabiala. "Thinking Otherwise About Africa: Postcolonialism, Postmodernism, and the Future of African Theology." *Exchange: Bulletin de Litterature Des Eglises Du Tiers Monde* 31, no. 4 (2002): 323–41.

Kesteloot, Lilyan. "The African Epic." *African Languages and Cultures* 2, no. 2 (1989): 208–9.

Kete, Asante. *The Afrocentric Idea*. Philadelphia: Temple University Press, 1987.

———. "Afrocentricity." Asante.net, April 13, 2009. http://www.asante.net/articles/1/afrocentricity/.

———. "The Creation of the Doctorate in African American Studies at Temple University: Knocking at the Door of Eurocentric Hegemony." Asante.net, August 5, 2009. http://www.asante.net/articles/7/the-creation-of-the-doctorate-in-african-american-studies-at-temple-university-knocking-at-the-door-of-eurocentric-hegemony.

———. "Discourse on Black Studies: Liberating the Study of African People in the Western Academy." *Journal of Black Studies* 36, no. 5 (2006).

———. "Why Afrocentricity?" *New York Times*, May 7, 2015. https://opinionator.blogs.nytimes.com/2015/05/07/molefi–kete–asante–why–afrocentricity/.

KillahManjaro. "Decolonising Our Universities – Molefi Asante." YouTube video, 28:31. May 28, 2016. https://www.youtube.com/watch?v=tgsbXajRBQw.

Kimambo, Isaria. "Establishment of Teaching Programmes." *Search of Relevance: A History of the University of Dar es Salaam*. Dar es Salaam: Dar es Salaam University Press, 2008.

Kimmerle, Heinz. "Afrikanische Philosophie in westlichenSprachen: Eine postkolonialeProblemkonstellation." *Polylog* 15 (2006): 47–74.
King Leopold II of Belgium. *King Leopold II of Belgium to Colonial Missionaries*, 1883. http://www.fafich.ufmg.br/luarnaut/Letter%20Leopold%20II%20to%20Colonial%20Missionaries.pdf.
Kioko, Angelina Nduku, Jayne Mutiga, Margaret Muthwli, Leila Shroeder, Helen Inyega, and Barbara Trudell. *Language and Education in Africa: Answering the Questions.* Nairobi: UNESCO, 2008.
Kishani, Bongasu. "On the Interface of Philosophy and Language in Africa: Some Practical and Theoretical Considerations." *African Studies Review* 44, no. 3 (2001): 27–45.
Ki-Zerbo, J. *Methodology and African Prehistory. Vol. 1 of General History of Africa* (Abridged ed.). Ibadan: Heinemann Educational Books, 1990.
Knowles–Borishade, Adetokunbo. "Paradigm for Classical African Orature: Instrument for a Scientific Revolution?" *Journal of Black Studies* 21, no. 4 (1991): 488–500.
Koch, Christof. "Does Brain Size Matter?" Scientific American, January 1, 2016. https://www.scientificamerican.com/article/does–brain–size–matter1/.
Koenig, H. G. "Religion, Spirituality, and Medicine: Research Findings and Implications for Clinical Practice," *Southern Medical Journal* 97, no. 12 (2004): 1194–1200.
Kolawole, Mary M. *Womanism and African Consciousness.* Trenton: Africa World, 1997.
Kolo, Jerry. "The Knowledge Economy: Concept, Global Trends and Strategic Challenges for Africa in the Quest for Sustainable Development." *International Journal Technology Management* 5, no. 1/2 (2009): 27–49.
Kozak, A. "Postmodern Changes in Marital and Family Life." *Journal of Education Culture and Society* (2011).
Kukolova, Monika. "Rethinking Representations of Identity in Contemporary Francophone West African Cinemas." PhD diss., University of Manchester, 2018.
Kunene, Mazisi. "Problems in African Literature." *Research in African Literatures* 23, no. 1 (1992): 27–44.
Langer, K. Susanne. "Language and Thought." In *The Human Perspective*, edited by Richard A. Alden, 23–31. California: CAT, 1988.
Lawrence, Bonita, and Enakshi Dua. "Decolonizing Antiracism." *Social Justice* 32, no. 4 (2005).
Le Gendre, Kevin. "Hip-Hop with Harps." The Guardian, February 15, 2008. https://www.theguardian.com/music/2008/feb/15/worldmusic.urban.
Le Silence de la Forêt. Directed by Didier Ouenangare and Bassek Ba Kobhio. Central African Republic, Cameroon, Gabon, France: Écrans Noirs, Nord–Express Productions, Centre National du Cinéma et de l'Image Animée, Films Terre Africaine, 2003.

Lee, Patrick, Samson Koromo, Julio Mercader, and Charles Mather. "Scientific Facts and Oral Traditions in Oldupai Gorge, Tanzania: Symmetrically Analysing Palaeoanthropological and Maasai Black Boxes." *Social Science Information* 58, no. 1 (2019): 57–83.

Lee, Tanya. "Fifty Years Later Native American Studies Still Evolving: 6 New Programs." *Indian Country Today,* May 21, 2014. https://newsmaven.io/indiancountrytoday/archive/50-years-later-native-american-studies-still-evolving-6-new-programs-VKG7SD29zU2thMVcvpBvyw/.

Leguy, Cécile, and Ruthmarie Mitsch. "Revitalizing the Oral Tradition: Stories Broadcast by Radio Parana (San, Mali)." *Research in African Literatures* 38, no. 3 (2007): 136–47.

Leiss, William. *The Domination of Nature*. Boston: Beacon, 1974.

Leong, Russell, ed. *Orientalism and the Legacy of Edward Said*. Asian American Studies Center Press, University of California, Los Angeles, 2005.

Lévi-Strauss, Claude. "The Structural Study of Myth." *Journal of American Folklore* 68, no. 270 (1955): 428–44.

Lewis, Desiree. "African Feminist Studies: 1980–2002." Review Essay for the African Gender Institute's "Strengthening Gender and Women's Studies for Africa's Social Transformation" Project. www.gwsafrica.org/knowledge/africa.

———. "African Gender Research and Postcoloniality: Legacies and Challenges." *African Gender Studies: A Reader* (2005): 381–95.

Lincoln, Yvonna, and Elsa González y González. "The Search for Emerging Decolonizing Methodologies in Qualitative Research: Further Strategies for Liberatory and Democratic Inquiry." *Qualitative Inquiry* 14, no. 5 (2008): 784–805.

Lindroth, James Daniel. "Zimbabwean Mbira Music and Modern Spirituality in the Western United States." MA thesis, Ohio State University, 2018.

Linnaeus, Carolus. *Systema Naturae*. Stockholm: Bokförlag Rediviva, 1758.

Love, Stephanie. "Decolonizing the Church/Decolonizing Language: Postcolonial Christianity, Language Ideologies, and the Morality of Teaching Vernacular Arabic (Darija) in Algeria." *Journal of Language, Identity & Education* 18, no. 1 (2019): 25–38.

Lloyd, Brown W. "The African Woman as Writer." *Canadian Journal of African Studies* 9, no. 3 (1975): 493–501.

Lord, Albert Bates. *Epic Singers and Oral Tradition*. Ithaca and London: Cornell University Press, 1991.

Luis, Lugo. "Tolerance and Tension: Islam and Christianity in Sub–Saharan Africa." Washington, DC, Pew Research Center 147 (2010).

Lusimbo, Richard, and Oguaghamba, Akudo. "Pan Africa ILGA Annual Report 2016–2017." *British Journal of Political Science* (2019): 1–20.

Luttmann, Ilsemargret. "Fashion and Fashion Development in Africa: An Introduction to the Main Research Fields." *Research Gate* (2010).

Madhok, Sumi. "Coloniality, Political Subjectivation and the Gendered Politics of Protest in a 'State of Exception.'" *Feminist Review* 119, no. 1 (2018): 56–71.

Mafeje, Archie. "Africanity: A Combative Ontology." *CODESRIA Bulletin* 1 (2000): 66–61.

———. "Africanity: A Commentary by Way of Conclusion." *CODESRIA Bulletin* 3/4 (2001): 14–16.

———. *Anthropology in Post–Independence Africa: End of an Era or the Problem Self–Redefinition*. Nairobi: Heinrich Boll Foundation, 2001.

———. "On the Articulation of Modes of Production." Journal of Southern African Studies 8, no. 1 (1981).

———. "Soweto and its Aftermath." *Review of African Political Economy* 5, no. 11 (1978): 17–18.

———. *The Theory and Ethnography of African Social Formations: The Case of the Interlacustrine Kingdoms*. Dakar: CODESRIA Book Series, 1991.

Makoni, Munyaradzi. "The Limitations of the Decolonization 'Moments.'" University World News, December 15, 2017. https://www.universityworldnews.com/post.php?story=20171215123042991.

Maldonado-Torres, Nelson. "On the Coloniality of Being." *Cultural Studies* 21, no. 2 (2007): 240–70.

———. "Thinking Through the Decolonial Turn: Post–Continental Interventions in Theory, Philosophy, and Critique – An Introduction." *Transmodernity: Journal of Peripheral Cultural Production of the Luso-Hispanic World* 1, no. 2 (2011): 1–15.

Malkmus, L., and R. Armes. *Arab and African Film Making*. London: Zed, 1992.

Mama, Amina. "Challenging Subjects: Gender and Power in African Contexts." *African Sociological Review* 5, no. 2 (2001): 63–73.

———. "Challenging Subjects: Gender and Power in African Contexts." In *Identity and Beyond: Rethinking Africanity*, edited by Suleymane Diagne, Amina Mama, Henning Melber, and Francis Nyamnjoh. Uppsala: Nordic Africa Institute, 2001.

———. "Is It Ethical to Study Africa? Preliminary Thoughts on Scholarship and Freedom." *African Studies Review* 50, no. 1 (2007): 1–26.

———. "Shedding the Masks and Tearing the Veils: Towards a Gendered Approach to African Culture." Paper, CODESRIA Workshop on Gender Analysis and African Social Science, Dakar, Senegal, 1991.

———. *Women Studies and Studies of Women in Africa During the 1990s*. Dakar: CODESRIA, 1996.

Mama, Amina, and Margo Okazawa-Rey. "Militarism, Conflict and Women's Activism in the Global Era: Challenges and Prospects for Women in Three West African Contexts." *Feminist Review* 101 (2012): 97–123.

Mamdani, Mahmood. "Between the Public Intellectual and the Scholar: Decolonization and Some Post-Independence Initiatives in African Higher Education." *Inter-Asia Cultural Studies* 17, no. 1 (2016): 68–83.

———. "Is African Studies a New Home for Bantu Education?" Remarks, the Seminar on the African Core of the Foundation Course for the Faculty of Social Sciences and Humanities, University of Cape Town, Cape Town, South Africa, 1998.

Mandara, Jelani, Noni Gaylord-Harden, Maryse Richards, and Brian Ragsdale. "The Effects of Changes in Racial Identity and Self-Esteem on Changes in African American Adolescents' Mental Health." *Child Development* 80, no. 6 (2009): 1660–75.

Mandela, Nelson. *Nelson Mandela's Favorite African Folktales*. New York: Norton, 2002.

Mapaya, Madimabe Geoff. "Indigenous Language as a Tool in African Musicology: The Road to Self-Assertiveness." *South African Journal of African Languages* 34 (2014): 29–34.

Mark, Andrew. "The Sole Mbira: An Ecomusicological Critique of Singularity and North American Zimbabwean Music." *Canadian Journal of Cultural Studies* (2017): 157–88.

Martin, Douglas. "Ali Mazrui, Scholar of Africa Who Divided U.S. Audiences, Dies at 81." *New York Times*, October 20, 2014. https://www.nytimes.com/2014/10/22/us/ali-mazrui-scholar-of-africa-who-divided-us-audiences-dies-at-81.html.

Masaka, Dennis. "The Prospects of Ending Epistemicide in Africa: Some Thoughts." *Journal of Black Studies* 49, no. 3 (2018): 284–301.

Mason, Ronald. "Archaeology and Native North American Oral Traditions." *American Antiquity* 65, no. 2 (2000): 239–66.

Matthews, Basil. *Black Treasure: The Youth of Africa in a Changing World*. New York: Friendship Press, 1928.

Maton, Karl. "Progress and Canons in the Arts and Humanities: Knowers and Gazes." In *Social Realism, Knowledge and the Sociology of Education: Coalitions of the Mind*, edited by Rob Moore and Karl Maton. London: Continuum, 2010.

Maulana, Karenga. "Founding the First PhD in Black Studies: A Sankofa Remembrance and Critical Assessment of Its Significance." *Journal of Black Studies* 49, no. 6 (2018): 576–603.

Mawere, Munyaradzi, and Tapuwa R. Mubaya. *African Philosophy and Thought Systems: A Search for a Culture and Philosophy of Belonging*. Cameroon: Langaa Research and Publishing Common Initiative Group, 2016.

Mayr, Ernst. *The Growth of Biological Thought*. Cambridge, MA: Harvard University Press, 1981.

Mazama, Ama. "African American Studies: The First Doctoral Program." In *Encyclopedia of Black Studies*, edited by Molefi Asante and Ama Mazama, 24–28. Thousand Oaks: SAGE, 2005.

———. "The Afrocentric Paradigm: Contours and Definitions." *Journal of Black Studies* 31 (2001): 387–405.

———. "Eurocentric Discourse on Writing: An Exercise in Self Clarification." *Journal of Black Studies* 29, no.1 (1998): 3–16.

Mazrui, Ali. *English in Africa After the Cold War*. New York: Multilingual Matters, 2004.

———. "European Exploration and Africa's Self–Discovery." *Journal of Modern African Studies* 7, no. 4 (1969): 661–76.

———. "Islam Between Clash and Concord of Civilizations: Changing Relations Between the Muslim World and the United States." Speech, Chatham House Meeting Record, January 16, 2007. https://www.chathamhouse.org/sites/default/files/public/Research/Arica/160107mazrui.pdf.

———. *The Political Sociology of the English Language: An African Perspective*. Berlin: Walter de Gruyter GmbH & Co KG, 2019.

———. *Political Values and Educated Class in Africa*. Berkeley: University of California Press, 1978.

———. "Towards Re–Africanizing African Universities: Who Killed Intellectualism in the Post-Colonial Era?" *Alternatives, Turkish Journal of International Relations* 2, no. 3–4 (2003).

Mba, Nina. *Nigerian Women Mobilized: Women's Political Activity in Southern Nigeria, 1900–1965*. Berkeley: Institute of International Studies, UC Berkeley, 1982.

Mbembe, Joseph. "Decolonizing the University: New Directions." *Arts & Humanities in Higher Education* 15, no. 1 (2016): 29–45.

McCall, John C. "The Pan-Africanism We Have: Nollywood's Invention of Africa." *Film International* 5, no. 4 (2007).

McCarthy, Teresa. "Empowering Indigenous Languages—What Can Be Learned from Native American Experiences?" In *Social Justice Through Multilingual Education*, edited by Tove Skutnabb-Kangas, Robert Phillipson, Ajit K. Mohanty, and Mianti Panda, 125–139. Buffalo: Multilingual Matters, 2009.

McCracken, John. "African History in British Universities: Past, Present, and Future." *African Affairs* 92 (1993): 239–53.

McDermott, Gerald. *Anansi the Spider: A Tale from the Ashanti*. New York: Holt, Rinehart and Winston, 1971.

McDougal, Serie. "Africana Studies' Epistemic Identity: An Analysis of Theory and Epistemology in the Discipline." *Journal of African American Studies* 18, no. 2 (2014): 236–50.

McFadden, Patricia. "African Feminist Perspectives of Post-Coloniality." *Black Scholar* 37, no. 1 (2007): 36–42.

McGreal, Chris. "Thanks China, Now Go Home: Buy–Up of Zambia Revives Old Colonial Fears." *Guardian*, February 5, 2007. https://www.theguardian.com/world/2007/feb/05/china.chrismcgreal.

Medie, Peace. "Women's and Feminists Activism in West Africa." 2016. http://www.researchgate.net/publication/303675840.

Mei, Zeng. "A Distinctive, Charming and Colorful Movement: African Epic Traditions." *Foreign Literature Studies* 28, no. 5 (2006): 150–57.

Merchant, Roland, Artemio Jongco III, and Luke Woodward. "Disclosure of Sexual Orientation by Medical Students and Residency Applicants." *Academic Medicine* 80, no. 8 (2005): 786.

Meyer, H. "Prejudice, Social Stress, and Mental Health in Lesbian, Gay, and Bisexual Populations: Conceptual Issues and Research Evidence." *Psychological Bulletin* 129, no. 5 (2003): 674.

Michrina, Barry. "Reflexive Ethnography: A Guide to Researching Selves and Others; Decolonizing Methodologies: Research and Indigenous Peoples." *Journal of the American Ethnological Society* 27, no. 1 (2008): 212–14.

Mignolo, Walter D. "Coloniality at Large: Knowledge at the Late Stage of the Modern/Colonial World System." *Journal of Iberian Research* 5, no. 2 (1999): 1–10.

———. "Coloniality Is Far from Over, and So Must Be Decoloniality." *Afterall: A Journal of Art, Context and Enquiry* 43, no. 1 (2017): 38–45.

———. "Cosmopolitanism and the De-Colonial Option." *Studies in Philosophy and Education* 29, no. 2 (2010): 111–27.

———. *The Darker Side of the Renaissance: Literacy, Territoriality, and Colonization.* Ann Arbor: University of Michigan Press, 1995.

———. *The Darker Side of Western Modernity: Global Futures De–Colonial Options.* Durham, NC: Duke University Press, 2011.

———. "Delinking: The Rhetoric of Modernity, the Logic of Coloniality and the Grammar of De-coloniality." *Cultural Studies* 21, no. 2–3 (2007): 449–514.

———. "Epistemic Disobedience, Independent Thought and Decolonial Freedom." *Theory, Culture & Society* 26, no. 7–8 (2009): 159–81.

———. "I Think Where I Am: Epistemology and the Colonial Difference." *Journal of Latin America Culture Studies: TRAVESIA* 8, no. 2 (1999): 234–45.

———. *Local Histories/Global Designs: Coloniality, Subaltern Knowledges, and Border Thinking.* Princeton, NJ: Princeton University Press, 2000.

———. "Prophets Facing Sideways: The Geopolitics of Knowledge and the Colonial Difference." *Social Epistemology: A Journal of Knowledge, Culture and Policy* 19, no. 1 (2006): 111–27.

———. "Putting the Americas on the Map: Geography and the Colonization of Space." *Colonial Latin American Review* 1, no. 1–2 (1992): 25–63.

Miller, Seumas, and Ian Macdonald. "The Role of Philosophy in South Africa." *Theoria: A Journal of Social and Political Theory* 73 (1989): 11–18.

Miranda-Mendizabal, A. "Sexual Orientation and Suicidal Behaviour in Adolescents and Young Adults: Systematic Review and Meta-Analysis." *British Journal of Psychiatry* 211, no. 2 (2017): 77–87

Mirra, Carl. "Countering Militarism Through Peace Education." *Encyclopedia of Peace Education* (2008): 93–98.

Mittelman, James. "A Better Intellectual Community Is Possible: Dialogues with Ali A. Mazrui." *African Studies Review* 57, no. 1 (2014): 153–70.

Mkhize, S. P. and Maharaj, P. "Meeting the Sexual Health Needs of LGBT Youth: Perceptions and Experiences of University Students in KwaZulu-Natal, South Africa." *Journal of Social Service Research* (2020): 1–17.

Mohamedbhai, Goolam. "Massification in Higher Education Institution in Africa: Causes, Consequences and Response." *International Journal of African Higher Education* 1, no. 1 (2014).

Mohammed, Razinatu. "Maternal Oppression of the Girl-Child in Selected Novels by Buchi Emecheta." *An International Multi–Disciplinary Journal*, Ethiopia 4, no. 2 (2010): 462–70.

Mohanty, Chandra. *Feminism Without Borders: Decolonizing Theory, Practicing Solidarity*. Durham, NC, and London: Duke University Press, 2003.

———. "Under Western Eyes." In *Third World Women and the Politics of Feminism*, edited by Chandra Mohanty, D. Russo, and L. Torres. Bloomington: Indiana University Press, 1991.

Moon, John Stanley. "African Children's Games." *Skipping Stones* 17, no. 3 (2005).

Moore, Gerald. "The Imagery of Death in African Poetry." *Africa* 38, no. 1–3 (1968): 57–70.

Moreira, Claudio and Marcelo Diversi. *Betweener Talk: Decolonizing Knowledge Production, Pedagogy, and Praxis*. Walnut Creek: Left Coast, 2009.

———. "Betweeners Speak Up: Challenging Knowledge Production Through Collaborative Writing and Visceral Knowledge in Decolonizing Times." *International Review of Qualitative Research* 5, no. 4 (2012): 399–406.

———. "Missing Bodies: Troubling the Colonial Landscape of American Academia." *Text and Performance Quarterly* 31, no. 3 (2011): 229–48.

Morgan, E. "Contemporary Issues in Sexual Orientation and Identity Development in Emerging Adulthood." *Emerging Adulthood* 1, no. 1 (2013): 52–66.

Morgenson, Scott. "Destabilizing the Settler Academy: The Decolonial Effects of Indigenous Methodologies." *American Quarterly* 64, no. 4 (2012): 805–8.

Morreira, Shannon. "Steps Towards Decolonial Higher Education in Southern Africa? Epistemic Disobedience in the Humanities." *Journal of Asian and African Studies* 52, no. 3 (2017): 287–301.

Morris, R. B. Seven *Who Shaped Our Destiny: The Founding Fathers as Revolutionaries*. New York: Harper and Row, 1973.

Morris, Rosalind, ed., *Can the Subaltern Speak? Reflections on the History of an Idea*. New York: Columbia University Press, 2010.

Motsoko, Pheko. "Effects of Colonialism on Africa's Past and Present." *Pambazuka News*, May 31, 2012. https://www.pambazuka.org/global-south/effects-colonialism-africas-past-and-present.

Mudimbe, Valentin. *The Invention of Africa: Gnosis, Philosophy, and the Order of Knowledge*. Bloomington: Indiana University Press, 1998.

Muller, Alex. "Scrambling for Access: Availability, Accessibility, Acceptability and Quality of Healthcare for Lesbian, Gay, Bisexual and Transgender People in South Africa." *BMC International Health and Human Rights* 17, no. 1 (2017): 16.

Murphy, Joseph. "Environment and Imperialism: Why Colonialism Still Matters." *Sustainability Research Institute* 20 (2009): 1–27.

Murr, Rachel. "'I Became Proud of Being Gay and Proud of Being Christian': The Spiritual Journeys of Queer Christian Women." *Journal of Religion and Spirituality in Social Work: Social Thought* 32, no. 4 (2013): 349–72.
Murrell, Peter. "Chartering the Village: The Making of an African-Centered Charter School." *Urban Education* 33, no. 5 (1999): 565–83.
Nadaswaran, Shalini. "The Legacy of Buchi Emecheta in Nigerian Women's Fiction." *International Journal of Social Science and Humanity* 2, no. 2 (2012): 146–50.
Naylor, Lindsay, Michelle Daigle, Sofia Zaragocin, Margaret Marietta Ramírez, and Mary Gilmartin. "Interventions: Bringing the Decolonial to Political Geography." *Political Geography* 66 (2018): 199–209.
Na'Allah, Abdul-Rasheed. *Globalization, Oral Performance, and African Traditional Poetry.* Cham: Palgrave Macmillan, 2018.
Nabudere, Dani. "Archie Mafeje and the Social Sciences in Africa." *CODESRIA Bulletin* 3–4 (2008): 8–10.
———. "Ubuntu Philosophy Memory and Reconciliation." *Texas Scholar Works* (2005): 1–20.
Nations Online. "Official and Spoken Languages of African Countries." Nations Online, n.d. https://www.nationsonline.org/oneworld/african_languages.html.
Ndimande, Bekisizwe. "Decolonizing Research in Post-Apartheid South Africa: The Politics of Methodology." *Qualitative Inquiry* 18 (2012): 215–26.
———. "Unraveling the Neocolonial Epistemologies: Decolonizing Research Toward Transformative Literacy." *Journal of Literacy Research* 50, no. 3 (2018): 383–90.
Ndlovu-Gatsheni, Sabelo. "A World Without Others? Specter of Difference and Toxic Identitarian Politics." *International Journal of Critical Diversity Studies* 1, no. 1 (2018): 80–96.
———. "Ali A. Mazrui on the Invention of Africa and Postcolonial Predicaments: 'My Life Is One Long Debate.'" *Third World Quarterly* 36, no. 2 (2015): 205–22.
———. "The Cognitive Empire, Politics of Knowledge and African Intellectual Productions: Reflections on Struggles for Epistemic Freedom and Resurgence of Decolonization in the Twenty-First Century." *Third World Quarterly* (2020): 1–20.
———. *Coloniality of Power in Post-Colonial Africa: Myths of Decolonization.* Dakar: CODESRIA, 2013.
———. "The Decolonial Mandela." *Journal of Developing Societies* 31, no. 3 (2015): 305–32.
———. *The Decolonial Mandela: Peace, Justice and the Politics of Life.* New York: Berghahn, 2016.
———. "Decoloniality as the Future of Africa: Decoloniality, Africa, Power, Knowledge, Being." *History Compass* 13, no. 10 (2015): 485–96.
———. "Decolonising the University in Africa." *Thinker* 51 (2013): 46–51.

———. "The Emergence and Trajectories of Struggles for an 'African University': The Case of Unfinished Business of African Epistemic Decolonization." *Kronos* 43, no. 1 (2017): 51–77.

———. *Empire, Global Coloniality and African Subjectivity*. New York: Berghahn, 2013.

———. "The Entrapment of Africa Within the Global Colonial Matricies of Power." *Journal of Developing Societies* 29, no. 4 (2013): 331–53.

———. "Genealogies of Coloniality and Implications for Africa's Development." *Africa Development/Afrique Et Développement* 40, no. 3 (2015): 13–40.

———. "Global Coloniality and the Challenges of Creating African Futures." *Strategic Review for Southern Africa* 36, no. 2 (2014): 182–202.

———. "Nationality of Power in Zimbabwe." In *Empire, Global Coloniality and African Subjectivity*, 156–166. New York: Berghahn, 2015.

———. "Power, Knowledge and Being: Decolonial Combative Discourse as a Survival Kit for Pan-Africanists in the 21st Century." *Alteration* 20, no. 1 (2013): 105–34.

———. "Revisiting the African Renaissance." In *Oxford Research Encyclopaedia of Politics*. Oxford: Oxford University Press. https://oxfordre.com/politics/view/10.1093/acrefore/9780190228637.001.0001/acrefore-9780190228637-720.

———. "Subjection and Subjectivity in South Africa." In *Empire, Global Coloniality and African Subjectivity*, 132–55. New York: Berghahn, 2015.

———. "When Did the Masks of Coloniality Begin to Fall? Decolonial Reflections on the Bandung Spirit of Decolonization." *Bandung* 6, no. 2 (2019): 210–32.

———. "Why Are South African Universities Sites of Struggle Today?" *Thinker* 70 (2016): 52–61.

———. "Why Decoloniality in the 21st Century." *Thinker* 48, no. 10 (2013): 10–15.

Ndlovu-Gatsheni, Sabelo, and Busani Mpofu, eds. "The End of Development and the Rise of Decoloniality as the Future." *In Rethinking and Unthinking Development: Perspectives on Inequality and Poverty in South Africa and Zimbabwe*. New York: Berghahn, 2019.

Neuberger Museum of Art. "Helmet Mask." Accessed August 5, 2019. https://www.neuberger.org/africanArtDetail.php?pid=89&catname=MASKS+AND+MASQUERADES.

News24. "Outrage Over Zuma's Africa Utterances." News24, October 23, 2013. http://www.citypress.co.za/politics/maharaj-apologises-withdraws-zumas-malawi-comments.

NewsClickin. "Samir Amin and Socialism in the 21st Century." YouTube video, 43:46. May 14, 2012. https://www.youtube.com/watch?v=RSvk8lms7Co.

Nii-Boye Quarshie, Emmanuel. "Self-Harm and Suicidal Behavior Among LGBTQ+ Young People: An Overlooked Public Mental Health Issue in Africa." *International Journal of Social Psychiatry* (2020).

Nkealah, Naomi. "Conceptualizing Feminism(s) in Africa: The Challenges Facing African Women Writers and Critics." *English Academy Review: Southern African Journal of English Studies* 134 (2006): 133–41.

———. "(West) African Feminisms and their Challenges." *Journal of Literary Studies* 32, no. 2 (2016): 61–74.

Nkrumah, Kwame. *Towards Colonial Freedom*. London: African Publication Society, 1962.

———. *Consciencism Philosophy and the Ideology for Decolonization*. New York: New York Press, 1964.

Nnaemeka, Obioma. "Bringing African Women into the Classroom: Rethinking Pedagogy and Epistemology." In *African Gender Studies: A Reader*, edited by Oyeronke Oyewumi. New York: Palgrave Macmillan, 2005.

———. "Feminism Rebellious Women, and Cultural Boundaries: Rereading Flora Nwapa and Her Compatriots." *Research in African Literatures*, no. 83 (1995): 80–113.

———. *From Orality to Writing; African Women Writers and the (Re)Inscription of Womanhood*. Bloomington: Indiana University Press, 1994.

———. "Introduction: Reading the Rainbow." In *Sisterhood, Feminisms, and Power: From Africa to the Diaspora*, edited by Obioma Nnaemeka. Trenton: Africa World, 1998.

———. "Nego–Feminism: Theorizing, Practicing, and Pruning Africa's Way." Signs: Journal of *Women in Culture and Society*, no. 376 (2004): 357–85.

———. Nsengimana, John Phibert. "How Africa Wins the 4th Industrial Revolution." *Forbes*, October 10, 2018. https://www.forbes.com/sites/startupnationcentral/2018/10/10/how-africa-wins-the-4th-industrial-revolution/#72d785e02f37.

Ntsebeza, Lungisile. "What Can We Learn from Archie Mafeje About the Road to Democracy in South Africa?" *Development and Change* 47, no. 4 (2016): 918–36.

Nuruddin, Yusuf. "Africana Studies: Which Way Forward—Marxism or Afrocentricity? Neither Mechanical Marxism Nor Atavistic Afrocentrism." *Socialism and Democracy* 25, no. 1 (2011): 93–125.

Nwabueze, Emeka. *Visions and Revisions: Selected Discourses on Literary Criticism*. Enugu: Abic, 2003.

Nwapa, Flora. *Efuru*. London: Heinemann, 1966.

Nyamnjoh, Francis. "Decolonizing the University in Africa." In *Oxford Research Encyclopedia of Politics*. Oxford: Oxford University Press, 2020. https://oxfordre.com/politics/view/10.1093/acrefore/9780190228637.001.0001/acrefore-9780190228637-717.

———. "From Publish or Perish to Publish and Perish: What 'Africa's 100 Best Books' Tell Us About Publishing Africa." *Journal of Asian and African Studies* 39, no. 5 (2004): 331–55.

Nyerere, Julius. *Ujamaa, Essays on Socialism*. Dar Es Salaam: Oxford University Press, 1986.

Nyoka, Bongani. "Mafeje and 'Authentic Interlocutors': An Appraisal of His Epistemology." *African Sociological Review/Revue Africaine de Sociologie* 16, no. 1 (2012): 4–18.

Obaji, Agbiji M., and Ignatius Swart. "Religion and Social Transformation in Africa: A Critical and Appreciative Perspective." *Scriptura* 114 (2015).

Obayemi, M. Ade. "The Phenomenon of Oduduwa in Ife History." In *The Cradle of a Race: Ife from the Beginning to 1980*, edited by I. A. Akinjogbin. Port Harcourt: Sunray, 1978.

Obonye, Jonas. "The Practice of Polygamy under the Scheme of the Protocol to the African Charter on Human and Peoples' Rights on the Rights of Women in Africa: A Critical Appraisal." *Journal of African Studies and Development* 4, no. 5 (2012): 142–49.

Odejide, Abiola. "Profile of Women's Research and Documentation Centre, Institute of African Studies, University of Ibadan, Nigeria." *Feminist Africa* (2002): 100–107.

Odey, O. Mike, John G. Nengel, and Okpeh O. Okpeh. *History Research and Methodology in Africa: Essays in Honor of Professor Charles Creswell Jacobs*. Markurdi: Aboki, 2007.

OECD/FAO. "Agriculture in Sub-Saharan Africa: Prospects and Challenges for the Next Decade." In *OECD-FAO Agricultural Outlook 2016–2025*. Paris: OECD, 2016.

Offen, Karen. "Defining Feminism: A Comparative Historical Approach." *Signs: Journal of Women in Culture and Society*, no. 14 (1988): 119–57.

Ogot, Bethwell, ed. Africa from the Sixteenth to the Eighteen Century. Vol. 5 of UNESCO *General History of Africa*. California: Heinemann, 1992.

Ogundipe-Leslie, Molara. "African Literature, Feminism and Social Change." *Malatu*, no. 23 (2001): 307–322.

———. "The Female Writer and Her Commitment." *African Literature Today*, no. 9 (1987): 5–13.

———. *Re-Creating Ourselves: African Women and Critical Transformations*. Trenton: Africa World, 1994.

Okagbue, Osita. *African Theatres and Performances*. New York: Routledge, 2007.

———. "Koteba (kote-tlon): Comedy and Satire of the Bamana." *African Theatres and Performances*. Abingdon, UK, and New York: Routledge, 2013.

Okara, Gabriel. "African Speech: English Words." *Transition* 10 (1963): 15–16.

Okebukola, Peter. *The State of University Education in Nigeria*. Abuja: National University Commission, 2002.

Okech, Anthony. "Multilingual Literacies as a Resource." *Adult Education and Development* (2002): 117–125.

Okeke, A. "Traditional Education in Igboland." *Journal of Igbo Language and Culture* 2 (1982): 15–26.

Okorobia, Mark. "The Neglect of History and Historical Scholarship in Nigeria as a Root of the Nation's Underdevelopment." Paper, International Conference on 'Nigeria at 50: Grappling with Governance, 1960–2010' by the Committee on Nigeria's Golden Jubilee Independence Anniversary, Abuja, Nigeria, September 26–29, 2010.

Okoth, Edwin. "Kenya: SGR Pact with China a Risk to Kenyan Sovereignty Assets." Nation, January 12, 2019. https://nation.africa/kenya/news/sgr-pact-with-china-a-risk-to-kenyan-sovereignty-assets-127328.

Oladejo, Mutiat. "Female Historians and Knowledge Production for Women's Studies: The Nigerian Example Since 1974." *International Journal of Gender and Women* 6, no. 1 (2018): 30–37.

Olaiya, Taiwo A. "Narrative of Governance Crisis in Nigeria: Allegories of Resource Curse and 'Emergence' from Tunde Kelani's Saworoide and Agogo-Èèwo." https://pdfs.semanticscholar.org/7853/54ec95750b1148b7ba2562b19419245afb3b.pdf.

Olatunji, O. Olatunde. *Features of Yoruba Oral Poetry*. Ibadan: Ibadan University Press, 2005.

Olayinka, Idowu. "The First Semester 2017/2018 Session Examination Results: Commendation and Recommendation." Accessed on July 23, 2020. https://web.facebook.com/idowu.olayinka.378/posts/2016351165054031.

———. "2016/2017 Sessional Examination Results and Matters Arising." Accessed on July 23, 2020. https://web.facebook.com/idowu.olayinka.378/posts/1758807610808389.

Olayinka, Wunmi. "The Oppressor Is Oppressed and in a Pathological State Too: Calix the Beyala and Buchi Emecheta's Male Characters." In *Language Literature and Criticism*, edited by Emmanuel N. Kwofie, and Babatunde Ayeleru. Ibadan: Zenith Book House, 2010.

Olukoshi, Adebayo, Lionel Cliffe, Peter Lawrence, and Katherine Salahi. "A Tribute to Archie Mafeje 1937–2007. A Giant Has Moved On." *Review of African Political Economy* 34, no. 112 (2007): 395–99.

Olorunyomi, Sola. *Afrobeat! Fela and the Imagined Continent*. Ibadan: IFRA, 2005.

Omolewa, Michael. "Educating the 'Native': A Study of the Education Adaptation Strategy in British Colonial Africa, 1910–1936." *The Journal of African American History* 91, no. 3 (2006): 267–287.

Omotoso, Kole. *Achebe or Soyinka? A Study in Contrasts*. Ibadan: Bookcraft, 2009.

Ong, Walter. *Orality and Literacy*. London: Routledge, 2013.

———. *Orality and Literacy: Technologizing of the Word*. New York: Routledge, 2002.

Online Etymology Dictionary. "Hunt." Online Etymology Dictionary, n.d. https://www.etymonline.com/word/hunt.

Onwuchekwa, Chinweizu, and Jemie Ihechukwu Madubuike. "Towards the Decolonization of African Literature." *Transition* 48 (1975): 29–57.

Opara, Chioma. "On the African Concept of Transcendence: Conflating Nature, Nurture and Creativity." *International Journal of Philosophy and Religion*, no. 11 (2005): 189–200.

Ortega, Mariana. "Decolonial Woes and Practices of Un-Knowing." *The Journal of Speculative Philosophy* 31, no. 3 (2017): 504–16.

Overton, John. "Decolonizing Methodologies: Research and Indigenous Peoples." *Development in Practice* 23, no. 4 (2013): 598–99.

Owino, Meshack. "'What Have We, Jo-Ugenya, Not Done? We Have Even Killed an Arab/Swahili Hermaphrodite': Constructing a History of the Jo-Ugenya-Arab/Swahili War by Means of a Saying." In *Africanizing Knowledge: African Studies Across the Disciplines*, edited by Toyin Falola and Christian Jennings, 103–124. New Brunswick and London: Transaction, 2002.

Owomoyela, Oyekan. "Language, Identity, and Social Construction in African Literature." *Research in African Literature* 23, no. 1 (1992): 83–94.

———, ed. "The Question of Language in African Literatures." *A History of Twentieth Century African Literatures*. Lincoln: University of Nebraska Press, 1993.

Owusu-Acheampong, Kwame. "The Adventures of Ananse the Trickster."Ananse Stories. http://www.anansethetrickster.com/ananse-stories.

Oyewumi, Oyeronke. "Conceptualizing Gender: The Eurocentric Foundations of Feminist Concepts and the Challenge of African Epistemologies." *Paper, CODESRIA Conference on African Gender in the New Millennium*, Cairo, Egypt, April 7–10, 2002.

———. "Decolonizing the Intellectual and the Quotidian: Yorùbá Scholars(hip) and Male Dominance." *Gender Epistemologies in Africa: Gendering Traditions, Spaces, Social Institutions, and Identities*. New York: Palgrave Macmillan, 2011.

———, ed. *Gender Epistemologies in Africa: Gendering Traditions, Spaces, Social Institutions, and Identities*. New York: Palgrave Macmillan, 2010.

———. *The Invention of Women: Making an African Sense of Western Gender Discourses*. Minneapolis: University of Minnesota Press, 1997.

Page, Robert Le. "Acts of Identity." *English Today* 8 (1986).

Parry, Milman, and Adam Parry, eds. *The Making of Homeric Verse: The Collected Papers of Milman Parry*. Oxford: Oxford University Press, 1987.

Passchier, Shmerah. "Lessons from New Nollywood: A Theory from the Global South." MA thesis, University of the Witwatersrand, 2014.

Patnaik, Prabhat, Jayati Ghosh, and C. P. Chandrasekhar. "In Memoriam: Samir Amin." International Development Economic Associates, September 1, 2018. http://www.networkideas.org/news–analysis/2018/09/obituary-samir-amin-1931-2018/.

Pattberg, Philipp. "Conquest, Domination and Control: Europe's Mastery of Nature in Historic Perspective." *Journal of Political Ecology* 14 (2007): 1–9.

Perdiagao, Yovanka Paquette. "Flora Nwapa and the African Woman's Struggle to Identify as Feminist." *The Nzinga Effect*, 2017.

Peters, Jonathan. "English Language Fiction in West Africa." In *A History of Twentieth Century African Literatures*, edited by Oyekan Owomoyela, 9–48. Lincoln: University of Nebraska Press, 1993.

Pietsch, Tamson. "Empire and Higher Education Internationalisation." *University World News* 20, no. 282 (2013).

Pillay, Navanethem. "Homophobia: The Violence of Intolerance." Africa Renewal. Accessed September 29, 2021, https://www.un.org/africarenewal/web-features/homophobia-violence-intolerance.

Pillay, Suren. "Decolonizing the University." *Africa Is a Country*, June 2015. https://africasacountry.com/2015/06/decolonizing-the-university.

Plato. *The Republic*. New York: Books, Inc., 1943.

Pindi, Gloria. "Beyond Labels: Envisioning an Alliance Between African Feminism and Queer Theory for the Empowerment of African Sexual Minorities Within and Beyond Africa." *Women's Studies in Communication* 43, no. 2 (2020): 106–12.

Poblete, Johanna. "Golden Rule." *Business World*, 2009.

Popkin, Richard. "The Philosophical Basis of Modern Racism." In *Philosophy and the Civilizing Arts*, edited by Craig Walton and John Anton. Athens: Ohio University Press, 1974.

Popper, Karl. *Conjectures and Refutations. The Growth of Scientific Knowledge*. New York: Basic Books, 1962.

Power, Jess E., David J. Tyler, and P. L. P. Disele. "Conserving and Sustaining Culture Through Traditional Dress." *Journal of Social Development in Africa* 26, no. 1 (2011).

Prasad, Pushkala. *Crafting Qualitative Research: Working in the Postpositive Traditions*. London: Routledge, 2005.

Price, Sally. *Primitive Art in Civilized Places*. Chicago: University of Chicago Press, 1984.

Pui Lan, Kwok. "Mercy Amba Oduyoye and African Women's Theology." *Journal of Feminist Studies in Religion* 20, no. 1 (2004): 7–22.

Quijano, Anibal. "Coloniality and Modernity/Rationality." *Cultural Studies* 21, no. 2–3 (2007): 168–78.

Quijano, Anibal, and Michael Ennis. *Coloniality of Power, Eurocentrism and Latin America*. Nepaulta: Duke University Press, 2000.

Radu, Sinita. "Africa Braces for the Fourth Industrial Revolution." *US News and World Report*, January 23, 2020. https://www.usnews.com/news/best-countries/articles/2020-01-23/the-stakes-for-africa-in-the-fourth-industrial-revolution.

Ramos, Mary, et al. "Attitudes of Physicians Practicing in New Mexico toward Gay Men and Lesbians in the Profession." *Academic Medicine: Journal of the Association of American Medical Colleges* 73, no. 4 (1998): 436–38.

Ramose, Mogobe B. "Discourses in Africa: The Struggle for Reason in Africa." In *The African Philosophy Reader*, edited by Pieter Hendrik Coetzee and Abraham Pieter Jacob Roux. 2nd ed. New York: Routledge, 2004.

Ramoupi, Neo. "African-Centered Education and African Languages: Content and Curriculum in Post-Apartheid Education and Training in South Africa." *Policy Brief* 56 (2011).

Raskin, Patricia, Stephanie Coard, and Alfiee M. Breland. "Perceptions of and Preferences for Skin Color, Black Racial Identity, and Self-Esteem Among African Americans." *Journal of Applied Social Psychology* 31, no. 11 (2001): 2256–74.

Resse, Scott. "Islam in Africa/Africans and Islam." *Journal of African History* 55 (2014): 17–26.

Rettova, Alena. "The Role of African Languages in African Philosophy." *Rue Descartes Philosophies Afracaines: Traversees Des Experiences* 36 (2002): 129–50.

Rindermann, Heiner, and James Thompson. "Cognitive Capitalism: The Effects of Cognitive Ability on Wealth, as Mediated Through Scientific Achievement and Economic Freedom." *Psychological Science* 22, no. 6 (2011): 754–63.

Rivera, Pauline. "Mis Recuerdos: The Quest for the Cities of Gold." *La Voz Nueva* (2004).

Robbins, Lawrence, Alec Campbell, Michael Murphy, George Brook, Abel Mabuse, Robert Hitchcock, Grace Babutsi, Mighty Mmolawa, Kathlyn M. Stewart, Teresa E. Steele, Richard G. Klein, and Christopher C. Appleton. "Mogapelwa: Archaeology, Palaeoenvironment and Oral Traditions at Lake Ngami, Botswana." *The South African Archaeological Bulletin* 64, no. 189 (2009): 13–32.

Robinson-Moore, Cynthia. "Beauty Standards Reflect Eurocentric Paradigms – So What? Skin Color, Identity, and Black Female Beauty." *Journal of Race and Policy* 4, no. 1 (2008): 66–85.

Rodney, Walter. *How Europe Underdeveloped Africa.* London: Tanzanian Publishing House and Bogle-L'Ouverture, 1973.

Rogers, Ibram. "Celebrating 40 Years of Activism." *Diverse Education*, June 28, 2006. https://diverseeducation.com/article/6053/.

Rosenkrantz, Dani, et al. "The Positive Aspects of Intersecting Religious/Spiritual and LGBTQ Identities." *Spirituality in Clinical Practice* 3, no. 2 (2016): 127.

Ross, Robert. "African Resistance to the Imposition of Colonialism: A Historiographical Review." *Itinerario* 3, no. 2 (1979): 89–96.

Rothchild, Donald. "A Review of Mazrui's Cultural Forces in World Politics." *African Studies Review* 35, no. 2 (1992): 145–46.

Rowley, Stephanie. "The Relationship Between Racial Identity and Self-Esteem in African American College and High School Students." *Journal of Personality and Social Psychology* 3 (1998): 713–24.

Rovine, Victoria L. "Style Migrations: South-South Networks of African Fashion." *South – South Axes of Global Art* 5, no. 2 (2016).

Russell, Letty. "God, Gold, Glory and Gender: A Postcolonial View of Mission." *International Review of Mission* 95, no. 368 (2004).

Rycoft, David. "Zulu and Xhosa Praise-Poetry and Song." *African Music* 3, no. 1 (1962): 79–85.

Said, Edward. *Orientalism.* New York: Vintage, 1978.

Samir, Amin. "The Election of Donald Trump." MR Online, November 30, 2016. https://mronline.org/2016/11/30/amin301116-html/.
———. "The Return of Fascism in Contemporary Capitalism." *Monthly Review* 66, no. 4 (2014): 1–12.
Sanogo, Aboubakar "In Focus: Studying African Cinema and Media Today." *Cinema Journal* 54, no. 2 (2015): 114–20.
Santos, Boaventura. "The World Social Forum: Toward a Counter-Hegemonic Globalization (Part I)." In *World Social Forum: Challenging Empires*, edited by Jai Sen and Peter Waterman. New Delhi: Viveka Foundation, 2004.
Savin-Williams, R. "Identity Development Among Sexual Minority Youth." *Handbook of Identity Theory and Research*. New York: Springer, 2011.
Sawyerr, Harry. "Issues of Educational Development in Africa: Towards the 21st Century." https://home.hiroshima-u.ac.jp/cice/wp-content/uploads/2014/03/2-2-2.pdf.
Scheufele, Dietram. "Agenda-Setting, Priming, and Framing Revisited: Another Look at Cognitive Effects of Political Communication." *Mass Communication and Society* 3, no. 2–3 (2000): 297–316.
Schlesinger, Arthur Jr. *The Disuniting of America: Reflections on a Multicultural Society*. New York: W. W. Norton, 1992.
Schneider, William. *So, They Understand: Cultural Issues in Oral History*. Logan: Utah State University Press, 2002.
Schneider, William, and Aron Crowell. *Living with Stories: Telling, Re-Telling, and Remembering*. Logan: Utah State University Press, 2006; repr. 2008.
Schreiber, Lisa. "Overcoming Methodological Elitism: Afrocentrism as a Prototypical Paradigm for Intercultural Research." *International Journal of Intercultural Relations* 24, no. 5 (2000): 651–71.
Schroeder, Leila. "Mother Tongue Education in Schools in Kenya: Some Hidden Beneficiaries." *Journal of Language Matters Studies in Languages of Africa* 35, no. 2 (2004): 379–89.
Segueda, Wendpanga Eric. "Imported Religions, Colonialism and the Situation of Women in Africa." *JungesAfrikazentrum der Universität Würzburg* (JAZ) 5 (2015): 1–20.
Sellers, Robert M., Nikeea Copeland-Linder, Pamela P. Martin, and R. L'Heureux Lewis. "Racial Identity Matters: The Relationship Between Racial Discrimination and Psychological Functioning in African American Adolescents." *Journal of Research on Adolescence* 16 (2006): 187–216.
Senghor S. Leopold. "Rapport sur la Doctrine et la Propaganda de Parti." *Discurso en el Congrès Constitutif du Parti du Rassemblement Africain* (1959).
Shaibu, A. Margaret. "Military History in Nigeria: A Discourse in Perspectives." In *Perspectives in African Historical Studies: Essay in xHonour of Prof. Chinedu Nwafor Ubah*, edited by Ojong Echum Tangban and Chukwuma C. C. Osakwe. Kaduna: Nigerian Defence Academy Press, 2013.

Sharp, John. "Mafeje and Langa: The Start of an Intellectual Journey." *Africa Development* 33, no. 4 (2008): 71–88.
Shava, Soul. "The African Aesthetic." In *The Sage Encyclopedia of African Cultural Heritage in North America,* edited by Mwalimu J. Shujaa and Kenya J. Shujaa, 11–16. London: SAGE, 2015.
Shiner, Larry. *The Invention of Art: A Cultural History.* Chicago: University of Chicago Press, 2001.
Shizha, Edward. "Rethinking Contemporary Sub-Saharan African School Knowledge: Restoring the Indigenous African Cultures." *International Journal for Cross-Disciplinary Subjects in Education* 4, no. 1 (2014): 1870–78.
Shohat, Ella, and Robert Stam. *Unthinking Eurocentrism: Multiculturalism and the Media.* London: Routledge, 2014.
Shujaa, Mwalimu, and Kenya Shujaa, eds. "The Nzuri Model of African Aesthetics." *The SAGE Encyclopedia of African Cultural Heritage in North America.* London: SAGE, 2015.
———, eds. "Oral Traditions as Communal Experience." In *The SAGE Encyclopedia of African Cultural Heritage in North America.* London: SAGE, 2015.
Silver, Marc. "If You Shouldn't Call It the Third World, What Should You Call It?" NPR, January 4, 2015. https://www.npr.org/sections/goatsandsoda/2015/01/04/372684438/if-you-shouldnt-call-it-the-third-world-what-should-you-call-it.
Simpson, Alaba. "Oral Tradition and the Slave Trade in Nigeria, Ghana, and Benin." *African Diaspora Archaeology Newsletter* 10, no. 1 (2007).
Skalnik, Peter. "Chiefdoms and Kingdoms in Africa: Why They Are Neither States nor Empires." http://www.ascleiden.nl/Pdf/chiefdomsandkingdoms.pdf.
Smart, Cherry-Ann. "African Oral Tradition, Cultural Retentions and the Transmission of Knowledge in the West Indies." *IFLA Journal* 45, no. 1 (2019): 16–25.
Smedley, Audrey, and Brian Smedley. *Race in North America.* 4th ed. Boulder: Westview, 2012.
Smith, Allan. "Ocasio-Cortez Reveals Her Jewish Heritage: 'I Knew It! I Sensed It!'" NBC News, December 10, 2018. https://www.nbcnews.com/politics/congress/ocasio-cortez-reveals-her-jewish-heritage-i-knew-it-i-n946041.
Smith, Andrew, and Chris Jeppesen, eds. "Development, Contingency and Entanglement: Decolonization in the Conditional." *Britain, France and the Decolonization of Africa,* 1–14. London: UCL Press, 2017.
Smith, Anthony. *National Identity.* London: Penguin, 1991.
Smith, David. "Why Africa is the Most Homophobic Continent," *Guardian,* February 22, 2014, https://www.theguardian.com/world/2014/feb/23/africa-homophobia-uganda-anti-gay-law.
Smith, Linda T. *Decolonizing Methodologies: Research and Indigenous Peoples.* 1st ed. New Zealand: University of Otago Press, 1999.
———. *Decolonizing Methodology: Research and Indigenous Peoples.* 2nd ed. London: Zed, 2012.

Smith, Nicola. "Neoliberalism." Encyclopaedia Britannica, June 28, 2019. https://www.britannica.com/topic/Protestant-ethic.

Smolen, Rafal. "Language Policy in Postcolonial Africa in the Light of Postcolonial Theory." *Studies of the Department of African Languages and Cultures* 50 (2016): 115–47.

Sogolo, Godwin. "Philosophy and Relevance within the African Context." *Journal of Humanities* 2, no. 1 (1988): 97–114.

Sophia, Mama. *The Woman in Me: The Struggles of an African Woman to Discover Her Identity and Authority.* Bloomington: Author House, 2010.

Souza, Aruna. "African History, Written in Africa." *Higher Education Research in Africa*, April 2019. https://www.carnegie.org/topics/topic-articles/african-academics.

Spivak, Gayatri, and Rosalind Morris. *Can the Subaltern Speak? Reflections on the History of an Idea.* New York: Columbia University Press, 2010.

Spurlin, W. "African Intimacies: Race, Homosexuality, and Globalization." *African Studies Review* 51, no. 3 (2008): 201–4.

Sramek, Jordan. "Seeking Common Ground through Oral Tradition." *Biblical Theology Bulletin* 43, no. 4 (2013): 212–20.

Stapleton, Sarah Riggs. "Oral Traditions, Changing Rural Landscapes, and Science Education." *Cultural Studies of Science Education* 12, no. 1 (2017): 189–98.

Steady, Filomena C., ed. *The Black Women Cross-Culturally.* Cambridge: Schenkman, 1981.

———. "An Investigative Framework for Gender Research in Africa in the New Millennium." Paper, CODESRIA Conference on African Gender in the New Millennium, Cairo, Egypt, April 7–10, 2002.

———. *Women and Collective Action in Africa: Development, Democratization and Empowerment.* Gordonsville: Palgrave Macmillan, 2005.

Stiftung, Friedrich Ebert. "Feminism in Africa: Trends and Prospects: Report on the International Workshop on Political Feminism in Africa." *FES Briefing Papers* 1 (2017): 1–15.

Stikkers, Kenneth. "An Outline of Methodological Afrocentrism, with Particular Application to the Thought of W. E. B. DuBois." *Journal of Speculative Philosophy* 22, no. 1 (2008): 40–49.

Stocking, George. *Race, Culture, and Evolution.* New York: Free Press, 1986.

Sturgeon, Noël. "The Politics of the Natural in US History and Popular Culture." In *From Inquiry to Academic Writing: A Text and Reader*, edited by Stuart Greene and April Lidinsky. 3rd ed. Boston and New York: Bedford/St. Martin's Press, 2015.

Sutherland, Peter. "Ancestral Slaves and Diasporic Tourists: Retelling History by Reversing Movement in a Counternationalist Vodun Festival from Benin." In *Africanizing Knowledge: African Studies Across the Disciplines*, edited by Toyin Falola and Christian Jennings. New Brunswick and London: Transaction, 2002.

Swart, Susan. "Beyond the Veil: Muslim Women Write Back." PhD diss., University of Pretoria, 1991.

Taglialatela, Jared, Jamie Russell, Jennifer Schaeffer, and William Hopkins. "Communicative Signaling Activates 'Broca's' Homolog in Chimpanzees." *Current Biology* 18, no. 5 (2008): 343–48.

Talton, Benjamin. "The Challenge of Decolonization in Africa." New York Public Library, 2011. http://exhibitions.nypl.org/africanaage/essay-challenge-of-decolonization-africa.html.

Tamale, Sylvia. "Introduction" In *African Sexualities: A Reader*, edited by Sylvia Tamale. Cape Town: Pambazuka, 2011.

———. "Exploring the Contours of African Sexualities: Religion, Law and Power." *African Human Rights Law Journal* 14, no. 1 (2014): 150.

———. "Point of Order, Mr. Speaker: African Women Claiming Their Space in Parliament." *Gender and Development*, no. 8 (2000): 8–15.

———. *When Hens Begin to Crow: Gender and Parliamentary Politics in Uganda*. Kampala: Fountain, 1999.

Tcheuyap, Alexie. "African Cinema(s): Definitions, Identity and Theoretical Considerations." *Critical Interventions: Journal of African Art History and Visual Culture* 5, no.1 (2014): 10–26.

Teasley, Martell, Jandel Crutchfield, Sheara Jennings, Annette Clayton, and Nathern Okilwa. "School Choice and Afrocentric Charter Schools: A Review and Critique of Evaluation Outcomes." *Journal of African American Studies* 20, no. 1 (2016): 99–119.

TED. "The Danger of a Single Story | Chimamanda Ngozi Adichie." YouTube video, 19:16.

October 7, 2009. https://www.youtube.com/watch?v=D9Ihs241zeg.

TEDx Talks. "TEDxFlanders – Olivia U. Rutazibwa – Decoloniser." YouTube video, 18:16.

September 27, 2011. https://www.youtube.com/watch?v=z0b6wfDGseU.

Teferra, Damtew. *Funding Higher Education in Africa: State, Trends and Perspectives*. Dakar: CODESRIA, 2014.

Thaut, Michael H. Rhythm, *Music and the Brain: Scientific Foundations and Clinical Applications*. New York: Routledge, 2005.

Thiong'o, Ngugi Wa. "The Commitment of the Intellectual." *Review of African Political Economy* 32 (1985): 18–24.

———. *Decolonising the Mind*. Portsmouth: Heinemann, 1981.

———. *Decolonising the Mind: The Politics of Language in African Literature*. London: James Currey, 1986.

———. "Europhonism, Universities, and the Magic Fountain: The Future of African Literature and Scholarship." *Research in African Literatures* 31, no. 1 (2000) 1–11.

———. "Freeing the Imagination." *Transition* 100 (2008): 164–69.

———. *Homecoming*. London: Heineman, 1982.

———. *Moving the Center: The Struggle for Cultural Freedoms*. Portsmouth: Heinemann, 1993.

Thompson, Paul, and Joanna Bornat. *The Voice of the Past: Oral History*. 4th ed. London: Oxford University Press, 2017.

Tiyambe, Paul. "African Studies and Universities Since Independence: The Challenges of Epistemic and Institutional Decolonization." *Transition* 101 (2009): 110–35.

Trevor-Roper, Hugh. *The Rise of Christian Europe*. London: Thames and Hudson, 1966.

Trinidad, Ruth. "Collective Memory of Violence of the Female Brown Body: A Decolonial Feminist Public Pedagogy Engagement with the Feminicides." *Pedagogy, Culture & Society* 24, no. 3 (2016): 343–57.

Tripp, Aili Mali. "Women in Movement: Transformations in African Political Landscapes." *International Feminist Journal of Politics* 5, no. 2 (2003): 233–55.

Trudell, Barbara, and Leila Schroeder. "Reading Methodologies for African Languages: Avoiding Linguistic and Pedagogical Imperialism." *Language Culture and Curriculum* 20, no. 3 (2007): 165–80.

Tucker, Andrew. "Geographies of Sexualities in Sub-Saharan Africa: Positioning and Critically Engaging with International Human Rights and Related Ascendant Discourses." *Progress in Human Geography* 44, no. 4 (2020): 683–703.

———. "Reconsidering Relationships Between Homophobia, Human Rights and HIV/AIDS." *The Routledge Research Companion to Geographies of Sex and Sexualities*. London: Routledge, 2016: 295–305.

Turner, Diane. "An Oral History Interview: Molefi Kete Asante." *Journal of Black Studies* 32, no. 6 (2002): 711–34.

Uchendu, Egodi. *Women and Conflict in the Nigerian Civil War*. Trenton: Africa World, 2007.

UNESCO. *Global Monitoring Report 2005. Education for All: The Quality Imperative*. Paris: UNESCO, 2004.

———. "Just 30% of the World's Researchers are Women. What's the Situation in Your Country?" UNESCO, n.d. https://en.unesco.org/news/just–30–world%E2%80%99s–researchers–are–women–whats–situation–your–country.

———. "Regional Overview: Sub-Saharan Africa." UNESCO. https://en.unesco.org/unesco_science_report/africa.

———. *The Use of Vernacular Languages in Education*. Paris: UNESCO, 1953.

———. *Why and How Africa Should Invest in African Languages and Multilingual Education: An Evidence– and Practice–Based Policy Advocacy Brief*. Hamburg: UNESCO Institute for Lifelong Learning, 2010.

United Nations. "World Population Day—11 July." United Nations. https://www.un.org/en/observances/world–population–day.

———. "World Population Prospects 2019 Highlights." https://population.un.org/wpp/Publications/Files/WPP2019_Highlights.pdf.

Uya, Okon. "Trends and Perspectives in Africa." In *Africa from the Sixteenth to the Eighteenth Century. Vol. 5 of UNESCO General History of Africa,* edited by Bethwell Ogot. California: Heinemann, 1992.

Van Allen, Judith. "'Sitting on a Man': Colonialism and the Lost Political Institutions of Igbo Women." *Canadian Journal of African Studies* 6, no. 2 (1972): 165–81.

Van Klinken, Adrian and Chitando, Ezra, eds. *Public Religion and the Politics of Homosexuality in Africa.* London: Routledge, 2016.

Vansina, Jan M. "Oral History and Tradition." In *Oral Tradition and Oral History in Africa and the Diaspora: Theory and Practice,* edited by E. J. Alagoa. Lagos: Centre for Black and African Arts and Civilization, 1990.

———. *Oral Tradition as History.* Madison: University of Wisconsin Press, 1985.

Vazquez, Rolando. "Translation as Erasure: Thoughts on Modernity's Epistemic Violence." *Journal of Historical Sociology* 24, no. 1 (2011): 27–44.

Verharen, Charles. "Molefi Asante and an Afrocentric Curriculum." *Western Journal of Black Studies* 24, no. 4 (2000): 223–38.

Vignoles, V., S. Schwartz, and K. Luyckx. "Introduction: Toward an Integrative View of Identity." *Handbook of Identity Theory and Research* New York: Springer, 2011.

Vrangalova, Zhana, and Ritch Savin-Williams. "Mostly Heterosexual and Mostly Gay/Lesbian: Evidence for New Sexual Orientation Identities." *Archives of Sexual Behavior* 41, no. 1 (2012): 85–101.

Vuyogo. "Chiwoniso." Vuyogo, May 21, 2018. http://vuyogo.de/chiwoniso/.

Wali, Obiajunwaka. "The Dead End of African Literature?" *Transition* 10 (1963): 13–16.

Wallace, Stephanie, James Nazroo, and Laia Bécares. "Cumulative Effects of Racial Discrimination on the Mental Health of Ethnic Minorities in the United Kingdom." *American Journal of Public Health* 106, no. 7 (2016): 1294–1300.

Wallerstein, Immanuel. "Eurocentrism and Its Avatars: The Dilemmas of Social Science." *Sociological Bulletin* 46, no. 1 (1997): 21–39.

Wanyande, P. "Mass Media–State Relations in Post–Colonial Kenya." *Africa Media Review,* no. 9 (1995): 54–75.

Washbrook, David. "The Global History of 'Modernity': A Response to a Reply." *Journal of the Economic and Social History of the Orient* 41, no. 3 (1998): 295–311.

Washington, Samantha. "Diversity in Schools must Include Curriculum." The Century Foundation, September 17, 2018. https://tcf.org/content/commentary/diversity-schools-must-include-curriculum/?session=1.

Waters, M. et al., eds. *Coming of Age in America: The Transition to Adulthood in the Twenty–First Century.* Berkeley: University of California Press, 2011.

Watters, Charles. "Three Challenges to a Life Course Approach in Global Mental Health: Epistemic Violence, Temporality and Forced Migration." In *The Palgrave Handbook of Sociocultural Perspectives on Global Mental Health,* edited by Ross G. White, Sumeet Jain, David M. R. Orr, and Ursula M. Read, 237–256. London: Palgrave Macmillan, 2017.

Webber, Sabra J. *Romancing the Real: Folklore and Ethnographic Representation in North Africa*. Philadelphia: University of Pennsylvania Press, 1991.

Wells–Gibbon, Rhonda, and Gaynell Marie Simpson. "Transitioning the Caregiving Role for the Next Generation: An African-Centered Womanist Perspective." *Black Women, Gender and Families* 3, no. 2 (2009): 87–105.

Werunga, Jane, Sheryl Reimer-Kirkham, and Carol Ewashen. "A Decolonizing Methodology for Health Research on Female Genital Cutting." *Advances in Nursing Science* 39, no. 2 (2016): 150–64.

West, Candace, and Don Zimmerman. "Doing Gender." *Gender and Society* 1, no. 2 (1987): 125–51.

Westefeld, J., M. Maples, B. Buford, and S. Taylor. "Gay, Lesbian, and Bisexual College Students: The Relationship Between Sexual Orientation and Depression, Loneliness, and Suicide." *Journal of College Student Psychotherapy* 15, no. 3 (2001): 71–82.

Wheeler, Andre. "Is Kenya's Mombasa Port Another Victim of China's Debt Diplomacy?" Splash 247, February 7, 2020. https://splash247.com/is-kenyas-mombasa-port-another-victim-of-chinas-debt-diplomacy/.

Whetung, Madeline, and Sarah Wakefield. "Colonial Conventions: Institutionalized Research Relationships and Decolonizing Research Ethics." In *Indigenous and Decolonizing Studies in Education: Mapping the Long View*, edited by Linda Smith, Eve Tuck, and Wayne Yang, 146–58. New York: Routledge, 2019.

Whipps, Heather. "How Gunpowder Changed the World." *Live Science*, April 7, 2008. https://www.livescience.com/7476-gunpowder-changed-world.html.

Whitman, Walt. *Leaves of Grass*. Mineola: Dover, 2007.

Willis, Thabiti J. "Negotiating Gender, Power, and Spaces in Masquerade Performances in Nigeria." *Gender, Place & Culture* 21, no. 3 (2014): 322–336.

Wiredu, Kwasi. "Conceptual Decolonization as an Imperative in Contemporary African Philosophy: Some Personal Reflections." *Rue Descartes* 2, no. 36 (2002): 53–64.

———. "An Oral Philosophy of Personhood: Comments on Philosophy and Orality." *Research in African Literatures* 40, no. 1 (2009): 8–18.

———. *Philosophy and an African Culture*. Cambridge: Cambridge University Press, 1980.

———. "Toward Decolonizing African Philosophy and Religion." *African Studies Quarterly* 1 (1998): 17–46.

Wolff, H. Ekkehard. *Pre-School Child Multilingualism and Its Educational Implications in the African Context*. Cape Town, PRAESA, 2000.

Wordsworth, William. "The Dungeon." April 1798. The Project Gutenberg Ebook, October 10, 2003. http://www.gutenberg.org/files/9622/9622-h/9622-h.htm.

———. "The Nightingale." April 1798. The Project Gutenberg eBook, October 10, 2003. http://www.gutenberg.org/files/9622/9622-h/9622-h.htm.

Workman, Daniel. "Zambia's Top Ten Exports." World's Top Exports, March 31, 2020. http://www.worldstopexports.com/zambias-op-10-exports/.

World Oral Literature Project. "Home." *World Oral Literature Project*. http://www.oralliterature.org/.

World Population Review. "Continent and Region Populations 2018." World Population Review. Accessed November 5, 2018, http://worldpopulationreview.com/continents/.

Wu, Jinting, Paul William Eaton, David W. Robinson–Morris, Maria F. G. Wallace, and Shaofei Han. "Perturbing Possibilities in the Postqualitative Turn: Lessons from Taoism (道) and Ubuntu." *International Journal of Qualitative Studies in Education* 31, no. 6 (2018): 504–19.

Yacob-Haliso, Olajumoke, and Toyin Falola. "Introduction: Gendering Knowledge in Africa and the African Diaspora." In *Gendering Knowledge in Africa and the African Diaspora: Contesting History and Power*, edited by Toyin Falola and Olajumoke Yacob–Haliso, 1–15. London: Routledge, 2017.

Yaszek, Lisa. "Afrofuturism, Science Fiction, and the History of the Future." *Socialism and Democracy* 20, no. 3 (2012): 41–60.

Young, Robert C. J. *Postcolonialism: A Very Short Introduction*. New York: Oxford University Press, 2003.

Zegeye, Abebe, and Maurice Vambe. "African Indigenous Knowledge Systems." *Review (Fernand Braudel Center)* 29, no. 4 (2006): 329–58.

Zeleza, Paul. "African Studies in the Postcolony." Keynote Address, Opening of the Centre for African Studies, University of Free State, November 5, 2007.

———. "The Decolonization of African Knowledges." Essay for the 9th Africa Day Lecture, University of the Free State, Bloemfontein, South Africa, n.d.

———. "Gender Biases in African Historiography." In *African Gender Studies: A Reader*, edited by Oyeronke Oyewumi, 207–32. New York: Palgrave Macmillan, 2005.

———. "The Intellectual Challenges." *Rethinking Africa's Globalization*. Trenton: Africa World, 2003.

———. "The Past and Futures of African History: A Generational Inventory." Seminar Paper, University of South Africa, Pretoria, South Africa, 2007.

Zenani, Nongenile Masithathu, and Harold Scheub. *The World and the Word: Tales and Observations from the Xhosa Oral Tradition*. Madison: University of Wisconsin Press, 2014.

Zinn, Howard. "A People's History of the United States: 1492 – Present, Part 1." In *Betweener Talk: Decolonizing Knowledge Production, Pedagogy, and Praxis*, edited by Claudio Moreira and Marcelo Diversi. New York: Harper Perennial Modern Classics, 2005.

Index

An italicized page number indicates a figure or table.

AAWORD, 17, 242, 321, 323
Aba Women's Riot, 442
aboriginal language, 28
academic freedom, 212, 350, 352, 360, 366, 369
acculturation, 319, 384
Achebe, Nwando, 311
activism, 226; intellectual, 204; political, 602; sociopolitical, 120; women, 295, 305, 314, 451
Ademowo, Adeyemi J., 105–7, 394
Adichie, Chimamanda, 76, 123, 456, 474, 477
Africa, cinematic experience, 500
Africa, recolonization, 279
Africa and the Fourth Industrial Revolution, 619
African academy, 349, 352, 368, 372–77, 555
African Americans, 49, 63, 71, 88, 300, 304, 363
African art, 153, 184, 377, 481–82, 496, 609
African artistic expression, 530
African civilization, 377, 436
African crafts, 153
African culture, 40, 89, 237–38, 303, 331, 345, 454, 481, 552; promoting, 497
African democracy, 235
African Development, 277, 368, 533, 535, 612–13, 615
African divination system, 558

African education system, 206, 211–12, 555
African emancipation, 23, 595
African epistemologies, decolonization, 9
African epistemology, 11, 91, 527, 529–31, 606, 609, 611; marginalization, 11
African fashion, 21, 481, 493–98; preservation, 495
African feminist movement, 330, 440
African feminist writers, 20, 241, 325, 438, 449, 455–56, 472–73, 476, 479
African films, 21, 498–99, 501–2, 504
African folktale, 175
African Futurism, 596n, 597, 601–5, 607
African healing systems, 547
African historiography, 2–4, 299, 364, 520, 524–26, 528
African identity, 23, 206, 209, 213, 507, 603, 608, 610; formations, 9
African indigenous languages, 13, 382–83, 385, 390
African knowledge economy, 211, 213, 559
African knowledge production, development, 365
African language, 19, 21, 105, 118, 155, 385, 412; decolonization, 431; resuscitation, 429–30; use, 110, 519, 582–83

African liberation and freedom, 533–34
African liberation struggles, 10
African literature, 122, 411, 426; decolonization, 431, 474; language, 498; modern, 427–29, 436, 609; obscurantism, 124; oral, 426, 434, 436, 579; traditional, 425, 427, 429
African militarism, 313
African multilingualism, 385
African music, 117, 120–22, 493; industry, 486; reclaiming, 485
African music scholarship, 121
African oral traditions, stigmatization, 182
African orature, 426, 435
The African Origins of Civilization: Myth or Reality? 363
African philosophical curriculum, 586–87
African philosophical thought, 582, 585, 591
African Philosophy, 568
African philosophy, 570; language, 581
African religion, practitioners, 70
African Renaissance, 2–3, 6–7, 515, 533, 601
African scholarship, Western hegemony, 320
African spirituality, 546–47, 549
African studies, Africanization, 293
African style, 496
African theater, 163
African traditional religion (ATR), 22, 538–40, 542–65; adherents, 548; components, 548, 552, 555; demonization, 539, 549, 564; healing system, 548–49; medicine system, 556; morality, 543; practices, 22, 539; sacredness, 542; worship, 562–63
African truths, 23, 590
African Union, 287, 366, 444, 535, 617
African Universalists, 577
African voice, 75, 485
Africanity, 98, 223
The Africans: A Triple Heritage, 240
Africa's epic belt, 171
Africa's multilingualism, 107–8
Africology, 16, 214, 217–18. *See* Afrocentricity
Afrocentric ideology, 66, 361; schools, 218–20
Afrocentricity, 77, 89–92, 214–15, 218
Afrocentrism, 66–68, 89–90, 125, 197, 204, 213–14, 216, 218, 220–21, 362
Afrofuturism, 23, 596–99, 622
Agency for Accelerated Regional Development (AFARD), 321
Agogo Eewo, 481, 507–10
Ahmadu Bello University, 6, 378, 530
Ake, Claude, 9, 15–16, 197, 232–33
Al-Baghdadi, Abu B., 64
Allen, Judith V., 238, 310–11, 441
altruism, 541
Amin, Samir, 6, 15–16, 42–43, 197, 227, 229, 231–32
animism, 541
antiquities departments, 530
Anzaldúa, Gloria, 85
apartheid, 96, 359, 485–86; fall, 536
Appiah, Kwame A., 598, 608
Arabic, classical, 406–7
Arabization, 404, 406, 408; policy, 409
Arbery, Ahmaud, 63
archaeology, 101, 191, 525
art, 94, 154; ancient, 480

artifacts, destruction of, 538
Asa, 21, 490–92, 510
Asante, Molefi, 15–16, 197, 214–16, 221–22, 242
Asian civilization, 377
aso oke, 493–94, 509
assimilation, policy, 355, 361
Association of African Universities (AAU), 365
authoritarian regimes, 369, 529
Awe, Bolanle, 17, 242, 295, 311, 315, 323

Badung Conference, 253
Bantu Education Act, 401
belief system, 609
Berlin Conference, 39, 80, 380
Bible, 14
Black Consciousness Movement (BCM), 516
Black Feminist Thought, 322
Black Lives Matter (BLM), 2–3, 7, 66, 66
Black pride, 2
Blyden, Edward, 363, 622
border epistemology, 263
border-thinking, 85, 87, 99–100, 189
The Boy Who Harnessed the Wind, 506
brain drain, 316, 352, 369, 615, 619
bridge, 472
British Advisory Committee on Education, 357
British Council, 392–93
Brown, Austin C., 52
buen vivir, 79

Cambridge History of Africa, 365
capitalism; decline, 227; European, 104; expansion of, 1; imposition of, 39; neoliberal, 249; role of, 43; senile, 229–32
Cartesian philosophy, 569

Cartesian subjectivism, 249
cartography, 258–59
Center for Advanced Social Science (CASS), 234
Chaka, Yvonne C., 21, 119, 485, 490
child marriage, 445, 477
Christian indoctrination, 546; symbolism, 258
Christianity, 353, 508; introduction, 40; spread, 60, 81
civil wars, 316–17
civilizations, 56, 60–61, 67; African, 436; American, 170,377; Asian, 377; Egyptian, 238; European, 246; human, 221, 536; industrial, 235; systems, 128; western, 436, 440
civilizing mission, 81, 416
clothing, 119, 158, 481, 493, 495
collective memory, 87, 190, 307
collectivism, value, 79
Colonial Development Welfare Fund, 355
colonial difference, 132, 257, 260, 269
colonial education policy, 356
Colonial Film Units, 500
colonial heritage, 135, 535
colonial historiography, 3, 520
colonial knowledge system, 362–63
colonial languages, 107, 122, 383, 386–87, 394; influence, 410
colonial matrix of power (CMP), 257, 259–62, 289
colonial philosophy, 115, 206
colonial university education, 360
colonialism, cultural, 296
colonialism; effects, 7, 20, 77, 383, 411–12; Eurocentric, 46, ideological justification for, 85; legacy, 102, 302, 421; mental, 117; psychological, 46; sexual, 18, 327, 340

colonialist Eurocentric traditions, 511
coloniality, 77; of being, 251–52, 603; economic 293; global, 16, 245, 247, 250, 252, 254, 519; of knowledge, 13, 251–52, 257, 271–72, 281, 603; of mind, 276; of nature, 252: power, 251, 257, 421, 603, 611
colonization, 37, 39
common language, 609
Common Sense, 284
communal focus, 41
comparative philosophy, 587–88
Confucianism, philosophy, 57
confused mentality, 289
Conrad, Joseph, 226, 303
consumerism, 83, 618
convivial scholarship, 529
cosmopolitan localism, 274, 580
cosmopolitanism, 84–85, 90, 248, 260–62
COVID-19, 68, 558, 618
creative expressions, 20, 473, 480–82, 583
Crethi, 28
criminal economy, 317–18
cultural diversity, Africa, 108, 132
cultural ethos, 14, 300
Cultural Forces in the World of Politics, 239
cultural identity, 137, 431, 607
cultural; emancipation, 609; familiarity, 114; ignorance, 299; kingdoms, 95; revivalism, 425, 435; servitude, 122; stasis, 392
culture, transmission, 103, 110
curricula, Africanization, 362

Dar es Salaam School, 4
dark continent, 511, 515
Daughter of Isis, 477
DAWN, 17, 242, 290, 324, 502

De Sousa, S. B., 15, 246, 270
decoloniality, 9, 27, 38, 77, 81–84, 89, 95; academic, 293; criticism, 276, 292; goal, 264–65; literature, 97; process, 579; tenets, 96; use, 250; voices, 243
decolonization theory, feminist, 242, 295
decolonization, 80; intellectual, 100, 424; political, 2–3, 7, 197, 519; process, 105, 116, 118, 125, 309, 323, 340, 514, 517, 563; strategy, 133
decolonizing research methodology, 134, 140
Decolonizing the Mind, 138
Decolonizing the Mind: The Politics of Language in African Literature, 425
deculturalization, 360
deity, 95, 543, 545, 609; woman, 461
democracy, 43, 197, 224, 232, 234–34; activism, 226; African, 235; American, 239; liberal, 234–35, 602; structures, 43
demonstration, 183
dependency school, 42
dependency theory, 2, 5, 280, 365
desilencing, 37
digi-Orature, 192
digital revolution, 503, 619
diglossia, 407
Dike, Kenneth. O., 3–4, 22, 513, 516, 522, 524–25
Diop, Cheik A., 363
Diviners, 552–53
Du Bois, W. E. B., 246, 363, 608
dual identity, 15, 207
Dussel, Enrique, 15–16, 262, 264–71, 273–74, 577–81, 588–90
dynamic homeostasis, 190

economic exploitation, 5, 198, 414

economic independence, 200, 603
economy, combat, 317; coping, 317–18
education, 615; decolonization of, 362, 368; eurocentric bias in, 59–60
education policy, 48; multilingual, 109; colonial, 356; French, 355
Efuru, 456, 458–62
ege, 174
egungun, 15, 159, 162, 174, 177, 545
Egyptian civilization, 238, 515n
Einstein, Albert, 56, 292
Elliot Commission, 354
El-Sadaawi, Nawal, 323, 476
Encyclopedia of African Religion, 540
English Language Teaching Support Project (ELTSP), 393
English language, 104, 122, 307–8, 381, 400, 434, 584n
English, broken, 398
epics, 151, 170–72
epistemic, delinking, 262–63; disobedience, 188, 191, 194, 256, 262, 579; violence, 13, 77, 85–89, 246
esa, 174, 177
essentialization, 209, 563
Ethiopianism, 516
ethnic studies, 48–50
ethnography, 129, 148, 129, 177, 188
ethno-philosophers, African, 580
ethno-philosophy, 23, 567, 570, 572–74, 576–79
Etiyeri, Eégún àgbà, *160*
Eurocentric capitalist system, 41
Eurocentric demonization, 540
Eurocentric gaze, 138
Eurocentric pedagogy, 88
Eurocentric values, 50–51, 204
Eurocentrism, 45, 50, 62, 350; ending, 62, 69; eradication, 73; first-order, 131, 148–49; instrumentalization of, 209; second-order, 131, 148–49; symptoms of, 89
Europe, 81
European colonization, 38, 405
European culture, 22, 67, 207, 416, 604
European hegemonic crusade, 64
European modernity, 41, 249, 252, 417, 419, 421
European Union, 35, 37, 287, 614
ewi, 174
exploitation, investment, 275
exploitation, trade, 278

failure of victory, 243
Falola, Toyin, *423*, 419
Fanon, Frantz, 19, 43, 130, 246, 284, 417, 424
faulty science, 32
Favorite African Folktales, 175
female genital mutilation (FGM), 93
femalism, 452, 455
femicides, 87
feminism, 300, 310, 330, 332, 440, 446; African, 20, 306, 331, 440; development, 438–39, 442; domestication of, 305; influence of, 444; nego-feminism, 454, 458; radical, 330; transformative, 462, 466; western, 300, 305, 450
Feminist Africa, 242
film production, 501
Floyd, George, 63, 65
fluid sexuality, 335
foreign grants, 289
foreign recordings, 183
France, 57, 64, 159, 355–56, 392, 439, 502, 600
French conscription policy, 180; education policy, 355

Garfield, jay, 132
gay rights, 328
gender, 301; inequality, 306; segregation, 11; stratification, 298
General Agreements on Trade in Service (GTS), 365
genocide, 490, 512
globalization, 130, 182, 248, 274, 335, 368; consequences of, 338; forces, 281; hegemonic and non-hegemonic, 275; knowledge, 371, 373; liberal, 231; policy, 84
God, 540, 542, 548
Gorge, Olduvai, 192
Gould, Stephen J., 55
Greek philosophy, 78, 221, 574
griot, 165; library, 534; modern-day, 473; performance of, 427
Grosfoguel, Ramon, 41

Haitian Revolution (1791–1804), 253
The Heart of Darkness, 112
Hegel, Friedrich, 207, 415–17, 592
Henry, Frances, 550, 564
hermitic hypothesis, 511
hetero-patriarchy, 31
heterosexuality, 328, 332
Higher Education Act of 1965, 48
historical consciousness, 21, 516, 531–33
historical subjectivity, 47
History of the Yoruba, 150, 522n19
history, economic, 525
history, imperialist, 12, 56
holistic thinking, 91–92
homophobia, 18, 332–33, 337; culture, 333; political, 340, 345
homophobic laws, 18, 338, 344
homophobic policy, African, 18
homosexuality, 327–29, 338–39, 448
Horn of Africa, 610
Hountondji, Paulin, 427

How Europe Underdeveloped Africa, 5, 198, 201, 351, 480
human rights issues, European Union (EU), 35
human rights, 18, 35, 326–29, 411, 445, 515, 534; abuse, 18
Human Rights Watch, 328
human subjectivity, 249
human trafficking, 317
humanism, 218, 251, 516
Hume, David, 55, 207, 209

Ibadan School of History, 4
Ifa divination corpus, 157
ijala ode, 174
illusion race, 608
I'm Still Here: Black Dignity in a World Made for Whiteness, 52
Imperial Manichean Misanthropic Skepticism, 252
imperialism, cultural, 181, 296–97, 307, 361, 450; European, 126, 198; neoliberal, 537
In My Father's House, 571
indigeneity, 254, 256, 261–62, 584
indigenous belief systems, 541
indigenous knowledge systems, 19, 101, 105, 210, 350, 352, 372, 376–78; destruction of, 350
indigenous languages: adoption of, 109; centralization of, 106; music in, 120; use of, 119–20, 137, 141, 387, 394, 400–401, 504
indigenous methodology, 13–14, 126, 133
indigenous responsibility, 147
individualism, 61, 201; philosophy, 544, 546
industrial slavery, 201
Information and Communication Technology (ICT), 367, 371, 614–18, 620

Information Technology Advisory Group's (ITAG), 616
insider-outsider status, 114
Institut Africain d'Education Cinematographique (INAFEC), 502
The Institute of African Studies, 324, 526
insularity, 135
intellectual blackmail, 73
intellectual property rights, 184
intellectual revolution, 67, 515, 533
International Lesbian, Gay, Trans, and Intersex Association, 330
international relations, 95
internationalization, 283, 367–68 *See* globalization
Islam, 237, 309, 406, 543
Islamic faith, preservation, 237
iyere, 174

Jaafari, Taoufik, 391, 393, 407–8
Jansen, Jonathan, 291
Johnson, James, 363, 521
Johnson, Samuel, 522n19
Journal of African American Studies, 220
Joys of Motherhood, 456, 462–65, 469
Julien, Eileen, 426–27
Jung, Carl, 186
Justice for Jamar Protest March, 8

Kasala praises, 157
Kelani, Tunde, 21, 482, 507–9
Kessi, Shose, 31, 33
King, Steve, 56
kinship ties, 41
Kioko, Angelina, N., 108–11
knowledge, 27; constellation of, 85, 189, 100; dearth of, 106; globalization of, 371, 373; production, 25, 534

Knowledge Economy Index (KEI), 614, 621
knowledge-as-emancipation, 271–72
knowledge-as-regulation, 271–72
Koteba, 159
kotket, 28
Kuti, Fela A., 120

lacanian void, 249
language, 29, 39, 102–3, 156; importance, 21, 138, 173; policy, 109, 400, 402–3, 41; power of, 11, 157; tone, 483
Laurent, Yves Saint, 496–98
laws, colonial antigay, 339
Le silence de la forêt, 505–6
legal reform, 340
Legitimation Code Theory (LCT), 82–83
Levi-Strauss, Claude, 186, 207
LGBTQ, 326; anti-LGBTQ sentiment, 327; community, 17–18, 326–30, 332–37, 339, 341, 344, 346; criminalization of, 333, 336; health issues, 337; human rights, 327, 329; physician, 340–34; pro-LGBTQ laws, 327; religious acceptance of, 344; stigmatization of, 336
liberation, intellectual, 75; philosophy, 16, 265, 268–71; socioeconomic, 5, 7
linguistic diversity, 108, 139, 155
Linnaeus, Carl, 55
Lion King, 193
logocentrism, 23, 143, 597

Madagascar, 285, 287, 549
Mafeje, Archibald Boyce Monwabisi, 15–16, 44, 197, 222–26, 241
magical thinking, 547

Makeba, Miriam, 21, 118–20, 484–87, 497
Makerere Conference of 1963, 253
Makerere University in Kampala, 19, 382
Makerere University in Uganda, 4
Mama, Amina, 17, 242, 295, 312, 323
Mamdani, Mahmood, 15–16, 197, 210–13, 359–60, 368–69, 372–74, 513
Mandela, Nelson, 96, 175, 284
Maraire, Chiwoniso, 486–88
Marinetti, Filippo, 596
Marxism, 5–6, 82–83, 201, 227, 310
Marxist school, 6
Marxist theory, 5
Mazrui, Ali, 15–16, 39, 197, *236*, 238, 240, 246, 361, 364
Mbembe, Achille, J., 15, 34–35, 197, 202–4, 206, 226, 372
media, Eurocentric bias, 70
mental health, 52, 86–87, 326, 333, 344, 346
Mignolo, Walter D., 9, 85, 254, 256–60, 580
militarism, 313
modern African literature, 427–29, 436, 609
Modern Standard Arabic (MSA), 407
modernity, 417
modernization theory, 2, 5, 10
Mohanty, Chandra T, 17, 242, 295
Monroe Doctrine, 61
Morgenson, Scott, 145
motherism, 452–53, 461
Mudimbe, V. Y., 15, 82, 197, 206–10, 585
multiculturalism, 37, 61, 90, 108, 397, 409, 584, 586
multilingual education, 109–10
music, 163

musicians, 21, 117–18, 120, 166, 170, 482–84, 493
myth of empty, 258
myths, 175–76, 186, 536, 567; production, 578
national archives, 4, 526
nationalism, spirit, 284, 422
nationalist liberation movements, 3
nation-states, 32–33, 80, 355, 405, 409, 534
Ndlovu-Gatsheni, Sabelo J., 16, 245–54, 288–92, 519, 602
negritude, 424, 472, 516, 533, 571, 599–603, 608, 622
negritude movement, 600
neocolonialism, 603
neoliberalism, 82, 338, 534, 602, 622
Nigerian film industry, 510
Nigerian University Commission (NUC), 287–88
Nkrumah, Kwame, 277, 283–84, 289, 422, 514–15, 603
North Africa, 19, 404–10, 498, 501
North African Berber community, 409
Nwapa, Flora, 446–47, 456, 458, 460, 477
Nyerere, Julius, 246, 277, 284, 364, 403, 422

Obama, Barack, 90
Ocasio-Cortez, Alexandria, 52–54
Oelofsen, Rianna, 420
ofo/ogede, 174
Olodumare, 540
Omar, Ilhan, 52
one localism, 274
oral literature, 153, 426, 428, 435, 481, 570, 578
oral lore, 143
oral tradition, 151–52, 523; informal, 162; recording, 161, 182–83

oral-based cultures, 143
oral-based education system, 102
orality, 143, 164, 177, 185, 426–27, 429, 567
oral-visual dyad, 142
ori aremo, 174
orientalism, 61–62, 114, 128, 351
oriki ,166, 174
orin Arungbe, 174
Orisha African religion, 550
oro, 177
Osun, 543
Otabil, Mensa, 606
Overton, John, 127
Oyewunmi, Oyeronke, 17, 137–38, 142–44

Paine, Thomas, 260, 284
Pan-African movements, 358
Pan-African University, 365–66
Pan-Africanism, 88, 90, 238, 513, 516, 533, 599–602, 622
patriarchy, 298, 302, 308, 312–14, 446, 456
peace rhetoric, 90
performance, African cultures, 158
Peterson, Derek R., 316–18
Pew Research Center's Forum, 541
phallic superiority, 463, 470
Phelps-Stokes Commission in 1922, 357
philosopher, 575
philosophy, development, 72
Philosophy of History, 207
philosophy, discipline, 591, 594
Pidgin English, 120–21; characteristic, 395; Ghanaian, 396–98; Nigerian, 395–400; West African, 395–99
Pillay, Suren, 59
Pindi, G. N., 331
pluralism, 39, 89, 430, 451

pluriversal: approach, 580, 587; globalism, 262; philosophy, 581n45
pluriversality, 31, 268, 274, 580, 584, 586–87
political independence, 4–6, 283, 514, 516, 533, 595, 600, 603, 622
political system, 63, 80, 276–77
politics of interpretation, 114
polyandry, 464
polygamy, 448, 463–65, 468
polygenism, 55
postapartheid African renaissance, 3, 6
postmodernism, 83–84, 272–74, 602–5, 622
postmodernism, role, 604
postracialism, 90
praise poetry, 154, 162, 166, 173–74, 178
Precolonial Black Africa, 363
Pressley, Ayanna, 52
primitivism, 71, 119
prostitution, 471
proverb, 75, 100, 173, 179
pseudoscience, 78
Purple Hibiscus, 456, 459–61

qongqothwane, 485
queer theory, 330, 332
Qur'an, 14

race, 608
racial: decolonization, 2; discrimination, 51–52, 204, 358, 513; identity, 35, 52; isolation, 219; pride, 51–52; supremacy, 417
racism, 50, 52, 62, 181, 257, 306
rara, 165, 174
regional integration, 375, 620
religion, 39; Abrahamic, 539, 541, 544, 610; ancestral, 555; non-European 55; weaponization, 332
religious fanaticism, 477

religious homophobia, 18, 332, 345
research, 111–12, 131, 286; designs, 134, 141–42, 146; goal, 139; language, 136, 138, 142; output, 283, 286, 370
Rhodes, Cecil, 7
Rhodes Must Fall (RMF), 7, 372
Rights of Man, 260
ritual, 79, 83, 94, 159, 162, 524, 560
RMF Statue Removal, *363*
Rodney, Walter, 5, 15, 197–202, 278, 351, 364, 480–81
Rutazibwa, Olivia U., 35–37, 224

sacrifice, 559–60
Said, Edward, 61, 114, 130, 351
Samir, Amin, *227*
Santos, Souse, 15–16, 246, 270–75
The Satanic Verses, 239
science, 32
The Second Sex, 440
Second World War, 2–3, 21, 228
self-expression, 11, 452
self-sabotage, 387, 392
sexism, 306–8, 444, 447, 455, 457
sexual appropriateness, 32
sexual identity, 17, 332, 334, 337, 340–44, 346, 450
sexual minorities, 18, 332, 342–43
sexual violence, 31, 33, 445
sexually transmitted diseases and infections, 335
Shanghaied organic intellectual, 44
signs, 156
singular epistemology, 76, 85, 99
Sissoko, Malian Ballake, 21, 490
Smith, Anthony, 421–22
Smith, Tihuwai, 126
snail-sense feminism, 452, 454
Social Darwinism, 238, 319
social responsibility, 98
Social Science as Imperialism, 233

social sciences, 92
sodomy laws, 338–39
Sojourner Truth's speech, 72
Soyinka, Wole, 123–24, 159, 425–26, 435–36, 506, 571
spiritual beliefs, disparity, 609
spiritual pain, 557
spirituality, 23, 79, 83, 177, 546–49, 597
Steady, Filomina, 17, 242, 316, 318–20, 323, 422, 442
stigmatization, 148, 181–82, 336–37, 340, 345, 560
Stiwanism, 452–53, 461
storyteller, 163; role of, 166, 508
Structural Adjustment Programs (SAPs), 81, 518
subaltern academics, 75–77, 100
subaltern epistemology, 13
subaltern literature, 96–97
subalterns, 12–13, 16, 77, 96–97, 288
subjectivation, technologies, 252
subjugation, financial, 64; physical 103, 384; spiritual, 103, 384
Swahili, 118, 155, 173, 193, 402–4, 484
symbols, 156
syncretism, 563, 570

taboos, 544, 556
Tanzania, 111, 327, 364, 388, 392, 400; language policy, 402
Taoism, 79
technology, 71, 192
theological dogmatism, 575
There Was a Country: A Personal History of Biafra, 433
A Theory of Political Integration, 233
Things Fall Apart, 124
Thiong'o, Ngugi wa, 19, 107, 122, 137, 246, 381–82, 425, 431, 483
Tlaib, Rashida, 52

Trade and Politics in the Niger Delta 1830–1885, 522–23
traditional African political systems, 553
traditional epistemology, 76, 98, 100
traditional medical practices, 101
traditional religious performances, 177
transatlantic slave trade, 21, 161, 180, 276, 512
translation, 87, 156, 307–8; barriers, 141; thick, 90
traveling theater, 504
Trevor-Roper, Hugh, 47, 70, 73, 170, 209, 415
triangular trade, 276, 281
tribalism, 90
Trinidad, 550–52, 563–64
Trump, Donald, 52, 70–71, 231

Ubuntu, 79, 491–92
Uganda, 4, 19, 211–12, 329, 345, 354, 382, 389, 392, 522
UNDP, 444–45
UNESCO, 79, 105–6, 108, 287, 365, 388, 514, 520–21, 549, 616
UNESCO General History of Africa, 365
UNICEF, 324, 490
United Nations, 80, 291
Universalism, 60, 74, 235, 261–62, 418, 420, 575, 587
Universalist African philosophers, 579
University College Ibadan, 354, 528
University of Ghana, 4
universities, 349–50
Usman, Bala, 6, 530
utopia, 30, 273

Vansina, Jan, 152
video recordings, 182

violence, ecological, 543
visuality, 133, 142–43
Wallerstein, Immanuel, 42, 55, 57, 61
Wanawake, Maendeleo Y., 443
wars, 72, 163, 312–18, 474, 500, 562, 619
Washington, Booker T., 363
Washington Consensus, 82
West African kingdoms, 57
Western culture, 15, 19, 84, 131, 170, 205, 361, 377, 453, 496, 499, 504, 517
Western filmmakers, 501
western hegemonic, 9, 204, 586
western languages, 19, 101, 108–10, 117, 263, 582–85
western pedagogy, 86, 133
western philosophy, 102, 299, 569, 571, 579
western science, 22, 86, 557, 559
Western supremacy, 203
Westernization, 21, 480; *See* globalization
Westphalian Peace Treaty, 80
white superiority, 11, 63, 304, 539
white supremacy, 59, 214, 217, 221, 549
wildlife management, 556
Wiredu, Kwasi, 424–25, 427, 542, 567, 570–72, 585, 591
womanism, 450–53, 469
women, 302–3; emancipation of, 439; government in, 445; muslim, 477; violent domination of, 470
WORDOC, 17, 242, 315, 323–24
World Bank (WB), 199, 279, 324, 392, 518, 529, 535, 612, 614–15
World Health Organization (WHO), 93, 558
World Oral Literature Project, 151, 182, 194

World Trade Organization (WTO), 365
World War II, 500–501, 521
The Wretched of the Earth, 43

xenophobia, 257
xenophobic narrative, 259–60

Yoruba culture, 21, 298, 307–9, 482, 491, 493, 509; Anglicization, 307

Yoruba masquerading, 504
Yoruba Orisha religion, 550–51, 562
Yoruba religious cosmology, 308
Yoruba scholarship, 299

Zambia, 279
Zeleza, Paul T., 59, 75, 310–12, 316, 375, 602–4

Printed in the United States
by Baker & Taylor Publisher Services